Take a Hike: San Diego County

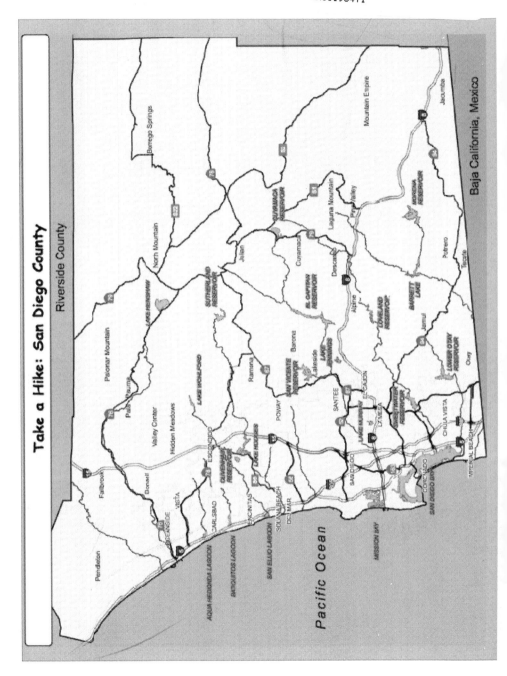

Riverside County

Baja California, Mexico

Pacific Ocean

TAKE A HIKE:
San Diego County

A HIKING GUIDE TO 260 TRAILS IN SAN DIEGO COUNTY

From Urban Oases to Backcountry Beauties,
from Sea to Forest to Desert

Explore one of the country's most diverse regions, and discover tales
of its past, flora and fauna of its present, and plans for its future.

PRISCILLA LISTER

ARCHWAY
PUBLISHING

Archway Publishing books may be ordered through booksellers or by contacting:

Archway Publishing
1663 Liberty Drive
Bloomington, IN 47403
www.archwaypublishing.com
1 (888) 242-5904

Because of the dynamic nature of the Internet, any web addresses or links contained in this book may have changed since publication and may no longer be valid. The views expressed in this work are solely those of the author and do not necessarily reflect the views of the publisher, and the publisher hereby disclaims any responsibility for them.

All photographs copyrighted by Priscilla Lister, except author photo by Chris Khoury, M.D.

ISBN: 978-1-4808-2539-0 (sc)
ISBN: 978-1-4808-2540-6 (e)

Library of Congress Control Number: 2015920794

Print information available on the last page.

Archway Publishing rev. date: 02/22/2016

Contents

Foreword
by Alison DaRosa

Priscilla Lister was born and raised in San Diego. She grew up in Point Loma, where she spent carefree childhood afternoons and weekends exploring canyons and wild open spaces of then undeveloped swaths of the peninsula. As a child of the '50s, she led playmates to neighborhood forts she built in the canyons of Loma Portal, she helped childhood buddies mine for treasure beneath scrub oaks on nearby hillsides, and she hunted four-leaf clovers and imagined herself soaring like the hawks that swooped overhead.

As she grew, Priscilla's sense of adventure and her inquisitive spirit grew with her, and they led her to a career in journalism. After earning a degree from Northwestern, she did an eight-year stint in Seattle, eventually writing the catalogue for REI, the outdoor adventure outfitter. By the time she was 30, Priscilla was back in San Diego, serving as editor and publisher of the weekly *La Mesa Courier*; and she was 35 when she became city editor of the *San Diego Daily Transcript*. During the 13 years she helped drive the editorial product at those newspapers, Priscilla gained an intimate, meticulous knowledge of our city and its workings—including its open spaces.

By then, Priscilla was hooked on hiking and spent virtually every free weekend in boots, trekking the region's developing trail system. Before long, she was as familiar with those trails as most of us are with the route to our favorite coffee shop.

Her love of the outdoors and off-the-beaten-track hikes flourished when Priscilla became a freelance journalist in 1993. She then had the freedom to explore around the world. Her travel stories appeared in the *San Diego Union-Tribune*, the *Los Angeles Times,* and other major newspapers and magazines across the country. Her stories almost always included an element of outdoor adventure; she led many a reader to explore on foot, usually on trails less traveled.

In 2008, Priscilla became a contributor to the *San Diego Union-Tribune*'s weekly Take a Hike column. Within a year or so, the column was exclusively hers, and it became her baby: When Priscilla wasn't out hiking and photographing San Diego trails, she was researching trail history and learning about the characters who'd lived that history. Her columns became far more than detailed hiking guides with rich descriptions of flora and fauna; they provided keen insights into the history and nature of the land as well as the men, women, and youngsters whose footprints preceded ours. Her columns were full of life.

After six years and more than 260 columns—each on a unique San Diego trail—Priscilla left the *Union-Tribune* to write this book. It's an updated, enhanced compilation of the best of her work—the only guide you'll ever need for exploring the best hiking that this region has to offer.

I've known Priscilla for more than a quarter-century, first as a competing colleague covering San Diego and inevitably as a friend. Like my friend, I'm a native San Diegan and an avid hiker. I thought I knew my way around, but I'm repeatedly surprised by how much I continue to learn from Priscilla. When I read what she writes about hiking, she makes me see and feel what it's like on the trail: I inhale the scent of wild lavender and sage, feel the healing warmth of the midmorning sun atop Cuyamaca or Mount Laguna, and see tracks of mule deer and jackrabbits imprinted on a dry, dusty path that disappears into the distance. When I'm on the trail, I allow my mind to wander, to play, to relive the stories I've learned from Priscilla about those who nurtured and loved this land long before either of us set foot here. Priscilla has taught me that the best hikes become journeys of the heart. Her guidance makes that happen.

Alison DaRosa is a native San Diegan and an award-winning journalist. She spent most of her career at the San Diego Union-Tribune, *first covering the city and then as a travel editor, writer, and photographer. During her tenure, she roamed the globe and was a six-time winner of the nation's most prestigious award for travel journalism, the Lowell Thomas Gold Award presented by the Society of American Travel Writers. Alison continues to write a monthly travel column for the newspaper. She also writes freelance travel stories for other publications, including the* Los Angeles Times.

Preface

Take a Hike: San Diego County was born in the pages of the *San Diego Union-Tribune* newspaper. For more than six years, I wrote a weekly hiking column, "Take a Hike," for the *U-T San Diego,* as it was named during those years. On many occasions, readers would ask me if my columns were compiled into a book.

Here it is. It is truly a labor of native love.

I was born and raised in San Diego. While growing up in Point Loma, my life as a child was centered more on the bay and the ocean because my father, Keith Lister, was an avid and accomplished sailor.

While living for nearly a decade in Seattle during my young adult years, I discovered the joys of hiking. When I returned home to San Diego, I brought that new pastime with me and began searching for hiking trails here. I found many of them, and I loved hiking every one. I figure I have hiked well over 1,000 miles of San Diego County, and I can identify more wildflowers, trees, birds, and mountain peaks than I ever thought possible.

Some trails are more beautiful than others, of course, but on every trail, I learned or saw something new, discovered another hidden corner of wonder, or simply enjoyed spending time outdoors.

When I began writing the column for the *U-T,* I used my journalism skills to tell tales of the trails, researching to find every interesting fact I could about each microcosm corner of our county. I have been a journalist for more than 35 years. I have traveled the world to write about it and photograph its beauties. But I have never found a greater passion for my writing and photography skills than my local hiking columns.

After more than 260 trails, I found that I had run out of trails I wanted to hike here. My efforts evolved into compiling my columns into this book.

My column lives on in this book. Even with the passage of time, these trails will still be there, awaiting your footfalls for years to come.

I still love hiking San Diego County's trails. Now I revisit my favorites. The breadth and range of this corner of the world is astonishing. I want you to discover it too.

Use this book over and over again. Plan out your hikes by downloading trail maps before you go. Get yourself a good hiking stick, and put some miles on it. You'll fall even more in love with San Diego County.

Introduction

Few places on the planet can boast the diversity of natural landscape found in San Diego County. When you consider the extreme low desert in Anza-Borrego, the more than 6,000-foot-high mountains of Laguna and Cuyamaca, the pastoral expanses between Julian and Warner Hot Springs, and the coastal wetlands of the Pacific Ocean, the breadth of our county's environment is downright remarkable.

"Nearly 2,100 plant species grow naturally on the land [of San Diego County]—more wild species than in any comparable area in the United States," states James Lightner in his book *San Diego County Native Plants*. Birds are bountiful here too. The San Diego Natural History Museum's *San Diego County Bird Atlas* "establishes a new benchmark for knowledge of birds in the region of the United States with more species than any other: 492."

More than 75 percent of the 2.7 million acres that make up San Diego County are undeveloped open space. Nearly half of the county's land is owned by government agencies, including the state's Department of Parks and Recreation, the U.S. Forest Service, the U.S. Bureau of Land Management, water districts, and the County of San Diego. Most of these lands are accessible to the public.

Miles of trails explore all our distinctive habitats, and because we enjoy sunshine most of the time, there are few finer places for hiking.

This Book's Focus

Take a Hike: San Diego County covers 260 trails that traverse our Pacific coastline, our urban and suburban communities, the pastoral foothills, our forested mountains, and the desert. There are harder trails out there than the ones covered in this book. I have omitted very popular trails like Iron Mountain, Cowles Mountain, and Mount Woodson because I prefer hikes that are less arduous and crowded. The trails I include here are all easily accessible by almost everyone; if I can hike them, most people can too. There are a few that are strenuous and many that are challenging, but generally these trails offer hikers very pleasant and rewarding excursions to almost every corner of our county. Get ready to explore many new destinations.

This book offers much more information about each hike than simply telling you to "turn left at the rock." Extensive research on every trail has uncovered its history, both cultural and natural. Read about the Kumeyaay and how they lived on this land for thousands of years, about the explorers and pioneers who transformed this region since the late 1700s, and about the present-day efforts to link trails among regions for even greater exploration opportunities. Learn about our local natural history with discussions of some of the flora, fauna, and geology present in our various habitats of chaparral, coastal sage scrub, oak woodlands, riparian, grasslands, coniferous woodlands, and desert wash scrub.

If you hike all these trails, as I have, you will surely enlarge your working knowledge of this remarkable region. Your appreciation for environmental protection of these natural places will increase, and you will learn something every step of the way.

When you don't feel like driving too far, check to see which trails are close to where you live—you might be surprised by how many there are. When you do feel like making an excursion out of your hiking plan, drive to Palomar, Cuyamaca, Laguna, or Anza-Borrego. These areas offer true wilderness experiences within very reasonable driving times, and even those delightful drives through the backcountry make you believe the journey can be as important as the destination.

Safety: Be Prepared on Trails

Enjoy our astounding scenery safely. Experienced hikers know how important it is to be prepared and aware. Here are several safety tips, compiled from several sources, including the National Park Service and the American Hiking Organization.

Before You Go:

Avoid hiking alone. Traveling with at least one companion adds to your safety margin.

Tell someone where you are going, and check in when you return.

Wear sturdy boots that are broken in and comfortable; know how they respond to slick surfaces.

Don't overestimate your abilities or the abilities of your companions. Know how hard the trail will be by estimating elevation gain and distance.

Find a map of the trail, and take it with you.

In Your Day Pack:

Water is the most essential item. Carry at least two quarts per person in every season. Experts recommend a gallon per person during a full day's hike in 70 or 80 degrees Fahrenheit in San Diego's arid backcountry.

Carry snacks for energy, a compass, a whistle, a flashlight, a basic first aid kit, and extra clothing that can stay dry.

Some say the most important safety item is your cell phone, but sometimes it won't get a signal.

On the Trail:

Carry a hiking stick. It can help with balance and help you navigate stream crossings. You can drag it or bang it against rocks to make vibrations to ward off snakes. You can use it to appear larger and more menacing if you should encounter a mountain lion. Some hikers prefer two hiking poles.

Don't climb on waterfalls. Injuries and deaths can occur on slippery, wet rocks.

Step over water bars, logs, or tree roots rather than on them. These surfaces can be slippery.

Heatstroke

You can lose a lot of fluid even over a two-hour period on a hot day. Heatstroke can kill, but it is preventable.

Do not overexert yourself, which causes dehydration.

Drink water before you feel thirsty—every half hour at least. For a seriously dehydrated person, encourage a few sips every 10 to 15 minutes even if he or she may not feel thirsty.

Heat fatigue is usually characterized by muscle cramps, strong thirst, and sudden and extreme fatigue. Heat exhaustion occurs when heat fatigue worsens. Symptoms include excessive sweating, dizziness, headache, nausea, and rapid heart rate.

Heatstroke is the most severe kind of heat-related illness. It is an extremely serious condition involving the total breakdown of the body's heat-control system. Heatstroke victims usually suffer from severe confusion, cannot sweat, and in some cases suffer complete nervous system failure.

In a serious situation, have the affected person lie down with his or her feet elevated to keep sufficient blood flowing to the brain. Place anything cold where major arteries are located: armpits, groin, neck. Add a wet bandanna on the forehead, and fan the person.

Your Dogs

Because of their fur, dogs can overheat more quickly than humans do. Don't overexert them, and don't forget to bring plenty of water for your dogs to stay hydrated, including a collapsible water bowl so they can access it.

Symptoms of heatstroke in dogs include rapid and frantic panting, wide eyes, thick saliva, and staggering. A dog's body temperature, normally 101–102 degrees Fahrenheit, is extremely dangerous over 106 degrees.

Apply flea and tick repellent before heading into woods or grasslands.

Leashes not only keep your dogs close; they keep your dogs out of harm's way and away from snakes, skunks, or other critters.

Be aware that if the ground is especially hot, the paw pads of your faithful companions can burn, so avoid long hikes in the hottest heat of the day with your pets, on black asphalt, in the desert, or anywhere temperatures soar.

Hazards

The two most dangerous natural hazards on San Diego County trails are rattlesnakes and mountain lions. It should be noted that in all my years of hiking San Diego County trails, I have never seen a mountain lion, and I saw a rattlesnake only once after it alerted me to its position by rattling its tail. I avoided hiking in the very early morning hours or very late afternoon hours, when snakes and mountain lions are more active.

Rattlesnakes

Five species of rattlesnakes live everywhere in San Diego County, from the coast to the mountains to the desert: western diamondback, red diamond, Southern Pacific, speckled, and sidewinder. The simplest way to identify a rattlesnake is by seeing or hearing its traditional rattle hiss, according to a pamphlet prepared by the County of San Diego Department of Animal Services. Some rattlesnakes can lose their rattles, however, so this is not a foolproof ID method.

All rattlesnakes have wide triangular heads that are much wider at the back than the front, with a relatively thin neck area. California's nonpoisonous snakes, by comparison, have heads roughly the same width as their bodies with no discernible neck region, and they have long pointed tails. Rattlesnakes can be brown, tan, yellow, green, gray, black, or dull red, and many have characteristic diamond or chevron markings on their backs or sides.

Rattlesnakes usually hibernate during fall and winter, waking up in spring (usually March and April). However, they can be found any time of year depending on the weather. Mild weather may draw rattlesnakes out of their hiding. Most snakebites here tend to occur in April and May.

Give the snake a chance to escape; leave plenty of room. If a rattlesnake senses your approach and can escape, it will do so, probably before you even see it. Startling a snake and attempting to pick it up or tease it are how most people get bitten. If the snake cannot escape, it will flatten its body and head and rattle its tail to give you a warning. If you hear that warning, stand still until you locate the snake, and then walk away from it calmly.

Rattlesnakes are deaf, so don't bother yelling at it.

Rattlesnakes also cannot crawl as fast as you can walk, so you should be able to leave the area. But they can strike in a split second, usually to defend themselves. They do not typically attack and only react to perceived threats.

Tips to Avoid Snakes
- Wear hiking boots.
- Stay on trails; avoid bushwhacking.
- Keep your dog leashed while hiking.
- Look for concealed snakes before you pick up rocks or wood.
- Carry a walking stick. If you encounter a snake, you can throw the stick so it may strike that instead of you or your pet.
- If you wear a hat, you can also throw the hat at the snake, which then may strike the hat instead of you or your pet.

If You Do Get Bitten
- Remain calm.
- If possible, immobilize the bitten extremity. Do not apply a tourniquet or constriction band. Do not apply ice to the wound. Do not attempt to cut the wound or suck out the venom.
- If a Sawyer Extraction Pump is available, apply suction to the wound using the pump. Do not cut the wound. Other types of snakebite kits are not

effective, according to the County of San Diego Department of Parks and Recreation.

- If alone, walk at a relaxed pace to the closest telephone reception or telephone and dial 911.

Mountain Lions

"About half of California is prime mountain lion country," says the brochure "Living with California Mountain Lions," produced by the California Department of Fish and Wildlife. They have always lived here, preying on deer and other wildlife, and they play an important role in our ecosystem.

The mountain lion is also known as a cougar, panther, or puma. It is tawny colored with black-tipped ears and tail, and it is one of North America's largest cats, weighing 65–150 pounds, depending on the sex and age. An adult male weighing 150 pounds may be more than eight feet long. Mountain lion kittens or cubs are covered with blackish-brown spots and have dark rings around their tails.

Mountain lions normally prey upon deer or bighorn sheep in our area, but they can also survive by preying on small animals. They usually hunt alone and at night, ambushing their prey from behind. They usually kill with a powerful bite below the base of the skull, breaking the neck.

"Their generally secretive and solitary nature is what makes it possible for humans to live in mountain lion country without ever seeing a mountain lion," says the brochure. They generally live where deer are plentiful. They are known to live in our mountain regions of Cuyamaca, Laguna, and Palomar but also in foothill areas that begin to encroach on our urban core.

Know that the potential for being killed or injured by a mountain lion is quite low compared to other natural hazards. For example, there is far greater risk of being struck by lightning than being attacked by a mountain lion.

Tips on Living in Mountain Lion Country
- Do not hike alone.
- Keep children close to you—within arm's length and always in sight.
- Most mountain lions will try to avoid confrontation. Give them a way to escape.
- Do not run from a mountain lion, because running may stimulate its natural instinct to chase. Make eye contact. If you have small children with you, pick them up so they don't panic and run. Although it may be awkward, pick them up without bending over or turning away from the mountain lion.
- Do not crouch down or bend over; in that stance you may appear more like a four-legged prey animal.
- Do all you can to appear larger. Raise your arms, and open your jacket. Throw stones, branches, or whatever you can reach without crouching or turning your back. Wave your arms slowly and speak firmly and in a loud voice to try to convince the mountain lion that you are not prey and may be a danger to it.

- Fight back if you are attacked. Fight back with rocks, hiking sticks, or bare hands. A mountain lion usually tries to bite the head or neck, so try to remain standing and face the attacking animal.
- If you are involved in a face-to-face encounter with a mountain lion, contact the nearest ranger's office or the California Department of Fish and Wildlife.

Poison Oak

This plant is actually not an oak but a sumac. It produces one of the most common allergic reactions in the United States. The oil in poison oak, called urushiol, is found in the sap of these plants. When it attaches itself to the skin after direct exposure, symptoms of allergic reaction will result, including rashes, oozing blisters, itching, and swelling.

Know what to look for to avoid contact.

"Leaves of three, let it be" is the mantra for poison oak. It is typically a shrub or can be vine-like as it climbs trees. Each leaflet consists of three leaves with rounded lobes that look similar to some oak leaves. Poison oak turns yellow and then red in the fall as it drops its leaves.

Wear protective clothing, including long pants and long-sleeved shirts, in brushy areas.

If you know you have been exposed, cleanse the area with plain soap and water to remove the urushiol before it can bind to the skin.

Find Fellow Hikers

Avoid hiking alone. That admonition is one of the most common pieces of safety advice offered by virtually every park and preserve.

If you find yourself unable to wrangle a companion to explore the amazing breadth of nature found in San Diego County, do not despair. There are many options available to join other hikers on the hundreds of trails here from the ocean to the desert.

Many of these groups are headed by seasoned naturalists, so chances are you will learn more about our natural wonders from these experts than you would on your own.

The Canyoneers

One of the oldest such organizations is the Canyoneers of the San Diego Natural History Museum. Founded in 1973 by Helen Chamlee Witham (an associate botanist at the museum, a teacher, and environmental activist), the group was first known as the Florida Canyoneers because it centered its activities in the Balboa Park canyon. By the early 1980s, Florida was dropped from the name, and the Canyoneers have guided hikes all over the county ever since.

Today, about 80 Canyoneers lead weekend hikes from September through late June. Canyoneers are museum volunteers who have completed a 13-week training course in natural history and who commit to leading 16 hikes over a two-year period.

Canyoneer hikes "are interpretive nature walks, not endurance hikes," and guides try to accommodate the abilities of all participants. The hikes are open to the public and are free, but destination parking fees may apply. Participants meet at the trailheads.

All Canyoneer hikes are ranked easy, intermediate, difficult, or extreme, with additional information about elevation changes and mileage. They usually take place every Saturday and Sunday, typically starting at 9:00 or 10:00 a.m.

For a calendar of upcoming hikes, go to http://www.sdnhm.org/education/naturalists -of-all-ages/canyoneer-hikes/.

Sierra Club

The San Diego chapter of the Sierra Club organizes frequent hikes all over the county. They're free, but participants must sign a liability waiver. Some of the hikes require advance sign-up because they limit the number of participants. Hikers meet at the trailheads, and carpool options are sometimes available.

Sierra Club outings are also ranked similarly to the Canyoneers', from easy to moderate, hard, strenuous, and very strenuous, with estimates on elevation changes and mileage.

For a calendar, go to http://sandiego.sierraclub.org/outings.

Anza-Borrego Desert State Park

Volunteer naturalists with the desert state park and the Anza-Borrego Foundation offer frequent outings. Spring wildflowers are one of the biggest draws there, and several walks to the best wildflower displays are scheduled through March and April. All programs are free.

Programs include Beginner's Bird Walk, a 1.5-hour walk around the visitor center with a volunteer naturalist to look for common birds of the desert; a 5-hour hike through the palm groves of Mountain Palm Springs; and an archaeological discovery tour of morteros with an archaeologist in Blair Valley.

For monthly calendar listings, go to the Anza-Borrego Desert State Park page, www.parks.ca.gov/?page_id=638, and click on the month's interpretive schedule.

San Dieguito River Park

One of the most active regional organizations dedicated to the conservation and preservation of the San Dieguito River Valley, the San Dieguito River Park sometimes offers guided hikes on its 65 miles of trails. Its centerpiece project is the Coast-to-Crest Trail, which one day will extend from Volcan Mountain near Julian to the beach at Del Mar.

San Dieguito River Park also invites volunteers to join weekend trail maintenance and habitat restoration projects. Check its monthly calendar for such opportunities: http://www.sdrp.org/wordpress/events/.

San Diego Audubon Society

The local chapter of the National Audubon Society conducts field trips almost every week to various locations around the county to search for birds. The guided excursions are usually free. Bring your own binoculars.

Check its web site for field trip listings: http://www.sandiegoaudubon.org/events/ field-trips.

State and County Parks

Virtually every state park, county park, and local preserve, from Cuyamaca Rancho State Park to Blue Sky Ecological Preserve to Cleveland National Forest's Laguna to Anza-Borrego Desert State Park, offers guided hiking opportunities. Check the websites listed for each of the hikes to see if there might be additional activities that interest you. You may be solo, but you don't have to hike alone.

Note about Web Page Addresses

Today you can find a satellite image for virtually every corner of the globe, including almost every inch of San Diego County. I give web page addresses with every hike so you can prepare yourself by downloading a trail map before you go. The web pages cited make it easier to locate that trail map that will keep you going in the right direction.

Web page addresses, of course, can change. If the web address cited no longer exists, and you are not automatically redirected, usually you can search for the agency, and that will bring up the website you seek. Most of the trails in this book are managed by governmental or public agencies that can easily be found by search engines.

Note about Trails

Like website addresses, trails can change too. Almost all of these trails are in areas or under jurisdictions that maintain them, so there should be few changes since I hiked them myself.

If you take a current trail map with you from the sources listed with each trail, you should have no major problems.

Your Rewards

Once you begin exploring San Diego County on foot, you will surely be astounded by its diversity, beauty and fascinating flora and fauna. The views are breathtaking. Wildflowers are wonderfully detailed and distinctive. Birds brighten the landscape with color and song. The stories of those who came before us offer plenty to ponder. The exercise afforded by hiking is far more fun than any gym session.

It turns out even those views translate into better health. Researchers from the University of California, Berkeley, have found that the positive emotions triggered by such awe-inspiring experiences as overlooking a scenic vista can boost immune systems and even help protect the body from heart disease, depression, and other chronic illnesses.

Go take a hike. You are in one of the most amazing places anywhere. Grab your walking stick, put on your hiking boots, pack your water and trail map, and explore the amazing richness of San Diego County's geographic wonders.

1. San Diego County Coast

San Diego County's coastline is dotted with lagoons that offer some of the best birding sites anywhere. Other coastal highlights include ocean caves and seaside bluffs that perch above the shoreline.

The centerpiece of coastal hiking here is Torrey Pines State Natural Reserve, where about eight miles of trails cover an oceanfront area that has been preserved for more than 100 years, offering a splendid landscape on the sea that will likely become a favorite hiking destination for you too.

1-1. Find Birds and Beach Dunes at Tijuana Estuary

The Tijuana River Estuary in Imperial Beach is prime birding territory. Some 370 bird species have been seen here, including the endangered white-bodied, black-headed California least tern; least bell's vireo; the beautiful red-throated California brown pelican; and the light-footed clapper rail, with its white-striped belly. Of those 370 species, only 50 live here year-round; the others are migratory. The adorable Western snowy plover, another endangered species, nests on the beaches here.

The estuary is part of the Tijuana River National Estuarine Research Reserve, which also includes the Tijuana Slough National Wildlife Refuge. It's one of only 24 wetlands in the entire United States to be designated a "wetland of international importance" by the international Ramsar Wetlands Convention. An estuary is a partially enclosed body of water that receives saltwater from the ocean and freshwater from rivers and rainfall. This one is located where the Tijuana River meets the Pacific Ocean.

**The North Beach Trail at the Tijuana Estuary looks toward
the sand dunes protecting the beach.**

It is one of the few salt marshes remaining in Southern California (90 percent have been lost to development), and it is subject to periods of drought that can leave it dry, as well as periods of flooding that can inundate the area. Because of these climatic extremes, the Tijuana Estuary is considered unique in the National Estuarine Research Reserve System.

In this part of the country, most rivers (including the Tijuana) flow only after rainfall. Daily tides push nutrient-rich water through the marsh, making estuaries some of the richest habitats on the planet. It is the only coastal lagoon in Southern California that's not bisected by roads and rail lines.

There are about three miles of trails here, but they aren't interconnected, so to explore the entire area requires some driving or separate trips. There are additional miles of trails farther south from the visitor center on the Tijuana Slough National Wildlife Refuge, where horses are allowed.

The best map of all the trails is on the estuary's website; go to www.tijuanaestuary. org. Note that the main trails leading from the visitor center are for hikers only—no dogs or bikes. Some trails do allow leashed dogs and bikes. The trails in the refuge are only for horses or hikers.

However you explore this coastal wetland, bring binoculars and look for those birds. I saw a couple of impressive great egrets, which are easy to spot because they are all white, and a juvenile heron watching for fish in the river.

This is one of the easiest places to hike in the county. It's entirely flat, and one of its special features is the stretch of undeveloped beach, complete with dunes, along the North Beach Trail. Obviously, the beach can offer prime shorebird watching.

The South Beach Trail on the refuge section is open to horseback riding on the beach—one of the only such opportunities around. Check out Happy Trails Horse Rentals at http://happytrailssandiego.com.

The Tijuana Estuary offers many activities, including guided bird walks every Sunday from 3:00 to 4:00 p.m.; nature walks every second and fourth Saturday from 11:00 a.m. to noon; Junior Rangers programs for students seven to 12 years old; a Saturday speaker series every third Saturday from 11:00 a.m. to noon; and lots of volunteer opportunities, including monitoring those endangered species after some training. Go to its website for more information.

Thomas Brothers Map: Page 1349, F-1.

Before You Go: Check the reserve's website for information: www.tijuanaestuary.org, or www.trnerr.org.

Trailhead: Take Interstate 5 south to exit 4, Coronado Avenue, in Imperial Beach. Turn right (go west) onto Coronado Avenue, which becomes Imperial Beach Boulevard, for about three miles. Turn left onto Third Avenue and follow the road around the corner with the visitors' center on your right.

Hours: The trails are open for hiking a half hour before sunrise and a half hour after sunset every day. The visitor center is open only Wednesday through Sunday, 10:00 a.m. to 5:00 p.m.

Distance/Difficulty: From 1.0 to 3.0 miles total; easy.

1-2. History, Downtown Views from Bayside Trail

The Bayside Trail on the edge of Point Loma in Cabrillo National Monument is an urban gem for its views of the downtown skyline and Coronado Bridge, as well as for its fascinating local history.

**The Bayside Trail at Cabrillo National Monument
has blue-water views of downtown's skyline.**

In 2013, San Diego's "only national park" celebrated its 100th birthday. Located atop the 422-foot-high peninsula, the Bayside Trail winds down toward San Diego Bay through mainly coastal sage scrub and southern maritime chaparral, two increasingly vulnerable habitats.

"The natural environment is much the same as when [Juan Rodriguez] Cabrillo came ashore here in 1542," says one of the many informational placards along the trail. The first European to set foot on the West Coast, Cabrillo had sailed from Mexico to claim land for the king of Spain, according to the brochure all visitors receive when they enter the national monument.

Cabrillo was greeted by native Kumeyaay Indians when he stepped ashore. "Some wore their long hair in braids with feathers or shells. Some of the men wore capes made of sea otter, seal or deer skin," says the brochure. Cabrillo observed in his journals that the locals looked prosperous and fished far out to sea in reed canoes. They made pottery, baskets, and shell jewelry, which they traded with their neighbors.

The Old Point Loma Lighthouse that sits on top of the peninsula, next to the trailhead for the Bayside Trail, was built in 1854 and lit San Diego's harbor until 1891. It was one of the original eight lighthouses on the West Coast of the United States. But standing atop that 422-foot crest, the lighthouse was too often enveloped in fog, so it was moved in 1891 to a lower elevation at Pelican Point, where it still operates today, down by the tide pools. The original lighthouse was fully restored in 2004 and is now open to view how the lighthouse keepers lived here in those rough, early years when San Diego was more than 10 miles away via a wagon road.

In 1852, the U.S. government recognized the importance of the Point Loma peninsula for its strategic views of the bay and ocean and so designated the area a military reserve. During the World Wars, military facilities on the point provided vital defense systems.

The Bayside Trail follows an old military defense road that heads down from the old lighthouse for nearly one mile. It's a moderately steep trail, with about 400 feet in elevation change, but the steep part is short, and those views are well worth the effort.

You'll learn a lot about the precious habitats here from the informational placards along the trail. Coastal sage scrub dominates these bluffs, with lots of California sagebrush and black sage, both of which fill the air with fragrance. "The roots of black sage and coastal sagebrush soften the soil for smaller shrubs like California buckwheat, deerweed and saltbush which form the ground cover in this miniature forest," says one placard. The buckwheat in spring is especially pretty in pink. You'll also see plants that fall in the precious maritime succulent scrub habitat on the driest, west-facing slopes, including cliff spurge, dudleya, and barrel cactus.

Lots of creatures live here too, from lizards and rattlesnakes to gray foxes, ground squirrels, and cottontail rabbits, as well as peregrine falcons, red-tailed hawks, hummingbirds, wrentits, and California quail (the state bird).

You'll pass by an old searchlight power station on the trail, built in 1919 to house and protect huge searchlights that lighted the harbor entrance during World Wars I and II.

The biggest appeal of this trail is in its views. On the clearest days, you can see the mesas and mountains of Mexico on the horizon. Downtown's skyline and the Coronado Bridge are almost always in view. On weekends, San Diego Bay is filled with boats of all types and sizes. You can also watch fighter jets and other aircraft landing at North Island across the water. Benches placed along the way invite a lot of lingering.

Try to imagine the scene here when Cabrillo and the Kumeyaay met more than 470 years ago. When you reach the end of the trail, where Ballast Point lies straight ahead on the eastern edge of the bay, picture the whalers who hunted gray whales off the point and processed them at Ballast Point from the 1850s to late 1880s. Imagine how hard life must have been for those early lighthouse keepers, including Robert Israel, who lived here with his family for almost 20 years in the late 1800s, hauling in firewood, water, and other supplies by wagon on a rough dirt road.

The climb back up Bayside Trail won't seem so hard.

Thomas Brothers Map: Page 1308, A-2.

Before You Go: Download a map from the national park pages (www.nps.gov/cabr), from the "Plan Your Visit" section.

Entrance to the national monument is open from 9:00 a.m. to 5:00 p.m. every day except Christmas Day. Entry for a regular passenger vehicle is $5 per vehicle.

The Bayside Trail is open only to hikers. Dogs are not allowed on the national monument grounds.

Trailhead: From Interstates 5 or 8, exit at Rosecrans/Highway 209, heading west on Rosecrans into Point Loma. Turn right onto Canon Street and then left onto Catalina Boulevard (also known as Cabrillo Memorial Drive). Head all the way to the end.

From the main parking area, walk to the Old Point Loma Lighthouse. To the west of its entrance is the trailhead for Bayside Trail.

Distance/Difficulty: From the main parking area, the round-trip is about 2.4 miles. The Bayside Trail itself from the lighthouse is about 1.8 miles round trip, with about 400 feet in elevation change. Easy to moderate.

1-3. Land and Sea Meet Beautifully at Sunset Cliffs Park

The 1.5-mile-long trail along the ocean at Sunset Cliffs offers one of our coastline's most beautiful walks.

The shoreline of sculpted sandstone is a dramatic meeting of land and sea, constantly changing with erosion.

This is Sunset Cliffs Natural Park, which includes a one-mile-long trail through Linear Park, encompassing about 18 acres on the coast. It connects to another half-mile or more of trails in Hillside Park, which covers about 50 acres. Hillside Park is designated a Multiple Habitat Preservation Area (MHPA), providing connectivity to the adjacent 650-acre Point Loma Ecological Reserve, a government-protected area around Cabrillo National Monument with very limited public access.

Linear Park begins at Sunset Cliffs Boulevard at Adair Street, and it sticks to the edge of the ocean as it heads south toward the end of Point Loma.

Hillside Park at Sunset Cliffs has trails on the bluffs above the ocean.

You'll pass by Spalding Point, one of the large rock protrusions that extend into the ocean; Osprey Point; Cormorant Rock offshore, where cormorants are constant visitors; peaceful No Surf Beach; and then Luscomb's Point, another sandstone extension that sits at the foot of Hill Street.

Luscomb's Point is a popular wedding venue. It was named for a local surfer, Rod Luscomb, who carved these waters, especially a surf break nicknamed Ab, in the late 1940s through the 1970s. Luscomb, who died in 2003, was also a local lifeguard. His son, Michael, has owned and operated La Jolla Kayaks since 1995.

You'll probably see those graceful gatherings of brown pelicans as they soar in formation above the waves, or surfers as they carve through breaks near Garbage Beach (named for lots of kelp there) below Hillside Park. If you take the stairs at Ladera Street down to the tide pools, especially during low tides, you might see anemones, limpets, and tiny fish.

The intertidal ecosystem, where the land and sea meet, harbors some of the greatest diversity of species on the planet, serving as a kind of nursery that includes crabs, clams, kelp, and baby fish. Step carefully around all these living creatures if you are in the tide pool area at low tide.

There are coves and arches carved in those sandstone cliffs and that very quiet No Surf Beach, which is accessed only by a steep, winding trail down its southern end. Ab Beach sits at the very southern end of Hillside Park, south of Garbage Beach.

While viewing the cliffs from the beach, look for evidence of their geologic beginnings. About 1 million years ago, according to the city park brochure for Sunset Cliffs, "tectonic action began to lift the peninsula of Point Loma above sea level. The 75 million-year-old Point Loma Formation is the bedrock of the park and most of the peninsula. This dinosaur-era shale is the dark gray geologic strata visible on the lower portion of the cliff face." This ancient rock formation extends into the sea, forming the ocean floor and creating reefs where waves break.

The sand-colored Bay Point Formation sits above the Point Loma Formation, forming the upper half of the cliff face. This porous sandstone layer is less than 120,000 years old and is "particularly vulnerable to erosion."

"It has a tendency to collapse and slump into the ocean, and as it disintegrates, it deposits sand onto beaches," says the brochure.

Do not underestimate the delicacy of these sandstone cliffs. Warning signs of potential danger on the unstable cliffs are posted frequently along the natural park. Over the years, many people have died while simply taking photographs when the cliff edges collapse without warning; in times of high surf, people have been swept off those extended formations when a surprise wave swallows them into the sea.

"Tides can change the sea level more than 9 feet within six hours," notes the brochure. Check tide tables.

The Kumeyaay probably knew the tides well. They lived seasonally in this area from more than 7,000 years ago, harvesting seafood from that intertidal zone and plants from the coastal sage scrub.

The park's southern boundary is shared with Point Loma Nazarene College, the latest incarnation of what once was the home of Madame Tingley and her Theosophical Community of Lomaland, founded on the bluffs in 1897.

In 1903, Albert Spalding (namesake of one of the coastal points) bought acreage north of Madame Tingley's property, including the 18-acre Linear Park section. He named the property Sunset Cliffs to attract attention during the 1915 Panama-California Exposition in Balboa Park. Spalding spent an estimated $2 million to install bridges, carved stairways, and cobblestone paths leading to the sandy coves. All those elements are gone now, as are most of the old homes that once had oceanfront spots here.

Most of the Linear Park land was acquired by the City of San Diego in 1926, and the Hillside Park's 48 acres were acquired by the city in 1968. The city purchased an additional two acres and dedicated the park in 1983.

The Hillside Park area is notably different from the Linear Park along the coast. Trails wind up into that bluff-top acreage for higher vantage points. There is also a demonstration garden here that aims to restore native plants in the park.

The park's master plan calls for removal of many of the old and diseased trees here to be replaced with native oaks and Torrey pines. The master plan even calls for a "Point Loma Trail" that will one day connect Sunset Cliffs to the Navy lands at the southern end of Point Loma below Cabrillo. That master plan invites everyone to take a hike along these coastal bluffs "and enjoy San Diego's natural coastal environment as it once was, free from the effects of man and intended to inspire the user to reflect on the grandeur of the sea and the beauty of the cliffs that are Point Loma."

Thomas Brothers Map: Page 1287, H-1.

Before You Go: Download a copy of the natural park's map at http://www.famosaslough.org/sc.htm, the website of the Sunset Cliffs Natural Park Council.

The city's parks page for Sunset Cliffs is http://www.sandiego.gov/park-and-recreation/parks/regional/shoreline/sunset2.shtml.

Trailhead: Take Interstate 8 west to its end and then follow Sunset Cliffs Boulevard south through Ocean Beach. Sunset Cliffs Boulevard ends at Ladera Street.

The Linear Park begins at Sunset Cliffs Boulevard at Adair Street. There is off-street parking at several places along the Linear Park.

Hillside Park begins at Sunset Cliffs Boulevard at Ladera Street. There is a lot of off-street parking here.

Distance/Difficulty: The Linear Park and Hillside Park oceanfront trail is about 1.5 miles one way. I hiked about 3.5 miles total, including exploration around Hillside Park. Easy.

1-4. San Diego River Mouth Is Rich in Bird Life

Some of San Diego's best birding can be enjoyed along the mouth of the San Diego River. Two spots at the river's end at the Pacific Ocean make for an easy meander along flat paths where waterfowl thrive all year round. In winter, many migratory species increase the fascinating bird life on view here. The best time to view birds here is October through March.

Begin at the Famosa Slough (pronounced slew), a 37-acre functioning wetland preserve. This small tidal marsh is managed by the City of San Diego and hosts year-round populations of egrets, herons, avocets, stilts, terns, hawks, and falcons, along with winter migratory species including lots of ducks. Notable here are sightings of the pretty blue-winged teal duck.

The trail around Famosa Slough is split by West Point Loma Boulevard. The southern section begins from there at Famosa Boulevard and skirts the edges of the tidal marsh along its western shore. You reach the end of this section at Valeta Street, and then you turn back the way you came.

Crossing West Point Loma Boulevard, hike the trail along the slough's northern section, which ends at Interstate 8. This northern section is prettier, but both are birders' delights. When I was there, I spotted several great egrets, snowy egrets, a kingfisher, a little blue heron, some elegant northern pintail ducks, some of those blue-winged teals with their brown spotted bodies and pale blue shoulder patches, and some lovely American wigeons with their green eye patches and pale blue bills.

"The first life on land probably crept from the same kind of ooze that stretches before you," says a placard at Famosa Slough. "Today, highly developed species—such as the egret, with its supple movements and complex hunting and mating patterns—share the marsh with their one-celled predecessors."

Some 95 percent of California's coastal wetlands have been destroyed. "What you see here is an attempt to halt further damage and an experiment in restoring a severely altered ecosystem."

Reaching the end of the slough's trail at Interstate 8, I turned around and headed back to my car. From here I drove to the San Diego River Flood Control Channel and Estuary, which includes the Southern Wildlife Preserve near the actual mouth of the San Diego River, where it empties into the Pacific. This part of the river is located in Mission Bay Park.

"The San Diego River area is a historical, archeological and biological treasure of statewide significance," says the San Diego River Conservancy. San Diego River has been called both the "Birthplace of California" and "California's First River" since the 1769 founding of the first European settlement on the West Coast along its banks, according to San Diego River Park Foundation.

"The San Diego River was the site of one of the first dam and water diversion projects undertaken by white settlers in what is now the United States," writes Philip Pryde in his book *San Diego: An Introduction to the Region*. "As early as 1792, a canal was constructed to bring water from upstream springs to the San Diego Mission de Alcala at the east end of Mission Valley."

When those first white settlers came here, San Diego River emptied into False Bay, the present-day Mission Bay. Some 50 years later, it altered course and began to empty into San Diego Bay. By 1877, a dam and a straightening of the river channel to the ocean created the river's mouth as we know it today.

Both the south and north sides of the San Diego River here have paved bicycle and walking paths that extend to the ocean. The south side's path begins in Mission Valley near Friars Road and Napa Street and extends about 3.75 miles to the ocean. I began on the north side of the river at South Shores Park, the access road just off Sea World Drive, and hiked about two miles one way to the river's end at the Pacific, turning around to retrace my route back.

San Diego River meets the Pacific Ocean right next to Mission Bay.

Someday, the San Diego River Park Trail will extend 52 miles from its headwaters near Julian to the Pacific Ocean here.

This final stretch of the San Diego River is sometimes known as San Diego's "Mile of Birds." Look for the magnificent osprey here as well as ruddy ducks, black brants, and red knots. I spotted many more great egrets, little blue herons, and lots of gulls. I spied flocks of ruddy ducks with their white cheeks and blue bills as well as buffleheads. Buffleheads are one of our cutest ducks; the males have a white triangle patch on the backs of their heads, and females have small white cheek patches. Both ruddy ducks and buffleheads migrate here for winter from their breeding homes in Alaska and Canada. According to a placard along the trail, they come on the Pacific Flyway, a major north-south route of travel for migratory birds extending from Alaska to Patagonia.

The Southern Wildlife Preserve, closed to boats, provides nesting and feeding grounds for both migratory and year-round birds. Of particular concern here are the light-footed clapper rail and the California least tern, both of which nest along this estuary.

The estuary of the river is where both seawater and freshwater intermingle where the river meets the sea. Estuaries are one of the most productive natural habitats.

One of the best times to go birding here is during low tides, when the mudflats are exposed and wading shorebirds, like the long-billed marbled godwits and curlews, dig for food stuff including crabs and shrimp.

Maybe you'll see a little blue heron stealthily nab a tiny crab for lunch, like I did.

Thomas Brothers Map: Page 1268, B-5 for Famosa Slough, B-4 for path along river at Quivira Boulevard.

Before You Go: Go to the San Diego River Park Foundation website, www.sandiegoriver.org/ river_trail.html, to get maps of various segments of the river trail currently open.

The estuary section, which also shows the location of Famosa Slough, is the last of the maps listed. Note that the north side of the river also has a paved trail from South Shores Park to the ocean.

San Diego Audubon has information on the San Diego River Estuary trails too: http://www. sandiegoaudubon.org/birding/local-birding-sites.

Dogs on leashes are welcome at Famosa Slough. At the San Diego River Channel in Mission Bay Park, leashed dogs are allowed on the shoreline trails only after 4:00 p.m. from November through March, after 6:00 p.m. from April through October, and in early morning hours before 9:00 a.m. year-round. Dogs can be leash-free at Dog Beach at the end of the southern side of the river channel in Ocean Beach.

Trailhead: To reach Famosa Slough, go to the western end of Interstate 8 and head south on Nimitz Boulevard. Turn left at West Point Loma Boulevard. When you reach Famosa Boulevard, you'll see the preserve on either side of the road. Park where you can.

To reach the estuary segment on the north side, head back to Nimitz Boulevard and head north, merging onto Sea World Drive. Turn right at South Shores Park and park along the access road that skirts the river. To reach this trailhead without going to Famosa Slough first, from Interstate 5, exit at Sea World Drive and head west, turning left (south) onto South Shores Park.

Distance/Difficulty: I hiked 1.25 miles in Famosa Slough, and then 4.0 miles round-trip along the estuary to the ocean. Flat, easy.

1-5. La Jolla Caves Revealed during Winter Low Tides

Fall and winter are the most opportune times to explore the La Jolla Caves on foot because extreme low tides occur during many of those afternoons.

When the tide is negative one foot or more—check local tide tables to find out when—hikers can navigate the exposed boulders and tide pools to reach several of the seven caves that dot these cliffs.

The largest cave is the best known because it's accessible to walkers through a manmade tunnel at the old Cave Shop at the northern end of Coast Boulevard. Frank Baum, author of *The Wizard of Oz,* named this cave Sunny Jim's Cave after a long-ago cartoon character. The other caves are named (west to east) Clam's Cave, Arch Cave, Sea Surprise, Shopping Cart, Little Sister, and White Lady. They are usually reachable only by water, making them a popular kayaking destination.

Begin the hike at least a half hour before the predicted low tide at the public beach access immediately south of The Marine Room Restaurant on Spindrift Drive. I started an hour before the low tide and finished an hour after that time, and I enjoyed a leisurely exploration without peril from the incoming tide.

As soon as the cliffs rise south of the Marine Room, the sand disappears and the boulders begin. A little cove of a beach features these tumbled rocks, perfectly rounded and smooth from eons of water action.

Aim for low tides to explore La Jolla Caves.

Next begin the tide pools that cover a large terrace of flat sandstone, covered by a carpet of sea grass that provides an easy walking surface. In the tide pools, look for sea anemones, hermit crabs, sea urchins, and little fish.

The little fish attract lots of waterfowl, the prettiest of which are the snowy egrets with their snow-white plumage and bright yellow feet. There are also the marvelous brown pelicans, who soar in formation with great grace, and of course lots of gulls.

Hanging out on the cliffs above the caves are dozens of black cormorants.

I had them in sight as I tried to make my way from the flat tide pools over the large, algae-covered boulders that must be crossed to get to the western caves. But these big green rocks foiled me and were too slippery. My first misstep landed me flat, so I decided against going any farther.

Dean Kaufman,19, from Poway reported to me that even though he slipped once too, he made it to the second big cave we could see. Youth always wins.

The tide pools proved a worthy reason to visit in themselves. The colorful rocks under the shallow water range from pink to green. Sometimes sea turtles stick their heads out of the water at the surf line. Watching the egrets pick their way gingerly through those rocks, grabbing a fish here or there, was great entertainment.

Scripps Institution of Oceanography's Birch Aquarium occasionally leads guided tours of these tide pools. Check its website, http://aquarium.ucsd.edu, for a calendar of such activities.

Thomas Brothers Map: Page 1227, G-5.

Before You Go: Check tide tables from the National Oceanic and Atmospheric Administration (NOAA) for La Jolla at its website, www.noaa.gov. Search for La Jolla tides at http://tidesandcurrents.noaa.gov/noaatidepredictions/NOAATidesFacade.jsp?Stationid=9410230.

Trailhead: From Interstate 5 heading north, exit at La Jolla Parkway heading west. At the fourth traffic light, turn right onto La Jolla Shores Drive. Go one block to Paseo Dorado, turn left, and park on the streets near the Marine Room.

From I-5 heading south, exit at La Jolla Village Drive heading west. At the third traffic light, turn left on Torrey Pines Road. At the fifth traffic light, turn right onto La Jolla Shores Drive. Go one block to Paseo Dorado, turn left, and park on the streets near the Marine Room.

Find the public beach access immediately to the south of the restaurant.

Distance/Difficulty: About 1.0 mile round trip; easy to moderate depending on those green boulders.

1-6. Scripps Coastal Reserve for Ocean Bluff Views: Paved Beach Access North

A moment after I stepped under the metal gate and found the trailhead to Scripps Coastal Reserve, an Audubon's cottontail rabbit hopped right across the path. I considered this an auspicious beginning to this pocket preserve along La Jolla's coastline.

Scripps Coastal Reserve is part of UCSD's Natural Reserve System (NRS), one of four natural ecosystems managed by the university, which include Dawson Los Monos Canyon Reserve, surrounding the Agua Hedionda Creek in North County; Elliott Chaparral Reserve, formerly part of Camp Elliott Military Reservation, located next to the Marine Corps Air Station Miramar; and Kendall Frost Reserve on the northern edge of Mission Bay.

The paved pathway to Black's Beach is part of Scripps Coastal Reserve.

The NRS was established by the University of California in the late 1950s by a group of scientists who "were weary of seeing wildlands that had once served as outdoor laboratories get bulldozed to build dorms and rec centers," says the NRS on its web page about its history. The scientists sought samples of natural ecosystems where they could study long-term.

"This is a state with enormous variety," said then UC President Clark Kerr. "Identifying the ecological areas and preserving them forever under university control is something that in the long run will loom as having been of increasing importance over the years."

Today, the University of California's Natural Land and Water Reserves System, known as the Natural Reserve System, consists of 39 reserves that include more than 750,000 acres across the state, available to researchers of every kind.

Known as the Knoll, the upper portion of Scripps Coastal Reserve is a coastal bluff that rises more than 300 feet above the ocean. The reserve also includes a marine portion that extends into the ocean to the depth of 745 feet into the tributaries of the Scripps and La Jolla submarine canyons. Scripps Pier, jutting 1,050 feet into the Pacific, provides access to those underwater habitats.

The loop trail around The Knoll takes only about 20 minutes to complete. The trail is terrific for its gorgeous coastal and eroded sandstone canyon views. Hikers may find brochures at the trailhead that will offer self-guided ecological tours coinciding with numbered markers on the half-mile trail.

The coastal scrub looks pretty toasty in summer, but according to a list of flora on the reserve's website, lots of wildflowers pop up in spring. Look for coreopsis, California everlasting, coastal sagebrush, broom, coyote brush, salt heliotrope, lotus, lupine, black sage, chia, and buckwheat.

The Knoll used to be home to Native Americans, as evidenced by archeological digs that have uncovered pottery shards and piles of shells. At the turn of the century, it was farmland, and in World War II it was a military lookout complete with foxholes and big guns.

Along the trail, you'll glimpse some of the multimillion-dollar mansions that are part of today's La Jolla Farms neighborhood—even William Black, who developed this neighborhood in the 1950s, would probably be amazed at the enormity of some.

There is no coastal access at the Scripps Coastal Reserve trail, but the bluff-side views take in the beach, Scripps Pier, La Jolla Cove, and even the kelp forests of La Jolla's underwater preserve. On a clear day, see if you can spot dolphins or leopard sharks from on high.

Less than a half mile north on La Jolla Farms Road is the paved access down Black's Canyon, which takes hikers all the way to Black's Beach. This is a well-known, clothing-optional beach, as well as the site of a popular surf break also known as Black's. This road to the beach is much easier and less dangerous than the longer and unpaved path that goes down to Black's Beach from the glider port. This paved trailhead begins where Black Gold Road dead-ends onto La Jolla Farms Road; a metal gate system alerts you to the public access. Still part of UCSD's NRS, the paved road to the beach here is steep, but switchbacks make it a little easier.

When you get to the beach, go north to the swimsuit-optional zone as well as the surf break. Heading south will take you to Dike Rock with its tide pools in about a half mile. Check tide tables before you go and aim for low tide.

Thomas Brothers Map: Page 1227, J-2.

Before You Go: Download a copy of the trail map at the Scripps Coastal reserve website, http://nrs.ucsd.edu/reserves/scripps.html.

No bikes, dogs, or vehicles are allowed here.

Trailheads: Find Scripps Coastal Reserve trailhead just 0.1 mile on La Jolla Farms Road after its intersection with La Jolla Shores Drive. La Jolla Farms Road is the first intersection west on La Jolla Shores Drive from Torrey Pines Road.

The paved beach access is also on La Jolla Farms Road, about 0.4 mile north from Scripps Coastal Reserve, where Black Gold Road dead-ends onto La Jolla Farms Road.

Parking is limited on the street.

Distance/Difficulty: The Knoll Trail is about a half-mile loop. The Black Canyon Road access to Black's Beach is about a half-mile one way. Easy.

1-7. Torrey Pines Reserve One of the County's Finest

Torrey Pines State Natural Reserve offers the most extensive trail system in a natural setting on San Diego's coast. Surely it ranks as one of the finest such recreational gems in all of Southern California. Lots of people think so: some 1.6 million visitors a year head to Torrey Pines.

George Marston and Ellen Browning Scripps would be pleased. City father Marston, along with botanists David Cleveland and Belie Angler, persuaded the city council in 1899 to set aside 364 acres of former pueblo lands as a public park. When the lands surrounding the park were in danger of being developed, local newspaperwoman and philanthropist Scripps bought two additional lots and willed them to San Diego in 1911.

The Torrey pine itself is the rarest native pine tree in the Americas, growing naturally only in this state reserve and on the island of Santa Rosa off Santa Barbara. The tree was officially discovered in 1850 when Dr. Charles Christopher Parry, a medical doctor and a botanist, was in San Diego as part of the U.S.-Mexico Boundary Survey. He studied why plants grew where they did and how Native Americans used them. He named the unique pine tree after his friend, Dr. John Torrey, a leading New York botanist at the time. The Parry Grove Trail remembers the good doctor.

The reserve has been part of the state park system since 1959; its official name was changed to Torrey Pines State Natural Reserve in 2007. It now counts about 1,000 acres in the main reserve with another 200 acres in Torrey Pines Reserve Extension (acquired in 1970), across Los Penasquitos Lagoon in Del Mar.

Guy Fleming, a naturalist and landscaper whose name graces one of the trails, was the park's first custodian in 1921. In 1922, Scripps hired architects Richard Requa and H. L. Jackson to design and build the Torrey Pines Lodge, styled after the Hopi Indian houses of Arizona.

That historic lodge is the reserve's headquarters today, and it is the best place to begin a hike. In the main room, which used to be the lodge restaurant, there are displays of animals and plants that make their home here as well as a small gift shop. Pick up the free brochures that offer excellent information on exploring Torrey Pines Reserve: common wildflowers along the trails, common plants along the trails, and the Torrey pine. The brochures suggest activities for learning on the trails. Hikers can try to find clues left by animals (scat, tracks, pathways, nests); identify the plants in the coastal sage scrub (low-growing, aromatic) community or in the maritime chaparral (dense, prickly) group; and learn the distinguishing characteristics of the Torrey pine (long-grooved needles, five per bundle).

There are six major trails covering about eight miles in the main reserve. The Guy Fleming and Parry Grove trials are more densely populated with Torrey pines, but many of these have been devastated by beetles.

The most popular trail is the Beach Trail. Longtime hikers may recall the Beach Trail was closed for a few years because of erosion safety issues. It's open again all the way to the beach, and now because of coastal erosion, it's actually easier to get to the sand. That ledge precipice at the end of the trail, once pretty scary, is bypassed altogether with a stairway to the beach.

You can take the Beach Trail down and climb back up along the Broken Hill Trail for a longer hike. Or you go back up the Beach Trail and turn north on the Razor Point Trail, which also takes you back to the parking area.

Torrey Pines' Beach Trail is the reserve's most popular trail.

The views from virtually any point in the reserve are so fantastic that it almost doesn't matter which route you choose.

One of the best times to explore Torrey Pines is when summer is over and the tourist crowds are gone. Fall and winter also offer some of the clearest weather, so get ready to gawk at one of the city's true wonders.

Thomas Brothers Map: Page 1207, G-2.

Before You Go: No pets, no food or picnics (except to carry to the beach), and no bikes. Download a copy of the trail map at www.torreypine.org. It is open 8:00 a.m. to sunset daily.

Entrance to the state park includes parking fees ranging from $10–15 depending on day of the week.

Trailhead: From Interstate 5, exit at Carmel Valley Road and head west for about 1.5 miles until you reach Coast Highway 101, where you turn left. After about a mile, the park entrance is on the right at the junction of Camino Del Mar and Torrey Pines Road, where they meet at the beach, between La Jolla and Del Mar. Drive through the park entry fee gate and head up the Torrey Pines Park Road to the top of the hill; there are two parking areas there near the visitor center. The Beach Trail begins near the second lot across the road from the visitor center.

Distance/Difficulty: The Beach Trail is 0.75 mile one-way, Razor Point Trail is 0.66 one way, and Broken Hill Trail is 1.4 miles one way. Easy to moderate.

1-8. See Oak Tunnel, Fossils on Torrey Pines' Broken Hill

"I never cease to have my breath taken away when I come to Torrey Pines," said Sarah Ontill, a visiting student from Cal Poly Pomona on the state reserve's Broken Hill Trail. It was slightly overcast that day, yet the path through the chaparral to the scenic overlook of the "broken hill" and the mesmerizing constancy of the ocean waves were as compelling as ever.

The Broken Hill Trail is the longest in the Torrey Pines State Natural Reserve. It has two forks. Reaching the beach from the north fork is 1.4 miles long, and it's 1.3 miles from the south fork. You can reach the Broken Hill overlook from either fork, and both trails converge just before reaching the beach.

Fall and winter are good times to hike in Torrey Pines because the summer crowds are gone, and you can more easily find parking on weekends at the top of the reserve.

The Broken Hill Trail is accessed along an old paved road about a quarter-mile south from the southern-most parking lot.

Torrey Pines' Broken Hill Trail is the state reserve's longest trail to the beach.

This old road, called Torrey Pines Park Road, was once part of the main highway between San Diego and Los Angeles, according to a placard placed there. It was built in 1910 and paved in 1915, all early years in the life of the state reserve.

In 1899, San Diego's city council set aside 364 acres of pueblo lands here for a public park. Local philanthropist Ellen Browning Scripps bought additional lots of pueblo land here between 1908 and 1911 and willed them to the people of San Diego. Guy Fleming of the San Diego Society of Natural History was appointed first custodian of the park in 1921.

The road's hairpin curve near the Guy Fleming Trail, at the northern end of the park, was the scene of so many accidents that local officials finally built a new roadway (the current Torrey Pines Road) in 1933, closing this end of the old road.

This part of Torrey Pines was also site of Camp Callan from 1941 to 1945, according to another placard along the old road. Stretching from the Broken Hill area south to UCSD, Camp Callan, an "instant city" for 15,000 residents, was a training camp for long-range artillery during World War II. The trails of Torrey Pines provided a natural obstacle course for soldiers, who dubbed the area Hell's Acres. The camp was dismantled in November 1945, and virtually no trace of it remains.

The Broken Hill Trail still offers a workout, but today it is considered a pleasant experience. It's a winding trail with little shade that meanders through an unusual form of chaparral habitat called maritime chaparral. One of the most common habitats in our county, chaparral is composed mainly of hard-leaved shrubs with thick, small, evergreen leaves; the plants are drought-tolerant and are specially adapted to survive wildfires. Maritime chaparral has been shaped by ocean winds and the extra moisture from coastal fog, according to Torrey Pines' website. You'll find one of the best specimens of the characteristic shrubs of this plant community on the Broken Hill North Fork trail. An old, twisty Nuttall's scrub oak shrub forms a thick canopy over the trail, creating a virtual tunnel.

The Broken Hill Trail also offers an excellent opportunity to observe the geology of Torrey Pines. The geology pages on the reserve's website state that all the rock layers at Torrey Pines are sedimentary and are divided into four formations according to age. The Delmar Formation and Torrey Pines Sandstone are the oldest at 48 million years old, followed by the Lindavista Formation (1 million years old) and the Bay Point Formation (120,000–400,000 years old).

Flat Rock, the distinctive landmark just off the coast at the end of this trail, is a sea stack remaining after wave erosion of the Delmar Formation. When you reach the beach, see if you can determine these layers and find their fossil shells.

The end of the Broken Hill Trail at the beach also converges with the reserve's most popular Beach Trail. You can choose to return to the top via the Beach Trail, which ends at the parking area, or go back the longer way on the Broken Hill Trail.

Thomas Brothers Map: Page 1207, H-3.

Before You Go: Download a map of the trails in Torrey Pines at its website, www.torreypine. org (note it is singular, not plural). There is a great deal of information on this website about its history, plants, animals and their tracks, and more.

Trailhead: From Interstate 5, exit at Carmel Valley Road and head west until you reach Coast Highway 101, where you turn left. The park entrance is on the right just before the highway begins to climb the Torrey Pines hill. There is a checkpoint entry here where you pay $10–15 per car per day. Continue uphill to the top of the mesa, where there are two parking areas. The first one to the east is closest to the historic visitor center, and the second to the west is nearest the old road to Broken Hill Trail.

Distance/Difficulty: From 2.0 to 3.0 miles round-trip, depending on your route. Easy.

1-9. Torrey Pines' Yucca Point Makes Fine Loop Trail

Make a loop of Yucca Point and Razor Point trails in Torrey Pines State Natural Reserve for a gorgeous seaside stroll on a priceless piece of coastal land that's been protected since 1899. Both these trails have been upgraded in recent years, following closures that resulted in major safety improvements on these bluff-top vistas.

If you're lucky, you might walk with one of the learned docents who complete several study sessions in order to share knowledge of this extraordinary place. When I was there in early August, Ken King, former Torrey Pines Docent Society president,

Yucca Point is an ocean bluff in Torrey Pines State Natural Reserve.

who is now a lifetime docent there, led me and a few other hikers down the trail to Yucca Point.

"Virtually all the trees here—and all the pine trees—are Torrey pines," he told us. The rarest native pine tree in the Americas, the Torrey pine grows naturally only in this area of the Torrey Pines reserve and on Santa Rosa Island in the Channel Islands off Santa Barbara. They probably originated on that island, but "no one knows why they're only there and here," King told me. "Birds or native peoples may have brought them over."

The Torrey pine, Pinus torreyana, was named in 1850 for Dr. John Torrey (one of the leading botanists of that time) by Dr. Charles Parry who was the first to describe it as a species.

The Torrey pine is distinguished by its long needles, usually in bundles of five. The needles are eight to 10 inches long and are grooved. "Their needles are so long so they can condense the fog," King said, adding that about 30 percent of the tree's water needs comes from that coastal fog.

The Kumeyaay who lived in this area near the Los Penasquitos Lagoon used the Torrey pine for many purposes, according to a pamphlet on the tree published by the Torrey Pines Docent Society. They harvested its pine nuts for food, used its pitch to repair cracks in pottery, and utilized its pine needles to weave baskets.

As we stood on top of the coastal bluff that is Yucca Point, King noted that metates and morteros, evidence of ancient peoples, are found "a couple miles out in the ocean. Less than 1,000 years ago, the shoreline was farther out there," he said. You might be able to see some of these ancient grinding sites on a very low tide in early winter.

Yucca Point is named for the mojave yucca that grows here. The only other yucca in the reserve is our lord's candle, King said, which sends out its single tall bloom before it dies. The mojave yucca, however, is not monocarpic (meaning it dies after it blooms); its cream-colored flowers appear every spring.

The mojave yucca was also used by native people to make rope and baskets, King noted.

"The only edible part is its fruit. All the plants in the reserve adapt to drought," King told us. "The scrub oak has tiny leaves, since it lives on only a few inches of rain a year. Chamise has oil on its leaves to help it retain water." If you spot a small red ball on a scrub oak here, that's a gall, a protective coating formed by an insect and the shrub that help insects protect their larvae, King told us as he pointed to one.

When you reach Yucca Point, you might note the trail has been moved back from the edge. Its former platform has been removed and new benches are in place.

Heading back up, take the first left at a trail T intersection to head north to Razor Point for another one of those bluff-top vistas. Then head northeast back uphill on the Razor Point Trail to the parking area

You'll note all the "badlands," those fascinating sandstone testaments to erosion that are characteristic of Torrey Pines reserve.

Very near the Razor Point trail end, look for a Torrey pine with an unusual growth in its branches, a very dense ball of Torrey pine needles.

"Those are called a witch's broom," King told me. "We have four in the reserve." The other three are nearer to the Guy Fleming Trail.

"They're not a parasite, but a mutation or something that irritated the tree, so it forgot to make branches," he said. "They are genetically the same, with the same five long needles per bundle."

The Torrey pine trees are widely used by the bird populations. Ravens, hawks, kestrels, woodpeckers, finches, sparrows, hummingbirds, bushtits, warblers, scrub jays, and quail make use of the trees for shelter, nesting, and food.

Another lifetime docent, Jack Friery, is a birding expert. San Diego County is a birding hotspot with some of the most sightings of any county in the country. "The most exciting bird here is the peregrine falcon," Friery told me. "They are the fastest animal in the world—three times faster than cheetahs, diving at 200 miles per hour." The favorite foods of these beautiful falcons are pigeons, doves, and ducks, Friery said. Males and females hunt in tandem as teams, and they build nests on natural platforms in the sandstone cliffs of Torrey Pines reserve that flank the beach. "We had four babies one year, three this year," Friery said. You might spot those babies around March.

The Torrey Pines Docent Society was formed in 1975—one of the oldest volunteer groups in the entire California State Park system—and today counts about 200 volunteers who lead walks, staff the lodge visitor center, and perform special projects from trail cleanup to publications. Docent training begins in February each year and runs through May (most Saturdays 9:00 a.m. to noon). For more information on becoming one, go to www.torreypine.org.

Thomas Brothers Map: Page 1207, G-2.

Before You Go: Download a trail map from the Torrey Pines State Natural Reserve website, www.torreypine.org. Trails are for hikers only.
   Note that this is a reserve, so no dogs are allowed, even on the beach. No food either, except on the beach.
   If you go to www.torreypines.org, you'll find the Torrey Pines Association, the nonprofit environmental organization dedicated to preserving this natural gem and founded in 1950 by Guy Fleming, the reserve's first custodian hired in 1921.

Trailhead: From Interstate 5, exit at Carmel Valley Road and head west until you reach Coast Highway 101, where you turn left. The park entrance is on the right just before the highway begins to climb the Torrey Pines hill. There is a checkpoint entry here where you pay $10–15 per car per day. Continue uphill to the top of the mesa, where there are two parking areas. Park near the visitor center in the historic Torrey Pines Lodge.
   From the lodge, head west across the road and the second parking area toward the trailheads, and begin on the Beach Trail. Then follow signs to Yucca Point. From Yucca Point, head north to Razor Point and then back up the hill to the parking area.

Distance/Difficulty: The Yucca Point/Razor Point loop hike is just shy of 2.0 miles total; easy with less than 200 feet elevation gain.

1-10. Combine Two Shortest Trails in Torrey Pines

The two shortest trails in Torrey Pines State Natural Reserve can be combined for an easy hike that still features some fantastic ocean views.

Start on the High Point Overlook. Just north of the historic Torrey Pines Lodge, the reserve's visitor center, High Point Overlook is a mere 100 yards long, most of it a series of steps up to the overlook.

The views from this short trail extend to the north, to the ocean and across the historic 1933 bridge over Soledad Creek and the railroad tracks that are part of Old Highway 101, as well as to the northeast across the flat, green Los Penasquitos Lagoon. Another vantage point here offers views directly east, across the lagoon and I-5 into Sorrento Valley.

A placard at this overlook commemorates beloved philanthropist Ellen Browning Scripps (1836–1932), who helped create Torrey Pines State Natural Reserve. "Although the City of San Diego had set aside some land to preserve the Torrey pines, the best and densest groves remained in the hands of developers who planned to subdivide and commercialize the area," reports the placard. "Miss Scripps bought these lots in 1908, 1911 and 1912" with the intention of preservation.

She built the Torrey Pines Lodge in 1922–23, designed by local architects Richard Requa and H. L. Jackson, to serve as a restaurant. She donated it to the people of San

Diego, and today it is the reserve's visitor center. Upon her death in 1932, Miss Scripps bequeathed these lands and their groves of Torrey pines to the City of San Diego, asking that they "be held in perpetuity as a public park." It became part of the California state parks system in 1959.

Just across the reserve's road—also historic, built in 1910, and paved in 1915 as the main route then between San Diego and Los Angeles—is the Parry Grove Trail. It's named after Charles Christopher Parry (1823–1890), who himself named the Torrey pine tree after his friend and fellow botanist, John Torrey. Like Torrey, Parry was a medical doctor who found he preferred botany to medicine, according to Hank Nichol's account on the Torrey Pines reserve's history web page. Parry was one of several botanists on the 1850 expedition that surveyed the new boundary declared after the U.S.-Mexican War of 1846–1848.

The view from Torrey Pines' High Point Trail
extends across Los Penasquitos Lagoon.

Although native peoples as well as settlers knew of the tree, Parry is considered the discoverer of the Torrey pine because he officially named it Pinus Torreyana. Its namesake, New Yorker John Torrey, never actually saw these groves. Parry also realized it was "endangered" as early as 1883 and wrote to the San Diego Society of Natural History of the need to protect them.

The Parry Grove Trail was once the home of the densest groves of Torrey pines, including the oldest specimens that were some 200 years old, according to Nichol's account. But drought and bark beetle infestations have devastated these stands so that only a few remain.

This trail is sometimes closed due to wet, rainy weather. At the beginning of this loop is a steep entry/exit climb of nearly 100 rugged steps that can be very dangerous if slippery, so park rangers close it during wet conditions. Even if you can't make it all the way down the Parry Grove loop, the Whitaker Garden at its trailhead makes an educational diversion. Here are specimens of common native plants, each identified with an informative sign that sometimes gives its Kumeyaay name as well as early native uses.

I learned, for example, on the sign for velvet cactus that cactus spines are actually modified leaves that help protect the plant from predators while also conserving water. The cliff spurge has the same poisonous milky sap as its relative the poinsettia, which can cause blindness if it gets in your eyes. The lemonadeberry's pink berries are coated with a sour, lemon-like substance that native Indians used to make a refreshing drink.

The Whitaker Garden is named for Dr. Thomas W. Whitaker, a conservationist dedicated to the preservation of Torrey Pines State Reserve in its natural state. He was president of the Torrey Pines Association from 1963 to 1985 and was instrumental in securing and preserving the 168 acres and their 1,500 Torrey pine trees in what is now known as Torrey Pines Extension, across Los Penasquitos Lagoon in Del Mar. Dr. Whitaker was a horticultural geneticist who also had been a research associate at Scripps Institution of Oceanography. A bench in this educational garden is also inscribed to Dr. Whitaker's wife, "Mary S. Whitaker Memorial Garden." Sit a spell and ponder the protected beauty of Torrey Pines State Natural Reserve.

Thomas Brothers Map: Page 1207, G-2, where North Torrey Pines Road hits the ocean; the turn west into the reserve is the dotted line there ...

Before You Go: Check the reserve's website, www.torreypine.org (yes, it is singular), for trail maps and closure information.

It costs $10–15 to park in the reserve's parking lots, payable at the guard station at the reserve entrance off North Torrey Pines Road.

Hikers only; no dogs allowed.

Trailhead: From Interstate 5, exit at Carmel Valley Road and head west until you reach Coast Highway 101, where you turn left. The park entrance is on the right just before the highway begins to climb the Torrey Pines hill. There is a checkpoint entry here where you pay $10–15 per car per day. Continue uphill to the top of the mesa, where there are two parking areas.

Park in either of the two lots at the top. To reach the trailheads for both the High Point Lookout and Parry Grove trails, head north from those parking lots a short way on the reserve road.

Difficulty/Distance: Combining the two trails results in a hike that's less than a mile. Easy, except for the steep steps in both trails.

1-11. Guy Fleming Trail in Torrey Pines Is Excellent Choice

"I try very hard to get people to hike the Guy Fleming Trail," wrote Hank Nichol in 1994 in "Notes from the Naturalist," on Torrey Pines State Natural Reserve's website. "I tell them how easy a walk it is. I tell them it has great views of the ocean. Ten minutes later, I see them out on the Beach Trail. The Fleming Trail is a much better choice if you come (in) flip-flops, or if you may have to lug a tired kid, or if you are as old as I am and can't hike so fast anymore."

As a matter of fact, the Guy Fleming Trail in Torrey Pines is the easiest trail in that natural reserve and is far less traveled typically than the popular Beach Trail. A loop of only two-thirds of a mile, it not only offers splendid views of the ocean, both south to La Jolla and north up Torrey Pines State Beach to Del Mar and the Los Penasquitos Lagoon, but it has more Pinus Torreyana—the park's namesake—than any of the other trails. The nation's rarest pine tree, the Torrey pine, grows only here and on Santa Rosa Island, the second-largest of the Channel Islands off Santa Barbara. Many of the trees extend their canopies right over this trail, and it's easy to learn to identify this tree that is closely connected with San Diego.

**Guy Fleming Trail in Torrey Pines is easy and features
many of the park's namesake pines.**

As an evergreen, Torrey pines typically have long needles (eight to 13 inches), five in every bundle, according to the National Audubon Society's *Field Guide to Trees, Western Region*. Their pine cones are four to six inches, egg-shaped, and bent down on stout stalks, with very large, edible seeds.

Groves of these pine trees were more abundant a few hundred years ago, but a plaque on the Fleming Trail points out that they were never plentiful enough to be a major food source to the indigenous people.

When Spanish explorers came to this area (AD 1500–1700), the trees were called Soledad Pines (Solitary Pines), according to the park's website. But in 1850, the tree was officially renamed after it was "discovered" by Dr. Charles Christopher Parry, for whom another trail in the park is named. Parry, a medical doctor, was in San Diego as a botanist for the U.S.-Mexico Boundary Survey that year, when California became a state. Parry named the tree for his friend and colleague, Dr. John Torrey of New York, who was a leading botanist at the time.

According to an informative plaque on the trail, the nearby ocean breezes literally prune the tops of Torrey pine trees, giving them distinctive, twisted shapes. The deeply furrowed bark on the trees helps defend it against bark beetles when rainfall is sufficient. However, drought stresses the trees, and the bark beetles can then kill them. One sign reports that a severe drought and bark beetle outbreak killed many trees in the mid-1960s. Strings of black funnels hanging from trees today are beetle traps.

There are also lots of wildflowers on this trail during spring and summer. In its coastal sage scrub and chaparral habitats, there are some 400 species of flowering plants. In late June, I spotted the yellow mariposa lily, purple sand verbena, yellow rock rose, white three-spot, white morning glory, golden yarrow, yellow sun cup, red Mexican pink, purple wild snapdragon, and the red Indian paintbrush.

Add the views of the ocean, when clear days may bring glimpses of dolphins cavorting in the waves (or at least surfers trying to catch them), and one must thank Guy Fleming, who was the park's first resident caretaker and began the trail system here. Born in Nebraska in 1884, Fleming came to San Diego at age 25 in 1909. He became chief guide for the plants and landscaping at the then new Balboa Park when the Panama-California Exposition took place there in 1915. He became interested in the unusual Torrey pine tree that grew on the coast just south of Del Mar, where the best specimens stood on land owned by Ellen Browning Scripps, noted historic philanthropist. She had bought the land specifically to preserve the trees and hired Fleming in 1921 to be custodian and naturalist.

Fleming also played a key role as well in creating Anza-Borrego, Cuyamaca, Palomar and Mount San Jacinto state parks. In 1950, he founded the Torrey Pines Association, dedicated to this day to preserving the trees and their habitat. He died in La Jolla at 75 in 1960.

Be sure to stop by the park's headquarters in the historic Torrey Pines Lodge, built in 1922 by Ellen Browning Scripps as a restaurant. You can pick up free trail maps and plant guides there.

Thomas Brothers Map: Page 1207, G-2.

Before You Go: Visit the Torrey Pines State Natural Reserve's website, www.torreypine.org (singular tense), for maps and other information. The park is open daily from 9:00 a.m. to 8:00 p.m. during summer, closing at sunset during winter. The visitor center is open from 9:00 a.m. to 6:00 p.m. during summer, and 10:00 a.m. to 4:00 p.m. during winter.

Parking Fees: It costs $10–15 for a day use fee to enter the park.

Trailhead: From Interstate 5, exit at Carmel Valley Road and head west until you reach Coast Highway 101, where you turn left. The park entrance is on the right just before the highway begins to climb the Torrey Pines hill. There is a checkpoint entry here where you pay $10–15 per car per day. Continue uphill to the top of the mesa; the Fleming Trail parking area is on the west side of the road before you reach the visitor center.

Distance/Difficulty: The Guy Fleming Trail is two-thirds of a mile in a loop trail. Easy.

1-12. Marsh Trail Winds through Los Penasquitos Lagoon

A lesser-known trail in Torrey Pines State Natural Reserve is the Marsh Trail that winds through Los Penasquitos Lagoon.

This trail actually lies within the Los Penasquitos Salt Marsh Preserve, part of Torrey Pines reserve, which manages the especially picturesque lagoon that lies between La Jolla and Del Mar.

Reach the trail across North Torrey Pines Road from Torrey Pines' South Beach entrance. You'll find the trailhead a bit south of this entrance on the east side of the road; look for the trailhead sign denoting no dogs or bikes allowed.

Los Penasquitos Lagoon and Marsh is designated a state preserve, which allows the most restricted usage, compared to a state park (free public access and recreational use) or a state reserve (restricted access and usage). Los Penasquitos Lagoon and Salt Marsh Preserve is closed to all boats and hiking is allowed only on the single Marsh/Flintkote Trail. The end of Flintkote Avenue is the trail's eastern gateway, located west of Sorrento Valley.

Los Penasquitos Lagoon's Marsh Trail is a lesser-known opportunity in Torrey Pines.

Beginning at the west end of the Marsh Trail, you'll wind around the western edge of the lagoon on the backside of the towering cliffs of Torrey Pines reserve. The entire trail is navigable now during this third year of drought; in wet years, some of it may be underwater.

The lagoon is formed where the Los Penasquitos River drains into the ocean. According to the Los Penasquitos Lagoon Foundation, a nonprofit formed in 1983 to manage the salt marsh preserve in partnership with the state parks, the lagoon was probably a bay 10,000 to 20,000 years ago after polar ice caps melted. Since then, sediment brought from the river has filled in most of the valley, forming extensive mudflats allowing relatively shallow channels.

"Until 1925, man had not greatly interfered with the normal lagoon drainage," says the foundation. But when the Santa Fe Railroad line was built, its tracks were built through the center of the lagoon valley, dividing it into its present northeast and southwest portions, significantly altering tidal currents. When the Pacific Coast Highway (North Torrey Pines Road here) was expanded in the 1930s, the lagoon entrance was shifted south to its present location near the old McGonigle Bridge.

The foundation's main function is to keep the lagoon's mouth open, restore habitat, and improve channel circulation.

I spotted several fish in those narrow channels. About 15 kinds of fish have been found here, the more common species being the California killifish, a small olive-green fish with a flattened head; the California halibut, a flatfish that uses the lagoon as a nursery; the bay topsmelt, with a greenish dorsal surface; and the mudsucker, a slender, yellow-bellied fish that hides in channel banks and hibernates in the bottom mud during the winter months.

After about the first mile on the Marsh Trail, you'll come very close to one of those channels where you might see those fish. You will also now be fairly close to the railroad tracks where Amtrak and Coaster trains fly by periodically.

You'll curve back west to edge closer to that backside of Torrey Pines reserve, where its eponymous Torrey pines, one of the rarest trees anywhere, dot the ridge line. You'll also see a few Torrey pines in this marsh area—usually lone specimens but some very old, big ones.

At about 1.75 miles, the trail becomes an old, paved road that keeps on going to that Flintkote Avenue in the industrial area of Sorrento Valley west of I-5. I went a short ways, and at about the two-mile point, I turned around and headed back.

The trail is lined in this upper marsh area with lots of yellow-blooming goldenbush as well as lemonadeberry shrubs. Back toward those lower-elevation channels of water, you'll find many salt marsh plants, including pickleweed and alkali heath. Look also for salt grass, sea lavender (pale violet flowers in midsummer), and California seablite with its small, greenish flowers and water-swollen leaves that turn orange in late summer.

In one lone part of the trail where it was quite wet, I saw a couple of fiddler crabs in the mud. These are small crabs easily recognized by their "stalked eyes and by the one large claw brandished by the males," according to "Natural Preserve and Lagoon," from the Torrey Pines State Natural Reserve's information on Los Penasquitos Marsh. "During courtship, this claw is waved back and forth, thus suggesting the crab's name."

I also saw snowy egrets with their yellow feet and black bills, great egrets with their yellow bills and black feet, a pair of osprey circling above the marsh, and a white-tailed kite perched on a wooden post deep in the lagoon. "The kites, which only a few years ago were in danger of extinction, are becoming commoner in the reserve," says "Natural Preserve and Lagoon."

When I reached my start, about four miles round-trip, I headed south on Torrey Pines beach to see whether I could spot any peregrine falcons. I had recently been told by Jack Friery, a docent at Torrey Pines, that these magnificent falcons ("the fastest animal in the world—three times faster than cheetahs—diving at 200 miles per hour") nest in the natural platforms and holes in the sandstone cliffs of Torrey Pines reserve that flank the beach. I didn't see any this time, but maybe they are more active in the early and late hours of the day.

One caveat about the Marsh Trail: I came home with several mosquito bites, so protect yourself.

Thomas Brothers Map: Page 1207, G-2.

Before You Go: Download a copy of the Marsh Trail map from Torrey Pines State Natural Reserve's pages on hiking trails: http://www.torreypine.org/img/activities/maps/trailmap-2-high.pdf. Go to the detailed map on the second page for the Marsh Trail.
This trail is open only to hikers and joggers.

Trailhead: From Interstate 5, exit at Carmel Valley Road and head west until you reach Coast Highway 101, where you turn left. The park entrance is on the right just before the highway begins to climb the Torrey Pines hill. There is a checkpoint entry here where you pay $10–15 per car per day. Enter the south beach parking area on your left.
The trailhead for the Marsh Trail is across Coast Highway 101 from the park entrance; watch for traffic before crossing the highway.

Distance/Difficulty: About 4.0 to 5.0 miles round-trip; easy.

1-13. Torrey Pines State Reserve Extension a Quieter Gem

Torrey Pines State Natural Reserve is one of the most beautiful hiking areas in the urban core, and as such it's well known and well traveled.

Far fewer hikers venture a few miles away to Torrey Pines State Natural Reserve Extension, which is well worth exploring. The extension is located across Los Penasquitos Lagoon from the main reserve. Though situated in a Del Mar neighborhood, once you enter the extension's pristine lands, you see very few people and very few houses along the upper cliff edges. The scenery here seems even a bit more beautiful than in the main reserve, perhaps because it is so little traveled or maybe because more trees live here.

There are a few trails in the extension, and some of them are marked at their beginnings. Connectors and other trails are not as well marked. Even so, it would be very difficult to get lost here because the extension isn't large, and any one of the trails covers only a mile or less. You can wander several of the pathways and spend a few hours here, or follow one of the trails for about two miles round-trip in about an hour.

From the extension entry at the cul-de-sac end of Del Mar Scenic Parkway, you will shortly come to a Y intersection where signs point right to the Margaret Fleming Nature Trail A, or left to the Margaret Fleming Nature Trail B, also known as the Mar Scenic Trail. Take the B left turn if you want to head toward ocean views.

The easy sandy trail goes through a natural wash of deep sand and continues past evidence of some old rock foundations. Right after the foundations, take a left at an unmarked trail spur. You are now heading to the West Ridge DAR trail, funded by the Daughters of the American Revolution.

Walk past the gnarly old Torrey pines, which you can identify by noting that each bundle has five needles; their needles are also notably long for pine trees. Note the sandstone cliffs that erosion has sculpted into fascinating forms.

The west DAR trail in Torrey Pines Extension leads to lagoon and ocean views.

After winding up the trail punctuated with a few old railroad ties for steps, you'll come to a T intersection. Now you can see the lagoon and the ocean spread out below, through those Torrey pine needles. Taking a right at the T intersection winds into a little hollow for a fairly short distance. Take the left at the T, and you'll head toward the DAR trail, which affords fantastic views of the lagoon and the ocean. From here you can also see the main Torrey Pines State Natural Reserve across the lagoon.

Wildflowers are abundant here, including wand chicory, buckwheat, and morning glory vines. Coastal scrub oak abounds, as does the chamise shrub. This entire area is a coastal sage scrub environment.

Rattlesnakes live here according to a sign at the trailhead informs, and they are an important part of the ecosystem. They "will not attack, but if disturbed or cornered will defend themselves. Give them distance and respect." If you do happen to see one on the trail, simply stop and give it plenty of time and space to leave.

Entry into the extension is free (there is a fee for the main part of the reserve). Hours are 7:00 a.m. to sunset. No dogs or bikes allowed.

Thomas Brothers Map: Page 1207, H-1.

Before You Go: Download a trail map of the extension from Torrey Pines State Natural Reserve web pages, www.torreypine.org.
     No dogs, bicycles or food allowed.

Trailhead: From Interstate 5, exit at Carmel Valley Road and head west. Turn right onto Del Mar Scenic Parkway and go to the end of this street, parking in the cul-de-sac.

Distance/Difficulty: About 2.0 miles round-trip; easy.

1-14. Margaret Fleming Trail's Nature Guide Found Again

"If we have the foresight to provide a network of urban forests, tangled stretches like the one proposed to extend Torrey Pines, then people will always have a place to go to find a sense of their source, and an escape from their crowded present," said Del Mar's Gloria Bates in 1967. She and her husband, Robert, were among the first activists to sound the clarion call in 1964 to protect the Del Mar canyon, which is now Torrey Pines State Natural Reserve's Extension Area. Several years later, with help from the Torrey Pines Association, donations came in from all over the country to purchase this precious stand of Torrey pine trees, preserving them from development.

In Del Mar, across Los Penasquitos Lagoon from the main reserve, Torrey Pines Extension adds almost 200 acres to the beloved natural reserve, protecting some 1,500 more of the Pinus Torreyana trees—the rarest pine tree in North America, which grows naturally only here and on Santa Rosa Island in the Channel Islands off Santa Barbara.

About three to four miles of trails traverse the TP extension. They are far less traveled than the trails in the main reserve, yet they offer a similar landscape complete with bluffs and ocean views. One of the least traveled of these trails, the Margaret Fleming Nature Trail, also offers some natural history lessons that enhance anyone's appreciation.

From the extension's entrance off Del Mar Scenic Parkway, head northeast on the Margaret Fleming Nature Trail, Trail A, and you'll soon encounter numbered posts, starting with No. 10. These posts were originally the brainchild of Del Mar Heights Elementary School teacher Carol Mason in the 1970s, who applied for a grant to create this trail where children could learn natural history in the field. The original posts are gone, but the ones there now were replaced by a local Boy Scout troop, according to Maryruth Cox. Cox's husband, Charles, is a professor emeritus of Scripps Institution of Oceanography, where he first started working as an oceanographer in 1948. She has lived near Torrey Pines Extension since 1953 and continues writing about its history.

The new numbered posts were moved a bit from the originals, so Maryruth Cox wrote the current guide in 2008. That guide, however, is out of print. I had to track her down to locate a copy, and I hope that readers will ask the state reserve to reprint it.

The Margaret Fleming Nature Trail was named for the wife of Guy Fleming, Torrey Pines' first park custodian, hired by Ellen Browning Scripps in 1921. Margaret Fleming, known as Peggy, lived for decades with her husband and children in a 1927 adobe not far from the main park's 1923 lodge, which is now its headquarters.

Post No. 10 on the Margaret Fleming trail sits in dry brush. Cox's guide points out how plants in the extension survive extended drought, because only rainwater sustains these plants here. "The lemonadeberry that sprawls to the south has tough leaves that resist water loss; its virulent red berries (visible in July) are covered with a sticky goo that no doubt helps conserve water," the guide says.

Look to the east of Post. No. 6. "The long ridge of red sandstone that lies across the canyon heads is called the Linda Vista (beautiful view) formation," Cox writes. "It caps the bulky beds of the yellowish-white Torrey Sandstone."

At Post No. 4, "No houses are visible from this post ... Smell the black sage, note the clusters of tiny white flowers on the toyon ... Plants in arid climates often have strong odors, such as California sage, black sage and yerba santa, all found here. Their pungent scents and brilliant blossoms compete to attract the scarce insects. In rain forests where insects are plentiful, plants often are without fragrance and with pale flowers."

Torrey Pines Extension's Margaret Fleming Trail once had numbered posts with guide.

Interestingly, the brilliant red scarlet larkspur is in full bloom during summer in the extension and is not found in the main reserve.

The trail no longer goes near Post. No. 1. After you reach Post No. 2, the trail reaches its highest point, with some fine ocean views. Keep to the right across the sandstone. At an unmarked junction, the trail to the right winds around the ball field of the elementary school and soon reaches a street. Go left at this junction, following a short ridge to a long wooden staircase. This unmarked trail is the Gully Trail, which crosses the extension to reach the main Mar Scenic Trail. Do not be deterred by the heavy grasses here; you can trudge through them.

When you reach the main trail, head north a short way to an intersection on your left. Take that to reach the Daughters of the American Revolution Trail, which will lead you as close to the ocean as this extension allows. Another connector trail heads east to take you back to the main trail; head south back to your starting point.

Thanks to those who saved this urban forest. "It is a treasure to be cherished in its natural state, a bit of the original Southern California environment that has been left unscarred by urban development," writes Maryruth Cox.

Thomas Brothers Map: Page 1207, H-1, where Del Mar Scenic Parkway ends.

Before You Go: Go to the website for Torrey Pines State Natural Reserve for more information and for trail maps. For a map of Torrey Pines Extension trails, go to http://www.torreypine.org/img/activities/maps/extension_trail_guide.pdf. One of the best maps for Torrey Pines Extension trails is the aerial one at the state parks' page, http://www.parks.ca.gov/pages/657/files/trailsextension.pdf.

The extension is open 7:00 a.m. to sunset; it's free here. No bikes, dogs, or horses allowed.

Trailhead: From Interstate 5, exit at Carmel Valley Road, heading west. Turn right onto Del Mar Scenic Parkway and park on the street where it ends.

Distance/Difficulty: Varies from 1.0 to 2.0 miles round-trip; easy.

1-15. For Sheer Variety, Hard to Beat San Elijo Lagoon

Instead of whizzing by on Interstate 5, wander through the San Elijo Lagoon Ecological Reserve for an exceptional glimpse of nature. Nearly 1,000 acres of precious coastal wetlands offer more than seven miles of trails through the home of nearly 300 species of birds, 26 species of mammals, 20 species of reptiles and amphibians, and six plant communities.

Coastal wetlands are among the most productive ecosystems in the world, according to the San Elijo Lagoon Conservancy, but they're also among the most threatened. The conservancy says more than 90 percent of Southern California's coastal wetlands have been destroyed since 1850, and all of San Diego County's 16 such habitats now depend on our help to survive.

The San Elijo Lagoon Ecological Reserve is one of the region's largest and most beloved coastal wetlands. It is formed where Escondido and La Orilla creeks meet the Pacific Ocean.

Hikers, joggers, and bird-watchers flock there. The six plant communities are coastal strand, salt marsh, freshwater marsh, riparian scrub, coastal sage scrub, and chaparral, encompassing more than 300 species of plants, some considered rare or endangered.

The Gemma Parks Interpretive Trail, a one-mile loop in the western part of the reserve named for a dedicated conservationist, passes through coastal sage scrub and salt marsh. Several signs identify some of the native species, including arroyo willow, black sage, California buckwheat, coyote brush, and laurel sumac. This trail connects to the reserve's longest trail, which passes under I-5 and continues east.

Eight trailheads provide access to the reserve's 7.5 miles of trails. The Santa Inez trailhead is a good midpoint start. You may cross the lagoon on the dike here, or you can head east or west for longer hikes. I headed west under I-5 so I could wander the western part of the reserve, including the interpretive trail. This made for a three-mile round trip that was especially thrilling for birding.

It's little wonder that the San Elijo Lagoon attracts bird-watchers from around the world. There's an amazing diversity of bird life because of the variety of habitats and mild climate. More than 100 species sighted at the lagoon are rare or uncommon migrants, and 74 are considered sensitive or endangered species. Many are lovely to see.

San Elijo Lagoon is a birder's delight.

During my afternoon, I photographed and then tried to identify what I saw by studying my bird books. I'm no birding expert, but I think I spotted a yellow, ruby-crowned kinglet; a ruby-crowned Hutton's vireo; a stilt sandpiper; American coots; several pairs of mallard ducks; gadwalls; American wigeons; greater scaups; northern shovelers and ruddy ducks; a snowy egret and its bigger version, the great egret; and the most impressive of all, a northern harrier. The northern harrier, which looks like a cross between a hawk and an owl, is a large predator that's a sight to behold.

The San Elijo Lagoon Conservancy offers free, guided nature walks at 10:00 a.m. every Saturday of the month, beginning at the Nature Center, an LEED-certified visitor center for the lagoon that opened in 2009. The Nature Center is an exceptional facility that offers interactive exhibits about the history and ecology of San Elijo Lagoon.

Right in front of the Nature Center is a separate, ADA-accessible, mile-long Nature Center Loop Trail that provides an overview of the lagoon, complete with informational placards along the way.

San Elijo Lagoon's website provides a wealth of information about the lagoon and its habitats and inhabitants. You can download a field checklist of its birds, learn the plants that make up each habitat, locate the various trailheads, and even choose to get involved in the preservation of this valuable natural resource.

Thomas Brothers Map: Page 1167, E-6 (Rios) and G-5 (Santa Inez)

Before You Go: Download a trail map at www.sanelijo.org. It's free to get in.
Dogs permitted only on leashes. No bicycles allowed.

Trailheads: To N. Rios trailhead: From Interstate 5, exit at Lomas Santa Fe, heading west. Turn right on N. Rios Avenue and drive to the end, parking on the street at the cul-de-sac.

To Santa Inez trailhead: From Interstate 5 heading south, exit at Lomas Santa Fe and turn left, going under I-5; take the first left on Santa Helena, then left on Santa Rosita, left on Santa Florencia, and left on Santa Inez to the end. From Interstate 5 heading north, exit at Lomas Santa Fe, continuing directly onto Santa Helena (do not turn on Lomas Santa Fe), then turn left on Santa Rosita, left on Santa Florencia, and left on Santa Inez to the end.

Distance/Difficulty: About 3.0 miles round-trip between Santa Inez and Rios avenues; easy.

1-16. The Quiet End Of San Elijo Lagoon

The eastern portion of San Elijo Lagoon offers a less-traveled trail that winds through forests of eucalyptus and a few Torrey pines before it emerges into the coastal sage scrub for glimpses of the namesake lagoon. This lagoon is also an estuary. It's fed by two freshwater streams, La Orilla Creek and Escondido Creek, that mix with seawater on their way to the Pacific Ocean. It's also one of only 16 coastal wetlands remaining in San Diego. Some 90 percent of coastal wetlands in Southern California have been destroyed by development since 1850, so the ones remaining are increasingly important to our region's biodiversity.

Coastal wetlands provide some of the most productive ecosystems in the world because they serve as breeding, resting, and nesting grounds for birds, and as hatcheries and feeding grounds for fish. Nearly 300 species of birds either live here or visit here during their long seasonal migrations. Some 20 species of fish live in the water, and 26 species of mammals live on the shore.

Of course, development always threatens coastal wetlands since the building of roads and railroads alters tidal flows, resulting in the buildup of sediment in the lagoon. San Elijo Lagoon began to see these impacts over 100 years ago, when the first railroad was built across the estuary's mouth in 1882; when the earliest version of Pacific Coast Highway, a wood-plank road, was built in 1891 (and was paved in 1932); and when Interstate 5 was constructed over it in 1965.

To help protect this coastal wetland, the County of San Diego and the California Department of Fish and Wildlife periodically open the lagoon mouth by dredging, so the freshwater and seawater can mingle as they would naturally.

I began my hike by first visiting the lagoon's visitor center at its western end, between Pacific Coast Highway and I-5, which opened in January 2009. There are informative displays and photographs that share the wildlife and habitats found here, as well as some of the area's history. Pick up free brochures that cover each section of the San Elijo Lagoon Ecological Reserve. The reserve covers nearly 1,000 acres and offers about 7.5 miles of hiking and equestrian trails.

The western section is more popular and offers more waterscapes and their accompanying waterfowl. The eastern end passes through more kinds of habitat and offers a serene wander through this rich resource. Equestrians are also welcome here.

I began my hike at the La Orilla trailhead at the eastern edge of the lagoon in Rancho Santa Fe. I saw hawks soaring above, great egrets, and American coots in the water, as well as a few cottontail rabbits on the trail.

San Elijo Lagoon East is quiet and features several habitats.

The first part of the trail passes through riparian woodland, which should feature lots of willow, sycamore, and cottonwood trees. You'll see many wild grape vines, but here, nonnative eucalyptus have invaded, competing with native plants for water. Their leaves also shed certain chemicals that inhibit the growth of other plants. When these eucalyptus trees die or are removed, the nonprofit citizens' land trust group, San Elijo Lagoon Conservancy, plants native trees to restore the riparian habitat.

The next habitat is the marsh, where cattails and reeds dominate along the edges of the lagoon's creeks and ponds. Mule deer graze here along the creek banks.

Chaparral is the next habitat. Scrub oak is abundant, and I spotted several bright blue western scrub jays.

The fourth habitat along this trail is coastal sage scrub, where low-growing shrubs like sage and buckwheat are plentiful. During winter, the bright red berries of toyon prove why they're often called the Christmas berry.

The trail continues through a power line easement, where some very large Torrey Pines are found. Identify them by noting their long needles and the grouping of five to a bundle.

The La Orilla trail is 3.5 miles from its eastern trailhead to the western end of the lagoon's trail system. I turned around at the flood control dike just before Interstate 5, which covers about 1.5 miles one-way.

Don't miss the unmarked, short loop spur on the northern side of the trail that takes you to Tern Point. You can't miss it; it's the only spur trail on the northern side. It features a couple of benches that invite you to see how many birds you can spot in the water. While retracing my way back, I saw several adorable cottontail rabbits on the trail, who stopped to ponder my intentions before they scurried back into the scrub.

Thomas Brothers Map: Page 1167, J-5, right where El Camino Real makes a 90-degree turn at La Orilla.

Before You Go: Go to the county's web page, http://www.co.san-diego.ca.us/parks/openspace/selr.html, or to the conservancy's web page, www.sanelijo.org, for more information and trail maps.
Open only to hikers and dogs on leashes.

Trailhead: For La Orilla trailhead, from Interstate 5, exit at Lomas Santa Fe, heading east. Turn left onto Highland Road at the four-way stop, then left onto El Camino Real. Look for the small parking area on the west side of the road, just before El Camino Real makes a sharp ninety-degree bend for a brief continuation on La Orilla Road.

Distance/Difficulty: About 3.0 miles round-trip; allow at least 1.5 hours. It's flat, easy.

1-17. Yellow Wildflowers, Birds Thrive at San Dieguito Lagoon

Walking along the wide path that is the San Dieguito Lagoon Trail in Del Mar, I saw a fish jump out of the blue water, just inches behind a pure white snowy egret that was foraging on the muddy banks.

Many yellow wildflowers are blooming in spring, including yellow cress, saltwort, some mustard, and crown daisies, sprinkled with bright orange California poppies, purple statice (sometimes known as sea lavender), delicate lavender clarkia, and an occasional patch of pickleweed with bright red flowers.

The trail follows the ocean end of the San Dieguito River, whose 346-square-mile watershed of streams and creeks that feed into it is San Diego County's largest. The river begins on Volcan Mountain, just outside Julian.

The San Dieguito Lagoon Trail is part of the Coast-to-Crest Trail that will eventually traverse 70 miles from the ocean to Volcan Mountain. The San Dieguito River Park (www.sdrp.org/wordpress/), a joint powers authority, was formed in 1989 by the County of San Diego and the cities of Del Mar, Escondido, Poway, San Diego, and Solana Beach to acquire, improve, and maintain the natural open space park along the San Dieguito River Valley. In concert, the San Dieguito River Valley Conservancy (www.sdrvc.org) is a nonprofit organization that helps to implement the river park and its Coast-to-Crest Trail. In addition, Friends of the San Dieguito River Valley (www. fsdrv.org) is an advocacy group for its open space conservation. All these entities offer lots of opportunities to involve yourself.

San Dieguito Lagoon is a 300-acre coastal salt marsh. It was once the largest of San Diego County's six wetlands, some 100 years ago extending east of El Camino Real.

Major filling projects over the years significantly changed the lagoon. The railroad was built across its mouth in 1881; the Pacific Coast Highway was constructed in 1912;

Del Mar's Coast Boulevard home plots began development in the 1920s; and Jimmy Durante Boulevard and the huge Interstate 5 project were built from 1965–67. Del Mar Fairgrounds was placed on 350 acres of wetland fill in the middle of the lagoon in 1936.

San Dieguito Lagoon is a wonderland of springtime wildflowers.

Today the lagoon is smaller than it once was, but some lost wetlands were regained in 2006. That was when San Dieguito Lagoon was selected for an $86 million Southern California Edison Wetlands Restoration Project that created 115 acres of wetlands, benefitting many species, including fish and endangered birds such as the brown pelican, Belding's savannah sparrow, California gnatcatcher, and the least tern.

Some 191 bird species are found in the lagoon, according to a full-color pamphlet produced by Friends of the San Dieguito River Valley. There are more species here during winter than other times of year, especially ducks that migrate during that time of year.

In addition to several snowy egrets (year-round residents), I also spotted a green heron (another full-timer) on the mudflats near the boardwalk portion of the trail, and some California thrashers (permanent residents) in chaparral. Most amazing to see were dozens of cliff swallows that come in the spring and summer to build and tend their nests underneath the I-5 bridge that crosses the lagoon. The trail goes under that freeway, and as soon as you pass it and continue west, the noise levels decrease dramatically.

You'll also encounter some informative placards that educate hikers about the importance of the river water as well as its inhabitants and their favorite foods. I learned that great blue herons eat not only fish but also mice and frogs, whereas the red-tailed hawk eats only mice and snakes.

The boardwalk along this western portion was begun in 2007 to allow hikers to get closer to the salt marsh as it continues the trail to the ocean. The boardwalk portion is open only to pedestrians, but the entire lagoon trail is also open to mountain bikers. Equestrians are allowed on the trail only east of I-5.

The San Dieguito Lagoon Trail ends at Jimmy Durante Boulevard, but you can walk about a block south on that street to reach the River Path Del Mar to continue your hike along the lagoon another quarter-mile. This is a very pretty, landscaped pathway that ends at the railroad tracks.

Retrace your steps back and take another look at those busy swallows.

Thomas Brothers Map: Page 1187, H-2

Before You Go: Download a map of the trail at http://www.sdrp.org/wordpress/wp-content/uploads/10.14-Trail-Map-Lagoon.pdf.
It's free and open to hikers and dogs on leashes.

Trailhead: Exit Interstate 5 at Via de la Valle in Del Mar, heading east. Turn right (south) at the light at San Andres Drive, just after the Albertson's shopping center. Continue to the end of this street and park on either side.

Distance/Difficulty: It's 1.63 miles one-way, including the 0.25-mile River Path Del Mar portion, making for a little more than 3.0 miles round trip. Easy.

1-18. Self-Guiding Markers on Batiquitos Lagoon Trail

Batiquitos Lagoon Trail in Carlsbad is one of the prettiest pathways along a precious coastal wetland because of an invader, the eucalyptus tree. Dozens of them rise high above the trail, providing welcome shade as well as their distinctive beauty.

The eucalyptus tree is native to Australia but has naturalized all over California. Its leaves and seed pods that fall to the ground contain oils that prevent other plants, including native coastal sage scrub, from growing underneath them, according to the self-guided trail guide that accompanies 25 markers along the lagoon trail.

Batiquitos Lagoon's trail in Carlsbad is shaded by many eucalyptus trees.

They're not all bad, however. The guide also points out that now the eucalyptus trees have become homes. "Great blue herons and both snowy and great egrets build their nests in trees. Look for nests and birds in the eucalyptus trees," states No. 21 in the guide.

The trail guide, which you can pick up free at the trailhead boxes, makes this nearly 2-mile round-trip walk even more interesting. It points out geology lessons through sediment layers, identifies several native and nonnative plants, discusses mudflat ecology (where worms and clams, snails and shrimp are all food for birds and other animals), and lists several birds and fishes that are commonly found here.

Over 180 species of birds have been sighted in Batiquitos Lagoon. At any time of year, you might spot the great blue herons and great and snowy egrets wading in the shallow waters. The American avocet is another wader. In winter, look for terns plunging for fish and mallard and green-winged teal ducks. The endangered California least tern comes here in late spring and summer on its migratory route. There are five man-made sand nesting sites on the other side of the lagoon for the California least tern and western snowy plover.

California Fish and Wildlife Department manages Batiquitos Lagoon as an ecological reserve today. The Batiquitos Lagoon Foundation, a nonprofit organization run entirely by volunteers, helps to preserve, enhance, and protect the lagoon through educational programs and events. Its website, www.batiquitosfoundation.org, is a wealth of information about the lagoon and its trail. You'll find lists with photos of plants, birds, and fish, as well as informative articles on its history, geology, and ecology. You can download that self-guiding trail guide from the website, but that version isn't as up-to-date as the free ones you pick up at the trailheads.

The foundation reports that nearly 200 prehistoric sites dating back 8,000 years have been found at Batiquitos Lagoon. The sites show that marine shellfish were harvested from the lagoon for thousands of years. "This means the lagoon must have been open to tidal flushing at least part of the year in order to allow marine shellfish to survive in the lagoon," says the foundation in its "History of Batiquitos Lagoon."

The Port of Los Angeles and the City of Carlsbad started restoration of that tidal flushing on the lagoon in 1994 through the Batiquitos Lagoon Enhancement Project. So with the health of the lagoon monitored and protected, take to this trail to marvel at its natural beauties. The lagoon is a little farther from this trail than, for example, the trail at San Elijo Lagoon a bit farther south, so you might need good binoculars to spot some of those waterfowl. However, you'll have those eucalyptus trees to view, along with glimpses of the expertly manicured greens of the Aviara golf course. This trail is so flat and wide that it's an easy pathway for wheelchairs and strollers as well.

Smell the aromas of the sage, sweet fennel, and lemonadeberry, as well as rotten eggs. The latter is caused by marsh bacteria that draw sulfur from dead plants and animals in the lagoon in order to decompose the dead materials. "If you smell rotten eggs, just be patient. It's good ol' bacteria at work," says a plaque along the trail.

Thomas Brothers Map: Page 1127, B-7.

Before You Go: Take a look at the Batiquitos Lagoon Foundation's website at www. batiquitosfoundation.org. You can download lists of birds, plants, and animals as well as the self-guiding trail guide and maps of the lagoon trail.

It's free to walk the lagoon trail. Dogs are allowed only on leashes. No bicycles or horses allowed.

Trailhead: There are several entry points to the main Lagoon Trail. The easiest starting point is near the lagoon's visitor center, open Monday to Friday from 9:30 a.m. to 12:30 p.m., and Saturday and Sunday from 9:00 a.m. to 3:00 p.m.

Exit Interstate 5 at Poinsettia Lane, going east. Turn right onto Batiquitos Drive, then right again onto Gabbiano Lane, and park in the designated parking spaces at the end of the cul-de-sac.

Distance/Difficulty: The main lagoon trail is a little less than 2 miles long from one end to the other, making for a 3.5- to 4.0-mile round-trip. Very easy.

1-19. Explore Agua Hedionda on Three Separate Trails

Three short trails explore different areas of Carlsbad's Agua Hedionda Lagoon, the county's busiest lagoon with water sports, the Encina power plant, the Hubbs-Sea World Research Institute hatchery, a YMCA aquatics park, and the Carlsbad Aquafarm (which raises mussels in the outer lagoon). That outer lagoon closest to the ocean is also popular with fishermen, who cast their lines from the shore in hopes of snagging halibut or sea bass.

The trails are currently very separate explorations. The Discovery Center Trail has views of the upland marshland area of the inner lagoon, the eastern-most part of that watershed. The Kelly School Trail runs along the northeastern border of the upland wildlife preserve, carving its way through a canyon. The Hubbs Trail runs along the north shore of the outer lagoon between Coast Highway and the railroad tracks, and it offers the most opportunities for spotting shorebirds.

I started at the Discovery Center Trail, which is a good place to begin because the center has a lot of interesting information about the lagoon. It even features a new aquarium for up-close looks at some locals. A native plant garden in front of the center offers a quick primer on several native plants and the birds and butterflies they attract. Placards placed here also share some history of this area.

People have lived along this lagoon for at least 10,000 years, says one placard. The Luiseño people spent winters here making salt and gathering shellfish for food, jewelry, tools, and trade. The Luiseño called this area Palamai, or "place of big water."

The Spanish expedition of Don Gaspar de Portola and Father Juan Crespi arrived here in 1769, greeted by the Luiseño with goodwill and curiosity, says one of the placards. The peaceful Luiseño were quickly assimilated into the Franciscan ways.

The soldiers of Portola's expedition are credited with naming this lagoon, which had been chosen for a rest stop. The scent of decaying fish and other debris inspired them to call it Agua Hedionda, or "Stinking Waters."

The Discovery Center Trail leaves from the overflow parking area just east of the center's main parking lot. It's a dirt road near the power lines that heads down to the eastern end of the lagoon (often quite dry) and continues northeast along this preserve area for only about a quarter of a mile.

The Kelly School Trail is the longest of the three, at about 1 mile. It follows a dirt road on the northeastern edge of the upland wildlife preserve above the eastern end of the inner lagoon. This trail carves through a canyon, where homes are scattered along the northern edge. This is the least scenic of the three trails because you can't see the lagoon from here.

The Hubbs Trail offers the most water views and skirts the edge of the outer lagoon itself, just inside Coast Highway from the ocean. It's about a half-mile long.

The Hubbs Trail at Agua Hedionda Lagoon has the most water views.

The tides in the lagoon ebb and flow twice a day, according to another placard at the Discovery Center. When the earth, sun, and moon are aligned, the moon is in its full and new phases, during which strong gravitational forces cause very high and very low tides; these are called spring tides (the seas springing out and springing back). When the sun and moon are perpendicular to the earth, the moon is in its quarter phases, and weaker gravitational forces result in smaller differences between high and low tides; these are called neap tides.

The pelicans fly in graceful formation during any of these tidal events, and you might also spot great blue herons, egrets, and of course gulls. We typically call them seagulls, but none is officially so named. There are 26 species of gulls listed in National Geographic's *Field Guide to Birds of North America*. Among the most common here are the Western gull with a white head, dark gray back, and pink legs; the Heermann's gull with a white head, black tail with a white band, and a red bill; and the California gull with a white head, yellow bill with black and red spots, and gray-green or greenish-yellow legs.

There are plans to connect these trails someday, eventually circling the lagoon, according to the Agua Hedionda Lagoon Foundation.

Thomas Brothers Map: Page 1126, J-1.

Before You Go: The city of Carlsbad has maps of trailheads at http://www.carlsbadca.gov/services/depts/parks/open/trails/locations.asp. Agua Hedionda Lagoon is on Carlsbad's North City map.

The Agua Hedionda Lagoon Foundation has more information about all three trails cited here: http://lagoon.aguahedionda.org.

Visit the Discovery Center, open every day but Monday, to learn more.

These trails are open only to hikers.

Trailhead: To reach the Discovery Center Trail first, from Interstate 5 exit at Cannon Road and head east about 1.7 miles. The center is on Cannon at Faraday Avenue, but you can't turn left into it from this direction. You'll have to make a right turn, and head back the other way on Cannon so you can then enter the center on your right.

To reach the Kelly School Trail, continue heading east on Cannon Road, turning left onto El Camino Real. Turn left onto Kelly Drive and go to the end of Kelly, where it intersects with Park Drive. The trail begins at the metal gates across from the school at this intersection.

To reach the Hubbs Trail, continue north along El Camino Real, turn left onto Tamarack, and head west all the way to the ocean. Turn left at Garfield, one street before Coast Highway, and go to the end of Garfield. Walk down the dirt access road to the lagoon-edge trail.

Distance/Difficulty: All three trails will total about 2.5 miles round-trip. Easy.

2. North County Coastal

Hike the canyons and ridgetops of Del Mar, Carlsbad, and Oceanside. Climb Carlsbad's highest point. Discover the extremely rare vernal pools on Carmel Mountain. You'll surely be surprised by these urban trails that tuck into little natural oases.

2-1. Crest Canyon Preserve Offers an Urban Respite

Crest Canyon Open Space Preserve provides a tranquil meander through coastal sage scrub and lots of Torrey pine trees, and it's right in Del Mar. There even seems to be more Torrey pine trees here than in some places in Torrey Pines State Natural Reserve. In fact, Crest Canyon was originally included in the plan for Torrey Pines State Natural Reserve, but it was omitted because of cost considerations. Today, Crest Canyon is part of the San Dieguito River Park, which will eventually include a 70-mile Coast-to-Crest Trail from the beach in Del Mar to Volcan Mountain in Julian.

San Dieguito River Park, born officially in June 1989, celebrated its 20th anniversary in 2009. Today more than 65 percent of the 92,000-acre San Dieguito River Park area is now in protected ownership, and nearly 45 miles of the Coast-to-Crest Trail and 20 miles of connecting trails are in place. The park includes trails in Crest Canyon and the Lagoon Boardwalk on San Dieguito Lagoon, Lake Hodges, Clevenger Canyon and San Pasqual, Pamo Valley, Santa Ysabel Open Space Preserve, and Volcan Mountain near Julian.

The Crest Canyon segment is open only to hikers (and dogs on leashes), and it offers nearly a mile of trails. There are two main trails that traverse the canyon north to south, connecting in a couple of places and diverging at both north and south entries to the canyon. The western-most trail is a wider, sandy path, and the eastern trail is narrower and a bit rockier and steeper. Both are easy walks through the canyon, with the northern point ending at San Dieguito Lagoon, one of the last remaining coastal wetlands in California.

The $86 million restoration of wetlands in the San Dieguito Lagoon in Del Mar on both sides of Interstate 5 continues. The San Dieguito River Valley Conservancy, a nonprofit dedicated to acquisition and preservation of river valley lands, oversees all of this planning. Crest Canyon will eventually be connected to the Riverpath Del Mar and the San Dieguito Lagoon Boardwalk, and there will be a wildlife viewing platform overlooking the restored lagoon west of I-5.

Crest Canyon was saved from development in the 1970s by local citizens who convinced the cities of San Diego and Del Mar to buy the land instead. It's also part of the County of San Diego's Multiple Species Conservation Program, which aims to preserve networks of open space to help protect biodiversity.

The coastal sage scrub habitat that surrounds our coastal wetlands includes drought-tolerant plants, an important complement to wetlands, according to the conservancy, which helps realize the visions of the San Dieguito River Park. The plants you'll see in Crest Canyon include the white and black sage, bush sunflower, California buckwheat, red-berried lemonadeberry bush, laurel sumac, and ceanothus (lilac). Then there are the lovely Torrey pines, our only native coastal evergreen, which grow naturally only in this area and on Santa Rosa Island in the Channel Islands off Santa Barbara. You can learn to distinguish a Torrey pine by observing its long needles in bundles of five.

Crest Canyon is full of Torrey pines.

The walk through Crest Canyon offers a lovely glimpse of the mostly natural landscape of eroded cliffs, with homes perched high on the edges above. Views through the lacy Torrey pines to the lagoon are worthy draws to this canyon. At the trailheads, the conservancy stocks pamphlets of "Crest Canyon Trails," "Plants of the San Dieguito River Valley," and "Birds of the San Dieguito Lagoon."

The conservancy organizes monthly habitat restoration events that attract volunteers who help remove invasive plants in the canyon. In 2007, the conservancy also partnered with the local Sierra Club chapter to form a Friends of Crest Canyon volunteer group. The conservancy sometimes offers guided hikes in the canyon.

To get more information on those activities in Crest Canyon, or to learn more about the entire San Dieguito River Park and conservancy, go to www.sdrp.org or www.sdrvc.org.

Thomas Brothers Map: Page 1187, G-4 and H-4 for north end; H-6 for southern end.

Before You Go: Download a map of Crest Canyon trails at www.sdrp.org/wordpress/.
Dogs on leashes are welcome. No bicycles or equestrians on Crest Canyon trails.

Trailheads: The south end of Crest Canyon is reached from Interstate 5. Go west on Del Mar Heights Road, then turn right (north) onto Durango Drive and parking at the end of that street.

The north end is accessible from I-5 going west on Via de la Valle, left (south) on Jimmy Durante Boulevard, past the Del Mar Fairgrounds, and then, just after the bridge over the river, left on San Dieguito Drive. Drive about a half-mile to the kiosk and park on the side of the road.

Distance/Difficulty: About 1.0 mile round-trip; easy.

2-2. Restored Lagoon Now Sports New Loop Trail

The newest trail open in the San Dieguito River Park is visible from Interstate 5, where it loops around the eastern end of the restored San Dieguito Lagoon. Now named the Dust Devil Nature Trail, this 1.7-mile loop trail is easy, short, and flat. It is a fine urban location for birding. Its terrain isn't the most beautiful in our county, but it does offer a look at years of work that restored the vital lagoon.

Begin from the trailhead just off El Camino Real by heading north on the 0.7-mile North Loop, which connects to the 0.6-mile West Loop as well as the 0.4-mile East Loop. You'll see acres of plantings and other man-made improvements that have helped to make the lagoon a productive, working estuary.

The Dust Devil Nature Trail gets close to restored lagoon.

For years the lagoon's mouth at the ocean had been allowed to plug with sand, effectively shutting off the natural tidal flow into the lagoon. Since the dredging, natural tidal flows have been restored between the ocean and hundreds of acres of new and existing habitat that depend on daily seawater tidal influences, according to Southern California Edison, the lead on the San Dieguito Wetlands Restoration Project along with SDG&E. Members of the San Dieguito River Valley Conservancy (SDRVC) and the San Dieguito River Park (SDRP) also contributed, as did scientists from University of California at Santa Barbara.

The project began in 1988 when plans began to restore San Dieguito Lagoon, which is located within the largest watershed (San Dieguito River) of the six San Diego coastal lagoons and was once the largest lagoon in the county.

According to a U.S. Coast and Geodetic Survey map drawn in 1889, San Dieguito Lagoon and its surrounding wetlands once extended as far east as El Camino Real. The surrounding valley floor was described as swamp and tidelands, according to the master plan for San Dieguito River Park and its Joint Powers Association.

The lagoon is a nursery for many oceanic fish, including California halibut and diamond turbot. Some fish live their entire lives in the estuarine environment, including anchovies and topsmelt, which are food for many waterfowl.

Endangered birds that use San Dieguito Lagoon wetlands include the light-footed clapper rail, Belding's savannah sparrow, California brown pelican, California least tern, and Western snowy plover. It's also a critical stopover on the Pacific Flyway for many birds, including Canada geese. Fifteen species of waterfowl are supported seasonally by the lagoon, including mallards, northern pintails, gadwalls, American wigeons, green-winged teals, northern shovelers, and blue-winged teals.

Scientists have documented nearly a tripling of bird species in the lagoon since restoration work began in 2006, according to SCE. The $90 million project was completed in late 2011, and another project to restore more wetlands here continues. SCE, SDG&E, and the City of Riverside's Public Utilities Department chose the lagoon restoration project to meet requirements to mitigate the impact on marine fish populations from the San Onofre Nuclear Generating Station. It has been one of the largest coastal restoration projects on the West Coast. Some 2 million yards of earth were excavated, much of which was moved from the mouth to the east of the lagoon, so that 116 acres of tidal wetlands were created on both sides of I-5. Interestingly, the excavation included the site of a former World War II navy blimp landing field to the west of I-5.

Steve Schroeter of the Marine Science Institute at UCSB is one of three principal investigators of the project, along with Mark Page and Dan Reed of the same institute. They continue to monitor the wetlands. "The mud flats are really good bird habitat," Schroeter told members of the SDRVC recently. "The white patches you see are nesting sites for endangered least terns and we hope for snowy plovers too."

Some 13.7 acres of sandy nesting habitat has been created or restored for California least terns and snowy plovers. Least terns like shallow waters near estuaries, and they lay their eggs along sandy beaches near these waters. Sand spits and beaches at river mouths are favored nesting spots for the snowy plovers. You'll also notice lots of coastal sage scrub plantings, including such endangered species as Del Mar mesa sand aster, Encinitas baccharis, and short-leaved dudleya.

Biologists have monitored the area for a year since the project completion and "found that the wetland supports a promising population of snails, crabs, amphibians, small mammals, birds and provides fish a place to spawn and grow," says SCE. "Terrestrial animals have also become visible, such as the burrowing owl, cottontail rabbit and various reptiles."

One area in the southern reaches still harbors eucalyptus trees and pampas grass, both considered invaders in the native coastal sage scrub habitat. These may someday be removed.

Future plans call for strategically placed trees or shrubs that will serve as blinds, allowing bird watching without disturbing them. Interpretive signs are also planned to explain the kinds of marsh visible from the trail. Meanwhile, see how many birds you can spot in the coastal sage scrub as well as on the eastern reaches of that blue lagoon.

Thomas Brothers Map: Page 1187, J-3, just across El Camino Real from Sea Country Lane.

Before You Go: Download a map of the Dust Devil Nature Trail from the San Dieguito River Park's trails page, http://www.sdrp.org/trails.htm.
This trail is open only to hikers and dogs on leashes. It's free to park here.

Trailhead: From Interstate 5, exit at Via de la Valle, heading east. Turn right (south) on El Camino Real and go uphill past the signal light at San Dieguito Road. The entrance to the parking area is on the right, just before you reach the signal light at Stallion's Crossing.

Distance/Difficulty: A 1.7-mile loop, this trail is very easy.

2-3. Nature Preserved on Shaw Valley Trail

The Shaw Valley Trail in Del Mar is a fairly easy single-track trail that is open to hikers and equestrians. At least some version of it has likely been there for a long time. It winds its way now through chaparral in a valley that has been farmed since at least the late 1800s. After nearly 2.0 miles one-way, it connects to Los Penasquitos Canyon Preserve, where another 20-plus miles of trails continue in these old canyon lands. From its beginning points, it also connects to the SR 56 bike route that goes all the way to Poway along that highway.

The Shaw Valley Trail, also known as the Shaw Trail, is now part of the Del Mar Mesa development plan adopted by the City of San Diego in the year 2000. It goes through Shaw Valley, which lies immediately south of the Grand Del Mar Hotel and its 18-hole golf course, which were part of that development plan.

Begin this trail off the hotel's Grand Del Mar Way just a short way in from Carmel Country Road or from the parking area on Clews Ranch Road. You'll see trail signs pointing the way to an unpaved trail. Because it's a relatively narrow trail, bikes are not allowed here, but dogs on leashes may accompany hikers or horses.

The trail is fairly flat through this valley that was a farming settlement in the late 1800s and early 1900s. Early settlers shared community interests in this region based on social and economic endeavors, according to the Del Mar Mesa Specific Plan filed by the city in 2000. According to the plan, in the 1950s "there appears to have been a brief endeavor to establish communal living on Del Mar Mesa." No other details were given.

When the railway was completed through Del Mar in the early 1880s, local farmers in this area were provided a means of transporting their goods to a broader market than sea transport had previously offered. Longtime residents included the families of Knecktel, Mecklenseck, and Neimann, who were all farmers in Shaw Valley. "Three generations of Knecktels have farmed Carmel Valley and Shaw Valley and several members of the family continue to live in the area," according to the plan. The Mecklensecks practiced dry farming in Shaw Valley and also had an egg business that remained in operation until 1984. The Neimanns built their home on Del Mar Mesa in 1895 and were among the first here to plant orchards. "The Neimann home remains intact as a component of Carmel Valley Ranch," according to the plan.

The Shaw Valley Trail winds through old farming valley.

The entire Del Mar Mesa area, including Shaw Valley, has been an important element in the city's Multiple Species Conservation Program. It's part of the Los Penasquitos Lagoon and Canyon/Del Mar Mesa core biological area, which encompasses one of the few intact natural open space areas in coastal San Diego County that is still linked to larger areas of natural habitat to the east—"hence, its tremendous significance." Areas such as these continue to provide wildlife corridors that can be critical to species' survival.

The trail winds through the valley with views of that green golf course. After about 1.5 miles one-way, you'll note an intersection that heads uphill to the left, with trail signs on the main trail for Shaw Trail and Equestrian Trail. Pass that intersection to continue on to the connection to Los Penasquitos trails.

In another quarter-mile or so, the trail goes under the bridge carrying Carmel Mountain Road and heads south into Los Penasquitos Canyon Preserve. At this point, I turned back to head up that other trail.

The uphill trail at the 1.5-mile point climbs up to the Grandview Loop Trail that heads down to the Grand Del Mar resort and golf course.

When I reached the top of the short hill, the trail intersects at a T; I headed to the right, climbing to the topmost knoll, where the trail ended after about a quarter-mile. The views from this point were long, spreading across the valley and the trail as well as the green golf course and the resort. On a clear day, you can probably see the ocean just 4 miles away.

From here I followed signs continuing on the Grandview Loop back to the resort to make a big loop. When you reach the resort, skirt around the tennis courts to reach the parking areas, where you can find the road to leave the resort and head back along Grand Del Mar Way to where you started.

Thomas Brothers Map: Page 1188, D-7.

Before You Go: Download a trail map of this portion of Shaw Valley Trail from The Grand Del Mar hotel's web page, http://www.thegranddelmar.com/assets/Uploads/Trail-Map.pdf.

You may also download the trails map at Los Penasquitos Canyon Preserve for the Shaw Trail as well as its connections to the preserve; http://www.sandiego.gov/park-and-recreation/pdf/penasquitoscanyon.pdf.

Trailhead: From Highway 56 heading east, exit at Carmel Country Road and take a right, going south. Turn right at Clews Ranch Road into the unpaved parking area, which also serves the State Route 56 bike trail.

An unpaved trail heads off from Clews Ranch Road, paralleling Carmel Country Road, taking you to Shaw Valley Trail. The trailhead from the resort is across Carmel Country Road at Grand Del Mar Way.

Distance/Difficulty: The round-trip loop from the trailhead to the beginning of Los Penasquitos and then back around the resort was about 4.5 miles; easy to moderate.

2-4. Del Mar Mesa Trail Connects to Preserve

The trail up Del Mar Mesa sits next to the road of the same name until it reaches a connector trail to Los Penasquitos Canyon Preserve. Most of this hike is therefore a suburban one, but it is a fine workout and has some scenic surprises.

For one, there are a few scattered horse ranches on this route, which reveal what this area looked like before development of multimillion-dollar homes here. The trail itself is nicely landscaped with split-rail fencing, and its soft surface is good for horses as well as hikers, bikers, and dogs on leashes.

Begin the trail where Del Mar Mesa Road intersects with Carmel Country Road. The trail follows the road on its right as you head up the hill into the semi-rural community. After about 1.1 miles, the scene becomes more rural as views extend east into Del Mar Mesa Preserve.

The eastern half of Del Mar Mesa is being conserved as open space under the City of San Diego's Multiple Species Conservation Program (MSCP).

Del Mar Mesa Preserve has been studied by biologists for many years, particularly because of its vernal pools. Like those on Carmel Mountain Preserve nearby, the vernal pools on Del Mar Mesa Preserve are extremely precious habitats for very rare species. "Vernal pools are considered to be sensitive habitat by local, state and federal governments, and it is estimated that over 95 percent of the vernal pool habitat in San Diego County has been destroyed," according to the city's resource management plan for both Carmel Mountain and Del Mar Mesa Preserves prepared by Recon Environmental Inc.

Del Mar Mesa protects rare vernal pools and open space.

Vernal pools are shallow, ephemeral wetlands. They fill with water during winter rains, and then the water evaporates after the rains end. You might mistake them for nothing more than puddles, but they actually support a lot of life. The San Diego fairy shrimp, the two-striped garter snake, and the Western spadefoot toad survive with vernal pools, as do sensitive plants including San Diego button celery and San Diego mesa mint.

The vernal pools on Del Mar Mesa have been severely impacted by unauthorized activity, especially by mountain biking and other vehicles, and so much of that eastern area is currently closed to trail users. Some trails here, however, have been recently opened, all having been realigned if necessary to avoid the vernal pools. These trails connect with other open spaces designed to be part of a regional trail system, according to the city's plan.

Both Carmel Mountain Preserve and Del Mar Mesa Preserve will connect to Torrey Pines State Natural Reserve. Carmel Mountain currently does connect via the Carmel Valley Recreational Equestrian Path (CVREP) on its north. Both preserves currently connect to each other (via the CVREP) and to Los Penasquitos Canyon Preserve. The preserves are also part of the 140-mile San Diego Trans County Trail, a.k.a. San Diego Sea-to-Sea Trail, that is currently about 70 percent complete from Torrey Pines to the Salton Sea.

Del Mar Mesa Preserve will also one day connect to Black Mountain Open Space Park through McGonigle Canyon and Carmel Valley. That would ultimately connect it to San Dieguito River Park and its eventual 70-mile Coast-to-Crest Trail from Del Mar to Julian's Volcan Mountain.

The current path along Del Mar Mesa Road continues until it dead-ends at Del Vino, after about 2.12 miles from the start. Here you'll see a road named Little McGonigle Ranch Road that brings up some history.

Ranching was the main occupation in this area from the late 19th to the early 20th century. The largest ranch in the area was owned by George McGonigle, for which McGonigle Canyon is named; this canyon stretches along Carmel Valley.

In 1899, the McGonigles sold more than 1,000 acres of land to the Sisters of Mercy, a Catholic order of nuns associated with Mercy Hospital. The nuns farmed and supplied vegetables and dairy products to Mercy Hospital, naming their property Mount Carmel Ranch, from which the valley took its name.

Within Del Mar Mesa Preserve, 38 prehistoric and historic archaeological sites have been recorded. The prehistoric sites, roughly from 8,000 to 2,000 years ago, are all listed as chipping stations or quarries, and they are determined from testing the cobbles (small rocks) that eroded out of the ridges, according to the city's plan. The historic sites also have several cobble features, including two cobble circles.

When you reach Del Vino, turn right. In a very short distance, the trail splits. It continues straight through a construction area, or winds to the left around a small vernal pool. Go left around that pool and head down on the single-track trail known as "The Cobbles." This trail is the connector to Los Penasquitos, and it is scenic. It passes through some stands of eucalyptus that may have been planted around age-old farmsteads in the late 1800s.

I turned around when I reached the Duck Pond, about 2.9 miles from the start, and headed back up the hill to retrace my route.

Be aware this is a popular mountain bike trail, and because it's a single track, keep your ears open for bikers.

Thomas Brothers Map: Page 1188, D-7, where Carmel Country Road intersects Del Mar Mesa Road.

Before You Go: Download a map of the Del Mar Mesa trail on the trail map for Los Penasquitos Canyon Preserve, http://www.co.san-diego.ca.us/reusable_components/images/parks/doc/Trails_Los_Penasquitos.pdf, from the County of San Diego's Parks & Recreation Dept.

Trailhead: From Highway 56 (Ted Williams Parkway), exit at Carmel Country Road and head south. Turn right at the first opportunity onto Clews Ranch Road, and park in this staging area for the CVREP. Walk south on Carmel Country Road about one block; cross the road to begin the trail that hugs the right side of Del Mar Mesa Road.

Distance/Difficulty: About 5.8 miles round-trip with about 575-foot elevation change; easy to moderate.

2-5. Wildflowers, Ocean Views in Del Mar's Gonzales Canyon

Gonzales Canyon is an open-space park just north of Carmel Valley and Highway 56 that offers several miles of trails in a natural setting amid development. This lovely canyon was preserved as open space when the Del Mar Highlands area began to be developed in the 1980s. Gonzales Canyon lies within the City of San Diego's Multiple Species Conservation Program, which sustains the biodiversity of our region and helps protect fragile wildlife and threatened species.

"By preserving an extensive network of habitat and open space, the MSCP will contribute to the region's quality of life," says the final MSCP plan, which was begun in 1991 with participation from the city, county, 10 additional city jurisdictions in the area, as well as California Fish and Wildlife and California Resources Agency. The MSCP area is bounded by the Mexican border to the south, national forest lands to the east, the Pacific Ocean to the west, and the San Dieguito River valley to the north.

It covers some 900 square miles within the 4,200-square-mile county.

Gonzales Canyon also falls within the City of San Diego's Parks and Recreation Department's Open Space Division, which manages more than 24,000 acres of open space.

It's also part of San Diego Canyonlands, a nonprofit corporation dedicated to preserving San Diego's special canyon spaces. San Diego Canyonlands grew out of the Sierra Club's San Diego Canyons Campaign in 1999 that was launched to preserve and protect these natural spaces within our urban core.

"San Diego's canyons are an escape to nature from an otherwise completely paved and urbanized environment," declares San Diego Canyonlands in a paper about its own history. "This visual treat helps soothe the mind and relieve the stress of modern

Gonzales Canyon is a fine swath of open space right in the city.

living with its fast pace and information overload. Singing birds, buzzing bees and the cry of soaring hawks replace the noise of traffic. The aroma of sage brush, twittering birds, flowering plants, butterflies and wildlife welcome the senses and curious eyes of urban dwellers."

You'll find all these sensations in Gonzales Canyon on its network of trails open to hikers, equestrians, bicyclists, and dogs on leashes. The main trail is the Torrey Pines

Loop Trail, about a 3-mile loop that begins just behind the restrooms and off-leash dog park at Torrey Highlands Park off Del Mar Heights Road at Lansdale.

When I was there in early May, there was an astounding abundance of wildflowers: yellow mustard, the brown-centered bush sunflower, white pearly everlasting, black sage, yucca, fuchsia-colored canchalagua, yellow-centered purple nightshade, scarlet monkeyflower, yellow pincushions, golden yarrow, white morning glory, white chamise, pink buckwheat, and lavender mariposa lily. One field was blanketed in yellow snakeweed near the eastern end of the loop trail, and at the west-side beginning of the trail from the dog park, you'll encounter a bounty of pink bush mallow blooms.

The loop trail winds down into the canyon. Near the trail's midpoint you cross a service road for the power lines that go through here. You could walk down this service road from the far northern end of the Torrey Highlands Park to reach the loop trail, but this service road is very, very steep. If you do explore this upper region of the canyon, you'll see ocean views at the overlook that lies just below that northern end of the neighborhood park.

After crossing the service road, the loop trail continues to the other side of the canyon. It goes through low elevation where arroyo willows live near a creek, and then it climbs the canyon walls again to head back up to the neighborhood park.

"In Gonzales Canyon, there were remnants of an adobe, constructed by Levi Gonzales in the late 1800s ... Gonzales had emigrated from Portugal and purchased land in the canyon where he grew a variety of crops," reports Project Clean Water on the San Dieguito River Watershed.

The trails in Gonzales Canyon will eventually connect with the San Dieguito River Park's trails just to the canyon's north. Once the connection is complete, the trail at the western end of Gonzales Canyon will go around Cavallo Farms and then connect with trails created by Rancho Valley Farms, a new Pardee Homes development at the top of Old El Camino Real.

Gonzales Canyon trail plans also call eventually for a connection to Los Penasquitos Canyon Preserve through McGonigle Canyon, which lies just south of Highway 56. These routes will also enhance the MSCP because they allow wildlife to migrate between open spaces.

Thomas Stuhr, a park ranger for the City of San Diego who manages six open space parks, including Gonzales Canyon, Crest Canyon, Clevenger Canyon and Black Mountain, observed evidence of that wildlife. "As I made my way to the eastern side of Gonzales Canyon, I noticed multiple wildlife tracks in a nearby shallow muddy water pond," he told Friends of Penasquitos Canyon for its January 2012 newsletter. "There were tracks made by deer, bobcat, raccoon, small rodents, and even the small tracks of a raven or two ... Wildlife corridors, undisturbed habitat are what wildlife needs to thrive in an urban setting ... It was a great sign to see those tracks in the mud right near the small natural pond."

Thomas Brothers Map: Page 1188, B-5, where Del Mar Heights Road intersects Lansdale Drive.

Before You Go: Download a trail map of Gonzales Canyon Open Space from the City of San Diego's park and recreation pages, http://www.sandiego.gov/park-and-recreation/pdf/gonzalestrailmap.pdf.

The trails here are open to hikers, bicyclists, equestrians, and dogs on leashes.

There is one wooden bridge on the main Torrey Pines Loop Trail's eastern portion that states no horses.

Trailhead: From Highway 56, exit at Carmel Country Road, heading north. Turn right onto Carmel Canyon Road, then left onto Del Mar Heights Road. Turn right onto Lansdale and take the first left to enter Torrey Highlands Park. Park here. The main trails begin just behind the restrooms and through the gates to the off-leash dog park.

Distance/Difficulty: The Torrey Pines Loop Trail is about 3.5 miles total with an elevation gain of about 500 feet; easy to moderate.

2-6. Carmel Mountain Home to Unusual Habitats

Carmel Mountain Preserve, a 400-acre mesa top, is truly one of San Diego County's remaining natural wonders. When you hike its several miles of trails, you will be treated not only to ocean views but to a landscape truly unlike any other. On its flat mesa top, there are huge patches of a hard gray moss, called ashy spike moss, that have a very interesting purpose. You'll also come upon puddles of water that settle in the mesa's depressions, which are actually vernal pools—an amazing environment that hosts species found nowhere else. The Chaparral Lands Conservancy has called it "a special Noah's Ark of nature surrounded by suburban development."

Every type of vegetation found on Carmel Mountain is "unique and imperiled," it says. Its habitats—southern maritime chaparral, coastal sage scrub, wet meadows, and vernal pools—support more than two dozen rare species, some of which have been listed as federally endangered.

Southern maritime chaparral is a habitat that occurs only on weathered sandstone formations that lie within the coastal fog belt, and it exists only in San Diego County from La Jolla to Carlsbad. "Only about 15 percent of Southern maritime chaparral that historically occurred in San Diego and Orange counties remains, and most of this is located on Carmel Mountain, in Torrey Pines State Park and in Carlsbad and Encinitas," says Rick Halsey of the California Chaparral Institute.

Characteristic species of this habitat include chamise, white coast ceanothus (a wild lilac that can grow into huge specimens here), and mission manzanita. Endangered species found only in San Diego and Orange counties include white-flowering Del Mar manzanita and Orcutt's spineflower. Threatened species include the yellow-flowering, big-leaved crown-beard and the shrubby Encinitas baccharis.

The vernal pools, though, are even more precious. Rarely more than six inches deep, the pools fill with water only after rainfall and rarely remain filled longer than 45 days at a time. When dry, they simply appear to be lifeless bare spots in chaparral or coastal sage scrub. Half of the plant species growing in California's remaining vernal pools are found nowhere else on the planet.

Carmel Mountain Preserve saves precious habitats.

"Because of their homely appearance, they provide an excellent example of how the importance of becoming familiar with native habitats and efforts to preserve them can violently collide with the desire to develop property by individuals unfamiliar with their value," says Halsey of the California Chaparral Institute.

Indeed, the Carmel Mountain Preserve was dedicated in 1999 after being saved from development by a coalition spearheaded by the Carmel Mountain Conservancy.

Some 97 percent of San Diego's vernal pools—which once covered some 28,500 acres in the county—have been destroyed, and that, naturally includes its rare species. Vernal pools, however, do also exist in Northwest Baja.

Both plants and animals of vernal pools must be able to withstand weeks of both winter rains and summer drought. Animals that live here include spadefoot toads and their favorite food, the San Diego fairy shrimp.

Living next to the vernal pools is the short-leaved dudleya, a tiny succulent that lives in only five places in the world, all in Del Mar and La Jolla, according to the Chaparral Lands Conservancy. When not in bloom, it looks similar to the marble-like iron pebbles that are also unique to North County coastal mesas, which helps it avoid being eaten by rabbits and rodents. When it blooms (more rainfall brings more blooms), tiny white and yellow flowers burst open. That ashy spike moss helps them thrive by preventing invasion of weeds and gophers, according to a placard on the trails. With such specialized species existing in what many would deem barren ground, it's more important here than ever to stay on the trails. "Take care not to trample on dry pool beds. Imagine the potential life hidden beneath the surface," says the placard near the vernal pools.

The trails crisscross the top of the mesa, with two major connecting trails heading downhill to join the preserve's Carmel Valley Recreational and Equestrian Path (CVREP) that generally follows Highway 56.

I started at the southwestern edge of the preserve at the corner of Longshore Way and Shorepoint Way, beginning the trek under the utility lines. This dirt road makes several up-and-down dips, some quite steep, as it follows the utility poles. When this main artery takes a final right away from the poles, you can take several trails (all unmarked so far) that wander around this mesa top. You can't really get lost, so feel free to explore all of these trails.

I headed east to reach the vernal pools, according to the map, and I eventually found them even though they were still quite dry in late fall. You'll know you've reached the pools when you see the informational placards and the stone borders that have been placed around the pools.

Hiking this mesa and learning about these truly unique habitats made for another fascinating day of discovery on San Diego County's trails. I can't wait to view the lovely, tiny blooms of that special dudleya after winter's rains.

Thomas Brothers Map: Page 1208, B-2.

Before You Go: Download a copy of the map of Carmel Mountain Preserve's trails at the City of San Diego's parks and recreation page, http://www.sandiego.gov/park-and-recreation/pdf/carmelmountaintrailmap.pdf.

For another map that shows street entrances to the preserve, go to the Friends of Los Penasquitos Canyon Preserve's page, http://www.penasquitos.org/map.htm.

For information about the Chaparral Lands Conservancy habitat restoration plan for the preserve as well as photos, go to www.chaparralconservancy.org.

For more information on vernal pools, go to the California Chaparral Institute at www.californiachaparral.com.

The preserve's trails are open to hikers, bicyclists, equestrians, and dogs on leashes.

Trailhead: I started hiking at the southwest entrance at the corner of Longshore Way and Shorepoint Way. From Interstate 5, exit at Carmel Mountain Road, heading east. Turn left (north) onto E. Ocean Air Drive, then left (west) on Longshore Way. Follow Longshore until it ends at Shorepoint. Park on the street near the utility lines, under which the trails begin.

Distance/Difficulty: I hiked nearly 4.0 miles; fairly easy.

2-7. Carmel Valley Two-Lane Path for Hikers, Bikers

The Carmel Valley Recreational and Equestrian Path (CVREP) is an excellent urban trail with both soft-surface and paved side-by-side trails able to accommodate a wide variety of users. The soft-surface path is intended for hikers and equestrians, and the asphalt-paved one is meant for bicyclists, baby strollers, and even wheelchairs. The separation makes it safer for everyone.

The trail runs 2 miles east from Interstate 5 at Carmel Valley Road to Carmel Country Road, but you don't have to stop there. According to a sign at the western end of the trail, the paved bike path continues 12 miles east to Poway. The whole bike path, including the CVREP, is known as the Highway 56 Bike Path.

The CVREP lies south of Highway 56, the Ted Williams Freeway. The rest of the bike path east of Carmel Country Road continues along that highway much more closely. The CVREP takes you a bit farther away from the traffic of the highway and invites a glimpse of this area the way it used to be.

There were once many ranches and equestrian facilities along this valley, but since development changed the landscape here beginning in the 1980s and 1990s, those ranches are far fewer today.

The CVREP is part of the Carmel Mountain Preserve, a 400-acre conservation preserve dedicated in 1999 following a unique agreement between conservationists and developers.

The CVREP is part of the Trans-County Trail.

The CVREP is part of the county's Multiple Species Conservation Plan (MSCP). "Every type of vegetation found on Carmel Mountain is unique and imperiled—Southern maritime chaparral, coastal sage scrub, wet meadows and vernal pools," according to the Chaparral Lands Conservancy, These habitats support more than 25 rare species, including the California gnatcatcher, San Diego fairy shrimp, and Del Mar Manzanita, all federally listed endangered species.

The wet meadows and vernal pools are found higher up on that Carmel Mountain Preserve's land. The CVREP follows Carmel Valley Creek with its very slow-moving water (hence the mosquito-spraying notices), which is filled with lots of cattails.

The median strip between the two paths on the CVREP is landscaped with Torrey pine trees, sycamores, and some very tall cottonwoods with their heart-shaped leaves.

I hadn't ever noticed before, but under those cottonwood trees here are lots of little white seed puffs that trees in the willow family shed each spring. They look like puffs of cotton, so the tree's name seems even more fitting. Also in that landscaped median strip are those lovely orchid rock roses, the bright purple blossoms with five black dots surrounding yellow stamens in the center.

The CVREP is also part of San Diego's Trans-County Trail. The Natural History Museum has a good map of that planned trail at http://www.sdnhm.org/archive/fieldguide/places/index.html.

I have seen the Trans-County Trail cited as both 110 miles and 140 miles when it is eventually completed from the ocean in Del Mar to the Salton Sea east of Borrego. Sometimes it has been called the Sea-to-Sea Trail, but that moniker appears outdated now, with Trans-County Trail the one to follow. About 70 percent of the trail is in place, using existing trails like the CVREP as well as trails through Poway, Sycamore Canyon, Oak Oasis Open Space Preserve, El Capitan Open Space Preserve, Cuyamaca Rancho State Park, Cleveland National Forest, and Anza-Borrego Desert State Park.

At about the halfway point on the CVREP, an intersection takes you uphill to Carmel Creek Road, where you can connect to other trails in the Carmel Mountain Preserve. I continued on the flat, easy CVREP end to end. Near the eastern end is the Clews Horse Ranch, a 40-acre equestrian facility where horses like to make themselves known to hikers and bikers; a sign fronting the trail says riding lessons are offered. "We have direct trail access allowing for hours of riding without ever crossing the same path twice," says the ranch's website, http://www.clewsranch.com.

At the western end of the trail, which goes under El Camino Real, the trail stops well short of I-5, with a wooden mile-marker post citing 2 miles. The mile markers, which log each quarter-mile along the trail, were the Eagle Scout project in 2010 by Alec Garton of Troop 717.

When I reached the western end, I turned around and retraced my way back, saving connecting trails for another day.

Thomas Brothers Map: Page 1188, C-7, Carmel Country Road, just south of Ted Williams Freeway.

Before You Go: For a map of all the trails in Carmel Mountain Preserve, including CVREP, go to the city's parks and recreation page for it, http://www.sandiego.gov/park-and-recreation/pdf/carmelmountaintrailmap.pdf.

Another good map I found of the CVREP is from a Sea-to-Sea Trail maps' page posted by Philip Erdelsky: http://www.efgh.com/c2c/c2ccarmelvalley.jpg. Erdelsky organizes a San Diego Day Hikers group through Meet-Up: http://www.meetup.com/sandiegodayhikers/.

Trailhead: From Ted Williams Parkway/Highway 56, exit at Carmel Country Road, heading south. Take the first right at Clews Ranch Road and park near the trailhead at the end of the road.

Distance/Difficulty: The one-way mileage for the CVREP is 2.0 miles, making a 4.0-mile round-trip. Easy.

2-8. Signs of Spring Abound in Manchester Preserve

Just a mile east of Interstate 5 in Encinitas lies the Manchester Preserve, a 123-acre open space that offers several miles of trails through coastal sage scrub and chaparral habitats. There are three or four trails here (depending on how you connect them) that pass through a gently sloping canyon and climb steep and eroded canyon walls to some fine vistas. The main trail essentially follows a major power line, and the preserve sits in the middle of suburban development; you're not in deep backcountry, but it's a remarkably pristine place to go hiking.

Manchester Preserve was established in 1996 when Techbilt Companies, a large residential development firm in Southern California, proposed the establishment of the Manchester Mitigation Bank. Presumably it was part of a deal to develop homes nearby.

Manchester Preserve mitigates home development.

Techbilt selected the Center for Natural Lands Management (CNLM) to both own and manage the preserve in perpetuity. "This site has been protected to be used as a mitigation bank, selling credits to surrounding developers to mitigate for habitat loss resulting from their projects," says the CNLM on its website. "Although small, it is a biologically rich site representative of the high diversity of San Diego County's natural habitats."

The CNLM, a nonprofit conservation organization based in Fallbrook, owns and manages this preserve, but the City of Encinitas has an easement over the trails, which means that the city maintains them for CNLM.

The CNLM protects the preserve in perpetuity for the conservation of natural resources, as it states on a sign along the trails. Manchester Preserve supports coastal sage scrub, southern maritime chaparral, and willow woodland. It is home to the endangered species of the coastal California gnatcatcher bird, San Diego thornmint (a tiny funnel-shaped, two-lipped, light violet flower that blooms in spring), and Orcutt's hazardia (a native shrub that blooms in late summer-early fall). Signs urge hikers to stay on the trails to help protect this natural habitat.

Manchester Preserve's trails are open to hikers, bicyclists, and horseback riders, but no motorized vehicles of any kind are allowed. Dogs are welcome but must be on leashes at all times.

When I was there in late March, a fellow hiker warned me that a rattlesnake was leisurely lying across one of the trails. Such a hazard is a good reason to keep your dogs on leashes. The fellow who spotted the snake had a beautiful golden retriever with him and was quick to pull his pet back, turning back on that trail so as not to disturb the rattler. Be aware that while rattlesnakes often hibernate during the cold fall and winter months; they awaken during the warm months of March and April, when they are most often seen countywide.

I always carry a strong walking stick, not so much to help me navigate the trails but to ward off snakes. Sometimes I drag the stick to make vibrations, thereby alerting the snake to get out of the way before it even sees me. I also like to think that the stick could help me appear larger and more menacing if I were ever to encounter a mountain lion. Get yourself a good stick.

I didn't need to see any rattlesnakes to enjoy the spring bounty in Manchester Preserve. The wildflowers are abundant. I'm no wildflower expert, but I took photos and then tried to identify what I saw using *San Diego County Native Plants* by James Lightner. Among the most arresting sights are the magnificent flowering stalks of the chaparral yucca. The canyon walls are covered in yellow bush sunflowers along with purple fragrant sage. Note the striking, extra long stamens on the purple parry phacelia, one of my favorites. There were patches of purple wild hyacinth, an occasional red-berried toyon, the bristly stemmed white forget-me-nots, scarlet monkeyflowers, light violet delicate clarkia, and yellow mojave stinkweed with its long, fuchsia-like blooms. Look even closer and see the very tiny yellow, white, and purple wildflowers that occasionally carpet the ground.

The main trail climbs to the top of the canyon where the power lines lie. There are good views down west through the canyon as well as east to the foothills of the mountains. Manchester Preserve is a marvelous escape smack in the thick of city development, and spring is an especially good time to visit.

Thomas Brothers Map: Page 1167, H-1&2.

Before You Go: Download a map of Manchester Preserve Trails at Encinitas' city government page: http://www.ci.encinitas.ca.us/modules/showdocument.aspx?documentid=3474. Note it is Trail Map No. 2 on the City of Encinitas' three trail map pages.

You may also go to www.cnlm.org, then to its page on Preserves, then to Manchester to view more information.

Open to hikers and dogs on leashes.

Trailhead: From Interstate 5, exit at Manchester Avenue, heading east for about one mile. Note that you must turn right to continue on Manchester when it intersects with El Camino Real, which continues straight ahead. Manchester Preserve's parking area is just before the intersection of Manchester and Trabant Ranch Road.

There is also a northern entrance into the preserve off Landquist Drive in Encinitas.

Distance/Difficulty: The several trails offer about 3.0 to 4.0 miles if you wandered around the entire preserve. The main trail is about 2.0 miles round-trip. Easy to moderate.

2-9. Bridges of Adventure in San Dieguito County Park

For a tiny touch of Tom Sawyer's Island, forego Disneyland and head to San Dieguito County Park. In this county park located just east of Solana Beach, there are a couple of miles of trails that offer a tiny treasure hunt for two old suspension bridges. When I came upon them, I immediately thought of my own childhood explorations on Tom Sawyer's Island in Disneyland, an adventure attraction that has captivated kids since 1956. The San Dieguito County Park version is a lot smaller and a lot cheaper, but also a lot of fun.

The suspension bridges are the best reward in this county park's trail system, but there's another worthy hunt here too. There are three lookout towers, and going from one to the other will take you not only to those suspension bridges but also on most of the trails, adding a little adventure in map reading and trail exploration.

San Dieguito County Park is a treasure hunt for kids.

The county park is just 125 acres, so it's pretty hard to get lost. It's nestled between the bustling boulevards of Lomas Santa Fe Drive and El Camino Real, yet it offers a natural chaparral habitat that makes a very pleasant outing. "Of all the distinct plant communities in California, only chaparral is found throughout the state and is said to represent the state's most characteristic wilderness," states a placard in the park. There are several signs along the trails that point out some of the native plants in the chaparral habitat and how the people who lived here hundreds of years ago used to use them.

The sages, including black sage, white sage, and fragrant sage (all members of the mint family) are very aromatic and give the chaparral its distinctive scent, reports another sign in front of some black sage. Butterflies and hummingbirds love the nectar of the sages.

The fruits of the prickly pear cactus, reports another sign, are called tunas (of all things), and they can be eaten raw or cooked, or dried and stored. Large cactus spines could be attached to sticks for spearing small fish.

I was mostly in pursuit of those lookout towers and their views. I picked up a map of the park and its trails at the entrance, but it's better to download that map before you go in case there aren't any in the box.

I parked in Area 3 and headed to the upper park and to the first of the three lookout towers, which are pinpointed on the map. From the parking area, I headed uphill to the right. Soon I was walking alongside Lomas Santa Fe Drive for a while. Horses are allowed on this part of the trails.

When I came to a small paved path offering a left turn from this street-side trail, I took it and was soon at the first lookout tower. It's constructed of old logs onto which you have to hoist yourself up and cross carefully, and it's a simple structure that offers sweeping vistas to the north and east.

After consulting the map, I headed a little bit back and to the left, going downhill into the center of the park and seeking the second lookout tower. This was where I came upon the suspension bridges, both classically shaky and just a little scary. It was a challenge just to climb onto that second lookout tower because of its log entry.

I continued downhill to the third tower, which offered much less of a sweeping view due to its lower elevation, but it still felt like an achievement in the treasure hunt.

While walking back up to the parking areas, I came upon Quentin Johnston, who was creating a fine plein-air oil painting of some of the lovely eucalyptus trees here.

Find your own attractions in San Dieguito County Park.

Thomas Brothers Map: Page 1167, J-6.

Before You Go: Go to the park's web page, http://www.sdcounty.ca.gov/parks/picnic/sandieguito.html, to download a copy of the trail map before you go.

Trailhead: From Interstate 5, exit at Lomas Santa Fe Drive, and head east. Turn left onto Highland Drive. The park entrance is on your right. There is a $3 day-use parking fee, payable only in cash at the entrance.

Dogs are allowed on leashes only.

Distance/Difficulty: About 2.0 miles of trails; easy.

2-10. Encinitas Ranch Trails Feature Torrey Pines

When part of the historic Ecke Ranch, a major poinsettia grower in Encinitas since 1923, was developed in 1994 as the 850-acre Encinitas Ranch, recreational trails were included in the design along with some 900 homes. The Encinitas Ranch Golf Course opened in 1998, and some of the trails border these greens. About 9.5 miles of trails here are open to hikers, equestrians, and bicyclists, as well as dogs on leashes, offering an amazing array of nature trails smack dab in the city.

I studied the trail map to carve out a round-trip hike of about 5 miles that surprised me with some of its beautiful features.

Encinitas Ranch offers miles of trails open to all users.

Beginning near the golf course at one of the housing development's entry points, I hiked up a hard-packed dirt path and quickly reached the top of a canyon rim, which afforded an amazing view east, over Rancho Santa Fe and all the way to the foothills toward Poway and Ramona. It's easy to imagine that this vast area was sparsely developed when Paul Ecke Sr. bought his ranch here for $150 an acre back in 1923.

Even earlier, the area's first inhabitants were native peoples called the San Dieguitos, the La Jollans, and the Dieguenos, according to the City of Encinitas' history page on its website. The Dieguenos were the missions' converts who helped Junipero Serra build his Spanish missions here and throughout California.

In 1769, Father Serra joined Gaspar de Portola, then governor of Baja California, on an expedition through San Diego to Monterey to build those missions, traveling along El Camino Real, or "the road of kings." Portola is said to be the one who named the area "Encina Canada," Spanish for "hills of live oaks."

Back in 1842, the area was part of a 4,434-acre Mexican land grant named Rancho Las Encinitas ("little oaks") given to Andres Ybarra. Encinitas' more modern history is traced to 1881, when the California Southern Railroad Company helped establish its historic downtown. It was used as a water stop for steam engines. Present-day Encinitas was incorporated as a city in 1986, combining the communities of Leucadia, Encinitas, Cardiff-by-the-Sea, and Olivenhein.

The first part of the trail I hiked lies adjacent to an agricultural parcel, recalling a time when almost all of Encinitas was devoted to agriculture, particularly flowers.

At the top of that ridge above Garden View Road is a long, straight grove of towering Torrey pine trees, which are distinctive because of their long needles, grouped five to a bundle. Shortly after, a spur trail heads down to Garden View Road, where it crosses and continues just a bit farther next to a housing development.

I walked down this spur and back up to the ridge, continuing south on the top of the ridge.

There is a parallel trail just below the ridge that could make an easy and short loop. I stayed on the top, following it as it eventually heads west toward the ocean, still skirting the housing development. Here, enormous eucalyptus trees become the dominant shade provider, and the trail heads down to the small community park called Las Verdes Park.

It's possible to make a loop by continuing north, just to the east of the golf course. I chose to go back the same way I came in order to revisit the shade canopies of the giant eucalyptus and Torrey pines.

Thomas Brothers Map: Page 1147, 4-E

Before You Go: Download a map of the Encinitas Ranch trails at the city of Encinitas' web page, www.ci.encinitas.ca.us. Go to its parks pages for trail maps. Encinitas Ranch trails are on Trail Map No. 1, http://www.ci.encinitas.ca.us/modules/showdocument.aspx?documentid=3476.
  Trails are open from sunrise to sunset to hikers, equestrians, bicyclists, and dogs on leashes. They're free.

Trailhead: From Interstate 5, exit at Leucadia Boulevard and head east. Turn south (right) onto Quail Gardens Drive. Turn east (left) onto Paseo de las Flores and go a short ways just until the housing development begins. Park on the street and note the trail markers on either side of the road. I started by heading uphill to the east.

Distance/Difficulty: My route was about 5.0 miles round-trip; easy.

2-11. Urban Path In Carlsbad Hugs Open Space Preserve

An urban trail that hugs preserved open space carves its way through the Bressi Ranch planned community development in Carlsbad. It's mostly paved and offers nearly a 5-mile loop for walking or biking, with views into that natural habitat.

I started on Gateway Road just off El Fuerte Street and made a loop along Alicante Road to Poinsettia Lane, west to El Camino, and then back along Poinsettia again to El Fuerte and up to Gateway. The prettiest part that veers into the open space off the roads lies along El Fuerte.

This trail, identified as the Bressi Trail in Carlsbad's trail system, can be connected to the Rancho Carrillo trails just to the east of El Fuerte on Poinsettia.

When beginning on Gateway and heading south on Alicante, you'll begin to see all that open space next to the trail that sits apart from but along the road. The open space that continues along Poinsettia and El Fuerte is all part of the Rancho La Costa

Preserve, a noncontinuous collection of some 1,500 acres managed by the Center for Natural Lands Management.

Rancho La Costa Habitat Conservation Area extends from El Camino Real to Elfin Forest within the cities of Carlsbad and San Marcos, as well as the County of San Diego. The site was set aside beginning in 2002 to offset impact from development projects, including Bressi Ranch, a 632-home master-planned community of eight neighborhoods that began selling homes in 2005. Bressi Ranch sits on 585 acres that was once a large working ranch.

The city of Carlsbad was the first city (and still the only city) in North County to establish a Habitat Management Plan (HMP), under the Endangered Species Act. An HMP is a scientific approach to preserving natural land for plant and animal species, linking nature preserves with regional and statewide preserves to create a natural network where species can thrive.

Most of this area of the preserve is covered in coastal sage scrub habitat, where threatened species include Del Mar manzanita, thread-leaved brodiaea, and the California gnatcatcher. Lots of birds and animals make their homes in these scrub lands, and I was delighted to see the yellow-

Bressi Ranch Trail offsets housing developments.

bellied western kingbird in that open space as well as a lovely American kestrel sitting atop a light fixture on the road.

As you walk along Alicante, you'll see the brand-new Alga Norte Community Park at the corner of Alicante and Poinsettia. This 32-acre park opened in January 2014 and features a new aquatic center with a 56-meter competition pool, with viewing bleachers; a 25-yard, 12-lane instructional pool; a smaller warm-water spa and a splash pad "spray-ground" play area for young children. There is an off-leash dog park (including obstacle course equipment) for canines, "about three times the size of the city's existing Ann D. L'Heureux dog park."

Alga Norte Park also offers a skate park larger than the Carlsbad Skate Park on Orion Way, says the city. Interestingly, Carlsbad was home of what many say was the world's first concrete skate park, Carlsbad Skatepark, which operated from 1976 to 1979. It was located next to the old Carlsbad Raceway, the site of which is home today to the Carlsbad Raceway Business Park off Palomar Airport Road in eastern Carlsbad.

Also at Alga Norte Community Park are three lit softball and baseball fields, a lit basketball court, picnic areas and barbecues, and a universally accessible playground.

Reaching Poinsettia Lane, head west as long as you like—all the way to the ocean, if you choose. The roadside trail ends a little west of El Camino Real. You'll pass a lot more of that open space, but signs are posted along the way prohibiting pedestrian entry.

When I reached El Camino, I turned around and headed back east along Poinsettia to El Fuerte, turning left (north) toward my beginning.

This segment of the Bressi Trail is its most natural, because although the trail is still paved, it actually heads a bit into that open space for a sense that you might not be exactly in the center of a city. But soon enough, upon reaching Gateway again, you'll be back in that urban setting, happy that open space parcels are set aside.

Thomas Brothers Map: Page 1127, G-2, where Gateway intersects with El Fuerte just south of Palomar Airport Road.

Before You Go: Download a copy of the trail map from the city of Carlsbad's trail pages: http://www.carlsbadca.gov/services/depts/parks/open/trails/default.asp.
This trail is open to hikers, bicyclists, and dogs on leashes.

Trailhead: From Interstate 5, exit at Palomar Airport Road and head east. Turn right (south) onto El Fuerte Street. There is no parking on El Fuerte. I took a right (west) onto Gateway from El Fuerte and parked on the street at Colt Place, the first available parking near the northern end of the trail.

Distance/Difficulty: The trail is officially 3.0 miles one-way. The route I carved out was about 5 miles total loop. Easy to moderate.

2-12. Ocean View Rewards Golf Course Trail

Carlsbad's Golf Course Trail is a 3.0-mile or 4.0-mile hike through an open-space preserve with an ocean view at its peak. It begins at the city's municipal The Crossings Golf Course. You'll see the trailhead placard at the far western end of the parking lots for the golf course, so park near there and begin the hike as it descends the hill toward some power lines.

This is a wide, unpaved trail that's fairly easygoing. The initial descent is steep for a short time, and the final ascent to the ocean view is somewhat steep for a short time as well, but the remainder of the trail is an easy meander. The trail is very well marked with wooden posts, so follow the arrows to stay on course.

When the trail reaches the bottom of the valley, the trail marker points to a right turn, toward the golf course ahead. The habitat along this part of the trail is Diegan Coastal Sage Scrub, which is the dominant vegetation community in all City of Carlsbad nature reserves. The most common plants in Diegan Coastal Sage Scrub habitat are California sagebrush (artemisia californica), buckwheat, and laurel sumac. "Overall, the habitat is moderately tall (5–6 feet in height) and dense, but areas locally dominated by laurel sumac and lemonadeberry typically exceed 8 feet in height," says the city's Preserves Management Plan.

As you walk along the wide trail through tall stands of laurel sumac and lemonadeberry, you'll see why those post markers are frequently accompanied by red signs that say, "Beware of Snakes." Along this part of the trail in late summer, I saw some of the biggest snake tracks I can recall. You can tell the snake tracks because they are typically horizontal across the path. In soft, sandy dirt, as the snakes make their way from the vegetation across the trail to more vegetation, they leave wavy lines behind. These wavy lines were large here. I also spotted lots of smaller horizontal tracks along other parts of the trail, but these big ones really caught my eye.

Beware of rattlesnakes on Carlsbad Golf Course Trail.

I was out in late morning under the hot sun, which is not a typical time for a rattlesnake to be out. "Rattlesnakes are ectothermic (cold-blooded) and have no control system for their body temperature, so they must stay underground in burrows, under rocks or in the shade to escape the hottest part of the day," says a brochure from the County of San Diego Dept. of Animal Services, "Rattlesnakes: A Guide for Living with Wildlife in San Diego County."

The most common species of rattlesnakes found in San Diego County are the Western diamondback, red diamond, Southern Pacific, speckled, and sidewinder. "Rattlesnakes usually hibernate during the fall and winter only to awaken in the spring months (usually March and April). They can be found, however, at any time of year depending upon the weather." Usually if a rattlesnake senses your approach, "it will leave the area probably before you even see it." But don't think if you make noise that will alert them. "Rattlesnakes are deaf," the brochure notes, but they do sense movement. It's one reason to carry a walking stick, which you can drag along as you walk to alert snakes that way. A snake might also strike the stick instead of you or your pet, so that's another good reason to use one. Rattlesnakes are one of the best reasons to keep your dogs on leashes, so that they won't go sniffing in those bushes or boulders where the snakes might be keeping cool.

After about a mile, you'll reach the golf course itself, a municipal course that opened in 2007. It took some 15 years for Carlsbad to build its city golf course, the Crossings, which was largely created on former agricultural lands. As part of the Crossings development project, 40 acres of new coastal sage scrub habitat were created as well, favored habitat for native bird species, least Bell's vireo, and the California gnatcatcher.

Michael Sweesy, a habitat restoration specialist and landscape architect with Dudek, an environmental consulting firm involved with the Crossings development, told Carlsbad planners in 2012 that before development of the golf course, the area was home to five nesting pairs of California gnatcatchers, "and as of last year, there were 19 breeding pairs," he said.

The trail crosses a big bridge over Macario Creek (and that riparian habitat), where it joins a golf cart path for a short way. After going through a tunnel below Faraday Avenue, the trail climbs up and then to the left of some eucalyptus trees through Veterans Memorial Park to that view of Agua Hedionda Lagoon and the Pacific Ocean to the west. From the top, circle back down to that tunnel again.

Here's where you can add that extra mile to the hike. After the Faraday Avenue tunnel at those eucalyptus trees, head to the right to climb another small hill that will eventually lead farther into a future part of Veterans Memorial Park slated for more trail development in 2020 or later.

Either way, retrace your route back, and watch out for those snakes.

Thomas Brothers Map: Page 1127, A-2, near where the golf course flag sign is off The Crossings Drive.

Before You Go: Download a copy of the Golf Course trail map at the City of Carlsbad's trails pages: http://www.carlsbadca.gov/services/depts/parks/open/trails/locations.asp.
This trail is open only to hikers, mountain bikers, and dogs on leashes.

Trailhead: From Interstate 5, exit at Palomar Airport Road and head east for about a mile. Turn left (north) onto The Crossings Drive, and continue to its end and into the clubhouse parking area on the right. Park at the western end of the parking lot near the trailhead placard.

Distance/Difficulty: This trail is a total round-trip of 3.0 or 4.0 miles, depending on which route to take east of the Faraday tunnel to the upper viewpoints. Easy to moderate with a total elevation gain of about 400 feet.

2-13. Carlsbad Oaks North Good for Lunch Hour

Carlsbad Oaks North Trail is a good place to head for your lunch hour if you work nearby. Hikers, bicyclists, and dogs on leashes are welcome on this soft-surface trail that winds through a conservation area set aside when Carlsbad Oaks North properties were developed for businesses. The 1.3-mile trail sits in 326 acres of the habitat conservation area; 108 acres of the western portion are owned by San Diego County, and the 218 acres in the eastern portion are owned by the Center for Natural Lands Management (CNLM), a private, nonprofit corporation dedicated to protecting and sustaining native species and their habitats.

The trail is maintained by the City of Carlsbad. It's a wide, old dirt road that sits a bit above the Agua Hedionda Creek, which runs through the site. Along that riparian habitat are lots of coast live oak trees as well as some willows. In the coastal sage scrub and chaparral habitats on the steep hillsides are such sensitive plants as San Diego thornmint and thread-leaved brodiaea. The California gnatcatcher lives here, as well as many red-tailed hawks.

"Much of the available habitat within the preserve is in good condition," says a report from CNLM posted at the south end of the trail. "To keep this condition, the preserve manager must regularly control weeds like Pampas grass, Mexican fan palm, sweet fennel and artichoke thistle, among others." I saw lots of that tall yellow sweet fennel at the very northern end of the trail, but this short part of the trail may as well be avoided.

I began at that northern end very near the corner of El Fuerte and Faraday, next to the pump station where there is a small parking lot.

From that parking area, you can see a faint trail through the brush below, which is where I started. This part of the trail is little traveled, thick with weeds and not very appealing. Start walking instead on the El Fuerte sidewalk, and about 100 yards south of the pump station, you'll see a "Trailhead 1" sign. The trail from here is that wider dirt road, which is far more navigable.

It's fairly flat for the first 0.75 mile or so as it skirts that creek bed to the north side of the trail. When you reach a trail

A Lorquin's Admiral butterfly on the Carlsbad Oaks North Trail.

signpost pointing to the right, the trail then begins a steep climb uphill. Very near this intersection is a large prickly pear cactus, a favored food source even today. Its flat and prickly pads are called "nopales" in Spanish and are common in Mexican food, as are its fruits, called "tunas" in Spanish and sometimes known as cactus figs. This specimen was loaded with fruits, whereas another prickly pear elsewhere on the trail had almost none.

The prickly pear fruits must be carefully peeled to remove the small spines on their skins. They have been used in Mexico for thousands of years to make jams, jellies, candies, and an alcoholic drink.

Erik Gronborg of the San Diego Cactus and Succulent Society presented a program in Balboa Park all about the prickly pear's botany and history. "The prickly pear was an important part of life for the indigenous people in America," said Gronborg in his program announcement. It's even "on the national seal of Mexico."

When you reach the top of that incline, you begin to descend to the buildings along Melrose Drive and finally to a pleasing park complete with flowing stream and picnic tables right next to the southern end of the trail, at the corner of Melrose and Palomar Airport Road. At this end, I turned around and retraced my way back.

The other highlight of this trail were the butterflies I saw on toyon bushes whose green berries haven't yet turned red (also called Christmas berry, the season when they are red). I saw a couple of different kinds of butterflies, some on laurel shrubs and some even landing on the dirt trail.

When I reached that intersection with the Trailhead 1 to the road and the less-traveled path through the weeds that I'd taken at first, I bypassed that overgrown path and headed straight to the road and back to the parking area.

Thomas Brothers Map: Page 1127, F-1 intersection of El Fuerte and Faraday.

Before You Go: Download a map of this trail from Carlsbad's trails pages on the web: http://www.carlsbadca.gov/services/depts/parks/open/trails/default.asp.
  Hikers, bicyclists, and dogs on leashes welcome.

Trailhead: From Interstate 5, exit at Palomar Airport Road and head east. Turn left on El Fuerte Street and head to its intersection with Faraday Avenue. Park in the small parking area next to the pump station at the southeast corner of Faraday Avenue and El Fuerte Street.

Distance/Difficulty: The trail runs 1.3 miles one-way for about a 2.6-mile round-trip hike; easy to moderate.

2-14. Ridgeline Trail Carves Up, Through La Costa Preserve

A fairly steep and rocky trail carves itself through the coastal sage scrub and chaparral of the Rancho La Costa Preserve, tucked within the city of Carlsbad. At the top of the Ridgeline Trail, reaching about 600 feet elevation, you earn a fine view of Batiquitos Lagoon and the ocean to the west.

The Ridgeline Trail is one of the Carlsbad's longest and most difficult trails, but it's not really terribly hard. It is a rocky, single-track trail that's open to hikers and mountain bikers, as well as dogs on leashes, and its difficulty lies more in that rocky terrain than the steepness. There's a total elevation gain of only about 350 feet, but because you go up and down through canyons, that gain is essentially doubled with the round-trip backtrack.

The trail follows the ridge above Box Canyon, a prime coastal sage scrub canyon that's been set aside as a preserve in perpetuity.

This part of the preserve covers about 500 acres, but the entire Rancho La Costa Preserve counts 1,500 acres in separate parcels extending from El Camino Real to Elfin Forest, through both Carlsbad and San Marcos. This Ridgeline Trail portion of the preserve was set aside in 2002 as mitigation for the development projects of La Costa Villages and University Commons. It is currently managed by the Center for Natural Lands Management (www.cnlm.org).

Climb Ridgeline Trail is great for ocean views.

Over 80 percent of this preserve is covered in coastal sage scrub and mixed chaparral, but most of what I saw was sage scrub. There are a few acres of cottonwood woodlands within Box Canyon, and when you cross San Marcos Creek on the trail, you'll see some of that riparian vegetation there. Box Canyon itself is off limits to the public in order to keep its habitats preserved, so stay on the trail.

The preserve is a wildlife corridor that connects Batiquitos Lagoon with Lake Hodges. Mule deer, coyotes, and bobcats all live here, but the only mammal I saw was a cute jackrabbit hopping across the trail. If you're lucky, you might spot an orange-throated whiptail lizard here, one of the threatened species this preserve helps protect. The red-diamond rattlesnake is another reptile here, but I happily didn't see one.

Golden eagles and northern harriers and kites, along with other raptors, are said to soar above this canyon, as do endangered species like the California gnatcatcher and the least Bell's vireo.

Spring wildflowers add lots of color to these canyons. When I was there just after the first day of spring, I saw golden California poppies, delicate purple wild radish, yellow deer weed, scarlet monkeyflower, pink and white buckwheat blooms, blue blooms of black sage, white morning glories, yellow wallflowers, and wide swaths of yellow and white daisies.

The trail begins off El Fuerte Street and heads into the natural canyons that are now surrounded by homes high on those ridges. It descends for the first foray down into Box Canyon, where that small stream flows across the trail at the bottom.

The trail then ascends somewhat steeply as you head toward a towering SDG&E power pole. When you reach the power pole, a short spur trail off the main trail offers a quick vista back over the lagoon to the ocean.

The trail continues uphill to the top of the ridge and then descends again into another canyon. About 1.5 miles from the trailhead, you'll reach some houses, where the trail becomes paved and continues another half-mile on the edge of a neighborhood until it reaches its eastern end at Corintia Street.

Go back the same way and see how many wildflowers you can spot in spring before enjoying that coastal view again.

Thomas Brothers Map: Page 1127, H-6.

Before You Go: Download a trail map of Rancho La Costa Preserve from the City of Carlsbad's trails page for south city trails: http://www.carlsbadca.gov/services/depts/parks/open/trails/default.asp.
    This trail is open to hikers, mountain bikers, and dogs on leashes.

Trailhead: From Interstate 5, exit at Poinsettia Lane/Aviara Parkway, heading east on Poinsettia. Turn right on Aviara Parkway and continue past El Camino Real, where Aviara Parkway turns into Alga Road. Turn right on El Fuerte Street (at top of hill, after about four miles on Aviara Parkway/Alga), go past the elementary school and park at the bottom of the hill, and you'll see the trailhead sign about 0.8 miles from Alga Road.

Distance/Difficulty: From 1.5 to 2.0 miles one-way, for a total of 3.0 to 4.0 miles round-trip. Moderate.

2-15. Carlsbad's East Ridgeline Is Easy with Lagoon Views

Here's a short, easy trail through a suburban preserve featuring blue-water lagoon views.

Rancho La Costa Preserve in Carlsbad has about 10 miles of trails in three separate parcels: The Ridgeline Trail, the city's longest and hardest one; Denk Tank Peak Trails, where a few routes will challenge hikers to the top; and East Ridgeline, where the Bobcat Trail joins it to form a path through chaparral and coastal sage scrub.

This time I hiked the East Ridgeline/Bobcat section, which sits above the steep walls of Box Canyon where San Marcos Creek winds through before joining Batiquitos Lagoon at the ocean. You cannot hike into Box Canyon—it's off-limits, and its walls are extremely steep. But at a viewpoint on the East Ridgeline Trail, you can peer down into the canyon to see a bit of the creek flow through its rocky environs.

The preserve stretches from El Camino Real to Elfin Forest and covers nearly 1,500 acres broken into various parcels. It's a wildlife corridor that connects Batiquitos Lagoon with Lake Hodges.

"The site is biologically rich and representative of the high diversity of coastal San Diego County's natural habitats," says the Center for Natural Lands Management (CNLM), a nonprofit organization that manages sensitive biological resources through science-based stewardship that aims to protect and preserve environmentally sensitive lands. Rancho La Costa Preserve was deeded to CNLM in 2002 as mitigation to offset impacts of development projects in the area.

In spring, the hills are alive with yellow and white crown daisies, bright orange California poppies, pale pink wild radish, white pearly everlasting, yellow and orange deer weed, new pink blooms of buckwheat, tiny purple-striped blue-eyed grass, and purple thistle.

Beginning on the East Ridgeline Trail from Cadencia Park, head west to reach that dead-end viewpoint overlooking the creek and canyon. Then head back up to the northeast, where the trail makes a boxlike loop. Upon reaching Old Santa Fe Road, paved here from Cadencia north to the fire station, turn left (north) until you reach the trailhead for the Bobcat Trail, which heads in a single track down to the west. It connects again to the East Ridgeline Trail, where you can head back the way you started.

East Ridgeline Trail heads to lagoon view.

Near the fire station are some informational placards sharing the story of the Harmony Grove Fire that burned through here in October 1996, "the most serious emergency event in Carlsbad's history," it says. The fire began east in Harmony Grove, but winds drove it west into this area. Several homes along Cadencia Street were among the 54 homes lost in Carlsbad that day. Santa Ana winds drove that inferno. "Linked often in literature and legend with bizarre behavior, the Santa Ana is an erratic, unpredictable, dry, hot, gusty wind that blows from the north and northeast, sucking moisture out of chaparral," says the placard. "Once a spark ignites the dry fuels, strong Santa Anas can quickly fan a small wildfire into storm-like proportions, shifting direction of attack in ways impossible to predict.

"A century ago, several small fires would burn during the summer, consuming older brush and leaving newer, moister vegetation untouched. Now the fire season has moved to fall, the season when Santa Anas reign. Instead of beginning 'naturally,' these fires typically arise by arson or accident … they are much bigger, burning larger areas of old, dried brush."

The Bobcat Trail is named after the cat species that is native but rarely seen here in the coastal sage scrub. Deer have been spotted here too. Perhaps they head for San Marcos Creek at the bottom of Box Canyon.

The San Marcos Creek watershed is the second-largest watershed within the Carlsbad Hydrologic Unit. Carlsbad's seven watersheds include Loma Alta Creek, Buena Vista Creek, Agua Hedionda Creek, Canyon de las Encinas Creek, San Marcos Creek, Cottonwood Creek, and Escondido Creek. They all empty into the four coastal lagoons of Buena Vista, Agua Hedionda, Batiquitos, and San Elijo. The largest of these watersheds is Escondido Creek, which empties into San Elijo Lagoon. Encinitas Creek joins San Marcos Creek, and both empty into Batiquitos Lagoon, which is owned and operated by the California Department of Fish and Wildlife as an ecological reserve.

When Lake San Marcos was formed by a dam on San Marcos Creek, and urban development continued to the sea, Batiquitos Lagoon was filling up with sediment by the late 1990s. A major project funded by the Port of Los Angeles in cooperation with the city of Carlsbad was completed in 1997, and it opened the lagoon to the ocean's tidal changes and flows. Today Batiquitos Lagoon is the pretty, blue-water wetland you see on this hike.

Thomas Brothers Map: Page 1127, J-7, Cadencia Park.

Before You Go: Download a copy of the Rancho La Costa Preserve trails map from Carlsbad's parks and recreation department: http://www.carlsbadca.gov/services/depts/parks/open/trails/preserve/default.asp.

Another good map of the East Ridgeline Trail network is on the Center for Natural Lands Management's website: http://cnlm.org/wp-content/uploads/Ridgeline-Trails-2014-bl-wh.pdf.

These trails are open to hikers, bicyclists, and dogs on leashes.

Trailhead: Begin at Cadencia Park in Carlsbad, where the East Ridgeline Trail starts from its northeast corner. From Interstate 5, exit at La Costa Avenue and head east. Turn left (north) on Cadencia Avenue and go about 1.5 miles to the park on the left. Park on the street; there are no facilities at Cadencia Park.

Distance/Difficulty: The East Ridgeline Trail is about 1.0 mile in length, and the Bobcat Trail is about 0.5 mile. Combining the two with a portion of the Old Rancho Santa Fe Road Trail, I hiked about 2.25 miles with very easy elevation gain of only about 180 feet total. Easy.

2-16. Carlsbad's Denk Peak Has Long Coastal Views

Coastline views from Camp Pendleton to La Jolla come into view on a fine clear day from Carlsbad's highest point, Denk Tank Mountain. Several trails covering about 10 miles reach the hilltop's viewpoint in the Rancho La Costa Habitat Conservation Area that encompasses Denk Tank Mountain. I took the Switchbacks Trail up and back for a 4-mile round-trip with a fairly easy grade, thanks to those switchbacks.

Rancho La Costa Habitat Conservation Area is managed by the Center for Natural Lands Management (http://cnlm.org) and covers a total area of about 1,500 acres in several parcels, extending from El Camino Real to Elfin Forest through Carlsbad, San Marcos, and the County of San Diego. The preserve was deeded to the CNLM in 2002 as mitigation for the area developments of La Costa Villages and University Commons. The preserve acts as a regional corridor connecting Batiquitos Lagoon and Lake Hodges, and it protects homes for mule deer, coyotes, and bobcats as well as golden eagles, red-tailed hawks, horned lizards, and orange-throated whiptail lizards.

Climb Carlsbad's highest point for long views.

Denk Tank Mountain is covered in coastal sage scrub and mixed chaparral, and so it offers virtually no shade. The plants are dense and dry in the fall, but the City of Carlsbad notes that in spring, this area "affords some of the best native flower blooms in March," notably California poppies and lupines.

The Denk Tank Mountain trails are very popular with mountain bikers, who don't seem to mind climbing up the steep grades and rocky trails to get those downhill thrills. I saw several bicyclists the day I was there, and thankfully I could hear them enough in advance to get out of the way on the single-track trail.

The Switchbacks Trail is one of the main routes up and is rated on the map at the top viewpoint as "easy grade." Signposts on the trail mark 0.5-, 1.0-, 1.5- and 2.0-mile points, the last at the end near the very top. There are several shortcut trails shortening the main switchback trail, but I stuck to the main trail up and down.

The trail passes and rises above the water tank that is presumably that Denk Tank. You reach the top after about a 550-foot elevation gain to its summit of about 1,065 feet.

The Denk family owned most of the mountain for nearly all of the 1900s. The family patriarch, Louis Denk, had been one of the first seven members of the Colony Olivenhain, who were invited in 1884 by the Kimball brothers, Warren and Frank, to purchase and settle about 442 acres of their 4,431-acre Rancho Las Encinitas.

The southern reaches of the Rancho La Costa Preserve extend to Olivenhain. According to a U-T article in 2005 by Diane Welch about Richard Bumann's book, *Colony Olivenhain,* published in 1981, this area, which lies beyond the end of Lone Jack Road, was the site of copper mining that began after a deposit was discovered here in 1887. The Encinitas Copper Mining and Smelting Co. constructed three vertical shafts and a small processing mill to concentrate the copper ore found. Processed ore was hauled by horse-drawn wagons to Cardiff, where it was loaded onto railroad cars and transported to Escondido.

Another vein of copper was discovered in 1897 by a copper mine then owned by C. W. Withan. "The mine is about six miles from Encinitas and is considered to be one of the richest discoveries of copper made in the West," reported the San Diego Union in 1897. Some 4 tons of ore were being removed daily. Eventually the Encinitas Copper Mine closed in 1917. One more local legend remains, giving Lone Jack Road its name: "A solitary jackass that once worked at the mines is said to have wandered the area for years following the mines' closure," wrote Bumann.

From the early 1920s to 1940, the area was also the site of open pit clay mines. Between mile 0.5 and 1.0 on the Switchback Trail, you'll note lots of rocks that have a blue-green tinge to them, from the copper that is present in those rocks.

The Switchback Trail earns its name as it climbs to the top, where an informational placard stands guard with a couple of benches. Linger up here to examine the view that extends 360 degrees. The Batiquitos Lagoon is one of the highlights, as well as the ocean from Oceanside to La Jolla. You'll see the high-rise buildings of University Town Centre. To the east, Black Mountain with all its antennae is a landmark. Housing developments fill in the rest of the landscape, but those several trails of this Rancho La Costa Preserve invite future exploration.

I returned the way I came, though you can study the map at the top and take a different (longer and/or steeper) route back down if you wish.

Thomas Brothers Map: Page 1148, B-1—the intersection of Camino Junipero and Corte Romero.

Before You Go: Download a map of most of the trails at the City of Carlsbad's trails page for Rancho La Costa Preserve: http://www.carlsbadca.gov/services/depts/parks/open/trails/preserve/default.asp.

Another good map of Denk Tank trails is at the Center for Natural Land Management pages: http://cnlm.org/wp-content/uploads/Denk-Overall_textbox.pdf.

The trail is open to mountain bikers, hikers, and dogs on leashes.

Trailhead: From Interstate 5, exit at La Costa Avenue and head east. Turn left (east) at Rancho Santa Fe Road, then right (south) on Camino Junipero. Go one block and turn left on Corte Romero. Park near the intersection of Corte Romero and Camino Junipero. The trailhead is at this intersection. Follow the signs uphill for the Switchbacks Trail.

Distance/Difficulty: The trail is 2.0 miles one-way, or 4.0 miles round-trip. With wandering at the top a bit, I covered about 4.5 miles total. Moderate.

2-17. Viewpoint Loop with Horned Lizard, Whiptail

Several trails reach Carlsbad's highest point, Denk Mountain, where views to Batiquitos Lagoon and the ocean spread west while Black Mountain and Palomar Mountain lie to the east. Some 10 miles over seven trails reach the viewpoint summit that lies in this Rancho La Costa Habitat Conservation Area. This conservation area covers nearly 1,500 acres and serves as a regional corridor connecting Batiquitos Lagoon and Lake Hodges. It is managed by the Center for Natural Lands Management (CNLM).

A loop up Carlsbad's highest point is easier with switchbacks.

This time, I headed up the Horned Lizard Trail to reach the viewpoint. Then I came back down the Whiptail Loop Trail for a loop of about 4.5 miles with about 650 feet in elevation change. Whiptail is a lizard, so look for them on these namesake trails.

Even though a monsoonal marine layer made the entire day gray, prohibiting long-range views, it also made a cooler summer foray up Denk Mountain, where chaparral and coastal sage scrub habitats offer no shade.

In summer, the only blooms you'll see are some late-blooming buckwheat, the scattered and spindly tiny yellow blooms of tarplant, and occasional conical clusters of the cream-colored flowers of laurel sumac, also known as the taco plant for its taco-shaped leaves.

To reach the Horned Lizard Trail, begin on the old dirt road called the La Costa-Junipero Trail, which follows power lines. You'll pass the trailhead for the Switchbacks Trail, another route up to the same viewpoint, as well as a couple of other unnamed trails. In about a half-mile on your left (north), you'll reach the obvious signposts that are posted at the beginning of the Horned Lizard Trail.

This trail is also full of switchbacks, but its grade is a bit more moderate than the Switchbacks Trail. At any trail intersection, follow the signs for Horned Lizard Trail to stay on course.

You'll pass signposts marking the 1.0-mile and 1.5-mile points on the trail, and then you'll reach the top, the viewpoint, at 2.0 miles from the start. From this vantage point there is an informational placard, bench, and open-air ramada. Stop a while to take in those lagoon and ocean views.

Head back down on the same trail, and shortly you'll come to the intersection with the Whiptail Loop Trail to the left (east), another moderate-grade descent with switchbacks that make it easier. These are both single-track trails that are also popular with mountain bikers. According to a notice at the viewpoint from the San Diego Mountain Biking Association, these trails offer "advanced technical features, steep grades and a narrow trail tread." Bikers should yield to pedestrians, and horses and bikes heading downhill should yield to bikes heading uphill.

When you head down the Whiptail Loop Trail, you'll see to the east a few more trails that lie in Copper Creek Canyon, an adjacent area in Rancho La Costa's conservation area.

While the single-track Horned Lizard Trail is open to hikers, mountain bikers and dogs on leashes, the Whiptail Loop Trail is closed to dogs. (Hikers with dogs may, of course, head back down Horned Lizard Trail.)

Dogs are not allowed on the Copper Creek trails because this secluded section "provides important wildlife habitat and access to water," notes the placard at the trailhead. "The connectivity to open space allows wildlife safe passage. Even when dogs are unsuccessful in catching the object of their chase, the potential prey has to expend significant energy in order to save their life," says the placard. "Since many animals are barely surviving with the limited resources available in the wild, expenditure of extra energy may push them over the edge." Also, don't forget that especially in summer, your dogs need water too. "If you are drinking water while hiking, then your dog should be drinking water, too," it says.

One really interesting aspect of hiking these trails up Denk Mountain is that the trail itself features a lot of soft dirt, which makes for excellent wildlife tracking opportunities. See if you can spot snake tracks (obvious wavy horizontal paths across the trail) as well as those of mule deer, bobcat, and other species. I saw lots of snake tracks along with those of birds and mule deer.

Another notable resident on these trails is ashy spike moss, a gray ground cover that virtually carpets many areas and appears nearly dead. According to the Soil Ecology and Restoration Group of SDSU, Ashy Spike Moss isn't really a moss but is more closely related to ferns. It can withstand intense drought and is an important ally against erosion in coastal sage scrub and chaparral habitats. "They green up and return to life within seconds of watering and can dry down and appear lifeless within hours as moisture levels drop," says SDSU. It's "an important component of the soil surface ecosystem in many parts of coastal San Diego and Baja California."

Denk Mountain derives its name from the Denk family that is said to have owned this area for most of the 20th century.

Also in this area, the Encinitas Copper Mining and Smelting Company mined "one of the richest discoveries of copper made in the west," according to an article in the San Diego Union in 1897. The copper mine was closed in 1917, but there are occasional reminders of that era in this conservation area.

Thomas Brothers Map: Page 1148, B-1, Camino Junipero at Avenida Maravilla.

Before You Go: Download a copy of the main trail map for Rancho La Costa Preserve from Carlsbad's city parks pages: http://www.carlsbadca.gov/services/depts/parks/open/trails/preserve/default.asp.

Another good map of Denk Tank trails is at the Center for Natural Land Management pages: http://cnlm.org/wp-content/uploads/Denk-Overall_textbox.pdf.

The single-track Horned Lizard Trail is open to hikers, mountain bikers, and dogs on leashes, but the Whiptail Loop Trail is closed to dogs. Go back down Horned Lizard with dogs.

Trailhead: From Interstate 5, exit at La Costa Avenue and head east. Turn left (north) at Rancho Santa Fe Road and then right (east) on Camino Junipero. Park on a side street (such as Avenida Maravilla) or at the end of Camino Junipero, and walk to the trailhead, which lies under the power lines that cross Camino Junipero.

Distance/Difficulty: Total round-trip for this loop is about 4.5 miles; moderate.

2-18. Aviara's Eucalyptus Trail Is Urban Natural Oasis

Carlsbad's Eucalyptus Grove Trail is one of those surprising finds in an urban setting: It meanders among Aviara neighborhoods but also features a hidden natural canyon or two. It's one of the longest trails in Carlsbad's Aviara Trails network at 2 miles. Although it stops short of connecting with the popular Lagoon Trail along Batiquitos Lagoon, you could easily combine with that trail by taking a short walk along Batiquitos Drive to a connector trail.

The Eucalyptus Grove Trail begins at its northern end just off Aviara Parkway on Kestrel Drive. You'll see a trailhead sign on the street. The first part is a steep decline down a short paved road. At the bottom of this canyon, the trail follows a gutter and heads toward the first eucalyptus grove. But the trail doesn't actually head into that grove. It takes a sharp left up a gravel path and begins to wind south around the backsides of the neighborhood.

As its name suggests, the trail does go through several fine eucalyptus groves, whose old trees soar high into the air. The fragrance of the eucalyptus pods wafts along the way.

The trail dips up and down for a few steep topographical challenges. At the first major trail intersection after about a mile, head downhill to the left, where the trail crosses Kestrel Drive and resumes on the other side of the street. If you go right at that intersection, you'll reach a dead-end bluff that affords your first ocean view. Also along that short spur trail are lots of lemonadeberry bushes bursting in summer with their sticky red berries.

Just after that first crossing of Kestrel, the trail hits the first bonus: a secret canyon oasis in the middle of an urban setting, where towering eucalyptus trees and lemonadeberry shrubs hide the fact you are smack dab in the city.

The lemonadeberry is in the cashew family, and mammals and birds like to eat these berries. The Kumeyaay used to soak the berries in water to make beverages.

The trail climbs out of the canyon and down to another street (Calidris Lane), where it crosses again. Signs at each of these street crossings alert hikers to the continuing trail. This last part of the trail is far more open providing little shade. Lots of yellow-blooming tarweed bushes line the sandy path as it climbs to the Eucalyptus Grove Trail Lookout Point. Glimpses of Batiquitos Lagoon lie straight ahead, with slivers of ocean to the west as well.

Tarweed is in the sunflower family, and along this trail, dense bushes of it paint the landscape yellow in summer. It's among the most common native herbs in San Diego County, according to James

Find a secret canyon in Eucalyptus Grove.

Lightner in his book *San Diego County Native Plants*. Interspersed among these yellow blooms are the fascinating pink blooms of a dudleya, sometimes called canyon live forever. A succulent, they shoot out long blooms in late spring and summer that feature several dark pink blossoms.

The plaque at the lookout point states that a rare habitat within Aviara is the Southern maritime chaparral with unique flora including Del Mar manzanita, summer holly, and coast white lilies.

The Eucalyptus Grove Trail ends just a short way down from this lookout point at another street (Savannah Lane), but you can walk west along Batiquitos Drive to reach a short connector trail to the Lagoon Trail. I turned around and retraced my steps back, happy to go into that secret canyon again.

Thomas Brothers Map: Page 1127, B-6.

Before You Go: Download a trail map at the Carlsbad web site for its Aviara trails: http://www. carlsbadca.gov/services/depts/parks/open/trails/aviara.asp.

Hikers, bicyclists, and dogs on leashes are allowed. It's free.

Trailhead: From Interstate 5, exit at Poinsettia Lane and head east. Turn right on Batiquitos Drive and continue past Kestrel Drive, about 0.5 miles to the first parking lot. The Eucalyptus Trail heads north from this parking area.

Distance/Difficulty: The Eucalyptus Grove Trail is 2.0 miles one-way, making a 4.0-mile round-trip. It's moderately easy.

2-19. Carlsbad's Hosp Grove Features Eucalyptus Trees

Among the most extensive in Carlsbad's citywide trail system are the Hosp Grove Trails. In this 5.5-acre park standing next to the very urban North County Plaza shopping area on Marron Road, you'll find 3 miles of trails that wind through huge old eucalyptus trees. The City of Carlsbad notes that these trees were planted many years ago to be used by the railroad industry in its construction of rail lines.

The towering eucalyptus tree has a love-hate history in the county and throughout California. Once considered an excellent protector against scale on grape vines, it was planted extensively in wine country from Napa and Sonoma to Escondido and El Cajon, according to Leland G. Stanford's 1970 article "San Diego's Eucalyptus Bubble" in *The Journal of San Diego History.* "Railroad construction, more than any other activity, caused continuous and prolific horn-tooting about the value of eucalyptus trees-for-ties," Stanford wrote.

From about 1875 to the early 1900s, Frank and Warren Kimball, brothers from National City who were leading railroad promoters here, planted thousands of eucalyptus along the Southern Pacific and Santa Fe railroad right-of-ways they'd help organize. By 1910, the Kimballs had planted 3 million eucalyptus trees in Rancho Santa Fe. "About the same time other persons, probably stimulated by the Santa Fe action, planted many acres of the trees in other parts of the county," wrote Stanford, who founded Balboa University here (now California Western).

We have a love-hate relationship with the eucalyptus tree.

It was soon discovered that eucalyptus timber rotted excessively, and its ties refused to hold railroad spikes. The trees were therefore no longer harvested for railroad ties.

It is not a native species, having been brought here from Australia in the 1800s. It tends to take over wherever it's planted so that few native species can survive along with it. The eucalyptus tree is "considered undesirable in natural areas," notes James Lightner in his book *San Diego County Native Plants*. Some nature preserves are actively removing eucalyptus trees, including parts of San Dieguito River Park.

However, many people love the majestic trees, which include some 600 species, for their shade and because they are fast-growing and drought-tolerant. Several species of birds, including Cooper's and red-shouldered hawks, nest in eucalyptus, according to the San Diego Natural History Museum. The enormous stand of eucalyptus trees in Carlsbad's Hosp Grove itself hosts the winter migration of the Monarch butterflies from the western side of the Rockies, according to San Diego County's chapter of the National Wildlife Federation.

Begin your foray through Hosp Grove's eucalyptus trees immediately west of the parking area off Jefferson Street. There are two trails here; take the one closest to the road, where a City of Carlsbad Regulations sign is posted. The other one nearest to a picnic table goes straight up to a T intersection connecting to the other trail. If you take the one closest to the road, you won't have to backtrack for lagoon views, as you loop up to that intersection and keep heading straight.

In the early part of the trail, you'll be able to see Buena Vista Lagoon immediately, on the north side of Jefferson Street. The trail winds up, gaining about 100 feet in elevation, passing through eucalyptus as well as meadows of green grasses and purple-and-white nonnative wild radishes.

From the trail's crest, you begin a descent down to Monroe Street, passing through fields of bright orange nonnative nasturtium. You'll also see here the yellow nonnative buttercup. Opt to take the low (road) trail that heads back to the Jefferson Street parking area, making for about a one-mile round-trip loop. Alternatively, cross Monroe Street to the eastern half of the Hosp Grove Trails. There's another parking area here as well with several trails that wind through more eucalyptus groves, covering a few more miles.

Hosp Grove, a lovely respite right in the center of a city, offers a chance to ponder how the eucalyptus, now ubiquitous statewide, is both treasured and reviled.

Thomas Brothers Map: Page 1106, E-3.

Before You Go: Get more information and download a good map of all the trails on both sides of Hosp Grove at the City of Carlsbad's web page: http://www.carlsbadca.gov/services/depts/parks/open/trails/default.asp.
Bicyclists, hikers, and dogs on leashes all welcome. It's free. Hours are 8:00 a.m. to 10:00 p.m.

Trailhead: From Interstate 5, exit at Las Flores in Carlsbad. Go west a short distance, turning right (north) onto Jefferson Street. Continue for about a half-mile. The Hosp Grove Park entrance is on the right (the twig sign on wood is a little hard to spot).

Distance/Difficulty: From 1.0 to 3.0 miles. Moderately easy.

2-20. La Costa Glen, Valley Trails Offer Urban Hike

For a nearby urban trail that accommodates wheelchairs, baby strollers, bicyclists, hikers, and dogs on leashes, consider the combination of two trails in southwest Carlsbad. La Costa Glen and La Costa Valley trails are two in Carlsbad's citywide trail system that lie less than a half mile apart. Put them together, and you get about a 4.5-mile workout on an easy, mostly level course. Have lunch between the two or after both in The Forum, a sprawling neighborhood shopping center, where you can also park for these trails.

I started on La Costa Glen Trail, an unpaved, soft-surface path that sits next to an open space corridor along Encinitas Creek.

The posted signs for La Costa Glen Trail say it's 2 miles for the entire one-way length, but my GPS gadget found it closer to 1.5 miles, making for about a 3-mile round-trip. (The city's brochure for La Costa Glen Trail also notes it's a mile and a half.)

Explore an urban respite along Encinitas Creek.

The area is sometimes called Green Valley. According to the city, it's a southern maritime chaparral habitat that supports critical populations of Del Mar manzanita and Encinitas baccharis, the latter a shrub in the sunflower family.

Spring wildflowers I spotted along the trail included black sage (which gave a strong and lovely scent to the air), white California everlasting, lots of yellow mustard, white and yellow sunflowers and daisies, pretty pink native California roses, pink bush mallow, and two especially eye-catching species I've found hard to identify. One I thought looked like a type of hibiscus or mallow while the other could be a type of clarkia primrose.

I asked local native plant expert, Tom Chester, to help identify them from my photos. His extensive expertise matched both: the first a "type of mallow, probably also a cultivated plant, your flower is a good match for Lavatera maritima," he told me. The other is likely a "non-native cistus (Cistus purpureus, or Orchid Rockrose) that is often planted as part of a drought-resistant landscape." Even though both plants are cultivated and not wildflowers, botanist Chester was able to make the match. He directed me to the extensive wildflower photos available on the web from http://calphotos.berkeley.edu. Chester's website is http://www.tchester.org.

Also on La Costa Glen Trail are some berry bushes, possibly the nonnative Himalayan blackberry, whose fruits were still small in mid-May. There are lots of willow trees that create canopies over parts of this trail. Several tall cottonwood trees with their heart-shaped leaves tower over it as well.

Peering down over the fence into that creek bed, I couldn't see any water, but the overgrown riparian habitat was evident, with lots of cattails and a few oak trees.

By far the best views from either of these trails come at the northern end of the La Costa Glen Trail. Housing developments lie just west of that trail for most of the way, but wide-open spaces take over near that northern end and Batiquitos Lagoon comes into view as well.

This northern end of the trail ends at La Costa Avenue; turn around and go back. Cross the road at Levante Street to continue on the trail, and again at Calle Barcelona (where you park at The Forum). Continue a bit farther south past the shopping center until you reach the end of the trail at Leucadia Boulevard. Turn around again and go back to Calle Barcelona.

Head east on Calle Barcelona less than a half-mile, passing El Camino Real and turning left onto Paseo Aliso. The entrance to the La Costa Valley Trail is here, across the street from El Camino Creek Elementary School.

La Costa Valley Trail loops around another open-space corridor surrounding another wetland habitat where you'll hear many birds calling.

La Costa Valley Trail also skirts residential neighborhoods along an unpaved path on its northern side with a paved path on its southern side. As you head east from Paseo Aliso, the trail ends at Avenida Helecho where you turn right to rejoin the trail on the south side of that open space. This part of the path is paved the whole way, where it connects to the paved bike and pedestrian paths along Calle Barcelona, which you follow back to your parking area at The Forum.

These are both easy, urban trails that protect and preserve open spaces, and they are popular with joggers, walkers, and strollers. Birdwatchers can look for California towhees, sparrows, and mourning doves.

Thomas Brothers Map: Page 1147, F-3.

Before You Go: Download a copy of the trails map from the City of Carlsbad's website. Both La Costa Glen and La Costa Valley trails are on the city's "South" trails map" section: http://www. carlsbadca.gov/services/depts/parks/open/trails/default.asp.

Hikers, bicyclists, and dogs on leashes welcome.

Trailhead: To begin on the La Costa Glen Trail, from Interstate 5, exit at La Costa Avenue and head east to El Camino Real. Turn right (south) on El Camino Real, then turn right again on Calle Barcelona and park in the northwest corner of the shopping center parking area.

The trail begins across Calle Barcelona from this parking area.

Distance/Difficulty: The La Costa Glen Trail is about 1.5 miles on-way; the La Costa Valley Trail is a 1.3-mile loop, making for about a 4.6- to 5.0-mile hike when combining both.

2-21. Trail Circles Lake Calavera and Even Includes a Maze

Carlsbad's Lake Calavera Preserve is the largest of that city's 13 managed nature preserves. Over 6 miles of trails open to hikers, mountain bikers, and dogs on leashes crisscross the preserve.

The 256-acre Lake Calavera Mitigation Bank Open Space area includes the 110-acre Calavera Nature Preserve that was set aside in the early 1990s by a developer in the area's history. The open space preserve surrounding Lake Calavera is bordered by housing developments to the north and south, but it is next to undeveloped natural lands to the east and west, making this preserve a big swath of open space in the urban core.

The 400-acre lake is a man-made reservoir managed by the Carlsbad Municipal Water District. Built in 1940, the earthen dam at the south end of the lake rises 67 feet high and 490 feet across. The lake stores 520 acre-feet of water.

Find over six miles of trails at Lake Calavera Preserve.

The preserve's main trail is a 1.9-mile loop that circles Lake Calavera. The main North Trail crosses the dam to continue along the main South Trail for that full lake loop. Just beyond the south end of the dam, a steep trail forks off to the south of that main South Trail. Take that trail uphill to reach the cliff side of Mount Calavera, the 513-foot-high summit centered in the preserve.

"Calavera means skull (in Spanish), which probably comes from the unusual shape of the area's centerpiece, Mount Calavera," says Preserve Calavera, a nonprofit citizens' organization formed in 2002 to protect this open space. Mount Calavera, says the organization, is not a mountain but rather a 22-million-year-old volcanic plug—a mass of volcanic rock that solidified in the volcano's vent millions of years ago. "When the volcano becomes extinct and starts to erode away, the 'plug' is all that is left." Mount Calavera is one of only three volcanic plugs in Southern California, it adds.

That cliff is evidence of mining done here in the early 1900s. It also seems to invite rock climbers, some of whom I saw. There have been several activities in this area for years that Carlsbad has been trying to eliminate, including motorized vehicles, swimming in the lake, rogue trails, dumping, and unleashed dogs running free. Since 2009, the city has partnered with the Center for Natural Lands Management to manage and patrol the preserve, install fencing and signs, fix trails and close unauthorized trails, survey plants and animals, and remove invasive plants, including mustard and fennel, which once thrived here.

When you reach the top of that short spur trail to Mount Calavera's cliff, head toward the entry opening in the chain-link fence. Just to the right of that opening is a surprising rock maze. You can't get lost inside this maze because you can step over one circle to the next. This concentric trail, like any contemplative labyrinth, invites one to ponder the journey rather than the destination. Nearby are rock arrangements that spell people's names and such.

Go back down to join the main South Trail around the lake. Just beyond a bench that looks out over the lake, the trail forks with the main trail on the low side and the Serpentine Trail (not currently marked with a sign) to the right. Take that right trail to head uphill. At a kiosk at the top, another trail heads up the top of that volcanic plug for the best views around. You can wander around these trails for several hours with very little chance of getting lost. However, take a map before you go to locate where you are, because many of the trails do not sport signs.

In winter, I saw lots of red-berried California toyon. In spring, wildflowers here include chamise, yucca, scarlet monkey flowers, fuchsia-colored conchalagua, and wild roses. On the lake I spotted several black, white-billed American coots. Others to look for include mallard ducks, cormorants, red-shouldered hawks, and scrub jays.

Thomas Brothers Map: Page 1107, 3C.

Before You Go: There are several entry points to Lake Calavera Preserve, which lies on the northeastern border of Carlsbad with Oceanside. Download a map at the city's trails pages: http://www.carlsbadca.gov/services/depts/parks/open/trails/default.asp.
 Hikers, bicyclists, and dogs on leashes welcome.

Trailhead: I entered the preserve at the Sky Haven West Trail, which is actually in Oceanside on the northern edge of the preserve.
 From Highway 78, exit at College Boulevard, heading south. Turn left onto Lake Boulevard and then right onto Sky Haven Lane. Sky Haven dead-ends at Azure Ladd Drive; park here on the preserve's side of the road.

Distance/Difficulty: From 2.0 to 4.0 miles, depending on route. Easy.

2-22. Carrillo Ranch Called Carlsbad's Sleeping Beauty

The 27-acre Leo Carrillo Ranch Historic Park offers about 4 miles of trails, divided into two routes on either side of Melrose Drive. The 2-mile trail on the west side connects with other trails through Bressi Ranch, and it has as its centerpiece the historic Leo Carrillo Ranch itself.

The easy trail is wide and well kept, paved in portions, and covered with gravel in others. It's available for hiking, bicycling, and walking dogs on leashes. You walk along the adobe wall that encircles the ranch for the first quarter-mile or so on fairly level terrain. As the adobe wall gives way to chain-link fencing, you can only glimpse the creek that runs through the middle of this property, once the vast valley home known as Agua Hedionda ("stinking waters") of the Luiseño people, who lived here for thousands of years.

A historic ranch still features plentiful peacocks.

A Mexican land grant of over 13,000 acres issued to Juan Maria Romouldo Marron in 1842 passed in 1865 to rancher Francis Hinton, whose ranch manager, Robert Kelly, inherited Rancho Agua Hedionda in 1870. The Kelly family named their land Rancho de los Kiotes, translated as Ranch of the Spanish Daggers (believed to refer to an agave plant known as the Spanish Dagger). They held onto much of this area, which eventually became Carlsbad, until the 1930s.

As the trail winds toward the ocean, you'll see lots of the yellow bush sunflower, some yellow pincushions, yellow wallflowers, and an occasional native white morning-glory.

After a little more than a half-mile, you'll come to a bridge that crosses that creek. The trail continues straight ahead for about another third of a mile, where it stops at El Fuerte Street, but there the Bressi Ranch trails continue.

While backtracking to the main bridge, I crossed and then continued north back toward the historic park entrance. Eventually the trail ends at Via Conquistador, a suburban street in the developments surrounding the park. You can walk along here until you turn left onto Carrillo Way to return to the park entrance.

Leo Carrillo offers a fascinating story. His ancestor, Jose Raimundo Carrillo, patriarch of one of the 12 original founding families of San Diego in Old Town, traveled in 1769 with Father Junipero Serra from San Diego north to establish the first missions. Later, Jose Raimundo Carrillo joined Don Gaspar de Portola on his journey north past Agua Hedionda to locate the Bay of Monterey. Serra, Portola, and Carrillo were the first names on a list of notables to pass by the Rancho Agua Hedionda.

Leo Carrillo bought 1,700 acres of Rancho de Los Kiotes from Charles Kelly in 1937 for $17 an acre, according to a plaque at the ranch. Carrillo bought another 840 acres two years later, holding about 2,540 acres. He named it the Flying LC Ranch—his brand is abundant on posts and pillars still standing.

Carrillo, whose grandmother was Josefa Bandini of San Diego's original Spanish American founders, was a very popular and successful movie and television actor. He appeared in over 90 movies but is probably best known as Pancho, the sidekick to the Cisco Kid in the 1950 TV series.

Carrillo was born in 1880 in Los Angeles, became a champion rough water swimmer, studied engineering in college, and worked on a Southern Pacific Railroad construction crew, where he became fluent in Chinese, Japanese, Italian, French and German, as well as his native Spanish and English. He was a cartoonist at the San Francisco Examiner, where he got to know William Randolph Hearst. In 1913 he went to New York, eventually appearing in 15 Broadway plays.

In his later years, Carrillo became one of California's most dedicated environmentalists. As a member of the State Beaches and Park Commission, he helped create Anza-Borrego Desert State Park. A yachtsman, fisherman, poet, and accomplished horseman, he was grand marshal for hundreds of parades. His prized palomino, Conquistador, is buried in some secret spot on his beloved Flying LC Ranch.

When he bought the property, he dedicated himself to recreating a grand old hacienda. His daughter, Toni, had sold off most of the parcels after Carrillo's death in 1961. But the 10.5 acres that remained were formally transferred to the City of Carlsbad in 1977, including all 18 major and minor structures.

Spring is the best time to view the peafowl, the male peacocks and female peahens who are descendants of Leo Carrillo's first six peafowl. Spring is their mating season, during which they emit plaintive, wailing howls while the males spread their gorgeous tail feathers, trying to attract the females.

Rancho Agua Hedionda, Rancho de los Kiotes, the Flying LC Ranch—by any name, the Leo Carrillo Rancho Historic Park is rightly known as Carlsbad's Sleeping Beauty.

Thomas Brothers Map: Page 1127, J-3,4

Before You Go: Visit the website www.carrillo-ranch.org for extensive information, including directions and a self-guided walking tour. You can pick up a copy of the trail map outside the ranch's store in the old Caretaker's Cottage.

You can also download the trail map at Carlsbad's city page: http://www.carlsbadca.gov/services/depts/parks/open/trails/default.asp.

Trails here open to hikers, bicyclists, and dogs on leashes.

Trailhead: From Interstate 5, exit at Palomar Airport Road. Head east about five miles and turn right onto Melrose Drive. After about a mile, turn right on Carrillo Way, then take the first right into the historic park.

The ranch grounds and trail are open Tuesday through Saturday from 9:00 a.m. to 5:00 p.m. and on Sunday from 11:00 a.m. to 5:00 p.m. It is free to park here and to walk the grounds and trail. Many of the buildings are open for guided tours on Saturdays at 11:00 a.m. and 1:00 p.m., and on Sundays at noon and 2:00 p.m.

Distance/Difficulty: About 4.0 miles round-trip; easy.

2-23. Oceanside's San Luis Rey River Trail Is Easy, Paved

For an urban, paved trail open to hikers, strollers, wheelchairs, skaters, and bicyclists, it's hard to beat Oceanside's San Luis Rey River Trail. The 9-mile-long trail is a class I bicycle trail, meaning it is separate from traffic with no stop signs or traffic lights. The City of Oceanside became the county's first city to receive a bronze award in 2009 from the League of American Bicyclists for being a bicycle-friendly town, largely because of this trail. The San Luis Rey River Trail is one of the longest such paved trails in the county.

The western end of the trail begins just a block from the ocean at the foot of Neptune Way. It goes under Interstate 5 and skirts Highway 76 within the first mile, but then it becomes surprisingly quiet as it follows the curves of the San Luis Rey River. I hiked for about 2.5 miles before retracing my way, going just a little past the point where it intersects with Benet Road and then reaches Oceanside Municipal Airport.

Nine miles of Class I bicycle trail sit next to river.

I could see the river itself only during the first part, near I-5. On the lookout for waterfowl in this estuary, I saw a great blue heron soar under the freeway, earning its name with its five-foot wingspan, and a group of snowy egrets (distinctively white with yellow feet) on the river's far bank.

The paved trail is very easygoing because it's almost entirely flat. It's about 10 feet wide with painted lines designating lanes; pedestrians are advised to keep to the right. Mileage is also painted every 0.2 miles, so if you feel like it, you could count your steps to measure how many you make in a mile.

The trail was built in the 1980s by the Army Corps of Engineers during levy construction along the river. At one point I could see a remnant of a former road, and I wonder if the trail follows some old route.

Its future is interesting. According to the San Diego Association of Governments (SANDAG), the San Luis Rey River Trail is eventually planned to extend all the way to Interstate 15, but this project is slated in bicycle lane plans that extend to 2050. That same timeline calls for a Coastal Rail Trail that will extend from Oceanside's San Luis Rey River Trail all the way to downtown San Diego's bayshore trail. Of that 44-mile dream, only about 10 miles are built so far with a future price tag of nearly $80 million to complete it.

The valley of the San Luis Rey River is distinctive here, with tall bluffs on both sides enclosing the major waterway. Although I couldn't see the water after those early glimpses, the riparian vegetation in this valley is thick. Along the trail itself were trees and plants not frequently seen elsewhere, but some are surely nonnative. The City of Oceanside has plans to remove non-natives from the area, but they are widespread here, including some feathery trees with long, narrow spikes of pink flowers—probably invasive tamarisk. Near the ocean end of the trail is a planted area of natives in a habitat restoration project, where lots of native yellow marsh evening primroses bloom.

While scanning the rocks that line the side of the trail toward the river, I noticed quite a lot of activity. I watched an agile roadrunner scramble over them, and I saw plenty of lizards that might have attracted him. Squirrels were also abundant. One bicyclist stopped me to ask about birds, reporting that he'd just seen a red falcon with a tiny mouse in its beak. I wonder if he saw an American kestrel, a jay-sized falcon with a rust-colored tail and back.

When I passed the 2.4-mile mark near Benet Road and a small community park, I turned around and hiked back, hoping to see at least one more roadrunner.

Thomas Brothers Map: Page 1085, J-7, where Neptune ends just to the east of the railroad, before Sea Cottage Way.

Before You Go: For a map of the entire nine-mile trail, go to Oceanside's web page for the San Luis Rey River Trail, http://www.ci.oceanside.ca.us/gov/ns/parks/amenities/trails.asp.
This trail is open to hikers, bicyclists, and dogs on leashes.

Trailhead: From Interstate 5, exit at Mission Avenue, heading west. At Coast Highway, turn north (right) and then turn left (west) at Neptune. The trail begins where Neptune ends right before the railroad tracks; park on the streets here.
Oceanside notes that this west-side trail entrance is just a few blocks from the Oceanside Transit Center, so you could get here via the Sprinter, Coaster, or Metrolink trains or NCTD buses.

Distance/Difficulty: The entire trail is about 9.0 miles long, with the east end near Oceanside's Mance Buchanon Park. I went about 2.5 miles one-way, for a 5.0-mile round-trip; easy.

2-24. A Lake, a Pond, Birds, and Easy Trails at Guajome

For an easy stroll around a pleasant lake, head to Oceanside's Guajome Regional Park. It's especially exciting there during winter, when migratory waterfowl visit the lake; some live there year-round. I saw lots of greylag geese, several mated pairs of mallard ducks, some American coots, and even a few cormorants. Sadly, one of the geese was limping because some fishing line had wrapped itself around his leg.

Sharon Rosiles, a volunteer at the park, told me that the good people from the humane society had been out to try to help that goose but were unable to catch him to remove the fishing line. "They are able to catch some of them and help," she said, "but some just fly away back into the water."

The lake is home to a variety of fish that are the draw for anglers. There are also 33 sites in a developed campground with partial hookups, playground facilities, grassy expanses, and even a basketball court.

About 4.5 miles of trails wander through the park's chaparral, wetlands and grasslands. I took the trail that encircles Guajome Lake—an easy, flat walk that takes only about a half-hour.

Lake and pond delight at historic Guajome County Park.

Then I took a loop trail to the Upper Pond, a small little water feature that is pretty much surrounded by cattails. The trails aren't really very well marked, but it's hard to get lost here. The best map for the trails is found on the San Diego County Parks and Recreation page for Guajome County Park: http://www.sdcounty.ca.gov/parks/ Camping/guajome.html. There are brochures near the parking area that also include a trail map, but I found that one harder to follow than the website's map.

Using either map, you head south from Guajome Lake past the campground, down a hill where you then see several dirt roads. Take the dirt road to the east that climbs uphill and keep going south until you reach the Upper Pond. On the website map, these trails (which are old dirt roads) are called Willow Trail and Summit Trail, though they may not be marked when you get there.

On the way back, take the west-side trail heading north, which is a loop back to Guajome Lake. Again, it may not be marked, but the direction back should be obvious; there aren't many choices.

When I reached the bottom of that hill south of the campground, I took the Nature Trail that headed back to Guajome Lake. The Nature Trail, according to its sign (one of the only signs), was refurbished by 6th and 7th graders from Roosevelt Middle School in 1997. It's a pleasant walk on a narrower path through eucalyptus and willow groves and the marshy areas.

Save time to visit the Rancho Guajome Adobe, a National Historic Landmark since 1970. You can hike there from the park, but I wasn't sure exactly how to do that, so I drove there. The website map gives a better idea of how to walk there from the park; it's a couple of miles from the park.

Rancho Guajome was originally given to two Luiseño Indian brothers by Governor Pio Pico when the area was part of Alta California, Mexico, in the early 1800s. The brothers sold the 2,219 acres to Abel Stearns of Los Angeles for $550. A few years later, Stearns gave the land to his sister-in-law, Ysidora Bandini, as a wedding gift. Ysidora had just married Cave Johnson Couts, who was an army lieutenant sent to California to help establish the U.S. and Mexican border. Couts and his wife moved into Rancho Guajome Adobe in 1853, raised 10 children there, and became one of the wealthiest families in Southern California through ranching and farming on this land.

The rancho remained in the Couts family until the County of San Diego's Parks and Recreation acquired the historic home and 566 acres of the original land grant in 1973. The 22-room, 7,000-square-foot adobe was restored, beautifully appointed with period furnishings, and opened to the public in 1996.

The Rancho Guajome Adobe grounds are open every day from sunrise to sunset. The Adobe House Museum is open Wednesday through Sunday, 9:30 a.m. to 4:00 p.m. Guided house tours take place Wednesday through Friday at noon and Saturday and Sunday at noon and 2:00 p.m.

Thomas Brothers Map: Page 1067, D7.

Before You Go: Check the website for the park, www.sdcounty.ca.gov/parks/Camping/guajome.html, and download the trail map.

Hikers, bicyclists, equestrians, and dogs on leashes are all welcome here, but the trail around the lake is not open to equestrians.

The website for the Rancho Guajome Adobe is www.sdcounty.ca.gov/parks/ranchoguajomeadobe.html.

There is a $3 day-use parking fee. Pay in the machine as you enter the parking lot.

Trailhead: From Interstate 5, in Oceanside take Highway 76 east. After about seven miles, turn right onto Guajome Lake Road. The park entrance is on your right.

To reach Rancho Guajome Adobe from the park, go back to Highway 76 and head west, turning left (south) at the next light onto N. Santa Fe Avenue. About two miles from there, the adobe is on your right.

Distance/Difficulty: The Guajome Lake circle trail is about a half-mile long, taking less than half an hour. The Willow and Summit trails to the Upper Pond and back are about 1.5 miles; easy.

3. Central County Coastal

Explore the historic canyons of old San Diego as well as a few charming neighborhoods. Some of our earliest trails are here, including those in Balboa Park. This section also takes in such urban pockets of contemplative nature as Los Penasquitos Canyon Preserve, where some 37 miles of trails invite exploration, and Black Mountain Open Space Preserve, where nearly 15 miles of trails take you to viewpoint peaks.

These trails are probably very close to your home base, wherever that may be. When you don't feel like driving very far, look here for trails right in the center of the city that will transport your mind and body into the joys of nature.

3-1. Interesting History for Chollas Lake

Stroll by Pebble Beach, Hidden Cove, and Turtle Point under the tall canopies of eucalyptus trees and enjoy one of the prettiest paths smack dab in the city. Chollas Lake Park truly is a "hidden treasure in an urban community," located on College Grove Drive near College Avenue. It offers a 2.5-mile loop that circles the blue-water lake as well as the 86 acres of open space called North Chollas Canyon. There is an additional quarter-mile-long nature trail above the lake trail that features a cactus garden.

I began the loop near the ranger's office and the main fishing pier. Interestingly, Chollas Lake is the only youth fishing lake in San Diego County. Fishing is free but is permitted only for children ages 15 and under.

In fact, professional angler Dean Rojas learned to fish on Chollas Lake as a young boy. "I have so many memories there. It's hard to believe that's where it all started, and now I'm on bass fishing's biggest stage, the Bassmaster Classic," he told the *U-T*'s Todd Adams in 2013.

Take a pretty loop around an old reservoir.

100

The lake is also home to lots of ducks and geese as well as egrets and herons, who are all fishing too.

The 1-mile loop around the lake passes plenty of picnic tables and playgrounds. Just before you reach the dam, head uphill a bit behind it to reach a Parcourse Fitness Circuit. This outdoor fitness sport offers nine stations where you perform specified exercises, spaced out along a walking or jogging path. Each fitness station describes and illustrates the specified exercise, such as a balance beam or a step-up. Near these fitness stations, look for the trail post marker that points the way to North Chollas Canyon. Head west from the lake.

This 1.4-mile loop traverses a large, open space where many more eucalyptus trees provide shade and a large ball field holds center court. There are lots of trails through here, with the main trail being the widest and most obvious. It heads up around the ball field and back down to a path that winds up behind the lake's dam.

The lake was dammed to form Chollas Reservoir in 1901 by the Southern California Mountain Water Company, which was then owned by the Spreckels Brothers. In 1906, the water company entered into a contract with the City of San Diego to provide from Chollas Reservoir up to 7.77 million gallons per day for 4 cents per 1,000 gallons (the lowest price paid for water anywhere in California at the time), according to the parks department's "History of Chollas Lake Park."

In 1912, a bond issue approved by voters for $2.5 million allowed the City of San Diego to buy Barrett Dam and its reservoir site, both Upper and Lower Otay Lakes, and Chollas Reservoir so the city no longer had to buy water from private companies. But by 1952, Chollas Lake was no longer used as a reservoir, and the water slowly dried up. The city in 1966 turned Chollas Reservoir over from the Water Department to the Parks and Recreation Department, and in 1971 it was designated as a children-only fishing lake.

Another really interesting fact about Chollas Lake is its role in the navy. In 1916, the world's first global Navy Radio Transmitting Facility (NRTF) was built just north of Chollas Lake at Chollas Heights. The transmitter, consisting of three 600-foot-high towers supporting the antenna, needed a lot of water to cool its tubes, and that's why it was built next to the lake. The NRTF at Chollas Heights broadcast the first news of the Japanese attack on Pearl Harbor on December 7, 1941. The NRTF ceased operations in 1992. The antenna was dismantled, and today 412 navy housing units occupy its former site. The original transmitter building remains with a small museum inside.

In 1991, the 12-acre site southwest of the lake, "Gloria's Mesa," was dedicated and named after former City Councilwoman Gloria McColl. The open space of North Chollas Canyon was opened with its maze of trails in 1997.

Next to the ball field there are many coast cholla, which I assume gave the area its name. "Most chollas are found in the desert, but three types (snake, cane and coast) are found near the coast," writes James Lightner in *San Diego County Native Plants*. The coast cholla, common in coastal sage scrub and maritime succulent scrub, combines in large colonies here. This cactus can reach six feet high, and these are among the biggest chollas I've seen. Blooms on the coast cholla are deep pink.

Winding back under the eucalyptus trees along the bright blue lake makes for a lovely urban outing.

Thomas Brothers Map: Page 1270, D-7.

Before You Go: Download a copy of the trail map at the city's parks page: http://www.sandiego. gov/park-and-recreation/pdf/programguide/chollaslake.pdf.
   Trails here are open to hikers, bicyclists. and dogs on leashes.
   The park opens at 6:30 a.m. and closes at 7:30 p.m. in summer, and it closes 4:30 p.m. in winter (an hour before sunset all year).

Trailhead: From Interstate 8, exit at College Avenue and head south on College. Turn right (west) onto College Grove Drive; entrance to the park is on the right.

Distance/Difficulty: About 2.5 miles total; easy.

3-2. Florida Canyon Started City's Major Hiking Group

Florida Canyon could serve as the very definition of urban oasis. This 150 acres of coastal sage scrub habitat within the 1,400 acres of Balboa Park is said to offer a glimpse of the original landscape of Balboa Park. It is mostly natural vegetation, having had little interference from the city in the last 100 years.

Several trails are scattered throughout Florida Canyon on both sides of Florida Drive. You'll find Florida Canyon east of the main part of Balboa Park, nestled in a natural canyon that's also a small earthquake fault aptly named Florida Canyon Fault, according to the San Diego Natural History Museum. On the east side of Florida Canyon is the municipal Balboa Park Golf Course.

Several trails crisscross Florida Canyon.

I sought the trail on the west side of Florida Drive, just below the Desert Garden and Rose Garden, off Park Boulevard. You can access this trail from the Desert Garden, but I found easier parking and another trailhead near the intersection of Upas Street and Florida Drive.

Starting from this trailhead, I passed through a verdant part of the canyon (not as natural) before reaching Morley Field Drive, where I crossed to continue the trail. In this first patch are several enormous eucalyptus trees and some interloping, albeit colorful, canna lilies.

Once past Morley Field Drive, the trail winds through a stand of coast redwoods, which seem a lot healthier here than elsewhere in Balboa Park. The trail quickly becomes exposed to the sun, and the coastal sage scrub habitat consists mostly of low-growing, aromatic, drought-deciduous shrubs. Common plants in this habitat include black sage, chamise, buckwheat, and prickly pear.

Sometimes the park rangers of Balboa Park and the Canyoneers of the San Diego Natural History Museum lead walks through Florida Canyon, identifying the native plants. In fact, the Canyoneers of SDNHM were originally named the Florida Canyoneers, because Florida Canyon was the first place where guided nature walks began through the museum.

During the summer of 1973, Helen Witham Chamlee, Nancy Inman, and Betty Robinson began the Florida Canyoneers by training volunteers regarding the plants, animals, geology, history, and Native American uses of the canyon, according to the SDNHM web page (http://www.sdnhm.org/education/naturalists-of-all-ages/canyoneer-hikes). Two years earlier, Lee Wolfram had coordinated trail-building in the canyon by Boy Scout groups as a community service project.

In November 1973, the Florida Canyon Nature Trails formally opened to the public, and 27 Florida Canyoneers graduated. Some 5,000 people participated in the hiking program by the next year. During the 1980s, several more hiking destinations were added to the group's schedule, and so "Florida" was dropped from the title; the group became simply the Canyoneers.

Today, Canyoneers (all museum volunteers) continue to be trained in San Diego's plant and animal life, geology, and Native Indian uses of their environment, according to SDNHM. "By leading public hikes at all points of the compass—San Diego's canyons, regional parks and preserves, lagoons, deserts and mountains—Canyoneers help the public to appreciate San Diego's special places," says the museum. Check the museum's calendar of guided walks at that web site.

I was on my own, and so I tried to observe the native plants along the trail. Many appeared dead during a heat wave of late September, but they are simply dormant for the season, and blooms will occur again in spring.

The trail winds through the canyon with periodic signposts pointing the way. It appears there are three different trails that converge here, according to those signposts: Trails No. 3, 5, and 12. Trails 3 and 5 are on the main Balboa Park Trails map for the Sixth and Upas Gateway. I followed Trail 12.

From the trail just past Morley Field Drive, I took the high road south, eventually reaching the end of this trail at Florida Drive. I retraced my steps, taking the low road on my return. My walk lasted about an hour round-trip.

There are several trails dotted throughout this area, including lesser ones that aren't marked. You can't really get lost here—Florida Drive is always in sight—but you can meander for several miles if you're so inclined.

It was interesting to note the dry stream bed of rocks at the bottom of Florida Canyon, suggesting there once was a river running through it. This wide expanse of natural landscape truly offers an easy respite right in the middle of the city.

Thomas Brothers Map: Page 1269, C-6, Upas at Florida.

Before You Go: Download a copy of the trail map from Balboa Park Hiking and Biking Trails pages (http://www.balboapark.org/in-the-park/hiking-and-biking-trails), and go to the Morley Field Gateway PDF map for the No. 12 trail through Florida Canyon.
This trail is open to hikers, bicyclists, and dogs on leashes.

Trailhead: From Interstate 5 heading south, exit at 10th Avenue. Turn left on A Street and then left again on Park Boulevard. Turn right onto Upas Street and park near its intersection with Florida Drive.
From Interstate 5 heading north, exit at Pershing Drive/B Street and take Pershing; then turn left on Florida Drive. Continue to Upas Street and park near the intersection of Upas and Florida.
From Highway 163 heading south, turn left onto Park Boulevard and then right onto Upas. Park near its intersection with Florida.

Distance/Difficulty: No. 12 trail through Florida Canyon is 2.4 miles one-way, or 4.8 miles round-trip; moderate.

3-3. See What Started in Switzer Canyon

Switzer Canyon was the start of something big. This open space preserve in North Park once faced the onslaught of a sewer line maintenance road—as did several other canyons in the city. When neighbors were informed about this project, several residents turned to the Sierra Club to help organize a response.

In October 1998, the Sierra Club guided about 60 residents on a tour of Switzer Canyon and organized the first canyon friends group, which soon became a model for more than 40 canyon friends groups throughout the county.

Ten years later, with the Sierra Club's endorsement, in 2008 San Diego Canyonlands was incorporated as a nonprofit to help preserve and protect San Diego canyons. Carrie Schneider, current vice president of San Diego Canyonlands' board, was one of the original participants behind the Switzer Canyon force. She remains the leader today of Friends of Switzer Canyon.

"Switzer Canyon is just gorgeous," said Schneider, a North Park resident with her husband, Bob Laymon. "I think of it as a place where there's always something interesting going on—every season there's something new to observe. It's a great place for hiking."

"San Diego is known for its beaches and the climate, but the feature that makes us unique among California coastal cities is (the) topography of our canyons," says San Diego Canyonlands on its website, http://sdcanyonlands.org.

Switzer Canyon started San Diego Canyonlands' preservation efforts.

"San Diego is an island botanically speaking," added Schneider. "It's surrounded by ocean, mountains and desert, so the vegetation is unique. We find all sorts of amazing plant communities in our canyons."

Explore Switzer for yourself and see why this island of nature in the middle of the city began such a valuable countywide movement.

Its western point begins from Balboa Park's golf course at 28th Street and Maple. and it goes about four blocks to 30th Street, which bisects it. Then it begins again at 30th for four more blocks to 32nd Street near Redwood. It's a pretty large swath of a natural canyon in the middle of North Park, and it took me a little more than an hour to walk both segments round-trip.

The western trailhead at 28th and Maple begins with the very green views into Balboa Park's golf course. After a steep decline, you enter Switzer Canyon and follow the trail, much of which appears to be an old rocky dry stream bed.

The Friends of Switzer Canyon have been working hard on canyon restoration, involving the removal of nonnative plants and the planting of natives. A couple of areas of habitat restoration are evident.

"One of the biggest problems natural habitats face is unchecked growth of some plants from other parts of the world," said Schneider, who is a biologist for a local biotech company. "They can become a different place, supporting different animals, making it less biologically diverse."

The San Diego Natural History Museum has compiled an exhaustive "Floristic List for Switzer Canyon," citing hundreds of plants and trees that make their home here. See http://www.sdnhm.org/research/botany/lists/switzer.html.

I caught wind of the lovely fragrance from black sage, marveled at the velvet leaves of yerba santa, and enjoyed the yellow blooms of the evening primrose. There are several towering eucalyptus trees here, especially in the eastern section between 30th and 32nd, where there are also several specimen queen palms. Also in that section are some lovely old pepper trees.

That eastern section is a bit easier to navigate because the trail isn't so much a rocky stream bed but more like an old dirt road. Be advised the trail doesn't go between the sections easily.

To exit the western section and reach 30th Street, watch for a graffiti-covered, old cement drainage tunnel. When you see that, go toward it and up the makeshift trail to 30th. Walk along 30th to the northern edge of the canyon and find another steep entry trail into that eastern section. The entries and exits off 30th are very steep and not actual trails, but you can make this connection between the two sections of Switzer Canyon. The official entries into the eastern section nearest 30th are at the end of Burlingame off San Marcos Avenue, or at the dead-end of Palm Street toward 31st.

You might even hear a coyote if a fire truck rolls down 30th. "They really love the fire trucks—even during the day, they'll start howling," noted Schneider.

You might also see the nests of dusky footed wood rats. "They make amazing collections of sticks for their nests. They like to collect shiny objects and build their nests under chaparral trees. Some of these nests are many years old," she said.

San Diego Canyonlands continues to develop friends groups to help protect these natural oases. The newest group has been formed in City Heights for the 47th Street Canyon.

And Switzer Canyon started it all.

Thomas Brothers Map: Page 1269, 7-D.

Before You Go: The best map of Switzer Canyon can be downloaded from http://www.sandiego. gov/park-and-recreation/pdf/switzertrailmap.pdf.
Dogs on leashes are welcome here.

Trailhead: From Interstate 5 heading south, exit at 10th Avenue. Turn left on A Street then left again on Park Boulevard. Turn right onto Upas Street and then right onto 28th Street. Park near the intersection of 28th and Maple Street.
From I-5 heading north, exit at Pershing Drive/B Street and take Pershing, then turn left on Florida Drive. Turn right onto Upas Street and then right onto 28th Street. Park near its intersection with Maple Street.
From Highway 163 heading south, turn left onto Park Boulevard, right onto Upas, and right onto 28th Street. Park near its intersection with Maple Street.

Distance/Difficulty: About 2.0 miles to cover both sections round-trip; easy.

3-4. 32nd Street Canyon Is Regional Role Model

Golden Hill's 32nd Street Canyon is one of the best-kept canyons in this mid-city neighborhood. It's also one of the best examples of the value such urban oases offer. Take a walk through its 12 acres of peaceful space in Golden Hill, bordered from Cedar Street to C Street, between 31st and 33rd. You'll smell the sage, ponder the leafy pepper trees, and trod a trail, much of which has been softened with loads of sawdust.

It wasn't always so inviting. "When we started, it had many signs of blight: diminishing native ecosystems, many invasive weeds, drug encampments, a fire and even signs of prostitution," said the Friends of 32ⁿᵈ Street Canyon. Mary Ann Sandersfeld and Laura Mays are two of the original members of the Friends of 32ⁿᵈ Street Canyon.

Thirty-Second Street Canyon is a fine example of neighborhood effort.

Tershia D'Elgin is not an original member but has been an active participant for several years. Sometimes she calls herself the "busybody of 32ⁿᵈ Street Canyon." She is listed as the contact person for Friends of 32ⁿᵈ Street Canyon on the San Diego Canyonlands website. I caught her in the canyon leading a group of fourth graders from Albert Einstein Academy on an exploration. "Five people started the [Friends of 32ⁿᵈ Street Canyon] group in 2000 to keep the [San Diego Unified] school district from developing the canyon," she told us. "That threat galvanized friends and neighbors."

Development threats are a common refrain among many of the friends groups of local canyons, which were originally sponsored by the San Diego Sierra Club and are now held together by San Diego Canyonlands (www.sdcanyonlands.org).

D'Elgin, an award-winning writer and editor, also serves on the City of San Diego's Forest Advisory Board. "I'm from Colorado," she said, "where there are forests. This kind of vegetation didn't mean anything to me." But now she'll pick a sage leaf and ask a child to smell its lovely fragrance. Or she'll point to the red berries of what appears to be a holly bush and point out its real name is toyon. "They named Hollywood after this berry bush, but it really should be Toyonland," she noted.

"When I moved to Golden Hill about a block away from the canyon, my friend Dave Buchanan was doing restoration here," said D'Elgin. "He taught me the value of native plants."

Native plants in this coastal sage scrub habitat are essential to a vibrant local ecosystem. The canyon's "self-sustaining carbon-sequestering greenscape also diminishes air and water pollution and offsets the 'urban heat island' effect," notes the 32ⁿᵈ Street Canyon Task Force. "Our coastal canyons are literally this region's life support, supplying fresher air and water, energy conservation and many other critical benefits."

To D'Elgin, the canyon isn't only about habitat. "It's also about human well-being," she said. "It has shown me the value of community, and how we can make a difference. Just like the way plants and animals help each other, this feels like a good model." She also noted that Golden Hill residents tend to respond to local needs and turn out to help.

That sawdust on the trail, for example, is a point of contention. "That mulch in the canyon, as an example, is its own story of poor stewardship," said D'Elgin. "The city has spent over $600,000 'revegetating' in 32nd Street Canyon, and there's not so much as one plant to show for it."

The neighbors have done a better job of "revegetating." Indeed, in just the last few years, nearly 10 tons of debris have been removed from 32nd Street Canyon, and some 4,000 native plants have been planted. Much of the labor comes from neighbors who live near it or from children who learn in it.

During fall when I was there, dozens of fourth graders from Albert Einstein Academy, a charter school at 30th and Ash Street just a few blocks away, were spending a half-day field trip in the canyon with D'Elgin and representatives from the Ocean Discovery Institute. They were planting native sage and buckwheat bushes while learning about this dry wetland and how important it is to the region's ecosystem.

There's a movement afoot to combine all the vital canyons that help define San Diego's topography—even its beauty. "Without canyons, San Diego would be a hotter, smoggier slab of humankind," notes the task force of the 32nd Street Canyon.

San Diego Civic Solutions goes even further. "The natural infrastructure of our place—the fundamental beauty—if not the uniqueness that makes San Diego special, are the canyons that connect all neighborhoods. We have significant quantity of these wonderful natural places; the question is, do we love them enough, do we appreciate them enough to sustain their presence," it states in a white paper proposing establishment of a Canyonlands Park throughout the San Diego region.

Take a walk through 32nd Street Canyon and see what natural beauty can do for you.

Thomas Brothers Map: For the Cedar Street at 31st entrance, Page 1289, E-2.

Before You Go: Download a map of 32nd Street Canyon from the San Diego County Parks and Recreation website: http://www.sandiego.gov/park-and-recreation/pdf/32ndsttrailmap.pdf. Dogs on leashes are welcome.

Trailhead: There are three main entrances to 32nd Street Canyon: on Cedar Street at 31st Street, at the dead-end of 32nd Street at B Street, and on C Street between 32nd and 33rd. Park anywhere on the streets near these entrances.

To reach Cedar and 31st, from Interstate 5, exit at Pershing Drive and head north on Pershing. Turn right onto 26th Street, left onto A Street, left onto Fern Street, and then right onto Cedar Street.

Distance/Difficulty: About 1.0 mile round-trip; easy.

3-5. Morley Field Gateway Offers Long Balboa Park Trail

The Morley Field gateway to Florida Canyon offers some of the longest continuous hiking trails in Uptown. For a bonus, there are even some fine views of the Coronado Bridge and the Coronado Islands.

There are two main trailheads for Balboa Park's Trail No. 13: one at the top of the trails (northern end) at Morley Field, off Morley Field Drive, and the other at the bottom of the trails (southern end) at the intersection of Pershing and Florida Drives and 26th Street. There really isn't any parking at that southern intersection, so it's better to start at the northern end where there's a generous parking lot at the trailhead.

You'll find that starting point at the off-leash dog exercise area next to the nature trail parking area, just east of Florida Street off Morley Field Drive.

There are over three miles of trails here along Florida Drive from Morley Field to 26th Street. The trails crisscross each other at points, so you can make a loop out of your journey.

The map at the trailhead shows a few points of interest that were cosponsored several years ago by the city and InSITE 97 to beautify this East Mesa area of Balboa Park through a combination of public art and native habitat restoration. I went in search of the Coiled Paths. I started from that northern trailhead, taking the high road, so to speak. I descended on the trail from the dog park area and soon took a left turn to go to the top of the mesa. From there I walked south all the way to 26th Street, walking part of that way along the edge of Pershing Drive. Here is the point where hikers get a fine view of the Coronado Bridge and two of the four Coronado Islands.

Then I took the low road back. According to the map, the Coiled Paths should have been off this southern area of the trails, near the intersection of Florida and Zoo drives. I asked a couple of regular

Some of Uptown's longest trails start at Morley Field.

hikers if they'd seen the Coiled Paths. Valentine Viannay had not, but she said she creates fabrics and plans to design one after Florida Canyon (check her website to see at www.vvfabrics.com). Gina Varela and her beautiful Golden Retriever, Betty, hike here often, and Gina had never seen the Coiled Paths either. It became a treasure hunt.

Regardless, the trail offered plenty of pleasure. It's a coastal sage scrub habitat here, so there aren't any trees to offer shade; in the summer it's very hot. But the trail is a marvelous escape from urbanization, and because it's open to dogs on leashes as well as bicyclists, it's a local favorite.

I finally returned to my starting point, still in search of those Coiled Paths. I drove through the Morley Field parking areas to the bicycle Velodrome, where there is another trailhead into these Florida Canyon trails. There I spoke to a park ranger, who solved the mystery: the Coiled Paths no longer exist. She said they had consisted of bales of straw meant to evoke ancient Kumeyaay designs. Because the public art projects originally incorporated native habitat restoration, the natives evidently won, and that public art project was absorbed into the landscape. The ranger began efforts to update those trailhead maps and to point out that the Coiled Paths are no longer there.

Imagine them, if you like, and enjoy that coastal sage scrub that makes Florida Canyon such an urban oasis.

Thomas Brothers Map: Page 1269, D-6.

Before You Go: Download a trail map from Balboa Park's hiking and biking trails pages (http:// www.balboapark.org/in-the-park/hiking-and-biking-trails), heading to the Morley Field PDF map. These trails are open to hikers, bicyclists, and dogs on leashes.

Trailhead: From Interstate 5 heading south, exit at 10th Avenue. Turn left on A Street then left again on Park Boulevard. Turn right onto Upas Street, right onto Florida Drive, and then left onto Morley Field Drive. Park near the nature trail and the off-leash dog area.

From I-5 heading north, exit at Pershing Drive/B Street and take Pershing, then turn left on Florida Drive. Continue to Morley Field Drive and turn left.

From Highway 163 heading south, turn left onto Park Boulevard, right onto Upas, right onto Florida, and then left onto Morley Field Drive.

Distance/Difficulty: A 3.3-mile loop; moderate.

3-6. 28th Street Has Historic Architecture and Nature

Stretching from North Park to South Park along the eastern edge of Balboa Park, 28th Street offers a splendid look at some historic Craftsman homes, sprinkled with a few Spanish eclectic and other architectural designs. There's a bonus on this historic neighborhood walk: a short connecting pathway through an open space preserve area that skirts the eastern edge of the Balboa Park Golf Course. You'll find both architecture and nature on this stroll with some pleasant surprises thrown in along the way.

Start near the intersection of Upas and 28th Street, where two Craftsman-style pillars mark an entry, declaring "Welcome to North Park, an Historic Craftsman Neighborhood." This small public art space blocks traffic from going through 28th Street, creating a quiet area to the north.

Head north from those pillars on 28th, where you'll find several homes built by David Owen Dryden, a builder in the Craftsman style who created more than 50 bungalows in this North Park neighborhood between 1911 and 1919. Another master builder in the North Park Dryden Historical District is Edward Bryans. Both Dryden and Bryans are named on a plaque by the pillars.

Born in Minnesota, Bryans came to San Diego in 1912 and built over 150 homes and apartment buildings by 1922, including over 22 apartment buildings along Park Boulevard in the 1920s. He also built the homes at 2829 28th Street and 3648 28th Street.

Hike a historic neighborhood as well as a pocket of nature.

Dryden, born in Oregon in 1877, moved with his oldest sister to Los Angeles County in the mid-1890s, where he was a carpenter in Monrovia. He and his wife, Isabel Rockwood of the William Judson Rockwood family of artists and craftsmen, moved to San Diego in 1911. While Monrovia's home-building industry was slowing at that time, it was booming in San Diego because of the Panama-California International Exposition in Balboa Park.

Dryden's Craftsman-style structures make "their neighborhoods significant examples of suburban communities in the era of the first World War," writes Donald Covington in *The Journal of San Diego History*'s winter 1991 issue. "As such, they typify the American Arts and Crafts movement."

Covington notes that a "Craftsman house expresses the close relationship between the earth and the shelter by use of natural materials as well as through the use of a low-pitched roof with deep overhang. The frame is exposed as much as possible with the heavy wooden beams and smaller rafters in full view, extending beyond the eave, while the body of the house is sheathed in redwood shingles or stream-washed boulders."

You'll especially want to look for Dryden's pagoda-style Craftsman at the corner of 28th and Capps, at 3553 28th Street. Its "oriental-upturned roof structure and heavily bracketed veranda columns add much to the exotic picturesque qualities of the house," writes Covington. This house was the first one Dryden built on 28th Street. Its original owners were George and Anna Carr. George Carr was a manufacturer and supplier of fine doors, mill work, and art glass. Their house was completed in 1915 for $6,550.

Dryden built his own home in 1915 at 3536 28ᵗʰ Street. He built a classic redwood board and shingle Craftsman in 1916 at 3446 28ᵗʰ Street, now honored with a historic plaque naming it for its original owner, the John Carman Thurston House. Thurston was a retired Chicago manufacturer whose yard in that house included citrus and fruit orchards, according to Covington.

Another Dryden home, now called the Kline/Dryden House, is located at 3505 28ᵗʰ.

Turn back and pass those pillars at Upas to continue south on 28ᵗʰ Street. Several historic homes here are adorned with plaques that give the names of their original owners and the years in which they were built.

At 3303 28ᵗʰ, enjoy the two mascots for the King Family Lion House, built in 1920, flanking sculptural lion guards named Scotty and Max.

The Sam and Mary McPherson/Hurlburt and Tifal House, at 3133 28ᵗʰ Street, was built in 1925. It is a smaller Spanish-style bungalow with a red-tiled roof, and it has an ornamental fountain at its side.

Notice the beautiful tile work at the red-tiled roof Spanish home at 3103 28ᵗʰ Street, the William R. and Julia Beers House, built in 1928.

The Paul E. Stake/George W. Schilling House at 3037 28ᵗʰ Street was built in 1935 and is a surprisingly modern, streamlined building.

The Emerson/Hurlburt and Tifal House at 2645 28ᵗʰ Street, built in 1924, is a splendid pink stucco Spanish eclectic gem.

The Josephine Shields House, built in 1923 at 2639 28ᵗʰ Street, features more of the flat-roofed Prairie style of architecture that Frank Lloyd Wright made so popular.

Walk all the way until 28ᵗʰ Street ends at Maple. Now you can begin the nature portion of this meander. Take the path into the Switzer Canyon Open Space, but don't actually enter Switzer Canyon to the east. Simply walk straight ahead here, as if you were continuing on 28ᵗʰ Street. You'll walk under a splendid oak woodland canopy, through groves of giant eucalyptus, all along the eastern edge of the Balboa Park Golf Course.

Eventually you'll reenter the land of sidewalks and 28ᵗʰ Street at Grape Street Park, now an off-leash dog park. You can either walk back north along Granada or 29ᵗʰ Street, a block or two blocks, respectively, east of 28ᵗʰ Street, where more historic homes reside. Or, you can retrace your steps back through the verdant green space and 28ᵗʰ Street.

For another bonus of this walk, walk along the west side of 28ᵗʰ Street on your way back, north from Maple. As you near Upas, you'll be fronting the eastern edge of Balboa Park's Morley Field area. A meandering sidewalk here is etched with the names of dozens of "San Diego Perching Birds," like the black-headed grosbeak, the western kingbird, and the violet-green swallow. You may even get a glimpse of the Coronado Bridge and downtown's skyline from this vantage point.

There's a lot to enjoy on 28ᵗʰ Street.

Thomas Brothers Map: Page 1269, D-6, Upas and 28ᵗʰ Street.

Before You Go: You may download a map of Balboa Park trails at http://www.balboapark.org/sites/default/files/bptrails_overall_maponly.pdf. This route isn't specifically traced on this map, but can you follow 28th Street along Balboa Park's eastern edge.

Dogs on leashes are welcome.

Trailhead: Begin at the intersection of Upas Street and 28th Street, along the eastern edge of Balboa Park. From Interstate 5, exit at Pershing Drive and head north on Pershing until you reach the intersection of Upas and 28th. Park on the street near here.

Distance/Difficulty: About 2.0 miles round-trip; easy.

3-7. Burlingame Is Home to Classic Bungalows

The Burlingame Historic District, a 10-block pocket roughly located between North Park and South Park, offers an easy stroll through a neighborhood rich in early century Craftsman and Spanish Revival bungalows. Burlingame's official boundaries are Redwood Street to the north, Juniper Street to the south, 30th Street to the west, and 32nd Street to the east, but most of the historic homes are located between Laurel and San Marcos Avenue to the north and Kalmia to the south, between 30th Street and 32nd Street. You can walk through this well-kept area in an hour or so.

Walk through "Tract of Character"

When its two partners, Joseph McFadden and George Buxton, first opened this land development in 1912, they called it "The Tract of Character." This high plateau just east of Balboa Park and south of Switzer Canyon offered 360-degree views back then, because little development existed to hamper those views.

"From the level acres of Burlingame, the eye sweeps over the wonderful panorama," reports the development's advertisement in the San Diego Union in 1912, according to a summer 1993 article by Donald Covington in *The Journal of San Diego History,* the San Diego Historical Society's publication. "In the foreground lies the park, its mesas and canyons soon to be covered with exposition buildings. Beyond, the silver sheen of the bay meets the white strip of sand that separates it from the blue Pacific ... to the south lies the city ... to the east the Cuyamacas, their peaks covered with snow in the winter."

During that first weekend, January 13, 1912, 34 lots were sold, about 20 percent of the total of 170 lots on 40 acres. Mule teams had graded the streets and paved them with crushed granite, and the sidewalks' concrete had been tinted a dull red. The neighborhood today is still known for its pink sidewalks. The developers enlisted several young builders and architects at the time to design homes in a variety of styles. "In the 10 years following the opening of the tract, Burlingame became a showcase of diverse architectural fantasies," writes Covington, a professor emeritus of design in the art department of San Diego State University.

The most notable architect of distinctive homes in Burlingame was William Henry Wheeler, who also designed the 1924 Balboa Theater downtown, among other civic buildings. Born in Australia in 1872, Wheeler emigrated in 1898 to San Francisco and studied engineering at UC Berkeley, where he was certified as an architect. After the 1906 earthquake, he moved with his wife and two sons to Arizona. His travels to Mexico during that time "significantly affected his aesthetic awareness," writes Covington, and he embraced many elements of Mexican and Spanish American architecture. After his first wife died, he moved to San Diego in 1912 and began working with McFadden and Buxton. One of Wheeler's two sons, Richard, also known as Dick, was a prominent architect himself for many decades in San Diego.

Wheeler's homes in the Burlington tract include the Moorish bungalow at 3128 Laurel, whose mirador tower was designed to take in the 360-degree view; a traditional Art and Crafts design at 3055 Kalmia; and another house at 2447 Dulzura described by Covington as "a yeoman's cottage style (that) is a transition in Wheeler's work from the traditional old-English style of the Kalmia house to the more modern Swiss chalet style he used on the house at 2457 Capitan." In 1912 Wheeler also designed the home at 3004 Laurel, whose first (and brief) owner was Dr. Harry M. Wegeforth, founder of the San Diego Zoological Society in 1916.

Other architects in the early years of the Burlington tract included Erwin Norris from San Francisco, who built the 10-room Craftsman house at 3170 Maple; Archibald McCorkle, who designed a modified Spanish Revival combining deep eaves and twin pergolas of the Craftsman style at 3048 Laurel; and Earl Josef Brenk, who designed two classic examples of California Craftsman bungalows at 2414 Dulzura and 2431 Capitan.

The home at 2525 San Marcos "was the most avant-garde house in the tract," writes Covington. It's an example of the Churrigueresque style, a substyle of Spanish Revival architecture featuring elaborate, complex curves and dramatic, sculptured stucco details. Wheeler also designed 10 houses on Kalmia, the first at 3171 Kalmia, a two-story Mission Revival house with a third-story mirador tower room.

Percival Benbough, an early mayor of San Diego and downtown retailer, bought nine of these Kalmia houses in 1913, persuading his family and friends to move there. "The Kalmia Street houses revealed a potpourri of current stylistic influences with mixtures of Mission Revival, Spanish Colonial Revival, American Colonial Revival, Prairie, Cubist, Craftsman and Italianate," writes Covington.

You'll find historic plaques on many of the homes in Burlingame citing their year of construction and sometimes their first owners as you ponder the beginnings of this neighborhood.

To read Donald Covington's entire article in *The Journal of San Diego History,* go to https://www.sandiegohistory.org/journal/93summer/burlingame.htm.

Thomas Brothers Map: Page 1269, E-7.

Before You Go: Download a copy of the neighborhood street map from the Burlingame Neighborhood Association's website, http://www.burlingamesd.com/wp-content/uploads/2010/02/Burlingame-Map.jpg.

Dogs on leashes are welcome.

Trailhead: To reach the intersection of 30th Street and Laurel Street, from Interstate 5, exit at Pershing Drive and continue onto Pershing. Make a slight right onto Redwood Street, then take a right onto 30th Street and a left onto Laurel.

Distance/Difficulty: About 1.0 to 2.0 miles, depending on how much you wander; easy.

3-8. Marston Hills Canyon Connects to Balboa Park

Marston Hills Canyon is a little-known finger of Balboa Park that offers a lovely trail through towering eucalyptus, olive, and pepper trees. Since the park renewed its emphasis on trails several years ago, this area has been mapped and signed. It's part of Balboa Park's Trail No. 5 and connects at the Upas Street bridge over Highway 163 to trails No. 4 and 3. You could wander on these trails for a couple of hours, if you choose to ramble from one trail to another.

I found the northeastern-most gateway to Marston Hills Canyon off Richmond Street near Brookes. Actually, there are two gateways here, one just north of Brookes and another just south, both on Richmond.

Taking the northern entry, the trail goes down some wooden steps into a really gorgeous canyon of old eucalyptus trees. During winter, the toyon bushes are ablaze with their red holly berries.

Old homes rise above the canyon's walls, and a high-rise or two from Sixth Avenue can be seen from the canyon floor, but otherwise it is a really pretty foray into nature here, right in the middle of Uptown.

After passing a couple of footbridges, the trail eventually runs into Highway 163. You can cross the pedestrian bridge at Upas to get to the other side of the highway, where the historic Marston House and those other trails await.

I stayed on the east side of the highway, heading uphill on a paved portion of the trail through another finger of the canyon. Eventually the trail ends at the corner of Upas and Vermont, near the Boy Scout headquarters.

Find a lesser-known canyon of Balboa Park.

I retraced my way back through the canyon and took the "high road" trail on the return route. The two trails essentially parallel their way through the verdant canyon, each offering a slightly different view of this natural oasis.

It's obvious that some attention has been recently lavished on this canyon. Several tree seedlings, including oaks and pines, have been planted throughout the area. A group of community volunteers came together a couple of years ago to make this park-wide system of trails more accessible. David Contois and Alyssa Wolven are credited with starting the project, according to Jeannette de Wyze's San Diego Insider blog (http://www.sandiegoinsidertours.com/blog). Contois and Wolven approached Balboa Park Senior Ranger Casey Smith about the need for such a project, and they appealed to the San Diego Community Foundation's Balboa Park Trust for funding.

There are five gateways to the park's trail system: Sixth and Upas, Morley Field, Park Administration at President's Way and Park Boulevard, Golden Hill, and Marston Point.

Downloadable trail maps at the Balboa Park website (http://www.balboapark.org/in-the-park/hiking-and-biking-trails) cover several areas of the park. This trail is on the Sixth and Upas Gateway page, where you'll see the canyon into Marston Hills at the northern edge of this map. The routes are all color-coded and marked, showing distance and degree of difficulty. The map says Trail No. 5 is the most difficult, but this section into Marston Hills Canyon isn't hard.

"The timeline for incorporating all the gateways is roughly the end of this year," wrote Contois in the spring 2009 newsletter of the Friends of Balboa Park (http://friendsofbalboapark.org/wp-content/uploads/2009/05/springnews09.pdf). "This vision is to then expand this series of trails beyond Balboa Park, affording fitness enthusiasts venues into downtown, by the harbor and through some of San Diego's diverse central neighborhoods."

The project in Balboa Park has certainly increased safety there, and cleanup for the trail system has also eliminated some hazards, including homeless camps.

Go see the improvements for yourself.

Thomas Brothers Map: Page 1269, 6-B.

Before You Go: Download a copy of the PDF map for the Sixth and Upas Gateway at Balboa Park's hiking and biking trails page, http://www.balboapark.org/sites/default/files/6th-upas_12-21-09_maponly_0.pdf.
This trail is open to hikers, bicyclists, and dogs on leashes.

Trailhead: From Highway 163 heading north, exit at Richmond Street and head east. Park near the intersection of Richmond and Brookes.
When heading southbound, from Interstate 5, exit onto Highway 163 north toward Escondido. Exit at Richmond Street and park near its intersection with Brookes.

Distance/Difficulty: The trail through Marston Hills Canyon is about a 2.0-mile loop; easy.

3-9. Habitat Restoration Calls to Friends in Juniper Canyon

Find some blue birds of happiness in Juniper Canyon. I saw several western scrub jays in this open space preserve in South Park. When you see their bright blue wings soaring through the air, it's a simple thrill of nature, much like Juniper Canyon itself.

Its main trail offers an easy walk through stands of scrub oak and the fragrant yerba santa. The coastal sage scrub habitat here is home to the endangered bird called the California gnatcatcher, which can sometimes be heard making its distinctive "kitten meowing" call during spring and summer nesting season, according to the city's Open Space Canyons and Parklands website.

Look for blue birds in Juniper Canyon.

Reach Juniper Canyon's main trailhead at the intersection of Nutmeg and Felton, several blocks east of 30th Street. This trail goes through the canyon until Juniper Street and then starts again on the other side of Juniper, ending a bit past Hawthorne Street. Find a good trail map at the city's parks and recreation website.

There's another disconnected piece of Juniper Canyon farther to the south. A couple of trails begin from the dead-end of Ash Street and Delevan Drive, according to the city's trail map. I found these trailheads by taking Fern Street south to C Street, turning left on C going east, and curving ahead until that street dead-ends (it turns into Delevan and Ash, but those aren't actually marked). You pass by an industrial area and are immediately west of I-15.

Back in the main section off Felton, it took me about 45 minutes to walk the entire length round-trip, crossing Juniper Street in the middle. It's a very pleasant walk through a natural space in the middle of the city.

Wes Hudson, who has lived on the canyon for about 16 years now, is one of the organizers of Friends of Juniper Canyon, a volunteer group that helps restore and preserve the canyon. Friends of Juniper Canyon is part of the San Diego Canyonlands organization, which exists to protect and preserve our city's open-space canyons. Eric Bowlby, executive director of San Diego Canyonlands, helped guide the new friends group when it started.

"We got together about two years ago because we were concerned about things going on in the canyon that were degrading it," said Hudson in 2009. By day he is a native garden designer. "Mostly we try to help preserve the native habitat that exists there. There are areas where native habitat is not pristine, but it's remarkably intact for something so close to a city."

Friends of Juniper Canyon, like other friends groups of local canyons, organizes trash cleanup, removal of invasive nonnative plants, and replanting native plants. "We're replanting scrub oaks, lemonadeberry, buckwheat, laurel sumac, manzanita, coast live oak trees. These are all things that exist in the canyon already, but we're trying to help it return where this habitat has been destroyed," said Hudson. The little flags by the new plantings alert people not to destroy these fledglings. "We've replanted two areas so far," he added. The group also has tried to remove arundo. "It looks like bamboo—it's incredibly tall grass that takes over waterways and crowds out all kinds of native plants, but doesn't contribute anything to the birds, insects and other animals there," Hudson pointed out.

Friends of Juniper Canyon meets periodically for trail cleanup and other events. Follow the group on Facebook or check the calendar at San Diego Canyonlands for the group's gatherings: www.sdcanyonlands.org.

Hudson said he's heard coyotes a lot. "They were gone for a while, but they've come back. It's actually exciting to have them around." However, coyotes will go after cats and small dogs, so keep your loved pets in check. Dogs on leashes are allowed in the canyon.

When asked what he loves about Juniper Canyon, Hudson gave a very personal response. "It has to do with meaning," he said. "When you understand how connected everything is in the habitat, how much it depends on everything else; when you see invasive plants or bad policies diminishing variety and connectedness there, they're taking away meaning. Parts of this canyon look the same as they did hundreds of years ago. It's worth preserving. It helps us feel something deeper about the area when you have native habitat."

When you add those bright blue wings in the air, it's hard not to feel happy in Juniper Canyon.

Thomas Brothers Map: Page 1269, F-7.

Before You Go: Download a copy of the trail map at the city's parks and recreation pages: http://www.sandiego.gov/park-and-recreation/pdf/junipertrailmap.pdf.
This trail welcomes hikers, bicyclists, and dogs on leashes.

Trailhead: From Interstate 5, exit at Pershing Drive and merge onto Pershing heading north. Turn right onto Redwood Street and then right onto Felton Street. Park where Felton dead-ends at Nutmeg.

Distance/Difficulty: The trails throughout the canyon total a bit more than 1.0 mile; easy.

3-10. Maple Canyon Trail Is an Urban Oasis

Towering eucalyptus trees, majestic Canary Island date palms, and lots of wild lilac adorn Maple Canyon, a restful retreat right in the middle of Bankers Hill. A trail traverses the canyon from the dead-end of Maple Street at Dove in Midtown to the Quince Street Trestle between Third and Fourth Avenues. It's an easy walk that takes less than an hour round-trip. You'll be viewing history along with magnificent trees. The eucalyptus alone are worth the walk; it's said that Kate Sessions was responsible for the early plantings in this canyon around 1911, so those trees are more than 100 years old.

You'll also experience two historic bridges in this canyon. The Quince Street Trestle, a wooden pedestrian-only footbridge, was built in 1905 to connect the community of Bankers Hill with the streetcar that used to run along Fourth Avenue.

The wooden bridge nearly faced demolition in the late 1980s, when its deterioration threatened its continuation. Termites and dry rot forced its closure in 1987. Local resident Elinor Meadows organized a movement to declare it historic, which the San Diego Historical Society's Site Board did. It was restored and reopened in 1990. It's a lovely wooden bridge that has inspired proposals and other special rendezvous over the last century.

As you walk from the trestle into Maple Canyon, you'll walk under the other historic bridge, First Avenue Bridge, a hinged truss arch steel bridge built in 1931 under the Improvement Act of 1911. It was originally known as the Peoples Bridge because it was erected due to demands of local property owners. The First Avenue Bridge was rebuilt for seismic security by the city several years ago. The project was approved in 2007 and included restoration of the bridge to its original 1931 appearance; "railings and light standards will be reconstructed and the structure will be painted with the original bronze color," according to city records.

Maple Canyon comes under the auspices of the city's Parks and Recreation Department's Open Space Canyons. There have been cleanup events in Maple Canyon in recent years, and I saw very little trash there, especially considering its inner-city location. This canyon is still available for adoption through the I Love a Clean San Diego, Adopt-A-Beach program (inland areas are now included).

The historic bridges of Maple Canyon may inspire you.

Volunteer opportunities include cleanup projects, invasive plant removal, habitat enhancement, and trail maintenance. If you'd like to get involved, contact the ranger in charge through the city's parks and recreation department, or check the I Love a Clean San Diego website, http://www.ilacsd.org.

Al Weiss, who lives in a condominium that looks into Maple Canyon, agrees it is beautiful. "But what bothers me most is the erosion there—street drainage is pushed into the area." Friends of Maple Canyon began to organize again in April 2015 through San Diego Canyonlands (www.sdcanyonlands.org) and the Bankers Hill Community Group. For more information, go to www.bankershillcommunity.org.

While you are in the neighborhood, you might also want to stroll the historic streets of Bankers Hill. The San Diego Historical Society offers two Bankers' Hill Walking Tours (http://www.sandiegohistory.org/tours/bankertour/bankertour1.htm), which focus on the classic homes there. Bankers Hill is made up of Hillcrest's "tree streets" north from Laurel through Upas, ranging west from Balboa Park to Curlew Street above Reynard Way Canyon.

Bankers Hill was named for "the important professionals who have had homes there since the area was developed in the 1890s," says the historical society.

The Bankers Hill No. 1 tour begins at First Street and Quince; No. 2 continues at Second Street and Walnut, and both tours point out historic Victorian, Craftsman, Revival, and Emerging Modern homes. In the Emerging Modern group are examples of "the most creative, cutting-edge architecture of 1905–1915, including designs by the world-renowned Irving Gill."

Find four Gill-designed homes in a row on Albatross near Walnut Street. Gill designed these and other cottages around Maple Canyon here, with original landscaping by Kate Sessions. "This early canyon grouping is an example of his commitment to creating simple, appealing and practical living conditions for everyone," says the historical society. The homes were originally rental properties for Alice Lee and Katherine Teats, whose main homes were among the historical properties known as Crittenden's Addition along Seventh Avenue, including the Marston House, also designed by Gill.

Maple Canyon remains the natural treasure that many of the homes in Bankers Hill still view today.

Thomas Brothers Map: Page 1269, 7-A.

Before You Go: Download a copy of the trail map from the city's parks and recreation pages, http://www.sandiego.gov/park-and-recreation/pdf/mapletrailmap.pdf.
This trail is open to hikers, bicyclists, and dogs on leashes.

Trailhead: From Interstate 5 heading south, exit at Sassafras Street/San Diego Airport and merge ahead onto Kettner Boulevard. Turn left onto Laurel Street, left onto First Avenue, and then right onto Quince Street. Park where Quince ends at Third Avenue.
From Interstate 5 heading north, exit at Sixth Avenue and turn right, heading north. Turn left onto Laurel, right onto First, and right onto Quince. Park near Quince and Third Street.

Distance/Difficulty: The Maple Canyon trail is about a half-mile long, making a 1.0-mile round-trip; easy.

3-11. Mission Hills Protects Its Historic Treasures

Mission Hills boasts some of the most beautiful historic neighborhoods in the entire city. It is an excellent place to find inspiration from its historic architectural styles. The Mission Hills Historic District, formally designated in 2007, was "the first resident-funded and resident-driven district in the City of San Diego," says Mission Hills Heritage, a group of local residents. This district includes 75 homes along the 1800 block of Sunset Boulevard, as well as all the houses along Lyndon Road and Sheridan Avenue. Adjoining this district, the Fort Stockton Line Historic District consists of 107 homes along parts of Fort Stockton Drive, West Lewis, and Pine Street, approved in 2007. A proposed extension of the Mission Hills Historic District includes 99 homes on the blocks between Sunset, Witherby, and Fort Stockton.

The area of the original Mission Hills Historic District was first known as Johnston Heights, when Captain Henry James Johnston bought 65 acres from the City of San Diego in 1869 for a total price of $16.25. A seafaring captain of the ship Orizaba, Johnston ferried passengers from San Francisco to San Diego. He wanted to build a home overlooking the harbor, but he didn't need as much land, so he sold 50 acres to a shipmate for $1 per acre, or $50 total. Sadly, he died in 1878 before he could build his dream home.

His daughter, Sarah Johnston Miller, did build that home in 1887, which became the first home built in Mission Hills. Though remodeled significantly from its original Victorian style into a Prairie style in the early 20th century, Villa Orizaba, as it is still called, stands today near the intersection of Orizaba and Miller Streets in that proposed historic district extension area.

Sarah's son, Henry Miller, subdivided his holdings in 1909, renaming Johnston Road Sunset Boulevard and calling the neighborhood Inspiration Heights. A marker naming this area still stands today on Sunset Boulevard.

Another syndicate was formed to buy and develop 60 acres in this area in 1908, with that parcel then costing $36,000. City leader George Marston also bought a 22-acre parcel bounded by Fort Stockton and Arden Way and gave the area its formal name of Mission Hills when his subdivision map was filed in 1908.

Kate Sessions made a mark on Mission Hills.

Kate Sessions, often called the mother of Balboa Park for her horticultural work, was also an early land owner in Mission Hills, where she lived from about 1903 until 1927. She played a major role in the area's development, which skyrocketed in the early 20th century when the city's streetcar extended to the intersection of Fort Stockton and Trias. Mission Hills Nursery, still located on Fort Stockton, was started by Kate Sessions in 1910. In 2010 it celebrated its 100th anniversary and its claim as the oldest nursery in the city.

These early civic leaders wanted to make Mission Hills one of the most exclusive areas in San Diego, and it did become the city's first restricted subdivision. Only single-family homes costing at least $3,500 could be built, and barns had to cost at least $500 each—during a time when the average worker made $10 a week.

Mission Hills quickly became known as an area of wealth and affluence. In the 1910s, Craftsman architectural styles predominated, with elements of Prairie and Pueblo styles continuing well into the 1930s. In the Mission Hills Historic District, you'll also find homes designed in Spanish Revival, Spanish Eclectic, Mission Revival, Dutch Colonial, English Tudor, and others. Several master architects of the time worked here, including William Hebbard (a longtime partner with Irving Gill), Richard Requa, and Nathan Rigdon.

You can easily walk the blocks of the Mission Hills Historic District by starting along that 1800 block of Sunset Boulevard and moving west along Sheridan Road and Lyndon Road. See if you can determine each unique home's historic architectural style: Craftsman, which comes from the title of a popular magazine published by furniture designer Gustav Stickley between 1901 and 1916, typically features wood, stone, or stucco siding; a low-pitched roof; wide eaves with triangular brackets; and exposed roof rafters with front porches. Prairie style, largely credited to Frank Lloyd Wright, was popular from 1900 to 1920 and is mainly characterized by strong horizontal lines, clerestory windows, overhanging eaves, open floor plans, and a low-pitched roof. Spanish Colonial homes feature stucco siding, decorative tiles, and red-tiled roofs. Dutch Colonial houses have gambrel-shaped roofs. Greek Revival usually features a symmetrical shape and an entry porch with columns. The Tudor style often features heavy chimneys and decorative half-timbering.

While walking in this charming neighborhood several years ago, we chatted with one longtime resident, Hugh McArthur, then 98, who had lived in his home here since 1955. A native San Diegan, he graduated from San Diego High School and told us he used to be a steel magnate. His company, Southern Equipment and Supply Co., distributed "all the steel in San Diego for 50 years," he said, "also helping to build Tijuana and Ensenada."

"The neighborhood has held up beautifully," he told us. "And we always get lots of sun." McArthur died at 103 in 2014. Inspiration Heights has obviously inspired many residents over the years to take care of their historic treasures.

To find lots of information about these historic districts and what they mean, visit http://missionhillsheritage.org, as well as http://sohosandiego.org and the city's page at http://www.sandiego.gov/planning/programs/historical.

You can view a list of historic sites throughout the city at http://www.sandiego.gov/planning/programs/historical/pdf/landmarklist.pdf.

Thomas Brothers Map: Page 1268, H-5.

Before You Go: Download a copy of the historic districts map at Mission Hills Heritage Organization, http://missionhillsheritage.org/districts.htm.
Leashed dogs are welcome here.

Trailhead: Take Interstate 5 to Interstate 8 and head east, exiting at Taylor Street toward Hotel Circle. Keep right to take Taylor Street ramp toward Morena Boulevard. Turn right onto Taylor Street. Turn left onto Juan Street. Turn left onto Sunset Road; Sunset Road becomes Sunset Boulevard. Continue to Sunset's intersection with Sheridan Avenue and park where you can.

Distance/Difficulty: You can wander for a mile or two or more, depending on how many blocks you choose to explore; easy.

3-12. Pioneer Park May Haunt You–At Least with Its Stories

Pioneer Park in Mission Hills is the perfect spot for a Halloween wander—if you dare. It once was the site of the Calvary Cemetery, a Catholic burial ground where some 4,000 bodies were laid to rest from about 1876 to 1960. The only evidence of the graveyard that remains today are nearly 150 tombstones that were saved and placed in the park's southeast corner. There is also a bronze memorial that lists many of the people buried there. When a new Catholic cemetery, Holy Cross, opened in 1919, Calvary Cemetery fell into disrepair, and burials there were rare. The last one was in 1960. By 1970, the city took over the site and transformed it into Pioneer Park, removing most of the headstones and "storing" them in a ravine at Mount Hope Cemetery, where they are today. However, most of the bodies remain interred under the lovely grassy expanse of Pioneer Park, also known as Mission Hills Park.

"There was supposedly a woman (ghost) who would rise up and walk around there," Valerie Goodpaster told a group of Grant Elementary School kids who did an impressive research project on Pioneer Park in 2005. Sadly, that research project, which included a few oral histories from people like Goodpaster, who grew up in Mission Hills, is no longer available online. Perhaps Missions Hills community leaders can investigate how to resurrect that project's online presence (pun intended).

"I get the creepiest feelings when I go there," said Sally Richards, founder of Ghosts Happen, a local group that investigates paranormal activity throughout San Diego County. "Over by the tombstones, I feel like I'm being watched." She said her electromagnetic field readers, a paranormal investigative device, "go off the charts there. And one of our people did get a photo of something walking through," she added. Go to the group's website (www.meetup.com/ghostshappen) to view photos; seek out one by Charles of Pioneer Park.

Pioneer Park has plenty of stories to tell.

"I definitely feel that if I were buried there and my grave was destroyed, I'd be haunting the place," said Richards. "At one time it was a beautiful graveyard, and now it's a beautiful park, a really friendly place during the day with people having a good time. But when the sun goes down, there's a different feeling to it."

Indeed, it is a lovely place during the day. The students at Grant Elementary right next door use it for physical education activities. It's a neighborhood favorite for picnics and dog walks. There are specimen eucalyptus trees as well as some lovely California peppers, ficus, and Chinese flame trees. Some of the huge old trees have surely been there since the cemetery days.

But it's the stories of the people buried there that still fascinate. Marna Clemons, a professional genealogist and president of the San Diego Genealogy Society, spent more than two years researching Calvary Cemetery. She was doing some research for her sister-in-law when she came upon a Bible on eBay that belonged to the John Stewart/Rosa Machado family, whose 1830s adobe home is today part of Old Town State Historic Park. It wasn't related to the research she was doing for her sister-in-law, but she thought it held a lot of San Diego history, and so she put together family information to give to the San Diego Historical Society.

"One thing led to another, which led me to learn about the history of Calvary Cemetery," said Clemons. "There was no complete record of who was buried there. I had the time, I started researching, and it led to a website." Her website, http://freepages. genealogy.rootsweb.ancestry.com/~clement/Calvary/home.htm, is an invaluable resource for information on the historic cemetery.

Many early city leaders were buried there, including John (Jack) Stewart, buried in 1892, and his wife, Rosa Machado, buried in 1898. Stewart, who lived to be 83 and had been a shipmate of Richard Henry Dana, well-known author of *Two Years Before the Mast*, had fought in the battle of San Pasqual and was active in other early incidents connected with this region, according to his 1892 obituary in the *San Diego Union*, which is linked on Clemons website.

Cave Johnson Couts, who was one of the wealthiest men in Southern California through his Rancho Guajome near Oceanside (now a historic site), was originally buried in the Old Town Cemetery in 1874 but was later moved to Calvary Cemetery. Couts had graduated from West Point Academy with Ulysses S. Grant and Robert E. Lee in 1843, and he served during the Mexican War. He married Ysidora Bandini.

Ysidora Bandini was buried beside her father, Don Juan Bandini, who had been married to Maria de los Dolores Estudillo, member of another prominent Old Town family.

Father Antonio Ubach presided over Ysidora Bandini's funeral, according to an 1897 *San Diego Union* obituary about the "impressive services over the remains of a pioneer," again linked through Clemons website.

Father Ubach was also buried in Calvary Cemetery. A priest in Old Town for 23 years beginning in 1860, he was called the Last Padre.

"There were a lot of children buried there, several murders, drowning, and many gruesome deaths involved trains, trolleys, and horses," said Clemons. She has even transcribed several letters between Charles Gooch and his wife, Julia, written during the Civil War. Many of these murder and accident cases were documented in the local newspaper at the time and are linked on her website. Go to the "Stories to Tell" section and click on highlighted names, or search the database alphabet for names of people buried there and click to see if they have a story to share from the old days.

You'll probably get caught up searching for all kinds of stories, which just might help you if you greet any of the players in the Pioneer Park at night.

Thomas Brothers Map: Page 1268, H-5.

Before You Go: There's a small map of Pioneer Park (a.k.a. Mission Hills Park) on the city's parks and recreation pages for Presidio Park: http://www.sandiego.gov/park-and-recreation/parks/regional/presidio/index.shtml.
For more information about Pioneer Park/Mission Hills Park, go to the city's page: http://www.sandiego.gov/park-and-recreation/parks/regional/presidio/missionhills.shtml.
Open to hikers and dogs on leashes.

Trailhead: From Interstate 5, exit at Washington Street, merging onto Hancock and taking the first left onto W. Washington Street. Turn left onto Goldfinch Street. Take the first left onto Fort Stockton Drive. Turn left onto Ingalls Street and then right onto Washington Place. The park is on the left.

Distance/Difficulty: The park is small and the hiking is easy.

3-13. Presidio Park Has History and Trails

Some call it the West's Plymouth Rock. Locals call it Presidio Park. This 50-acre oasis in Mission Hills stands on the hill recognized as the site where California began.

"It was here in 1769 that a Spanish Franciscan missionary, Father Junipero Serra, with a group of soldiers led by Gaspar de Portola, established Alta California's first mission and presidio (fort)," says the San Diego Historical Society.

Some 160 years later in 1929, the Junipero Serra Museum and Presidio Park were dedicated by the 79-year-old George Marston, who had personally spent over 20 years and his own money to buy the land to preserve this historic site and to build a museum to house the San Diego Historical Society and its collections.

Today the Serra Museum remains the historical society's most important venue. It is open after Labor Day through May on Saturdays and Sundays, and from June through Labor Day on Fridays, Saturdays, and Sundays, at 10:00 a.m. to 5:00 p.m.

Presidio Park is a jewel among city parks. If you've only just driven by, you might have glimpsed wedding parties under its classic wisteria-covered colonnade. It's also a favorite place for picnics among its several grassy expanses shaded by old magnolia, eucalyptus, pine, and palm trees. It offers views of San Diego Bay, Mission Bay, and Mission Valley.

You may not know it also has over 2.0 miles of trails that meander between Mission Hills and Mission Valley. These trails begin behind the museum and the grassy areas. There are a couple of entry points to the network that covers the less-developed hills behind the well-kept park grounds.

I have lived here all my life and never knew these trails existed, even though I've picnicked in Presidio for decades. While wandering the trails recently, I marveled at the native and nonnative plantings, including lots of blooms in full color. I counted among the flower show many orange nasturtiums, big yellow sunflowers, blooming prickly pear and barrel cacti, pink raphiolepis, blue plumbago and ceanothus (wild lilac), purple pride of Madeira, yellow trumpet vines, aloes, and hibiscus. The trails wander up and down, but it's relatively easy going and a true escape right in the center of the city.

Search for statues in pretty Presidio Park.

The developed areas in the park are equally alluring. There are Inspiration Point on its western summit with sweeping views, which reminds us of its earlier military importance; Palm Canyon and Eucalyptus Grove, both below the museum and across Presidio Drive; and the Arbor, where all those weddings take place, next to the Bowl. You can find nooks among the various grassy knolls for plenty of privacy.

It's also fun to try to find all the statuary in the park. Just below the museum is Presidio Wall, which was recreated close to the original presidio location, where some crumbled adobe ruins remain. Near there is the large bronze Indian statue created by the late Arthur Putnam, a noted sculptor. Across Presidio Drive from there is the Serra Cross, built in 1913 from fragments of original Spanish tiles. Behind the cross is the famous bronze statue of Father Serra, also created by Putnam.

Near Inspiration Point, just to the west of the intersection of Presidio Drive and Cosoy Way, you'll find a statue and mural commemorating the Mormon Battalion, whose journey from Council Bluffs, Iowa, to San Diego in 1846 to help win California for the Union is still the longest infantry march in history.

In the eastern section near Cosoy Way is the statue of a Mexican cowboy on horseback, donated to the City of San Diego in 1969 by the president of Mexico, Gustavo Diaz Ordaz, to celebrate the 200th anniversary of the founding of San Diego by the explorer Cabrillo.

Find the treasures in Presidio Park.

Thomas Brothers Map: Page 1268, G-4 for lower entry; also Page 1268, G-4, for intersection of Presidio Drive and Cosoy Way.

Before You Go: Download a copy of the map of Presidio Park at the city's parks and recreation pages: http://www.sandiego.gov/park-and-recreation/parks/regional/presidio/index.shtml.

There are a couple of entries to the trails of Presidio Park. Find them behind the Serra Museum and the Bowl, which lies to the west of the museum at the eastern end of Cosoy Way. You may also begin the trails at their bottom if you park off Taylor Street just before it intersects with I-8 in Mission Valley.

Dogs on leashes are welcome.

Trailhead: From Interstate 8, exit at Taylor Street, taking the Taylor Street ramp toward Morena Boulevard. Turn right onto Taylor. Park at the bottom of the park here at Taylor near its intersection with I-8. To continue to the upper portion of the park, from Taylor Street, turn left onto Presidio Drive, and park in the parking areas.

Distance/Difficulty: The trails cover 2.0 miles; easy.

3-14. Little Traveled Trail in Balboa Park Has History

Far from the madding crowds in the center of Balboa Park is a trail in its southwest corner that takes you to a little-known historic building, through a grove of coast redwoods, and under the boughs of some beautiful old trees.

It's a part of trail No. 5 on the map of Balboa Park Trails (http://www.balboapark.

Some beautiful old trees live on Balboa Park's No. 5 trail.

org/in-the-park/hiking-and-biking-trails). The entire trail system in Balboa Park for hikers and bicyclists and dogs on leashes offers 65 miles of trails of various difficulty and scenery, including those that travel through the park's remote reaches as well as those that lead to museums.

The entire Trail No. 5 covers a lot of ground in the park—6.6 miles of it, in fact. Of course, you don't have to walk the entire trail in one fell swoop. I covered just the southwest corner and found a lot to enjoy.

Located between Sixth Avenue and Highway 163, this area southwest of Cabrillo Bridge is little traveled and still seems to harbor some sad realities. Nearest to downtown and culminating in the flagpole at Marston Point, this part of the park attracts some homeless campers, whose deep-canyon digs can sometimes be seen from the trail here near Highway 163.

However, the city continues to make efforts to keep the homeless from making permanent camps in the park. They are allowed to sleep overnight but are not allowed to camp in one place for long periods of time.

I parked just south of Laurel Street and El Prado on Balboa Drive and began my meander on the concrete walkway to the west of Balboa Drive.

Right away was the first attraction here: old Brazilian pepper trees bending over the walkway along with yellow-blooming Chinese flame trees, all making marvelous shadows. I passed the Horseshoe Pits and headed down to Marston Point. Views of much of the downtown skyline are afforded here because it's really close to these very same buildings.

The flagpole that marks Marston Point was dedicated there by the Free Masons of San Diego County in 1927. That was the same year the city fathers chose Robert Snyder's Spanish Colonial design for the Fire Alarm Building, which opened in 1928. Few people know about this historic building, and it was kind of intended that way from the beginning.

"First of all, it was located on city park property, but far enough removed from the highly visible Panama-California Exhibition Buildings to afford privacy," wrote Alex Bevil in his 1988 article "Forgotten Sentinel on Marston Point: The History of the San Diego Fire Alarm Communications Building, 1928–1971," for *The Journal of San Diego History* for the San Diego Historical Society (http://www.sandiegohistory. org/journal/88fall/forgotten.htm). Second, Bevil wrote, since the building was on city park property, it wouldn't be threatened by public or private buildings nearby for a long time. Third, it had a commanding view of the city and could be easily reached by fire department headquarters then located at 10th Avenue downtown.

Snyder's architectural partner was William Templeton Johnson, who had designed the San Diego Fine Arts Gallery building in the park (now San Diego Museum of Art) in the same Spanish Colonial style in 1926. For over 40 years, Snyder's building served as the fire alarm telegraph station for the city. The fire alarm communications network was finally moved in 1970 to the city hall complex downtown. Today, the Fire Alarm Building by Marston Point is home to the city's Parks and Recreation Department's administration.

Continuing along the walkway past the Fire Alarm Building, I encountered the chain-link fencing that protects the seasonal home of the Haunted Trail, an annual Halloween event in Balboa Park (http://www.sandiego.org/events/holidays/haunted-trail-of-balboa-park.aspx). While walking along the back side of this fencing, I eventually hooked up to the part of Trail No. 5 that's not paved, and I headed down into the canyon through which Highway 163 whizzes. It's a steep stairway down through a very natural part of the park. To see the historic Cabrillo Bridge from below is an interesting sight.

After wandering back up into the park from the north side of that bridge, I continued on an unpaved trail and then hit the redwood trees. Coast redwoods are not really well-suited for our climate, and you can see that they aren't as hardy here as they are in Northern California. Some have had to be cut down when they died, but many of these mighty evergreen trees survive, having been planted for the 1915 exposition.

Lots of that historic nature makes Balboa Park the multifaceted gem that it is, and Trail No. 5 shares a little more of it.

Thomas Brothers Map: Page 1289, B-1.

Before You Go: Download a trail map from Balboa Park's hiking and biking trails pages, zeroing in on the PDF map for the Sixth and Upas Gateway: http://www.balboapark.org/sites/default/files/6th-upas_12-21-09_maponly_0.pdf.
 This trail is open to hikers, bicyclists, and dogs on leashes.

Trailhead: From Interstate 5 heading south, exit at Sassafras Street/San Diego Airport and merge onto Kettner Boulevard. Turn left onto W. Laurel Street and head into the park just past Sixth where Laurel turns into El Prado. Turn right from El Prado onto Balboa Drive and park on the street here.
 From Interstate 5 heading north, exit at Sixth Avenue, turning right onto Sixth and then right onto Laurel. Then proceed as above.

Distance/Difficulty: The total mileage for Trail No. 5 is 6.6 miles and is rated difficult, but you can do this shorter, moderate version for about 2.0 to 3.0 miles.

3-15. Dogs and Birds Both Love Fiesta Island

Walk around the entire perimeter of Fiesta Island on Mission Bay for a sparkling blue-water hike of nearly 6 miles. This is a very easy, flat walk along the sandy shoreline of the island's northeastern and northwestern edges, across a rocky and shell-strewn beach at the southwestern edge, and around the favorite leash-free dog area of the southern edge, where the trail heads up along a ridge overlooking the entire island. Views of downtown's skyline are the bonus at the southern edge, where that ridge-line trail also looks down into the brushy island interior. After curving around calm coves, you'll come full circle to your starting point.

There are a lot of shore birds wading and floating along the sandy beaches. The calmest areas along the eastern flank of the island draw the highest numbers of waders, whose reflections in the calm early-morning waters make for pretty pictures.

I spotted lots of 18-inch marbled godwits, with their very long, half-pink, half-black bills; 15-inch smooth gray willets, with their thick gray and black bills and gray legs; eight-inch pale gray sanderlings; and western and least sandpipers, the smallest of the waders at around six inches wearing white breast feathers.

And of course, there are lots of gulls. I learned a while ago that there is no official bird named seagull. They are all gulls, and there are dozens of species of gulls: the *San Diego County Bird Atlas* by Philip Unitt and the San Diego Natural History Museum lists 21 species.

The western gull is the only gull species that nests here and stays all year long. It's a large gull, up to 27 inches tall, and has a white head, yellow bill with red dot, dark gray back and wings, and pink legs. Heermann's gull stands at 16 to 18 inches, and Unitt says is the "most distinctive and attractive of North American gulls." It is a very dark gull with a red bill. The 18- to 20-inch California gull has a white head and body with gray wings and black wing tips, greenish-yellow legs, and black and red spots on its yellow bill. The glaucous-winged gull, also large at 27 inches, has gray wings with no black markings and pinkish legs.

Fiesta Island is a favorite for dogs.

The northern and southern ends of Fiesta Island are fenced to protect the endangered California least terns that nest on open sandy beaches. These are among four nesting sites for that bird on Mission Bay, a program now 13 years old that aims to protect these lovely birds. The least tern is a small tern, around nine inches, with a black cap and white forehead, a white and gray body, and a relatively long, yellow bill with a black tip.

In the coastal chaparral in the island center, I also saw the Say's phoebe with its rust-colored belly, and the yellow-eyebrowed savannah sparrow.

Fiesta Island is surely a dogs' paradise because they can run leash-free on the entire island—and into the bay. A fenced area along the southern end is especially popular for dog owners; their dogs are a bit more contained, even though they're free to run.

Mission Bay Park is the largest man-made aquatic park in the United States, covering 4,235 acres, with 46 percent of it land. There are 27 miles of shoreline and 14 miles of bike paths along Mission Bay. It was developed into its present-day beauty over many years, from the 1940s to 1960s. Juan Rodriguez Cabrillo called it False Bay in 1542, when it was little more than a tidal marsh where San Diego River emptied into the Pacific. The first dike along the south side of the river was built in 1852 by the U.S. Army to drain San Diego River more predictably, but this dike failed soon after it was built. It wasn't until 1944 that the city's chamber of commerce recommended developing this area into a tourist attraction, but dredging and filling didn't begin until the late 1940s.

Fiesta Island came to be around 1956 when it was essentially made the disposal area of all the dredged materials. Over the years, it was made more attractive, and today is a great place to walk, ride bicycles, or even horseback ride on a 2.5-mile loop on part of the island—one of the only county beaches where horses can go in the water.

Fiesta Island is also one of the few beaches left with fire rings on the sand. No alcohol is allowed.

Stay into a summer evening to view Sea World's fireworks shows almost every night in July and August, along with some weekends in June and September.

Thomas Brothers Map: Page 1268, 3-D.

Before You Go: For more information about Fiesta Island and Mission Bay Park, go to the city's parks page at http://www.sandiego.gov/park-and-recreation/parks/regional/missionbay/fiestaisland.shtml.

Download a copy of Mission Bay Park's map at http://www.sandiego.gov/park-and-recreation/parks/regional/missionbay/facilities.shtml.

Open to hikers, bicyclists, equestrians, and dogs (with off leash allowed).

Trailhead: From Interstate 5, exit at Sea World Drive and head west. Follow signs to the one road onto Fiesta Island off East Mission Bay Drive.

Distance/Difficulty: Walk along the perimeter of the entire island for about a 5.75-mile loop; very easy. Follow the main road or head to the sandy beach or inland ridge trails.

3-16. Trails at Kate Sessions Offer Sweeping Views

Kate Sessions Memorial Park in Pacific Beach is well known to those who play soccer on its grassy fields, attend occasional outdoor music concerts on summer Sunday afternoons, or watch their kids swing and slide on the playground equipment. But few know that most of the park—60 of its nearly 80 acres—is left undeveloped and interlaced with a couple of hiking trails.

Panoramic bay, ocean, and downtown views revealed from Kate Sessions Park.

One of the biggest reasons to go to Kate Sessions, for its park grounds or these trails, is for the panoramic views. Sweeping from the Pacific Ocean to the west to the peaks of the eastern horizon, this 350-foot-high hilltop looks over all of Mission Bay, the downtown skyline, and the Coronado Bridge. It is truly one of the great vistas in the city.

Born on San Francisco's Nob Hill, Kate Sessions was an important horticulturalist who came to San Diego at age 28 in 1885 and remained here until she died in 1940. In 1892 she leased what was then city park land for a nursery, making a deal to plant 100 trees there each year as well as 300 trees elsewhere in the city. That city park became Balboa Park in 1902 through the efforts of Sessions and her friends George Marston and Mary B. Coulston.

Sessions lived in Pacific Beach near her namesake park and also owned a nursery at the corner of Garnet and Pico. Here at the site of her former nursery, she planted a Tipuana tree, which is now a California Registered Historical Landmark.

The trails in Kate Sessions park are not marked and are not even very well kept. Be mindful that some lead to what appear to be former or current homeless hangouts hidden in the brambles. Avoid the trail beyond the green chain-link fence that separates just a little bit of the wild area to the east of the playground area. Instead, find the trailhead that starts at the very northeast edge of the playground area, behind the memorial benches; look for Robert Gordon's memorial bench and walk northeast behind it. This trailhead takes off from the dirt where you can see the vast undeveloped area beyond the bushes.

The coastal scrub here doesn't offer much variation. Mostly you'll find lots of mock orange bushes that offer a lovely scent when blooming in the spring, and a few rogue pampas grasses. There are virtually no trees in this undeveloped area, so there is little shade. There are splendid specimen trees in the developed park; Kate Sessions is well remembered there.

The main trail is an obvious dirt one that meanders up and down rocky ravines of erosion. It's not really difficult, but there are some steep patches where you need to watch your step. At the top of the hill, another trail takes off toward the eastern part of this undeveloped area. Or you can just linger here and marvel at the city spread out below.

Thomas Brothers Map: Page 1248, A-4.

Before You Go: Though it is a city park, there is no online map from the parks and recreation department for Kate Sessions Neighborhood Park. Here is a case where a Google satellite map fills the bill. Go to San Diego Coast Life's website, http://www.sandiegocoastlife.com/attractions/san-diego-coast/parks-kate-sessions.html, and click on the map. Make it a satellite image map, and you'll see all the trails.

No bikes or motorized vehicles are allowed. Leashed dogs are welcome.

It's open dawn to dusk and is free.

Trailhead: Located at 5115 Soledad Road, San Diego 92109. From Interstate 5 heading south, exit at Balboa/Garnet; from Interstate 5 heading north, exit at Grand/Garnet. At the major intersection of Mission Bay Drive and Garnet/Balboa, head west on Garnet. Turn right onto Soledad Mountain Road, left onto Beryl, and then right onto Lamont. The park is on the right.

Distance/Difficulty: About 1.0 to 2.0 miles round-trip; easy to moderate.

3-17. Kumeyaay Village, Lots of Birds in Tecolote Canyon

This canyon was slated to become a landfill in the 1950s, but community protests scrubbed that plan. Then it was slated for various subdivision developments throughout the 1960s, including the last one for about 600 homes and a concrete-lined flood channel.

But when the bulldozers began to roll, "the community was outraged," wrote M. Eloise Battle, who spearheaded formation of Citizens to Save Open Space in the early 1970s to preserve Tecolote Canyon in Bay Park. After years of wrangling City Hall as well as the canyon's neighbors, Battle and her fellow conservationists realized the formation of the Tecolote Canyon Park District in 1974, and the City of San Diego acquired the nearly 900 acres for a natural park. In 1978, Tecolote Canyon Natural Park was dedicated, and it was one of the earliest preserved open spaces within the urban core.

In 1994, the Tecolote Canyon Nature Center was built, and one of its classrooms is dedicated to Battle and her decades-long commitment to save this natural canyon.

The Kumeyaay thrived here for centuries. One of the first settlers in the canyon was Judge Hyde who began farming here in 1872, according to the city's parks page. As late as 1953, cattle were still grazing in the canyon.

Visit the nature center to see a rare recreation of a Kumeyaay village, including a hut and shelter made from willow branches. A native plant garden here also features and labels several of the species common in chaparral, coastal sage scrub, and riparian habitats like those in the canyon.

Learn about Kumeyaay at Tecolote.

Inside the nature center, marvel at all the animals, both live and preserved, as well as informational displays on the geology and animal and plant life here. There are beautiful specimens of Kumeyaay baskets, like those made from willow, which had a natural insect repellent so stored acorns would not spoil. There are also examples of morteros and metates, the deep and shallow holes ground in rock by native women making meal from acorns.

Just beyond the center, you'll find some 6.5 miles of hiking and biking trails. I took the southern trail from the center, and I followed it through the chaparral and then along the southern edge of Tecolote Canyon Golf Course, winding uphill via power line access roads to reach broad views back down into the big canyon, which is home to many animals and birds, including coyotes, opossum, weasels, gray foxes, bobcats, snakes, lizards, California quail (our state bird), roadrunners, hawks, sparrows, hummingbirds, and butterflies.

Tecolote Canyon is named for the owls that live here; pre-Colombian Native Americans called the owl tecolote, according to the park.

You will likely spot lots of birds in the canyon, both year-round residents as well as migratory ones. Because it's close to Mission Bay, the birds found there and along its shoreline that are usually not found in the chaparral and riparian habitats can be seen here. I saw many yellow-bellied kingbirds and several kinds of sparrows. You might also see gulls and terns, mourning doves, woodpeckers, western scrub jays, western bluebirds, and even least Bell's vireo, an endangered species that nests here.

The riparian habitat features some very old sycamore and live oak trees along Tecolote Creek, which empties from here into Mission Bay near Fiesta Island. You'll pass under a couple of oak canopies on that southern trail route.

Several blooms are still brightening the trail in summer, including toyon, whose white flowers will turn into those bright red berries in fall and winter. Also in summer, look for the blue berries of Mexican elderberry, from which the Kumeyaay made a tea to treat headaches and fever. Birds like these berries too. You'll see lots of lemonadeberry with its dense clusters of sticky reddish berries that natives used to make a lemonade-like drink to treat colds and coughs. Laurel sumac shrubs are blooming in summer in white conical clusters at the top ends of branches. This shrub is sometimes called the taco plant because its leaves seem shaped like taco shells. The fragrances of white and black sages, as well as California sagebrush, fill the air. Tall, yellow blooms of hooker's evening primrose line the trail at one point.

Take the single-track trail off the main road near the beginning of the southern route, and you'll see the blue dome and other buildings of University of San Diego up on the canyon rim. This trail joins the main dirt road, which also serves as the trail.

Follow the road or take any side trails instead. I stayed close to the fence of the golf course until I wound up at the top of the canyon near Kearny Mesa Community Park, where I turned around and retraced my way back.

Tecolote Canyon Natural Park offers lots of programs and classes. Of special note is its annual Baskets and Botany: Kumeyaay Cultural Experience in Tecolote Canyon, held the second Saturday in October every year. This free, family event celebrates Kumeyaay traditions and invites kids to make their own baskets and pottery.

Thomas Brothers Map: Page 1268, G-2.

Before You Go: Download a copy of the trail map at the city's parks page, http://www.sandiego.gov/park-and-recreation/pdf/tecolotetrailmap.pdf.

The trails are open to hikers, mountain bikers, and dogs on leashes.

For more information about programs and classes, go to the city's parks and recreation page for Tecolote activities: http://www.sandiego.gov/park-and-recreation/centers/recctr/tecolote.shtml.

Trailhead: From Interstate 5, exit at Tecolote Road/Sea World Drive and head east onto Tecolote Road. Cross Morena Boulevard and continue until Tecolote Road ends at the parking area for the Nature Center. The trail begins just to the left of the center.

Distance/Difficulty: I mapped about 4.5 miles round-trip with about 555 feet total elevation gain in both directions. The first mile is easy and flat, but that second mile and a half or so climbs some steep power-line access roads about 400 feet to the canyon rim. Easy to moderate.

3-18. Rose Would Still Love His Fine Canyon Today

When you hike the 3-mile trail through the middle of Rose Canyon, you are treading on a lot of local history. You'll also see lots of wildflowers, a cottontail rabbit or two, a bobcat if you're lucky, and maybe even a mule deer. Coyotes make their home here too.

Don't miss its marvelous tunnels of trees: old oaks, sycamores, and willows at the eastern end of the canyon make graceful canopies that completely envelop the trail, creating natural, people-sized "rabbit holes" that practically beg you to explore.

It's hard to imagine this canyon was once was home to a Kumeyaay village, a vineyard, a cattle ranch, coal mines, a brick factory, and an important corridor for the first railroad.

In the middle of Rose Canyon is Rose Creek, a local water source that has attracted wildlife as well as people through the ages.

"Rose Canyon was formed when water following the Rose Canyon Fault Zone carved out layers of sedimentary rock laid down 46 million to 55 million years ago," says a fine publication on Rose Canyon by the San Diego Archaeological Center. The Rose Canyon Fault Zone is a system of faults that extends about two-thirds of a mile wide from offshore La Jolla into San Diego Bay. This fault zone is responsible for forming

Alluring tree tunnels invite hikers to Rose Canyon.

both Mount Soledad and San Diego Bay, says the center, and the zone is still active, having "moved about 29 feet in the last 8,000 years."

Rose Canyon has made a natural corridor for millennia, and it still does today. Rose Canyon lies between the intersection of Interstate 5 and Highway 52 at the west to Interstate 805 at Governor Drive to the east, and today both the Coaster and Surfliner rail operations pass through this open-space park of about 400 acres.

The earliest archaeological sites in Rose Canyon date from about 7,000 years ago. "Just as today, San Diego was a very nice place to live 7,000 years ago," says the center publication. "Fresh water was plentiful … deer, fowl and rabbit were probably hunted and seed-producing plants were available most of the year. Walking around Mount Soledad would lead people to the shore for fishing and shellfish gathering."

Many stone tools from this era were made from quartzite, abundant here as smooth, rounded river cobbles.

The canyon is named for Louis Rose, a German Jewish immigrant who arrived here in 1849 in search of gold. At one time he owned nearly 4,000 acres in San Diego, more than any other resident. His first investment was 80 acres in what is now Point Loma, naming it Roseville-on-the-Bay; he hoped it would become the future site of New San Diego.

An active member of the community, Rose owned 1,920 acres by 1856 in Rose Canyon, establishing a vineyard, cattle pasture, and tannery. He had tried to bring the railroad to San Diego for 20 years, but it wouldn't come until 1881. Rose Canyon later became a cattle ranch under Gustavus Fischer from 1853 to 1868, then George Selwyn from 1868 to 1894. From 1894 to 1936, George Gilbert and Joseph Richert established a dairy. By 1936, most of Rose Canyon was part of George Sawday's cattle ranch until housing demands replaced the cattle as late as the 1960s.

When Louis Rose died in 1888 at age 80, his only surviving daughter, Henrietta, recalled her father "especially loved animals, flowers and trees." He would love Rose Canyon today. Many wildflowers bloom here in spring and summer. I marveled at close-ups of pretty pink buckwheat, toyon blooms that will become red berries in December, wide white flowers of jimson weed, tiny stalks of purple and white salt heliotrope, white horse-nettle that's really purple, sweet fennel, bristly ox-tongue, sunflowers (including rock and ox-eye daisies), and matilija poppies. Look for coyote melons too, which might be a legacy from former farmers. Rose would have loved the trees—giant old sycamores, coast live oaks, and willows—especially where they form irresistible tunnels near the east end of the canyon.

I began at the dead-end of Regents Road, where I took the main path to the west all the way to its end at Highway 52. The path heads west through the canyon with views to Mount Soledad and then winds up a ridge that looks down on I-5 and the railroad tracks. After crossing a couple of wooden footbridges over the creek, the trail ends shortly after reaching Highway 52.

I turned around and retraced my way back, passing my entry to head to the eastern end at Genesee Avenue. A secondary trail continues east along University City High School to the canyon's end at I-805 for another three-quarters of a mile.

At the southwest end near the junction of I-5 and Highway 52, you can hike under the freeways and connect with Marian Bear Memorial Natural Park that lies on the southern side of Highway 52. Rose Canyon, Marian Bear, and Tecolote Canyon Natural Park make up what is called Tri-Canyon Parks, three open-space parks that cover 1,500 acres for hiking, biking, and bird-watching.

I hiked only the main trail, posting a round-trip of about 6 miles, and I marveled at the life that still thrives in Rose Canyon.

Thomas Brothers Map: Page 1228, C-5.

Before You Go: Download a copy of the Rose Canyon Open Space trail map from the city's parks pages: http://www.sandiego.gov/park-and-recreation/pdf/rosecanyontrailmap.pdf.
Hikers, bicyclists, and dogs on leashes are welcome.

Trailhead: From Highway 52, exit at Regents Road and head north to its dead-end, past Governor Drive. There is ample off-street parking near the kiosk at the trailhead.

Distance/Difficulty: The main trail section from Highway 52 at I-5 to Genesee Avenue is 3.0 miles one-way, making for a 6.0-mile round-trip. Easy.

3-19. Adventure, Education in Marian Bear Park

Thanks to a community activist, San Clemente Canyon is an urban natural oasis instead of a freeway. Marian Bear (1912–1979), was an active community leader who worked tirelessly to preserve San Diego's canyons in their natural state. She was the driving force behind moving State Route 52 from the canyon floor to its northern hillsides, thereby preserving a remarkably alluring landscape that today is home to lots of wildlife. Marian R. Bear Memorial Park, which had been designated San Clemente Park in 1968 after the highway was begun in 1966, was renamed for her when she died in 1979.

The park covers some 472 acres in San Clemente Canyon alongside State Route 52, and it offers loads of learning opportunities in addition to its trails. There are about 4.0 miles of trails in the park, popular with hikers, joggers, bicyclists, and dogs on leashes.

The main trail runs about 3.2 miles from its western terminus west of Regents Road to its eastern end near the Interstate 805 intersection with SR 52. There are a few spur trails off of it, as well as some narrower trails that parallel the main trail along the San Clemente Canyon creek.

Several informative placards along the trail present facts and photos about the park that make visits there even more engaging, especially for children.

One set of photos offers a sort of treasure hunt for a dead oak tree whose main trunk has been left standing for the birds, for "bee" trees, for holes bored in tree trunks by acorn woodpeckers who store acorns there, for a rock in the fork of an old sycamore whose bark has grown around it, and for a pile of sticks that is actually a wood rat nest. Another set of fact sheets talks about three kinds of spiders: tarantulas, who secrete digestive enzymes on its prey to dissolve it so it can suck in the liquefied meal in its small mouth; trapdoor spiders, who make nests with ground-level entrances that have a lid hinged on its uphill side like a trap door, and who can resist a pull 38 times their weight; and eight-eyed wolf spiders, so named because they were once thought to hunt in packs.

Lots to learn in Marian Bear Memorial Park.

Thoughtful gardeners may learn from the lists of nonnative plants that can catch and spread fire, including eucalyptus, pine trees, and giant bamboo. "Oak trees are an example of a fire zone-compatible plant," says another sheet. "Oaks have bulky water-laden trunks which are difficult to ignite." Some native shrubs that are fire zone-compatible include toyon, holly-leafed cherry, lemonadeberry, and coffeeberry. "California fuchsia is also a fire-retardant plant with scarlet flowers that attracts hummingbirds." Native verbena, with blue, fragrant flowers, will guard against fire and erosion.

A page about the area's history notes that Native Americans lived in this area for 10,000 years; look for morteros in the canyon where they once ground those acorns. Cattle grazed here in the early 19th century. The area was named Clemente Canyon in the late 19th century for a Native American rancher.

I hiked from the western end to the eastern end, logging about 2.75 miles one-way, and then I turned around. I marveled at the fine old coast live oaks—especially in one verdant grove on a short spur trail that intersects about halfway along the main trail—and the stately sycamores that seem like sculptures in winter when their leaves have dropped.

Look for large oak trees that have natural large holes in them. "Cavity trees in oak woodlands provide shelter and breeding sites for many oak-woodland wildlife." Most cavities occur in large, living, mature trees that usually have wounds or dead branches. Raccoons, some owls, and reptiles use cavities in oaks, as do western bluebirds, acorn woodpeckers, and ash-throated flycatchers.

Very early on the trail I spotted a magnificent great blue heron, who seemed to follow me as I hiked east. After a few close encounters, another woman and I were watching it, and we both thought it appeared injured. She called Project Wildlife, and a little later I phoned the number for the park on one of the placards to report this injured bird; I also told a police officer I encountered in a parking area.

Within a remarkably short time, Park Ranger Andy Quinn was searching for the bird, as were Officer Gold of the city's Department of Animal Services and Tamara, a volunteer with Project Wildlife, all of whom came to the park after hearing about the injured bird. The experts determined the bird could fly and feed, so they thought he was okay. I was duly impressed with the quick and concerned response from all these people.

After that exciting adventure, as I returned to the western parking area, I continued farther west along the half-mile Self-Guided Nature Trail with numbered posts accompanied by a brochure that identifies and discusses nine native plants, including coast live oak, western sycamore, toyon, buckwheat, and elderberry.

Marian Bear would surely be delighted with all the adventure, education, and natural beauty so easily accessible in her canyon park.

Thomas Brothers Map: Page 1228, C-7, immediately south of 52 and west of the Regents Road exit.

Before You Go: Download a copy of the trail map at the city's Parks and Recreation Department page for Marian Bear Memorial Park: http://www.sandiego.gov/park-and-recreation/pdf/marianbeartrailmap.pdf.
  It's free and is open to hikers, joggers, bicyclists, and dogs on leashes.

Trailhead: From Highway 52, exit at the Clairemont Mesa Boulevard/Regents Road exit, heading west on Clairemont Mesa. Almost immediately, turn right into the parking area.

Distance/Difficulty: I went a total of about 6.6 miles on mostly flat terrain; easy.

3-20. Los Peñasquitos Is an in-City Treasure

Find a big swath of country right in the city in Los Peñasquitos Canyon Preserve. One of the biggest open spaces left in our urban sprawl, Los Peñasquitos lies between Mira Mesa and Rancho Peñasquitos, covering about 4,000 acres stretching some seven miles between the merge of Interstate 5 and Interstate 805 to a bit east of Interstate 15. Jointly owned by the city and county of San Diego, the preserve encompasses both Peñasquitos ("little cliffs") and Lopez canyons, each of which holds a namesake creek.

The main trails, open to equestrians, mountain bikers, hikers, and dogs on leashes, are found on both sides of Peñasquitos Creek, with one short spur leading into Lopez Canyon, which is named for homesteaders who raised cattle here for 100 years starting in the 1840s.

One of its best natural attractions is a waterfall that cascades just a few feet down volcanic rock.

There are several entry points into the preserve, but I began my hike near Peñasquitos Creek Park, at the junction of Park Village Road and Camino del Sur (once noted on older maps as Camino Ruiz). From there, I stayed on the main trail on the north side of the Peñasquitos Creek.

The waterfall is a big attraction at Los Peñasquitos Canyon Preserve.

Near the trailhead, I met a rim resident, Nancy Walters, and her leashed 4-year-old silver Weimaraner, Dieter. She told me she has hiked here regularly for nearly 15 years. I was very glad to encounter her because she gave me some valuable advice about avoiding rattlesnakes, which are common in this canyon in the warmer months.

"Stay on the main trail, avoiding the single-track trails," she advised. "You'll be perfectly safe that way." As their name implies, the single-track trails, closed to mountain bikers, are much narrower cuts through the tall grass—great places for snakes to linger. She also showed me how to spot snake tracks, drawing a rock on the sandy trail to demonstrate what it looks like.

Sure enough, on that main trail, I then spotted several wavy tracks crossing the trail horizontally, straight across from side to side getting back into that grass. I didn't see any snakes, happily. Nancy said she's seen them here, though she has avoided nasty encounters. She's also spotted deer, including a buck, as well as bobcats, coyotes, and rabbits.

The preserve is an excellent example of the impressive biodiversity found in San Diego County. According to the city's website on the canyon, it is home to "more than 500 plant species, more than 175 types of birds, and great variety of reptiles, amphibians and mammals." It hosts 14 habitats, including the riparian stream-based corridors that are home to forests of giant live oaks and sycamores; a fresh-water marsh attracting great blue herons, egrets, and ducks; and the grassy hillsides that surround the canyons.

Following Nancy's directions, I stayed on that main trail, headed straight ahead under the power lines to the waterfall, and ignored one junction where a trail sign pointed right. About two miles later, the sign to the waterfall pointed to the left, and very shortly I could hear the cascading water. Scrambling on the giant rocks to view the water was difficult. When it was time to go, I simply retraced my way back.

Little wonder that remains of prehistoric culture can still be found in this canyon, and according to the city, Native American history here dates back 7,000 years.

Rancho de los Peñasquitos was the first Mexican land grant in California. "In 1823, one league (4,243 acres) of land was awarded to Captain Francisco Maria Ruiz, a commandant of the San Diego Presidio," according to the Friends of Los Peñasquitos Canyon Preserve. Ruiz built a one-room adobe here in 1824. The restored historic remains of that adobe, Rancho de los Peñasquitos, lie at the eastern end of the preserve at 12020 Black Mountain Road, and it is open for tours on Saturdays at 11:00 a.m. and Sundays at 1:00 p.m. This adobe was expanded in 1862, and today it is the oldest private standing structure left in San Diego. The ruins of another home, the El Cuervo Adobe (circa 1857), lie at the west end of the preserve.

During the 1840s, the main highway between Old San Diego and Yuma ran through Los Peñasquitos Canyon by Rancho Peñasquitos, then known as Alvarado's Place after Ruiz's grandnephew, who had inherited it. General Stephen Watts Kearny and his starving army rested here after their defeat in the historic Battle of Mule Hill in San Pasqual in 1846. The road was designated the first county highway and was part of the first Transcontinental Mail Route. By the early 1960s, the Peñasquitos ranch covered over 14,000 acres. Facing a future as residential development, it was purchased by the county and city of San Diego for park and open space use.

Friends of the Los Peñasquitos Canyon Preserve was formed in the early 1980s to protect as much of the old ranch lands as possible. Its members continue that advocacy role while they lead nature walks, restore habitat, teach wildlife tracking skills, and publish a newsletter. Check out the website at www.penasquitos.org.

Thomas Brothers Map: Page 1208, A-7—at junction of Park Village Road and Camino del Sur, just west of Peñasquitos Creek Park.

Before You Go: Download a trail map at the city's website on the preserve: http://www.sandiego.gov/park-and-recreation/pdf/penasquitoscanyon.pdf.

Find the city's page on the open space park for more information: http://www.sandiego.gov/park-and-recreation/parks/osp/lospenasquitos/penasq2.shtml.

The trails are open from 8:00 a.m. to sunset for hikers, bicyclists, equestrians, and dogs on leashes. It is often closed during and after heavy rains; check the website of the Friends organization for trail closures.

Trailhead: To reach the entrance at Peñasquitos Creek Park from Highway 56, exit onto Black Mountain Road and head south. Turn right onto Park Village Road and then left onto Camino del Sur (formerly Camino Ruiz). Park in the parking area next to the trailhead.

Distance/Difficulty: Varies. There are almost 20 miles of trails here, but my hike of 2.0 miles one-way was easy.

3-21. Grand Sycamores Tower in Penasquitos' West End

Some of our grandest sycamore trees can be found in the western end of Los Peñasquitos Canyon Preserve. At around 4,000 acres, it is one of the largest open spaces in the urban core, and it's only about 15 miles from downtown San Diego.

The California sycamore, also known as the western sycamore, is one of the largest native trees (along with coast live oak and Torrey pine) that grow in lower elevations near the coast in our county. Sycamores are common in riparian habitats because they require lots of water, and Los Peñasquitos Canyon is centered on the year-round Peñasquitos Creek, so they like it here. Sycamores can reach 80 feet tall with massive, spreading branches and huge lobed leaves that resemble those of the maple. Their mottled bark of white and gray is one of the easiest ways to identify them.

In winter in Los Peñasquitos ("little cliffs"), those large leaves of the deciduous sycamore have dropped, offering lots of opportunity for stomping on dried piles of them like you did when you were a kid. It's also easy during winter to spot the huge growths of mistletoe in the bare sycamores. A parasite, the big-leaf mistletoe is common here on native deciduous trees. Birds eat mistletoe berries and then deposit their seeds on tree branches. Heavy infestation can kill trees, but mistletoe is also a native plant here that provides food and nesting sites.

Some enormous specimens of the sycamores are one of the draws to this end of Los Peñasquitos, where I took the western entrance's main south trail heading east to the canyon's waterfall. It's a wide path that is sometimes rocky. It is open to hikers, bicyclists, equestrians, and dogs on leashes, and it's popular with lots of outdoor enthusiasts, young and old.

Sycamores thrive in Los Peñasquitos Canyon.

The trailhead on that western end begins near the confluence of Peñasquitos Creek and Lopez Creek. I had wanted to visit the El Cuervo Adobe Ruins near here, but that short spur trail to that site was closed when I was there. Trails in Los Peñasquitos are closed during and after heavy storms. Some years rains wreak havoc here, closing several trails in winter as well as some Peñasquitos Creek crossings that allow hikers to move from the main south to the north trails. To check on the status of the trails before you go, go to http://www.Peñasquitos.org/ranger.htm. This website of the Friends of Los Peñasquitos Canyon Reserve posts the ranger's update.

The El Cuervo Adobe Ruin is part of the home built in 1857 by Diego Alvarado, son of Francisco Maria Alvarado, who inherited the original land grant—the first Mexican land grant in San Diego County—that was owned by his great uncle, Captain Francisco Maria Ruiz, a commandant of the San Diego Presidio. Ruiz was awarded 4,243 acres (one league) in this canyon in 1823 but, according to the Friends' web page, asked for another league of land for better cattle grazing to the west, which he was awarded. He called it El Cuervo ("the crow"). The adobe ruin is also called the Ruiz-Alvarado Adobe, and it reportedly includes remains of old outbuildings and a corral.

I missed seeing that historic site this time, but I continued on the main south trail to the waterfall, a 2.7-mile hike one-way. The waterfall plunges over a jumble of volcanic rock that seems to appear out of nowhere in the otherwise wide-open valley. It's a picturesque destination from either end of the preserve.

The preserve is home to "more than 500 plant species, more than 175 types of birds, a great variety of reptiles, amphibians and mammals," reports the city's website on the canyon. On the back of the map placard near the Wagon Wheel Crossing (the first one across Peñasquitos Creek from the western end of the preserve) is a poster describing some of these plants and animals here. Budding naturalists will also want to find replicas of animal footprints on some of the mile-marker wooden posts.

I noticed lots of caterpillars on the trail. The larva stage of butterflies, caterpillars come in as many colors and patterns as butterflies. The ones I saw were probably those of tiger moths, according to a comprehensive website that helps identify such things (www.discoverlife.org).

See what you discover in this grand open space preserve.

Thomas Brothers Map: Page 12-8, D-5.

Before You Go: Download a copy of the trail map at http://www.sandiego.gov/park-and-recreation/pdf/penasquitoscanyon.pdf.
    For more information, go to the city's park and recreation page on Los Peñasquitos Canyon Preserve: http://www.sandiego.gov/park-and-recreation/parks/osp/lospenasquitos/penasq2.shtml.
    Hikers, bicyclists, equestrians, and dogs on leashes all invited.
    It's free to park here. Hours are 8:00 a.m. to sunset.

Trailhead: To reach that parking area, from Interstate 5 or Interstate 805, exit at Sorrento Valley Road or Vista Sorrento Parkway (depending on which direction or freeway you're on) and make your way to Sorrento Valley Boulevard, which heads east very near the merge of I-5 and I-805. The entrance to the preserve is on the south side of Sorrento Valley Boulevard, about one mile east from Vista Sorrento Parkway.

Distance/Difficulty: The south main trail from that western entrance is 2.7 miles one-way to the waterfall, for about a 5.4-mile round-trip hike. Easy to moderate.

3-22. Eastern End of Peñasquitos Offers Urban Core Workout

The trail along the eastern edge of Peñasquitos Creek in Los Peñasquitos Canyon Preserve offers a workout within the urban core. It isn't traversing the prettiest terrain even within the preserve, but this trail is far less traveled than other trails in that 4,000-acre oasis, and it also leads to one of San Diego's oldest and most historic homes that's open for view.

This eastern-most trail in the preserve follows the creek for about two miles east from Black Mountain Road. From the preserve's eastern parking area, the trail goes under Black Mountain Road. The creek water can be surprisingly deep here, but the trail stays high and dry to the right. After skirting around Canyonside Stables, where horses are boarded and Horsebound LLC offers lessons and summer camp opportunities, the trail continues along the creek.

You can't see Peñasquitos Creek for most of the way, but its thick riparian vegetation, including dense beds of cattails, lets you know it's there. The oak and willow trees remain down by the creek, so there's little shade along this trail.

After almost a mile, the trail crosses the creek, where it tumbles over a concrete slab. I walked across it here, getting my feet a little wet because the flowing water was a few inches deep.

The trail continues, heading straight into Ridgewood Park, a community park in Rancho Peñasquitos, while also heading north (left) up a steep hill.

Climb the hill at the eastern end of Peñasquitos for views.

I took the left up the hill to see the views. After climbing up to the top, I turned around when the trail hit two fences closing off its access at the street of Calle de las Rosas. The views from that ridge looked south and west over Peñasquitos, both the community as well as much of the eastern end of the canyon preserve. I could see evidence of a trail heading up another ridge beyond Ridgewood Park.

I retraced my route back along the trail that follows the southern side of Peñasquitos Creek. I noticed a hiker and her dog on the northern side of this eastern portion of Peñasquitos Creek. There is a trail there too, but it dead-ends at Black Mountain Road, so if you take that option, you'll have to backtrack to get back to the southern-side trail to reach your car and the main trails of the preserve.

When I reached the eastern parking area where I began, I continued on the main trail into the preserve to the historic Ranch House, which lies only about a half-mile away. Portions of Los Peñasquitos Ranch House date from 1823, making it San Diego's earliest surviving adobe. Most of this historic rancho was built in the 1860s.

The original 4,243-acre Rancho Santa Maria de los Peñasquitos was the county's first land grant, awarded by the first Mexican governor of California, Luis Antonio Arguello, to Captain Francisco Maria Ruiz, commandant of the Presidio, in 1823. Ruiz conveyed the ranch in 1837 to his grandnephew, Francisco Maria Alvarado, a politically active leader in the young town of San Diego in the 1830s and 1840s.

Inside the historic adobe are detailed displays about its various owners and families, including old photographs. There are also even older artifacts, including acorn-grinding holes in granite, used by earlier inhabitants in this river canyon, the Kumeyaay.

Captain George Alonzo Johnson, a riverboat captain along the Colorado River in the 1850s, married Alvarado's daughter, Estefana, who was also the niece of California's last Mexican governor, Pio Pico. Johnson and his family then owned half of Rancho Peñasquitos and expanded the ranch house in 1862.

Several other people owned the ranch over the years, which by 1962 spanned some 14,000 acres. In 1974, the County of San Diego acquired the area around the ranch house, ultimately developing it into the Los Peñasquitos Canyon Preserve. The county still operates the ranch house and about a mile of the preserve's eastern section. The City of San Diego maintains most of the trails along the rest of the 6-mile-long preserve.

The displays in the historic Ranch House are open from 8:00 a.m. to 4:00 p.m. daily, but you can only peek into several of the other rooms. Docents lead tours through the house on Saturdays at 11:00 a.m. and on Sundays at 1:00 p.m.

Thomas Brothers Map: Page 1189, D-7, at intersection of Black Mountain Road and Mercy Road.

Before You Go: Download a trail map at the city's parks page: http://www.sandiego.gov/park-and-recreation/pdf/penasquitoscanyon.pdf.

For more information about the historic adobe, go to the county's page: http://www.sdcounty.ca.gov/parks/openspace/Peñasquitos.html.

It's open to hikers, equestrians, and mountain bikers (except on single-track trails). Dogs on leashes are also welcome.

There is a $3 day-use parking fee here.

Trailhead: To reach the east parking area for Los Peñasquitos Canyon Preserve, from Interstate 15, exit at Mercy Road and head west. Turn right on Black Mountain Road and then left at the first light. Follow the entry road to the Ranch House parking area.

Distance/Difficulty: This trail covers about 4.0 miles round-trip, and except for the hill at the eastern end, it is easy and flat.

3-23. Stately Sycamores Color Penasquitos' Lopez Canyon

Lopez Canyon in Los Peñasquitos Canyon Preserve has one of the loveliest and largest stands of native sycamore trees in the county. Known as western or California sycamore, the massive trees are deciduous and are found in riparian habitats (along stream beds in valleys and mountains). In Lopez Canyon, they have lived for probably hundreds of years along Lopez Creek. In fall, their broad lobed leaves turn yellow and orange before falling to reveal sculptural trunks.

Some of these Lopez Canyon sycamores rise 100 feet tall with multiple trunks that seem to span more than 20 feet in circumference. The champion of this species was measured in Santa Barbara in 1945, at 116 feet tall with a 27-foot trunk circumference and a 158-foot crown spread, according to the National Audubon Society's *Field Guide to Trees, Western Region.* I'd say one or two of Lopez Canyon's specimens might give that record a run.

The Lopez Canyon Trail begins at the West End parking and staging area of Los Peñasquitos Canyon Preserve. Follow the sign as it forks to the right at the main trail intersection into the preserve.

The trail follows the creek for about a mile and then comes to a fork with a trail sign pointing to the right. That right fork trail climbs up, past a sign noting "Old Lopez Road, Passable for Pedestrians and Equestrians Only," and in short order it reaches its end at commercial buildings on top of the hill near Pacific Center Boulevard. There are some worthy views from atop this knoll looking back into the canyon.

Ponder the past in Lopez Canyon.

Somewhere near here is where Ramon Lopez Sr. built a wooden house and barn and ran a dairy farm, a pursuit his family carried on in the canyon for more than 100 years, according to Will Bowen, PhD, a walk leader for Friends of Los Peñasquitos Canyon Preserve. Ruins of the old house and barn are said to exist, but I didn't see them. Bowen often leads hikes into this area and talks about the Lopez family and their dairy farm. Check the Friends' website, http://Peñasquitos.org, for schedules.

Lopez acquired his land of 160 acres in this canyon in 1895, but he was settled here long before that, says Bowen. Los Peñasquitos' history says the Lopez family tended livestock here from the 1840s.

Ramon was one of several children of Bonafacio Lopez, who had bought the original Rancho Soledad land grant from Cave Couts in 1853. Couts had bought it that same day from Francisco Maria Alvarado, who claimed it had been given to him as a Mexican land grant in 1838. Alvarado was then the owner of the original Rancho de los Peñasquitos, the county's first Mexican land grant, awarded in 1823 to Francisco de Maria Ruiz, who gave it to Alvarado in 1827 when his health was failing. Peñasquitos Canyon emptied into Soledad Valley, which is what we now know as Sorrento Valley. Bonafacio Lopez was known as "the King" in Old Town, where he was a family member of Francisco Lopez, who had built Casa de Lopez there in 1835. Bonafacio was "a rotund, flamboyant horseman," says Bowen, and an early leader in Old Town's Presidio.

When you've ponder this protected canyon area's former occupants, return back down to that fork and take the left lower trail farther into Lopez Canyon. For a little more than a half-mile, a well-tended trail continues to follow the creek, even though this trail isn't on the preserve map.

After crossing the stream a couple of times, this part of the trail continues along that sycamore-laden valley until it empties into a wide rocky wash that continues to the visible concrete overpass of Camino Santa Fe. I wandered around those rocks for a spell but then turned back to retrace my steps.

The Lopez Canyon Trail never does connect with other trails in Los Peñasquitos. Lopez Canyon Trail remains on the south side of Sorrento Valley Boulevard, and the main trails in the preserve are north of that street. However, Lopez Canyon is one of the prettiest, least traveled of the preserve's trails, and it's greatly enhanced by those stately sycamores. It was also among the friendliest of trail experiences: I had three conversations with others who were jogging or hiking Lopez Canyon. Perhaps because it's right in the city and attracts regular visitors, especially from Qualcomm and other companies above it, people feel at home here. The Lopezes might like to know that.

Thomas Brothers Map: Page 1208, D-4—where the Lopez Canyon trail goes off to the right from the main preserve trail.

Before You Go: Download a map of Lopez Canyon Trail at the San Diego city parks' page for Los Peñasquitos Canyon Preserve: http://www.sandiego.gov/park-and-recreation/pdf/penasquitoscanyon.pdf.

This trail is open to hikers, mountain bikers, equestrians, and dogs on leashes. The preserve is open from sunrise to sunset, and it's free to park in the staging areas.

Trailhead: To reach that parking area, from Interstate 5 or Interstate 805, exit at Sorrento Valley Road or Vista Sorrento Parkway (depending in which direction or freeway you're on) and make your way to Sorrento Valley Boulevard, which heads east very near the merge of I-5 and I-805.

The entrance to the preserve is on the south side of Sorrento Valley Boulevard, about one mile east from Vista Sorrento Parkway.

Go the West End parking and staging area of Los Peñasquitos Canyon Preserve and follow the main trail, which soon offers a right fork into Lopez Canyon.

Distance/Difficulty: Hiking on both forks of Lopez Canyon's trails is a total of 3.5–4.0 miles round-trip. Easy with one moderate hill.

3-24. Lusardi Creek Loop Rolls Up, Down a Green Canyon

The Lusardi Creek Loop Trail just east of Fairbanks Ranch invites exploration of an open space canyon that preserves nature within urban development. Remarkably green with long views, Lusardi Creek's canyon features riparian habitat along the creek itself, surrounded by chaparral and coastal sage scrub hills. The trail itself is somewhat hilly, and it's popular with mountain bikers but is also traversed by hikers and equestrians.

Lusardi Creek trails connect to others in Black Mountain.

As part of the Santaluz Open Space that was required of the Santaluz development here, this Lusardi Creek parcel became part of the Black Mountain Open Space Park in 2006, when the city acquired it. The Lusardi Creek Loop Trail itself is a 9.7-mile loop connecting with other Black Mountain trails, where some 20 miles total invite outdoor recreation in a fairly pristine landscape. Black Mountain is the park's namesake and centerpiece at 1,554 feet high; spot this peak immediately to the south; it's the one with all the microwave towers.

Black Mountain Open Space Park is owned and managed by the City of San Diego, and it currently covers 2,352 acres. The city may expand this urban park in the future, it says.

Don't confuse this trail with the shorter one that's part of the County of San Diego's 194.5-acre Lusardi Creek Preserve, acquired in 1999 for inclusion in the county's

Multiple Species Conservation Program (MSCP) preserve system. The county's Lusardi Creek Preserve sits above the northern boundary of the City of San Diego, just east of Rancho Santa Fe, and just north of this Lusardi Creek part of Black Mountain Open Space.

When I hiked Black Mountain's Lusardi Creek Loop Trail, I could see evidence of another trail to the northeast high on the canyon ridge. I didn't see a connecting trail to that area, and the maps I found don't suggest these two systems connect. They are both centered on the same Lusardi Creek, which just northwest of here empties into the San Dieguito River.

There was once a community known as Lusardi in this area in the 1880s and 1890s. Sitting between the huge Mexican land grants of the 1840s, Juan Maria Osuna's Rancho San Dieguito to the west and English trader Joseph Snook's Rancho Bernardo to the east, this area was available for homesteading after the U.S.-Mexican War of 1848, the resulting Land Act of 1851, and the Homestead Act of 1862, according to county documents.

Peter (Pietro) Lusardi from Italy was a homesteader here. He came to California during the Gold Rush, started a sheep ranch on Palomar Mountain in 1866, and homesteaded in this La Jolla Valley area with his brother Francisco in 1887. They opened a school and post office in 1889, but the post office closed in 1911. The Lusardis were sheep ranchers here, eventually amassing 3,000 acres. They also grew hay and oranges.

The beginning of the Lusardi Creek Loop Trail follows what was probably an old ranch road through lots of native grasslands. It meanders up and down the canyon, eventually reaching Lusardi Creek itself, where riparian habitat takes over. There are very few trees here, however. Most of the vegetation consists of typical chaparral shrubs including lemonadeberry, laurel sumac, coffeeberry, and chamise. California lilac promises lots of blue blooms in spring. Coastal sage scrub natives here include sagebrush, black sage, and lots of California sunflowers. This trail features several signs identifying native plants. Harbingers of spring were already blooming when I was there in early February, including gold poppies and a few bright purple lupine.

The trail continues on that old ranch road until it reaches Lusardi Creek. After the wooden foot bridge over the creek, the trail becomes a single-track, narrower dirt trail. In another eighth of a mile or so from that creek crossing, the trail goes under the vehicle bridge of Camino Del Sur. About eight inches of water covered that concrete creek crossing when I was there, so I didn't cross it and chose to turn around. At that moment, however, some bicyclists came to that creek crossing under the bridge from another trail connecting to the Lusardi Creek Loop Trail right there. Perhaps that narrow dirt trail eventually connects to the other preserve; I don't know.

At the San Dieguito Trailhead of the Lusardi Creek Loop Trail, there is a posted document describing the entire 9.4-mile loop trail, especially for bikers.

My hike was 1.8 miles one-way, 3.6-mile round-trip, all in a pastoral oasis seemingly far from urban sprawl.

Thomas Brothers Map: Page 1168, J-5

Before You Go: For more information, go to the city's page: http://www.sandiego.gov/park-and-recreation/parks/osp/blackmtn/index.shtml.

Download a copy of the trail map at http://www.sandiego.gov/park-and-recreation/pdf/blackmountaintrailmap.pdf.

Hours are dawn to dusk. Dogs on leashes are welcome.

Trailhead: To reach the San Dieguito trailhead for Lusardi Creek Loop Trail, from Highway 56, exit on Camino Del Sur and head north a few miles. At San Dieguito Road, turn left (west); the trailhead is 0.5 miles on your right.

There's a small dirt parking area here that is free.

Distance/Difficulty: From San Dieguito Trailhead to the Camino Del Sur bridge is 1.8 miles one-way, 3.6 miles round-trip. Some steep hills make it easy to moderate.

3-25. From Mountains to Islands, Black Mountain Has Views

Pick a clear day when you hike to the 1,554-foot-high summit of Black Mountain, and you'll have a remarkable, 360-degree view of Palomar Mountain to the east, Mount Woodson to the southeast, and the Pacific Ocean to the west. On the clearest of days, you may also see the skyscrapers of downtown San Diego to the south and even San Clemente and Catalina islands off the coast.

Black Mountain is the centerpiece of Black Mountain Open Space Park, 2,352 acres of chaparral, coastal sage scrub, and occasional riparian habitats that are home to more than 80 species of birds, big and small mammals from mule deer to wood rats, rattlesnakes and lizards, and even Pacific chorus frogs.

There are over 20 miles of trails throughout the park, including 10 miles of trails surrounding the Santaluz Development that were the most recent acquisition. This area lies northwest of the main portion of the park centered on Black Mountain itself.

Choose a clear day to climb Black Mountain.

Another recent acquisition is the 538 acres known as the Montana Mirador parcel, located to the south of the main park area. There are no plans to develop trails in this area because its primary purpose remains biological resource protection.

The trail to Black Mountain's summit is a fairly steep loop, climbing nearly 900 feet in its roughly 2-mile ascent.

Black Mountain is located in the geological area known as the Poway Quadrant and consists of rock units called Santiago Peak Volcanics, which are composed of metamorphosed volcanic and sedimentary rocks that are extremely hard, according to the park's management plan filed with the City of San Diego.

Located in a chain of "relatively high coastal peaks" stretching from northern Baja California to Camp Pendleton, Black Mountain is characterized by steep ridges and canyons. "Most of the site is greater than 25 percent slope and much of the remainder is more than 10 percent."

Chaparral dominates the north and east sides of the mountain, where vegetation is greener and denser. Plants in this habitat include lemonadeberry, chamise, manzanita, laurel sumac, toyon, and lots of California lilac (ceanothus), which can paint the landscape blue with its spring blooms.

The dominant habitats in the dryer south- and west-facing slopes of the park are coastal sage scrub and sage-chaparral scrub, and they feature such native plants as artemisia californica (California sagebrush), fragrant black and white sages, and buckwheat.

One of two informative placards on the Nighthawk Trail points out that leaves and branches of California sagebrush were commonly used by native Kumeyaay (who called this area home for thousands of years) as floor coverings to repel fleas and ticks. Fresh sagebrush leaves were also mashed and applied to wounds, and tea made from its leaves was used to treat colds.

Another interesting thing to observe here are the "whitewashed" rock outcroppings that indicate they are used as perches for raptors, including red-tailed hawks, American kestrels, northern harriers, Cooper's hawks, and turkey vultures. When you reach that summit, you might be at the same level with some of those hawks soaring over the landscape.

Owned by the City of San Diego, the park originated in 1964 when the city acquired it under the Recreation and Public Purposes Act of 1926. Today the park is considered a "core resource area," where corridors allow wildlife to connect to bigger areas. Wildlife corridors link Black Mountain to the Del Mar Mesa corridor to the northeast and to the Lusardi Creek corridor to the north and northwest, which links to San Dieguito River Park trails and Lake Hodges.

Begin this loop at the Hilltop Community Park's trailhead for the Nighthawk Trail. This trail has some very steep portions that are also quite rocky. To reach Black Mountain's summit, stay to the left at any intersection, followings signs to stay on the Nighthawk Trail. Shortly after the first mile, the Nighthawk Trail will connect to the old service road that continues the trek to the top where all those microwave communication towers are located. When you reach the top, walk around those towers to take in all those views.

Then head back down, and this time continue to the bottom via the old service road. This route down is not as steep and rocky as the Nighthawk Trail, so this is an easier descent. As you head down, scope out your return route back to Hilltop Community Park. You'll see a section of the service road heads southwest to enter a housing development, where you walk one block on the sidewalk to reach the final portion of the trail that heads steeply back up to Oveido Way and the park where you began.

See how far you can see from Black Mountain on a clear day.

Thomas Brothers Map: Page 1189, E-2.

Before You Go: Download a copy of the trail map at the City of San Diego's parks pages: http://www.sandiego.gov/park-and-recreation/pdf/blackmountaintrailmap.pdf.

This loop trail to Black Mountain's summit is open to hikers, bicyclists, and dogs on leashes. For more information, go to the city's open space parks page on Black Mountain: http://www.sandiego.gov/park-and-recreation/parks/osp/blackmtn/index.shtml.

Trailhead: To reach the park, from Highway 56, exit at Black Mountain Road and head north. Turn right on Oviedo Street and right again on Oviedo Way. Hilltop Community Park is at the top of the hill on your right.

Begin on the Nighthawk Trail that heads north from Hilltop Community Park. From the Nighthawk Trail, connect to the old service road to reach the summit; then take that service road all the way back down to Hilltop Community Park again.

Distance/Difficulty: This loop hike is about 4.7 miles total with an elevation gain of nearly 900 feet; moderately strenuous.

3-26. Little Black Loop Climbs High, Just Short of Black Mountain

The 1,554-foot summit of Black Mountain usually offers a 360-degree view from the ocean to the west and mountains to the north and east. Even the 1,200-foot summit of Little Black typically reveals far-reaching views. On the October day I was on the Little Black Loop Trail, from about 11 a.m. to 2 p.m., the fog never lifted. It wafted across those chaparral and sage scrub hills and obscured any long views. But it also made for a far cooler climb up those hills, where there are no trees to provide shade.

It's a pretty steep climb up that Little Black Loop Trail. In this part of Black Mountain Open Space Park, the trails sport a 30 percent slope, making them among the steeper climbs for their mileage.

I began on the Nighthawk Trail, which also heads up to Black Mountain Summit itself. But instead of going to that microwave-towered summit, I headed east up the Little Black Loop and the South Point View Trail. The views were actually better from Little Black than that South Point, even if the fog hadn't been there.

Black Mountain Open Space Park originated in 1964 when the City of San Diego acquired it under the Recreation and Public Purposes Act of 1926, a federal policy administered by the Bureau of Land Management. The City of San Diego owns and manages the 2,352 acres.

Fairly steep climb up Little Black brings views.

A couple of placards on the way up give some interesting facts about this coastal peak. The first one suggests hikers look up in search of Black Mountain's birds, including cliff swallows, black ravens, and red-tailed hawks. If you're really lucky, you might spot a golden eagle.

The second one notes that you are on a "Trail to the Past," where the Kumeyaay lived for thousands of years. Evidence of their village lives is found in this open space park, mostly in the creek beds of its northwestern area: morteros and metates on the rocks reveal where Kumeyaay women would grind acorns into meal.

The chaparral and coastal sage scrub vegetation on the Little Black Loop and South Point View trails is dominated by laurel sumac, toyon, ceanothus, and black sage. Sage was particularly important to the Kumeyaay. They would spread its leaves and branches on the floors of their dwellings to repel fleas and ticks, according to the placard. Fresh leaves were mashed and applied to wounds, and they were sometimes used to flavor food, including that bland acorn mush. Tea made from sage leaves was used to treat colds and bronchial infections.

Today, if you simply rub its leaves between your fingers, you'll enjoy its fine fragrance.

Lining both sides of Little Black and South Point View trails were lots of laurel sumac, its blossoms turning nearly black in October. Orange berries of the toyon, sometimes called Christmas berry, added color to the harvest season before they turned red for the holiday season.

I saw a couple of desert cottontail rabbits. Coyotes, mule deer, and bobcats also live here, and a sign at the trailhead noted a mountain lion had been spotted recently.

More than 80 species of birds are found here, including the California gnatcatcher and northern harrier.

I connected to the Little Black Loop Trail from the Nighthawk Trail by taking it in a counterclockwise direction. It's a steep climb no matter which way you go. Once you reach the top of Little Black and then connect to the South Point View Trail, that latter trail is fairly flat as it heads straight south along a 1,100-foot-high ridge.

After hiking back along the South Point View Trail and reconnecting with the Little Black Loop heading left, I rejoined the Nighthawk Trail back to the trailhead at Hilltop Community Park in Rancho Penasquitos, making for about a 3.5-mile round-trip.

The city says there may be a trail someday that will connect Black Mountain with Los Penasquitos Canyon Preserve.

Thomas Brothers Map: Page 1189, 2-E, Hilltop Community Park.

Before You Go: Download a copy of the trail map at the City of San Diego's parks pages: http://www.sandiego.gov/park-and-recreation/pdf/blackmountaintrailmap.pdf.
This loop trail is open to hikers, bicyclists, and dogs on leashes. It's free here.
For more information, go to the city's open space parks page on Black Mountain: http://www.sandiego.gov/park-and-recreation/parks/osp/blackmtn/index.shtml.

Trailhead: To reach the Nighthawk Trail, from Highway 56, exit on Black Mountain Road, heading north. Turn right on Oviedo Street and then right again on Oveido Way. Park at Hilltop Community Park. The trailhead is just to the north of the parking area.

Distance/Difficulty: My route made for about a 3.5-mile loop that is moderately difficult. Total elevation gain is about 500 feet to Little Black, but with steep ups and downs, it's harder than it might suggest.

3-27. Bees Buzzing on Black Mountain with Abundant Wildflowers

The bees are buzzing on Black Mountain. The wildflowers are so abundant during spring that you'll find lots of color in this 2,400-acre oasis in the urban landscape. There are some 20 miles of trails in this city open space park, where the centerpiece is the 1,558-foot-high Black Mountain.

I chose the more moderate experience by taking the Miner's Ridge Loop Trail, and I ended up forging my own loop when I joined the Glider Point Trail. I generally enjoyed the climb to points where views extended 180 degrees. On a clear day from these elevations, one can see all the way to the Coronado Islands to the south and the Channel Islands to the north. It wasn't that clear when I was there, but I still marveled at the landscapes below—some highly developed with housing tracts, others still wide open or agricultural.

The Miner's Ridge Loop Trail is sometimes referred to as Black Mountain North Slope. It's a 2.5-mile loop around the lower north-facing slopes of Black Mountain, where thick chaparral offers nearly impenetrable safety for such wildlife as rabbits and rattlesnakes. I didn't see either one.

The trail gets its name from some Black Mountain history. In the 1920s there was a short-lived boom in white arsenic because it was part of a pesticide that attacked a boll weevil infestation in Southern cotton crops. A local rancher, rodeo cowboy, and actor, Frank Hopkins of Escondido, used his Hollywood contacts to fund an arsenic mine on the north slope of Black Mountain. Several years of very cold winters and dry summers in the South effectively eliminated the boll weevils, so demand for white arsenic fell. The mine was abandoned in 1927, but its concrete dust chamber, shafts, and oven remain there today. I didn't see them, but I was thrilled with all the blooming wildflowers in spring.

Look for wildflowers on Miner's Ridge Loop.

I had to check my native plant book when I got home. On the trail, I saw blooms of white and yellow yarrow, yellow wallflowers, a smaller species of mustard, blue-blooming black sage, red penstemon, purple indigo, and white chamise. The bees were really happy here.

The trail climbs up about 400 feet in elevation, going up and down and around along the way. Some parts are pretty steep. The park says most of the land here has a 25 percent or greater slope, so be advised it's not very flat, though this trail is easier than the main one to the summit.

There are signs to keep you on the Miner's Ridge Loop Trail, but after about a mile and a half, I was unsure which way a sign was pointing. This juncture occurs where an opening in the wooden fence goes right. The main trail appears to continue left, where a big sign points. I took that left fork for a while but decided it didn't seem right. Now I think it was. Take the left fork to continue the Miner's Ridge Loop Trail.

I entered the opening in the wooden fence (the right fork) and ended up on a steep descent down to the trailhead for Glider Point Trail, which is located in an entirely different parking area from Miner's Ridge. This mistake—or, rather, right fork choice—did provide the best western views, so that was a good thing. When I ended up in the wrong parking area, I had to walk along Carmel Valley Road for about a half-mile, climbing up the paved entry into the main Black Mountain Open Space parking area to return to my car. The map doesn't indicate that these trails connect, but indeed they do.

Whichever route you take on Black Mountain's north slope, you'll enjoy the colorful show in spring.

Thomas Brothers Map: Page 1169, E7.

Before You Go: Download a copy of the trail map at the City of San Diego's parks pages: http://www.sandiego.gov/park-and-recreation/pdf/blackmountaintrailmap.pdf.

It's free here.

Dogs on leashes are welcome. Mountain bikers and equestrians are allowed in Black Mountain Open Space, but the Miner's Ridge Loop Trail is better for hikers because parts of it are too rocky, narrow, and steep for others.

For more information, go to the city's open space parks page on Black Mountain: http://www.sandiego.gov/park-and-recreation/parks/osp/blackmtn/index.shtml.

Trailhead: From Highway 56, take the Black Mountain Road exit, heading north on Black Mountain Road to where it ends at Carmel Valley Road. Turn right onto Carmel Valley Road. In about 0.3 miles from that intersection is the first parking area to Glider Point Trail. Continue about a half mile farther to the main Black Mountain Open Space parking area to reach Miner's Ridge Loop Trail.

Distance/Difficulty: About 2.5 miles in a loop; moderate.

4. South County Coastal

Rivers and bays dominate the trails in South County Coastal, including Tijuana River Valley, Otay Valley River Park and even an eastern portion of the Sweetwater River, which may introduce you to the San Diego National Wildlife Refuge system.

4-1. Birds, Butterflies At Tijuana River Valley

At its Bird and Butterfly Garden, one of the best features of the Tijuana River Valley Regional Park, I saw a remarkably high number of butterflies: painted ladies, pale swallowtails, monarchs, and pairs of orange sulphurs doing their midair mating dance. Plants here were specifically chosen to attract these gorgeous winged creatures, and they seem to be doing a great job.

Walking paths in this small, special garden wind through tall and stately podacarpus trees, also known as fern pines; silk oaks, a species of oak totally unlike the live oaks we're familiar with here; and aleppo pines, a species not often seen in the wild here. The aleppo is native to Mediterranean sites including Syria, Morocco, and Algeria, and thrives on even poor soil in deserts and seacoasts.

Find birds and butterflies near Tijuana River.

The garden labels all these trees, along with many of the shrubs, including springtime bloomers red salvia, strawberry guava, pyracantha (a.k.a. firethorn), and red cane honeysuckle, where I caught an iridescent green hummingbird sticking its long bill deep into the red blossom.

The Tijuana River Valley is one of the county's best spots for birding according to San Diego Audubon, particularly the Dairy Mart Pond, in the northeast corner of the park, and the Bird and Butterfly Garden, which has been recognized as a backyard wildlife habitat by the National Wildlife Federation. More than 340 bird species have been seen in the valley. My best sightings were a couple of roadrunners, a couple of red-tailed hawks soaring above, a couple of adorable rabbits, and a couple of cute squirrels.

I began at the park's ranger station in its southeast corner. From there, I hiked a bit farther east along Monument Road until the trail began adjacent to that road on its northern side immediately opposite Clearwater Way.

I headed east until a trail marker pointed the way to the northwest. The map I carried really made a difference since there are several trails around. And though the county parks' map names most of the trails, they are not necessarily marked by name in the field. I basically headed north and west until I reached Hollister Street. I approached the Tijuana River itself at one point fairly early on, where I had my worst sighting: trash. When I hit Hollister Street, I had to walk a short way, crossing the river's road bridge to reach the Bird and Butterfly Garden. I saw a lot more trash in the river.

It's getting a lot of attention, however. The Tijuana River watershed is classified as a Category I (impaired) watershed by the State Water Resources Control Board due to a wide variety of water-quality problems, according to Project Clean Water, a San Diego Region water quality resource. "The Tijuana River watershed encompasses a region of approximately 1,750 square miles on either side of the California-Baja California border, and in terms of water quality degradation is probably the most severely impacted watershed in San Diego County," says Project Clean Water on its website (www.projectcleanwater.org). Its problems are largely the result of "non-point agricultural sources on the U.S. side of the border and a large variety of point and non-point sources on the Mexican side," it says. "The Tijuana Estuary, a National Estuarine Sanctuary that supports a variety of threatened and endangered plants and animals, is threatened by inflows from the Tijuana River containing high concentrations of bacteria, sediment, trace metals, PCBs and other pollutants."

It has been estimated that hundreds of thousands of pounds of trash and waste-tires are carried across the U.S.-Mexico border by the Tijuana River during winter months, according to Wildcoast, an international conservation organization (www.wildcoast.net). A lot of the trash is said to come from Tijuana neighborhoods that don't have trash collection.

There are substantial efforts afoot to address the problem on both sides of the border, in order to keep all that trash from not only harming the river valley itself but also from entering the ocean. The Surfrider Foundation organized 300 volunteers from both sides of the border who hauled out more than 6 tons of trash, including around 600 tires, from the Tijuana River Valley on a weekend. The Environmental Protection Agency has recently awarded grants to help remove the trash and sediment to keep the river flowing freely and also avoid flooding that can occur. Since 2008, the Tijuana River Valley Recovery Team, a consortium of dozens of organizations including those noted above, as well as the San Diego County Water Authority, the California Coastal Commission, the California Department of Fish and Game, Scripps Institution of

Oceanography, and many more, have put together a plan to reclaim and restore the entire Tijuana River Valley in partnership with Mexico.

From my starting point, I reached the Bird and Butterfly Garden after 2.5 miles of hiking along fairly flat, wide trails through coastal sage scrub. The park's central staging and parking area is located next to this garden, so I would recommend starting there instead of where I began. This central staging area is off Hollister Street just past Sunset Avenue. Trails from here also head to the beach and the river's estuary.

Hollister Street is home to lots of horse ranches, so these trails are very popular with equestrians. Bicyclists will also enjoy the wide, flat trails.

There are about 22.5 miles of trails in the 1,800-acre regional park. A $1.5 million grant from the California Coastal Conservancy has recently been awarded to fund habitat restoration and new trails.

For now, find a map and plot your course for the Bird and Butterfly Garden on Hollister or the Dairy Mart Pond for the best experiences.

Thomas Brothers Map: Page 1350, B-4 for Hollister near Sunset or D-5 for Dairy Mart Road at Clearwater.

Before You Go: Download a copy of the trail map from the county's parks and rec page for Tijuana River Valley Regional Park: http://www.co.san-diego.ca.us/reusable_components/images/parks/doc/Trails_TJRVP.pdf.

I picked up an even better map in the county parks' Tijuana River Valley Regional Park brochure at the ranger station.

Trails are open to hikers, bicyclists, equestrians, and dogs on leashes.

Trailhead: To reach the park's ranger station, from Interstate 5, exit at Dairy Mart Road and head west. After Dairy Mart Road becomes Monument Road, the ranger station will be on the left (south) side of the road, just past Clearwater Way.

To reach the central staging area near the Bird and Butterfly Garden, from Interstate 5, exit at Tocayo Avenue and head west to Hollister Street. Then turn left (south) until you reach a three-way stop-sign intersection with a sign pointing right (west) to Trail Staging Area and the Bird and Butterfly Garden.

Distance/Difficulty: I went a total of about 4.5 miles; easy, mostly flat.

4-2. Otay Valley's Easy Path Features Historic Ponds

There are about 8.3 miles of trails in the Otay Valley Regional Park, including this very easy loop of nearly 4.0 miles in its western area along the Otay River. The trail skirts the river, which is dry in late summer, along with four small ponds that were created long ago for salt and gravel mining operations here. The ponds today make for some appealing viewpoints as well as good spots for birding.

More than 200 species of birds have been spotted in the park year-round, including great blue herons, snowy egrets, American coots, ducks, least Bell's vireo, coastal gnatcatcher, and the southwestern willow flycatcher.

Because it's very near the coast, most of the habitat along this western portion of the park is maritime scrub and coastal sage scrub. Smell the sage as you walk along the trail, and in late summer, note the abundant yellow blooms of coastal goldenbush, common around river mouths and salty marshes, according to James Lightner's *San Diego County Native Plants*.

Ponds feature many bird species along Otay River.

Though Otay River is dry in late summer today, it wasn't always so. Some 13,000 years ago, Kumeyaay people populated this river valley year-round, living on its abundant resources and free-flowing water that emptied into San Diego Bay, according to a history of Otay Valley at University of San Diego. "Otai" is the Kumeyaay word for brush. Father Junipero Serra chose the Otay River Valley as his first camp when he traveled north to establish the missions in what is now California, according to the park.

By the early 1800s, Spanish ranchos took over the area and cattle grazed around the river. Commercial salt production began here in the 1850s. In 1897, the first Lower Otay Dam was built by the Southern California Mountain Water Company, then owned by E. S. Babcock and John D. Spreckels, with the intention to supply Coronado and the Hotel del Coronado, built by Babcock in 1888. The Upper Otay Dam followed a bit later.

But in 1916, after Charles Hatfield, the notorious rainmaker, had been hired in December 1915 by the city of San Diego to bring some rain, the disastrous flood of January 1916 completely destroyed the Lower Otay Lake Dam and flooded the entire Otay Valley. It destroyed the commercial mining companies begun in Otay Valley in 1912 by Henry G. Fenton, who had been a muleskinner (driver of mules) who hauled sand and rock for Babcock and his Coronado Beach Company. By 1915, Merrill Nelson bought property near Fenton and started another sand and gravel company, Nelson & Sloan, with partner Paul Sloan. Both companies rebuilt after the flood, and sand and gravel production in the valley continues to this day, though now on a very limited basis. The salt works operation that you can still see there today originated in this part of San Diego Bay in 1871 by Shaffer and Stone. In 1902, the Western Salt Co. was founded there by Graham Babcock, son of E. S. Babcock. Fenton eventually took over salt mining here in 1922.

One of the ponds you see on the trail is named Fenton Pond after the longtime businessman in this area.

This pond sits next to Willett Grove, where a monument to its namesake, John Willett, also stands. Willett, a World War II veteran and the father of Chula Vista's Mayor Cheryl Cox, was awarded in 2009 (at age 88) for his long service in making the Otay Valley Regional Park the beauty that it is.

In the early 2000s, the valley was filled with garbage, including refrigerators and abandoned cars, according to an article written for the *U-T San Diego* by Katie Westfall in 2009. Willett's cleanup efforts resulted in the removal of some 700 tires and 1,200 tons of trash in the river valley. As chairman of the Otay Valley Citizen's Advisory Committee, Willett organized many volunteers in this effort. His leadership and dedication made it all happen.

Today the Otay Valley Regional Park is a multijurisdictional effort by the County of San Diego and the cities of Chula Vista and San Diego, begun as a Joint Exercise of Powers Agreement in 1990. The trails weren't really as attractive as they are today until just a few years ago.

There are several trailheads in this regional park, which you can identify when you download the map. The soft-surface trails and their intersections are not well marked on-site yet, but you can't really get lost here. Still, you'll want to take a map with you. You'll pass through a commercial nursery and spot some of those old salt and gravel operations from afar.

The ponds are the blue gems here, so take your time at them.

Thomas Brothers Map: Page 1330, C-6, where Beyer Boulevard crosses Otay Valley Regional Park.

Before You Go: Download a copy of the trail map at www.ovrp.org. All the trails are open to hikers and bicyclists, with portions open to equestrians as well. Dogs on leashes are welcome.
    Also check the County of San Diego's park page for Otay Valley: http://www.co.san-diego. ca.us/parks/openspace/OVRP.html.

Trailhead: The main trailhead and the ranger station are located on Beyer Boulevard. From Interstate 5 heading south, exit at Main Street and go east about 0.75 miles, turning right onto Broadway, which turns into Beyer Boulevard. The entrance to the park and the ranger station is about 0.5 miles on the right.

Distance/Difficulty: From Beyer Boulevard, I headed west and then backtracked, crossing the river a couple of times to reach Beyer Way, before heading back to Beyer Boulevard for about 3.9 miles; very easy.

4-3. Snake Season and Blue-Water Views

On my midday hike around Lower Otay Lake in late April, a king snake slithered across the trail. A little later, a rattlesnake, coiled and very hard to see on the edge of the trail in the shade, alerted me to his presence with that rattle.

Rattlesnakes are more often seen in spring (March through May), when the weather warms. "They are less active during cool times than during warm ones," says the San Diego Natural History Museum. "They can come out at any time, day or night, if it's warm enough for them to be active."

Like all reptiles, rattlesnakes cannot regulate their own body temperature, and so they select locations where they can find sun or shade, depending on what they need. If it is very hot—say, over 100 degrees Fahrenheit—they can overheat and die if they cannot find a cool place (shaded rock or bush). "So it's temperature, not time of day, that determines how active a rattlesnake is," says SDNHM.

They are seen much less often in the cooler months, when they may be hiding underground. We see the most bites during May, but bites can occur generally from April through October.

Lower Otay Lake is one of county's oldest reservoirs.

Remember that rattlesnakes don't attack people; they strike only in self-defense. The one I saw—or rather, didn't see until it started rattling—let me know not to bother it. As soon as I heard that unmistakable sound, I bolted backward, checking behind for others. Then I kept going that way. Rattlesnakes are the only venomous snake in San Diego County. That king snake I saw was harmless.

There are four kinds of rattlesnakes commonly found here, according to SDNHM: in coastal and mountain regions, they are the southern pacific, the southwestern speckled, and the red diamond. In the desert is the Colorado desert sidewinder.

Here are rattlesnake tips from SDNHM as well as San Diego County.

- Always wear hiking boots with socks when hiking in grassy or rocky areas—no open-toed shoes.
- Carry a walking stick. You can throw the stick, and the snake will strike the stick instead of you. I also sometimes drag the stick to create the vibration to alert the snake to vacate before I see it.
- Avoid tall grass or underbrush where you cannot see the ground.
- Don't put your feet or hands under or around logs or rocks without checking to see if any snakes are hiding there.
- If you do get bitten, walk as slowly and calmly as you can to get help at the nearest emergency room as soon as possible, or call 911 for help.

The snake encounters were a little alarming but those blue-water views along the western side of Lower Otay Lake were calming.

I began on the trail immediately south of the Olympic Training Center that uses the reservoir for rowing sports. Park on the wide shoulder areas off Wueste Road south of its intersection with Olympic Parkway. You'll see gates that block dirt roads there, which is a good place to start. When you reach the trail along the lake, you'll see the sign posting trail rules.

I headed north, wandering through the patches of tall eucalyptus trees and the yellow mustard lining the dirt path. This trail is very popular with mountain bikers, so watch out for them, especially on weekends.

At about 1.5 miles from my start, I had nearly reached the northern end of the trail when I encountered the rattlesnake and turned back. On my return, I went a bit farther south from my starting point and reached the Olympic center's dock on the lake. From there, signs were posted to keep out from this part of a wildlife preserve area, so I headed back to my car, posting about 3.65 miles total.

The lake is a longtime reservoir. The first Lower Otay Dam was built in 1897. At the turn of the 20th century, about 18,000 people were living in San Diego, according to Joseph Hill in "Dry Rivers, Dammed Rivers and Flood," a 2002 article written for the San Diego Historical Society's *Journal of San Diego History*. By 1910, nearly 40,000 lived in the city, with nearly 75,000 by 1920.

Drought conditions prevailed during the first 15 years of that century, Hill said. "City fathers offered a local rainmaker named Charles Hatfield $10,000 if he could cause enough rain to fill Morena Reservoir (built in 1895)." On January 1, 1916, Hatfield built towers near Morena Reservoir and released "strange and secret vapors into the atmosphere." On January 14, 1916, a massive storm rolled in, and for the next six days, Southern California was deluged. Just a few days later, another storm brought a second deluge. In all, Old Town received more than seven inches of rain that month; Cuyamaca received 32 inches.

Otay Dam was a total loss. The wave of water flooded "in a canyon of gigantic proportions." Downstream, water was at about 20 feet high; every structure was destroyed, and many people died. That 1916 flood was the worst in San Diego County history. After the flood, Hatfield eventually tried to collect his fee, but the city attorney determined if he collected the fee, then he was also responsible for flood damage. He did not collect and disappeared. The Otay Dam was rebuilt in 1918 and renamed Savage Dam.

The Lower Otay Lake today is about 67 percent full of its capacity of almost 50,000 acre-feet. Its shoreline measures 25 miles, but the trail goes nearly seven miles only along the western edge.

Fishing and boating are popular on the lake but are permitted only on Wednesdays, Saturdays, and Sundays. The trail is accessible anytime, dawn to dusk.

Thomas Brothers Map: Page 1293, map 1312, 7-A.

Before You Go: For more information about the lake and its concessions, go to the city's water pages on reservoirs: http://www.sandiego.gov/water/recreation/reservoirs/lowerotay.shtml. For a map of the lake, go to the county's parks pages for Otay Lakes County Park, at the southern end of the lake: http://www.sdcounty.ca.gov/parks/picnic/otay_map.html.

For a trail map, go to Google Maps for a satellite image of the trail along the west side of the lake.

This trail is open to hikers, bicyclists, and dogs on leashes.

Trailhead: From Interstate 5 heading south, exit at Highway 54 East and then Highway 125 South (a toll road, $2.50 per car). Exit at Olympic Parkway and head east. At Wueste Road, turn right (south) and go just past the Olympic Training Center. Park on the road's east-side shoulder.

Or you could turn left (north) on Wueste Road and park at Mountain Hawk Park, heading to the lake trail from there.

Distance/Difficulty: From the rules sign to the upper end of the lake at Otay Lakes Road is about 1.75 miles one way, for a 4.0-mile total round-trip from there to the Olympic Training Center dock. Easy.

4-4. Easy Rice Canyon Trail Home to Endemic Cacti

There are several reasons to recommend hiking at Chula Vista's Rice Canyon Open Space Preserve. It is a very easy and pleasant 2-mile-long trail that is fairly flat and open to just about everyone—hikers, bicyclists, equestrians, and dogs on leashes. It hosts lots of wildflowers and native cacti, some of which are "narrow endemic species," meaning they occur here naturally more than anywhere else. The trail's gateway is home to a demonstration garden that aims to encourage low-water and fire-resistant beauties that may inspire you to give up that lawn.

This wide, unpaved trail begins just across Rancho Del Rey Parkway from Discovery Park. Take a look at that demonstration garden at the trailhead. In spring and summer, the yellow blooms of the few palo verde trees, distinctive because of their green trunks, wave over the cacti, agave, and succulents whose blossoms are always stunning surprises.

Head on into the canyon, which has been carved here by Rice Creek. There is virtually no history available on this canyon or its namesake that I could find, but it has been suggested the area was formerly home to cattle ranching.

Look for endemic cacti in Rice Canyon.

The Rice Canyon Open Space Preserve was formed in the 1980s after neighboring developments, including Rancho Del Rey, began building homes on the canyon's ridges. Today Rice Canyon is home to more coast cholla than just about anywhere else. Snake cholla, another twisting form of that tubular cactus, is one of those "narrow endemic species" that are protected here as part of the county's Multiple Species Conservation Project (MSCP). Others are Otay tarplant, San Diego thornmint, and variegated dudleya. There are big patches of these chollas, sprinkled with a few prickly pear cactus. They are present here in the habitat known as maritime succulent scrub, dominated by jojoba, shore cactus, coast cholla, snake cholla, and Mohave yucca. These plants are integral to the lives of sensitive wildlife species such as the coastal cactus wren.

The City of Chula Vista began a five-year land management program in 2009 to restore and enhance the degraded habitat for the coastal cactus wren and other species in Rice Canyon, which included restoring patches of coast cholla as well as the Otay tarplant and San Diego thornmint. Current evaluations show that these sensitive plants have made significant comebacks in Rice Canyon.

Another major habitat here is Diegan coastal sage scrub, a favorite of the California gnatcatcher and wood rat that is dominated by California sagebrush, California buckwheat, broom, encelia, goldenbush, and lemonadeberry.

Along the Rice Creek bed in the riparian habitat are some tall cottonwood trees as well as sycamores and willows, all of which attract birds, including the yellow warbler. A sprinkling of big old pepper trees provide about the only occasional shade here.

I counted lots of yellow blooms on the prickly pear cacti as well as many magenta blooms on the coast cholla. The fanciful yellow blooms of bladderpod were notable with their dangling fruit pods; when dried, the pods may have been used as rattles for Kumeyaay babies centuries ago. The tiny blooms of salt heliotrope, which always attract bees, are summertime marvels that require close-ups.

Rice Canyon's trail is punctuated by the telltale yellow-topped posts that mark the California Riding and Hiking Trail, of which this must be an offshoot. Other wooden post markers declare it the Rice Canyon Loop Trail.

The trail heads west from Discovery Park for about 1.65 miles, when it reaches the Rancho Del Rey Parkway's looping road again. Cross the road, and you'll soon see the yellow-topped post marker and the continuation of the trail downhill. It continues for another one-third of a mile until it reaches its apparent end at H Street. I retraced my route back.

If you're wondering about that "loop" designation, there is another fork in this trail. Very near its western end at H Street, the trail intersects with a steep, uphill portion, where you'll see those yellow-topped markers continuing north. I didn't go there, but a placard at the trailhead shows this route is open to hikers and equestrians. The trail continues north, past Terra Nova Drive, and then east through another canyon that ends at Rancho del Rey Parkway. It appears that you continue through Marisol Park and then south on a trail that heads back down to Rice Canyon, where you would then head east again to get back to Discovery Park.

In case you're wondering who the bronze statue in front of Discovery Park depicts, it's Christopher Columbus. It was donated by the developers of the Rancho Del Rey neighborhood in 1990, but its plaque is missing.

Thomas Brothers Map: Page 1311, A-5, Discovery Park.

Before You Go: You'll find a trail map for Rice Canyon in Jerry Schad's *Afoot and Afield San Diego County.*

But the best map to download for this trail would be to go to a satellite hybrid map from Google or National Geographic. Zoom in on Rice Canyon, which heads west from Discovery Park, and you should be able to see the route described above from the trailhead placard.

This trail is open to hikers, bicyclists, equestrians, and dogs on leashes.

Trailhead: Park at Discovery Park. From Interstate 805, exit at H Street and head east. Turn left onto Paseo Ranchero and then right on Rancho del Rey Parkway. At Buena Vista, turn right to park in Discovery Park.

Cross Rancho del Rey Parkway to reach the Rice Canyon Open Space Preserve to the west.

Distance/Difficulty: This 4.0-mile round-trip is practically flat; easy.

4-5. An Easy Loop around South Bay Golf Course

Here's an easy loop around a green golf course, where the bonus is birds. Rohr Park in Chula Vista is one of the prettiest parks in that South Bay city, complete with gazebos, playgrounds, picnic areas, and even a model railroad track. The park sits next to the

Chula Vista Municipal Golf Course. A 3.3-mile loop trail winds around that golf course and through the park.

This is a very easy amble on the outside edge of the golf course, which is separated by chain-link fencing. Still, there are plenty of signs warning to watch out for errant golf balls. The soft-surface trail is open to everyone—hikers, bicyclists, equestrians, and dogs on leashes.

Make a fine loop around pretty South Bay Park.

It's actually located in Bonita, an unincorporated community bounded to the south by Chula Vista. Bonita stretches along five miles of the Sweetwater River. The trail passes under lots of old and stately eucalyptus, oaks, cottonwoods, and palms. It passes over a couple of wooden bridges over the Sweetwater River and attracts a fair number of exciting birds to see.

I spotted a Nuttall's woodpecker, a black-and-white speckled and striped beauty that is almost entirely restricted to California alone. The male has a small red crown, and the female's crown is black. It is named for Thomas Nuttall (1786–1859), an English botanist who spent years in America joining various natural history expeditions. He published *Manual of Ornithology of the United States and Canada* in 1832. In 1836 he landed in San Diego, where he met Richard Henry Dana, Jr. An interesting tidbit: the character of "old curious" in Dana's *Two Years before the Mast* is said to be based on Nuttall.

I also saw a whizzing Anna's hummingbird with its iridescent green body and the rose-colored crown that seems to appear only when the sun lights it. In another batch of tall eucalyptus perched a pretty western kingbird with its pale yellow belly, gray breast, and head, and white throat. On the three ponds on the golf course, look for mallard ducks as well as American coots.

The trail begins and ends at Rohr Park. It circles the outside of the golf course around Sweetwater and Bonita Roads. When you reach the municipal buildings along Bonita Road, you might want to detour through the Bonita Museum and Cultural Center.

The Bonita Museum, founded in 1987, collects items of historical significance to the area once known as El Rancho de la Nacion. This rancho was a Mexican land grant given in 1845 by Governor Pio Pico to his brother-in-law, John Forster, of 26,632 acres that today encompass National City, Chula Vista, Bonita, Sunnyside, and western Sweetwater Valley.

Interesting items on view at the museum include artifacts from the area's dominant dairy and cattle ranches, as well as those from its agricultural roots in oranges, lemons, and olives. It also displays older artifacts from Kumeyaay days, such as metates and manos, the mortars and stones used to grind acorns. Over 1,000 historic photographs are part of its collections.

Rohr Park is named for its benefactor, Fred H. Rohr, an important figure in Chula Vista's history. Born in New Jersey in 1896, Rohr and his family moved to California two years later, according to a pamphlet about him published for Chula Vista's centennial in 2011 by the Altrusa Club of Chula Vista (with the Chula Vista Elementary School District and the Chula Vista Public Library). Rohr's father opened a sheet metal shop, where young Rohr apprenticed. He moved to San Diego in 1924 and started his own sheet metal shop. He began making fuel tanks for planes being built by Ryan Aeronautical Company and soon became sheet metal foreman at Ryan, where he met Charles Lindbergh. Lindbergh contracted with Ryan, who formed a "Night Hawk" team that included Rohr, to build his *Spirit of St. Louis* plane that would fly nonstop from New York to Paris in 1927.

Rohr started Rohr Aircraft Company in 1940, soon leasing 10 acres on Chula Vista's bay front. While working nonstop during World War II years, the company had nearly 10,000 employees by 1945 and was one of the factories employing women who became known as Rosie the Riveter. Fred Rohr died in 1965, but his company continued to prosper throughout the 20th century. It was sold to BF Goodrich in 1997.

In the center of Rohr Park sits Rohr Manor, a two-story wood-and-brick house that was built in 1938. Rohr Aircraft Corp. purchased the home and surrounding land in 1955 as a recreational facility for its employees. The park and the old home are owned by the City of Chula Vista today. Rohr Manor has been fenced off and boarded up for years now, declared unsafe and deteriorating. Sadly, due to budget constraints, there are no plans to renovate the old house.

Make that loop around the park and golf course. and afterward, you might still be able to ride the little model railroad run by the Chula Vista Live Steamers in Rohr Park. Volunteers keep it rolling once a month on the second Saturday.

Thomas Brothers Map: Page 1310, H-2.

Before You Go: Download a copy of the trail map at Chula Vista's pages on its citywide Greenbelt Trail: https://sphinx.chulavistaca.gov/City Services/Development Services/ Planning Building/Planning/documents/Greenbelt Trail Map.pdf?s=952669C37A4EF731 98015C6F10CB374615A0ACC5. That web address is so unwieldy, so just do a search for "Greenbelt Trail Map, Chula Vista," and you'll find it.

You can also download a trail map at the city's parks pages on Rohr Park: http://www. chulavistaca.gov/departments/public-works/operations/parks. Rohr Park is No. 43 on this map. Open to hikers, bicyclists, and dogs on leashes.

Trailhead: From Interstate 5 heading south, exit onto CA-54 East. In about 4.4 miles, exit at Briarwood Road and turn right (south) onto Briarwood. Where the road stops at Sweetwater Road, turn right (west) onto Sweetwater. Rohr Park will be on your left.

Distance/Difficulty: The entire loop is 3.3 miles; very easy.

4-6. Wildlife Refuge Trail Educates In Wilderness

The Sweetwater Interpretive Loop Trail on the San Diego National Wildlife Refuge offers a great introduction to our region's collection of wildlife refuges. It's an easy hike that mostly follows the Sweetwater River and includes informational placards about special species that are protected here.

San Diego National Wildlife Refuge was established in 1996 and covers 11,152 acres stretching from Jamul to Spring Valley and eastern Chula Vista. There are a handful of separate parcels that protect the slopes and canyons of Mount San Miguel and McGinty Mountain, as well as this corridor along the Sweetwater River. Other refuges within San Diego County include Tijuana Slough and parts of San Diego Bay.

The Sweetwater Interpretive Loop begins just beyond the historic 1929 steel Sweetwater Bridge, off Campo Road. Follow the trail that hugs the south side of the Sweetwater River until you come to a large wooden bridge that crosses the river. Across that wooden bridge, the trail continues a short way to a dam on the river, but it stops shortly after that. The trail continues past the wooden bridge on the south side of the river, and the refuge says it continues all the way to the Sweetwater Reservoir.

Learn from placards during hike through local National Wildlife Refuge.

However, the Sweetwater Reservoir Trail from its trailhead in Sweetwater Summit Campground is currently closed to protect the fairy shrimp in the very rare vernal pools located there—one of the protected habitats in the refuge complex.

I stopped on this trail when it seemed to dissipate on a rocky ledge above the river, and I turned back. Just before that wooden bridge, there is a trail intersection that forms the loop. Follow this "high road" trail back that leaves the river and climbs just a bit into the foothills of Mount San Miguel, which you'll recognize from its collection of communication towers on top. The loop trail eventually connects back to that historic steel bridge.

The placards that make this trail "interpretive" are genuinely informative. With illustrations of each species described, they invite hikers to take note of why refuges like these are important to species they protect.

One can learn about:

- San Diego ambrosia, an endangered plant with feathery gray-green leaves that lives only in southwest San Diego County;
- the endangered least bell's vireo, a small greenish-gray bird that arrives here from March to October and lives in the riparian habitat of willows and cottonwoods along the river;
- the endangered arroyo toad, whose loud trill can be heard in late winter and early spring after rains;
- the Southwestern willow flycatcher, a small bird with white throat, pale olive breast, and pale yellow belly that comes in late May;
- the Hermes copper butterfly with its orange-yellow coloration with black spots that lives only in San Diego County and northwest Baja, and whose larvae feed only on spiny redberry (several of which are near this sign);
- the quino checkerspot butterfly, with its checkerboard-like wing pattern in cream, rusty red, and black, and that was once one of Southern California's most abundant butterflies but now is in danger of extinction, though a small population lives on this refuge;
- the threatened San Diego thornmint that rabbits eat;
- and the threatened California gnatcatcher, a small, native songbird that's dark gray on top and light gray on bottom and sounds like a kitten mewing.

When I was reading about thornmint, a rabbit ran into the brush. I saw a beautiful butterfly munching on some purple wild radish. And a red-tailed hawk soared above me.

San Diego National Wildlife Refuge, administered by the U.S. Fish and Wildlife Service, is part of the National Wildlife Refuge System that today comprises more than 520 units in all 50 states and American Samoa, Puerto Rico, the Virgin Islands, and other Pacific Islands. There are more than 93 million acres preserved under the 1997 National Wildlife Refuge System Improvement Act. This collection of wildlife refuges traces its earliest beginnings to 1864, when Congress transferred the Yosemite Valley from the public domain to the State of California. It was later returned to the federal government and established as a national park. In 1903, President Theodore Roosevelt established Florida's Pelican Island National Wildlife Refuge, which became the first official refuge. The refuge system really began at that moment, and it celebrated its centennial in 2003.

The San Diego National Wildlife Refuge offers monthly guided hikes with a ranger on various trails within the local complex. Check the local refuge website for guided hike dates and trailheads.

Thomas Brothers Map: Page 1271, J-6, Singer Lane and Campo Road.

Before You Go: Note: This trail is open to hikers, bicyclists, equestrians, and dogs on leashes.
Visit the San Diego National Wildlife Refuge website: http://www.fws.gov/refuge/ San Diego. For the Sweetwater Interpretive Loop, go to http://www.fws.gov/refuge/san diego/ visit/plan your visit/Sweetwater Interp Loop.html. On this page, you may download a Google satellite image map of the trails.

Trailhead: Take Highway 94 East to Jamul/Rancho San Diego. When Highway 94 turns into a stoplighted road that leads to a large shopping center, turn right at Campo Road to continue on Highway 94. In about a quarter mile, turn right onto Singer Lane, a small road just across from the McGrath Family YMCA. You will see the big steel bridge with a small parking area half-paved; there are no signs, but park here and walk across the bridge. Immediately past the bridge, turn right onto the trail, which will lead to a refuge kiosk.

Distance/Difficulty: I wandered around the trails, sticking mostly to the main loop itself, for about 3.8 miles total. Easy.

5. North County Foothills: Vista/ San Marcos/Escondido

Trails in the North County Foothills areas of Vista, San Marcos, and Escondido may be within the urban core of the county, but they offer some fine forays into such preserved gems as Daley Ranch and Hellhole Canyon Preserve, both in Escondido. The City of San Marcos has developed an impressive system of trails that extend to small peaks for views, as well as Discovery Lake and a pretty creek or two.

5-1. Alta Vista Gardens Focuses on Plants, Art

Tucked on a hillside overlooking Vista's Brengle Terrace Park is Alta Vista Gardens, a 14-acre botanical garden with a couple of miles of trails. Years in the making, the public "living museum" intends to integrate nature, education, and art. Today, it boasts the largest concentration of public art in Vista, with some 20 outdoor sculptures and artworks placed among the themed garden spaces. Among the specimen trees, shrubs, and flowering plants are several that are very rare and many that are simply beautiful.

I began to hike through the garden on a Saturday morning when Bryan Morse, president of the garden's board and chief visionary, was tending to chores. He amiably offered me a guided tour, pointing out several of the garden's special residents. "A botanical garden was in the city's plans in the 1960s," he told me. But it took several decades for this one to emerge.

Alta Vista is a "living museum" of plants.

After the Brengle family donated its 39 acres to Vista for park use in about 1968, the adjacent 14-acre parcel, then owned by the Paul Smitgen family, was eyed for future acquisition. The City of Vista bought the Smitgen property in about 1990, but it took nearly 10 more years for a botanical garden to come to fruition.

Morse, who is a landscape contractor with his own firm, Expanding Horizons, became involved with the garden in about 2003. "I've personally made every trail here with my tractor," he said. The Boston native has lived in Vista about 30 years, having graduated from UCSD. He has masterminded the shape of Alta Vista Gardens today and even has visions for how it might evolve over the next 50 years. Lots of plans are in the works, but with everything donated and done by volunteers, funds are needed to implement some projects.

About 20 themed garden spaces are in existence or are being planned. One of the first I encountered near the entry is the Children's Garden, with its Jeffrey Stein Children's Music Garden. Here are several musical instruments, including an amadinda (an African xylophone), a piano pebble chime that makes lovely tones when small pebbles are placed in its holes, a whale drum, and a chime wall. Also in the Children's Garden are a "tube tunnel" (made of several huge cement pipes placed in a meandering pattern) and several colorful sculptures, *Tail Spin* by Melissa Ralston, *Miro Kite* by Mindy Rodman and Paul White, and *The Constellation Tree* by Fritzie Urquhart.

One of the garden's most recent creations is its medicine wheel in the Desert Garden. With help from Native American Craig Kessinger, Morse designed and placed the rocks and plants that define the medicine wheel. "The whole circle is 32 feet with four-foot trails and four quadrants," Morse said. "Sacred geometry makes a difference, and it respects the four elements: air, water, earth, and fire." In the center is a stacked rock monolith. Each quadrant features plants in a certain color: black, white, yellow, and red. "Craig uses dousing rods to find energy fields and says there is a vortex in the right quadrant," Morse added.

Another special place is the garden's labyrinth. Built around the *Broken Link* granite sculpture by Tony Imatto, the labyrinth consists of a single path that circles the center five times, with circuits planted from the inside to outside in succulents, Mexican feather grass, sweet pea bushes, lavender, and rosemary.

Labyrinths, which date to Celtic times, are said to enhance right-brain activity. One simply walks in the circles to the center and then back out again. I've always thought they help to illuminate the joy of the journey as well as the destination.

Just below the labyrinth is the cycad garden with its Wollemi pine, a purchase of this rare "living fossil" tree that has lived since dinosaurs roamed the planet. This pine tree was auctioned in 2005 in Australia and brought to Vista, where its dark green, bottle-brush foliage is a treasure of the garden. The neighboring cycads, including sago palms, also date back to the Jurassic era and can live very long lives.

Work has begun on the Japanese garden, which Morse envisions will one day include a traditional tea house and a large pond. Today, some conifers are planted that will sit outside the pond, along with several red cherry trees and several types of bamboo.

There are currently two ponds in the garden: a large one in the ceremonial garden with a new lotus plant, centered by Lia Strell's *Golden Torsion* sculpture; and the lower pond and patio, filled with water lilies and overlooking a fine view down into the park and across to the horizon.

"On the clearest days in December, you can even see San Clemente and Catalina islands from here," Morse said.

He has deliberately added plants to attract butterflies, including milkweed, the host plant of the monarch, and passionflowers, which are favored by fritillary butterflies.

In October, the garden hosts its annual Fall Fun Festival. Lots of activities are typically scheduled, which in the past have included demonstrations on how to make truck-sized bubbles, music by the bluegrass North County Boys, Mary-Joy Neuru playing her crystal alchemy bowls, garden tours, and a plant sale. For a complete list of festival activities, go to http://www.altavistagardens.org/html/fall_fun_festival.html.

Head to the gardens anytime to walk its peaceful trails and admire its colorful collections of specimen plants and outdoor sculptures.

Thomas Brothers Map: Page 1088, A-5.

Before You Go: Go to the gardens' website to download a copy of its trail map: http://www.altavistagardens.org/html/trail_map.html.

It's a $2 donation per person who visits the garden, payable at its entry under an honor system. Hikers and dogs on leashes are welcome.

The gardens are open Monday through Friday 7:00 a.m. to 5:00 p.m., and on Saturday and Sunday from 10:00 a.m. to 5:00 p.m.

Trailhead: From Highway 78, exit at Vista Village Drive and head north. Vista Village Drive turns into East Vista Way. At Vale Terrace Drive, turn right. Continue past the main entrance to Brengle Terrace Park and turn left at the second entrance to the park on the Jim Porter Parkway. The address is 1270 Vale Terrace Drive, Vista 92084.

Distance/Difficulty: I wandered about 1.5 miles along several trails; very easy.

5-2. Anstine-Audubon Saves Native Plants and Birds

Since 1999, volunteers with the San Diego Audubon Society have been hard at work on an 11.6-acre preserve in Vista that features four different plant communities. Restoration of the southern part of the site was completed in 2011, and the first trails were open to the public. Today the Anstine-Audubon Nature Preserve offers a short, easy trail that covers less than a mile. The trail may be short in distance, but it is long on education. There are labels that identify most of the plants that are natives of California's distinctive habitats, and periodic classes on-site help visitors learn about incorporating these plants into their own gardens to create water-saving, low-maintenance yards that naturally attract birds and wildlife.

The Anstine-Audubon Nature Preserve is open only on Saturdays 10:00 a.m. to 4:00 p.m. Typically visitors will also be guided by volunteers, so the educational aspect increases.

Anstine-Audubon offers native plant education.

Becky Wilbanks, the resident caretaker of the property, was there the day I visited, and she escorted me around the existing trails with some forays into the northern areas, where more trails will eventually be created. We started our walk at the portal that leads to the trails, named the Claude G. Edwards Habitat Restoration Trails. "He set the groundwork," Wilbanks told us. A professional biologist and native plant birding expert, Edwards is a native San Diegan and has aided several organizations and individuals over the past 40 years. With his partner Michael Klein, the two continue Klein-Edwards Professional Services here, which offers field trips in birding and insect identification as well as an annual sensitive butterfly workshop. For more information, go to www.klein-edwards.com.

When San Diego Audubon Society took over management of the Anstine property, "there were tons of junk, old cars, and flat grounds of dirt," said Wilbanks. It took countless hours of volunteer effort to clear the junk and plant species to restore the native habitats here. Nonnative plants have been removed, and more than 2,000 native plants have been added, resulting in a land that now features thriving coastal sage scrub, willow riparian, oak woodland, and marshland habitats.

The trail begins in an area that once was nothing but dirt, but today it is a coastal sage scrub habitat filled with dark green black sage, silvery white sage, and lighter green Cleveland sage shrubs, along with coyote bush and buckwheat. "This is what California smelled like when the Indians were here," Wilbanks said. "You can't help but relax." We inhaled those lovely sage fragrances.

The sage scrub habitat is one of the most endangered in Southern California, and so volunteers began by planting those species. "We lost less than 10 percent of the plants we planted," Wilbanks said, "because we planted them in communities, not just as individual plants. They feed each other; fungus connects their root systems, so they work together to survive."

The native plants naturally attract birds and wildlife. About 100 bird species have been identified at Anstine-Audubon. "We have cedar waxwings, a mated pair of red-tailed hawks, and two coveys of California quail," Wilbanks said. Also sighted here have been Cooper's hawks, red-shouldered hawks, American kestrels, white-crowned sparrows, red-winged blackbirds ("year-round at the pond"), California and spotted towhees, and even a great blue heron near the dam spillway.

John and Lois Anstine bought the property in the 1940s and planted a small orchard on their 11-acre farm. The Army Corps of Engineers built an earthen dam to create the 1.5-acre pond as a water source for agriculture. Upon their deaths, the couple left their property to San Diego Audubon Society to assure protection for the birds and other native animals they loved. That pond was filled with cattails when I was there, but not for long. Plans are in place to remove most of the cattails to restore an area of open water, attracting more water birds.

A bridge will be built across the dam spillway, where a new trail will offer access to the northern part of the property. When all the trails are completed, there will probably be only about 1.5 miles, but they will offer a lovely short course in all those habitats. "It's still a work in progress," said Wilbanks. "But I just love it here."

Be sure to compare your arm span to the wingspan of six birds painted on a wall near the trail entrance. Crystalyn Alford painted the nine-foot wingspan of a California condor, the seven-foot span of a bald eagle, the five-foot span of a great horned owl, the four-foot span of a red-tailed hawk, and the much smaller spans of a scrub jay and a tiny hummingbird.

There are several periodic events to watch for at Anstine-Audubon Nature Preserve, including a wilderness awareness class that offers instruction in bird languages, mammals and plants, and a native plant workshop that involves hands-on projects and field work.

Thomas Brothers Map: Page 1087, H-1, just north of Osborne on Hutchinson.

Before You Go: Download a map of the trails from San Diego Audubon Society's website on Anstine: http://www.sandiegoaudubon.org/images/PDF/AnstineTrailGuide1.12_for_web.pdf.

For more information on the nature preserve, go to http://www.sandiegoaudubon.org/our-work/sanctuaries/anstine-nature-preserve. The nature preserve is open only on Saturdays 10:00 a.m. to 4:00 p.m., October through June. It is open only to hikers.

Trailhead: Heading south on Interstate 5, exit at Highway 76, heading east. Turn right on East Vista Way and then right on Hutchison. Follow Hutchison around the curve; the preserve is on the left after the wooden fence.

Heading north on Interstate 5, exist at Highway 78, heading east. Exit at Vista Village Drive, heading north over freeway. Turn right onto Santa Fe Avenue and then right onto Osborne. Then left onto Hutchison; the preserve is on the right.

Anstine-Audubon Nature Preserve is located at 2437 Hutchison Street, Vista 92084.

Distance/Difficulty: So far it's only about 1.0 mile of trail; very easy.

5-3. Easily Reached Oak Grove In Vista's Buena Vista Park

For an easy walk through a really lovely old oak grove along a year-round stream, head to Buena Vista Park in Vista. As one of the only Vista parks with hiking trails, Buena Vista Park offers a surprising patch of nature easily accessible to urban dwellers. An entertaining duck pond marks the beginning and end of this easy loop trail that covers about 2.5 miles in the 146-acre open space park.

On the pretty pond, I saw several pairs of mallard ducks, lots of American coots, some Greylag geese or perhaps hybrid domestic swan geese, some ducks that looked like a hybrid between mallards and northern shovelers, and a single great blue heron wading close to shore.

There are a handful of trails in Buena Vista Park, Pond and Open Space, all of which link up to each other, so you can take any route you like. Begin just beyond the duck pond. Right away, you have a choice to take an uphill climb or wander straight ahead; the uphill trail will come back down to join the main trail in fairly short order, so if you want a bit more exertion, add that hill. The main trail is fairly flat the whole way, and even though it is unpaved, it's easy even for baby strollers.

A wonderful oak grove lives in Vista's Buena Vista Park.

The first part of the main trail is open-space country with little shade, though you are right next to the riparian oak grove that flanks both sides of Agua Hedionda Creek. The Agua Hedionda Creek is the main arterial for the watershed of the same name that winds some 10.6 miles from the San Marcos Mountains to the Agua Hedionda Lagoon and the Pacific Ocean. It's part of the Carlsbad Watershed Network. Including the main Agua Hedionda Creek and all its tributaries, more than 70 miles of creeks feed into this watershed.

After about 0.65 mile on the main trail, it crosses under the cement bridge of South Melrose Drive and soon gets closer to that live oak grove.

Buena Vista Park's oak grove is an excellent example of this beautiful habitat, with several specimens that are surely more than 100 years old. The limbs of these coast live oak trees span across the trail or across the creek, forming a shade canopy and habitat that hosts many creatures, including squirrels, jays, quail, and swallows. I saw a few bright blue western scrub jays and some white-crowned sparrows in these old oak woodlands; they all like to feed on the acorns.

There is also plenty of poison oak too, so be on the lookout for those "leaves of three," and "let them be." The only time you have to worry about that poison oak is when you try to cross the creek, but that will become easier soon.

After about 1.3 miles, the trail ends at a fence. There was a bridge that crossed the creek here, but it was removed in 2009 for safety concerns. A worker there in 2013 told me a new bridge should be in place again by spring of that year.

A short way before that fence, you'll see a rope swing that hangs from an old oak limb. Cross the creek right before that swing for the easiest way to forge your way across. You'll reach the trail that follows the other side of the creek for that full loop.

You'll also note another smaller trail that heads off to the left from the main trail right after you've crossed the creek. It heads to the far reaches of the park and offers a lovely wander through this small valley, and it eventually connects with the main trail on this southern side of the creek.

Either way, this trail ends when you reach a huge oak that has fallen over the trail, requiring hoisting yourself over its limbs. There's a fence here that impedes going any farther. Go down and cross the creek back to the other northern side trail. The trail continues along a southern route just shy of the main trail you began on, and it winds through some very tall eucalyptus groves as it makes its way back to the duck pond.

At the end here you'll see a sign designating this the Arroyo Vista Trail by the Woman's Club of Vista on Earth Day in 1991. The Woman's Club of Vista, founded in 1916, was recognized in the 1990s by Keep America Beautiful for planting more than 700 oak tree seedlings in local parks, including the lovely Buena Vista Park.

The park takes its name from one of the original land-grant ranchos in the Mexican era. Rancho Buena Vista was originally issued in 1845 by Governor Pio Pico to Felipe Subria, a Luiseño Indian, according to Vista's history pages. The property changed hands many times until it was sold to Cave Couts for $3,000 in 1866. Couts then owned neighboring Rancho Guajome because that land grant was given to his wife, Ysidora Bandini. The combined Rancho Guajome and Rancho Buena Vista became the center of social activities, including grand parties. The historic Rancho Buena Vista Adobe on the original Rancho Guajome, several miles from here on the other side of Highway 78, was acquired by the City of Vista in 1989 and is currently operated by the San Diego Parks Department.

Thomas Brothers Map: Page 1107, H-5, where Antigua Drive intersects Shadowridge Drive.

Before You Go: Download a Google satellite map of Buena Vista Park's trails at the City of Vista's Parks and Facilities page: <u>https://www.google.com/maps/d/viewer?mid=zlHJDW4crbb8.</u> <u>k2SoQC0Mt9-U&msa=0</u>.

For another map of Vista's parks, check <u>http://www.cityofvista.com/home/showdocument</u> <u>?id=32</u>.

These trails are open to hikers, bicyclists, and dogs on leashes.

Trailhead: From Interstate 5, exit at Palomar Airport Road and head east. Turn left onto College Boulevard, right onto Faraday Avenue, then left onto S. Melrose Drive, left onto Shadowridge Drive, and then left onto Antigua to enter the park's parking area.

Distance/Difficulty: About a 2.5-mile loop; easy.

5-4. Discovery Creek, Lake Offer Scenic Exercise

Discovery Creek and Discovery Lake trails in San Marcos can be combined for a fairly easy 3-mile loop hike with very pleasant views. Even though they're in an urban area—included as part of the Discovery Hills housing neighborhood—these trails offer some very natural scenes along the way. They're both multi-use trails open to hikers, bikers, equestrians, and dogs on leashes. They feature soft-surface and hard-surface paths that are often side-by-side.

I began on the Discovery Creek Trail from the Lakeview Park, which sits next to Discovery Lake. From that parking area, when facing the trailheads, take the trail to the right (west), heading down a steep hill paralleling Discovery Creek.

Discovery Lake offers a pretty exercise route.

You'll note trails on either side of the creek, the soft-surface trail on its south side and the hard-surface trail on its north. I took the soft-surface trail, but you can take either one and, when reversing course, take the other on the way back.

Several trails connect here, giving several options, including the trail to Double Peak, a 5-mile round-trip from Discovery Lake with a 1,000-foot elevation gain, as well as the 3-mile round-trip Cima Trail that intersects along Discovery Creek.

I stayed on Discovery Creek Trail's southern soft trail as it wound through the backcountry of a neighborhood. The creek was mostly dry in mid-August, when the heat levels were also very high in this valley that was discovered in 1797 by Spaniards pursuing a small band of local natives, according to the San Marcos Historical Society. The Spaniards named it Vallecitos de San Marcos, or "Little Valleys of Saint Mark," to honor April 25, St. Mark's Day (the day they found it).

The Discovery Hills development that surrounds these trails began in the early 1990s, when population growth in San Marcos boomed. From a total of some 2,500 people in 1956 when Colorado River water arrived here, it became the third-fastest growing city in the state with 17,479 by 1980. During the 1980s, population almost doubled to 33,800, and today it's 82,743.

Just after the Discovery Creek trail crosses Applewilde Drive, it splits with one segment heading across the creek and another continuing toward the hills. I took the left toward the hills here. Shortly, the trail takes a steep left up the hill at Cima Drive at Via Vera Cruz, where it becomes the Cima Trail and heads up to a water tank. It also connects to the Double Peak Trail.

I took a right onto Via Vera Cruz to find the trail on the other side of the creek for my return. I walked just a couple of blocks and found the trail heading off from either side of Via Vera Cruz, and I took the one heading farther ahead instead of heading back.

This hard-surface trail continues just another quarter-mile or so until it dead-ends near Discovery Elementary School at McNair and La Noche. From here I turned around and headed back, taking that hard-surface route on the other side of Via Vera Cruz.

An interesting placard at this trail entry gives some facts about sycamores and oaks, both residents of this creek's riparian habitat. Sycamores are also known as the buttonwood or buttonball tree for the round fruits that hang from these mottled-barked trees in fall and winter. Deciduous sycamores can be among the largest of our local native trees, reaching heights well over 100 feet and up to 175 feet tall with multiple trunks that can be over 8 feet in diameter. The coast live oaks along this creek habitat feature shiny dark green leaves that are stiff, leathery, and convex with their edges tending to roll under, according to the placard. Their slender and pointed acorns take one year to mature and are held in a "turban-like cup which is very fuzzy inside and fairly shallow."

This trail continues on the southern edge of Discovery Creek. It connects again with the soft-surface trail, but either one will take you back to Discovery Lake, a small, five-acre reservoir also developed in the early 1990s. Fishing is popular here, as is bird-watching, especially for all the ducks.

A sign posted at the Discovery Lake trailhead points out that the distance around the lake is about three-quarters of a mile, so five laps total 3.63 miles and 10 laps total 7.25 miles. Many people use this trail for exercise.

One notable fact about Lakeview Park's fountain: you're encouraged to splash around and feel good about it. "The fountain is also a water-conscious way to maintain Discovery Lake," says the city of San Marcos. "A deep well feeds the fountain which in turns trickles into the lake that has had a history of evaporating away in drought years." The fountain bubbles up for 15 minutes every day at 11:00 a.m. and at 12:30, 2:00, 3:00, and 5:00 p.m.

Thomas Brothers Map: Page 1128, G-2, Lakeview Park at Foxhall and Poppy.

Before You Go: Download a map of both Discovery Creek and Discovery Lake trails at San Marcos' trail pages: http://www.ci.san-marcos.ca.us/index.aspx?page=257.
It is open to hikers, bicyclists, equestrians, and dogs on leashes.

Trailhead: From Interstate 5, exit at Palomar Airport Road, heading east. At almost three miles, it becomes W. San Marcos Blvd. Turn right onto S. Bent Avenue, which becomes Craven Road. Turn right on Foxhall Drive and continue just past Poppy Road, to Lakeview Park at the end of Foxhall.
For Discovery Lake, from this park, head straight ahead. For Discovery Creek, head on the trail to the right (west).

Distance: The total loop I covered was about 3.0 miles; fairly easy.

5-5. Double Peak Wows with Views, Birds

On a very clear day, hike up Double Peak in San Marcos and scope out an amazing view that includes snow-capped San Jacinto to the northeast and San Clemente and Catalina islands to the far west, with a lot of North County spread out in between.

Those kinds of clear days are more common in winter, and those colder temperatures also make the uphill trudge a bit easier. Even if the skies are not the clearest, you will still find views worth the effort.

Double Peak sits at 1,644 feet in elevation, the second highest peak in the Cerro de las Posas Mountains of San Marcos. The San Marcos Mountains are part of the Peninsular Ranges that extend more than 300 miles from the Santa Ana and San Jacinto Mountains of Orange and Riverside Counties to the Sierra San Pedro Martir in Baja California, according to Wayne's Word (http://waynesword.palomar.edu), "an online textbook of natural history" site created by Wayne Armstrong, an adjunct professor of biology and botany at Palomar College. The Peninsular Ranges also include Laguna, Cuyamaca, and Palomar.

As you climb to the top, you might also notice some striking and rare endemic plants in San Diego County that grow in the reddish soil that decomposes from San Marcos gabbro, a dark, basic intrusive rock that contains a lot of iron and magnesium. These plants include southern mountain misery (chamaebatia foliolosa), a bright green shrub, and chamaebatia australis, an endemic shrub in the rose family. Armstrong says southern mountain misery gets its name "perhaps because of the strong-smelling resin that gets on your clothing as you hike through thickets of this shrub." Spring wildflowers here should include lemonadeberry, ceanothus (wild lilac), monkeyflowers, white and black sage, bush mallow, and more.

Climb Double Peak for views.

What I noticed most on this trail besides the panoramic views were all the birds in the chaparral and on Discovery Lake, where this hike begins. Susan Heller, a San Marcos resident and former member of the city's trails committee, wrote to me a while ago to suggest the Double Peak Trail. "If you want a good workout with terrific views, start at Discovery Lake and climb 2.5 miles to the top—it's higher than Cowles Mountain and has fantastic views 360 degrees from Mexico up to San Jacinto," she wrote. She sent detailed instructions, which I carried with me and which really helped navigate the way.

Begin at Lakeview Park on Discovery Lake. "To start your hike," she wrote, "take the park access on the right by the billboard kiosk to a path that goes over the dam at the end of the lake. You'll see the trail/paved fire road going up the hill ahead, with wooden post fencing along it. The trail winds up the hill, coming to a housing development; stay left or simply stay on the road (Stoneridge Way), and you'll see the trail paralleling it up the hill. At the top of the hill, stay left—you'll see the trail entrance. You'll pass a water tower and finally a decomposed granite trail takes off steeply to your left. You are now on your way up Las Posas Mountain. This small section is the steepest, so don't despair! It takes a sharp turn to the right, and now you can breathe easier for the rest of the hike to the top."

The trail is quite steep for that first three-quarters of a mile, gaining about 500 feet. But then it really is easier the rest of the way. When you come to a T intersection, turn right, and the trail switchbacks gradually up the hill.

You'll eventually intersect a paved trail, marked to the right as the Ridgeline Trail. Turn left here and continue to the paved road that goes to the top of the mountain (yes, you could have driven up here). Walk on the trail alongside the road to the top of the mountain. Just before you reach a sign that says, "Warning: Steep Trail Ahead," you'll see an unmarked dirt trail that heads off to the left. You'll take this on the way back. First, follow the paved road to the top.

Now those panoramic views are laid out below you. Surrounding the telescope are inlaid renderings of all the distant horizons, identifying San Clemente and Catalina islands, Batiquitos and Agua Hedionda lagoons, and the Encina Power Plant in Carlsbad; Lake San Marcos; San Jacinto, San Bernardino, and Palomar Mountains; and downtown San Diego and Tijuana.

Turn back to go down the way you came, but this time take that "secret trail" back, a narrow, rocky, and steep trail. "It goes east across this part of the mountain, eventually joining another trail, which you go left on, that will take you back to the T-junction you originally turned right on," wrote Heller. Another tip: when you reach a bench at an intersection on this Secret Trail, stay to the left. You'll spot small South Lake from this trail.

"We fought like mad to prevent [developers] from putting a hotel or luxury homes up there," wrote Heller. "Craig Sergeant-Beach was head of the Parks Department then (he recently retired)—he was amazing, taking on all those developers who didn't want to put in trails (the city required them to conform to the master trail plan). Then they all turned around and used the trails to hype their developments."

On the way down, I spotted the bright blue flash of a western scrub jay, the yellow belly of a tiny Pacific slope flycatcher, and the long, down-curved bill of a California thrasher. On Discovery Lake at the bottom, I watched several mallard pairs, American coots, a common moorhen with its bright red bill and long greenish legs, a bufflehead duck, and a black-and-white western grebe.

Double Peak Trail was a good workout. The views were fantastic, and the birds were bountiful.

Thomas Brothers Map: Page 1128, G-2. Lakeview Park lies at the junction of Poppy Road and Foxhall Drive.

Before You Go: Heller recommends finding the trail on Google Maps of the Discovery Lake area.

You can also download a copy of the Double Peak Trail map from the City of San Marcos' trails pages: http://www.ci.san-marcos.ca.us/index.aspx?page=257. The "Detail Map of the South City Trails" shows the Secret Trail on the map as well as the main trail.

This trail is open to hikers, bicyclists, equestrians, and dogs on leashes. Parking is free.

Trailhead: Park at Lakeview Park, which lies at the junction of Poppy Road and Foxhall Drive. From Highway 78, exit at San Marcos Blvd., heading west. Turn left (south) on Bent Avenue, which soon turns into Craven. Turn right on Foxhall and go to its end at the park.

Walk across the northern edge of the lake where it is dammed. Then follow the instructions above.

Distance/Difficulty: It's about a 4.5-mile round-trip hike with a 1,000-foot elevation gain. Moderate.

5-6. Las Posas Road to Chaparral Then Palomar Arboretum

Take a hike on the San Marcos' Las Posas Borden trail, which combines an attractive two-lane, soft- and paved-surface route along Las Posas Road with a single-track trail through undeveloped chaparral. Add an excursion or continue your hike to Palomar College for a wander through its wonderful arboretum, and you'll enjoy an excellent urban exploration of nature.

The City of San Marcos has some remarkably fine urban hiking trails, now covering some 60 miles throughout the community just east of Carlsbad and Vista, all developed within the last 20 years.

Plans call for a projected 72 miles of trails connecting residential neighborhoods with local parks and schools, also designed to connect with the wider regional trail systems planned by neighboring cities.

This fine San Marcos trail leads to a splendid arboretum.

The city's goal is to provide an alternative means of non-motorized travel while also encouraging a "Go Play and Get Fit" theme to encourage healthy lifestyles, it says.

Begin at Cerro De Las Posas Park, a 12-acre community park developed in 1993 that also operates a public 25-yard lap pool from early April through September. From the park, head north on Las Posas Road along the two-lane paved and unpaved pathways.

The urban portion of this hike passes under some pretty pepper, pine, and bottlebrush trees, with lots of blue agapanthus in bloom during summer. I spotted a red-crowned Nuttall's woodpecker on one of those pepper trees.

After about 0.85 mile, Las Posas Road ends, and the trail continues through chaparral, with the Agua Hedionda Creek just below it. A few oak trees provide a little shade, but mostly this trail is shade-free as it joins some old dirt roads through lands that are largely undeveloped. The city plans other trails through this area eventually.

In this stretch of nature, I was delighted to see a pair of red-breasted house finches, a yellow-bellied ash-throated flycatcher, and a blue western scrub jay.

I continued back along the same route, turning off Las Posas and onto W. Borden Road for a ways until I returned to my car at Las Posas Park, marking nearly 3 miles. You could walk east along Borden Road from here to Palomar College Arboretum, adding another 3 to 4 miles round-trip. I drove to the college on a very hot day instead.

On the mid-July Saturday I was there, the parking lots were empty. But any day, campus visitors are required to go the Palomar College police station near the main entrance off Mission Road to obtain a no-cost visitor's pass with instructions on where to park.

I found Palomar College Arboretum near the northeast corner of the campus, behind the bookstore, cafeteria, and geodesic dome that is its gymnasium. The arboretum is a lovely place that officially opened in 1973, and today it is home to more than 519 plant species, including flowering trees, shrubs, palms, bamboo, pines, and agaves. Plants from all major continents are represented in this arboretum. There are enormously tall magnolias, ficus, pines, and palms. Most of them are labeled with name and country of origin. Some beauties include the California incense cedar, southern magnolia (southeast United States), gingko biloba or maidenhair tree (China), white silky oak (northeastern Australia), Guatemalan holly (Central America), paper mulberry (southeast Asia), pink snowball (Africa), Queensland bottle tree (Australia), and silk floss tree (South America).

I was especially thrilled to hear the screeching of a trio of red-tailed hawks. I watched one for a long time eating its lunch on a limb of a huge Moreton bay fig tree. Most of the specimen trees are labeled with "M-#," like the M-34 for this one, which corresponds to a listing of them on Wayne Armstrong's website, http://waynesword. palomar.edu/pcarbor1.htm. Armstrong is a retired botany professor at the college who was on the very first committee that established the arboretum in the early 1970s. Many of the plants here have been acquired or donated by the Huntington Botanical Garden, Los Angeles County Arboretum, and San Diego Zoo.

Just south of the arboretum on Palomar College's campus is also its cactus and succulent society garden. "If you consider all the plants in the arboretum (over 500), all the plants on campus (at least 250), all the plants in the Palomar cactus & succulent society garden (at least 200), and all the plants in the native coastal sage scrub northeast of the campus (about 200), the total number of different species is (over) 1,000," said Armstrong on the arboretum website. "This is one of the greatest concentrations of plant diversity within a relatively small area in San Diego County, rivaled only by Balboa Park, the Wild Animal Park and Quail Botanical Gardens."

With all the bird sightings, as well as a cottontail rabbit in the arboretum, this was a delightful urban hike.

Thomas Brothers Map: Page 1108, E-5, Cerro de las Posas Park.

Before You Go: Download a copy of the map of Las Posas/Borden Trail at the City of San Marcos' trails pages: http://www.ci.san-marcos.ca.us/index.aspx?page=257. For a map of Palomar College, go to http://www.palomar.edu/maps/campusmapOct2014.pdf.

For a satellite map of the entire route, including the undeveloped area, zoom in on a Google map of San Marcos.

The Las Posas/Borden trail is open to hikers, bicyclists, and equestrians, as well as dogs on leashes.

Trailhead: Begin at Cerro De Las Posas Park, at the southeastern corner of N. Las Posas Road and W. Borden Road in San Marcos. From Highway 78, exit at Rancho Santa Fe Road, heading north. Turn right (east) onto W. Mission Road, then left (north) on N. Las Posas Road, then right (east) on W. Borden Road; park your car inside the park. Begin walking north along Las Posas Road.

Distance/Difficulty: I went about 3.0 miles round-trip on Las Posas and into the undeveloped area, then another mile in Palomar College Arboretum; easy.

5-7. Urban Loop Trail from San Marcos to Carlsbad

This 3-mile loop hike combines a trail in San Marcos with another in Carlsbad for an urban jaunt through an open-space creek corridor. From its perch atop San Marcos' Simmons Family Park, the Rancho Dorado Trail begins at an elevation of about 800 feet high, where ocean views add allure on a clear day. As you peer north, you can see the trail below as it switchbacks down around power lines, dropping into an open space corridor centered on a seasonal creek.

Within about 0.6 mile, the trail drops about 450 feet, making for a very steep descent—and ascent on the way back. But the rest of this loop has little elevation change, so it's only this first part that is difficult.

When you are near the bottom after that descent, you'll come to an intersection with a sign pointing left (west) to join the Rancho Carrillo Trail in Carlsbad. If you turn right at this intersection, you will continue into San Marcos' trails system, where you can connect with other urban trails; San Marcos' existing urban trails cover 65 miles. I turned left to head toward Rancho Carrillo and soon came into a big view of that open space corridor.

As you enter Carlsbad, you'll be on the southern section of the east-side Rancho Carrillo Trail, also known as the Melrose Drive North and South routes. As you hike along the southern soft-surface path, you'll see the northern route on the other side of the creek bed.

The water flow in this seasonal creek is actually hard to see because it's covered by cattails and other vegetation. But it is there, providing nesting habitat and protective cover for many birds, including the California gnatcatcher, a high conservation priority in the avian world here. It was federally listed as a threatened species in 1993.

"The entire world's population of the California gnatcatcher occurs in Baja California and coastal southern California year-round where it depends on a variety of arid scrub habitats," says the National Audubon Society. Pairs of California gnatcatchers are monogamous and fledglings tend to stay within about six miles of where they were born, acquiring a mate within several months. They eat mostly spiders, beetles, and other bugs. Look for this tiny gray songbird with its long black tail with white tips and fine white edging. Its song sounds a little like a kitten mewing.

Hike from San Marcos into Carlsbad on this urban loop.

When you enter Carlsbad's portion of this loop, you'll notice lots of pretty pepper trees. Both Peruvian and Brazilian pepper trees, the two species typically found here, are naturalized but not native, according to James Lightner's *San Diego County Native Plants*. On this trail, you'll see the Peruvian pepper tree, which prefers sage scrub habitat, like the coastal sage scrub here. They were introduced here more than 100 years ago for landscaping purposes, and they have gradually naturalized, largely propagated by wildlife eating the berries (when harvested and dried, they become pink peppercorns).

Another big pink berry plant spotted on this trail is the lemonadeberry shrub, a native that's abundant here, especially along the coast and in urban canyons. It is "valued by wildlife for food and cover, larger mammals as well as birds," writes Lightner.

At about 1.25 miles from the start, the trail reaches Melrose Drive, where you turn right to connect to the northern section of this Rancho Carrillo Trail that skirts the other side of the open space you've been hiking along. At the trailhead for the Melrose Drive North access of the Rancho Carrillo Trail, there is room for a few cars to park. You could hike along this north-south loop of the Rancho Carrillo Trail from here if you want an easier, shorter route, avoiding that climb back up to Simmons Family Park back in San Marcos. On the other side of Melrose Drive to the west, you can head to the Leo Carrillo Ranch Historic Park, where the Rancho Carrillo trail has a western loop of another two miles or so. If you go to the historic park, to the former home of Leo Carrillo, who played Pancho in the 1950s TV series *The Cisco Kid*, you'll see many of the descendants of Carrillo's colorful peacocks (male peafowl; females are called peahens), who spread their plumage to attract mates throughout spring and summer.

After continuing back on the Melrose Drive North section of the Rancho Carrillo loop, you'll quickly come to a high road versus low road choice. Take either one; they end up at the same place, which is a paved road you should recognize from when you crossed it earlier. Turn right here on your way back; this road essentially marks the boundary between Carlsbad and San Marcos. Shortly, you'll see the entrance on the left to the San Marcos trail that brought you here earlier.

You'll climb back up that steep switchback to Simmons Family Park. Perhaps the clouds will have lifted to reveal the ocean.

Thomas Brothers Map: Page 1128, A-3, Simmons Family Park.

Before You Go: Download copies of maps for both the Rancho Dorado Trail in San Marcos (http://www.ci.san-marcos.ca.us/index.aspx?page=271) as well as the Rancho Carrillo Trail in Carlsbad (http://www.carlsbadca.gov/services/depts/parks/open/trails/carrillo.asp).
This loop trail is open to hikers, mountain bikers, and dogs on leashes.

Trailhead: To begin at Simmons Family Park in San Marcos, from Interstate 5, exit at Palomar Airport Road, heading east for about 5.8 miles. At the intersection with Business Park Way heading north and White Sands Drive heading south, turn right (south) onto White Sands Drive. Turn left onto Coast Avenue, left onto Island Drive, and then left onto Rocky Point Way, where Simmons Family Park lies at the end.
The trail heads downhill from the northern end of the park near a big water tank.

Distance/Difficulty: This loop hike is about 3.0 miles round-trip, with a total elevation gain of about 700 feet; easy to moderately strenuous.

5-8. Horsey San Marcos Plans Trails Festivals

The city of San Marcos sports 65 miles of trails, including 44 miles of multi-use trails that are specifically designed to welcome equestrians as well as hikers and bicyclists. These multi-use trails typically provide a 10-foot-wide paved pedestrian and bicycle path separated by a double-rail fence from a 10-foot-wide decomposed granite path designed for horses. "These trails are set up well so horses have their own space," Robin Bond, a San Marcos horse trainer, told me.

Carolyn Read, a longtime San Marcos resident and horsewoman who founded California Horsetrader publication in 1979, now headed by her son, Warren Wilson, invited me to join her, Bond, Buck Martin (San Marcos' community services director), and Martin's assistant director Holly Malan near Walnut Grove Park to showcase their city's trails. Walnut Grove Park even features a free public arena for equestrians to use.

"The equestrian community has a very positive impact on our community," Martin told me. San Marcos adopted its Master Trails Plan in 1991, a detailed guide for a system that one day will feature 72 miles of trails, including 21 miles of urban trails for pedestrians and bicyclists as well as the 51 miles for pedestrians, bicyclists, and equestrians.

"Many communities now close to buildout are struggling to retrofit a trails system, having missed the opportunity as they grow," said San Marcos' trail plan in 1991. "San Marcos is in a position of being able to implement the system now, as it grows, putting a significant recreational resource in place for the future." Its multi-use trails have helped San Marcos maintain its rustic appeal. Trails view or wind through the city's prominent land features, including the Merriam Mountains, San Marcos Mountains, Cerro de las Posas, Double Peak, Owens Mountain, Twin Oaks Valley, and San Marcos Creek.

I watched Bond, Martin, and Malan ride from Deer Springs Equestrian, the largest boarding facility in North County. Deer Springs has new owners, Ted and Elaine Olsen, and their expert trainers, Eric Antman and Austin Eversman, have really spruced it up. It was especially interesting to watch Bond hit the rider-level horse-picture button on the stop lights at Twin Oaks and Deer Springs to give them the go signal. They walked their horses along the multi-use trails and around Walnut Grove Park.

San Marcos has several multi-use trails.

Carolyn Read is especially concerned about trail users following proper multi-user safety rules. The number one rule to remember is that hikers and bicyclists always yield to equestrians. All users should keep to the right of the trail, and if encountering horses and their riders, bicyclists and pedestrians should slow, be respectful of horses and their innate fears, and whenever possible be on the low side of the trail compared to horses on the high side.

I followed Read to her home, where she lives on five acres with five horses and a border collie in the oldest house in San Marcos. One of those multi-use trails passes her pastoral property. Her home is now known as the Borden-Read House, named for Reynold Bascomb Borden (who built it in 1882) and for her. Read bought the two-story farm house in 1963 and raised her four children there.

Borden had come west by wagon train in 1874 and eventually homesteaded here on 330 acres next to the Los Vallecitos de San Marcos Spanish rancho, according to an article written about him by Warren Wilson. Borden lived in the home for 36 years, and he and his family grew grain and raised bees. Richland Elementary School stands where his grain once grew.

Borden Road, named for him, was once a wagon trail the Bordens traveled to reach the only year-round freshwater source at Indian Rock Springs, four miles away.

In honor of Borden and Read, I hiked the Richland Road loop trail from that elementary school. It winds through this northern edge of San Marcos, offering some of its characteristic combo of suburban and rural views. Highlights of this loop include the Borden-Read House on Richland Road and the Grace Episcopal Church on Rose Ranch Road, which consists of two 1880s churches that were combined in 1902 at the corner of Pico and San Marcos Boulevard, then given by San Marcos Historical Society to Grace Episcopal and moved to its present site in 1984.

This soft-surface trail winds behind homes, where views extend to Double Peak and some of its trails. The trail turns into normal sidewalk along Mulberry Drive, where it passes by the historic San Marcos Cemetery founded in 1894. Then it heads onto Rose Ranch Road.

Just before Rose Ranch Road hits Richland Road again, take the multi-use Olive Hills Trail that turns right (south). This trail soon branches off to head to two separate small parks, Mulberry Park to the north and Hollandia Park to the south.

I headed to Mulberry Park and then retraced my steps back to Rose Ranch Road, where a foot path above the elementary school directly across the road from that Olive Hills Trail brought me to my start.

You might want to hike a San Marcos trail on National Trails Day, the first Saturday in June.

San Marcos Annual Horse Heritage Festival usually takes place in October at Walnut Grove Park. San Marcos Trails Day is another annual community event that raises funds for the city's trails. Check the city's event calendar for dates and times.

Thomas Brothers Map: Page 1109, B-5, Richland Road near Richland Elementary School.

Before You Go: Download a map of San Marcos' North City trails from the city's trails pages: http://www.ci.san-marcos.ca.us/Modules/ShowDocument.aspx?documentid=660. South City trails map is document ID #659.

For a brochure on all of San Marcos' trails, go to http://www.ci.san-marcos.ca.us/Modules/ShowDocument.aspx?documentid=1474.

Trailhead: For the Richland Loop, from Interstate 15, exit at El Norte Parkway, heading west; El Norte becomes Borden Road. Turn right (north) onto Richland Road and park on the street near the trail above the school.

Or from Highway 78, exit at Barham Drive/Woodland Parkway and head north, turning left (west) onto Borden and then right (north) onto Richland.

Distance/Difficulty: The Richland Loop as described above is about 3.2 miles with an elevation gain of about 500 feet; easy.

5-9. Ocean and Lake Views from Two Winning Communities

When San Elijo Hills, a 1,921-acre, 3,400-home, master-planned development in San Marcos, began in the mid-1990s, more than half of its acreage (1,115 acres) was set aside as permanent open space. When its first residents moved in during the year 2000, their neighborhood's amenities included 18 miles of hiking, biking, and horseback riding trails, which also welcome leashed dogs.

The highest peak in North County is reached on one of those trails, the Double Peak Trail. I explored another trail in the San Elijo Hills system that afforded amazing views virtually 360 degrees around. I enjoyed a splendidly clear day in early November. That kind of clear weather is more common in fall and winter, so grab your hiking stick and head for these hills.

I carved out a loop trail that began at the Sunset Trail at the northern edge of San Elijo Hills Park, a 19-acre community park that fronts the town square. This park is also the main trailhead for that 18-mile network of trails.

Most of the trails are paved, and my route followed the hills and valleys of this canyon-dotted terrain, making for some semi-strenuous ups and downs.

After heading out on the Sunset Trail, School House Way Access, I descended a short way to a T intersection, where I turned right (north), hiking down and up some canyons. You'll see a huge power tower ahead, which is basically where I headed.

The Sunset Trail eventually hits a suburban street, where gates prohibit vehicular access to these trails. Take a right here past another gate across the road, then walk a short way up to the continuation of the trail on your left, made from decomposed granite.

This trail winds up, again heading for that power tower. The grade is so steep that a sign here asks bikers to walk their bikes uphill, and an alternate switchback trail immediately to the right takes hikers up to the same spot more gradually.

As you look around, you can see the Batiquitos and Agua Hedionda lagoons, the power plant on the ocean in Carlsbad, and even a faraway glimpse of high-rises that are in the UTC area. You can also see San Elijo Hills, a community development inspired by Southern California's neighborhoods of the early 1900s and designed by New Urbanist Peter Calthorpe of Berkeley and San Diego architect Roger Basinger of Architects BP Associates. Their town center and home designs borrowed from the architectural styles of American Arts and Crafts, California Bungalow and Craftsman, French Country, English Country, Spanish Colonial, Mission, and California Monterey to create a community that has won some of the most prestigious awards in the building industry, including a gold award for master-planned community of the year from the National Association of Home Builders.

At the top of that switchback, the trail hits another intersection: left to Lake San Marcos trails and right to the Ridgeline Connector Trail. I took the left to see that lake. After going up and down again, I soon saw glimpses of Lake San Marcos, created in 1946 from a dam built on the south end of San Marcos Creek. In 1962 the Frazar brothers bought 1,648 acres from the Clemson and Wells families, who had owned the land since 1927. The Frazars, who had built some 6,000 homes in Riverside and San Bernardino, created their 2,500-home, master-planned community here around that lake. Interestingly enough, it won the award for best planned lakeside community in the nation from the National Homebuilders Association Convention in 1967.

Reach ocean views from San Marcos' Ridgeline Trail.

You can continue to the Lake San Marcos Trails, but I took a sharp right turn onto the Ridgeline Connector Trail to continue my loop. This is the final climb up to that power tower on the top of the ridge. I saw the only interesting wildlife here, a roadrunner. But from this elevation, I was also at almost the same height as the soaring hawks. From here I had that 360-degree view all the way to Palomar and the ocean.

The Ridgeline Trail continues for 2.25 miles; it's part of this trail system's 10K running loop. However, I stayed on the Ridgeline Connector to get back to the Sunset Trail and my starting point. Note that where a large sign declares the trail straight ahead is "Not a Trail, No Neighborhood Access," the Ridgeline Connector takes a right turn and heads back down to that switchback part and the Sunset Trail back to the park.

Thomas Brothers Map: Page 1128, D-6, San Elijo Park.

Before You Go: Download a copy of the trail system map at http://www.ci.san-marcos.ca.us/index.aspx?page=193. The Ridgeline Trail is on the South City map.

Or visit the community's visitor center, open 10:00 a.m. to 5:00 p.m. every day, at 1215 San Elijo Road, San Marcos 92078, and pick up a pocket-sized trail map.

This trail is free and is open to hikers, bicyclists, equestrians, and dogs on leashes.

Trailhead: To reach the Sunset Trail, from Interstate 5, exit at La Costa or Leucadia, heading east to Rancho Santa Fe Road, where you turn north (left). Then turn right onto San Elijo Road and left onto School House Way. You can also reach San Elijo Road and Twin Oaks Valley Road off Highway 78.

San Elijo Park is at the public end of School House Way, right before a gated neighborhood continues. There is ample free parking at the park; park at the northern end of the lot where the trail begins.

Distance/Difficulty: My loop was about 3.5 miles round-trip. Moderately strenuous.

5-10. Surprises Await on Twin Oaks Valley Trail

The Twin Oaks Valley Trail, an urban trail in San Marcos, has several surprises. It is a flat, soft-surface trail that sits next to a paved trail, right next to city streets, including Twin Oaks Valley Road. Both the unpaved and paved paths are great for strollers, wheelchairs, bicyclists, equestrians, hikers, and dogs on leashes.

The first surprise is that this urban trail is so naturally inviting, even though it sits right next to a busy road. For most of the way along Twin Oaks Valley Road, you can hear the traffic, but you can't see it. The soft-surface path, which I followed, sits below the paved path and the road, and it is lined with tall sycamores and oaks, which form canopies over the trail, shading it and making it remarkably attractive.

On the other side from the road, the paths follow the Twin Oaks Valley Golf Course, providing extra green vistas along the way. The riparian habitat along the golf course was "revegetated with native plants to mitigate the Civic Center project," says the City of San Marcos.

A very inviting suburban trail awaits in San Marcos.

These native plants include many California roses, blooming in spring with pink wild roses; lots of purple-flowered Mexican sage; and some laurel shrubs, also in bloom in spring. On the Sycamore Drive portion, look for marsh evening primrose featuring yellow flowers. Another surprise I encountered was a great egret, standing in the water at the city runoff facility that sits next to La Cienega Road. These impressive white birds are usually found closer to the ocean or on inland lakes, but just this little bit of water evidently attracted this one. He was there when I made my way back as well.

This trail begins at Walnut Grove Park in the northern reaches of San Marcos, in front of the Williams Barn, also known as the Red Barn. Originally located where San Marcos City Hall and Library are today, the barn was purchased by the city in 1973, moved to Walnut Grove Park in 1992, restored in 1993, and is now used for public events. It was built in 1952 by Fred and Frances Williams; Fred was the first volunteer fire chief of San Marcos. They held square dances and other community festivities in the Red Barn.

The San Marcos Historical Society is headquartered right next to Walnut Grove Park in Heritage Park, where two other historic buildings were moved. The 1888 Cox House and the 1890 Bidwell House, both restored by countless volunteers since they were moved here in 2000 and 2002, respectively, are open for docent-led tours on Tuesdays, Wednesdays, and Thursdays from 2:00 to 6:00 p.m. Admission is $3 for adults.

Jacob Uhland built two houses in 1888 on what would eventually become Cox Road; the Cox family bought them in 1923. One house burned down that year, but the Cox family lived in the remaining house for 55 years, raising chickens and dairy cows and delivering milk, butter, and eggs to the neighborhood through the 1930s.

Uhland also built the Bidwell House. Bought by Colonel John Bidwell about 1921, this house is built mostly of redwood.

In front of the two historic houses is a native plant garden, installed in 2008. Native plants including salvia (like that Mexican sage), Mojave yucca, basket bush, and golden currant are planted here, and a walking path highlights the cultural uses of the plants used by the Native Americans that used to live in this area.

The Twin Oaks Valley was a land of homesteaders in the 1800s, where they ranched, farmed, and kept bees. The area was named for the Twin Oaks tree, which had two trunks growing from the same base. The original tree died of old age after living more than 200 years.

The city's pocket guide for its trails (usually available at trailheads) says this park area was pastureland for the original Twin Oaks Valley Horse Ranch. Horse facilities remain in Walnut Grove Park, inviting equestrians to practice in the two arenas before heading out on the trail.

The trail begins in front of the Williams Barn and follows Sycamore Drive to the south. Turn right on La Cienega Road and look for the egret. Turn left (south) on Twin Oaks Valley Road, staying on the east (lower) side of the road. The trail ends just before Borden Road. Turn around the go back the way you came.

The trail along Twin Oaks Valley Road is said to follow one of the early horse-and-buggy routes through this area. You might still see some horses on it today.

Thomas Brothers Map: Page 1108, J-1, Walnut Grove Park.

Before You Go: Download a map of the trail from the City of San Marcos' page: http://www.ci.san-marcos.ca.us/Modules/ShowDocument.aspx?documentid=725. Also pick up a brochure for San Marcos Parks and Trails at the trailhead.

For a brochure on all of San Marcos' trails, go to http://www.ci.san-marcos.ca.us/Modules/ShowDocument.aspx?documentid=1474.

Trailhead: From Interstate 15, exit at Deer Springs Road, heading west. In about 2.2 miles, turn left onto Sycamore Drive. Turn right to continue on Sycamore. Walnut Grove Park is on the right.

If you miss the Sycamore Drive turn, from Deer Springs Road, turn left onto Olive Street, follow signs to Walnut Grove Park, and turn left onto Sycamore.

Distance/Difficulty: The map says this trail is 2.0 miles one-way. My GPS unit measured it closer to 2.34 miles one-way, making about a 4.7-mile round trip. Very easy.

5-11. Daley Ranch Trail Offers Oaks, Ponds, and History

In 1996, the City of Escondido halted plans to develop the historic Daley Ranch by buying its 3,058 acres as habitat preserve. The city manages Daley Ranch "in perpetuity for preservation of a biologically unique and diverse habitat area of regional importance," it says. Habitats found on Daley Ranch include oak woodland, coastal sage scrub and chaparral, grassland, and riparian. Over 20 miles of trails on six main routes are open to hikers, mountain, bikers, equestrians, and dogs on leashes. They offer wide-open views of colorful meadows, three year-round ponds, and lots of lovely oak trees.

Daley Ranch is a natural oasis right in Escondido.

Most of the oaks are Engelmann or coast live oaks, both of which are used by over 300 species of birds, including raptors, according to the city's Daley Ranch website. The ponds attract aquatic birds, including cranes and osprey, but I saw only a few coots.

The Engelmann oak woodlands were once relatively widespread but now are one of the most endangered in California. The most common habitat here is chaparral, and typical plants of this habitat include chamise, scrub oak, black sage, and ceanothus (wild lilac).

There are also big boulder outcroppings on the ranch that provide homes for many reptiles, including rattlesnakes. I saw a few snake tracks (wavy lines cutting horizontally across the dirt road), including a couple that looked like some big specimens had slithered their way back into the brush.

The boulder caves, as evidenced by their soot stains, provided homes to the native Kumeyaay and Luiseño tribes for centuries here, the city's website say. Metates (shallow holes) and morteros (deep holes), used for grinding oak acorns into flour, are also found here.

Daley Ranch is one place where it really helps to print out a copy of the trail map before you head out. There are lots of intersections and loops, and it makes a difference when you can consult the map on the trail. I carved out a route that covered mostly moderate trails for a total of about 3.5 miles round-trip. To help determine my route,

I also consulted the map on the placard at the trailhead that showed which trails were moderate or more difficult.

From the ranch's southern parking area at the end of La Honda Drive, I started out on the Ranch House Trail, which goes uphill for the first third of a mile or so, on an old paved ranch road. After about three-quarters of a mile, I came to the old Daley ranch house itself.

Built in 1928 out of single-board heart redwood, the ranch house is currently undergoing complete restoration. The workers told me it would take another two years to complete the city's project, and then the house would be open to the public in some form.

Robert Daley was the first European settler to come to this valley as a young immigrant from England. He settled here in 1869 and built a small log cabin, which now sits at the bottom of the one of the ponds. Around 1880 he moved to a small pine house, which still stands (although not sturdily, it appears) on a knoll across from the main ranch house. The Daley family farmed and raised horses here.

After Robert Daley died in 1916, his family moved to Jamul but continued to use the Daley Ranch as a dairy and summer getaway. The 1928 ranch house's massive fireplace was built with cobblestones brought here by clipper ship.

From the ranch house, I continued on a short part of the Jack Creek Meadow Loop to reach Sage Trail, which took me to the big Mallard Pond and afforded fine views to the southwest overlooking the lower ponds.

I backtracked here to the ranch house and then took the East Ridge Trail to the Middle Pond Trail, which passed between those lower ponds and connected to the main Ranch House Trail to the parking area.

Naturalists lead guided hikes throughout Daley Ranch on a regular basis. Check the park's website for a calendar: http://www.escondido.org/daley-ranch-hikes.aspx.

Thomas Brothers Map: Page 1110, C-3, where La Honda Drive dead-ends at Daley Ranch.

Before You Go: Download a copy of the trail map at http://www.escondido.org/daley-ranch.aspx.
The trail is open daily from dawn to dusk, is free, and is open to hikers, mountain bikers, equestrians, and dogs on leashes.

Trailhead: From Interstate 15, exit at El Norte Parkway and head east. Just past the light at Midway, you'll see signs for Daley Ranch and Dixon Lake, pointing to take the left turn at La Honda Drive. La Honda Drive ends at the Daley Ranch parking area.

Distance/Difficulty: My loop was about 3.5 miles; moderate.

5-12. Boulder Loop Trail Lives Up to Its Name

The 3,058-acre Daley Ranch in Escondido preserves important natural habitat that has changed little over the last hundred years. More than 20 miles of trails open to hikers, mountain bikers, equestrians, and dogs on leashes offer an opportunity to explore this beautiful, historic terrain.

The City of Escondido bought this old ranch in 1996 to preserve its biologically diverse area of regional importance, saving it then from development plans. It was a working ranch since 1869 when English immigrant Robert Daley became the first European settler in this valley. Evidence of earlier people here, including the Kumeyaay and Luiseño, is found in the soot-stained ceilings of boulder caves and the metates and morteros used to grind acorns into meal. Lowell and Diana Lindsay, authors of the comprehensive *The Anza-Borrego Desert Region* guidebook, define the difference between metates and morteros as essentially slicks versus holes. Using hand-sized smooth rocks called manos, Kumeyaay women would grind seeds or dried plants in holes (morteros) pounded out in granite boulders or by using roller-pin action to create slicks or slabs (metates). One of the best trails on Daley Ranch to try to find these old proofs of historic inhabitants is the popular Boulder Loop Trail, a 2.5-mile loop that climbs high for some awesome views as it winds through big boulder country.

Boulder Loop Trail in Daley Ranch is very popular.

Be wary if you try to wander around those boulders; snakes like that habitat too. While I was on the trail in midday, one of those locals crossed the trail a few dozen yards ahead of me. It was a harmless garter snake, but I still stopped for it to pass; it looked at me a while until it continued across the trail into the brush.

The Boulder Loop Trail begins about a half-mile from the La Honda trailhead, adding another mile to the hike. That first half-mile offers help in identifying several native plants. Markers along that paved road, an old ranch road, point to plants including poison oak, mountain mahogany, deer weed, buckwheat, laurel sumac, goldenbush, a coast live oak, and an Engelmann oak. The signs identifying an Engelmann oak and a coast live oak might help in learning to distinguish the two species. Engelmanns are generally fewer than coast live oaks. Engelmanns have thin, scaly, light gray bark and oblong leaves that are rounded at the ends. Coast live oaks tend to be much bigger, reaching 80 feet with wide spreading limbs, deeply furrowed bark, and oblong leaves with spiny teeth. (Black oaks, by comparison, have deeply lobed leaves.)

There are three main habitats on Daley Ranch: oak woodlands, coastal sage scrub, and chaparral. All of these have "been greatly reduced in Southern California due to urban sprawl," says a fine brochure of native plants here produced by Friends of Daley Ranch (available at the trailhead for a $2 donation). "Daley Ranch plays an important role in preserving" these important habitats, it says. Many wildlife species depend on these natural habitats for shelter as well as food sources, including mountain lions, coyotes, bobcats, gray foxes, brush rabbits, wood rats, snakes, lizards, and birds.

A coyote captured my eye as it emerged from the riparian creek area when I was near the end of the loop. You'll note the riparian (stream-centered) habitat when you see the much lighter green willow trees next to the old oaks.

The first half of the Boulder Loop trail climbs up to long views to the west and northwest, where much of North County can be seen toward the ocean. The trail crosses old grasslands (evidence of that ranching past) too, and there are lots of colorful wildflowers, including yellow and red monkeyflowers, bright fuchsia canchalagua, yellow rush roses (a type of rock rose), sages, and ceanothus. When the trail loops back toward its beginning, the views look east over the Daley Ranch lands all the way to layers of distant peaks, including Palomar Mountain.

Mountain bikers may find the trail challenging, because there are some seriously deep ruts to navigate. Some have been filled in with bales of hay, but not all of them.

Boulder Loop Trail offers a classic Southern California natural landscape with its giant granite boulders, oaks, and wildflowers—the way it's been for centuries.

Thomas Brothers Map: Page 1110, C-3, where La Honda Drive ends.

Before You Go: Daley Ranch is open daily from dawn to dusk, and it's free. Dogs are allowed on leashes. For a trail map, go to the City of Escondido's Daley Ranch website: http://www. escondido.org/daley-ranch.aspx.

Trailhead: From Interstate 15, exit at El Norte Parkway, heading east for about four miles, turning left onto La Honda Drive. Look for Daley Ranch and Dixon Lake signs, because La Honda Drive is not a major intersection. Go about a mile to the end of La Honda Drive and park in the parking area for Daley Ranch.

To reach Boulder Loop Trail, take the main Ranch House Trail from the main parking area for 0.47 miles. The Boulder Loop Trail is on the left and is well marked.

Distance/Difficulty: A total of 3.5 miles, easy to moderate.

5-13. Rare Engelmann Oaks On Daley Ranch Trail

The Engelmann Oak Trail in Daley Ranch is a 4.75-mile total loop in the northern section of that historic property. It is far less traveled than other trails there.

Escondido's Daley Ranch dates to 1869, when Robert Daley, a young English immigrant, settled in this valley to farm and raise horses. Today it is a 3,058-acre conservation area that the City of Escondido acquired in 1996 to preserve its biologically important habitat. There are some 20 miles of trails that traverse this old ranch land where grasslands, ponds, and oak woodlands beckon.

The Engelmann Oak Trail passes through chaparral habitat and a few fine oak woodlands, and it climbs several hundred feet for some sweeping views.

Engelmann Oak Trail honors those rare natives.

Those atmospheric oak woodlands found near streams feature old, 70-foot-tall coast live oaks that form shady canopies above the trail. The namesake Engelmann oaks, on the other hand, tend to stand more singly on the higher mesas. Engelmann oaks are natives here, even valued as "regional endemic" trees. "Central San Diego County [is] the epicenter of the species," notes James Lightner in his book *San Diego County Native Plants*. They're far rarer here than coast live oaks or canyon live oaks (which tend to be the biggest of the three in this part of the world), but they're even rarer outside San Diego County. There are some other populations, Lightner says, near Pasadena, central Orange County, south Riverside County, Catalina Island, and Baja California just south of Tecate.

Over 300 species of animals and birds in California use Engelmann oak and coast live oak woodlands, according to a report on Daley Ranch's habitat at the City of Escondido's website.

Engelmann oaks are smaller than coast or canyon live oaks. Engelmann oaks reach about 40 or 45 feet tall compared to the 75-foot height that coast live, canyon live, and black oaks can attain.

The leaves of Engelmann oaks tend to be lighter green or even blue-green in color compared to coast live and canyon live oaks. Engelmann leaves are also flat, oblong, and toothless, whereas coast live and canyon live oaks have oblong leaves that have tiny, spiny teeth.

You'll find most of the Engelmann oaks on this trail near the top of the loop. This loop trail is accessed by starting out on the Cougar Ridge Trail at the northern entrance to Daley Ranch. After walking through meadows thick with buckwheat, you reach the first of the oak woodlands, where the trail crosses a small stream. These big old oaks are coast live oaks.

At 0.71 miles, the Cougar Ridge Trail intersects with the Engelmann Oak Trail on the left. The Engelmann Oak Trail then climbs more than 300 feet to reach the top of the ridge. The entire elevation gain of the trail is about 550 feet, reaching nearly 1,900 feet in elevation, according to William Sherrard's e-book," (http://daleyranch.info/styled-6/page35/daley-ranch-engelmann-oak-trail.html).

After that climb, the trail meanders more gradually through chaparral. There are few wildflowers here, but the Engelmann oaks are scattered alongside the trail.

At about 1.6 miles from the beginning, you'll come to a wooden bench beside the junction with the single-track Bobcat Trail that reconnects to the Cougar Ridge Trail if you want to make this hike a bit shorter. I kept going straight ahead on the Engelmann Oak Trail, which is an old ranch road, where it's far easier to spot snakes ahead than on those single-tracks. After that bench, the trail becomes quite sandy, which might provide a chance to see some wildlife tracks; I think I saw coyote tracks there, and I have seen a coyote on Daley Ranch before. Other possibilities include tracks of foxes, bobcats, and even snakes.

The trail continues its loop, offering some views to the east including Palomar Mountain, and then it passes an old water tank. After about two miles, it reaches an intersection with Hidden Spring Trail, which is its high point in elevation. The Engelmann Oak Trail begins to descend here, and it passes through another fine coast live oak grove. There are also more boulder outcroppings on this part of the trail, which are important denning, nesting, and perching sites for coyotes, bobcats, ringtail cats (a kind of a raccoon), rattlesnakes, and raptors.

In a little more than a half-mile, the trail ends at its southern intersection with Cougar Ridge Trail, where you go right to return to your starting point.

This part of the Cougar Ridge Trail descends steeply and is very heavily rutted, which is a note to mountain bikers and equestrians, who are welcome on this trail.

You get to pass through that first lovely oak grove once again, crossing that small creek to return to the parking area.

Thomas Brothers Map: Page 1090, H-4, the northwestern boundary of Daley Ranch.

Before You Go: Daley Ranch is open dawn to dusk every day. It's free and is open to hikers, mountain bikers, equestrians, and dogs on leashes.
Download a trail map at the City of Escondido's website for Daley Ranch: http://www.escondido.org/daley-ranch.aspx.

Trailhead: To reach the northern entrance to Daley Ranch, from Interstate 15, exit at El Norte Parkway, heading east. Turn left onto Broadway, go about 4.2 miles, and turn right onto Cougar Pass Road, which is a graded dirt road (you do not need four-wheel drive). After about 1.2 miles, park on the left across the road from the gated entrance to Daley Ranch.

Distance/Difficulty: The entire loop of the Cougar Ridge-Engelmann Oak trails is 4.75 miles; moderate.

5-14. Sweeping Views, Lake from Daley's Caballo

A hike up the Caballo Trail in Escondido's Daley Ranch is a heart-healthy workout worthy of special appreciation for its natural setting in an urban surrounding. It climbs uphill to survey the northeastern section of the city, with largely undeveloped views extending to its north and layers of hills lining the horizon to the south. Make it all the way to Dixon Lake and throw in a beautiful blue-water vista.

Daley Ranch is called the Jewel of Escondido for good reason. This naturally and culturally historic 3,058-acre park narrowly escaped a 1,700-home development in the mid-1990s, when Escondido bought the land in 1996 in a complicated deal with developers who had bought it from the Daley family in 1992.

Today Daley Ranch is a habitat preserve "managed in perpetuity for the preservation of a biologically unique and diverse habitat area of regional importance," says the City of Escondido. It offers over 20 miles of trails open to hikers, bicyclists, equestrians, and dogs on leashes.

Caballo Trail climbs to birds-eye views.

Nature enthusiasts can download check lists of more than 75 species of birds, including those frequenting the waters of Dixon Lake, as well as owls, raptors, woodpeckers, perching birds, and flycatchers. There are also hundreds of plants populating the coastal sage scrub, chaparral, and oak woodland habitats. The ranch is also home to snakes, lizards, mountain lions, bobcats, gray foxes, coyote, rabbits, and deer.

In its earliest days, the area was home to the I'pai ti'pai people, also known as the Diegueño and Kumeyaay, who lived off the land, hunted for game, and ate native plants. The smoke-darkened caves they used as shelters are found on the ranch, as are metates and morteros in the bedrock they used to grind acorns, a diet staple.

English immigrant Robert Daley "squatted" on the then federal land from 1869 to 1875, when he made a legal claim to it. He farmed here and raised cattle and horses, and subsequently the Daley family operated a dairy farm, holding the land in the family for more than 120 years.

The Caballo Trail (caballo being Spanish for horse), heads uphill steeply at the beginning, gaining about 500 feet in elevation in the first 1.5 miles. It's steep enough that signs at the beginning warn equestrians to be experienced riders and to watch for ruts as well.

Once you reach the intersection on the right at about 1.35 miles with the single-track Quail Run Trail, the going gets much easier for the rest of this route, gaining only another 100 feet or so. At the intersection with the Sage Trail at about 1.65 miles, turn left and continue on to Dixon Lake, which you'll be able to see about 2.15 miles from the start.

It's hikers only from the Sage Trail to the Dixon Lake area. At that 2.15-mile point, where the trail takes a sharp left to begin its descent to the lake, I stopped at a boulder viewpoint, where I finally saw the lake below. As I gazed at the lovely lake from this vantage point, a redheaded turkey vulture soared immediately above me. From here, I turned around and retraced my route back.

The Caballo Trail runs through primarily chaparral and coastal sage scrub, with virtually no shade along the way, making it especially hot in summer. Carry a lot of water for both you and your horses or dogs.

Friends of the Daley Ranch, an all-volunteer, nonprofit organization dedicated to conserving this preserve, publishes an excellent, small guide to native plants of the ranch; you can sometimes find it at the ranch's main La Honda Road trailhead for $2. It helps to identify and distinguish such common plants as white sage from black sage. White sage leaves are pale gray-green, and the flowers are white to pale lavender, blooming on opposite sides of the stalk. Black sage leaves are dark green above and lighter underneath with pale blue flowers that grow like pompoms along the stalk. The dried dark stalks and flower whorls that remain on black sage after flowering give it its name.

Black sage is especially evident on the Caballo Trail, as are buckwheat, chamise, laurel sumac, and sugar bush.

The Caballo Trail takes off near the Escondido Humane Society, so you might even spot a wonderful dog with a dedicated volunteer hiking the trail, as I did. There is a sign at the trailhead here that cautions hikers to take care of their dogs on the trails, especially during summer heat. "Dogs cannot sweat to cool off and can die from heat stroke," it warns. Symptoms of heat exhaustion in dogs include dry mouth and nose, lack of urine, weak muscles or shakes, drooling, glazed eyes, dilated pupils, difficulty walking, vomiting, and diarrhea. The even more deadly heatstroke symptoms include rapid and erratic pulse, rapid breathing, struggling for breath, exaggerated panting, suddenly not panting, very high body temperature, collapse, and seizures leading to coma and death.

First aid tips to save your dog include shade, offer a little water, soak body with cool water, fan the dog, and carry dog to get medical treatment. Also be aware of dogs' paws, especially on hot pavement. Keep your dog on a leash at all times, especially to keep it away from rattlesnakes.

Thomas Brothers Map: Page 1110, E-5, near Mayflower Dog Park.

Before You Go: Download a copy of the trail map of Daley Ranch from the city of Escondido's website: http://www.escondido.org/daley-ranch.aspx.

The Friends of Daley Ranch's website address is http://daleyranch.org/.

The Caballo Trail is open to hikers, bicyclists, equestrians, and dogs on leashes. The Sage Trail and Dixon Lake are hikers only.

Trailhead: From Interstate 5 heading south, exit at El Norte Parkway, turning east (left onto Valley Parkway. From Interstate 5 heading north, exit at Via Rancho Parkway, which turns into Bear Valley Parkway, turning east (right) onto Valley Parkway. From Interstate 15, exit at Valley Parkway and go northeast for about five miles.

From Valley Parkway, turn west (left or right, depending on which way you are coming) onto Beven. It ends very shortly. Turn right toward Escondido Humane Society and park in the dirt parking area by the trail kiosks.

Distance/Difficulty: I went about 4.3 miles round-trip with a total elevation gain of about 750 feet. Moderately difficult.

5-15. Lovely Lake with Signs That Inform Along Way

A loop hike around the northern shore of Escondido's Dixon Lake includes a nature trail segment with informational placards, making for an educational, blue-water-view outing. The views of this lovely lake would be reason enough to hike here, and if you time it in winter, you might be rewarded with lots of water fowl sightings as well.

Summer is hot in this shallow valley surrounded by rocky hills, and it is known as Escondido, or "hidden" in Spanish. Although you are not allowed to swim in Dixon Lake, a freshwater source for the City of Escondido, its blue hue may cool you along with breezes wafting from its shores.

Blue-water views abound around Dixon Lake.

Dixon Lake sits immediately next to Daley Ranch, the 3,058-acre, open-space recreational gem that offers some 20 miles of trails open to hikers, mountain bikers, equestrians, and dogs on leashes. You can continue from the trail around Dixon Lake into Daley Ranch and hike away. However, note that Dixon Lake and its trails are open only to hikers—no bikes, dogs, or horses here. The Dixon Lake recreational area was created in 1971 when the dam was completed.

I began from the Jack Creek Picnic Area, which lies just to the east and below the Hilltop Picnic Area that's the first you'll see when you enter the Dixon Lake recreational area. If you park within the Dixon Lake area, you pay $5 at that entry station. You may also park in the Daley Ranch lot just across the street, which is free, and you can walk in for free.

I started on the Jack Creek Nature Trail, which heads down to the lake from that picnic area. I found a trail entry just opposite a large shade shelter at the bottom of the Jack Creek Picnic Area, where a wooden footbridge crosses a dry creek. That trail winds down to the northwestern end of Dixon Lake for your first water views. Follow the trail to the left as it winds along the lake's north shore. You'll soon pass Pier 3, one of four fishing piers on the lake that are popular on weekends.

The lake's main concession stand, where you can rent motorboats and rowboats, lies across the lake on its south shore. There are also 34 camp sites here. Anglers fish for rainbow trout, bluegill, channel catfish, and largemouth bass. Some 34,000 pounds of trout and 13,000 pounds of catfish are stocked annually.

There's a big story of the one that got away at Dixon Lake. Dottie, a huge largemouth bass, almost made the record books but instead just made history. Three lifelong friends from Carlsbad, Mac Weakley, Mike Winn, and Jed Dickerson, grew up fishing here. In 2003 Dickerson thought he'd broken the world record largemouth bass mark of 22 pounds and 4 ounces when he pulled in the bass and immediately weighed her at around 23 pounds. But it took Fish and Game officials three hours to verify it as a record, and they say the fish was stressed by then, weighing in officially at only 21 pounds, 11 ounces. They noticed she had a black dot on her chin and named her Dottie. They released her back into the lake.

Weakley caught her again in 2006 and weighed her at 25 pounds, but she had been unintentionally "foul hooked" (not hooked in the mouth), so she couldn't be counted. She was found floating dead in the lake in May 2008, weighing 19 pounds. Her story is known in fishing circles everywhere.

As the trail continues on the north shore, you'll pass by Catfish Cove before reaching Pier 4. Then you'll pass by Whisker Bay, a particularly tranquil, small cove near the dam that marks the lake's eastern edge.

When you reach the dam, the trail ends. But a spur trail heads uphill to the left. You could simply turn around and retrace your steps back along the lake for an easy, flat hike. Or you can take that spur trail to a dirt road, where you'll be rewarded with the best views of the lake as well as eastern panoramas of Escondido and faraway horizons.

The dirt road takes you into Daley Ranch and all its trails. When you reach the top of the hill, about 250 feet above the lake, you'll come to an intersection that begins those Daley Ranch trails. A sign points to "Rattlesnake" to the left with "Sage" trail to the right. You could go left and straight back to the parking area, but I suggest you continue toward Sage to the right. Very soon you'll see a trail heading off on the left, signed "Nature Trail, Hikers Only." This trail will also take you back to your parking area but with those bonus informational placards along the way.

You'll learn about Native Americans' use of yucca (they ate its flowers, stalks, and seeds and made cordage out of its leaves); the "oak apples or oak galls" on scrub oaks that are reactions to irritations caused where gall wasps lay eggs; the red-barked mission manzanita, whose berries are eaten by coyotes and then passed as seeds ready to resprout; and wild lilac, whose blossoms were used by native peoples as soap or shampoo. Several other placards offer more interesting chaparral facts.

The trail emerges at that Jack Creek Picnic Area, just inside the Dixon Lake area across from the parking for Daley Ranch.

Thomas Brothers Map: Page 1110, C-4.

Before You Go: The Dixon Lake Recreation Area is open every day from 6:00 a.m. to dusk (8:00 p.m. in summer). It's $5 to park inside, or it's free to park in the Daley Ranch parking area across the street from the Dixon Lake entry.

Download a map of Dixon Lake, including this hiking trail, from the City of Escondido's page: http://www.escondido.org/dixon-lake-fishing-map.aspx. Download another map of Daley Ranch trails at http://www.escondido.org/daley-ranch.aspx.

The trail around Dixon Lake is for hikers only.

Trailhead: From Interstate 15, exit at El Norte Parkway, and head east about three miles. Turn left onto La Honda Drive, which dead-ends at the Daley Ranch parking area, across the street from the Dixon Lake entry station.

Distance/Difficulty: The loop trail I hiked totaled about 3.0 miles; easy to moderate.

5-16. Elfin Forest's Variety Offers Lessons, Views

For an excellent self-guided primer on our region's typical plant communities, as well as sweeping views over Escondido's backcountry, head to Elfin Forest Recreational Reserve. There are some 11 miles of trails in the 784-acre reserve, which opened in 1991. In November 2010, San Diego County bought an additional 145 acres in the middle of the reserve, once slated for the development of 17 homes, to be set aside as open space.

The reserve is owned by the San Diego County Water Authority and managed by the Olivenhain Municipal Water District. One of the trail system's viewpoint destinations, the Ridgetop Picnic Area, overlooks the Olivenhain Dam and Reservoir, the county's first major new dam and reservoir in 50 years. Opened in 2003, it can store 24,000 acre-feet of water and is part of the county water authority's emergency storage project, which also includes Lake Hodges, another reservoir visible from some of Elfin Forest's trails.

From the main parking area on Harmony Grove Road in the rural community of Elfin Forest, the main trailhead for the Way Up Trail crosses Escondido Creek. Instead, head to the left of that trailhead for the Creek Viewing Area and then the Botanical Trail. The Creek Viewing Area is a short, boulder-studded, sandy walk to the edge of Escondido Creek, which flows year-round from Lake Wohlford all the way to San Eljio Lagoon. In fall, the beautiful sycamore trees' leaves are golden.

Botanical Trail offers lots to learn in Elfin Forest.

Go back the way you came to the creek and head east, up the wide road to the Botanical Trail. Be sure to pick up a Botanical Trail Guide in the box at the start. There are 27 numbered posts along the trail that are explained in the trail guide. It identifies elements of the three main habitats here—chaparral, coastal sage scrub, and riparian—and many of their resident plants. Post No. 2 describes chaparral, one of the most common habitats in San Diego County. Trees and shrubs here are dwarfed, rarely reaching more than 20 feet tall, and they often have waxy leaves that help them reduce water loss in our summer's hot and dry season.

Post No. 4 explains that "riparian" is simply a word that means "with water." Riparian habitats occur next to creeks and streams and often feature the beautiful sycamore and oak trees. You'll locate a coast live oak tree at No. 6. Post No. 8 points out an "ecotone," a dividing line between one plant community and another; in this case, you have just walked out of a live oak riparian forest and into the hotter, drier chaparral.

Other markers point to black sage, Mojave yucca, mountain mahogany, chamise, laurel sumac, lemonadeberry, and wild lilac (ceanothus), all of which are common native plants in our county.

Lots of wildlife lives here too, says marker No. 20, including bats, raccoons, brush rabbits, mule deer, bobcats, wood rats, barn owls, turkey vultures, horned lizards, and rattlesnakes. I saw only a couple of adorable cottontail rabbits munching on some very green grass.

The Botanical Trail winds up about three-quarters of a mile to an intersection with the Way Up Trail, where I turned left to join that trail to higher viewpoints. You can also return here to the parking area for a one-mile loop.

The Way Up Trail from this point switchbacks steeply up the ridge and is very rocky most of the way. Although it's open to mountain biking and equestrians as well, it looked really scary when I saw a couple of brave women biking their way down (and sometimes screaming just a little).

When you reach the Harmony Grove Overlook at 1,010 feet high, the most difficult climbing is over. But keep going up, stay straight ahead on the Way Up Trail, and pass intersections for the Me-xal Trail and the Equine Incline Loop Trail. Then cross the Ridgeline Maintenance Road to reach the Ridgetop Picnic Area, 1,140 feet in elevation. Here are several picnic tables, drinking water, restrooms, and lovely views over the Olivenhain Reservoir's 8 billion gallons of water.

I turned around at this point and gingerly picked my way back down the Way Up Trail's rocky, steep path. There are other trails that continue from the ridgetop, if you're so inclined, including one that follows the maintenance road for a while to connect to the Lake Hodges Overlook Trail.

The reserve offers several guided hikes each month, usually on Saturdays and Sundays. Check its website for these events.

Thomas Brothers Map: Page 1149, A-1.

Before You Go: Download a trail map of the Elfin Forest Recreational Reserve at its website: http://www.olivenhain.com/elfin-forest-recreational-reserve.

Download a copy of the Botanical Trail Guide at https://www.olivenhain.com/files/docs/Park/Botanical%20Trail%20Guide.pdf.

These trails are open to hikers, bicyclists, equestrians, and dogs on leashes.

Trailhead: From Interstate 15, exit in Escondido at 9th Ave/Auto Parkway, heading west, where you soon turn left onto 9th Avenue. After crossing Valley Parkway, the road bends sharply left and becomes Hale. Turn right onto Harmony Grove Road, making the first two lefts to stay on Harmony Grove Road. In another 3 miles, between mile markers 6.0 and 6.5, turn left into the Elfin Forest Recreational Reserve.

It's open daily from 8:00 a.m. to 5:00 p.m.

Distance/Difficulty: My route covered about 2.0 miles one-way, or 4.0 miles round-trip. Moderately strenuous.

5-17. Tough Climb Rewards with Wildflowers, Water Views

For a hearty workout, blue-water views, and a plethora of pretty wildflowers, head to Del Dios Highlands Preserve in Escondido. The blue-water views may include the Pacific Ocean, but only if the skies are really clear. Much closer and always in view are the blue waters of Lake Hodges and the Olivenhain Reservoir.

When I was there in mid-May, the wildflowers were casting their colors with abandon. I spotted large swaths of golden yarrow and yellow wallflower shrubs, as well as the blue blooms of fragrant sage and the darker blue clusters of ceanothus (also known as wild lilac). With eyes peeled for close-ups, I marveled at the beauties of bright magenta canchalagua, scarlet monkeyflowers, purple wild pea, yellow sunflowers, yellow rock roses, red Mexican pinks, yellow and orange deerweed, white morning glories, and bright white daisies.

Views of two reservoirs are seen from Del Dios Highlands trail.

These amazing blooms are worthy rewards for a fairly tough climb straight uphill, with at least a 500-foot elevation gain in just the first mile. But even if you make it only for just the first half mile, you'll see those views back toward Lake Hodges. Make it the 1.3 miles all the way to the top, and you'll see the Olivenhain Reservoir. Go another 1.8 miles to the Lake Hodges Overlook, and you'll see the Olivenhain Reservoir on one side and Lake Hodges on the other.

The Del Dios Highlands Preserve is 774 acres of open space consisting of coastal sage scrub and chaparral habitats, as well as this 1.3-mile trail. The County of San Diego, partnering with the Escondido Creek Conservancy and the San Dieguito River Park Joint Powers Authority, acquired this parkland in 2004 as part of its Multiple Species Conservation Program. The MSCP preserves San Diego's unique, native habitats, and wildlife in a unique regional conservation effort. It also protects watersheds and water quality, and both the Olivenhain Reservoir and Lake Hodges are part of our county's water storage.

The Olivenhain Reservoir was built between 1998 and 2003, the region's first major new dam constructed in 50 years. A connection between it and the Lake Hodges Reservoir makes Lake Hodges water available to the region when needed, according to the San Diego County Water Authority. "It is the cornerstone of San Diego County Water Authority's Emergency Storage Project, helping to protect the region from severe water supply shortages."

The Del Dios Highlands Preserve trail straddles both the San Dieguito and Escondido Creek watersheds. When you reach the top of that uphill climb after 1.3 miles, you'll connect with the Elfin Forest Recreational Reserve trail system, which is managed by the Olivenhain Municipal Water District. That connecting parkland offers 11 more miles of trails.

Both the Del Dios Highlands and Elfin Forest Reserve's trails are open to hikers, mountain bikers, equestrians, and dogs on leashes.

After the workout of that Del Dios Highlands trail, I reached the top and passed through the gate that separates it from Elfin Forest. Just after that gate, opposite a sign to the right for the Quail Trail, take a left onto the maintenance road to head to the Lake Hodges Overlook Trail. First, note the fine views of that Olivenhain Reservoir with its bright blue water, 24,000 acre-feet, enough for 50,000 families for a year.

The Lake Hodges Overlook Trail begins just after the Escondido Overlook viewpoint. This trail is a narrow, single-track that switchbacks and winds around through the chaparral for eventual views of Lake Hodges. You'll see a sign noting that this part of the area was burned in the 2007 Witch Creek Fire, but it's making an amazing comeback.

Those wildflower shows continue, and soon you'll see expansive views of Lake Hodges, a reservoir created by the Hodges Dam on San Dieguito Creek in 1918. Lake Hodges has 27 miles of shoreline and a water storage capacity of 30,251 acre-feet.

I didn't make it all the way to the overlook itself, but I saw the lake after about the first mile or so of that trail. I retraced my way back for a total hike of between five and six miles.

Thomas Brothers Map: Page 1149, E-1

Before You Go: The Del Dios Highlands Preserve is open to hikers, mountain bikers, equestrians, and dogs on leashes every day from 8:00 a.m. to a half hour before sunset. There is no fee.

For more information and a trail map, go to the county parks' page: www.co.san-diego.ca.us/parks/openspace/deldios.html.

For a map of the connecting Elfin Forest Reserve's trails, go to the Olivenhain Municipal Water District's page: http://www.olivenhain.com/elfin-forest-recreational-reserve.

Trailhead: From Interstate 15, exit at Via Rancho Parkway, heading west. After four miles, at the dead-end at Del Dios Highway, turn left (south). The parking area for the preserve is about a quarter mile down on the right.

Distance/Difficulty: The Del Dios Highlands trail is 1.3 miles one-way; the Lake Hodges Overlook Trail is 1.8 miles one-way after that. This is a moderately strenuous hike of 5.0 to 6.0 miles round-trip.

5-18. Hike Hellhole Canyon Trails through Important Preserve

Hellhole Canyon Preserve in Valley Center is a lot more inviting than its name suggests. The 1,907-acre, open-space preserve features a flowing stream in its center complete with mature oak and sycamore trees, views across an undeveloped valley, and (for the peak baggers) the 3,886-foot-high Rodriguez Mountain, where you might even see the ocean. The 13.5 miles of trails here are open to hikers and equestrians, as well as dogs on leashes. No bikes are allowed.

The main trail descends from the staging area into the riparian habitat of that stream, where little cascades flow over boulders most of the year. Oak and sycamore trees provide the only shade you'll encounter.

There are over 13 miles of trails in Hellhole Canyon.

It's a drop of several hundred feet down to Hell Creek, as it's called, in about three-quarters of a mile. That fairly steep descent requires the ascent on this same trail back up, but that's the only difficulty; the rest of this trail is flat and easy.

The first part of the trail also features several plant identification signs, which were the work of Nate Brown earning his Eagle Scout badge in 2007. Learn to distinguish the white flowers of the California buckwheat from chamise, two of the most abundant bloomers during spring and summer in our native chaparral habitats. The buckwheat's blooms form rounder little bouquets, and chamise's white flowers cluster more conically on the ends of its evergreen stems.

The first placard reports the effect the disastrous fires of October 2003 had on Hellhole Canyon Preserve. The Paradise Fire, which occurred at the same time as the huge Cedar Fire of 2003, burned 95 percent of the preserve. The Poomacha Fire of 2007 burned part of the preserve again. The placard notes that oak woodlands are fire adapted, meaning they often survive fire compared to the less hardy pines. Oak trees resprout along their branches as opposed to their stumps.

Once the trail leaves the Hell Creek riparian area, it continues along a ridge where there are no trees for shade, but there are lots of chaparral shrubs and wildflowers, including yellow and orange deerweed, red monkeyflowers, purple Cleveland sage, and so many yellow wallflower shrubs that they often obscure the narrow trail.

Hell Creek, the centerpiece of Hellhole Canyon, is part of the San Luis Rey Watershed, one of 12 major watersheds in San Diego County, reports another placard along the trail.

Shortly past the watershed placard, the trail intersects with the Horse Thief Trail loop, which I took to the right. Almost immediately is another intersection; head left to continue on the Horse Thief Trail loop. The trail to the right heads uphill to both the Paradise Trail and Rodriguez Peak Trail—both harder climbs, which I didn't take.

The loop continues to wind along the ridge overlooking the valley. It's hot here during the summer, so bring plenty of water. Another placard showcases photos and foot-track renderings of mountain lions, coyotes, deer, and bobcats. "Hellhole Canyon Preserve is surrounded by undeveloped land and facilitates animal movement in all directions," it says.

Friends of Hellhole Canyon Open Space Preserve, a volunteer, not-for-profit land trust and educational organization, continues work to enlarge this preserve to protect its wildlife connectivity. The Friends group was successful in garnering funds to buy an additional 190 acres in the preserve's center, along Hell Creek, in 2005. "The canyon has over 3 miles of creek bed and provides a critical, but threatened habitat and wildlife corridor connecting Rancho Guejito, Cleveland National Forest, Bureau of Land Management and southern inland areas of the county ... the area represents the last inland connection between the north and south parts of the county west of the inland mountains," it says.

Just behind that placard about wildlife linkages, I noticed a clear wildlife trail through the grasses. The last placard points to the cut along the ridge you see above Hell Creek. It's not a trail but a path where the old wooden Escondido Flume built in 1895 used to carry water from the San Luis Rey River to the reservoir at Lake Wohlford. When a steel siphon was constructed here in the early 1900s (still in use today), the wooden flume was removed.

Docents lead hikes (sometimes horseback rides) through Hellhole Canyon Preserve on the third Saturday of every month except August; meet at 9:00 a.m. at the staging parking lot. Check the Friends' calendar on its website: www.hellholecanyon.org.

Thomas Brothers Map: Page 1091, H-3.

Before You Go: The preserve is open only Friday through Monday. It is closed Tuesday, Wednesday, and Thursday, as well as from August 1 to September 4 because of extreme heat. It's free. Trails are open only to hikers, equestrians, and dogs on leashes.

Download a trail map at the county parks' page: http://www.co.san-diego.ca.us/reusable_components/images/parks/doc/Trails_Hellhole.pdf.

Go the Friends' page, www.hellholecanyon.org, to download a copy of the Self-Guided Trail Guide of the flora found here.

Trailhead: From Interstate 15, exit at Valley Parkway, heading east about 5.5 miles. Follow Valley Parkway signs through downtown (because you'll be on Grand), then Second before joining Valley Parkway again. Turn right onto Lake Wohlford Road. After about 6.0 miles, turn right onto Paradise Mountain Road. After about 3.5 miles, turn left onto Kiavo Road, following signs to the preserve, turning uphill onto Santee to the parking area.

Distance/Difficulty: The 1.3-mile (one-way) Hell Creek and 1.5-mile Horse Thief Loop trails combine for about a 4.0-mile round trip; easy to moderate.

5-19. Lake Wohlford Trail Good for Birding

The Kumeyaay Trail around the northern edge of Escondido's Lake Wohlford is an easy walk with sparkling water views and lots of water birds. The trail skirts a little above the lake for most of the way, but you can also try to navigate walking along the shoreline with all the folks fishing.

From the main parking area, the trail going to the southwest (to the right when facing the lake) is named the Osprey Trail, which goes only about a quarter-mile or so to the orange West Buoy Line that marks a closed area of the lake.

Retracing your steps back, the Kumeyaay Trail begins to the left of the main parking area (when facing the lake) and climbs up just a bit above the water line. I walked along the shoreline for quite a way here until some big boulders and too many tall stinging

nettles made that too hard. Near the first group of big old oak trees, I went uphill to connect with the main trail. The trail winds through several small groves of ancient coast live oaks that frame views of the water.

Parts of the trail are a bit overgrown, but it's still easy to follow. Keep looking for the red arrows painted on the rocks that show the way. After about a mile, the trail intersects with a road that leads from the eastern parking area. You'll note a portable toilet here. A trail leads down to the lake directly across from that facility. Continue straight ahead to stay on the main trail, where it continues at the end of that road past the toilet facility.

You'll soon see an old dam construction among towering oak trees. Keep following those red arrows; the trail eventually ends at the East Buoy Line on the lake. Before that, though, I went down to the water's edge to

Find birding bounty at Lake Wohlford.

try to get closer to a large gathering of water fowl near that eastern end of the lake. I saw more lovely white great egrets than I can recall seeing anywhere else. They were joined on that shore, away from all the people, by great blue herons and many mallard ducks and western grebes.

Ranger Myron Wells told me a bald eagle makes his home year-round at Lake Wohlford, but I didn't see him. Wells thinks the eagle lives in the oaks along the southwestern edge, on the other side of the lake from these main trails. Wells also told me to be on the lookout for the biggest rattlesnake he'd ever seen here, along that Kumeyaay Trail, but I didn't see him either. Just watch where you walk, especially among the rocks; snakes will want to avoid you too.

Retrace your way back, following those red arrows to the main parking area.

Lake Wohlford was Escondido's first reservoir, with the dam completed in 1895. Water was brought to it from the Escondido Canal, which diverted flow from the San Luis Rey River basin. It was originally called the Bear Valley Reservoir, but the name was changed in 1924 to honor Alvin Wohlford, who'd died that year. Wohlford was an engineer who created the water supply system that resulted in the canal and lake. He was also the founder of the Bank of Escondido, and his descendants continue to contribute to Escondido today.

In 1969, the Indian Bands of the San Luis Rey Indian Water Authority, which includes the La Jolla, Pala, Pauma, Rincon, and San Pasqual bands, sued the City of Escondido and the Vista Irrigation District for diverting water from the San Luis Rey River basin. In 1988, the bands negotiated a partial settlement compensation of $30 million through the San Luis Rey Indian Water Rights Settlement Act. However, delivery of water to the reservations remained "caught up in the long delays of trying to resolve the much larger problem of Colorado River water users," says the San Luis Rey Indian Water Authority. It appears a settlement was reached with all parties in December 2014.

Fishing is very popular on Lake Wohlford. It stocks 1,500 pounds of rainbow trout in May and catfish in June and July. Bluegill, largemouth bass, and black crappie are also caught here. You can't bring your own boats here, but you can rent them: rowboats are $17 a day, motor boats are $35 a day, and bass boats are $50 a day. Fishing licenses are required and are available at Smokey's Lake Wohlford Cafe.

Lake Wohlford is open seven days a week from mid-December to the weekend after Labor Day, from 6:00 a.m. to 7:30 p.m. It's open Saturdays and Sundays only from September to mid-December.

Thomas Brothers Map: Page 1110, J-2, where line goes to lake from Lake Wohlford Road.

Before You Go: Download a copy of the trail map for Lake Wohlford from the City of Escondido's website: http://www.escondido.org/Data/Sites/1/media/pdfs/LakeWohlfordFishingMap.pdf.

It's free to park here. This trail is open only to hikers and bicyclists; no dogs are allowed in the park.

For more information, check Lake Wohlford's website: http://www.lakewohlford.com.

Trailhead: From Interstate 15 heading north, exit at Via Rancho Parkway heading east; it becomes Bear Valley Parkway. Turn right onto East Valley Parkway, right onto Lake Wohlford Road, and then right into the lake's parking area.

From Interstate 15 heading south, exit at East Valley Parkway. Go east about eight miles, turn right on Lake Wohlford Road, and then right into the lake's main parking area.

Distance/Difficulty: About 2.85 miles round-trip; easy.

5-20. Kit Carson Trails Lead to Lake and Disc Golf Course

Kit Carson Park is the largest regional park in Escondido with about 285 acres, which include a few miles of trails through natural habitat. Begin walking the unpaved paths (mostly wide dirt roads) that lie straight ahead from the park's main entrance, just beyond its youth baseball and softball fields.

You'll quickly come to Sand Lake, one of three small lakes in the park; the others are Tree Lake and Duck Lake that lie at the western edge. The park has become "a particularly good birding spot in Escondido for wintering birds," says the San Diego Audubon Society. Palomar Audubon Society, based in Escondido, conducts regular bird-watching outings in Kit Carson Park all year round; check its website (http://palomaraudubon.org) for calendar listings.

San Diego Audubon notes that "possible (wintering) species one might see are pine siskin, cedar waxwings, and American goldfinch." When I was there in mid-August, I watched a lovely snowy egret catch some fish in Sand Lake, a great egret fly over it and land near the cattails, and a red-beaked common moorhen ply the waters with an American coot.

Birding, magic, and disc golf are all in Kit Carson Park.

From Sand Lake, the unpaved trail continues to an intersection, where you may go north or south. I headed south as far as it took me, across a foot bridge to Loop Road, which sits very near Westfield Shopping Center. Along that southern trail were a large, marshy area filled with yellow-blooming marsh evening primrose and a small oak grove where limbs leaned over the trail.

Upon reaching that southern end, I turned back until I took the main uphill road to the western edge of the park. This trail reaches the high point a couple of hundred feet in elevation from the start, affording some views across the park to the distant peaks of Poway. The trail then dips farther down toward the west, where a couple of parallel paths carve out another loop.

The park, acquired by Escondido from the City of San Diego in 1967, was named for Christopher (Kit) Carson, the legendary fur-trapper scout who guided Captain John C. Fremont in 1842 from Missouri to Oregon and California. In 1846, Carson led the forces of U.S. General Stephen Kearny from New Mexico into California to fight in the

Mexican-American War's Battle of San Pasqual, which took place just a mile southeast of this park. Carson died at age 59 in 1868 in Taos, New Mexico, where he is buried.

After heading back toward the park and connecting again with that main trail, you reach the Iris Sankey Arboretum with its Queen Califia's Magical Circle Sculpture Garden. The sculpture garden was the last major project created by Niki de Saint Phalle, the French artist whose distinctive, mosaic-covered, whimsical animal forms grace other places in San Diego, including UCSD, where her *Sun God* was commissioned in 1983 for the Stuart Collection, and a few other pieces in front of the Mingei International Museum in Balboa Park. De Saint Phalle lived in La Jolla for the last eight years of her life, which ended here at age 71 in 2002.

Queen Califia's Magical Circle consists of nine mosaic sculptures inspired by the artist's interpretations of early California history, myths, and legends of Native Americans and Mesoamericans, as well as the study of indigenous plants and wildlife, according to Escondido's website on the sculpture garden (http://www.escondido.org/queen-califias-magical-circle.aspx).

The sculpture garden's centerpiece is Queen Califia standing on the back of a five-legged eagle, encircled by eight totemic sculptures, all surrounded by a 400-foot-long snake wall entry maze.

As I was continuing along the main path, I saw families riding bicycles, hikers walking with their dogs, and teams of people playing disc golf. Kit Carson Park has an 18-hole disc golf course that's free to the public and covers a little more than a mile in length. "The first five holes play over rough open space with tight OBs (out-of-bounds markers where penalties apply if disc lands there). The balance of holes meander through a section with a creek, oaks, sycamores and manicured grass," says the DG Course Review website (www.dgcoursereview.com).

"It's actually a very good course, designed by people who are quite good," a couple of players told me. A shop at the park's Sports Center sells and rents the discs used for disc golf, which are a little smaller than a normal Frisbee.

San Diego's first disc golf course is located at Morley Field in Balboa Park. Others are found at the Sun Valley Golf Course in La Mesa; Sunset Park, and Montiel Park in San Marcos; Cal State at San Marcos; Center City Golf Course at Goat Hill in Oceanside; and San Diego Aces Disc Golf Course at Brengle Terrace Park in Vista.

I returned back to Sand Lake at the end of my hike, where I saw that same snowy egret patiently wading for lunch.

Thomas Brothers Map: Page 1150, C-2, Entrance Drive at Mary Lane.

Before You Go: Download a copy of the map of Kit Carson Park at Escondido's park page: http://www.escondido.org/kit-carson-park.aspx.
   The trails are open from sunrise to sunset to hikers, bicyclists, and dogs on leashes.

Trailhead: From Interstate 15, exit at Via Rancho Parkway and head east; the road soon turns into Bear Valley Parkway. At Mary Lane, turn left (west) onto Entrance Drive into Kit Carson Park.

Distance/Difficulty: I went about 3.0 miles total with about 285 feet elevation gain; easy.

6. Central County Foothills

The Central County Foothills areas of Scripps Ranch, Poway, and Ramona are highlighted by the many splendid trails in the San Dieguito River Park, home of the Coast-to-Crest Trail that one day will extend 70 miles from Volcan Mountain near Julian to the beach at Del Mar. Poway is another one of the county's forward-thinking cities that has put an emphasis on trail planning throughout development; even some of its center-city trails are remarkably appealing. Pamo Valley just outside downtown Ramona is one of the county's most scenic areas. From Lake Poway to Bernardo Mountain to Ramona Grasslands, this area may become a nearby favorite.

6-1. Shepherd Canyon Is Easy in-City Trail

For much grander surroundings than the inside of a gym, head to Shepherd Canyon in Tierrasanta for some exercise. Open to hikers, joggers, bicyclists, and dogs on leashes, this fairly flat trail offers just under three miles through open space of sage scrub habitat with lots of lovely old eucalyptus trees. There's even a little pond (actually a reservoir) surrounded by cattails that harbored two pairs of mallard ducks when I was there.

It's part of the Mission Trails Regional Park, according to that park's trail map on its website, and it connects to MTRP's North Perimeter Trail to the northeast and to its Suycott Valley Trail to the southeast.

I remained only in Shepherd Canyon and found it a really lovely foray into nature right in the middle of the city. Although houses rim both sides of the canyon, sometimes you see only the tall trees.

The sign at its trailhead calls it Greenbelt Canyon, and the sign at the pond calls that Dishwasher Pond. But most organizations refer to it as Shepherd (or Shepard) Canyon and Shepherd Pond. The MTRP calls it the Shepherd Pond Loop Trail.

Whatever its real name, it's a wide, unpaved trail through native and nonnative vegetation, including some very tall eucalyptus trees, several old palms, and willows. Some of those eucalyptus trees are

Shepherd Canyon is popular
for walking and jogging.

especially attractive with fairly smooth bark that's mottled with cream and red. The trail is also lined by chaparral broom and the occasional red-berried bush that might be either a lemonadeberry or some type of sumac.

If you happen to see anything metal, don't touch it. This area was once part of Camp Elliott, a marine corps training center for over 40 years. During World War II, Camp Elliott was a major installation for tank and parachute training as well as infantry, scout, mortar, and sniper schooling, according to the Tierrasanta Community Council website (http://www.tierrasantacc.org/history-of-tierrasanta).

On its more than 30,000 acres, Camp Elliott provided three permanent camps, four bivouac areas, 41 combat or firing ranges, and over 75 miles of secondary roadways. Perhaps this trail was once one of those roadways.

In keeping with that military history, you'll surely hear, as I did, the loud roar of the jets from nearby Miramar when you see them soar overhead. Camp Elliott was closed in 1961, but since then, over 5,000 ordnance items (small arms and larger munitions) and nearly 25 tons of ordnance debris have been removed from Tierrasanta and Mission Trails. It's very unlikely that you'll see any such thing, because the areas have been swept many times to clear them from such dangers. The U.S. Army Corps of Engineers continues to monitor these areas at least every five years.

There are several smaller spoke trails off the main trail, but I stayed on that wide path, which was very easy to follow. When I reached the pond, the main trail splits into a V. I took the right path closest to the pond and continued east to the end of this canyon; then I simply turned back and retraced my steps. This end of the trail hits Via Valarta Street, where there is another entry point.

Thomas Brothers Map: Page 1249 H-1—the little Remora Street off Santo Road (just north of Clairemont Mesa Blvd.).

Before You Go: To download a map from the Mission Trails Regional Park website, go to http://www.mtrp.org/aaapopups/trail_maps/new_trail_map.html. The Shepherd Pond Loop Trail is in the West Fortuna section.

This trail allows dogs on leashes, hikers, and bicyclists. It's free.

Trailhead: To reach the trailhead, from Highway 52, exit at Santo Road, heading south. At Remora Street (one block before Clairemont Mesa Blvd.), turn left. Park on Remora and walk a short way north on the sidewalk of Santo Road to the Greenbelt Canyon trailhead. You can also get there by taking Interstate 15, exiting at Clairemont Mesa Blvd. and heading east, then take left on Santo Road and right on Remora.

Distance/Difficulty: About 2.8 miles round-trip. Easy.

6-2. Hike around All of Lake Miramar

A walk or jog or bike ride around Lake Miramar in Scripps Ranch is a very pleasant, easy outing with constant blue-water views. Miramar Reservoir is owned and operated by the City of San Diego's water department, storing some 6,682 acre-feet of water for the northern part of the city. The dam and reservoir were completed in 1960 as part of the second San Diego Aqueduct project that brings water from both the Colorado River and the California Aqueduct.

A paved road goes around the entire lake, and several unpaved portions sit below the road closer to the water. Those unpaved portions don't continue around the entire lake but can make for some fine detours along the shoreline under enormous old eucalyptus trees.

It's an easy walk around all of Lake Miramar.

The community of Scripps Ranch is known for its eucalyptus trees, which were a source of controversy just a few years ago. Some 300 homes in Scripps Ranch were burned in the disastrous 2003 Cedar Fire, still the state's largest wildfire in recorded history. After claims from fire officials that eucalyptus trees might be a fire hazard, the city began cutting down many of the stately specimens in the summer of 2009. The community protested this action, and the city stopped ridding the area of the trees.

A group of concerned residents fought that removal and posted their fact findings on a website, http://scrippscentral.com. Among their claims is that most of Scripps Ranch is forested by red gum eucalyptus, a variety said to burn only under extraordinary heat and wind conditions. Blue gum specimens are sometimes thought to explode in fires, but that type is confined in Scripps Ranch to a single area near Pomerado Road, says the group.

The eucalyptus forest of Scripps Ranch was originally planted in 1909 by E. W. Scripps, the community's namesake. E. W. (1854–1926) had worked with his older half-brother, James, when he founded *The Detroit News* in 1873. E. W.'s half-sister, 18 years his senior, was Ellen Browning Scripps (1836–1932), who also had worked with brother James at *The Detroit News*. After splitting with James, E. W. and Ellen formed their own newspaper publishing company that eventually counted 35 daily newspapers in the Scripps-Howard company.

E. W. and Ellen first came to San Diego in 1890 after visiting a sister, Annie, in Alameda, California, and another brother, Fred. Annie and Fred had come to California in search of cures for their aching joints, possibly from rheumatic arthritis, according to the San Diego History Center's article by Molly McClain about the Scripps Family in San Diego. E. W. and Ellen liked the climate and the potential for San Diego growth, and so they settled here then. They first bought 400 acres in what is now Scripps Ranch, and eventually they added more land that totaled around 2,000 acres in the area.

In 1891, E. W. and his brothers Fred and Will, along with Ellen, began building a ranch house on the property overlooking the Linda Vista mesa. They named it Miramar ("sea view" in Spanish), a rancho-style home with four one-story wings around a central courtyard. "By the time the house was completed in 1898, it had 49 rooms—most with their own fireplace—running water and a telephone line," wrote McClain. Miramar was also a "utopian experiment" where several family members and their spouses and children would have spaces of their own.

Ellen, who never married, moved in 1895 to La Jolla, where she built a home on the seaside designed by Irving Gill that eventually became the site of the Museum of Contemporary Art San Diego. Ellen also became a well-known philanthropist here, donating land for Torrey Pines State Natural Reserve as well as Scripps Park in downtown La Jolla, founding Scripps Institution of Oceanography, the Bishop's School, and Scripps Memorial Hospital, and supporting many other organizations, including Balboa Park, La Jolla Woman's Club, and others.

Miramar, that enormous ranch house built by the Scripps family, was demolished in 1973. The name remains at the reservoir that locals and visitors alike enjoy.

The trail around the lake is marked by quarter-mile posts. You'll pass by other markers that note the names of the fingers of the lake—San Diego Arm, Escondido Arm, Poway Arm, and Penaquitos Arm, along with other spots including Elliot Cove, Starvation Cove, Miramar Point, and Woodson Point. There are 18 barbecues and 48 picnic tables spread around the lake.

At Natalie Park, on the opposite side of the lake from its main entrance, a short nature trail follows the paved road on its uphill side. Boats can be launched here and are also rented at the main concession stand at the entrance. Fishing for largemouth bass, bluegill, catfish, and sunfish is popular. Naturally, the lake is awash with birds, including cormorants and ducks like mallards, gadwalls, and northern shovelers. The ones I really enjoyed viewing when I was there were a family of geese, domestic swan geese, or perhaps Chinese geese, a breed descended from the wild swan goose. Whatever their name, these geese floated together as a family of five, led by their fully white, orange-billed leader; the rest were brown-bodied, sporting large black knobs on the upper part of their black bills.

Thomas Brothers Map: Page 1209, G-4, where Miramar Reservoir Road intersects at lake.

Before You Go: Visit the city's website for Miramar Reservoir: http://www.sandiego.gov/water/recreation/reservoirs/miramar.shtml.

The path around the lake is open to hikers, bicyclists, strollers, and dogs on leashes.

You may download a copy of the map of the lake from http://fishingnetwork.net/socal/images/miramar2.gif.

Trailhead: From Interstate 15, exit at Mira Mesa Boulevard and head east. Turn right onto Scripps Ranch Boulevard and then left on Scripps Lake Drive. The entrance to the reservoir parking area will be on your left.

Distance/Difficulty: The entire loop around the lake is 4.92 miles. Very easy.

6-3. Poway's First Cardio Hike Is Del Poniente Trail

Poway's Del Poniente Trail winds through suburbia but feels wilder than you might imagine. As it heads toward the west, its environment becomes increasingly more natural amid lots of open space. The trail starts off Del Poniente Road and heads north for just a quarter-mile. Then it turns west and goes almost straight for a couple of miles until it reaches the Pomerado Trail and Pomerado Road.

At about a half-mile, the trail intersects with the north-south Avocado Trail. If you head south on the Avocado Trail, you will soon reach the Twin Peaks Trail. Head

All users welcome on Poway's Del Poniente Trail.

north, and in one mile you'll hit Lake Poway Road. This intersection on the Del Poniente Trail is marked with a big directional sign.

Poway has some 65 miles of city-maintained trails that are generally open to hikers, bikers, equestrians, and dogs on leashes, all of which are welcome on the Del Poniente Trail.

Del Poniente translates from Spanish to mean roughly "of the west," which fits because the trail heads directly west. Bookending the trail are views to the east of Mount Woodson and views to the west of Black Mountain. The trail has several short, steep stretches, so it offers a workout.

In fact, the Del Poniente Trail is home to Poway's first official "cardio hike." Covering two miles along the Del Poniente Trail and part of the Pomerado Trail, the cardio hike sports markers every quarter-mile. Volunteers from Poway's Temple Adat Shalom installed all these mile markers. The cardio hike is two miles one-way, for a four-mile round-trip.

"From Marker 1 (about 200 feet east on the Pomerado Trail just southeast of the intersection of Pomerado Road and Bernardo Heights Parkway), you will continue east, then southeast along the Pomerado Trail," reports *Poway Today,* a quarterly municipal newsletter for Poway residents. "The first mile of the hike consists of mild changes in elevation as the trail meanders smoothly along the base of the foothills to the southeast, then transitions to a much more aggressive climb to the east as you begin mile number two. The second half of your second mile rewards you with a series of gentler ups and downs."

I started from the opposite direction and saw the two-mile cardio hike marker (its eastern end) at about three-quarters of a mile from my east-end start. This eastern end of the Cardio Hike lies near the intersection of Midland Road and El Camino Entrada in a private gated community.

The Del Poniente Trail passes by some backyards, but the trail itself is surprisingly wild and quite pleasing. It passes under some old eucalyptus groves with very tall trees, crosses a stream that is diverted underneath it, and after a little more than a mile, heads into truly undeveloped open space when you begin to see those views of Black Mountain and its communication towers almost directly to the west. There are even a handful of rope swings under an old pepper tree next to a picnic table on this trail. There's really only one specimen oak tree on this trail in that open space, but you'll see lots of laurel sumac whose bright green leaves are shaped like taco shells and many white sage bushes that waft their lovely fragrance in the air.

You'll see Pomerado Hospital when you reach the end of the Del Poniente Trail at Pomerado Trail. I turned around and retraced my way back from here.

At a high point of elevation in that wilderness section, you can see hikers on Twin Peaks Trail when you look to the south. I watched a big black turkey vulture soar above me here and saw several white-crowned sparrows with pinkish-orange bills. I was especially enamored by a yellow-rumped warbler with its bright yellow throat and flanks, who posed for me on a fencepost.

Heading back east, those views of 2,894-foot-high Mount Woodson in all its rocky glory were on view. That horizon reveals the peaks from Mount Woodson to 2,696-foot-high Iron Mountain to its south.

The trail heads almost in a straight line for most of the way, and you can also get fine views of your path. I thought this was a surprisingly sweet suburban trail with real touches of wilderness, and I found the workout a worthy bonus for my heart, just like those mile markers say.

Thomas Brothers Map: Page 1170, G-7, Del Poniente Road at Crestview Court.

Before You Go: Download a copy of the trail map at the City of Poway's website on trails and hiking: http://poway.org/502/Trails-Hiking.

The Del Poniente Trail is No. 8 on the Poway trails map. It is open to hikers, bicyclists, equestrians, and dogs on leashes.

Trailhead: Heading north on Interstate 15, exit at the Ted Williams Parkway, and head east. Turn right (east) on Twin Peaks Road, left (north) on Espola Road, and then left (west) on Del Poniente Road. Go just a short distance to the trailhead, which is on the north side of the road just before Crestview Court.

Heading south on Interstate 15, exit at Rancho Bernardo Road, which turns into Espola in Poway. Turn right (west) onto Del Poniente Road and follow directions above.

Distance/Difficulty: This trail is about 2.06 miles long, for about a 4.12 mile round-trip. Elevation gain is about 700 feet. Moderate.

6-4. Garden Road Trail and Coyotes in "City in Country"

Poway's Garden Road Trail is an easy meander through dry creek beds filled with sycamores in this "city in the country." The trail begins along Garden Road itself, just past Sycamore Valley Road. Soon the trail heads north into that creek bed area, behind the few homes in this neighborhood.

When you reach the junction of Garden Road and Quiet Valley Lane, cross the street to continue on the path that sits right next to the road. You'll pass the small Sycamore Creek B Park as the trail continues east along Quiet Valley Lane. At the end of the cul-de-sac, the trail heads into the wilderness along Poway Creek, which is totally dry during this drought.

At this point on the trail, still in a suburb but heading toward open space, I saw a small coyote ahead of me. He didn't see me and kept walking on the trail until he turned into the brush.

Find a quiet trail into backcountry at Garden Road.

I wondered how this drought was affecting this skinny creature, who was probably searching for water. News reports throughout Southern California in 2014 have cited the drought as a reason coyotes and other wild animals are venturing closer into human territories. Valuable tips on coexisting with these wild animals are easily found from Project Coyote (www.projectcoyote.org), as well as the Humane Society of the United States (www.humanesociety.org/animals/coyotes). Project Coyote started 14 years ago in Marin County to teach us how to coexist with wild animals. "They have not only shown it can be done, they have proven we have much to gain by doing so," said the EcoReport on a public radio broadcast in August 2014.

"Humans and coyotes need to learn to live together," said Gina Farr of Project Coyote. The animals are not very big—18 to 35 pounds, typically—and can be trained to avoid humans and their homes.

Both Project Coyote and the Humane Society of the United States recommend "coyote hazing," which calls for scaring coyotes off so they learn to avoid people. Hazing consists of using deterrents such as noisemakers (even pots and pans), small projectiles, or a hose to move the coyote out of a specific area, including your yard. If you do encounter a coyote, make eye contact, stand your ground, and advance toward the coyote with your hazing tools or anything to make you appear as big and noisy as possible. Don't stop until the coyote is gone.

Teaching coyotes to avoid us is more effective than trying to eliminate them, both organizations say. "You kill the stable resident population, and transients come into the new territory where they don't know to stay away from people," Farr said.

Other tips include keeping your pets indoors, especially at night when coyotes are more active, but anytime they are around; feeding your pets indoors only; and maintaining fencing that's over six feet high and ideally solid with no visibility to inside. Bury the fence six to 12 inches underground to prevent coyotes from digging underneath. Coyote rollers and wire extensions on top of fencing can also discourage them from jumping into your yard.

I saw only that one coyote as I continued along this lovely, easy trail.

Lots of sycamores and coast live oaks, native trees, line some of these dry creek beds. Views extend to the east into the wilderness that lies along the ridges and canyons between Poway and Ramona.

The trail, open to hikers, bicyclists, equestrians, and dogs on leashes (especially with coyotes around) is well groomed in the beginning and quite wide. As it heads into the undeveloped areas, it narrows considerably. After about a mile, the trail starts to climb some very rocky, very steep ridges. At that point in the summer heat, I turned around and headed back.

From the trail's high points, you can see far to the west into the neighborhoods of Poway. The sycamores, which give many areas in Poway their names, are turning orange and gold in late August as they lose their leaves for winter. Also revealed then are lots of their round, spiky seed balls, which give the trees their nickname "buttonball tree."

This trail, according to a sign at the trailhead, is adopted by the McNelly family. Poway invites volunteers to keep trails safe and clean, matching people with trails or parts of trails. For more information on the Adopt-a-Trail program, go to Poway's trail pages.

Thomas Brothers Map: Page 1191, A-4.

Before You Go: Download a copy of the Garden Road Trail map from Poway's trail pages: http://poway.org/502/Trails-Hiking. The Garden Road Trail is No. 26 on Poway's main trail map. This trail is open to hikers, bicyclists, equestrians, and dogs on leashes.

Trailhead: From Interstate 15, exit at Poway Road. Turn right onto Garden Road and head east. Park along Garden Road near Sycamore Valley Road, where you see the trail heading north from the road.

Distance/Difficulty: The trail goes for at least 1.0 mile for a 2.0-mile round trip, unless you explore the narrowing path farther. Easy.

6-5. Poway Trail Now Links Major County Trails

The Old Coach Trail in Poway marks a recent milestone in the county's trail map. In early October 2011, a final half-mile of that trail was created to link it with the San Dieguito River Park's San Pasqual Valley Trail, part of that park's Coast-to-Crest Trail. The extensive trail system in the City of Poway also now links the Old Coach Trail to the Trans County Trail that currently runs east-west through south Poway.

The new link means that the 45 continuous existing miles of the Coast-to-Crest Trail can now be linked to the 14 existing miles of the Trans County Trail through about eight miles of the Poway Trail system. Poway alone currently has about 65 miles on 32 trails throughout its city, some more urban than others.

Old Coach Trail now connects to San Dieguito River Park.

The Old Coach Trail winds through some rural backcountry, though it occasionally skirts some housing neighborhoods and follows the southern edge of the Maderas Golf Club, one of the county's leading public golf courses where local residents get special rates. But mostly, this trail follows an old dirt road and single-track dirt trails that wind up and down some hills, dipping into some old-oak riparian stream beds and offering some fine backcountry views from those elevation gains.

I began the hike from the southern staging area in Poway for the Old Coach Trail. Off Old Coach Road, where there is no parking at all, the staging area is the only place you can park to reach the southern trailhead. From that parking area, I walked a short way down along the west side of the street, crossing to the east side to begin on Justin's Trail. Justin's Trail follows Old Coach Road along its east side.

Naturally enough, Old Coach Road was once the old stage coach route that went from Poway to Escondido. Stage coaches first began carrying mail, money, and passengers in San Diego in 1852, and they were important vehicles until the railroad came here in 1882. Stagecoaches eventually lost out not so much to the railroad but to automobiles and buses by the early 20th century.

At 0.6 miles on Justin's Trail, Old Coach Trail itself begins on the other side of Old Coach Road. A trail signpost points to the left, and though "Justin's Trail" is still on that post, the "Old Coach Trail" sign is missing. You'll note a "Pedestrians Use Trail" sign at the juncture, and across the street another sign, "Old Coach Trail Entrance."

After skirting the edge of a neighborhood, the trail follows an old dirt road along a riparian stream bed of Sycamore Creek. Some of Poway's oldest oaks, the city says, are along the Old Coach Trail.

Past the 0.5 mile marker for the Old Coach Trail, it climbs up and down, winding through another of those splendid old oak groves. Here's where things can get a bit tricky. Near the end of that oak grove, the trail splits. On the right is a sign noting a bridge is out and is scheduled for reconstruction. On the left, the trail jumps across a small creek crossing and continues uphill to a ridge that at the top skirts several houses.

This junction isn't marked currently, but I believe the main Old Coach Trail continues to the right where that bridge is out. It climbs up the ridge for another few miles to reach the new half-mile link to the Coast-to-Crest Trail.

I took the left at this junction, which I believe is the Lomas Verde Trail in Poway's trail system. Again, there were no signposts to tell me, but the Google maps offered on Poway's website for its trails confirmed that was what I took.

I wound up that ridge and at the top went to the right, following the trail for another half-mile or so, where I enjoyed wide views over the backcountry, that golf course, and even the Old Coach Trail itself. After having gone about two miles total, I chose to turn around and retrace my way for a four-mile round-trip hike that had plenty of ups and downs for me.

Poway doesn't give mileages for its individual trails, but I think the whole Old Coach Trail is about four miles long one-way.

Thomas Brothers Map: Page 1170, F-2, just past Butterfield Trail on Old Coach Road.

Before You Go: Download a map of Old Coach Trail as well as Lomas Verde Trail from Poway's website for its trail system: http://poway.org/502/Trails-Hiking.

Old Coach Trail is No. 1 on Poway's main trail map. It's open to hikers, bicyclists, equestrians, and dogs on leashes.

Go to San Dieguito River Park's page, http://www.sdrp.org/projects/Heritage/Oldcoach detail3.pdf, for a map of the new link to its Coast-to-Crest Trail. If you want to reach the new northern staging area of the Old Coast Trail near that link; it's at 12460 Highland Valley Road near the Evergreen Nursery in Escondido.

Trailhead: To reach the southern staging parking area for Old Coach Trail, from Interstate 15, exit at Rancho Bernardo Road heading east. That road turns into Espola Road once you reach Poway city limits. Turn left onto Old Coach Road, and just past Butterfield Trail, the staging area is on the left. Cross the road to find Justin's Trail; cross the road again after 0.6 miles to begin Old Coach Trail.

Distance/Difficulty: From 4.0 to 8.0 miles round-trip; moderately strenuous.

6-6. South Poway Trail Part of Trans-County Trail

The South Poway Trail climbs over the undeveloped ridge of Poway between Scripps Poway Parkway and Poway Road. The main section from Pomerado Road to Sycamore Canyon Road covers about five miles one-way.

The views from this ridge extend from the Pacific Ocean to Mount Woodson and the other rocky peaks that rise to the east of Poway. At its highest point of nearly 800 feet in elevation, the trail has a good view of the ocean on a really clear day.

The best place to access this trail is its equestrian staging area off Metate Lane, just a quarter mile west from Community Road. There is ample, easy parking here.

The trail climbs up the ridge and soon reaches a T intersection. I went to the right (west) to see if those ocean views got better. If you don't plan to hike the entire length of this trail, I'd recommend going to the left here (east), where the views are actually more interesting.

South Poway Trail traverses suburban ridges.

As I hiked toward the ocean, the trail climbs up and down the ridge, crossing some small riparian stream pockets. At the first of these, I spotted an impressive roadrunner, its crested head highlighted by a small red patch behind its eye.

The greater roadrunner gets its name because it really runs on the road; it needs open ground for running to capture its favorite food of lizards and snakes. "The greater roadrunner is one of the only animals known to attack rattlesnakes," says *The Sibley Field Guide to Birds of Western North America*. "Pairs sometimes hunt rattlesnakes cooperatively; one bird distracts the snake while the other sneaks up and pins its head. They then kill the snake by bashing its head against a rock." I didn't see any of that action, but the big bird did run right into the stream's willow thicket.

The trail climbs up and down as it continues west toward Pomerado Road. Although houses are never far from view, the ridge remains in a natural state—very dry chaparral in autumn with no trees for any kind of shade. The one high point in flora were the toyon, sometimes called Christmas berry because its bright red berries appear in fall and winter.

There are some additional trails carved through this area, but I generally kept to the main, wide trail, which is open to mountain bikers, equestrians, and dogs on leashes. The map I had with me seemed to show the trail ending at Pomerado Road, so I turned around when I reached it, which was about 1.3 miles from the trailhead. But the City of Poway's trail map shows the South Poway Trail continuing another 2.0 to 3.0 miles west of Pomerado, following Poway Creek.

I headed back, and when I reached my original starting point at that T intersection, I pressed ahead farther east for another three-quarters of a mile or so. The communication towers of Mount Woodson are distinctive, as are all the other rocky peaks (including Iron Mountain) that rise above Poway toward Ramona.

At the crest of the ridge—the highest point of nearly 800 feet—as you survey the terrain from mountains to the sea and look down on a lot of the trail itself, know that you are also on the Trans-County Trail. Also known as the Pines to Spines Trail, it will be about 110 miles long when eventually completed, from the pines of Torrey Pines State Reserve to the spines of Anza-Borrego Desert State Park. According to the San Diego Natural History Museum, which posts a map of the entire trail incorporating existing trails (http://www.sdnhm.org/archive/fieldguide/places/index.html), some 70 percent of it is now open to public use. "In other areas, the route still needs to be acquired or the trail built; in those places the trail is not yet open," it says. Check out the museum's report of a 1998 "Spines to Pines" expedition that was "the first ever to follow the 114-mile route of the Trans-County Trail," even though all of it is not yet completed.

The City of Poway's trail system, an integral portion of the Trans-County Trail, consists of more than 65 miles of trails so far, with another 15 miles or so planned. Its trail guide lists 30 trails and grades them for difficulty. A true highlight for me on the South Poway Trail was a close-up view of a northern harrier perched on one of the wooden fence posts that line some of the trail. When I got really close to it, it took off, soaring above the dry terrain with its head down, hard at work to find lunch. It was a rare sight to be above the bird of prey while it was hunting, adding excitement to another fine hike.

Thomas Brothers Map: Page 1190, 5-E, just 0.25 mile west of Community Road on Metate Lane.

Before You Go: Download a copy of the South Poway Trail map at the City of Poway's trails website: http://poway.org/502/Trails-Hiking.

The South Poway Trail is No. 28 on Poway's main trails map. It is open to hikers, bicyclists, equestrians, and dogs on leashes.

Trailhead: From Interstate 15, exit at either Poway Road or Scripps Poway Parkway. From Poway Road, turn south onto Community Road; from Scripps Poway Parkway, turn north onto Community Road. From Community Road, turn west onto Metate Lane and go about 0.25 miles; park in the South Poway Trail staging area.

Distance/Difficulty: My total mileage on this trail was 3.65 miles with an elevation gain of nearly 700 feet; easy to moderate.

6-7. In Search of a Trail and Other Hazards

Rattlesnake Canyon in Poway features a riparian habitat along Rattlesnake Creek, where oaks and sycamores spread some lovely shade. It's a surprisingly pristine canyon near populated Poway, where you may really feel away from it all. A highlight of this hike near the tree-shaded creek is a mortero, one of those deep holes pounded by the Kumeyaay, who ground acorns here hundreds of years ago.

Look for this mortero about a half-mile from the start of the main trail off to its right (south). It's just a single deep, round hole in a single large, granite boulder, but such a find reminds us of life here among local native people who thrived for thousands of years before the European settlers changed the region in the late 1700s.

Poway was known in Kumeyaay as Pauwai, which means "meeting of the creeks" — Poway Creek and Rattlesnake Creek — according to history records at the Kumeyaay-Ipai Interpretive Center in Poway.

During some years, Rattlesnake Canyon is also the site of splendid wildflower shows, but not so much during years of drought.

Rattlesnake Canyon leaves suburbia for backcountry.

Orange California poppies, our state flower, and purple lupine can be especially plentiful here after winter rains. These blooms also appear after wildfires, which occurred in this canyon both in 2003 during the Cedar Fire and in 2007 during the Witch Fire. "One of the most amazing phenomena in nature's remarkable recovery from fire is the brilliant display of wildflowers that appears with the onset of winter and spring rains," writes Wayne Armstrong, a longtime life sciences professor at Palomar College who posts an extensive website on local natural history (http://waynesword.palomar.edu/index.htm). "Seeds of some wildflowers may lie dormant for decades, and then germinate by the millions following fire," he writes. "The developing wildflowers thrive in the ash."

Fire-following wildflowers usually disappear after a few years following a fire, however, because the native plants of chaparral and sage scrub take over.

On Rattlesnake Canyon Trail in a recent spring, I saw only a single patch of a few orange California poppies next to a scattering of purple phacelia and some white wild radish blooms. But back in a big way after the fires are the fragrant California sagebrush (artemesia californica) and white sage (salvia apiana), two characteristic plants of coastal sage scrub. These sages were known as "cowboy cologne," according to Friends of Rattlesnake Canyon.

Also characteristic of this part of our county are lots of boulders dotting the landscape. Rattlesnakes like to hang around boulders because they can provide cover. I didn't see any rattlesnakes on this trail, but I did think about them, especially when I lost the trail.

I believed I was following directions given by the lamentably late, great Jerry Schad from his 2009 column on Rattlesnake Canyon in the *San Diego Reader*. I also had trail maps with me. But at one intersection or another, I took a wrong turn and kept going. I ended high up in the wilderness of this area with no trail in sight. I wasn't really in danger of being lost, because Poway Road was still visible up on the ridge. But I was not really comfortable bushwhacking my way around these boulders in search of a trail.

After studying my GPS unit's map of where I hiked, I went east along the Middle Fork of the creek, which is noted on Poway's Rattlesnake Canyon Trail. That trail eventually just ends. Eventually I had to turn back and head toward trails I could see far down below. There were a few very steep, rocky spots that had me scrambling backward or sliding down on my bottom, and those thoughts of rattlesnakes were ever-present.

So what if you find yourself in such a situation? Friends of Yosemite Search and Rescue offers lots of hiking safety tips at http://www.friendsofyosar.org/safety/hikingSafety.html. Some valuable ones include telling someone where you are going so they know if you don't return. Also, bring essential safety gear, including a whistle, plenty of water, a flashlight, extra clothing, a compass, and a cell phone. However, don't count on cell phone coverage everywhere.

California Parks also offers important hiking safety tips (http://www.parks.ca.gov/pages/23997/files/2008_CampingandHiking_Tips.pdf), as does the National Park Service (http://www.nps.gov/isro/planyourvisit/upload/Safety%20Tips%20for%20Hiking-2.pdf).

For example, step over wet logs or tree roots, which can often be slippery (but see note below about logs). If falling, try to avoid landing on your hands, elbows, or knees; landing on the side of your body is much safer. Sometimes you can stop the slide with a hiking stick.

As for those rattlesnakes, here's good advice from the Blue Sky Ecological Reserve, also in Poway: http://www.blueskyreserve.org/snakes.html. "Never reach under rocks or logs. If there is a fallen log on the trail, always look over the other side. Step way out and over as a snake may be lying on the other side."

Wear long pants, long sleeves, and sturdy hiking shoes.

"If you do come upon a snake, take two giant steps backwards … then give it a very wide berth and move on."

If you do happen to get bitten, use your cell phone if possible to summon help. If you must hike out, do so fairly calmly and slowly, reaching the nearest hospital as soon as possible. Never apply a tourniquet or ice to the wound, and do not attempt to cut the wound or suck out the venom.

"Rattlesnakes are quite shy and do not come after people," says the San Diego Natural History Museum in its fact sheet about rattlesnakes (http://www.sdnhm.org/archive/research/herpetology/resources4b.html). "They will strike only in self-defense." The more you know about them, the better equipped you are on the trails here. I like to stay on obvious trails for obvious reasons.

I eventually found the trail here again; no harm done. But I'll leave the bushwhacking to others.

Thomas Brothers Map: Page 1190, H-2, where Rattlesnake Creek crosses Range Park Road.

Before You Go: Download a copy of the Rattlesnake Canyon Trail map from Poway's trail pages: http://poway.org/502/Trails-Hiking.

Rattlesnake Canyon Trail is No. 21 on Poway's main trails map. It is open to hikers, bicyclists, equestrians, and dogs on leashes.

Trailhead: From Interstate 15 heading south, exit at Camino del Norte. From Interstate 15 heading north, exit at Ted Williams Parkway, and head east from either exit. At Twin Peaks Road, turn and continue heading east. Past Espola Road, near the end of Twin Peaks Road, turn right (south) onto Range Park Road and go a short way until you see the trail entrance on the left (east) of the road. Park on the road.

Distance/Difficulty: I ended up heading east through Rattlesnake Canyon on what the map calls Middle Fork. I hiked a total of about 3.5 miles, and it was moderately strenuous.

6-8. Poway's Twin Peaks Trail Offers Views on High

The Twin Peaks Trail in Poway is a classic trail in that "City in the Country." It winds through suburban neighborhoods as well as open spaces, and it affords long views to Mount Woodson and Iron Mountain in the east and Bernardo Mountain in the west, as well as Poway spread out below.

Begin hiking this trail off Tierra Bonita Road, where you'll walk above the adjacent athletic fields of Twin Peaks Middle School. For the first mile or so, you'll be winding past the backsides of suburban homes, as the unpaved trail climbs up and down along the route of power lines. There are several steep sections along this trail open to hikers, bikers, equestrians, and dogs on leashes. Some gravelly parts can make the steepness a bit slippery, but they tend to flatten out quickly enough so there are plenty of respites.

There are several trail intersections along the way as well, but if you follow the directional arrows as I did, you can easily stick to the main path with no fear of getting lost.

After that first mile or so when you head into that pristine open space, you might start noticing red-tailed hawks soaring above the landscape.

Twin Peaks Trail fits "City in Country."

This mix of country in the city is a hallmark of Poway. Ever since it became a city in 1980, one of its primary goals has been to retain the country lifestyle known to generations of Poway residents, reports *Poway Today*, a city newsletter. "All elements of the General Plan reinforce a single basic philosophy that Poway should retain its rural atmosphere," it said in its winter 2005 edition.

In addition to the rules of its General Plan, Poway has made a concerted effort to preserve important "heritage lands" throughout the city, maintaining them in their natural state and acquiring them when possible. One of those purchases in 2005 was the 40-acre parcel making up the top of Twin Peaks, a 1,308-foot-high promontory that has become a city landmark. The hillsides, ridgetops, and mountains of Poway (including Mount Woodson and Iron Mountain) are integral to Poway's views, which from some of these high points can extend all the way to the ocean.

I couldn't see the ocean the day I hiked Twin Peaks Trail, but it might be possible on the clearest days to see just a peek of the Pacific from here.

As the trail winds uphill toward the top, you will encounter intersections with other trails that likely lead to some of the same destinations or to other trail entry points. Download a Google satellite map if you want to see where they all go.

I followed the arrows pointing the way along the main trail, and when I reached the end at Sagecrest Drive, a bit more than two miles from Tierra Bonita, I turned around and followed the same arrows back.

Like many of Poway's trails, Twin Peaks Trail also connects with other bona fide Poway trails, so you could extend this hike a lot farther.

When I neared my starting point, about a third of a mile from Tierra Bonita Road, I hiked up the Avocado Trail for a short ways. On the Twin Peaks Trail, there is a post marker pointing to the Avocado Trail, where you turn north to join it. The Avocado Trail extends all the way to the junction of Lake Poway Road and Espola Road for probably a bit more than two miles, but I went just a short way through some very pretty groves of old eucalyptus trees.

At my beginning at Tierra Bonita Road, I also continued a bit farther on the Tierra Bonita Trail, which begins immediately opposite the trailhead for Twin Peaks Trail. You could make an additional loop here, combining the Tierra Bonita Trail heading east from Tierra Bonita Road for a short way until it turns north and then west on Del Poniente Road. It intersects with the Avocado Trail there, where you could head south to its intersection with Twin Peaks Trail. Check the Poway trails map to see this route.

This time I stuck to the main Twin Peaks Trail, enjoying the views as well as the climbs in this "City in the Country."

"Poway is a city where you can look all around and see beautiful hills, unscarred mountains and native open spaces that are not covered with homes and developments," said *Poway Today*. "These open spaces are something to preserve and pass on to future generations of Powegians."

Thomas Brothers Map: Page 1190, G-1, Twin Peaks Road at Tierra Bonita Road.

Before You Go: Download a map of Twin Peaks Trail from Poway's trails pages: http://poway. org/502/Trails-Hiking. Twin Peaks Trail is No. 23 on Poway's main trails map. This trail is open to hikers, bicyclists, equestrians, and dogs on leashes.

Trailhead: From Interstate 15 heading south, exit at Camino del Norte; from Interstate 15 heading north, exit at Ted Williams Parkway, and head east from either exit. At their junctions with Twin Peaks Road, head east on Twin Peaks Road. At Tierra Bonita Road, turn left (north). You'll see the Twin Peaks trailhead on the left (west) side of the road, just beyond the middle school. Park on the street near the trailhead.

Distance/Difficulty: I went a total of about 5.0 miles round-trip; moderately strenuous.

6-9. Blue Sky Reserve Is County Microcosm

Blue Sky Ecological Reserve in Poway offers one of the county's best hiking destinations because four native habitats coexist here.

- Chaparral, also called The Elfin Forest, a hot, dry environment. Plants have thick leaves to minimize water loss, and animals have thick fur to protect them from rough undergrowth.
- Coastal Sage Scrub (a.k.a. the Scented Forest), featuring low-growing, aromatic shrubs including white sage, buckwheat, and laurel sumac.
- Riparian, a canyon oasis that centers on a creek, where sycamores, willows, and cottonwoods give shade to wild roses and poison oak as well as wildlife.
- Oak Woodlands, just away from the water source, where magnificent live oaks spread their mighty branches between the riparian corridor and the chaparral.

Each of these habitats has its own beauty, and when you toss in the elevation gains heading to both the Lake Poway and Lake Ramona dams, you find wonderful views, grand boulderscapes, and notable quiet.

Views, habitats, and lakes are draws in Blue Sky.

The trail begins on the Green Valley Truck Trail, a wide, unpaved road where only official vehicles are allowed. This road continues for 0.9 miles to the first turnoff, and it is popular for equestrians as well as hikers with their dogs on leashes. No bikes are allowed in the preserve.

About a quarter-mile from the trailhead, a smaller, narrower trail heads left into an oak grove along the creek, aptly named Oak Grove and Creekside Trail. This trail meanders along the creek through the black-limbed oaks and white-trunked sycamores for about a half-mile, and then it connects again to the main Green Valley Truck Trail. No horses or dogs are allowed on the Creekside Trail, which protects the wildlife while also protecting your pets, because there are thickets of poison oak along this trail. Stick to the trail and learn how to identify poison oak so you can avoid it: "Leaves of three, leave it be."

At 0.9 miles from the trailhead, a main fork heads right to the Lake Poway Trail, and in about 1.3 miles you will reach the lake. If you were to go straight instead of taking that right turn to the Lake Poway Trail, you would head toward Lake Ramona, a steeper climb to that lake in about 1.4 miles.

I took the right turn to Lake Poway, passed a campground, and then began the switchback climb toward the dam that created Lake Poway. Once you reach the top of the dam, you can access more trails around Lake Poway itself, including a trail up Mount Woodson. This trail up to Lake Poway is much narrower and steeper than the Green Valley Truck Trail, so you won't see any vehicles. Be sure to take plenty of water because it can be very hot and dry here as you enter that chaparral.

The reserve was saved from development in the early 1990s, and now the 700-acre canyon is managed by the City of Poway, the California Department of Fish and Game, and the County of San Diego's Department of Parks and Recreation.

Docent-led hikes take place just about every weekend and meet at the south end of the parking lot; they're free and no reservations are required. Check Friends of Blue Sky website for details: www.blueskyreserve.org. You'll also find some interesting articles on these pages, including one by noted San Diego birding expert Claude G. Edwards, "Hiding in Plain View, Our Chaparral Birds." Edwards notes that "chaparral is often subtle and understated," and the same can be said for birds that live in chaparral. "Most of the year, such (chaparral) plants as wild lilacs, scrub oaks, manzanitas and chamise maintain the same appearance, not wilting or losing foliage when it is hot and dry," he says.

Several species of birds that live in Blue Sky Canyon also share "generally somber coloration. Most of them wear shades of brown. Some are patterned with combinations of black, gray, rust, white or olive. Such qualities help these birds blend into their surroundings." Typical chaparral-dwelling birds include the California quail, Bewick's wren, California towhee, wrentit, and California thrasher, all "generally grayish brown." You can learn to identify them by their sizes and shapes, their bills, and their calls and voices.

Edwards says the California thrasher's downward-curving beak allows it to toss around dry leaves, for example, whereas the short-beaked towhee uses its feet to do this.

California quails have a perky crest of crown feathers, and males have a very black throat bordered by white. "They often give a three-part song that goes something like 'chi-CA-go' or 'mu-CHA-cho,'" writes Edwards.

You can become a docent here. Training includes two Wednesday evening sessions and seven Saturday mornings over a three-month period. Blue Sky also has its own tracking team with members learning the skill through the San Diego Tracking Team.

Thomas Brothers Map: Page 33, B-2.

Before You Go: No bikes, but horses and dogs on leashes are allowed. Entrance is free.

To download a copy of the trail map or for more information, go to the Friends of Blue Sky's website: www.blueskyreserve.org.

Poway also has a website on Blue Sky (http://poway.org/337/Blue-Sky-Ecological-Reserve), including lists of mammals, birds, and plants seen here.

The state department of fish and game also has a page dedicated to Blue Sky: https://www.wildlife.ca.gov/Lands/Places-to-Visit/Blue-Sky-ER.

Trailhead: From Interstate 15, exit at Rancho Bernardo Road and head east for 1.6 miles, where it becomes Espola Road in Poway. Continue east on Espola Road for about 1.7 miles. Where Espola Road starts curving south, look for the reserve's parking entry on east side of road.

Distance/Difficulty: The trail up to Lake Poway is about 4.4 miles round-trip; moderate.

6-10. Ramona Dam Hike Can Be Easy or Strenuous

The hike to Ramona Dam in Poway's Blue Sky Ecological Reserve has two distinct parts that offer some options. The first mile or so meanders on a fairly flat, old dirt road through some lovely old oak groves. The second mile or so climbs above those riparian creekside and oak woodland habitats in a steady ascent of nearly 800 feet to reach Lake Ramona, where views stretch back to Lake Poway, Mount Woodson, and distant layers of hills. If you seek an easy stroll through a fine forest of live oaks, cover just that first level mile and return for a two-mile round-trip. For a heartier workout, go the distance where that blue-water Lake Ramona is a rewarding sight in itself.

Hundreds of coast live oaks live in Blue Sky Ecological Reserve. They can live to be 200 years or more, and they provide homes in their hollows for owls and squirrels and acorns to feed orioles and woodpeckers.

Ramona Dam rewards with lake views.

Those acorns were also consumed by the local Kumeyaay-Ipai people, who lived here for at least 1,000 years before the turn of the 20th century, when their hunter-gatherer community began assimilation into the settlers' culture that had arrived here in the mid-1800s. The area that is now known as Poway was called "Paguay," according to Mission San Diego de Alcala records from 1828, a name derived from the local Dieguo and Luiseño Indian language that was prevalent at the time. Paguay is generally translated to mean "the meeting of little valleys" or "end of the valley," according to Poway history.

Today the local Kumeyaay call this place Pauwai. You can visit the Kumeyaay-Ipai Interpretive Center at Pauwai, located at 13104 Ipai Waaypuk Trail in Poway (off Silver Lake Drive just south of Poway Road), to see recreated elements of an ancient Kumeyaay village, including milling stations where women would grind acorns, some native gardens, and an 'ewaa (Kumeyaay house). The oak groves along that first leg of this hike—the Green Valley Truck Trail, an old dirt road—would have been a prime location for people for possibly thousands of years here.

Just 0.2 miles from the trailhead, a sign points to the Oak Grove and Creekside Trail to the left. This narrow, single-track trail runs parallel to the Green Valley Truck Trail through a riparian habitat for about a quarter-mile before rejoining the main GVTT.

The Oak Grove goes off to the left of that Creekside Trail for a short stroll through some mighty old oak trees. A large sign was posted when I was there, noting high bee activity, so if you're allergic, you might want to avoid this short spur trail. I risked it and did hear and see a very active hive in one of those oak hollows, but the bees didn't bother me.

Along the rest of the Creekside Trail, you'll also spot some native sycamore trees mixed in with the oaks. Here I also heard and saw a redheaded acorn woodpecker preparing a hole to stash an acorn or two. At about 0.9 miles from the trailhead, a right turn will take you up to Lake Poway, where you can continue to the top of Mount Woodson, if you're game for an 11-mile round-trip strenuous climb. The hike to Lake Poway from Blue Sky is about 2.2 miles one-way.

Continue straight ahead for Lake Ramona. At about 1.1 miles from the trailhead, the GVTT splits with the left fork heading uphill to Lake Ramona, beginning the ascent. This old dirt road winds around chaparral scrub, where you'll find no trees for shade now. But you will begin to enjoy those sweeping views.

In late February, a few signs of spring to come added a touch or two of wildflower color. I spotted a fuchsia-colored wild pea, some gold California poppies, some yellow wallflowers, orange monkeyflowers, and orange and yellow deerweed.

When you reach the paved road that heads straight up to Ramona Dam, you'll encounter the steepest incline from here to that lake. Press ahead to reach that blue-water sight.

Lake Ramona is a reservoir built here in 1988 to provide water primarily to commercial avocado and citrus growers. You may not swim or boat on Lake Ramona, but you may carry your fishing equipment (and fishing license) along with you to try to catch some of the stocked bass. I enjoyed the view of that lake surrounded by the huge boulders that are common in this area.

The hike back down seemed a lot easier than that final trudge uphill.

Thomas Brothers Map: Page 1170, G-3, entrance to Blue Sky Ecological Reserve off Espola Road.

Before You Go: To download a copy of the trail map or for more information, go to the Friends of Blue Sky's website: www.blueskyreserve.org.

Poway also has a website on Blue Sky (http://poway.org/337/Blue-Sky-Ecological-Reserve), including lists of mammals, birds, and plants seen here.

The state department of fish and game also has a page dedicated to Blue Sky: https://www.wildlife.ca.gov/Lands/Places-to-Visit/Blue-Sky-ER.

The reserve is open every day from sunrise to sunset. Bicycles are not allowed in Blue Sky, but trails are open to hikers, equestrians, and dogs on leashes.

It's free to park here.

Trailhead: From Interstate 15, exit at Rancho Bernardo Road, heading east. That road turns into Espola Road once you've entered Poway city limits. The Blue Sky Ecological Reserve is located at 16275 Espola Road—a left turn when heading east on Espola.

Distance/Difficulty: The round-trip to Ramona Dam is about 4.8 miles; easy to moderately strenuous.

6-11. Lake Poway Loop Circles Blue Water Views on High

The Lake Poway Trail dips into the backcountry and circles that blue reservoir for some really wonderful waterscape views, all in the urban core. The loop trail is about 2.8 miles total, but it also connects to several other trails if you want to make a longer trek. The Blue Sky Ecological Reserve Trail connects at the 1.0-mile point on the Lake Poway Trail, which can also take you 1.6 miles more to Lake Ramona. At the 1.9-mile mark on the Lake Poway Trail is the Mount Woodson Trail for an elevating climb of about another 2.0 miles.

The Lake Poway loop begins just to the left of the lake's concession building and boat dock, where you can rent fishing or pleasure boats or grab some grub from the grill.

Lake Poway makes beautiful views from its loop trail.

I started there for a counterclockwise loop, which I think is a little easier in terms of steepness than going the other way around. There are a few spots of moderate elevation gain (about 400 feet), all the better for the views that extend west to (from the southern end) 1,306-foot Twin Peaks, 1,552-foot Black Mountain, 2,140-foot Starvation Mountain, and 1,150-foot Bernardo Mountain.

From that trailhead, begin next to the lake and then quickly start a short, steep climb. When you reach the top, looking down on Lake Poway's dam, there is a junction of two trails. Take the trail on the right that begins a descent into the backcountry, below the dry side of the dam.

That dam was completed in 1971, after nearly 12 years of planning and three attempts (1963, 1966, and the successful 1969) to pass bond issues to support its construction from local taxpayers. By 1972, Lake Poway had become a multipurpose lake with a 300-foot boat dock, a 100-foot fishing pier, a concession building, and restrooms, along with 17 acres of landscaped picnic areas, boat ramps, and parking areas.

Lake Poway is 120 feet deep and stores 3,800 acre-feet of water, holding about 1 billion gallons. It has 64 surface acres with a 2.5-mile shoreline. Its water comes from the county's first aqueduct, built in 1945, which brings water to the region from the Colorado River.

Lake Poway's log-boom about halfway from the dam keeps humans out of that area to protect the underwater aeration system. Rainbow trout, catfish, and bass are all stocked and fished from the lake.

As soon as you reach that first high point and begin the descent behind the dam, you'll see to the north the dam that creates Lake Ramona, another storage reservoir built in 1988, which also holds water from the first aqueduct.

This first part of the Lake Poway loop trail descends a series of steep switchbacks into that backcountry behind the dam. Near its low point is the connecting trail to Blue Sky Ecological Preserve and Lake Ramona. At that junction, take the high road up to continue the Lake Poway loop. In a more gradual climb, you'll soon be higher than the dam, so you'll see the lake again. Just before you reach scenic Pine Point, you'll note some placards with mileage to points along the trail as well as some lake history.

There used to be numbered signposts accompanying an interpretive brochure along the Lake Poway loop trail, but those wooden posts burned down in the 2007 Witch Fire that claimed most of this chaparral habitat. It's amazing to see the healthy state it's in now, just four years later. Park rangers report that local Eagle Scouts are working to restore those signposts, so perhaps more learning opportunities will resume on the trail.

Just past Pine Point is the lovely Hidden Bay, the most secreted of the coves in the lake, where bass like to hide, according to the placard about the lake's history. Boulder Bay, just beyond Hidden Bay, sports a lovely beach. Extending into the lake just past Boulder Bay is Jump-Off Point, where trout may be found. The trail climbs a bit just past Hidden Bay, where it intersects with the Mount Woodson Trail. Just a bit farther, the trail also connects with the Sumac Trail, which climbs into open space and then the High Valley development area, and which loops back to the Lake Poway Trail, adding a little less than a mile more if you want to take it.

I kept to the Lake Poway loop, marveling over those fantastic blue-water views on a crystal clear autumn day.

Thomas Brothers Map: Page 1170, H-4.

Before You Go: Download the best map of the Lake Poway Trail at the City of Poway's website: http://ca-poway.civicplus.com/DocumentCenter/View/1260.

You may also download the main Poway trails map: http://poway.org/502/Trails-Hiking. The Lake Poway Trail is No. 13 on the main Poway trails map.

Note there is a $5 day-use parking fee for non-Poway residents from on weekends and holidays. The trail and park are open every day November through May from sunrise to sunset, and from June through October from 7:00 a.m. to sunset. Fishing and boating on the lake are closed all year on Mondays and Tuesdays.

The Lake Poway Trail is open to hikers, equestrians, mountain bikers, and dogs on leashes.

Trailhead: From Interstate 15, exit at Rancho Bernardo Road, heading east. This road turns into Espola Road once you reach Poway city limits. From Espola Road, turn left onto Lake Poway Road and enter the park.

The northwest trailhead is immediately to the left of the boat dock when facing the lake.

Distance/Difficulty: The entire lake loop trail is about 3.2 miles. Moderate.

6-12. Oaks, Boulders, Views on Fine Fry-Koegle Trail

The Fry-Koegle Trail that stretches from Ramona to Poway offers a few of my favorite things: atmospheric live oak groves, gargantuan boulders, and sweeping views from one of the county's high points. It's a steady climb up the northeast flanks of Mount Woodson, which rises to 2,894 feet. Although the Fry-Koegle Trail stops a few hundred feet short of that mountain's high point, you can join two other trails to reach the top of Mount Woodson, if you like. You can also connect to other trails that take you down to Lake Poway.

I stuck to the Fry-Koegle Trail alone, and it was enough of a workout for me at about 6.6 miles round-trip. If you want to connect to the Lake Poway trails, you might consider a two-car, one-way effort.

The Fry-Koegle Trail is far less traveled than the trails to Mount Woodson from Lake Poway or even Highway 67. Even though it's also open to equestrians and mountain bikers, the Fry-Koegle Trail is a fairly rocky, narrow trail with several switchbacks, not to mention a few skinny passages between those boulders that surely make it a lot harder for horses and bikes than for hikers and dogs on leashes.

I picked up the trail on the west side of Archie Moore Road near Mount Woodson Estates. A wooden fence separates the trail from the road. The trail skirts the edge of that development's golf course and then begins a climb uphill alongside the backyards of several homes in that community.

The trail climbs up behind those homes for about the first mile. Just past the collection of birdhouses hanging from fruit trees, the trail descends into the first of two fine coast live oak groves. The sound of trickling water accompanies this riparian hideaway, where lots of towering oak trees spread their canopies over the trail made softer by fallen leaves. This first oak grove made that initial climb well worth the effort.

Fry-Koegle Trail is one of best ways up Mount Woodson.

In another third of a mile or so, you'll see a large water tank near where the trail makes a sharp left turn to head uphill some more. Now you begin to enter that land of gigantic boulders. Jerry Schad, in his hiking guidebook *Afoot and Afield in San Diego County*, reports that Native Americans used to call Mount Woodson "Mountain of Moonlit Rocks," whereas early white settlers called it "Cobbleback Peak." The slopes you're climbing are covered with the giant boulders that give this area such a distinctive landscape; they are a granitic bedrock known as Woodson Mountain granodiorite that weathers into surprisingly smooth and rounded boulders.

You'll see a huge split rock boulder shortly past that water tank, and then the trail will meander among and between some of these behemoths as it continues its climb. You'll enter another lovely coast live oak grove, punctuated with some of those boulders, as the trail takes an occasional dip down before heading up again.

After about two miles, the trail starts revealing those panoramic views to the north across Ramona. You can see part of the Lake Ramona reservoir all the way to Palomar Mountain on the horizon. The nearby hills are covered in those vanilla-colored boulders that sometimes combine in fantastic tableaus. As you wander closely around some of them, you might find yourself feeling a little like Jonathan Swift's Gulliver in Brobdingnag.

At 2.7 miles, according to an intersection sign, you'll reach the Old Fry-Koegle Trail that heads up another 1.5 miles to the Mount Woodson Summit. The Fry-Koegle Trail continues another 0.6 miles to the Mount Woodson Trail that comes up from Lake Poway. I continued straight ahead on the "new" Fry-Koegle Trail, which gets its name from Mike Fry and Norman Koegel, who constructed this trail in 1990.

The trail continues to reveal those views with no trees providing shade or obstruction as you wind around the flank of Mount Woodson. After 0.6 miles, you reach its end, where it intersects with other trails that head up 1.3 miles to Mount Woodson's summit, as well as 2.8 miles downhill to Lake Poway. From this vantage point, another remarkable view spreads itself to the northwest over Poway.

I turned around here to retrace my way back. The views were even easier to appreciate on the way back down, the oak groves were just as inviting the second time around, and the boulders continued to impress. I really liked this trail.

Thomas Brothers Map: Page 1171, F-3, intersection of Archie Moore Road and Rancho de la Angel Road.

Before You Go: The Fry-Koegle Trail is part of the City of Poway's trail system, and it can be located on its trail map (http://poway.org/502/Trails-Hiking). The Fry-Koegle Trail is No. 17 on the main Poway trails map.

The best map I found for it is the National Geographic topographic map on the website: http://www.mountainbikebill.com/MtWoodson.htm.

This trail is open to hikers, bicyclists, equestrians, and dogs on leashes.

Trailhead: From Highway 67 heading east into Ramona, just past the main east-side trailhead up Mount Woodson, turn left onto Archie Moore Road. You'll see the Fry-Koegle Trail begin on your left at the intersection of Mount Woodson Way, but that road enters the gated community. Go a bit farther on Archie Moore Road to Rancho de la Angel Road, turn right there, and park off the road at that intersection. Cross Archie Moore Road, and hike left onto the trail bordered by the wooden fence on the west side of the road.

Distance/Difficulty: About 6.6 miles round-trip; moderate with an elevation gain of about 1,000 feet.

6-13. Poway's Warren Canyon Requires Lots of Water

The hike up through Warren Canyon from Lake Poway is about half as difficult as the intersecting trail to the top of neighboring Mount Woodson. Although the Mount Woodson trail climbs some 2,300 feet to reach the summit, the Warren Canyon trail climbs just over 1,000 feet up that same Mount Woodson trail when you reach the Warren Canyon trailhead.

You'll pass the one-mile wooden post marker for the Mount Woodson trail as you keep climbing. Shortly, you'll reach the well-signed intersection to Warren Canyon. From this intersection, Mount Woodson's summit is still 1.9 miles away. Warren Canyon heads east from here for 2.3 miles to its end at Highway 67. Both of these trails start with about 1.0 mile first on the Lake Poway Trail that goes around the entire reservoir, so you've gone about 2.0 miles before you reach the Warren Canyon trailhead.

That view of Lake Poway is surely one of the beauties of all these trails. As you climb, more panoramas reveal themselves all the way to the ocean. Even the first part of the Warren Canyon trail is steep in parts as it winds through this distinctive boulder country that is so characteristic of Mount Woodson. Soon enough you will see almost the entire route of this trail as it weaves through the canyon. You'll also see Highway 67 in the distance.

Those boulders distinguish Mount Woodson from several neighboring peaks. Early settlers called it Cobblestone Peak. In about 1875, Dr. Marshall Clay Woodson; his wife, Mary Ann Pell Woodson; and their children moved here from Kentucky and homesteaded on 320 acres at the base of what would become known as Mount Woodson. According to the San Diego Historical Society's *Journal of San Diego History,* Dr. Woodson was a

physician who had served the Confederate army in the Civil War as a surgeon. "Finding it impossible to make a lucrative living as a physician, Woodson became a successful apiarist and horticulturist," according to the journal's summer 1982 issue.

Those boulders are as big as buildings strewn all over Mount Woodson and are outcroppings of its particular granitic base, called Mount Woodson granodiorite. This kind of light-colored granite, filled with white feldspar and clear quartz, has weathered into smooth boulders. Local rock climbers consider Mount Woodson one of the best local spots for bouldering.

Start on the Lake Poway Trail, which leaves the main concession area, and head to the east counterclockwise on this lakeside trail. After about a mile, you'll reach the junction for both Mount Woodson and

Take plenty of water to Warren Canyon.

Warren Canyon trails, where you continue east. I went only a short way into Warren Canyon before I stopped because it was so hot and the way up had been rather strenuous.

Several signs at the trail's beginnings warned, "High Heat Advisory: Be Sure to Bring Enough Water." I was disturbed by how many hikers did not seem to heed that warning and in some cases had no water at all. Always take plenty of water on any hike, but especially during the hot summer months. Heatstroke can kill.

"Even a top athlete in superb condition can succumb to heat illness if he or she ignores the warning signs," says MedlinePlus, a medical encyclopedia from the National Institutes of Health. "Heat cramps (caused by loss of salt from heavy sweating) can lead to heat exhaustion (caused by dehydration), which can progress to heatstroke. Heatstroke, the most serious of the three, can cause shock, brain damage, organ failure and even death."

Early symptoms include profuse sweating, fatigue, thirst, and muscle cramps, followed by headache, dizziness, weakness, nausea and vomiting, and cool skin.

Subsequent heatstroke symptoms include irrational behavior; extreme confusion; dry, hot, and red skin; rapid breathing; seizures; and unconsciousness.

If any of this occurs, have the person lie down and raise his or her feet about 12 inches. Apply cool, wet cloths to the skin, and fan to lower body temperature. If the person is alert, give him or her purified water, salty water or Gatorade to drink, but do not give the person anything by mouth if he or she is vomiting or unconscious.

Always take plenty of water with you. Most recommendations call for a gallon per person for a full day's hike in 70 to 80 degrees—that's eight 16-ounce bottles. Take at the least a half-gallon up Mount Woodson per person.

Carry some of that water (and a collapsible bowl) for your dog too. Dogs can suffer the same heat illnesses and should not be overexerted or lacking water on hard summer hikes.

Pay attention to how you feel; if you need to rest, do so. Then you will enjoy those mountain-high views above Lake Poway.

Thomas Brothers Map: Page 1170, H-4.

Before You Go: Download a copy of the trail map from the city of Poway's trail pages: http://poway.org/502/Trails-Hiking. The Warren Canyon Trail is No. 16 on the main Poway trails map.

This trail is open to hikers, bicyclists, equestrians, and dogs on leashes. On weekends and holidays only, there is a $5 parking fee for non-Poway residents in the Lake Poway parking areas. Poway residents show proof of residency at the office.

Trailhead: From Interstate 15, exit at Rancho Bernardo Road and head east. Rancho Bernardo Road turns into Espola Road after entering Poway. Continue east on Espola, and then turn left (east) onto Lake Poway Road into the Lake Poway Recreation Area.

From the main parking area, head to the trailhead above the lake's southeastern shore. Begin on the Lake Poway Trail, connecting to the Mount Woodson Trail, and then to Warren Canyon Trail. Retrace your way back. You might then want to take the "low road," the trail closer to the lake, on the way back.

Distance/Difficulty: The total Warren Canyon Trail round-trip would be about 8 miles (about the same as the hike up Mount Woodson) with an elevation gain of at least 1,000 feet, compared to 2,300 for Mount Woodson. I went a total of only about 4.5 miles, which included about a quarter-mile one-way on Warren Canyon's trail.
Fairly strenuous.

6-14. Wind through Canyon, History at Goodan Ranch

Equestrians, mountain bikers, and hikers get along very well on the hard-packed trail through the Goodan Ranch Open Space Preserve in Poway. Once a working farm where cattle, dairy cows and horses coexisted with a few hardy people, the 325-acre ranch preserve sits next to the 2,270 acres of Sycamore Canyon Open Space, where both pristine places offer about 10 miles of trails.

I meandered down the main trail of Goodan Ranch, a wide and easy path that was formerly a dirt ranch road. It can be a loop trail of a bit more than 3.3 miles when joined with the nearby, narrower West Boundary Trail, but I stayed on the main trail both ways (for about 3.0 miles round-trip) in order to avoid rattlesnakes. The wide, clear path makes visibility much better when on the lookout for those creatures.

History is on view at Goodan Ranch.

When you reach the southern end of the main trail, you arrive at the Goodan Ranch Center, a modern facility designed for low site impact and high energy efficiency (LEED certified) with exhibits and ranger staff offices. This facility was built after the devastating 2003 Cedar Fire that destroyed 95 percent of Goodan Ranch and Sycamore Canyon lands. The fire also claimed the historic stone house that was built here in 1937–38 by May and Roger Goodan, the ruins of which sit next to the modern building.

Roger Goodan owned the Los Angeles Furniture Company, and he and his family bought this land to be a country retreat, according to one of the exhibits in the ranch center building. May was the stepdaughter of Harrison Gray Otis, the first publisher of the *Los Angeles Times,* and the daughter of Harry Chandler, who eventually took charge of that newspaper.

The Goodans would come on weekends and holidays, and they operated the ranch as a working farm with cattle, dairy cows, and pigs. Their ranch hand, Ernest Allbee, was hired in 1941 and lived on the ranch for more than 50 years. Even after the Goodans sold the property in 1985, Allbee was secured with lifetime residency; Allbee died in 1998 at age 101.

Classic San Diego habitats of coastal sage scrub, chaparral, and one fine oak woodland are found here, but Goodan Ranch also has native and nonnative grassland, where those cattle used to roam. These days, those grasslands reveal distinctive wildlife paths—narrow trails tamped down through the grass surely made by the mule deer, bobcats, mountain lions, and coyotes that roam here now. See how many of these wildlife trails you can spot.

In the ranch center, preserved animals are exhibited that reveal the breadth of wildlife found here.

Goodan Ranch is part of the Multiple Species Conservation Program (MSCP), a comprehensive, long-term habitat conservation program that aims to preserve San Diego's native habitats and wildlife. A regional effort, the MSCP is a partnership of local, state, and federal agencies, including the U.S. Fish and Wildlife Service, the Bureau of Land Management, County of San Diego, and the cities of Poway and San Diego, as well as other entities.

A comprehensive 2002 field guide prepared by Carol Crafts and Kathy C. Young for Friends of Goodan Ranch lists many of the plants and animals found here. It also shares the ranch's colorful history. Go to http://goodanranch.org/pdf/Field_Guide.pdf. It lists several endangered and threatened species, including the orange-throated whiptail lizard, Poway mint (a thorn mint), mission manzanita, and several birds, including the California gnatcatcher, least Bell's vireo, and all raptors. I saw a splendid American kestrel soar above the grasslands when I was there.

The ranch center hosts several programs throughout the year. For more information, check the program guide for Goodan Ranch at http://www.sandiegocounty.gov/parks/openspace/Sycamore_Goodan.html.

Thomas Brothers Map: Page 1191, C-7.

Before You Go: Download the best map at http://www.goodanranch.org/map.html.
It is open to equestrians, mountain bikers, hikers, and dogs on leashes. It's free.

Trailhead: From Interstate 15, exit at Poway Road/Rancho Penasquitos Blvd., heading east on Poway Road. After about five miles, turn right onto Garden Road. In another mile, turn right onto Sycamore Canyon Road, which ends at the Goodan Ranch preserve parking area, 16281 Sycamore Canyon Road.

Distance: The main trail is about 3.0 miles round trip; easy.

6-15. Martha's Grove Abloom in Wildflower Colors

Step into spring in Sycamore Canyon. Martha's Grove Memorial Trail, located in that open-space preserve, winds through hills and canyons covered in native plants common in coastal sage scrub and chaparral habitats. Those natives dress up from mid-March through April. Most impressive here are the dense blue flowers of ceanothus, also known as wild lilac. When you're viewing from the top of this trail down into the canyons, clusters of these shrubs cast a pale blue hue across the landscape.

Fragrant sage is also a spring bloomer with blue flowers, their sweet aroma a special bonus. There are several patches of bright yellow golden yarrow, delicate yellow rock roses, and yellow and orange deerweed. Dashes of white morning glories enliven the scene along with some occasional bright red scarlet larkspur. Keep your eyes peeled for the lovely lavender bush mallow and the bright pink checkerbloom too.

Martha's Grove is one of the best trails for wildflowers in the Goodan Ranch/Sycamore Canyon Preserve, an open-space preserve administered by the County of

San Diego near Poway. Sycamore Canyon Preserve consists of nearly 2,300 acres of hills surrounding the 325-acre Goodan Ranch, where grasslands and riparian habitats dominate.

Martha's Grove Trail is one of the best for wildflowers.

Another year-round reason for hiking this trail is the Martha Harville Memorial Oak Grove, which sits at the bottom of Sycamore Canyon; Sycamore Canyon Creek trickles along with you. The trail is named for Martha Shawn Harville, a county park ranger from 1978, when she was just 21, to 1988, when she died of malignant melanoma at the tender age of 31. Named a supervising park ranger in 1983 at Felicita Park in Escondido, she was also a training officer in the park department's headquarters. She was especially interested in the history of the parks she supervised, and she sought out old-timers to hear their stories of the areas. She worked with county parks historians to document places and artifacts, and she was well versed in the history of Native Americans here. The memorial oak grove named for her was regularly visited by Native Americans for centuries.

Harville was appointed acting district park manager for North County parks in 1986 at age 28, "possibly the youngest ranger ever appointed to this responsible position," says the county plaque with her picture in the oak grove. The biography on view here was written by Martha's mom, Verdie Harville. Martha's ashes were placed in Sycamore Canyon beneath an oak tree planted in her memory.

Her namesake oak grove is a lovely, verdant gathering around the stream of old oaks that remarkably survived the devastating Cedar Fire of 2003, the largest wild land fire in California history. The Cedar Fire burned over 380,000 acres (about 15 percent of the county), including over 95 percent of the Sycamore Canyon Preserve. Oaks are fire adapted, which means they usually survive after a fire. The Cedar Fire destroyed only about 14 percent of our oak species countywide, compared to 95 percent of conifers, according to a California State Parks study completed by Linnea Spears of San Diego

State University. Ceanothus and other wildflowers have obviously rebounded beautifully as well.

This trail leaves from the Goodan Ranch Staging Area and heads immediately east from the parking lot. It's a one-way trail also used by equestrians and mountain bikers. That one-way limitation is good here because the trail is quite narrow, rocky, and sometimes steep, so it's better that multiple-use traffic is all going in the same direction.

It can be a dangerous trail for mountain bikers; when I was on the Goodan Ranch trail, a biker had fallen and had to be airlifted to a hospital.

The one-way part of Martha's Grove Trail lasts for about 1.7 miles. A short way after the oak grove, the trail emerges onto an old dirt road through the flat pasturelands that once were active with cattle on Goodan Ranch. An old dammed area here turns Sycamore Creek into a small pond.

The trail then intersects with the Main Crossing spur trail back to the main trail to the Goodan Ranch Staging Area, both of which cover about another 1.3 miles, making a 3.0-mile loop hike.

Thomas Brothers Map: Page 1191, C-7, right where "Sycamore" runs into park boundary.

Before You Go: Check the county parks page for Goodan Ranch/Sycamore Canyon Preserve: http://www.co.san-diego.ca.us/parks/openspace/Sycamore_Goodan.html. The best map of the trails can be downloaded from the website of Friends of Goodan Ranch and Sycamore Canyon Open Space: http://goodanranch.org/map.html.

This park also offers several free programs and guided hikes throughout the year. Check the county park's program guide at http://www.co.san-diego.ca.us/reusable_components/images/parks/doc/destinations.pdf.

It is open to hikers, bicyclists, equestrians, and dogs on leashes.

Trailhead: Note there are two staging areas for this open space preserve. The Goodan Ranch Staging Area is where Martha's Grove Memorial Trail begins its one-way ascent/descent into the canyon. To reach this staging and parking area, from Interstate 15, exit at Poway Road, heading east. Turn right onto Garden Road and then right again onto Sycamore Canyon Road, which ends at the parking area. Martha's trail heads uphill immediately east of the parking area. The main trail to Goodan Ranch and the visitor's center heads straight ahead from the parking area.

The other staging area is off Highway 67 in Lakeside at 13920 Highway 67.

Difficulty/Distance: A 3.0-mile loop trail, moderate.

6-16. Sycamore Canyon's Ridge Filled With History, Scrub

Hike the Ridge Trail in Sycamore Canyon to get a bird's-eye view of an enormous swath of open space. The trail is located in the Goodan Ranch Sycamore Canyon Preserve, a 2,272-acre preserve that is surrounded on all sides by open-space lands, so the views extend much farther than just the preserve.

The trail goes up and down the ridgeline until it finally dips down to the valley where the old Goodan Ranch once was home to a hundred cattle. You'll see the historic ranch below you as you wind through this undeveloped area.

Most of the preserve (1,830 acres of it) is southern mixed chaparral with another 126 acres of coastal sage scrub, the dominant habitats you'll hike through on this ridge. There are 10 habitat types, including oak woodland and riparian areas, which lie at lower elevations in the valley.

Sycamore Canyon's Ridge Trail has extensive views.

The preserve is managed by San Diego County's Department of Parks and Recreation that had a biodiversity study completed in 2008 to help develop resource management plans. According to that study, 313 plant species were identified along with 73 bird species, 30 mammal species (including 11 bats, 10 small mammals, and nine medium and large mammals; the mountain lion was not included in the original survey but has been spotted here), 16 reptiles (including rattlesnakes), and 46 invertebrates.

On the Ridge Trail in late winter, I saw lots of black sage, a common and very fragrant shrub in the coastal sage scrub habitat, as well as the distinctive felt-leaved yerba santa, which was just beginning to bloom. I also spotted chamise and buckwheat, both common in coastal sage-chaparral scrub. Common plants in the chaparral habitat seen here include wild lilac (ceanothus), scrub oak, and manzanita. Some of the manzanita were just beginning to bloom.

You can get a list of the plants here from the San Diego Natural History Museum's Plant Atlas project, an impressive survey of the entire county's plant species in undeveloped areas. Go to http://www.sdplantatlas.org, and you'll find a wealth of information, lists, and photographs of virtually every native plant in the county. One especially cool feature of the SDNHM Plant Atlas online is the ability to draw a small map on the countywide map to see what plants were collected there, or to see what plants were found in any given ecological region. "The Plant Atlas project began in 2003 and has increased our knowledge of the flora in San Diego in ways never imagined," says the museum on the project's website. "Not only have we added over 55,000 specimens to our collection, but we now have amazing resources available to the general public." Volunteers are trained to do all the collecting, if you're interested in participating.

While you ponder the flora in the Ridge Trail, consider the history here too. The Kumeyaay lived in this valley for thousands of years according to archaeological evidence found, including mortero grinding sites, pottery remnants, and even arrowheads.

The Kumeyaay boiled black sage leaves and stems to use them in bathing for the flu, rheumatism, and arthritis, according to the San Diego Archaeology Center's list of the ethnobiology of local plants. Yerba santa leaves were used to make tea, according to James Lightner's *San Diego County Native Plants*.

In 1884, families began to file homestead claims in Sycamore Canyon, forming the town of Stowe, according to Carol Crafts and Kathy C. Young, who wrote a field guide to Goodan Ranch Sycamore Canyon preserve in 2002. Those early settlers were largely farmers of orchards, vineyards, and grains. In 1889 the post office for Stowe opened, and in 1890 the Stowe School was opened. But the school was closed in 1903, and the post office shut in 1905. Extreme weather with torrential rains and intermittent droughts during those years, as well as a decision to stop a railroad spur in the area, contributed to the demise of Stowe, says Crafts. Among the historic buildings still on Goodan Ranch is the old caretaker's house.

When you've gone about 1.25 miles on the Ridge Trail, it takes a sharp right turn to go down into the ranch valley. In another 0.6 miles or so, it reaches the bottom and connects to the Stowe Trail, according to the post marker. But at the bottom, direction is given to a connection with the Western Trail. Perhaps this was renamed as part of the historic Stowe Trail? Stowe Trail does not appear on Goodan Ranch Sycamore Canyon Preserve trail maps.

The Stowe Millenium Trail was said to be dedicated a Community Millennium Trail in 2000 by the White House Millennium Council, and it connects Sycamore Canyon with Santee and Mission Trails Park. It is said to be a 16-mile-long trail that follows the old Survey Road 55 once used to transport raisins in the area, part of it going through Marine Corps Air Station Miramar. Negotiations to use that part of the trail appear to be ongoing with the county. I have not found any map of this trail or any official designation of its completion, and I would appreciate hearing if it is now open and exactly where it goes.

Thomas Brothers Map: Page 1191, E-5, where Sycamore Park Drive intersects Highway 67.

Before You Go: The trails on Goodan Ranch Sycamore Canyon Preserve are open to hikers, equestrians, bicyclists, and dogs on leashes. It's free to park at either the Goodan Ranch staging area off Sycamore Canyon Road in Poway or at the northern staging area off Highway 67.

Download a copy of the trails map at the county's parks' page: http://www.co.san-diego.ca.us/parks/openspace/Sycamore_Goodan.html.

The best map of the trails can be downloaded from the website of Friends of Goodan Ranch and Sycamore Canyon Open Space: http://goodanranch.org/map.html.

Trailhead: To reach the Ridge Trail, head to the Highway 67 staging area of the preserve. From Highway 67, turn west onto Sycamore Park Drive. You cannot turn left onto this road when heading north on Highway 67, so in this case, turn right at Scripps Poway Parkway, make a U-turn, and go back south on Highway 67 to turn right onto Sycamore Park Drive. The road—much of it dirt but negotiable by standard cars—goes about 1.25 miles before the parking area.

Distance/Difficulty: The Ridge Trail is about 1.8 miles one-way, for a 3.6-mile round-trip, with about 900 feet in elevation gain. It's slow going on this rocky, steep trail. Moderately strenuous.

6-17. The Site of Bloody Battle Has Pastoral Views Today

An easy hike with long views above San Pasqual Valley surveys the site of the bloodiest battle fought in California during the U.S.-Mexican War of 1846. It's about a 1.5-mile round-trip hike above the San Pasqual Battlefield State Historic Park museum, and it climbs to a small summit, from which you can see nearly 360 degrees—clearly a good spot for watching out for combatants.

Imagine this trail as a battlefield lookout.

It also has some tough terrain. The trail is brushy and overgrown, though still easy to follow. It passes through some of the thickest colonies of prickly pear cactus I've seen here. Such a forbidding landscape makes the vision of men fighting on horseback with muskets, bayonets, and small cannons pulled by mules even more disturbing.

The skirmish here between the American forces seeking to take California and the Mexican forces seeking to keep it ultimately led to both sides claiming victory, according to the brochure about the historic state park published by California State Parks. General Stephen W. Kearny led a contingent of First Dragoons into battle with several Californios, who were people of Hispanic descent living in California after the Mexican revolution. Captain Andres Pico, brother of Pio Pico (one of the last governors of Mexican California), led the Californios against the Americans. The Pico brothers owned Rancho Santa Margarita, which was near San Pasqual Valley, close to Fallbrook, and it had been a Mexican land grant to them in 1841. At the time of this battle, the native northern Kumeyaay, known as the Ipai, were living in a secularized mission established by the Mexican government here in 1835.

After President James K. Polk declared war on Mexico, Kearny and his soldiers were ordered by him to take Santa Fe for the United States, which they seized peacefully. Kearny then led his men to California, where he met frontier scout Kit Carson, who told him that Commodore Robert F. Stockton had raised the American flag over San Diego, so California was now in American hands. Kearny therefore sent most of his troops back to Santa Fe. Kit Carson guided Kearny and about 100 men to San Diego.

The Pico forces were camped in San Pasqual (then Pascual) Pueblo on December 5, 1846, when Kearny's scouts were fired upon. "The Dragoons and their mounts, exhausted by their desert trek, were in no condition to fight. The riders' cold hands could barely maintain a grip on their reins. Wet gunpowder made their weapons useless and the low-lying fog obscured their vision," says the brochure.

Early on December 6, 21 Americans fell while Mexican forces lost only one man, though several were wounded. The next day the two sides battled again on Mule Hill, just a few miles west in the San Pasqual Valley. By December 11, Stockton's troops arrived from San Diego to escort Kearny's remaining men to San Diego. Then on December 29, a combined force of Stockton's and Kearny's men set out for Los Angeles. On January 10, 1947, the Mexicans surrendered to the Americans, and Andres Pico signed the Articles of Capitulation, ending the war for good.

This state park has had its own recent battle. It was one of two in San Diego County, along with Palomar Mountain State Park, slated for closure in 2012 because of state budget woes. But both parks avoided that ax, and San Pasqual Battlefield State Historic Park remains open, albeit only on Saturdays and Sundays.

The trail is still accessible on weekdays even if the gates are closed, however. I parked out front and then walked around the gates and up the road to the picnic areas. The half-mile Nature Trail begins here and intersects with the longer Battle Monument Trail. There are a few remaining numbered signposts along that Nature Trail that point out native flora, including an Engelmann oak sprouting anew, some white sage, and all that prickly pear cactus. Download a copy of the San Pasqual Nature Trail Guide to carry along for more information: http://www.parks.ca.gov/pages/655/files/SanPasqualNatureTrailGuide_FINAL120314.pdf.

The first post points to the monument that depicts Lt. Edward F. Beale and Kit Carson hailing Commodore Robert Stockton. Beale had accompanied Carson to San Pasqual to get help for Kearny and his troops stranded on Mule Hill.

Look for the Engelmann oak at post No. 2. The guide notes that its acorns, as well as those of other oaks, were a diet staple for native tribes throughout California because they are high in fat, carbohydrates, protein, and vitamins and minerals, and they are an excellent source of fiber. Sounds like a super food today.

Look for wild buckwheat (post No. 4), white sage (No. 5), laurel sumac (No. 6), and sagebrush (No. 7). Prickly pear (No. 11) fruits were eaten fresh, and its pads were boiled or fried. One prickly pear cactus on the Battle Monument Trail was far taller than all the rest, reaching a height of at least eight feet with very large yellow fruits (called tunas in Spanish). It is still a popular edible treat today, especially in Mexico.

The views from the small summit reveal signs of the 21st century, but many agricultural lands still remain in this valley, much like there would have been 169 years ago.

Interesting wildlife lives nearby. There is an ostrich farm just a few miles west on Old Milky Way road, and the San Diego Zoo's Safari Park is about 1.5 miles west.

Thomas Brothers Map: Page 1131, B-7.

Before You Go: The state parks' website offers that history lesson as well as a good trail map: http://www.parks.ca.gov/pages/655/files/SanPasqualFinalWebLayout101209.pdf. Right next door, also on state park property, is the San Diego Archaeological Center.

It is open to hikers and dogs on leashes.

Trailhead: The historic state park is located about 1.5 miles east of the San Diego Zoo's Safari Park and about 8.0 miles east of Escondido on Highway 78.

From San Diego, head north on Interstate 15, exiting at Via Rancho Parkway and heading east. Continue ahead as that road turns into Bear Valley Parkway South. Turn right on San Pasqual Road. Turn right onto Old Milky Way/Old Pasqual Road. Just east of where Old Milky Way Road intersects Highway 78, the state historic park is on the left.

Distance/Difficulty: About 1.5 miles round-trip; easy.

6-18. Geocaching Treasure Hunt on Highland Valley Trail

Enjoying nature is often reward enough from hiking, but now there's a global game called geocaching that adds a little high-tech treasure hunting to the activity. A few of us joined park rangers Ken Colburn and Jacob Gibbs of San Dieguito River Park during winter a few years ago for a geocache hunt on the Highland Valley Trail, and we discovered an amazingly fun new pastime.

Geocaching is a global phenomenon that began in May 2000. On May 2, 2000, "the great blue switch" that controlled selective availability was pressed by the government, essentially upgrading 24 satellites around the globe so that the accuracy of GPS technology improved exponentially, according to the book *The Complete Idiot's Guide to Geocaching.*

On May 3, 2000, Dave Ulmer, a computer consultant, wanted to test the new accuracy, so he hid a container in the woods near Beaver Creek, Oregon, and posted its GPS coordinates on an Internet GPS users' group page. Inside his container he placed a logbook and pencil and some prizes, including videos, books, and a slingshot.

Within three days, two readers used their GPS devices to find the container and shared their experiences online. Mike Teague, the first person to find Ulmer's stash, began gathering online posts of coordinates around the world, documenting them on his personal home page. The original "GPS Stash Hunt" soon became geocaching, and a new game began.

Trail treasure hunting is now a global game called geocaching.

Today all players throughout the world register their geocaches' coordinates on www.geocaching.com. There are more than 2.5 million documented geocaches around the globe now, and the numbers rise staggeringly every single day. There are several rules of etiquette involved in geocaching. View videos of the game and its rules at www. geocaching.com, as well as http://www.rei.com/learn/expert-advice/gps-geocaching. html; REI is an outdoor equipment store that sells geocaching materials.

The most important rules are: (1) Leave the geocache better than you found it; If you take something from the geocache, put something of equal or greater value back in it. (2) Be mindful of nature when placing and retrieving so as not to disturb the environment. (3) Sign your name on the log inside each geocache. (4) Put the geocache back exactly where you found it.

Additionally, there are "travel bugs," which are essentially numbered dog tags made for this sport that are meant to be taken and moved to another cache. The person who finds a travel bug logs its number on the website and agrees to move it to another cache, so the original owner can trace its movement—sometimes thousands of miles around the world.

Geocaches are typically placed in various waterproof containers, from metal boxes to film canisters to Altoid cans. Some avid players make their own containers or affix rocks to them so they are easier to conceal. Now there are tiny containers the size of thimbles, sometimes magnetic, that can make discovery even harder. Players name their geocaches, sometimes giving clues; they can be very creative in hiding them.

Ranger Colburn had placed five geocaches on the Highland Valley Trail, the first four offering clues to each subsequent one. It was a geocache game he called "The

Mystery Witch Hunt." One of the items in the final geocache treasure box is a laminated sheet documenting some of the effects the Witch Creek Fire had on San Dieguito River Park just over a year ago. "You can make it as difficult as you want," said Colburn. "You can try to stump people. It's pretty fun."

There are even a few acronyms accompanying the new sport. CITO means "Cache In, Trash Out," which refers to a global initiative to clean up parks while geocaching. FTF means "first to find"—the first person to find the geocache gets to be FTF in the logbook. ROT13 refers to hints that are encrypted, whereby each letter is rotated 13 characters up or down the alphabet. TFTC means "thanks for the cache."

Colburn and Gibbs both noted that sometimes there is enormous competition to be FTF among aficionados, who may even receive alerts on their cell phones as soon as a new geocache in their area is registered.

To place geocaches in San Dieguito River Park, go to its website, www.sdrp.org, and follow its rules. You must register with the park to place any geocaches there. The most important rule in the park is that geocaches must be placed along the trail—no bushwhacking off trail, so that sensitive habitat will not be harmed. Illegal geocaches that aren't approved by the park will be removed by the rangers in efforts to protect the park.

At the SDRP website about geocaching, go to "bookmark list" to find current geocaches on the park's trails ready to be discovered. The Mystery Witch Hunt on the Highland Valley Trail appears to have ceased, but lots more treasures are out there today.

"It's really fun solving these little mysteries," said Colburn. "And kids are whizzes at this."

Thomas Brothers Map: Page 1150, B-5.

Before You Go: Check www.geocaching.com to locate hidden geocaches wherever you want to search. For the list of current geocaches hidden on San Dieguito River Park trails, go to http://www.sdrp.org/wordpress/trails/geocaching and click on "bookmark list."

Trailhead: Highland Valley Trail is a lovely trail even if you don't search for the geocaches. It runs along Highland Valley Road in Rancho Bernardo through an agricultural area, a pastoral scene filled with many oak trees that miraculously survived the Witch Creek Fire. Find the trailhead at the intersection of Highland Valley Road and Pomerado Road, the latter an exit off Interstate 15.

Distance/Difficulty: The Highland Valley Trail is 2.0 miles one-way; easy.

6-19. Lots to Learn on Highland Valley Trail

One of the easiest, loveliest, and most accessible trails in the San Dieguito River Park takes you through Highland Valley in Rancho Bernardo, where views extend into the San Pasqual Valley agricultural preserve. The Highland Valley Trail is a bonus of sorts in the SDRP. It will not be part of the Coast-to-Crest Trail, the 70-mile trail planned from the San Dieguito River's headwaters on Volcan Mountain in Julian to the ocean at Del Mar. About 45 miles of the Coast-to-Crest Trail have been completed so far, and the river park currently includes a total of about 65 miles of trails, including auxiliary trails like Highland Valley.

The trail through Highland Valley passes through some lovely old oak groves and boulder-strewn meadows while it meanders alongside Highland Valley Road. The road is never far from view, but the trail takes in vistas to the west to Bernardo Mountain and to the east to Poway peaks.

Lessons are available on Highland Valley Trail.

The Highland Valley Trail is accompanied by numbered post markers that correspond to a pamphlet of "Discovery Points," aimed especially at children but equally informative for adults. The Ruth Merrill Children's Interpretive Walk is dedicated to the longtime San Dieguito River Park Conservancy and UNICEF volunteer, and it teaches us all the importance of a river. Discovery Point 1 asks hikers to scan the surrounding area to locate the San Dieguito River. "You won't see the river from this trail, but you will see the effects of the river," it says. "The river is found where you see the thickest growth of trees and plants." The trees and plants that grow along a river create a "riparian habitat," it continues, which is very important to wildlife for water and shelter.

The interpretive pamphlet, which can be downloaded, asks hikers to stop and listen for birds. "Each bird has its own special call," it says. "Red-tailed hawk: 'Kee-ee-arr'; house finch: "Chi-chuwee'; black phoebe: 'Tee-hee Tee-hoo.'"

It shows examples of animal tracks, which are fairly easy to spot on the sandy dirt trail. I saw lots of tracks, including those of deer, snakes, and a large bird that might have been one of those red-tailed hawks or even a wild turkey. Snake tracks are easy to spot because they typically cross the trail horizontally in wavy lines.

Discovery Point 5 is situated in an "ecotone ... the area where two types of habitat meet," it says, in this case coastal sage scrub and riparian woodland. Watch out for poison oak, it adds, with a picture of the three-leaved plant.

Discovery Point 6 discusses the Kumeyaay, "often called the Indians of the Oaks." Oak trees were very important in that native culture because acorns were ground into flour for an important food source. "The Kumeyaay helped nurture the oaks by moving saplings to the best growing areas."

Some of the huge boulders are a type of granite called gabbro, the pamphlet informs. Gabbro is formed by volcanic action deep under the earth's surface and then brought to the surface by geologic forces.

There are 15 Discovery Point markers along the trail. But there are also several quarter-mile mile markers, so don't be confused when you reach the end of the trail and spot a marker with "2.0" on it—it's a mile marker this time. At the trail's end, where a picnic bench sits under an oak and sycamore tree, simply turn around and head back.

Look for lichens that "grow where nothing else will grow," such as on rocks. That green stuff on the rocks is actually a composite organism made up of fungus and algae. "What makes lichen unique is the symbiotic relationship between the fungi and algae," says the pamphlet. "In this case, the fungus benefits from the algae through photosynthesis and, in turn, the algae receive protection from the sun and water absorbed by the fungus."

Perhaps you'll see a big pile of neatly stacked sticks and twigs. You may have discovered the home of a wood rat, another important food of the Kumeyaay, says the pamphlet.

The most noticeable wildflower on this trail in June is buckwheat, which lines the trail heavily in several places. Also on sporadic view is datura, the large white flower that is part of the nightshade family. Look for the tiny pink, red-stem filaree. Near the eastern end of the trail, look for the yellow blossoms of what looks like a kind of squash.

Learning really can be fun on the Highland Valley Trail.

Thomas Brothers Map: Page 1150, B-5, note dotted line of Highland Valley Trail.

Before You Go: Download a copy of the map at the San Dieguito River Park website: http://www.sdrp.org/wordpress/trails/.

Download the pamphlet for the Ruth Merrill Interpretive Walk at http://www.sdrp.org/kidswalk.htm.

The Highland Valley Trail is open to hikers, equestrians, bicyclists, and dogs on leashes. There is no fee.

Trailhead: From Interstate 15, exit at West Bernardo Road/Pomerado Road and head east. Turn left onto Highland Valley Road and then make an immediate right into the trail parking and staging area.

Distance/Difficulty: The round-trip is about 4.2 miles with an elevation gain of only about 150 feet; easy.

6-20. Bag Bernardo Mountain for Blue-Water Views

Hike up Bernardo Mountain on a clear winter's day, and you'll earn panoramic views, from Palomar Mountain, Volcan Mountain, and Mount Woodson to the east as well as Lake Hodges and the blue Pacific to the west. It's truly a stunning view. The hike up the 1,150-foot-high mountain, a landmark in North County, is actually only moderately taxing until the last mile of the 3.3-mile, one-way climb, when it gets pretty steep. Bernardo Mountain is No. 46 on the Sierra Club San Diego County's Peaks List, rated as class one, among the easiest of our peaks to climb. The rocky trail can create a bit more difficulty, but when you see those views, it all seems like a walk in the park.

And it is. Most of Bernardo Mountain is part of the San Dieguito River Park now, and the trail to its peak is maintained by that joint powers operation. The joint powers of SDRP, formed in 1989, are the County of San Diego and the cities of Del Mar, Escondido, Poway, San Diego, and Solana Beach.

Beautiful Lake Hodges views revealed from Bernardo Mountain.

Bernardo Mountain was saved from development in 2002 by SDRP and its conservancy partner, San Dieguito River Valley Conservancy. Plans for development of up to 82 homes were on the books since 1983 with the City of Escondido, but after a rallying cry to preserve what was then left of the landmark (its northeastern quarter was already developed) a consortium of groups, including SDRP, SDRVC, the City of Escondido, and the Nature Conservancy, raised the $4.1 million to buy the 232 acres remaining to preserve them. The whole mountain is about 400 acres and is covered with chaparral and inland sage scrub habitats. The SDRVC says there are 14 kinds of mammals that make their home here, including mule deer, bobcats, coyotes, and ringtail cats, a protected species. I saw deer tracks on the trail.

The Bernardo Mountain Summit Trail intersects with the 8.0-mile-long North Shore Lake Hodges Trail, which can be accessed at several points. The summit trail, which totals 1.95 miles one way, is reached after about 1.35 miles from the parking area noted here. The summit trail also passes through an oak riparian woodland when you reach the Felicita Creek, one of the tributaries that empties into Lake Hodges.

There are at least 55 species of birds that live on the mountain, including golden eagles. Lake Hodges, that beautiful blue body of water that swirls around the mountain's south and west flanks, is a Globally Important Bird Area, so named in 1999 by the American Bird Conservancy, conferring its highest level of recognition on Lake Hodges, the first site in California to be so formally recognized. One of the reasons Lake Hodges was honored as an avian resource is the large number of threatened California gnatcatchers that make their home on Bernardo Mountain. Additionally, more than 200 bird species live or visit Lake Hodges each year, and winter is prime bird migration time. Though the lake is fairly far away from the Bernardo Mountain trail, I saw a few uncommon white pelicans on its shoreline. I also spotted an osprey on top of a tree stump when crossing the bridge over Lake Hodges from the parking area to reach the North Shore Lake Hodges Trail that connects to the Bernardo Mountain Summit Trail.

The lake's level is low now during these drought years, at only about 39 percent capacity in 2015, so when you cross that Stress Ribbon Bridge, opened in 2009, you won't see water below but lots of vegetation during drought periods.

Lake Hodges is a City of San Diego—owned reservoir, created in 1918 when Hodges Dam was built on San Dieguito River.

The Kumeyaay lived on this river for thousands of years before the first Europeans came here in 1769. This part of San Diego County was under Spanish rule from 1769 to 1821 under authority of missions, according to the Rancho Bernardo Historical Society. The mission fathers bestowed the names that appeared on the first written maps in the early 1800s. This area was named El Paraje o Canada de San Bernardo, or "the place or canyon of Saint Bernard."

When Mexico won its independence from Spain in 1821, the mission lands came under Mexican control. From 1842 to 1845, the Mexican government granted the 17,763-acre Rancho San Bernardo to Don Jose Snook, an English sea captain who became a Mexican citizen. Snook married Maria Antonia Alvarado, and they raised cattle, sheep, horses, and mules on Rancho San Bernardo. The land passed through various hands after they died.

Water men Ed Fletcher and William Henshaw owned the remaining 5,800 acres of the old Rancho San Bernardo in the 1920s, and they began leasing it to George Daley, a pioneer rancher in Escondido. Daley bought Rancho San Bernardo in 1943. In 1961, the Daley heirs joined with developer Harry Summers to develop the ranch into a planned community called Rancho Bernardo.

You'll see that city from your perch atop Bernardo Mountain as well as all the other sights that make this climb worth the effort. Retrace your route back, remembering to make a sharp right turn when you reach that "Welcome to Bernardo Mountain Summit Trail" sign at the bottom of its northern flank.

Thomas Brothers Map: Page 1150, 5-A, where "W" in W. Bernardo Drive hits Piedras Pintadas Trail.

Before You Go: Go to the San Dieguito River Park's trail maps page and download a copy of the Bernardo Mountain Summit Trail (http://www.sdrp.org/wordpress/trails), which is on the North Shore trail map.

Also download a copy of the Piedras Pintadas Trail map for the best parking location used here. This trail is open to hikers, bicyclists, equestrians, and dogs on leashes.

Trailhead: I parked at the West Bernardo Drive parking area for the Piedras Pintadas/Bernardo Bay trails of SDRP. This parking area cuts about a half mile from the hike compared to parking at the Via Rancho Parkway/Sunset Drive parking area, from where the round-trip is about 7.2 miles.

Distance/Difficulty: From the West Bernardo Drive parking area, I logged a little more than 3.3 miles one-way, for a little more than 6.6 miles round-trip. My GPS unit measured 826 feet in elevation gain at the peak, noting a total of just over 1,000 feet by the end.

6-21. Bolted Chairs Are Unusual Reward in Clevenger Canyon

Near the end of a fairly strenuous hike up Clevenger Canyon in the San Dieguito River Park, take a seat in the two wire-mesh chairs bolted onto boulders and review your route from on high. The Clevenger Canyon South trail climbs about 1,100 feet to reach a peak that stands 1,755 feet in elevation, offering sweeping views of San Pasqual Valley to the west, all the way to the ocean on a very clear day, and over Boden Canyon to Palomar Mountain, Volcan Mountain, and the Cuyamacas to the east. On that eastern horizon, you are even able to locate the three peaks of Cuyamaca, from left to right: North Peak at 5,993 feet high, Middle Peak at 5,883 feet, and Cuyamaca Peak with its two humps at 6,512 feet high. It wasn't the clearest day when I was there, but the views were still well worth the effort to reach them from that highest point.

Clevenger Canyon is just south of the Santa Ysabel Creek and a little north of the Santa Maria Creek. When both those creeks join in the San Pasqual Valley, they then become the San Dieguito River, one of the county's major watersheds.

Some of best views of San Pasqual Valley are from Clevenger Canyon ridges.

Clevenger Canyon North and South trails are part of the San Dieguito River Park, a Joint Powers Authority created in 1989 by the County of San Diego and the cities of

Del Mar, Escondido, Poway, San Diego, and Solana Beach. They are auxiliary trails in the proposed 70-mile Coast-to-Crest Trail that will eventually extend from Volcan Mountain near Julian to the beach in Del Mar. About 45 miles of that trail have been completed, and about 65 total miles of trails within the river park's boundaries are open for public use. Many of the SDRP trails are open to bicyclists and equestrians, but the steep Clevenger Canyon trails are open only to hikers and dogs on leashes.

Hiking up Clevenger Canyon affords some of the best views of this river valley, because you can see all the way from Volcan Mountain across San Pasqual Valley. There are very few trees along the steeply sloped canyons, which are formed along a local fault, according to the SDRP. Huge granite outcroppings "are the upper margins of a batholith, an immense chunk of granitic rock which underlies most of the region," it says. A batholith is a large convergence of rock, often granite, that forms from cooled magma deep under the earth's crust. The boulders emerge on the surface after tectonic plate movements. One huge example is the Sierra Nevada batholith, where Yosemite's Half Dome is a granite monolith. The granite outcroppings near the top of the Clevenger Canyon South trail may appear fairly small when you start out, but when you stand next to them eventually, they are truly quite large.

After switchbacking up the trail for the first half-mile, you come to a fork. The right or west fork reaches a high peak at 1,550 feet in another 0.9 miles. The left or east fork, which I took, goes for another 1.7 miles to reach two view peaks at 1,755 and 1,635 feet, where you'll find those bolted chairs and the best views at the end. A short way after that first intersection, when you're on that east fork, you'll come to a riparian respite from the tree-less slopes. A creek runs through a grove of coast live oak trees, offering a shady waypoint.

Then the trail climbs up again until you reach those two chairs, an unusual sight on any of our local trails. From this vantage point, as you survey the San Pasqual Valley to the west, you might consider John Clevenger and his family, who settled this land in 1872 to farm wheat and dairy cows. Thanks to the SDRP and its partner, the San Dieguito River Valley Conservancy—local pioneer organizations in creating an east-west regional trail network—this area has been largely conserved.

The east fork of the Clevenger Canyon South trail ends after 2.2 miles from its trailhead. Retrace your steps back and enjoy those views.

The Clevenger Canyon North trail heads north from Highway 78 and is said to be steeper and harder during its 2.0-mile, one-way ascent of about 1,300 feet to 1,879 feet in elevation.

After your hike, you might want to stop in at the nearby San Diego Archaeological Center, which is 3.2 miles west from the trailhead on Highway 78. This small museum, located at 16666 San Pasqual Valley Road, displays artifacts that share the story of how people have lived here over the past 10,000 years, from Native American hunter-gatherers to immigrant settlers.

Thomas Brothers Map: Page 409, G-11, where 78 takes sharp turn to right.

Before You Go: Download a trail map for Clevenger Canyon South at San Dieguito River Park's website for its trails: http://www.sdrp.org/wordpress/trails/.
    This trail is open only to hikers and dogs on leashes. It's free and is open from dawn to dusk every day.

Trailhead: Heading east on Highway 78, also known as San Pasqual Valley Road, the trailhead for Clevenger Canyon South trails is on the right, 5.3 miles east of the San Diego Zoo Safari Park entrance, or 3.2 miles east of the San Diego Archaeological Center.
    Reach Highway 78 (San Pasqual Valley Road) from Interstate 15, exiting at Via Rancho Parkway and heading east. Turn right onto San Pasqual Valley Road.

Distance/Difficulty: It was 4.4 miles round-trip; fairly strenuous.

6-22. North Clevenger Tough but Rewards with Views

The steep trail up North Clevenger Canyon immediately east of San Pasqual Valley is a workout that surveys a beautiful, dramatic stretch of backcountry. The trail is part of the San Dieguito River Park (SDRP), which will one day complete its 70-mile-long Coast-to-Crest Trail from Julian's Volcan Mountain to the beach at Del Mar. The two Clevenger Canyon trails, North and South, are auxiliary trails in SDRP, not actually part of the Coast-to-Crest linear route. However, these Clevenger Canyon trails offer sweeping views of much of that trail's path, notably the agricultural San Pasqual Valley that lies below the canyon's steep walls.

Clevenger Canyon itself developed over a local fault, according to the City of San Diego's Open Space Parks website on the canyon and its trails. "This area is known for its peaks and steeply sloped canyons," it says. "An immense amount of granite lies under most of the region. Reddish, coarse, sandy loam covers the hillsides as a result of weathered remains from exposed batholith."

North Clevenger is a steep trail with long views.

The trail up North Clevenger Canyon climbs one of those steep slopes, studded by lots of granite boulders, some quite large and others precariously perched so that you hope this fault isn't active while you're there.

The terrain is covered in southern mixed chaparral, dominated by chamise, ceanothus, and scrub oak. There is really no shade on the trail except in the short stretch of riparian habitat that exists along the Santa Ysabel Creek at the canyon bottom.

A notable plant to look for here is the spice bush, also known as bush-rue, which is a low-growing (three to five feet high), spreading, rounded shrub with tiny green waxy leaves that have a lovely aroma similar to orange blossoms. It is actually a member of the citrus family and is a native to Southern California, appearing almost entirely only in this region. In late winter and early spring, it sports small, four-petaled white flowers and then later lots of small red berries. It will color the hillsides with gold, so that's another way to spot it. Rub some of those leaves between your fingers to inhale that citrusy fragrance.

Also here are rare Engelmann oak trees, which you can usually spot by their lighter green color compared to coast live oaks. Engelmann oaks also are usually more adapted to less water, and so they can often be found a bit farther from a creek compared to the riparian coast live oaks. Look for Engelmanns near the Santa Ysabel Creek riparian ribbon.

The trail begins with a 200-foot descent to that creek, which is currently bone dry. My hiking companion on this trail, Chris Khoury, who is a San Dieguito River Valley Conservancy board member and avid SDRP hiker, told me that in 2012 this creek was flowing so abundantly it was impossible to cross its 60-foot-spread of five-foot-deep water.

With ongoing drought conditions, the trail crossing is quite dry at the creek. From that low point, the trail climbs fairly steadily to reach the 1,879-foot elevation at the top. The trail winds up with switchbacks to make that grade a bit easier, but note there are several false trails that have been cut through the switchbacks. These can be notably steep, slippery, and hard to navigate, also causing greater area erosion, so you'll want to try hard to stay on the main trail. There are also plenty of narrow wildlife trails that cut across the canyon walls. These trails were used by the Kumeyaay people who once lived in this area. The city's parks page says historians believe these trails allowed them to collect more than 12,000 native plants for food and medicinal uses.

Clevenger Canyon is named for John Clevenger, a dairy and wheat farmer who settled in the San Pasqual Valley in 1872 with his father, wife, and five children. The Clevenger home was San Pasqual Valley's oldest until it was lost in the October 2007 wildfires that roared through here.

The original trail up North Clevenger Canyon was 10 miles long one-way, but today much of it has been obliterated. We climbed up to the top of the canyon after about 2.3 miles one-way to its summit on a large granite outcropping. We continued a little farther north reaching the boundary between this BLM land and the private Rancho Guejito (no trespassing) that lies to the north. Then we headed back down the main trail.

The views across San Pasqual Valley are splendid from the top. Large crops of citrus and avocado spread below. To the east on the horizon are clear views of Cuyamaca's peaks (from south to north): Cuyamaca, Middle, and North. Just to the north of them is the saddle of Volcan Mountain, the source of this river valley. Santa Ysabel and Santa Maria creeks in this valley ultimately join to form San Dieguito River.

You'll have a view just like the red-tailed hawks you see soaring.

Thomas Brothers Map: Page D, in the San Pasqual open space between map pages 1131 and 1152.

Before You Go: Download a copy of the trail map from San Dieguito River Park website: http://www.sdrp.org/wordpress/trails/.

You may also go to the city's open space pages in the Parks and Recreation Department for a trail map: http://www.sandiego.gov/park-and-recreation/parks/osp/sanpasqual.shtml.

Note that this steep trail is open only to hikers and dogs on leashes—no bicyclists or equestrians allowed.

Trailhead: From Interstate 15, exit at Via Rancho Parkway and head east. Turn right onto San Pasqual Valley Road and follow signs to San Diego Zoo's Safari Park on Highway 78. The parking area for the North Clevenger Canyon trail is 5.8 miles east on the north side of Highway 78 from the Safari Park entrance. The north trailhead staging area is 0.5 miles east of the Clevenger Canyon South trailhead staging area.

Distance/Difficulty: We went a total of about 5.25 miles, and my GPS unit logged a total elevation gain of just over 2,000 feet. Strenuous.

6-23. Boden Canyon a Pristine Preserved Natural Space

Hiking along the old dirt road that goes through Boden Canyon Ecological Reserve takes you through a nearly pristine natural canyon in the foothills of San Diego County. The trail winds through several kinds of habitat, including chaparral, coastal sage scrub, oak woodland, and riparian areas. The Santa Ysabel Creek flows through some of the canyon.

"While Boden Canyon is not an inherently unique feature in the landscape, most of the low-lying canyons similar to Boden Canyon have been irreparably damaged by long histories of heavy agriculture and urban fringe development," says the California Department of Fish and Wildlife on its website about this reserve. The CDFW, as well as the City of San Diego and San Diego County, own and manage the ecological reserve, which also lies within the San Dieguito River Park. "Few such canyons remain as intact representations of San Diego County's natural communities," it says.

The 2,068-acre Boden Canyon is also part of one of the longest natural wildlife corridors occurring within coastal San Diego County, which extends east to Pamo Valley and north to Riverside County through U.S. forest lands.

When I was there in 2012, I saw a posted camera with a sign informing visitors that it documents movements of bobcats, coyotes, and other passersby as part of Megan Jennings' PhD research project for the SDSU Biology Department. "I've been getting photos of some of the pretty standard species we expect to see there, including bobcats, coyotes, people, and dogs—but not too many skunks and no mountain lions," said Jennings during a phone interview. She focused primarily on bobcats, she said, to learn "how bobcats respond to burned landscapes after fire, and whether there's enough movement—connectivity between habitats." She selected bobcats as her focus because "they're more abundant than a mountain lion that needs a lot of area, and more sensitive than a coyote who may be willing to go into small canyons adjacent to homes." Her project examined whether the animals can physically travel safely between several preserves from west to east along Highways 56, 67, and 78, with the goal of advising how to improve that connectivity. She also trapped and captured bobcats to collect genetic samples and track the animals.

Natural wildlife corridor remains in Boden Canyon.

Too bad her research is no longer available to view online; she had remarkable photos from the 36 cameras she had in preserves, including Los Penasquitos, Sycamore Canyon, Goodan Ranch, Pamo Valley, and Boden Canyon. You don't often see bobcats on the trails because they're elusive and stealthy. "But look for them in the fall when they're in breeding season and their hormones are going a little crazy—that's when we get the most sightings," said Jennings.

The trail descends through nearly treeless chaparral and sage scrub to reach the creek bed. Look for blue-blooming ceanothus (wild lilac), orange monkey flowers, California poppies, yellow wallflowers, and white morning glories, all of which I spotted in mid-March.

After about a mile, you'll come to Santa Ysabel Creek, which you have to cross to continue. The water level was low enough to cause no problem for me, but it might be roaring through here sometimes. The trail then ascends and passes through a lovely oak woodland. As you reach some higher elevations, the views extend long into those natural corridors to the north and east.

The San Dieguito River Park plans to help preserve and protect Boden Canyon while also eventually constructing a segment of its Coast-to-Crest Trail through lower Boden Canyon to connect it to Pamo Valley and Lake Sutherland, among other goals. Check http://www.sdrp.org/projects/boden.htm for more details.

After about 2.5 miles, I passed through another oak woodland when the trail took another sharp turn. I headed back the way I came, making for a 5.0-mile round-trip hike. However, you may continue if you wish; this trail keeps going for a full 3.4 miles to reach Pamo Valley, offering a 6.8-mile round-trip.

Even though Boden Canyon was burned about 35 percent in the 2003 Cedar Fire and about 60 percent in the 2007 Witch Creek fires, it seems its habitats have survived, along with those beautiful bobcats.

Thomas Brothers Map: Page 409, G-11, right where Highway 78 takes that sharp downturn.

Before You Go: Download a map of Boden Canyon's trail from the California Department of Fish and Game's website: https://www.wildlife.ca.gov/Lands/Places-to-Visit/Boden-Canyon-ER. The topo map is the best one for the trail.

The trail is currently open only to hikers and dogs on leashes; mountain bikes and horses are not allowed.

It's free to park here.

Trailhead: From Interstate 15, exit at Via Rancho Parkway, head east, and follow the signs to the San Diego Zoo's Safari Park, which will take you to Highway 78. From the entrance to the Safari Park, go seven miles on Highway 78, turning left into the entrance to an unmarked gated dirt road, which is the trail. This trailhead is also located five miles west on Highway 78 from the Highway 78/67 intersection in Ramona.

Distance/Difficulty: I went for a round-trip of 5.0 miles; easy to moderate, with about 500 feet in elevation gain.

6-24. Fascinating History Awaits on Mule Hill

Mule Hill Historic Trail in Escondido offers one of the best trail stories of yesteryear in the county. It's a lovely trail through boulder-strewn grasslands along the northern edge of Lake Hodges, which was formed in 1918 when the San Dieguito River was dammed. The trail is part of the San Dieguito River Park and connects to the San Pasqual Valley Agricultural Trail. Both trails are part of the park's Coast-to-Crest Trail, which will eventually traverse 70 miles from Volcan Mountain in Julian to the coast in Del Mar.

The Mule Hill Historic Trail is about 1.5 miles long before it becomes the San Pasqual trail. Along Mule Hill, several placards tell its gripping story. "On Dec. 6, 1846, California's bloodiest battle of the Mexican War took place at San Pasqual five miles east of here," says the first placard. On December 7, American soldiers under command of Brigadier General Stephen Watts Kearny were attacked from the rear by Mexican forces. This move forced the Americans to withdraw to higher ground, where they were attacked for the next four days by the Mexican forces that had surrounded them at the bottom of the hill.

The Mexicans were called Californios, being residents of California at the time who descended from Mexican and Spanish colonists. "These men, mostly ranchers and vaqueros, were excellent horsemen and very adept with their primary weapon, an 8-foot lance," says the sign.

The Americans were short on food and resorted to eating their mules, which gave the hill its name.

There is interesting history on Mule Hill Trail.

One of the legendary scouts involved in this battle was Kit Carson. On December 8, Carson, Navy Lt. Edward Beale, and an unnamed Native American were dispatched to sneak through enemy lines to reach San Diego to seek help. On December 11, 180 troops from San Diego arrived and outnumbered the Mexican forces, who withdrew. General Kearny and his remaining men marched to what is now Old Town, "thus completing a 2,000-mile march from Kansas," notes the sign.

More history lessons on the trail tell about the earliest days of Rancho San Bernardo, a rancho land grant from Mexico in 1842 to Don Jose Francisco Snook. From 1820 to 1870, this trail was part of an overland route from San Diego to Yuma, and it was used by stagecoach for years. During this time, the town located here was known as Bernardo, "a popular stopping-off place for people traveling from Ramona to Escondido to San Diego."

Mule Hill Historic Trail is popular today with hikers, joggers, bicyclists, and equestrians. I saw a few of each, including Nola Michel on her beautiful walking horse, Bailey, and Lori Weiss on her sweet spotted blond Pony of the Americas, Rocky.

The San Pasqual Valley Agricultural Preserve Trail winds through acres of organic farms, which are compatible with healthy wildlife populations, another sign reports.

Several red-shouldered hawks soared above the trail, and I also saw four adorable jackrabbits scurry across the path. The hawks obviously didn't see those guys. The area is also now a favorite habitat for the golden eagle.

The natives, and later the pioneers, knew this area as a valley of eagles. The In-ke-pah tribe called this valley Mo-culoch-culoch, meaning "one stone on top of another."

At the trailhead, you'll also note the ongoing restoration of the Sikes Adobe Historic Farmstead. The San Dieguito River Park Joint Powers Authority purchased this site from the City of San Diego in 2008. One of the oldest structures in San Diego County and one of the few remaining adobes, the Sikes site represents the farming and ranching history of the county. It fell to the Witch Creek fire in 2007, but it has been fully restored (again; it had been restored in 2004 as well).

Zenas Sikes and his wife, Eliza, bought a 2,400-acre portion of the former Rancho San Bernardo for $2,500 in 1868. They built a one-room adobe for themselves and their six children by 1872, adding additions in wood until 1881. The family had been wheat farmers here until Zenas died after being kicked by a horse in 1881. Dairy operations were begun after their wheat farming declined. In 1897, the family had to sell the property to August Barnett for $10 to pay off the mortgages he held on it.

Few trails offer as much information about life here during the last 200 years. Add the picturesque landscape, which is especially green after rains, and you have an excellent trail exploration in store.

Thomas Brothers Map: Page 1150, 3-B—right where Sikes Adobe site shows the trail that winds east along Lake Hodges.

Before You Go: Download a map of the Mule Hill Historic Trail and its continuation as the San Pasqual Valley Agricultural Trail from the San Dieguito River Park's website: http://www.sdrp. org/wordpress/trails/. The organization's website also includes a lot of information on the Sikes adobe project and its history.

It is open to hikers, bicyclists, equestrians, and dogs on leashes.

Trailhead: To reach the main staging area for the Mule Hill Historic Trail, exit Interstate 15 at Via Rancho Parkway, heading east. At the first intersection, turn right onto Sunset Drive; continue to Sunset's dead-end and the parking area. There is no fee to park here.

Do not make the mistake I made and head onto the paved trailhead at the entrance to the parking area; it stays right next to the freeway. Rather, the trailhead for Mule Hill is across the street from the parking area, where you walk toward the historic Sikes Adobe, complete with windmill.

Distance/Difficulty: The Mule Hill Historic Trail is about 1.4 miles long for a 2.8-mile round-trip. The San Pasqual trail continues for another 8.85 miles one-way and is more difficult due to elevation gains.

6-25. Del Dios Gorge Trail Connects to Lake Hodges

One of the newer trail segments in the San Dieguito River Park offers a 2.0-mile hike through Del Dios Gorge with lovely views of the San Dieguito River. This Del Dios

Gorge Trail for hiking, horseback riding, and biking now connects to the North Shore Lake Hodges Trail at the Lake Hodges Dam. It's part of the park's plan to create the 70-mile-long Coast-to-Crest Trail that will someday link trails from the river's source in the forests of Volcan Mountain near Julian to the Pacific Ocean at San Dieguito Lagoon, between Del Mar and Solana Beach.

About 65 percent of the land within the planned Coast-to-Crest Trail system is now in public ownership. "The vision of the San Dieguito River Park reaches out to the future with ideals of preservation and protection of the beautiful rural character of the San Dieguito River Valley," according to the park's website (http://www.sdrp.org/wordpress). The park is the mission of The San Dieguito River Valley Regional Open Space Park Joint Powers Authority, a collaborative agency of the County of San Diego, the City of San Diego, and the cities of Del Mar, Escondido, Poway, and Solana Beach. The agency was formed in 1989.

The San Dieguito River Valley Conservancy is a nonprofit citizens organization formed three years earlier, in 1986. It is dedicated to managing the San Dieguito Watershed, acquiring land to complete the San Dieguito River Park, and extending segments of the Coast-to-Crest Trail. Its 1,200 members seem to be among the county's most active supporters of such an important natural resource. Check out its website: http://sdrvc.org.

Opening this Del Dios Gorge segment was no easy task, and members of all the entities mentioned above were important players. Besides completing about another mile of trail, some of which incorporates SDG&E maintenance roads, a 180-foot-long steel truss bridge had to be installed over the river. The bridge was manufactured in Colorado, shipped here in three pieces, and placed into position by three huge cranes.

The trail begins just east of Rancho Santa Fe off Del Dios Highway (S6). It winds above the river itself, affording views of the river gorge as well as the mostly uninhabited hills that surround the river valley. The trail follows S6, so you do hear that traffic noise,

Del Dios Gorge Trail connects to Lake Hodges trails.

but it's still a lovely walk through nature. There are lots of eucalyptus trees down by the river, but not for long; they are nonnative invaders that will be removed. When I was there, workers from the California Conservation Corps, a state agency that provides jobs for young people between 18 and 25, were removing some of them at the western end of the trail. The San Dieguito River Valley Conservancy has received more than $900,000 in grants over the last two years to control invasive species and restore natural habitat throughout the 94,000-acre San Dieguito River Park. "Riparian habitat in the San Dieguito River below Lake Hodges is severely impacted by eucalyptus trees and other non-native species," wrote William Proffer, former president of the board of directors, on the SDRVC website in 2009. "Eucalyptus effectively displaces native vegetation, eliminating the dense cover upon which riparian birds depend for forage and nesting habitat. To accomplish the project goals, 5.5 acres of non-native trees will be removed." Replanting of native vegetation will take place where possible by volunteers. Some of the birds that will benefit include least Bell's vireo and southwestern willow flycatcher, both endangered species, as well as the yellow warbler and yellow-breasted chat, both species of concern in California.

Along the trail a few placards offer other interesting information. One talks about bats and how they unfairly get a bad rep. They are good neighbors, says the placard, because they each eat about two thousand bugs a night.

Another sign points out that in 1916, the San Dieguito River flooded and destroyed agricultural land owned by the Santa Fe Railroad. The railroad's W. E. Hodges supported local developer Col. Ed Fletcher's ambition to build a dam that would provide water for future population growth while protecting downstream land from flooding. The dam was built in 1918, forming Lake Hodges, and since 1925 it has been owned and operated by the City of San Diego.

One sign points out the Hodges Flume that you can still see above Highway S6 from the trail. Another informs us that this area is known as the Harris Site, once owned by C. W. Harris; Malcolm Rogers, curator of San Diego's Museum of Man from 1930 to 1945, excavated several archaeological sites. Artifacts dating from three prehistoric cultural periods were found here, proving that this rich river valley has been home to people for over 9,000 years.

The people dedicated to this river park today are helping it remain a rich natural resource.

Thomas Brothers Map: Page 1148, J-7, just east of Calle Ambiente, a faint street that goes south off S6.

Before You Go: Download a map from the river park's website: http://www.sdrp.org/wordpress/trails/.
Horses, hikers, and bicyclists are allowed in the trail, as are leashed dogs. There is no fee.

Trailhead: There is trail parking at the southern end of this segment, at the Santa Fe Valley and Del Dios Gorge trailheads. Exit Interstate 5 at Via de la Valle in Del Mar and head east on S6. In Rancho Santa Fe, S6 takes a right turn at a stop sign, turning into Paseo Delicias and then Escondido Del Dios Highway. Pass Bing Crosby Boulevard, and then immediately past Calle Ambiente, turn right just before a yellow shed onto a small road. The trail parking area is down this road a short distance.

Distance/Difficulty: This trail is about 2.1 miles one-way. Retrace your steps back. Easy.

6-26. Lovely Learning on Piedras Pintadas

One of San Diego County's most informative trails, the Piedras Pintadas path near Lake Hodges features placards that share fascinating information about the Kumeyaay, who lived in this area for thousands of years. Many panels provide drawings of native plants and their Kumeyaay names and uses. Others talk about general habitat management by the Kumeyaay as well as the natives' sources of food and its preparation. Add the lovely landscape with views of the lake and the boulder-strewn hillsides surrounding it, and you have a splendid hiking experience.

Piedras Pintadas means "painted rocks" in Spanish, paying tribute to some remarkable rock art created in this area by the Kumeyaay some 500 to 1,000 years ago.

It is very hard to spot, especially in competition with scattered graffiti that has sadly been added far more recently. Shockingly, some appears to have been drawn on top of the historic rock art, showing no regard for this treasure.

Lots to learn on Piedras Pintadas Trail.

One of the placards on the trail points out that "numerous rock art panels are found in the area, painted on faces of freestanding granitic boulders." Large-scale and painted almost entirely in red ochre, the Kumeyaay rock art is abstract and geometric. "The most characteristic motif is a maze-like design of parallel lines joined at right angles. Other motifs include fret patterns, diamonds, zigzag lines, chevrons and cross-hatching." Its meaning "is undoubtedly tied to ritual and ceremonial activities."

Begin at the Rancho Bernardo Community Park and follow the main trail, heading to the left (south and west) at early major intersections. The other direction heads to the Bernardo Bay Trail. In about a half-mile, you'll cross the Green Valley Creek Bridge, which was rebuilt after the 2007 Witch Creek Fire that scorched more than 50,000 acres of the San Dieguito River Park. Head right after you cross the bridge.

After about 1.0 mile, you'll reach a fenced portion prohibiting entry that overlooks the rock face of a waterfall. There is no water there now during our drought-stricken years, but you can see where it falls when rains come. You'll also see some of that graffiti on the rock faces near the waterfall, even though posted signs indicate $10,000 fines for trespassing in this protected area.

Past the waterfall, the trail winds through a riparian area and reaches a split, where a panel tells of "Kumeyaay Resources Management Practices." This is the final loop of the Piedras Pintadas trail. I headed clockwise.

Other informative panels in this area talk about the three kinds of rabbits found here, which were important food sources for the Kumeyaay, as were wood rats, squirrels, and deer, all of which are still found here. Birds were also a food source for the native people. As you gaze over to Lake Hodges, a City of San Diego reservoir today that was created in 1918, look for western grebes, great egrets with their yellow bills and black legs, and cormorants.

You'll soon reach one of the only coast live oaks on this trail, a fine, big, old one. "A key species in traditional Kumeyaay life," says its placard, the oak tree's acorns were ground for food, and its bark was burned for fire and boiled to medicate sores.

Right next to the panel here depicting the metate, mortar, slick, and other elements of Kumeyaay "food processing," you'll see one of the actual granite boulders with its deep morteros once used for grinding those acorns. Shortly after this oak and morteros, head to the right at the trail intersection to stay on the Piedras Pintadas loop.

"The vicinity around the Piedras Pintadas trail had the largest indigenous population in the County of San Diego when the Spanish missionaries arrived," said Chris Khoury, longtime board member of the San Dieguito River Valley Conservancy. "Excavation of the middens in the area revealed that the most commonly found bone was of the southwestern pond turtle. This suggests that the Indians created a series of dams and shallow ponds along the San Dieguito River to create habitat for an important source of food. The area around the loop portion of the Piedras Pintadas trail often has one of the county's most prolific and diverse displays of wildflowers at the end of the rainy season."

In spring look for blooms of white sage, "a very important plant used in a number of ways," says a placard on the trail. Its young stalks were eaten as vegetables, the leaves were boiled for tea for serious cases of poison oak or respiratory ailments, and the leaves also burned in cooking fire coals to freshen homes. You may also see cream cups, white everlastings, shooting stars, wild lilac, sunflowers, and monkeyflowers. Several panels depict such wildflowers as blue-eyed grass, boiled for tea to relieve cramps; flat-top buckwheat, boiled for tea to ease stomach ailments; blue elderberry, whose fruit was eaten fresh or dried, and whose blossoms were boiled for tea to combat fever; and deer weed, which was used to thatch over a home.

Few trails offer as much to learn as Piedras Pintadas. Meanwhile, San Dieguito River Valley Conservancy (SDRVC) invites volunteers to participate in a program called Citizen Science. Periodic outings will gather data to help monitor plants, wildlife, and other elements of this splendid natural resource. The SDRVC has also partnered with San Diego Zoo Global Institute for Conservation Research to develop a citizen-science app called wildsd.org that provides materials on how to do field work; it can be downloaded onto iPhones. For more information, go to www.sdrvc.org.

Thomas Brothers Map: Page 1150, 5-A.

Before You Go: Download a copy of the trail map from San Dieguito River Park's website: http://www.sdrp.org/wordpress/trails/.

You can begin this trail from either the trailhead parking area just southwest on West Bernardo Drive from the Pomerado Road exit, or from Rancho Bernardo Community Park, which lies immediately south from that parking area.

This trail is open to hikers, bikers, equestrians, and dogs on leashes.

Trailhead: From Interstate 15, exit at West Bernardo Drive/Pomerado Road in Rancho Bernardo, heading west on West Bernardo Drive. Shortly, you'll see the trailhead parking area on the right of West Bernardo Drive, right before the entrance on the right into the community park.

Distance/Difficulty: The Piedras Pintadas Trail is 2.2 miles one-way; beginning at the community park, I logged just under 4.0 miles total. Starting from the Rancho Bernardo Community Park cut about 0.4 miles from the total mileage.

6-27. Peek into the Past in San Pasqual Valley

The San Pasqual Valley Agricultural Preserve Trail carves through that historic valley, offering sweeping views of inland North County where remarkably little has changed in 200 years. Farming has always been conducted here, even before California became a state in 1850, according to an informative plaque at the Ysabel Creek trailhead. Local natives farmed here for generations, but by the end of the 19th century, pioneer farmers were introducing more mechanization as well as better transportation and refrigeration, all of which developed the valley's agrarian success.

When you hike along this trail, which largely follows an old dirt road, it's amazing to see so much undeveloped acreage in the middle of urban sprawl. The plaque notes that although Southern California experienced a land boom in the 1880s, the San Pasqual Valley never became an urban center, leaving such distinction to nearby San Diego and even Escondido.

Today, the 11,000-acre San Pasqual Valley Agricultural Preserve is owned and managed by the City of San Diego, allowing farming to continue here so close to urban centers.

The trail is mostly an easy meander. I headed west from the Ysabel Creek trailhead. For the first quarter-mile or so, it follows Bandy Canyon Road, and then it dips down a bit heading northwest into the valley. After about the first mile, the trail climbs a few hundred feet as it skirts around the 1,000-foot-high Raptor Ridge. Look for hawks soaring. The views from this vantage point cross the agricultural holdings and their ponds, taking in the foothills on the horizon to the north and east.

After about 2.0 miles at the top of the ridge, a picnic table and viewing areas scope the valley views to the west, including the San Dieguito River.

The entire San Pasqual Valley Trail, including the 1.4-mile Mule Hill, covers 10.25 miles one-way, beginning at the San Pasqual Trailhead (where Highway 78 intersects with Bandy Canyon Road) and ending at the Mule Hill Trailhead on Via Rancho Parkway at Interstate 15. It's open to hikers, bicyclists, equestrians, and dogs on leashes.

San Pasqual remains agricultural zone.

It's part of the San Dieguito River Park, a regional greenway that stretches from Volcan Mountain in Julian to the beach in Del Mar. Eventually a trail will cover that entire 70 miles.

The top of the ridge offered me a good point to turn around, making for about a 4.0-mile round-trip hike. At the east end of San Pasqual Valley you'll pass the Bandy Canyon Ranch on that namesake road. Originally homesteaded by John D. Bandy in the late 1870s, the ranch once held more than 4,500 acres and included the entire San Pasqual Valley.

The 2007 Witch Creek Fire heavily damaged the property and burned more than 50,000 acres in the San Dieguito River Park, but the Bandy Canyon Ranch has been restored and now is open to the public as a wedding venue, as a private or corporate retreat with several cottages, and as a place to board your horse or take a trail ride on one of theirs. Check www.bandycanyon.com for more information.

Also nearby is the San Pasqual Battlefield State Historic Park, which commemorates the bloody exchange on December 6, 1846, between U.S. forces led by General Stephen W. Kearny and the Californios led by Major Andres Pico during the U.S.-Mexican War of 1846. The historic San Pasqual battle, also very well documented along the Mule Hill Historical Trail at the west end of this trail, was one of the bloodiest and most controversial during the war. The U.S. Army of the West had marched from Kansas to Santa Fe, New Mexico, and Kearny had erroneously been told that California was secure in American hands. He sent two-thirds of his men back to Santa Fe and continued west with only 100 men, including scout Kit Carson. They crossed the perilous, exhausting desert, arriving near what is now Ramona on December 5, 1846.

Pico's Californio forces were camped at the Native American pueblo of San Pasqual, ready for battle. At dawn on December 6, the two sides burst into battle in this trail's very valley, where the Californios' superior horsemanship and agility with lances proved advantageous over the U.S. troops' short swords and clumsy rifles. Twenty-one Americans were killed here to one Californio, it is believed. Some of the deceased soldiers were buried here.

Check that state park after you've hiked in the same storied land.

Thomas Brothers Map: Page 1151, B-1, right where Bandy Canyon Road intersects with Ysabel Creek Road. (You'll see dotted trail alongside Bandy Canyon Road).

Also Page 1131, F-6, where the dotted line (the trail) begins at the intersection of 78 (San Pasqual Valley Road) and Bandy Canyon Road.

Before You Go: Download a copy of the trail map from the San Dieguito River Park at http://www.sdrp.org/wordpress/trails/.

For more information about the San Pasqual Battlefield State Historic Park, go to http://www.parks.ca.gov/?page_id=655.

This trail is open to hikers, bicyclists, equestrians, and dogs on leashes.

Trailhead: The trail actually starts near the intersection of Highway 78 (San Pasqual Valley Road) and Bandy Canyon Road, but most of that first 2.75 miles follows Bandy Canyon Road. I started at the Ysabel Creek Staging Area, with plenty of parking at the intersection of Bandy Canyon Road and Ysabel Creek Road.

To reach the Ysabel Creek Staging Area, exit Interstate 15 at Pomerado Road/West Bernardo Road, heading east. Turn left onto Highland Valley Road, continuing for four miles. Turn left at Bandy Canyon Road and then left at Ysabel Creek Road; the parking area is at this intersection.

Alternatively, from Highway 78/San Pasqual Valley Road, turn south onto Bandy Canyon Road, travel about three miles, and turn right at Ysabel Creek Road.

Distance/Difficulty: Total length 8.85 miles one-way. I went about 2.0 miles, for a 4.0-mile round-trip. Easy to moderate.

6-28. Santa Fe Valley Trail Cuts through History

The Santa Fe Valley Trail along the San Dieguito River offers a very pleasant walk through coastal sage scrub, with occasional views of that river and its riparian habitat. The 2.0-mile-long trail cuts through the river valley, where significant troves of local history have left their mark.

First, you'll notice lots of eucalyptus trees, especially right along the river. They are descendants of the millions of eucalyptus planted in the early 1900s by the Atchison, Topeka, and Santa Fe Railway, which had bought most of the Rancho San Dieguito land grant in 1906 from Juan Osuna. Osuna, the Mexican Alcalde of the Pueblo of San Diego, was awarded an 8,825-acre land grant (then called Rancho San Dieguito) in 1845 from Mexico. The land included much of what is Rancho Santa Fe today, according to the Rancho Santa Fe Association, which was formed in 1928 by local homeowners.

The railway company, through its subsidiary Santa Fe Land Improvement Company, planted the eucalyptus in hopes of using the timber for railroad ties, but the wood soon proved itself unsuitable for that purpose. "However, the eucalyptus plantings forever changed the character of the area," notes the association. "Despite the fact that eucalyptus trees have called San Diego home for more than 150 years, they are not native to the area and have replaced native habitat, particularly in riparian areas," says the September 2009 newsletter of the San Dieguito River Valley Conservancy (www.sdrvc.org), a volunteer organization dedicated to improving and protecting the San Dieguito River Valley. Fallen eucalyptus leaves are essentially toxic to many other plants. The conservancy is working to remove the eucalyptus trees from the Del Dios Gorge and Santa Fe Valley areas, which includes this part of the river. It says when these invasive nonnative plants are removed, at least 29 species of natives will likely thrive again, including the beautiful western sycamore trees. Such habitat improvement will also likely benefit two federally endangered bird species, the least Bell's vireo and the southwestern willow flycatcher.

Santa Fe Trail winds through local history.

Another interesting historical fact is that this area of the San Dieguito River Valley hosts "one of the most important archaeological sites in the United States [that] has been placed on the National Register of Historic Places," notes the San Diego Archaeological Center (www.sandiegoarchaeology.org), which opened in 2002 in Escondido near the San Diego Zoo Safari Park. Though not visible from the trail because its exact location is kept under wraps, this archaeological site is known as the C. W. Harris Site Archaeological District.

Malcolm Rogers, an orange farmer from Escondido who was also an avid amateur archaeologist, started exploring this area in 1919. When a flood in 1927 exposed more artifacts in the San Dieguito River Valley on a farm owned by C. W. Harris, Rogers and others began an additional 10-year excavation project. Their studies and others over the last 70 years have proved that people lived in this area for over 9,000 years. The three main prehistoric cultural periods are all represented here: the San Dieguito, whose people lived from 7,000 to 10,000 years ago; the La Jolla, who lived from 4,000 to 6,000 years ago; and the Late Prehistoric, ancestors of the Kumeyaay, who lived from 1,000 to 3,000 years ago.

Less than 10 years ago, the Harris Site received even better protection when the Starwood Capital Group in 2001 developed the Crosby at Rancho Santa Fe, a 722-acre development of 443 homes on an 18-hole golf course. Starwood's development included environmental protection of the river valley open space that borders it, keeping 170 of its 722 acres as preserved open space. In fact, Starwood built the Santa Fe Valley trail along the length of its property. The company has also partnered with the conservancy on that eucalyptus removal, and it built a 340-foot bridge over the river to minimize encroachment.

The Santa Fe Valley Trail passes under that bridge and continues right next to the golf course in several places. At its western end, the trail switchbacks up a few hundred feet to reach the top of a hill where power lines lie. When you reach that viewpoint, you can see miles of this pristine river valley bordered by that golf course, as well as expansive equestrian and agricultural estates. People have loved living here for a long, long time.

Thomas Brothers Map: Page 1148, J7, the dotted line road just east of Calle Ambiente that goes south to the dotted trail line along the river.

Before You Go: Download a map of the Santa Fe Valley Trail from San Dieguito River Park website: http://www.sdrp.org/wordpress/trails/.

The Santa Fe Valley Trail is open to hikers, equestrians, mountain bicyclists, and dogs on leashes. It's free.

Trailhead: Exit Interstate 5 at Via de la Valle in Del Mar and head east on S6. In Rancho Santa Fe, S6 takes a right turn at a stop sign, turning into Paseo Delicias and then Escondido Del Dios Highway. Pass Bing Crosby Boulevard, and then immediately past Calle Ambiente, turn right just before a yellow shed onto a small road. The trail parking area is down this road a short distance.

Distance/Difficulty: The Santa Fe Valley Trail is about 2.0 miles one-way; retrace your steps for a 4.0-mile round-trip hike. The trail connects with the Del Dios Gorge Trail, offering another 2.0-mile length north to the Lake Hodges Dam. Easy.

6-29. North Shore Lake Hodges One of Best for Birding

Birders flocks to Lake Hodges for its avian bounty. When I hiked the North Shore Lake Hodges Trail in mid-October, I saw several impressive birds in the oaks and eucalyptus along the shore as well as many waterfowl wading and gliding on the lake. At the beginning of my hike, I saw three redheaded, two-foot-tall turkey vultures resting in some eucalyptus trees, occasionally soaring in search of a carcass. They ride columns of warm air called thermals to save energy, covering miles of territory, according to the National Audubon Society's *Field Guide to Birds, Western Region*.

Sweet little song sparrows darted in and out of the coastal sage scrub shrubs. Near the boat dock, I saw majestic white great egrets standing at the shoreline; these lovely "stately fishermen" are also year-round residents here, according to "The Birds of Lake Hodges," a brochure produced by the San Dieguito River Park. Just beyond the boat dock, I saw a beautiful red-tailed hawk. Red-tailed hawks, American kestrels and red-shouldered hawks are year-round residents who also breed here. During courtship, the red-tailed hawk performs "spectacular aerial acrobatics," says the brochure.

Lake Hodges is one of the world's best birding sites.

Crystal Burlington, assistant reservoir keeper of Lake Hodges, told me the large birds I spotted in the oak trees near the boat dock are among the 12 resident black-crowned night herons who live in those trees. Down by the water were several pairs of mallard ducks, lots of black American coots with their distinctive white beaks, gulls, and even a wintering whimbrel with its long legs and down-curved bill.

The western grebe is "arguably the bird most readily associated with Lake Hodges," according to the river park's brochure. Burlington told me their mating ritual is fascinating to watch as a pair flies above the water and then plunges down, essentially in a dance.

More than 200 species of birds are year-round or winter residents on Lake Hodges. In fact, the winter months are some of the best times to visit because of the thousands of migratory birds.

Lake Hodges is designated a Globally Important Bird Area by the National Audubon Society and American Bird Conservancy. It was so named in 1999 after efforts by the San Dieguito River Park and Palomar Audubon Society submitted extensive documentation of the lake's avian resources. The Important Bird Area (IBA) program was launched in the United States in 1995 with ascending levels of state, national, continental, and global designation; Lake Hodges was the first site in California to be designated at that highest level. One of the birds that helped secure that designation is the California gnatcatcher, a threatened species that thrives in the 2,300 acres of coastal sage scrub habitat surrounding the lake.

Lake Hodges is owned and operated by the City of San Diego Water Department, and it's a man-made reservoir built in 1918. Some 300 square miles of watershed feed the lake, which holds 30,251 acre-feet of water covering 1,234 surface acres. At full capacity, Lake Hodges is 6.5 miles long with about 27 miles of shoreline.

Its longest trail is the 8.2-mile North Shore Lake Hodges Trail that extends from the Lake Hodges Dam to Interstate 15. I covered the middle half of the trail, starting at the parking area at the end of Rancho Drive, just below Hernandez Hideaway restaurant in Del Dios.

The first 1.2 miles from my starting point to Del Dios Community Park is a wide-track dirt trail that passes through verdant groves of oaks, eucalyptus, pepper, and occasional sycamore trees. It's also popular with mountain bikers; stay to one side so you don't get run over.

After the park, the trail continues another 1.1 miles to the boat dock, offering far less shade as it gets a bit farther from the water. I went just a bit farther after the boat dock, where the trail narrows into a single track and gets closer to the water. Watching fishing boats, small sailboats, and kayakers on the water was almost as much fun as the birding. The lake is open for fishing and boating Wednesdays, Saturdays, and Sundays during fishing season from February through October, and only by a permit purchased near the boat dock.

The trail is open year-round, and the birds are always beckoning.

Thomas Brothers Map: Page 1149, E-4, end of Rancho Drive at the water, where dotted line intersects.

Before You Go: Go the website for the San Dieguito River Park, (http://www.sdrp.org/wordpress/trails), to download a map of the North Shore Lake Hodges Trail.

It is open to hikers, bicyclists, equestrians, and dogs on leashes.

For information about fishing and boating on the lake, go to http://www.sandiego.gov/water/recreation/reservoirs/hodges.shtml.

Trailhead: From Interstate 5, exit at Via de la Valle in Del Mar and head east on S6. In Rancho Santa Fe, S6 takes a right turn at a stop sign, turning into Paseo Delicias and then Escondido Del Dios Highway.

From Del Dios Highway, turn right (east) off S6 onto Rancho Drive. There is a parking area at the end of Rancho Drive, just below Hernandez Hideaway Mexican Restaurant.

Distance/Difficulty: I went about 2.4 miles one-way, turning around and retracing my route for a round-trip of 4.8 miles. The trail is mostly flat; easy.

6-30. Oaks, Views at County's Luelf Pond Preserve

Relatively new to San Diego County's Open Space Preserve collection is Luelf Pond Preserve in Ramona. It's a day-use only area of nearly 90 acres that includes 2.0 miles of trails. The best reason for hiking on this trail is walking through the oak woodland habitat at its beginning. For about one-third of a mile, the trail takes you through a verdant landscape under a canopy of dense coast live oak trees. It's surely one of San Diego County's loveliest habitats, and the oak woodland example on the Luelf Pond trail is excellent.

Oak grove and views are found at Luelf Pond Preserve.

The coast live oak, an evergreen, can typically reach 250 years old. We have some live oaks in the county that are older than that. Here on the Luelf Pond trail, these specimens have probably survived well over 100 years. They withstood the catastrophic Cedar Fire of 2003, which burned over 380,000 acres countywide—some 15 percent of county land. A placard on this trail reports that over 95 percent of this 90-acre preserve was burned in that fire. "Oak species are fire-adapted, which means that they survive after a fire under normal conditions," says the placard. It's an amazing recovery. Though the trunks may be charred still, the trees are alive and well. Many small mammals and birds thrive in oak woodlands, where acorns provide food and branches provide shelter.

After a lovely stroll through this oak woodland, the trail comes to an intersection of sorts. A steep trail to the right climbs up the hill. The main trail continues straight ahead for a very short distance to a locked gate, where it ends. You can enjoy this fairly flat, easy walk through the oak trees and turn around for a short hike, or you can opt for the right turn to seek some higher views.

This part of the Luelf Pond Preserve trail is much harder going. It doesn't incorporate switchbacks and basically climbs straight up nearly to the top of the ridge for about another 1.5 miles.

Now you are walking through chaparral habitat, "one of the most widespread vegetation communities in San Diego County," says a placard on the trail. Plants in the chaparral community are typically dense, hard-stemmed, leathery-leaved shrubs that can reach 10 feet tall. Cacti may be included, but typical chaparral plants are manzanita (with its pretty red bark), scrub oak, chamise (with its white flowers), mimulous (brilliant red flowers), and several kinds of ceanothus, also called California wild lilac, which should burst into bloom in the spring.

"Chaparral has adapted to wildfire by either resprouting from underground roots after a burn or regrowing from seeds after a fire. This new growth has less competition for resources such as nutrients, sunlight and water and thrives once a fire has cleared an area," the placard says. After a fire like the Cedar Fire of 2003, the plants in this habitat reach their full height in about 10 years, but they won't reach their full density until about 20 years later.

This part of the trail, as is typical of chaparral, offers much less shade than oak woodland, so will be especially hot in the summer. The trail keeps climbing up, reaching an elevation gain of about a few hundred feet at the top. You'll recognize the top of the trail when you encounter enormous slabs of granite that offer a perfect perch to peer at the wide-open vistas to the south. Although you can see Ramona housing communities to the east, the south and west are notably free of development. The topography is a layered one of hills and valleys with lots of boulders.

I couldn't find any information about who Luelf might have been or how this parcel was acquired by the county, but some Internet research turned up some likely explanations. According to a 1958 article in the *Vista Press* newspaper, an Oscar Luelf of Ramona was a member of the county's Farm Bureau. Another citing of the name noted that the Luelf Ranch was developed into estate homesites beginning in 1978. I guessed Luelf was a Ramona rancher whose land once held the little pond.

After my column appeared, James W. Hodges, an attorney in Pacific Beach, responded, solving the mystery of Luelf Pond's namesake. He says Oscar and Evelyn Luelf (pronounced "elf" with an "L" in front) headed "an old-time chicken ranching family back in the 1940s and 1950s in Ramona ... Their old home is still there on the top of the knoll." Mr. Hodges was a 1960 Ramona High graduate along with Oscar and Evelyn's son, Steve. Joe and Danny Luelf were Steve's younger brothers. Oscar and Evelyn moved to Arkansas in the 1960s.

"Steve and I went on to college and law school, both graduating in 1967 ... we still remain in touch. He worked as an attorney with a Los Angeles firm until summer of 1979 when he quit, stopped by my home in Escondido to say good-bye (in his Jaguar with skis on the roof), and moved to Arkansas where he resides to this day." Steve Luelf then subdivided his family's Ramona property, "where Luelf Pond is located, saving the beautiful oak and pond area where we used to hike as kids." Many thanks, Mr. Hodges.

Once you reach the top elevation of the trail, it has become more like an old road and levels off. I recommend that you turn around here at the top by the big slabs of granite, before the trail descends as it continues. I continued a little farther, looking for that pond. When the trail starts to descend a bit, you'll come upon some large boulders with old spray-painted "No Trespassing" on them.

I continued, believing the signs were not current and that I was on county open-space land. I soon arrived at a very small pond that appeared more like someone's backyard. That homeowner also responded after my column ran and asked hikers not to trespass or sit on his chairs. He has since posted more obvious no-trespassing signs.

Thomas Brothers Map: Page 1172, E-4.

Before You Go: You can download a simple map of the preserve as well as driving directions from the county's parks page: http://www.sdcounty.ca.gov/parks/openspace/luelfpond.html.
⠀⠀⠀This open-space preserve is open to hikers, bicyclists, and equestrians; dogs are not allowed on open-space preserves.

Trailhead: From Interstate 15, exit at No. 17, the Scripps Poway Parkway exit. Head east on Scripps Poway Parkway for 8.6 miles. Turn left onto SR-67 and go 7.9 miles. Turn right onto Dye Road. After 1.0 mile, turn right onto Southern Oak Road. After another mile, turn right onto Willow Oak Drive, which turns into Duck Pond Lane. Park in the cul-de-sac by the Luelf Pond sign.

Distance/Difficulty: About 2.0 miles one-way, 4.0 miles round-trip; moderate.

6-31. Old Cattle Ranch Offers Oaks, Views, and Flowers

Barnett Ranch Preserve in Ramona is a 728-acre open space that offers two trails through lovely grasslands and oak woodlands, awash in wildflower blooms during spring. The property was purchased by the San Diego County in 2002 to be included in the Multiple Species Conservation Program (MSCP) to preserve sensitive species. Some of the sensitive species that thrive in these riparian, oak woodland, and coastal sage scrub habitats include the Southern California rufous-crowned sparrow, loggerhead shrike, white-tailed kite, and orange-throated whiptail lizard. Much of the vegetation here is native and nonnative grassland, because the property was a working cattle ranch for over 100 years.

Barnett Ranch has loads of spring wildflowers.

Augustus Barnett and his wife, Martha, had come west from New York. Augustus first established himself as a prominent businessman in Cleveland from about 1825 to

1840, according to an article published in the *San Diego Union-Tribune* in 2007 by Vincent Nicholas Rossi. The Barnetts moved to California in 1869 and to San Diego County in 1875. They established the Barnett Ranch in Ramona in 1877, which eventually grew to more than 1,300 acres and produced cattle as well as honey.

Augustus and Martha Barnett are important players in Ramona history, especially for the 1894 construction and gift of the Ramona Town Hall on Main Street, listed on the National Register of Historic Places. Ramona Town Hall, one of the largest and oldest adobe structures in Southern California, was designed by famed architect William S. Hebbard, who would eventually partner with Irving Gill, another famous local architect during the early 1900s.

Augustus Barnett died in 1906, but his family has continued ranching on Barnett Ranch for generations. His grandson Jimmy, who died at 87 in 1990, was a lifelong rancher there. His great-great-grandsons, Phil and Dan Parker, continue to run part of the original Barnett Ranch, according to a 2003 *U-T* article by Ruth Lepper.

There may also be plenty of descendants of Augustus' bees, because many were buzzing on the bright purple lupine. We also tried to identify several other wildflowers along the trail, using James Lightner's book *San Diego County Native Plants* and other sources. We spotted tall spiky purple gilia, curving yellow fiddlenecks, densely packed and short yellow brass buttons, lots of blue phacelia, and some very tiny apricot-colored ground cover.

There are two trails that take off from the trailhead. I took the Rattlesnake Trail/Oak Loop Trail that offered a 2.8-mile round-trip hike along an old ranch road. It's an easy walk through the old grasslands sprinkled with live oak trees that gather near the San Vicente Creek. The trail crosses the creek, which can be full with water, but a detour pathway through the grass circumvents getting your feet wet. You'll also see a small pond that was dammed from the creek that probably was a former cattle watering hole. Here the surrounding ground is covered in those tight yellow buds of brass buttons. A couple of picnic benches scattered on the trail hold court under the old oak trees so you can relax in some shade. The Rattlesnake and Oak Loop trails, which separate only a short way at their ends, culminate at viewpoints that survey a swath of open space in this foothill country. You backtrack on the same trail.

The trails are open to hikers, bicyclists, equestrians, and dogs on leashes. I encountered three horseback riders, Yvonne Mendoza on Amigo, Gloria Coleman on Fickle Rose, and Ray Spence on Duro. Spence, who said he's "cowboy'd all my life," used to work with Phil Parker on Barnett Ranch with the Hereford cattle.

Today Spence still works with ranchers and their cattle, and he trains horses and their riders at San Diego Country Estates' stables. He said he takes people on trail rides through nearby Riviera Oaks Resort.

The second trail on Barnett Ranch Preserve is the Valley View Trail that offers a 2.6-mile round-trip hike. You can easily combine the two for a little more than 5.0 miles round-trip.

Thomas Brothers Map: Page 1172, G-5

Before You Go: Download a trail map at the San Diego County parks' page: http://www.
sdcounty.ca.gov/parks/openspace/Barnett_Ranch.html.
  It's open to hikers, bicyclists, equestrians, and dogs on leashes.

Trailhead: Heading east on Highway 67, in downtown Ramona, turn right onto Tenth Street,
which turns into San Vicente Road. Go about 2.5 miles and turn right into the Barnett Ranch
Preserve parking area on Deviney Lane.
  It's free.

Distance/Difficulty: From 2.6 to 5.4 miles round-trip, depending on the trails you choose. Easy.

6-32. Dos Picos Trail Adds Educational Element

The nature trail in Ramona's Dos Picos County Park is not only a pleasant walk through
oaks and boulders; it also offers some education along the way. There are two short trails
in the county park, and 75 campsites are also tucked among old oak trees, along with
a large picnic area with many tables and a lovely little pond with lots of ducks.

The trails add up to no more than a mile, but you may wander around them for
an hour or two and contemplate the lessons staked out on the main nature trail. The
shortest of the two trails takes off from the parking lot furthest east and winds up
above the pond. You can connect to the main nature trail from the south end of the
pond just west of its dam.

Find this fine trail at Dos
Picos County Park.

Before you head out, be sure to ask at the
ranger station for a headset with the tiniest
iPod to play the narration that accompanies
12 numbered posts along the main nature
trail. When you start on the nature trail
from that southwest side of the pond, the
numbered posts will go from 12 to one; the
beginning of the trail, conversely, is at the
westernmost end of the campsites, if you'd
rather go from one to 12 with the posts.

The numbered posts and narration are
an Eagle Scout project by Hunter Owens
in 2008.

Post No. 1 asks hikers to stop, close
their eyes, and listen. "Focus your senses on
the sounds, smells, and movements around
you," the speaker says.

Also available are laminated sheets by
the ranger station to bring along with you
that point out sights, sounds, and clues.

If you hear a bird "laughing" at you in a tree, it just may be a redheaded acorn woodpecker. If you hear a sharp sound near the ground that goes "deek! deek! deek!" see if you can find a ground squirrel.

If you see a bunch of acorn shells on top of a rock, a bird might have placed them there while knocking them open for the seeds inside. If you find a little gray wad of fur and bones, you may have found an owl pellet. "Owls gulp down their food whole and regurgitate what they can't digest," the narration says.

Notice holes in the ground under trees. Snakes don't dig those holes, but they may go inside them for food or shelter. If the hole is as big as a fat burrito, it was probably made by a ground squirrel; if it's smaller, like a hot dog, is was probably dug by a gopher.

A numbered post points out the granite formations of the boulders along the trail. "Almost all rocks here are granite formed from molten material deep below the earth's surface," the narrator says. Movement of the earth's crust has brought them to the surface.

The posts will identify sugar bush, whose berries made a pleasant drink enjoyed by local Kumeyaay; scrub oak, whose acorns are a prime food source for birds and small mammals; manzanita, Spanish for "little apples," for the small fruits it bears on its reddish branches; thick-leaved yerba santa, with its woolly leaves that were brewed into medicinal cures for ancient people here; lichen, the living algae and fungus on rocks; and the mainstay plants of our local chaparral: California lilac, mountain mahogany, chamise, buckwheat, and poison oak.

Two different species of the wild lilac bloom here in spring: the very common chaparral whitethorn ceanothus, which blooms in blue, and the cup-leaf ceanothus, which blooms in white.

Dos Picos means "two peaks" in Spanish, derived from two prominent peaks nearby. Though unidentified, I think the two peaks, which you can see from the trail, are nearby Iron Mountain and Mount Woodson. Mount Woodson is especially obvious, covered in boulders with communication towers on top.

The coast live oak and Engelmann oak trees here make the picnic and camping areas especially inviting; some of them are said to be 300 years old. As the nature trail winds up into the hills, you'll encounter more scrub oaks.

Another informative sheet near the ranger station points out that a mature oak tree can absorb up to 50 gallons of water a day. Some oaks don't produce acorns until they are 20 years old, and when they are over 100 years old, acorn production starts to slow.

There are a few leftover remnants from the 1970s of an exercise area near the pond.

The main attraction is that oak-studded, boulder-strewn trail where views extend to those two peaks, as well as to Ramona and mountains on the horizon to the east. See what your senses will uncover at Dos Picos.

Thomas Brothers Map: Page 1171, H-5.

Before You Go: Download a map and brochure about Dos Picos County Park at the San Diego County Parks page: http://www.sdcounty.ca.gov/parks/Camping/dos_picos.html.

There is a $3 day-use fee, payable at the entrance.
The hiking trails are open only to hikers and dogs on leashes.

Trailhead: From Highway 67 heading east into Ramona, turn right onto Mussey Grade Road, following the signs to Dos Picos County Park. After about a mile, turn right onto Dos Picos Park Road and enter the park after about 0.8 miles.

To reach the beginning of the nature trail, head to the southwestern end of the campsite area. Or, from the eastern end of the park, begin with the smaller trail above the pond and head up the nature trail from the southwest edge of the pond.

Distance/Difficulty: About 1.0 mile total; easy.

6-33. Holly Oaks for Horses and Luelf Pond Oaks

Holly Oaks Park in Ramona is really dedicated to equestrians, but hikers can enjoy an outing here too. From the park, follow a soft-surface suburban trail along a neighborhood road; then connect to an open-space preserve to Luelf Pond Preserve and its wonderful old oaks.

The Holly Oaks Park staging area sits at the intersection of Southern Oak Road and Dye Road. There is an arena complete with barrels for training and working horses, and several corrals are secured with white-painted fencing. Volunteers of the Ramona Trails Association (RTA) developed this facility, which members and others use for special events and weekend workouts. Opposite its entry, there's a gate at the far end of the white fencing that takes hikers and horses out into the open space preserve part of Holly Oaks, where a short loop trail traverses the 25-acre scrub.

Holly Oaks also features a trail system of pathways that begins along Southern Oak Road, where I headed out from the park.

This trail leads to oaks in Ramona.

This unpaved pathway next to the road continues all the way to the end of Southern Oak Road, about 1.2 miles from the arena area.

Before its end, at Southern Oak Road's intersection at Oak Shade Lane on the right (west), continue down that short spur street to its end, where a trail heads into more open-space preserve and a fine stand of oaks. "Thanks to years of determined effort by Planning Group member Patrick Uriel and Holly Oaks resident George Eastwood," this area was opened to the public in 2004, according to the RTA.

Continue through the oaks here to Duck Pond Lane and then head left along that lane to the entrance to Luelf Pond Preserve. The magnificent oaks in this lower section of Luelf Pond Preserve have been estimated at some 200 years old. They form beautiful canopies over the road and make for a worthy reward on this suburban trail.

They are all mostly coast live oaks here, "the most common large tree in the county," according to James Lightner's *San Diego County Native Plants.* "Woodlands arise in valleys, where water is plentiful but not constant," says Lightner. When the waters are flowing in Luelf Pond's oak valley, equestrians like to take their horses here to get them used to walking through water, says the RTA.

Oak trees provide welcome shade for hikers as well as lots of woodland creatures. Their acorns were a favored and important food source for the Kumeyaay people, who lived on our lands for thousands of years before the arrival of Europeans. "After removing the shell, they ground the seeds into meal, which was washed to remove the bitter taste, and boiled into mush or baked in ashes as bread," according to the National Audubon Society's *Field Guide to Trees, Western Region.*

Oak woodlands are extremely important to wildlife, according to the U.S. Forest Service. Some 110 bird species live in oak woodlands during breeding season. Oaks' acorns are a prime food source for many species, including the acorn woodpecker, our state bird the California quail, and the lovely blue western scrub jay, as well as bighorn sheep, black bears, chipmunks, and squirrels, cottontail rabbits, mule deer, raccoons, opossums, and wild pigs.

There are 2.0 miles of trails in Luelf Pond Preserve, including one that heads sharply uphill to reach panoramic views of the backcountry east of Ramona. Check for my separate column on Luelf Pond. This time, I stuck to the flatlands of that lovely oak woodland before turning around. After heading back the same way I came, I walked through the Holly Oaks subdivision again.

Just before you reach Mesa Oak Court on the east side of Southern Oak Road, an entrance into the Holly Oaks open-space area lies on the west side of Southern Oak Road. Follow that into the scrub land where that loop trail winds through this open space. This is dry land with virtually no shade except for a cottonwood tree or two.

I followed this dirt trail back to the white-fenced arena and parking area where I began.

Thomas Brothers Map: Page 1172, D-4, Holly Oaks Park.

Before You Go: Check the county's parks page for Holly Oaks Park and download a copy of the trail map at http://www.co.san-diego.ca.us/parks/picnic/hollyoaks.html.

More information and another trail map is also found at Ramona Trails Association's page on Trials and Camps: http://www.ramonatrails.org/trails-camps.

These trails are open to hikers, equestrians, mountain bikers, and dogs on leashes.

Trailhead: From Highway 67 heading north into Ramona, turn right (east) onto Dye Road. Proceed to Southern Oak Road on the right, where the Holly Oaks Park staging area and arena are located. The pathway along Southern Oak Road, as well as the loop trail from the arena, begin here.

Distance/Difficulty: From about 3.5 to 5.0 miles round-trip, depending on how much ground is covered in Luelf Pond Preserve and in the open-space preserve of Holly Oaks. Fairly easy.

6-34. Ramona Grasslands Trail One of County's Newest

One of the newest trails in the county covers a 4.0-mile loop in a small portion of the Ramona Grasslands Preserve. Opened in June 2011, the trail traverses an important grassland ecosystem that supports several habitats, including grasslands, coastal sage scrub, and oak woodlands, as well as rare animals such as the Stephens' kangaroo rat and the arroyo toad.

Particularly special here are the "spectacular number of hawks," which spend the winter here, says the county. Many year-round residents include red-tailed hawks, red-shouldered hawks, and some rare pairs of golden eagles.

The Wildlife Research Institute (www.wildlife-research.org), which has its headquarters next door to Ramona Grasslands, conducts "Hawk Watch" events each year on Saturdays in January and February, inviting the public to view these splendid soaring birds.

More trails are likely in Ramona Grasslands' future.

The county notes that more than two-thirds of what was once an extensive grassland ecosystem here in Santa Maria Valley has been lost to development. Golden eagles are primarily a grasslands species and have fallen from a recorded 104 pairs in the late

1800s to about 46 breeding pairs in 2008, according to WRI, "primarily due to lost habitat which were grasslands or combinations of grasslands and other open plant communities."

WRI was one of the principal sponsors to preserve the Ramona Grasslands. It began a campaign in 1996, and with help from several local volunteers, including Carol Angus, Tom Carr, Janet Gilbert, and Bruce and Regina Wilson, it garnered support from the Nature Conservancy, California Fish and Game, U.S. Fish and Wildlife Service, and the County of San Diego to protect this endangered habitat. Over the next 10 years, the Nature Conservancy acquired several parcels to create this Ramona Grasslands Preserve. Among them was the 419-acre Cagney Ranch, owned by William Cagney, brother of the actor James Cagney; the 1,231-acre Eagle Davis Ranch; and the 1,400-acre Gildred Ranch. The preserve now counts 3,521 acres.

"The Ramona Grasslands is far from complete," says WRI on its website. It "should be as big as 7,000+ acres when complete, including conservation easements, all county airport and Ramona Water District lands and connective lands ... to ensure the Ramona Grasslands do not become an island but rather include corridors where wildlife can travel."

The preserve has also proved valuable for archaeological evidence of Kumeyaay villages. Native Americans occupied the Santa Maria Valley for thousands of years prior to the arrival of the Spanish in 1769, and rare finds of entire villages have been undisturbed and preserved here, according to a management and monitoring plan for Ramona Grasslands Preserve prepared for The Nature Conservancy. Nine major village locations have been studied, and several "contain stacked rock architecture ... the remains of several structures built by the Kumeyaay, including a unique ceremonial structure," says the report.

The 4.0-mile loop trail circles around a 480-acre western portion of the preserve. The rest of the preserve is not yet open to the public, but additional trails are planned, says the county. The current trail does not come near those archaeological sites, perhaps helping to preserve them.

Much of the trail follows an old ranch road, and hawks soaring above are nearly always on view. The soft dirt of the trail also reveals many footprints. You might see not only the hooves of visiting horses and paw prints of dogs but tracks of local residents such as bobcats, coyotes, and mountain lions. I saw a few snake tracks that often tend to cross the trail horizontally, including a big one that would have been a formidable sight in the flesh.

From the parking area, I took a left at the trailhead, beginning a clockwise route on the 0.8-mile Meadow Loop. I noticed several wildlife trails that take their own paths off the main path through the grasslands. This trail then hits a connector trail. Turning left takes you to the main 2.0-mile Wildflower Loop Trail. I took the right arm of this loop trail, beginning a counterclockwise route. This trail winds through some wonderful oak woodlands, especially along the Santa Maria Creek (dry in late summer and fall), and it gains a little elevation to offer some fine views to the south and east beyond Ramona and its airport.

When the loop trail rejoins that connector, take a left to reach the connector trail back to the parking area. But first, take a short detour to the right, and you'll come to a pretty pond, where I also found black cattle spending their afternoon.

Instead of heading right to go back on the Meadow Loop again, go straight ahead to the parking area.

Thomas Brothers Map: Page 1151, 7-G—just a mile east on Highland Valley Road from Archie Moore Road intersection.

Before You Go: The county parks' website has a Ramona Grasslands Preserve page, but there is no trail map yet: http://www.sdcounty.ca.gov/parks/openspace/Ramona_Grasslands.html. You will find a trail map at the trailhead placard.

On another county parks page for Ramona Grasslands Preserve, you'll find an aerial view of the area: http://www.sandiegocounty.gov/content/dam/sdc/common_components/images/parks/doc/RG_Aerial.pdf.

The preserve is open every day from 8:00 a.m. to 5:00 p.m. in fall and winter, and from 8:00 a.m. to 7:00 p.m. during daylight savings time.

Hikers, mountain bikers, equestrians, and dogs on leashes are invited. It's free to park here.

Trailhead: From Highway 67 heading east, just past Mount Woodson, take a left at Archie Moore Road; go 1.6 miles and continue straight ahead onto Highland Valley Road East. In about 1.0 mile, the preserve will be on your left.

Distance/Difficulty: A 3.0- to 4.0-mile loop, depending on your route. Fairly easy.

6-35. Forest Road to Oaks and Picturesque Pamo Valley

A hike up the lower section of the Upper Santa Ysabel Road not only takes you to a gorgeous live oak grove, but it also affords wide views of the particularly picturesque Pamo Valley. Pamo Valley is one of San Diego County's prettiest places, and it captures your attention as soon as you descend Pamo Road from Ramona into the pristine landscape. It really hasn't changed much since the mid-1800s, when it was largely a cattle ranch, which most of it remains today.

The nomadic Diegueño people lived here in the summers for hundreds of years before the 1800s. Pamo is an Indian word roughly translated to mean "hole in rock worn by water," according to a 2006 *U-T* article on the area by J. Harry Jones.

Among Mexico's land grants in the 1840s, this valley was part of the 17,708-acre Santa Maria Rancho, also called Valle de Pamo, granted in 1844 to Mexican soldier Narciso Botello and later passed to Jose Joaquin Ortega, according to *The History of San Diego* by Richard F. Pourade. The town of Ramona was in the center of the Santa Maria Rancho.

Today, Pamo Valley covers about 4,300 acres. Its centerpiece is the Santa Ysabel Creek, a tributary of the San Dieguito River. That brings up another interesting fact in its history. Most of the valley today has been owned by the City of San Diego's Water Department since the 1960s, when a plan to build a reservoir would have turned Pamo Valley into a lake. The dam plan was dead by the late 1980s, with little possibility it will ever be resurrected.

Oaks and pastoral views await above Pamo Valley.

Today the land is leased by Bob Neal, a cattle rancher who has operated the Foster Ranch in the valley for years. The Foster family began ranching in Pamo Valley when A. B. Foster first purchased land there around 1903. Descendent Raymond Foster, who died in 2002, sold the land to the city in 1964, leasing it back for cattle ranching.

Lying within the watershed of the San Dieguito River, Pamo Valley will one day be included in a 12-mile segment of the Coast-to-Crest Trail, which will eventually cover 70 miles from Volcan Mountain to Del Mar. The Coast-to-Crest Trail, a project of the San Dieguito River Park and its partner, the San Dieguito River Valley Conservancy, consists of about 45 miles of trails today, with the remaining segments awaiting completion. There are a total of about 65 miles of trails within the San Dieguito River Park today.

The conservancy recently announced it bought 40 acres in Pamo Valley that had been owned by the Hodges Family for more than 60 years. This property sits just above the planned Pamo Valley segment of the Coast-to-Crest Trail "and is the last remaining wild land there still in private hands," said Rand Newman, president of the board of the San Dieguito River Valley Conservancy. "We have generally laid out the route for the trail (through Pamo Valley), but there are still a few issues," Newman told us. It is very hard to predict when the Pamo Valley trail will be completed.

"There is also the possibility the conservancy would use the (newly acquired) property to create a spur trail that would branch off the Coast-to-Crest Trail and afford beautiful panoramic vistas of Pamo Valley," said Chris Khoury, an SDRVC board member, in the organization's winter 2012 newsletter.

The 12-mile section through Pamo Valley will eventually consist of the existing Lower Santa Ysabel Truck Trail (3.4 miles from Boden Canyon to Pamo Road), the existing Upper Santa Ysabel Truck Trail (6.0 miles from Pamo Road to Lake Sutherland), and a 3.0-mile section between the two truck trails paralleling Pamo Road.

Hiking on that Upper Santa Ysabel Truck Trail (a.k.a. road) is a fine foray. The Upper Santa Ysabel Road climbs uphill from Pamo Road and is a forest service road in Cleveland National Forest. It travels about 5.0 miles east from Pamo Road to Black Canyon Road.

I went only about 2.0 miles from Pamo Road, in search of that oak grove. At about the 1.5-mile mark, Upper Santa Ysabel Road intersects with Black Mountain Road, which climbs uphill about 5.6 more miles to the 4,051-foot summit of Black Mountain. We passed that intersection to continue on the Santa Ysabel Road.

In another 0.3 miles or so, the oak grove envelops the road, where a small creek descends to join Santa Ysabel Creek. This riparian habitat is filled with fine old oaks and sycamores and is one of the loveliest such groves you'll find.

I turned back after the grove, and as I wound down the dirt road, those amazing views of Pamo Valley became the focus. With the valley surrounded by the forested hills, it might have been a good reservoir site, but the birds, squirrels, cows, and hikers are happier this way.

Thomas Brothers Map: Page 1152, 1-G–to the end of Pamo Road, which goes off this map onto Page D.

Before You Go: Download a copy of the map of Upper Santa Ysabel Truck Trail from Road from the Ramona Trails Association website: www.ramonatrails.org/trails-camps.

This dirt road is open to hikers, bicyclists, equestrians, and dogs on leashes. Occasional cars and motorcycles can be used here too, so be aware.

You must post an Adventure Pass in your car to park on Cleveland National Forest lands. Buy a $5 day pass or $30 annual pass at CNF ranger stations, or at outdoor stores such as REI or Adventure 16. For more information about the CNF Adventure Pass, go to http://www.fs.usda.gov/main/cleveland/passes-permits.

Trailhead: From Highway 78 near the eastern end of downtown Ramona, turn left (north) onto Seventh Street, which soon becomes Elm Street. When Elm hits the T intersection at Haverford Road, turn right. Haverford Road takes a sharp left bend and becomes Pamo Road, which descends into the valley. After Pamo Road turns into a dirt road, go about 1.5 miles to the intersection with the Upper Santa Ysabel Road on the right. Park off Pamo Road on the shoulder.

Distance/Difficulty: I went about 4.0 miles round-trip with about an 800-foot elevation gain; moderate.

6-36. Hike from Pamo to Boden for Gorgeous Oak Groves

Pamo Valley is one of the prettiest places to hike in San Diego County. This broad valley, which stretches before you when you descend Pamo Road, surrounds the confluence of the Santa Ysabel and Temescal Creeks. This hike travels the Lower Santa Ysabel Truck Trail that heads west from Pamo Valley and reaches Boden Canyon in about 3.4 miles.

The San Dieguito River Park's proposed Coast-to-Crest Trail, which will one day cover 70 miles from the beach at Del Mar to Volcan Mountain in Julian, will include this leg of the Lower Santa Ysabel Truck Trail; then it will join a 3.0-mile segment paralleling Pamo Road and will connect to the existing Upper Santa Ysabel Truck Trail for six more miles to Lake Sutherland.

The Lower Santa Ysabel Truck Trail is an easier hike than the Upper SYTT due to less elevation change. Although the Upper SYTT's climb affords some panoramic views across Pamo Valley, the Lower SYTT offers some mighty views of Santa Ysabel Creek's meander toward Boden Canyon, and it also winds through some outstanding old oak groves.

Wonderful old oaks have shaded people here for a long, long time.

In a very short distance after Pamo Road reaches the valley floor, park off the western side of Pamo Road, where a cattle guard and gateway mark the paved road to the Lower Santa Ysabel Truck Trail. Walk along this paved road until it comes to a T intersection; to the right is the Orosco Ridge Road, and to the left is the unpaved Lower Santa Ysabel Truck Trail, where you begin.

The Lower Santa Ysabel Truck Trail follows Santa Ysabel Creek, which is a tributary of San Dieguito River. The Temescal Creek flows into San Luis Rey River. Most of Pamo Valley is owned by the City of San Diego's water department; the area was once considered for a much-debated reservoir. However, the hillsides surrounding the valley are part of Cleveland National Forest.

The Lower SYTT climbs a few hundred feet within the first 1.33 miles, when it reaches a locked gate, prohibiting motor vehicles as well as equestrians from heading farther here. But hikers can easily walk around the gate. Once you reach the gate, you'll see traffic on Highway 78 a few miles ahead where this road ends at Boden Canyon.

Before you reach this gate, you will already have passed under some glorious coast live oak trees, whose canopies drape across the road.

You will also have already spotted lots of spring wildflowers. On this hike in mid-April, I was treated to countless yellow-and-white tidy tips, purple filaree, blue dicks, orange monkeyflowers, white pearly everlasting, lavender and white Chinese houses, caterpillar phacelia, purple wild pea, white forget-me-nots, yellow mustard, and purple owl's clover.

I also saw a 20-inch-long night snake, which froze on the trail, and a flock of wild turkeys that crossed the road ahead of me. I see lots of wild turkeys in the rural reaches of our county, especially in Cuyamaca and Laguna Mountains. Today they are likely descendants of about 230 birds released countywide in 1993 by California Fish and Game and hunting enthusiasts with the San Diego chapter of the National Wild Turkey Federation. Today local wild turkeys are estimated at 15,000 to 20,000. Wild turkeys thrive in the backcountry according to John Massie, a retired wildlife biologist with California Fish and Game and a local leader in the wild turkey federation chapter. The iridescent birds roost at night in trees because they are able to fly 20 feet up into the branches, and they root for nuts, leaves, and insects by day.

This area was also much favored by the Northern Diegueño Indians, who lived here nomadically for hundreds of years before the Spanish explorers first found Pamo Valley in the late 1770s. The Northern Diegueño people are believed to have traveled between here and the coast with the seasons.

The word Pamo probably comes from the Diegueño word "paamuu," according to *California Place Names* by Erwin G. Gudde and William Bright. The word roughly translates to mean "hole in rock worn by water," according to a 2006 *U-T* article on the area by J. Harry Jones.

Pamo Valley holds the remains of at least three Diegueño villages from historic and prehistoric times, as determined from rock paintings and etchings and from many morteros and metates, the grinding holes in bedrock used by women to mash oak acorns, a food staple. Tools, broken pottery, and cremation burials have all been discovered here, especially when the valley was the subject of scrutiny during the reservoir proposal.

You'll see a mortero at the very beginning of this hike on the paved road just off Pamo Road, before you reach the T intersection with Lower Santa Ysabel Truck Trail. Look for others as you hike the old road. The area between the road and the creek likely holds a lot of village evidence in the many bedrock boulders that are scattered throughout the green valley.

It's easy to imagine why the Diegueño would want to settle in this lovely place, where oaks provided acorns and creeks provided plenty of water. The big boulders could also provide some shelter.

When I reached a particularly lovely gathering of oaks and sycamores on the road after about 2.4 miles, I turned back and retraced my route, marveling at the views, the wildflowers, and especially the magnificent oaks.

Thomas Brothers Map: Page 1152, H-1, just beyond the map here where Pamo Road continues north.

Before You Go: Download a copy of the National Geographic topo map from the Ramona Trails Association (horseback enthusiasts) website: http://www.ramonatrails.org/trails-camps.

This trail is open to hikers, bicyclists, equestrians (but note that gate), and dogs on leashes.

You need an Adventure Pass to park here on Cleveland National Forest lands. Purchase a $5 day pass or $30 annual pass at outdoor recreation stores including REI, Adventure 16, and Sports Chalet; at CNF ranger stations; or online through the forest service (www.fs.usda.gov/adventurepass).

Trailhead: Heading east on Highway 67 in downtown Ramona, turn left (north) on Seventh Street, which quickly turns into Elm. Continue on Elm until it intersects with Haverford Road, where you turn right. Turn left onto Pamo Road and continue 2.6 miles to the entrance on the left to the Lower Santa Ysabel Truck Trail. Park off Pamo Road here and walk a short way on the paved road to the T intersection, where you turn left to begin on Lower Santa Ysabel Truck Trail.

Distance/Difficulty: This hike totaled about 4.8 miles round-trip, with about 518 elevation gain. Fairly easy.

7. East County Foothills

The East County Foothills region steps still farther toward the backcountry, but it keeps a foot inside the city. Mission Trails Regional Park, one of the county's largest open spaces with more than 40 miles of trails, offers much local history as well as favored rock-climbing sites.

Head into Lakeside for a trail around one of the only real lakes in the county, or take a turn around a reservoir such as Lake Murray, El Capitan, or Lake Morena.

7-1. Oak Canyon Trail Is a Jewel in MTRP

It's been called the third jewel in the City of San Diego's park system, after Balboa Park and Mission Bay. It's also one of the largest urban parks in the country. The 5,800-acre Mission Trails Regional Park (MTRP), only 8.0 miles from downtown San Diego, has over 40 miles of trails, boating on Lake Murray, camping at Kumeyaay Lake, numerous guided hikes every week, and a very nice Visitor and Interpretive Center. Its website (www.mtrp.org) is equally informative, offering many pages of history covering some 8,000 years, as well as listings of flora and fauna found here.

One of its loveliest trails is the Oak Canyon Trail. It follows Oak Canyon Creek, a tributary of San Diego River, which the creek flows into near the beginning of this trail.

One of MTRP's prettiest trails winds through Oak Canyon.

Although there is water in the San Diego River, Oak Canyon Creek is often completely dry. Perhaps it will flow again in spring, as normally happens in non-drought years. Try to mark your mental calendar to walk on this trail in February, when the California lilacs (ceanothus) are usually in full purple bloom all along this canyon. With the creek dry, picking your way along its rocky environs is easier. You'll miss the few cascades of water that flow over the granite slabs in the wet season. The bonus during fall is that touch of color in the sycamore and cottonwood trees. The coast live oaks don't lose their leaves in winter, but the sycamores and cottonwoods do, and during fall their foliage is ablaze in yellows and oranges.

You'll learn about some of that interesting history at the very beginning of this trail. It starts at Old Mission Dam, a nationally registered historic landmark. A few informational placards and models of the dam tell of its construction from 1809 to 1815. It was a project organized by Father Junipero Serra, the Franciscan priest, to secure a dependable water source for the Mission San Diego de Alcala, which lies about 6.0 miles to the west of MTRP. Mission Gorge was identified as an ideal location for a dam, and construction on it began using Indian labor from the mission and local villages.

"While all of the California missions had some sort of water delivery system, the dam and flume constructed for the Mission San Diego de Alcala was by far the most ambitious," says the MTRP website. The 244-foot-long, 13-foot-thick, 13-foot-wide dam was built of stone and cement on bedrock across the head of Mission Gorge, creating a permanent reservoir behind it. Water was released into a 6.0-mile-long, gravity-fed, tile-lined flume down to the mission.

After the missions were secularized in 1833, the dam and flume fell into disrepair, and the flume tiles were carried off to be used in pioneers' homes. The floods of 1916 washed away most of the flume itself. The dam is still very much in evidence at the beginning of the Oak Canyon Trail.

The trail begins at an iron footbridge that crosses the San Diego River. The trail is well marked with signs; follow those that direct you to Oak Canyon Trail and be sure to stay on the main trail. You'll pass by some of those western cottonwood trees sparkling in the sun, lots of California sycamores with their mottled bark and lobed leaves, and many splendid evergreen coast live oaks, whose acorns were a favorite food source for the Kumeyaay. There are a couple of coast live oaks on this Oak Canyon Trail that are simply massive, probably well over 100 years old with enormous limbs rising every which way to reach some 70 feet tall. The deep roots of the coast live oak allow them to survive drought years, and they seldom die in fires. A lot of this area was burned badly in the Cedar Fire of 2003, but these oaks obviously survived.

After about a mile from the trail's beginning, you'll reach an intersection with a service road. Walk a short way to the left on this road until you see an "Oak Canyon Trail" sign on your right. Follow that sign to the continuation of the trail, which is now referred to as Upper Oak Canyon Trail.

Continue to follow the dry stream bed and all its granite rocks. Soon you'll see the overpass that is Highway 52 ahead. Just before that overpass is a jumble of almost blue granite boulders that make for seasonal waterfalls during the rainy seasons. The trail here crosses the stream in a few places, but because it's dry now, that's no problem. If it's wet, be careful.

When I reached the Highway 52 overpass, I simply turned around and retraced my steps back. I marveled at the feeling of wilderness so close to the urban core. While you see that Highway 52 overpass and a few antennae, there is no other evidence of urban development.

Plans for MTRP began in the 1960s, when development throughout the city was advancing. The City of San Diego decided an urban park was needed, and a plan was begun to set aside 1,765 acres of open space that included Fortuna Mountain, Mission Gorge, and Old Mission Dam. The federal government also transferred some of its excess military lands, and some of Camp Elliott here, a U.S. Marine Corps training area, was transferred to the City of San Diego in 1963. In 1974, Cowles Mountain was purchased by the city, county, and Navajo Community Planners together, and the park was coming together. A community-wide contest in 1979 resulted in the park's name: Mission Trails Regional Park. With about 3,000 acres combined under various public ownerships and an additional 2,500 acres bought by 1984, the park was established. In 1995, the visitor center opened.

Guided hikes throughout MTRP are conducted almost every Wednesday, Saturday, and Sunday from 9:30–11:00 a.m. Check the website's event calendar for locations and details.

Thomas Brothers Map: Page 1230, F-6

Before You Go: Download a trail map from Mission Trails Regional Park's website: www.mtrp. org. There is no fee to park or hike the trails. It is open to hikers, bicyclists, equestrians, and dogs on leashes.

There is another good trail map from the city's park and recreation pages: http://www. sandiego.gov/park-and-recreation/pdf/missiontrailstrailmap.pdf.

Trailhead: From Interstate 8, exit at Mission Gorge/Fairmount. Turn north onto Mission Gorge Road and then east at Friars Road junction to stay on Mission Gorge Road, following it for 4.2 miles. Just past the Jackson Drive intersection, turn left onto Father Junipero Serra Trail. Proceed 1.8 miles, past the first pipe gate, and just past the stop sign at the second pipe gate. Enter Old Mission Dam parking on the left. If the parking area is full, there is parking on the road shoulder nearby.

From Highway 52, exit at Mast Boulevard in Santee. Turn north onto Mast and then right at first traffic light onto West Hills Parkway. At Mission Gorge Road, turn right; go 0.2 miles and merge right onto Father Junipero Serra Trail. Proceed 0.7 miles down this road to the Old Mission Dam parking lot on the right.

Distance/Difficulty: The Oak Canyon Trail is 1.7 miles one-way, for a 3.4-mile round-trip. Moderate. Elevation gain is only about 200 feet, but the rocky trail makes it a little harder.

7-2. Climbers Loop Adds Oaks and Morteros

In the middle of Mission Trails Regional Park, combine a few short trails to create a history lesson with views. Start at the visitor center, which opened in 1995 to serve the 5,800-acre park, one of the largest urban parks in the nation. Before you hit the trails—there are about 40 miles of them in the park—consider watching one of the videos presented daily in the 94-seat theater, including "Stewardship through the Ages" about the Native Americans, Spanish, Mexicans, and Americans that have cared for this land, and "Mission Trails Regional Park: A Natural Beauty," showing flora and fauna highlights of the park.

For this route, combine a portion of the visitor center Interpretive Trail, the Grinding Rocks Trail, the Climbers Loop Trail, and the Oak Grove Loop Trail for a hike of about 3.0 miles total.

Begin on the visitor center Interpretive Trail North Loop Trailhead, just east from the center's entrance. This interpretive trail is a 1.4-mile loop that features informational

Climbers Loop is one of best in county for rock climbing.

placards identifying many of the native plants. Walk along this trail only until the first junction to the Grinding Rocks Trail; then turn right (east). You'll pass under some mighty coast live oaks until you reach the edge of the San Diego River.

The San Diego River carves its way right through the center of Mission Trails. The Kumeyaay were the first people to live extensively in this area, from about 1100 BC to AD 1822, according to history articles written by archaeologist Ruth Alter on the MTRP website. "To the Kumeyaay, the land itself and all its features and resources were and are powerful living entities," she wrote. "In exchange for receiving the benefits that the land, plants and animals provided, people had certain responsibilities toward them. The land had to be kept clean, which meant burning off the understory beneath the oaks each year; and in particular, water courses were specially cared for, with banks and river beds kept free of debris."

The Kumeyaay pounded acorns and grass seeds to make mush and flour for breads, and at Grinding Rocks, you'll see "an ancient food processing site." In the flat granite slabs, look for an 'ehmuu (mortar or mortero), a bowl-like depression worn into the rock from grinding with a hand-held stone (called a hepechaa, or pestle), and an 'ehpii (metate), a flat, sometimes portable, grinding surface used with a flat, hand-held grinding stone called a habiichaa (mano).

Continue ahead on the trail to reach Father Junipero Serra Trail, the main, paved road. Directly across the road is the south trailhead for the Climbers Loop Trail, a 1.0-mile loop that climbs about 400 feet in elevation in the first third of a mile. This is a steep trail that climbs up 17 switchbacks, including several stair sets, to reach the top. Pick up a map of this specific trail at the trailhead.

The Climbers Loop Trail is popular with rock climbers. The Mission Gorge area, carved by that San Diego River over the past 35 million years or so, features steep walls and many granite boulders.

The Climbers Loop Trail heads up the western slope of 1,194-foot-high Kwaay Paay Peak. It does not connect to the separate Kwaay Paay Peak Trail, which begins near the Old Mission Dam. Climbers Loop Trail takes climbers to the oldest established climbing area in San Diego County. "The rock is metamorphosed granite, unique to the county, and is extremely hard and water-polished," says www.rockclimbing.com. "The cliff offers a mixture of both crack and face climbing, and is steep, slick and strenuous, often requiring creative palming, pinching and counterbalance maneuvers. Most routes are 40 to 80 feet high."

After about a third of a mile and many of those switchbacks, you are near the high point on the loop trail. This first area is known as Middle Earth, and some climbers start here. Beware of false trails here: The trail appears to continue straight ahead, but this very rocky portion is not the main trail and will dead-end or send you on a very steep shortcut down. If you keep going east on the rough and rocky trail leading to more climbing sites, you'll stay on this loop trail. For hikers, the views start here. Look back to see many of the park's trails, its riparian areas along the river, and its several peaks, including South Fortuna, the nearest at 1,094 feet high, and North Fortuna, 1,291 feet high.

After that Middle Earth area, you'll reach the Limbo Area and Underworld Area after only 0.18 miles, and then the Main Wall Area about 0.75 miles from the start. The trail then heads back down to its north trailhead. With only nine switchbacks and 328 feet, it's easier going down than that south trailhead going up.

At the bottom, head south back toward the visitor center on the paved Father Junipero Serra Trail. Look on your left (east) for the trailhead for the Oak Grove Loop Trail. When you reach the small oak grove on this trail, you'll also see a recreated 'ewaa, a traditional Kumeyaay dome home made from willow branches.

This last loop is an easy mile that will take you back to your start.

Thomas Brothers Map: Page 1250, 2-D, Mission Trails Visitor & Interpretive Center.

Before You Go: Go to Mission Trails Regional Park's website, http://www.mtrp.org, and download a copy of the trail map. Or pick up a copy at the visitor center when you get there.

There is another good trail map from the city's park and recreation pages: http://www.sandiego.gov/park-and-recreation/pdf/missiontrailstrailmap.pdf.

Trails in MTRP are open to hikers, bicyclists, equestrians, and dogs on leashes. Some trails are open to hikers only, however, including the Climbers Loop Trail.

Trailhead: From Interstate 8, exit at Mission Gorge/Fairmount and head north onto Mission Gorge Road. After about 4.2 miles, look for the large wooden park sign and turn left onto Father Junipero Serra Trail. Park near the visitor center.

From Highway 52, exit at Mast Boulevard and head east, turning left onto Mast Boulevard. Go under the freeway to the first traffic signal and turn right onto West Hills Parkway. At Mission Gorge Road, turn right and go 2.4 miles, past the Father Serra Trail entry to Old Mission Dam. Turn right onto Father Junipero Serra Trail to the visitor center.

Distance/Difficulty: The visitor center loop, Grinding Rocks trail, and Oak Grove Loop are all easy; the Climbers Loop Trail is moderately strenuous. Combine them to make about 3.0 miles total.

7-3. It's a Hard Climb with Worthy Views

It may be a tough climb, but on a clear day from Kwaay Paay Peak in Mission Trails, you can survey the county from the Cuyamaca Mountains to the Coronado Islands. It is a sweeping view that takes in 6,512-foot-high Cuyamaca Peak to the east, its slightly doubled peak a clue on the horizon. Nearer is the rocky promontory that is Mount Woodson, as well as its neighbor, Iron Mountain.

To the northwest you'll see the trails up Mission Trails' Fortuna Mountain. To the west, look for Mount Soledad in La Jolla at the northern end of the ocean views, all the way south to downtown, the Coronado Bridge, and those offshore islands.

One of MTRP's hardest trails has the best views.

Spot at least three of the four Coronado Islands on the ocean's horizon. The largest (at about 450 acres) is officially called South Coronado, the middle one (at about 35 acres) is Central Coronado, and the third (about 114 acres) is North Coronado. The fourth is named Pilon de Azucar (Pile of Sugar) and is very small, at 17 acres.

The Coronados lie about 15 miles south of the entrance to San Diego Bay, but it is only 8.0 miles from Tijuana; they belong to Tijuana and are a popular destination for yellowtail fishermen. They were named Los Cuatro Coronados, or the Four Crowned Ones, in 1602 by Spanish explorers to honor four martyrs.

South Coronado is the only one with a bay and lighthouses. During Prohibition in the United States in the 1920s, its northeast cove was used by alcohol smugglers. There was so much traffic there at that time, a casino flourished and the spot was named Smugglers Cove. Only the foundation of that casino remains. Today, the islands are a Mexican wildlife refuge, and humans are not allowed to land on them (except the few who work there).

The land you hike up to reach these remarkable views features a steep grade. Though only the fourth highest peak (at 1,194 feet) in Mission Trails Regional Park—the highest is 1,594-foot-high Cowles Mountain—Kwaay Paay is considered the hardest climb there. The 1.5-mile trail climbs 865 vertical feet (my GPS unit actually measured just over 1,000 feet up) to reach the peak, and there are no switchbacks here; it's a hard slog on a steep, rocky trail to that top. Only hikers and dogs on leashes are invited to make this climb.

Kwaay Paay is a Kumeyaay word meaning leader, according to MTRP. The Kumeyaay and the San Dieguito people before them occupied the area of Mission Trails for thousands of years before the European explorers entered the scene in 1769. There are more than 30 Kumeyaay sites in the park.

One bright spot you'll see from the Kwaay Paay Trail is Kumeyaay Lake, just below the trail to the north. Kumeyaay Lake is near the Kumeyaay Campground, the only such facility in MTRP. Overnight camping is available there only on Friday and Saturday nights.

From the peak trail, you can also see the trails through the grasslands in the park and in both the South Fortuna and North Fortuna mountain areas. Try to spot the Old Mission Dam just below the west side of the peak.

There is virtually no shade on this trail because it winds through chaparral and sage scrub habitats. Native plants here include chamise, ceanothus (wild lilac), red-trunked manzanita, scrub oak, and toyon (red Christmas berries). When you reach the peak, you might also be level with birds that soar above the park, including hawks and crows.

In July 2014, 95 acres near and including the summit of Kwaay Paay were burned in a wildfire. MTRP rangers and a 12-person crew from AmeriCorps restored this fire-damaged area.

MTRP offers several guided walks in the park. Many take off from the main visitor center, which is farther down Junipero Serra Drive from the campground. The campground is nearer to the Kwaay Paay Peak trailhead.

Free activities include guided nature walks on Wednesdays, Saturdays, and Sundays. Every second Friday from 7:00 to 10:00 p.m., meet at the campground to join members of the San Diego Astronomy Association (SDAA) to view the stars and planets from their telescopes. The SDAA also presents speakers on astronomy topics at the visitor center. Check MTRP's website, www.mtrp.org, for event listings.

Thomas Brothers Map: Page 1230, G-6.

Before You Go: Download a copy of the Kwaay Paay Peak trail's map from the Mission Trails Regional Park website: http://www.mtrp.org/aaapopups/trail_maps/new_trail_map.html.

There is another good trail map from the city's park and recreation pages: http://www.sandiego.gov/park-and-recreation/pdf/missiontrailstrailmap.pdf.

This trail is open only to hikers and dogs on leashes.

Trailhead: From Highway 52, exit at Mast Boulevard in Santee; when driving east on 52, turn left onto Mast Boulevard and go under the freeway; when driving west on 52, turn right onto Mast. Then turn right (west) onto West Hills Parkway and right (west) onto Mission Gorge Road. Take the first right onto Father Junipero Serra Trail into MTRP.

From Interstate 8, exit at Mission Gorge/Fairmount, turning north onto Mission Gorge Road. Proceed 6.5 miles to the northern (Kumeyaay Lake) MTRP entrance on the left via Father Junipero Serra Trail.

Park in the dirt lot at Bushy Hill Drive, opposite the entrance to the Kumeyaay Campground. Walk a short way down Junipero Serra Trail to the Kwaay Paay trailhead on your left.

There is another trailhead for this peak trail about 0.3 mile farther on Father Junipero Serra Trail on the left across from the Old Mission Dam parking lot. This second trailhead is said to be a little less steep than the first trailhead. Both of these merge at about 0.3 miles on the trail, so they both make that hard climb to the top.

Distance/Difficulty: About 3.0 miles round-trip; strenuous.

7-4. Ocean Views from West Area of Mission Trails

The largest municipally owned park in California, Mission Trails Regional Park encompasses 5,800 acres of open-space preserve within the City of San Diego, where more than 40 miles of trails beckon. There are five major areas in Mission Trails, each offering a different set of trails. They are Lake Murray, Cowles Mountain, Mission Gorge, East Fortuna, and West Fortuna.

I hiked the West Fortuna area on a clear day in February that afforded sweeping views across the city to the south and west, all the way to the blue Pacific. I could see from Point Loma to Mount Soledad on the coast from a high elevation of about 850 feet above sea level.

Rim Trail takes you to ocean views.

There are a few trailheads for each of the five major areas on Mission Trails. I began at Tierrasanta's Colina Dorada trailhead, a name to remember to find one's way back.

The trails are generally well marked, but there are some intersections where you choose your direction. I was headed for the Rim Trail, but signage from the Colina Dorada trailhead didn't immediately point the way there. After following signs for the Quarry Loop Trail, I headed north to connect to the Rim Trail, and eventually signs for it told me I was on the right track.

When you descend a steep part of the trail, still heading basically north, you'll come to a big intersection of trails, with one heading west to Clairemont Mesa, one heading east to South Fortuna and the visitor center area, and one heading north toward the "Twin Towers," two pale blue structures that are part of the San Diego Aqueduct. Head toward those towers, generally north.

As its name implies, the Rim Trail generally keeps to a ridgeline where those clear-day views are a bonus. As you begin climbing toward the north, you'll see the grasslands of the large Suycott Valley to the east, backdropped by Fortuna Mountain, whose north peak rises to 1,291 feet high; its south peak reaches 1,094 feet high.

Some 1,000 years ago, the Kumeyaay began to establish several small villages where Mission Trails Regional Park lies today, writes archaeologist Ruth Alter on the park's website. "There are more than 30 Kumeyaay sites in the park, all overseen and protected by park staff," she writes. "To the Kumeyaay of the past and traditional Kumeyaay of today, the land itself and all its features and resources were and are powerful living entities.… People were part of the natural world and in exchange for receiving benefits that the land, plants and animals provided, people had certain responsibilities toward them." They burned off the understory beneath oaks each year, killed large game animals with respect and ritual, and cared for and kept clean all their water courses and river beds. "They dammed rivers to create bathing pools for themselves and places for turtles and fish to live," she writes. Tule reeds and willow branches along the San Diego River became rafts or house thatching; flat granite rocks became kitchen grinding surfaces, and quartz was carved into arrow tips.

Father Junipero Serra and his fellow Catholic missionaries from Spain established the first of 21 California missions near here, Mission San Diego de Alcala. A 244-foot-long, 13-foot-thick dam was constructed of stone on the San Diego River here at Mission Gorge by 1815, creating a permanent reservoir to serve that mission. The Old Mission Dam in the park's Mission Gorge region is now a nationally registered historic landmark.

After continuing on the Rim Trail, I ultimately reached Shepherd Pond, a small water basin on the ridge top where those ocean views spread out to the west. Most of the habitat in the West Fortuna area is California sage scrub or chaparral. In the sage scrub, typically at lower elevations on slopes facing south or west, look for sunflowers, lemonadeberry, laurel sumac, buckwheat, and California sagebrush (artemisia californica). In the chaparral, usually at higher elevations here on slopes facing north or east, one can look for chamise, Ramona lilac, scrub oak, redberry, mission manzanita, mountain mahogany and toyon.

After the Spanish (1769–1822) and then Mexican periods (1822–1846) here, when the United States prevailed in the Mexican-American War, the area became home to ranchers and farmers until the 1960s. Beginning in about 1873, this region was also home to several granite mines, and some of the blocks of granite from Mission Gorge were used to construct the breakwater in San Diego Bay. Sand and gravel mines were home here too, including those of the Kenneth Golden Company, H. G. Fenton, V. R. Dennis, and J. B. Stringfellow.

The park began formation with the purchase in 1974 of Cowles Mountain by the City of San Diego. In the 1980s, additional acreage was purchased and the San Diego City Council and San Diego County Board of Supervisors approved a plan in 1985 for the regional park. The visitor center was opened in 1995.

We hiked a short distance past Shepherd Pond and then turned around and retraced our way back, following those signs for the Colina Dorada Trailhead.

Mission Trails Regional Park offers many activities, including guided nature hikes on Saturdays, Sundays, and Wednesdays, as well as art and nature classes for children.

Thomas Brothers Map: Page 1250, B-2, intersection of Colina Dorada and Calle de Vida.

Before You Go: Download a copy of the trail map from the Mission Trails Regional Park website: http://www.mtrp.org/aaapopups/trail_maps/new_trail_map.html.
There is another good trail map from the city's park and recreation pages: http://www.sandiego.gov/park-and-recreation/pdf/missiontrailstrailmap.pdf.
There are equestrian trails in Mission Trails, but this Rim Trail is not one of them. The Rim Trail and most of the other trails in the West Fortuna area are open to hikers, mountain bikers, and dogs on leashes.

Trailhead: From Interstate 15, exit at Tierrasanta Boulevard, heading east. Travel about two miles and turn left on Colina Dorada. Drive one mile north to the intersection of Colina Dorada and Calle de Vida and park on the streets near the trailhead.

Distance/Difficulty: I hiked a total of about 4.5 miles with a total elevation gain of about 680 feet. Moderate.

7-5. Easy Lake Murray Loop Good for Birding

The hike around Lake Murray's perimeter road is a popular pastime any day of the year. The paved road is also open to bicyclists, strollers, and dogs on leashes, and it's an easy walk around the reservoir. Winter is a good time to go to view many migrating water fowl making good use of the lake and all its fish. Lake Murray is also open for fishing for the stocked largemouth bass, bluegill, catfish, black crappie, and trout. Anglers need fishing licenses, which are available at the lake's concession, and boats are rented there as well.

The main hiking trail, which follows that perimeter road, begins at the eastern end of the main parking lot off Kiowa Drive. It winds around the eastern, northern, and western shores of the lake for 3.2 miles to the dam gate, where you turn around and head back the same way for a 6.4-mile round-trip.

There is good birding on Lake Murray.

The dam that created this reservoir was actually first called La Mesa Dam and was built in 1895, according to Philip Pryde's book *San Diego: An Introduction to the Region.* It was one of the earliest dams, creating reservoirs built here in the late 1800s. The very first dam was what today is called the Old Mission Dam, now just a remnant that lies in Mission Trails Regional Park, where Lake Murray is situated as well. The Mission Dam was built in 1807 at the eastern end of Mission Gorge on the San Diego River by the missionaries who sought water at the San Diego Mission de Alcala, the first of 21 California missions established by Junipero Serra in 1769. By the 1860s, however, the Mission Dam was in disrepair, according to Pryde.

Major dam building then began. The La Mesa Dam corralled the water of Alvarado Creek in 1885, the same year the Escondido Dam was built on Escondido Creek. The La Mesa Dam was eventually submerged by Lake Murray when its new dam was built in 1918. Similarly, the Escondido Dam was rebuilt as the Wohlford Dam in 1924.

The Sweetwater River Dam and Sweetwater Reservoir were built in 1886; Cuyamaca Dam on Boulder Creek, where Lake Cuyamaca sits, was built in 1887; the Lower Otay Dam on the Otay River was begun in 1887 (and rebuilt in 1919 after the disastrous 1916 flood destroyed it); and the Morena dam and reservoir on Cottonwood Creek was begun in 1895. Lake Hodges was formed by a dam on the San Dieguito River in 1918. Today there are 17 major dams in the county.

Lake Murray is named after James A. Murray, a Montana capitalist who joined with Ed Fletcher, whose Cuyamaca Water Company had already built Cuyamaca Dam and was delivering water to San Diego through a 35-mile-long wooden flume. Murray bought that flume system, according to Richard Pourade's "The History of San Diego" at the San Diego Historical Society, and he built Murray Dam on the old La Mesa Dam site. The City of San Diego owns and operates Lake Murray today.

One of the sights you'll see from the trail is the Spanish Colonial bell tower of the Alvarado Treatment Plant, one of three major filtration systems for Colorado River water that comes to Lake Murray from the California Water Project aqueduct; the other two are at Miramar Lake and Otay Lake. If you make it all the way to that fence at the dam, you'll note a sign with a red target on it that says, "Touch the Bulls-Eye or Your Lap Doesn't Count." Everyone touches it.

You'll also note in the distance to the southwest Mount San Miguel, a landmark at 2,566 feet with all its communication towers.

Most notable at the beginning of the trail, though, is Cowles Mountain, at 1,591 feet high a major promontory—the highest point in the City of San Diego. It is a popular 3.0-mile round-trip hike to the top. Cowles Mountain, like Lake Murray, is also in Mission Trails Regional Park, one of the largest urban parks in the country.

Mission Trails offers more than 40 miles of trails, including Lake Murray's and Cowles Mountain's, and it contains the deepest gorge (along the San Diego River) found within any major city in the United States, says Pryde. The Lake Murray trail also skirts the public Mission Trails Golf Course.

One of the great attractions at Lake Murray are the birds. About 180 species have been seen here, and dependable sightings according to San Diego Audubon include osprey, California gnatcatcher, tricolored blackbird, California thrasher, green heron, and, in the summer, Bullock's oriole and western kingbird. Look for the huge osprey nest high atop some power poles near that golf course on the lake's northern shore. When I was there, I delighted in watching several western grebes, some large double-crested cormorants, several pairs of mallard ducks, and lots of lesser scaups, the black-and-white ducks with blue bills. Duck-like American coots with their black bodies and white bills, one of the most common of our water fowl all year, were also abundant.

If you take note of all the signs along the trail that name the lake's major fingers, you'll have to hunt for the last one. There are nine signs, a 2003 Eagle Scout Project by Brett Nieman, that point out Del Cerro Point, Del Cerro Bay, Cowles Point, Cowles Bay, San Carlos Point, San Carlos Bay, Padre Point, and Padre Bay, but the No. 1 sign is off that beaten path. You'll find the sign for Alvarado Bay on the southern edge of the lake, near its Kiowa Drive entrance, where shorter trails also head to the dam from that other direction.

Thomas Brothers Map: Page 1250, F-7, where Kiowa Drive ends at the lake.
Also see Page 1270 for Kiowa Drive's intersection with Lake Murray Boulevard.

Before You Go: Go to the Mission Trails Regional Park page for Lake Murray: http://www.mtrp.org/lake_murray. For a map, go to MTRP's map page: http://www.mtrp.org/aaapopups/trail_maps/new_trail_map.html.
This trail is open to hikers, bicyclists, and dogs on leashes.

Trailhead: From Interstate 8, exit at Lake Murray Boulevard, heading north. Turn left on Kiowa Drive, which ends at the main parking area at Lake Murray.

Distance/Difficulty: The main route is 6.4 miles round-trip. Easy.

7-6. Backcountry Trails in Urban Oasis Just East of El Cajon

Just a few miles east of El Cajon lies the Crestridge Ecological Reserve, a 2,800-acre oasis in the middle of million-dollar equestrian suburbia. There are several miles of trails suitable for hiking, mountain biking, or horseback riding, and the trails meander through the coastal sage scrub and chaparral habitats.

It was once the site of a Kumeyaay village. According to the Earth Discovery Institute (EDI), three prehistoric archeological sites have been identified here, including a village-like site consisting of extensive numbers of grinding features—metates and morteros, the (shallow and deep, respectively) holes in granite boulders created by native women to grind acorns into flour and meal.

Crestridge is an urban oasis.

In 1845, Pio Pico granted 48,800 acres here—the third largest land grant in San Diego County, known as El Cajon de San Diego—to Maria Antonia Estudillo de Pedrorena. That land was known as El Cajon de San Diego, "the box," which referred to the pass between two hills. The land ultimately became El Cajon, Lakeside, Santee, Bostonia, and Flinn Springs.

The land served a cattle ranch in the early 20th century, and then it was bought just before World War II by local water and land developer Ed Fletcher. In 1990 the land was set aside as open space as part of a 92-home project by Gatlin Development. In 1999 the Nature Conservancy purchased the property, and today it is overseen by the California Department of Fish and Wildlife (CDFW).

As I walked along the old dirt roads that make up most of the trail system, I was buzzed overhead by a soaring Cooper's hawk, I marveled at the extensive stands of wild lilac, just about to bloom with buds of white and blue, as well as lots of white-blooming chamise. Indeed, according to the CDFW, Crestridge is home to the largest known population of Lakeside ceanothus (a rare wild lilac), and it is also important to the California gnatcatcher (an endangered bird) and many native butterflies.

When I was there in late June, several teenagers working through the Urban Corps of San Diego County were removing nonnative plants and planting native species to replace them. They were also involved in restoring and repairing the trails. "For many of them, it's their first job," noted supervisor Joe Whitley. The students working with Urban Corps were also nearly done building a kiosk designed by James Hubbell, the famed artist and designer from Julian. The kiosk is made from straw and mud, said Whitley, and inside its floor is constructed of bricks laid out in concentric circles. In addition, the EDI has partnered with the Cajon Valley Union School District to provide fourth through sixth graders with learning and service experiences at the reserve.

The trails are easygoing because they follow old truck roads. I began at the entrance to the reserve off Horsemill Road. I passed the kiosk to my right, continuing on a dirt road to a stand of several Engelmann oak trees on my left. I kept to the right of the trees, and at a T intersection I took the road to the right up the hill past a small house.

The trails climb, and it shortly affords panoramic views northeast over El Cajon valley. I continued ahead, and signs of urban development diminished as the trails went farther into the backcountry.

At the top of the ridge on this trail, just about a mile from its beginning, there is another intersection. A right turn here will take you back on a long loop to the trailhead, through lots of that wild lilac. Continuing straight ahead on the trail will take you farther into the boulder-strewn landscape, down into a ravine, and up over another ridge, with trails clearly viewed from the ridge. I followed that trail straight for a while and then retraced my steps back to the intersection to go back on the loop.

As you drive through the community of Crest to reach the reserve, note the homes on this part of the county's precipitous ridges; they must have amazing views.

Thomas Brothers Map: Page 1232, J-7.

Before You Go: For more information, go to https://www.wildlife.ca.gov/Lands/Places-to-Visit/Crestridge-ER or the Earth Discovery Institute (www.earthdiscovery.org/projects).

For the best map to download ahead of your visit (there should be trail maps available at the information kiosk on-site), go to a Google map of Crestridge: www.google.com/maps/place/Crestridge+Reserve+Visitor+Center/.

These trails are open to hikers, bicyclists, equestrians, and dogs on leashes.

Trailhead: To reach the trailhead, from Interstate 8, exit at Greenfield Drive and head south for a half-mile. Turn left on La Cresta Road, left on Mountain View, and then left on Horsemill Road, which dead-ends at the entrance to Crestridge Ecological Reserve.

Distance/Difficulty: From 2.0 to 4.0 miles round-trip; easy to moderate.

7-7. Water Birds Galore During Stroll Around Santee Lakes

Just 20 minutes from downtown San Diego are the seven Santee Lakes, the world's first example of how a community's wastewater can be reclaimed and reused by the people while providing plentiful recreation at the same time. The 190 acres of this peaceful, water-based playground provide opportunity to fish for trout and bass, glide in a canoe or kayak, or walk, jog, or cycle its paved pathways. The pathways are marked for fitness buffs and offer three routes: a 1K (0.62 miles), a 3K (1.86 miles), or a 5K (3.1 miles) loop.

While you're walking around these manmade lakes, you should notice a bounty of waterfowl. Winter is the best time to see them because many are migratory birds that come here only then. I spotted numerous pairs of mallard ducks, dozens of American coots, several majestic great blue herons, a few all-white great egrets, gorgeous wood ducks, cormorants, and more.

Go birding at Santee Lakes.

If you're really lucky, you might spot an osprey, a large bird of prey that is a winter resident here. According to one of the many informative placards on the pathways, ospreys feed almost exclusively on fish, diving feet-first into the water to catch their meal. Cute black-and-white bufflehead ducks also make their winter home here before migrating to Canada and Alaska to breed. They often remain with the same mate for years. Mallards live here all year. Look for their tiny baby ducklings in the spring.

I've never been so close to the large, 4-foot-tall great blue herons anywhere else. Often seen walking on the shoreline, they're one of the largest birds here, living at Santee Lakes all year round. They catch their fish with their sharp yellow bills.

Santee Lakes themselves almost didn't hatch. In December 1961, the Santee County Water District (Padre Dam MWD) announced that Santee Lakes were to be the subject of an important research project backed by the U.S. Public Health Service, California State Department of Water Resources, the State Water Quality Control Board, San

Diego County Department of Public Health, and other agencies. Funding from state and federal sources was nearly cancelled, but Santee Water District General Manager Ray Stoyer wrote to President John F. Kennedy explaining the long-term benefits of water reclamation. The project was approved, and the first four lakes were created.

After determining the lakes were safe for the public's health, boating and fishing were allowed on Lake 4 by June 1961. By 1966, Lake 5 was built, and by the 1980s, Lakes 6 and 7 were created along with the public campground.

In the 1960s, the lakes were the site of the Festival of the Lakes every June, which included a sailboat regatta, games, craft booths, and a parade through the center of town complete with the Queen of the Lakes. Some 10,000 people attended these festivals, but they no longer take place.

Santee Lakes now hosts outdoor summer movies and an enormous egg hunt in the spring. Its trout season runs from November through March, and some 13,000 pounds of rainbow trout are stocked then. From April through October, it's catfish season when 24,000 pounds of channel catfish are stocked in the lakes. You can rent rowboats, pedal boats, kayaks, and canoes from the general store, ranging from $7-$14 depending on the boat and whether you take it for a half-hour or an hour.

There are also five playgrounds and one "sprayground," which is especially popular in the summer when temperatures can reach the triple digits.

Even with all these activities, a stroll around the lakes might be the most appealing. It's suitable for wheelchairs too, so almost anyone can navigate these pathways. Get up closely and personally to all those water birds.

Thomas Brothers Map: Page 1231, 5-A.

Before You Go: Check the website for more information: http://www.santeelakes.com.
Download a trail map at the website's fitness pages: http://www.santeelakes.com/walking-running/.
The trails around the lakes are open only to hikers and bicyclists; no dogs are allowed in the day-use areas.
There is a $3 day-use parking fee during weekdays, or $5 on weekends.

Trailhead: Go east on Highway 52, exiting at Mast Boulevard. Turn left onto Mast, proceed for about a mile and a half, and turn right onto Fanita Parkway. The entrance to Santee Lakes is on your right.
From Highway 52 heading west, exit at Fanita Drive and turn right onto Fanita Drive, then right onto Mission Gorge Road, left onto Carlton Hills Boulevard, left onto Carlton Oaks Drive, right onto Fanita Parkway, and then left into Santee Lakes.

Distance/Difficulty: From 1.0 to 5.0 miles, depending on which route you choose. Very easy.

7-8. Stroll along San Diego River in Santee Park

Take an easy amble along the San Diego River in Santee under the shade of sycamores and oaks, and you might spot a turtle. Western pond turtles are the only turtle species to live in our local rivers; look for them basking in the sun on a log. "Turtles are the oldest living group of reptiles, dating back to the time of the earliest dinosaurs," says the National Audubon Society's *Field Guide to California.* "California turtles hibernate during the winter, in air pockets in mud at the edge of pond bottom."

The river attracts lots of water fowl too. I saw a majestic great blue heron with a beak full of food, a white snowy egret with black bill and yellow legs, several pairs of mallard ducks and many American coots. I also spotted a perching lesser goldfinch, a red-breasted house finch, a Nuttall's woodpecker, and a willow flycatcher (an endangered species).

There are about 25 endangered species of plants and animals here, now protected by law, including least Bell's vireo and the California gnatcatcher. "The San Diego River in Santee is primarily a freshwater aquatic ecosystem bordered by a community of plants known as riparian," says one of the informative placards along the trail. Besides the sycamores and oaks, riparian trees here also include the cottonwoods (with their heart-shaped leaves) and willows.

Look for turtles in Santee's segment of San Diego River.

It wasn't always this pretty, according to a couple I met on the trail, Dave and Wendy Mastronardi. Dave has lived in this area since 1958 and told me the river area here used to be dry and dusty, because most of the land was used by a cattle dairy. In the last 50 years, as Santee has developed, the river has been restored with more of its native species.

Santee began its city life as Cowleston, named for one of its earliest settlers, George Cowles, for whom nearby Cowles Mountain is named. He bought 4,000 acres here in 1877 for his vineyards. He died in 1887, and his widow, Jennie Cowles, married Milton Santee, a local surveyor. In 1891, Jennie received permission to operate the post office under her husband's name, and in 1893 the city "followed her lead and changed the town's name to Santee," according to the Santee Historical Society.

Meanwhile, Hosmer McKoon's 9,543-acre Fanita Ranch was subdivided, and 7,000 acres were sold to the Scripps family of newspaper fame in 1898. The Scripps raised cattle here. In 1958, 4,300 of these acres were purchased by the Santee-Carlton Company for development; the company's early president was Bill Mast, for whom the boulevard and park are named.

River restoration has been a long, ongoing project. Water primrose, a vine-like plant that grows in thick mats on the river's surface and reduces oxygen levels and raises water temperatures, is one invasive plant that the city of Santee has tried to eliminate for the last several years. Youths from Urban Corps, a nonprofit organization that provides job training to disadvantaged young adults, have helped get rid of water primrose for the past several years.

The trail along the river here is also still being developed. Mast Park West Trail, which heads under Carlton Hills Boulevard just west of Mast Park, was completed in 2011, adding about a half-mile through the 43-acre Carlton Oaks Preserve to the Carlton Oaks Golf Course. This portion of the trail is decomposed granite and passes next to the river through a riparian forest. Sadly, it was the site of a fire in late April 2014 that burned parts of the trail's wooden fencing as well as trees and shrubs.

The delightful, hand-painted murals under the street, which mark the beginning of the Mast Park West Trail, were not harmed. They were the 2011 work of Boy Scout Troop 51, led by Chance Kawar. You'll also find those informative placards on this part of the trail as well as a small native plant garden complete with labels. The Mast Park West Trail earned a Merit Award in 2012 from the California Trails Conference Foundation.

When you reach the end of Mast Park West Trail at the golf course, you'll see a sign for "Future Home of the San Diego River Trail," where the old road continues alongside the golf course. There are plans to create a trail easement around the golf course that will eventually connect this San Diego River Trail to Mission Trails Regional Park.

Additionally, in 2011 the City of Santee purchased 105 acres of property to create the Walker Preserve along 1.3 miles of San Diego River frontage between Magnolia Avenue and Lakeside's baseball fields on Marathon Parkway. This property, which once was used for sand mining here for more than 60 years, is the site of a new trail.

Eventually the San Diego River Park Trail will extend from El Capitan Reservoir to Mission Trails Regional Park.

Thomas Brothers Map: Page 1231, 6-B, Mast Park.

Before You Go: Download a copy of the trail map from the San Diego River Park's website: http://sandiegoriver.org/river_trail.html. Go to Santee River Park, and you'll see the current trail as well as the Walker Preserve extension.

This trail is open to hikers, bicyclists, and dogs on leashes. There's also a leash-free fenced area in Mast Park for dogs.

Trailhead: From Highway 52 heading east, exit at Mission Gorge Road and turn left, heading east. Turn left (north) onto Carlton Hills Boulevard. Turn right (east) into park, just before Carlton Oaks Drive.

From Highway 52 heading west, exit at Fanita Drive. Turn right onto Fanita, right onto Mission Gorge Road, and left onto Carlton Hills Boulevard. The park is on the right.

The mostly paved trail winds along the San Diego River, currently ending at Town Center Community Park at Cuyamaca Street in the east. For Mast Park West Trail, head west from the park under Carlton Hills Boulevard, stopping at Carlton Hills Golf Course where the current trail ends.

Distance/Difficulty: This route is a little more than 4.0 miles round-trip with fairly flat elevation; easy.

7-9. Oaks and Water Views in Boulder-Strewn Oakoasis

Just off Wildcat Canyon Road in Lakeside are several open-space preserves. The smallest of them, Oakoasis Open Space Preserve, offers nearly 400 acres of boulder country with two very special draws: an oak oasis and sweeping views of the San Vicente Reservoir. The acreage was a gift to the county from the Margaret Minshall Family in the late 1980s. Margaret had been a physical education teacher at Hoover High and had built a cabin here in 1936. She later operated a summer camp with horseback riding. Her old cabin burned to the ground in the devastating 2003 Cedar Fire, which consumed 95 percent of this preserve. Today, the oak trees are spreading their shade again, and recovery appears well underway.

View San Vicente Reservoir from Oakoasis trails.

From the parking area, begin on the trailhead marked Trans-County Trail. This preserve will eventually become part of the Trans-County Trail, sometimes called the Pines to Spines Trail, which will cover 110 miles from Torrey Pines State Reserve to Anza-Borrego Desert State Park. Nearly 70 percent of this route uses existing trails, which are already open for public use; the remainder needs to be acquired or built. Federal, state, county, and local governments are working together to connect existing trails. The San Diego Natural History Museum has a good map and information about this future Trans-County Trail; go to http://www.sdnhm.org/archive/fieldguide/places.

The Oakoasis trail is about a 2.5-mile loop through oak riparian and chaparral habitats. You'll know you're in the oak riparian habitat when you reach the preserve's namesake area. A placard at the trailhead informs that chaparral has dense, hard-stemmed, leathery-leaved shrubs that can be up to 10 feet tall. Typical plants in the chaparral habitat, which can include cactus, are the red-barked manzanita (which takes much longer to recover from fire), scrub oak, chamise (which bloom profusely in spring with white flowers), and lots of ceanothus (wild lilac).

It's a good idea to study the map at the trailhead to try to get your bearings. Basically, head counterclockwise on the loop, avoiding short spur trails. When you hit the first T intersection in the trail, it looks like a marker points to the right turn, but ignore that marker and turn left. (The right turn is not the trail; it goes to a private residence).

Just after a bench, you will hit another intersection, this one with a marker pointing left for the Trans-County Trail, and right for Trail. Take the right turn for Trail. Generally you will want to follow the signs for Trail, because the Trans-County Trail isn't part of this loop.

Soon you will be in that oak oasis. The trunks may be blackened, but life has returned to this oak-covered ravine, providing welcome shade in the summer heat. Look for birds here.

Shortly after the oak oasis, you'll hit another marked intersection. Trail goes left, and Upper Meadow goes right. Take the right turn to Upper Meadow. It's a little steep here but is worth the views you'll soon see. At the top of the ridge is a short spur marked "Scenic Outlook." Take this trail for the best views of the San Vicente Reservoir. Notice how low the water level appears. Even so, the blue water is a lovely sight among the boulder-strewn landscape dotted with a few homes.

In 2008 the San Vicente Reservoir was closed to recreational activities, including fishing and boating, for a dam-raising project that will increase its water storage capacity. The latest estimate for it to reopen for fishing and boating is late 2015, but it could be delayed to 2017. For more information about the reservoir, go to the city's water department pages (http://www.sandiego.gov/water/recreation/reservoirs/sanvicente.shtml), or to the San Vicente Dam Raise Project (http://www.sdcwa.org/san-vicente-dam-raise).

Continue on the main Oakoasis Trail and keep following signs, heading right in that counterclockwise loop. For your final reward, you'll encounter a field of lavender-blooming lupine abuzz with bees, just before you go back into that oak oasis area.

Follow the last markers to parking, and you'll reach your car.

Thomas Brothers Map: Page 1212, F-3–immediately opposite–to the left of–Blue Sky Ranch Road (dotted lines).

Before You Go: Check the map on the Oakoasis Preserve page at the county's open space program: http://www.sandiegocounty.gov/parks/openspace/oakoasis.html.

Download a copy of the trail map at http://www.sandiegocounty.gov/reusable_components/images/parks/doc/Trails_Oakoasis.pdf.

This trail is open to hikers, bicyclists, equestrians, and dogs on leashes.

Trailhead: While heading east on Interstate 8, go north on Highway 67. Just after the freeway portion of Highway 67 ends, turn right onto Maple View Street. After 0.3 miles, turn left onto Ashwood, which turns into Wildcat Canyon Road. At 4.2 miles from the Ashwood intersection, turn left into the driveway for Oakoasis Preserve, immediately opposite Blue Sky Ranch Road. Go 0.1 miles on paved road to parking area.

Distance/Difficulty: About 2.5 miles total loop; moderate.

7-10. Lakeside Linkage Trail Leads to Stone Home

The trail through Lakeside Linkage Preserve leads to a historic rock house, whose owners donated it to the county with these words: "For all of you who come to our beloved hilltop, bring your joys or sorrows, tears or laughter, and find strength, healing, serenity, a belief in miracles, quiet and a place to meditate and dream your dreams."

Begin your journey at the trailhead that lies along Los Coches Road some 750 feet below the hilltop destination. This is the main trail through the Lakeside Linkage Preserve, a 134-acre open space preserve acquired as part of San Diego County's Multiple Species Conservation Program (MSCP). Parcels in this three-part preserve were acquired by the county beginning in 1948. The central property where this trail lies includes the Hilltop House property, which was donated to the county to be preserved in perpetuity as a park in 1994. Final pieces of this preserve were acquired by 2000, with another originally acquired in 1932 by the Department of Public Works added to the preserve in 2003.

Lakeside Linkage Trail draws lots of butterflies.

"The preserve is essential to the South County MSCP because the three properties function as a corridor linkage for coastal California gnatcatchers from conserved lands to the south of Interstate 8 (Crestridge Conservation Bank) to conserved lands to the northeast (lands around El Capitan Reservoir)," reports the Final Area Specific Management Directives for Lakeside Linkage Open Space Preserve, prepared in 2008 for the county's Parks and Recreation Department.

The dominant habitat here is coastal sage scrub, and most of the shrubs you'll see are California sagebrush (artemisia californica), California buckwheat, and laurel sumac. You'll also spot white sage, deerweed, broom, sunflowers, and blue elderberry bushes, especially in spring and early summer.

I most enjoyed seeing here the tiny Behr's metalmark butterflies, with only a one-inch wingspan, munching on all the buckwheat. Near the top of the ridge, I also marveled at a soaring red-tailed hawk.

The trail climbs quite steeply in a few places, but it quickly offers plenty of respite as you climb that 750 feet or so to the top in about 1.4 miles. There are other, lesser trails that head off from the main one, but stick to the main trail, following the green-painted wooden post markers with white-painted tips. Keep heading uphill toward the power lines. Near the power lines, the trail veers off to the left (north) from a dirt road and climbs a bit higher. You generally head east to reach the Whitakers' Hilltop House, which you'll finally see on its hill when you begin a descent to its winding drive where you then head uphill again. At the bottom where that drive intersects the trail, the trail continues uphill to the left (north) of the drive just past some eucalyptus trees.

Hale and Mildred Whitaker built their beloved Hilltop House themselves and lived there until they died. Their perch has wraparound views, extending to Lindo Lake as well as the flat-rock face of El Capitan. Hale, born in Illinois in 1905, had lived in Lakeside since 1908. Mildred came here with her mother in 1931. Mildred worked for the San Diego Harbor Department from 1932 until 1940. The local story goes that they met at a party in Lakeside in 1933, fell in love, and married in secret because married women in those days were not allowed to work at the Port District. Hale had served in the navy and was a heavy-equipment operator for the County Road Department for 47 years.

Their labor of love on their stone home was said to be inspired by designs they'd seen by Mary Jane Coulter, including her Bright Angel Lodge and Hopi House at the Grand Canyon, near where the Whitakers were married. The couple made rock-lined pathways around their home, taking in the amazing views in every direction. They planted trees beginning in 1940. The trees include two pyracantha formosa trees directly in front of the house that bloom with bright crimson berries, and a now 15-foot-tall night-blooming cactus that features more than 1,000 blooms in summer, and whose cuttings have also been planted around the property. The Whitakers planted pines and cypress around the south end of the property in 1944 and nearby eucalyptus trees in 1946, a green-trunked palo verde tree at the northeast corner of the house in 1940, and a Chinese pistachio tree in 1971.

Mildred's mother, Nellie Scharnke, had lived with them there, and when she died in 1955, she was buried at the north edge of the home under the stately eucalyptus trees with views east to Lindo Lake. Hale died in 1980, and Mildred passed in 1992. Both are buried next to Nellie under those eucalyptus trees.

The home serves as offices today for county park rangers. It is often open during the Christmas season for historic home tours, and its lighted star can be seen during that time of year from miles around.

Return the way you came and look for more butterflies.

Thomas Brothers Map: Page 1232, B-6 & C-6, Los Coches Road between Ha Hana Road and Los Coches Court.

Before You Go: For more information about this county open space, go to its county parks page at http://www.sandiegocounty.gov/parks/openspace/Lakeside_Linkage.html. Download a copy of the trail map there.

The trail is open to hikers, equestrians, and dogs on leashes; no bicyclists.

Trailhead: From Interstate 8 heading east, exit at Los Coches Road and head straight north for about one mile. The trailhead is on the east side of the road between Ha Hana Road and Los Coches Court. Park along Los Coches Road.

Distance/Difficulty: The round-trip hike is about 2.8 miles total with about 900 feet total elevation gain; moderately difficult.

7-11. Easy, Flat Trail on San Diego River

In 2008 a new trail opened along the San Diego River in a restored riparian habitat known as Lakeside River Park. This flat trail offers a very easy walk through cottonwoods, sycamores, eucalyptus, and pepper trees with a fine view of West Pond, where a bounty of birds congregates all year long. Much of the trail also skirts the Willowbrook Country Club golf course.

The river park is a fairly recent addition to the county's Multiple Species Conservation Plan (MSCP), which sets aside large habitat areas and connects them with natural corridors for protection of wildlife. "San Diego has the highest number of species in danger of extinction of any county in the lower 48 states," says a placard at the trail's West Pond overlook. "Over 200 plants and animals are endangered, threatened or rare. The River Park is a vital linkage. In the midst of suburban industry, it connects natural places together so wildlife can find an unrelated mate and protected nest."

Some 50 species of migratory birds come to nest here during spring (March-July), says another placard. Resident species include egrets, blue herons, and red-tailed hawks.

Look for osprey nest in Lakeside River Park.

Special residents now include the osprey, a large raptor with a five-foot wingspan that dives into ponds for fish. In November 2012, a Boy Scout troop from Coronado completed a 22-foot-high nesting platform hoping to attract the magnificent birds. The scouts should be congratulated because today that platform holds the characteristic nest of huge sticks. Ospreys' nesting season is typically around February and March, according to the *San Diego County Bird Atlas* by Philip Unitt and the San Diego Natural History Museum.

The pond supports lots of wildlife and is an important feature today of San Diego River. San Diego River flows about 52 miles from its headwaters near Julian to the Pacific Ocean in Ocean Beach. It's one of the most important watersheds for San Diego County, supplying 5 percent of the county's water. The other big watersheds in the county are San Juan, Santa Margarita, San Luis Rey, Carlsbad, San Dieguito, Penasquitos, Pueblo, Sweetwater, Otay, and Tijuana, according to the county's Project Clean Water (www.projectcleanwater.org). The El Capitan Dam on this river was constructed in 1935. The San Vincente Dam was built in 1943 to help serve San Diego's growing population, states another placard along the trail.

The Kumeyaay lived all along San Diego River in clans of five to 15 families for some 12,000 years before the Spanish arrived in 1769, according to another placard. The Kumeyaay were hunter-gatherers who walked footpaths here, perhaps very near this trail. "Kumeyaay called this the 'upside-down river' because surface water flows would disappear in the summer heat," says a placard.

During the last half of the 20th century and continuing today, the sand and gravel industry worked this part of the river establishing brick, concrete, and asphalt plants. These operations are nearing an end as they are mined out, which will create new opportunities for Lakeside River Park.

Lakeside's River Park Conservancy was established in 2001. The organization acquired this 100 acres for the park from former sand mining operations. Hanson Aggregates Inc., which still operates next to the trail, has committed to donating its 22 acres to Lakeside River Park when its mining operations end, allowing expansion of the recreational opportunities.

The Hanson property is marked by the Hubbell Monument Gateway, designed by local artist James T. Hubbell. The monument depicts a great egret with wings spread overlooking a mosaic stream of fish created by Lakeside schoolchildren, and it will someday be the main entrance to the river park.

There are currently two main entrances to this trail. The western entrance is off Channel Road, and the northern entrance is off Riverside Drive. You can also enter the park immediately south of that Hubbell gateway, just before the intersection of Channel Road and Lakeside Avenue.

You'll see many memorial plaques donated by local residents next to native trees planted along the trail. As the invasives such as eucalyptus, arundo, and tamarisk are thinned out or removed, native species are being replanted, including mulefat, willows, sycamores, and scarlet monkeyflowers.

Birds you might see include roadrunners, goldfinches, yellow warblers, sparrows, black phoebes, and hummingbirds. At a small overlook onto an area of the river filled with cattails and reeds, look for the red-winged blackbird. On the pond are plenty of mallards and American coots with occasional egrets and herons—and ospreys now.

Thomas Brothers Map: Page 1231, H-3 for northern entrance. Page 1232, A-2, for eastern entrance.

Before You Go: Download a copy of the trail map from the Lakeside River Park Conservancy website: http://www.lakesideriverpark.org/Info/trailmap.htm.

The trail is open to hikers, mountain bikers, equestrians, and dogs on leashes from dawn to dusk every day.

Trailheads: The northern entrance is located across from the intersection of Rio Camino and Riverside Drive. Park on surface streets of Rio Camino and adjacent streets and cross Riverside Drive to the trailhead next to the River Run East industrial park. Do not park in that industrial parking lot.

The eastern entrance is immediately south of the Hubbell Monument Gateway, immediately south of the intersection of Channel Road and Lakeside Avenue. Do not park at this entrance either, but on surface streets nearby.

To reach the northern trailhead, from Highway 67, exit at Riverford Road in Lakeside. Go north on Riverford to the first light and turn right on Riverside Drive. Park on side streets Rio Camino or Vista Camino.

To reach the western trailhead, from Highway 67, exit at Riverford Road and head north to the first light. Turn left onto Mast Boulevard and then left onto Marathon Parkway. Proceed to the dead-end at the Lakeside Baseball Fields. The trailhead is located at the southeast corner of the parking lot.

Distance/Difficulty: The current trail is about 2.0 miles in length for a 4.0-mile round-trip. Very easy.

7-12. Full Circle Views of Lake Jennings

In our semi-arid region, our lakes are a true life source. Most of the lakes in San Diego County are man-made reservoirs. The only natural lakes here are believed to be Big Laguna Lake, the swampy area that became Lake Cuyamaca, and Lakeside's Lindo Lake. Lakeside's other lake, a reservoir, is Lake Jennings, and a 5.0-mile hike around its perimeter is especially appealing in warmer months, even if you can't go swimming in it since it's a source of drinking water.

There is a road that encircles Lake Jennings, and it is the main hiking path as well as the route for fishermen to various locations along the shore and campers to the campground. There are also several shoreline trails that have been created mostly by those fishermen. There is no shoreline trail that goes entirely around the lake. If you choose to dip down to that water line, you'll have to keep going back to that road to continue.

I began my hike by parking near the dock at Siesta Point, which lies a bit north and below the bait and tackle shop at the lake entrance, where you pay your daily use fee.

I started to hike counterclockwise from here, which coincides perfectly with the trail's mile markers encountered on the route.

From this starting point, the road is paved for about 2.0 miles. Just after you reach Eagle Point on the northern shore, the road is unpaved for the next mile or so until you reach the campground area.

Hike around all of Lake Jennings.

For those first miles of paved road, the lake is lined with lots of old eucalyptus trees, many of which are growing right out of the water. Look for several large birdhouses in these trees, which have been placed here for owls and eagles. There are also some 14-foot-high nesting platforms for red-tailed hawks and great horned owls. Both bald eagles and golden eagles have been spotted here. You can view several videos on YouTube of bald eagles in flight over Lake Jennings.

The eagles are just two of the 195 species of birds spotted at Lake Jennings, according to a bird checklist on the Lake Jennings website. The variety of bird life here is great because many species are found both on the water and in the surrounding chaparral. When I was there, I spotted a bright redheaded house finch, several mallard ducks (including some variants with purple instead of green heads), a great blue heron, and an enormous redheaded turkey vulture with a wingspan of nearly six feet, soaring right above me as I crossed the Chet Harritt Dam.

The Chet Harritt Dam was completed to create Lake Jennings in 1962. Harritt was general manager and chief engineer in 1926 of the La Mesa, Lemon Grove, and Spring Valley Irrigation District, the precursor of today's Helix Water District, which owns and manages Lake Jennings and Lake Cuyamaca.

Lake Jennings is named for William H. Jennings, a water lawyer who lived in La Mesa until he died in 1983. Born in 1899, Jennings had grown up on his family's farm near Lakeside, where he learned the importance of water firsthand. He served as secretary and general counsel to the San Diego County Water Authority for 26 years, and he also served on the state's California Water Commission for many years, including as vice chairman. Jennings was one of the instrumental proponents of the State Water Project that began in the late 1950s to bring water from Northern California to Southern California, as well as securing part of the Colorado River Water for San Diego County in the 1960s. Lake Jennings filled what was formerly known as Quail Canyon in Lakeside.

According to the lake's website, in addition to the trail around the lake, there is a 5.0-mile trail that takes off from the north side of the lake and follows the old flume along the ridge of El Monte Valley, which once carried water between this lake and El Capitan Reservoir. I couldn't find this trail, and when I checked back with the ranger on duty, he said it was mostly overgrown now but was located near Half Moon Cove, which you can spot on the lake map.

Half Moon Cove is just before Sentry Point, one of the prettiest parts of the lake where a peninsula juts into the water. When you reach Sentry Point, the unpaved road ends, and you now must climb uphill into the campground area to reconnect to the paved road that will continue across that dam and back to the starting point.

Lake Jennings may not be open for swimming, but it is open for fishing Fridays, Saturdays, and Sundays; you must bring a valid fishing license with you because they are not sold here. It also rents motor boats ($30 for half a day, $40 for a full day), row boats ($14 for half a day, $19 for a full day) and paddle boats ($10 per hour). Private boats may be launched here for $8 a day. Entrance to the lake for fishing costs $8 for adults, $3 for kids 8-16 and free under 8. Lake Jennings stocks 26,000 pounds of trout and 8,000 pounds of channel catfish every year.

Note that the perimeter trail is open to hikers only during those days the lake is open for fishing (Fridays, Saturdays, and Sundays).

Thomas Brothers Map: Page 1232, F-4, Lake Jennings Park Road to Harritt Road to Bass Drive for lake entry.

Before You Go: Download a copy of the map of Lake Jennings from its website: www.lakejennings.org.
   The route around the lake is open to the public for hiking only on Friday, Saturday, and Sunday. Registered campers there may hike the perimeter trail seven days a week.
   Day-use fee for hikers is $2, payable at the bait and tackle shop near the entrance.

Trailhead: From Interstate 8, exit at Lake Jennings Park Road and head north. Turn right on Harritt Road and head straight into Lake Jennings Park.

Distance/Difficulty: The hike around the lake is about 5.5 miles. It is fairly easy with about 375 feet total elevation change.

7-13. Wander Flinn Springs Trails into Hills

Flinn Springs County Park has a gazebo that's popular for weddings, a year-round creek surrounded by old oaks and sycamores, and 2.5 miles of trails that head off into the hills. Begin by wandering around the pretty park itself, which is centered on Los Coches Creek, sometimes called Flinn Springs Creek here. Several footbridges cross the year-round creek in the 40-acre park, which also features a couple of softball fields, a few play areas (including several swings), and barbecue and picnic areas.

The prettiest part of the park is that creek, where big boulders make for climbable explorations, and lots of fine old coast live oaks and sycamores provide plenty of shade as well as roosts for owls and hawks.

The creek hugs the northern edge of the park nearest Olde Highway 80. Olde (sometimes just Old) Highway 80 was once known as the "Broadway of America" because this true intercontinental highway ran from downtown San Diego to Savannah, Georgia, according to Jack Brandais's *Weekend Driver San Diego*. Highway 80 still takes travelers east from Dallas, but west from Dallas, the highway was ultimately decommissioned between 1964 and 1974, when Interstate 8 took over. US 80 was the first all-weather, coast-to-coast route available to auto travelers, and it was among the first U.S. highways commissioned in 1926. Parts of it were already in place in San Diego starting as early as 1909.

Flinn Springs traces its history back to the early ranchos awarded to local residents by the Mexican government, when it held California from 1819 to 1846, before the Mexican-American War ended. California became part of the United States in 1848 and became a state in 1850.

Head to the hills at Flinn Springs.

In one of his last gifts of land, in 1845 Mexican Governor Pio Pico awarded 48,800 acres—the second largest of the Mexican land grants in San Diego County next to the 58,875 acres of Old Mission lands encompassing San Diego—to Maria Estudillo, wife of Miguel Pedrorena. That Rancho El Cajon encompassed present-day El Cajon, Bostonia, Santee, Lakeside, Flinn Springs, and the eastern reaches of La Mesa.

Flinn Springs ultimately got its name from the William Flinn family, who settled along the Los Coches Creek in 1865, according to *This Was Yesterday*, a brief history of the area written by his granddaughter, Julia Flinn De Frate, self-published in 1953 and shared by the El Cajon Historical Society. Born here in 1876, Flinn De Frate describes how her grandparents traveled west from Texas and acquired the ranch land along Los Coches Creek and called it La Vinita. It was just 4.0 miles away along the same creek from La Canada De Los Coches Ranch, which was settled by her maternal grandparents, the Julian Ames family, in 1859. The Flinns soon gave the area the name of Flinn Valley, which eventually became Flinn Springs by the 1920s. It sat in the shadow of a mountain the Indians had long called Montebanna, meaning "sleeping woman," for its shape.

The trails that meander across the park's western reaches head up into that mountain area and into Crestridge Ecological Reserve, a 2,800-acre reserve administered by the California Department of Fish and Wildlife. Check the map placards at the park for the most detailed map of the trails. Once you get out there, they aren't well marked, but it shouldn't be hard to find your way. Behind the large ball field located at the southwestern part of the park, you'll see a placard discussing the 2003 Cedar Fire that scorched a small portion of the park. Behind that placard is a trail that heads uphill into the backcountry.

In a short way up the hill, you'll see a sign noting the boundary of the ecological reserve. The trail continues to climb up here, but I didn't go much farther. I believe the trail eventually connects to Crestridge, though there are some private properties that lie in between, so a true easement between Flinn Springs Park and Crestridge trails has yet to materialize.

I headed back to the wildlife placard and continued east through the park's southern reaches. Several trails crisscross around here. Wander through this coastal sage scrub habitat and note the views that look east to the mighty rock face of El Capitan on the horizon.

You can take one of several trails that head back down into the park, which you can see from this elevation in the hills as it spreads out below. Enjoy those oaks and sycamores a little longer along Los Coches Creek, which ultimately joins San Diego River.

Thomas Brothers Map: Page 1232, J-4.

Before You Go: Download a copy of the map of Flinn Springs County Park at the county's parks pages: http://www.sdcounty.ca.gov/parks/picnic/flinnsprings_map.html.

For general information on the park and all its facilities, go to http://www.co.san-diego.ca.us/parks/picnic/flinnsprings.html.

These trails are open only to hikers and dogs on leashes, and dogs on leashes are also allowed on Crestridge Ecological Reserve trails. For more information on Crestridge, go to https://www.wildlife.ca.gov/Lands/Places-to-Visit/Crestridge-ER.

Trailhead: From Interstate 8 heading east, exit at Lake Jennings Park Road and head straight ahead on Old Highway 80 until you reach Flinn Springs County Park on the right.

From Interstate 8 heading west, exit at Dunbar Lane toward Harbison Canyon. Turn right onto Dunbar and then left at the first cross street onto Olde Highway 80. The park will be about 2.5 miles later on your left.

Distance/Difficulty: I hiked around the park and its trails for about 2.0 miles total with an elevation gain of about 350 feet; easy.

7-14. El Capitan Trail Has Challenges

The trail to Conejos Creek along the eastern shore of El Capitan Reservoir has those pretty water views backdropped by layers of rocky hillsides, including El Capitan itself.

But it's not the easiest of trails to navigate, and much of it is overgrown with scratchy shrubs, so be prepared for those difficulties if you tackle this trail; perseverance and long pants are recommended.

When you reach the blue-water reservoir's parking area on its western shore, you'll easily see the trail cut into the hillside on the opposite eastern shore. This 3.0-mile stretch is actually the remnant of an old redwood-planked flume that brought water from the Cuyamaca Mountains to La Mesa and other western cities in the early 20th century, according to Jerry Schad's hiking guidebook, *Afoot and Afield, San Diego County*. That flume once traversed 36 miles. The 9 million board feet of redwood used to build the flume and its 300 trestles "were scavenged a long time ago," he wrote. That would have been after the El Capitan Dam created the reservoir in 1935, so the flume lost its purpose and was abandoned.

Find your way to old flume path at El Capitan.

El Capitan Reservoir is the largest in the City of San Diego's reservoir system. When full, it has 1,562 surface acres, storage capacity of 112,806 acre-feet, a maximum water depth of 197 feet, and 22 miles of shoreline.

Boating and fishing are popular here when the reservoir is open, Friday through Monday from 6:00 a.m. to 6:00 p.m. Boats are available for rental, and bait may be purchased for trying to catch largemouth bass, crappie, bluegill, catfish, sunfish, and carp.

Waterskiing, wakeboarding, and personal watercraft (including jet skis and kayaks) are also permitted here. There's an 85-boat limit on the lake. Boaters may bring their own watercraft here, but there are posted, strict rules on leaving the lake and cleaning boats to minimize the spread of invasive quagga mussels that have infested El Capitan Reservoir. Quagga mussel infestations have been documented in California since early 2007, according to the Department of Fish and Wildlife. They have spread to many Southern California lakes and reservoirs that receive raw water from the Colorado River via the Colorado River Aqueduct. Infested reservoirs in San Diego County include

Lower Otay, San Vicente, Lake Murray, Lake Miramar, El Capitan, Sweetwater, Dixon Lake, Olivenhain, Lake Jennings, Lake Ramona, and Lake Poway. Five that are not infested yet, according to the San Diego Public Utilities Department, are Lake Hodges, Morena Reservoir, Barrett Reservoir, Upper Otay Reservoir, and Lake Sutherland.

El Capitan Reservoir has daily spot checks during its busy season (June through September) to ensure boaters comply with rules intended to minimize the spread, including draining and drying all water from outboard motors and ballast tanks.

To reach that trail on the eastern shore, hikers must head to the very southern end of the lake and make their way across its muddy bottom. Here you'll see evidence of the mussel infestation because the mollusks have affixed themselves to limbs and trees that lie high above the water, pointing out how much higher that water level can rise. It's an odd sight to see trees covered in these tiny mussels.

To reach that southern end, follow the old road that leaves the parking area heading south. Quickly leave that road and make your way down to the end of the lake. There isn't an obvious route at this southern end, so you have to pick your way to that muddy bottom and then climb up the sandy shoreline to reach hard ground. I was there in mid-September, when the area was probably a lot less muddy than it can be in rainier seasons.

You'll encounter trails then that offer sketchy paths to reach that old flume cut above the eastern shore. When you finally get to the eastern shore, the trail is obvious, if overgrown with buckwheat and sage. That sage offers a lovely, strong fragrance here, so that is a pleasant reward. The views across the blue water to the layers of hills are fine too. El Capitan is the sheer southern face of El Cajon Mountain, which is 3,675 feet high and looms above the lake along its western edge.

The trail follows the old flume path for about 3.0 miles until finally reaching Conejos Creek. I didn't make it all the way on the very hot day I was there, turning around after about 1.7 miles from my start where the trail seemed to become even more overgrown.

After making my way back through that muddy bottom along the southern end, I climbed back up to the dirt road and hiked another half-mile or so as it continued west toward Interstate 8. That stretch was a lovely bonus because the road passed under boughs of old oak trees and secreted some lovely oak-shaded grounds to its left. From there, I retraced my way back to the parking area.

Thomas Brothers Map: Page 1233,G-1.

Before You Go: For a satellite map of El Capitan Reservoir and this old eastern trail, go to the California State Parks Division of Boating and Waterways website: http://www.dbw.ca.gov/maps/facilityinfo.asp?facilityID=226.

For information about El Capitan Reservoir and its boating and fishing rules, as well as a general map, go to http://www.sandiego.gov/water/recreation/reservoirs/elcapitan.shtml.

This trail is open only to hikers. Leashed dogs are allowed here but must be 50 feet away from the water, and part of this hike gets closer.

There is an $8 day-use fee per person at the entry gate.

Trailhead: From Interstate 8 heading east, exit at Lake Jennings Park Road and head north for about 1.4 miles to El Monte Road, where you turn right and continue about 8.0 miles to the end of the road and the reservoir's entry gate.

Distance/Difficulty: We went a total of 4.0 miles. If you take the trail to its end at Conejos Creek, according to Schad, it continues about 3.5 miles for a 7.0-mile round-trip, not including the road. Mostly easy.

7-15. Stroll Lindo Lake and Picture Past

Walk the easy 1.5-mile loop around Lindo Lake in Lakeside and imagine the scene hundreds of years ago. Lindo Lake is one of San Diego County's only natural lakes (Big Laguna is another), so it was a homesite for Kumeyaay people for thousands of years. These native people would migrate between here and the desert according to the seasons. "They lived a peaceful life of hunting, fishing and gathering acorns, mesquite beans, pinon seeds and berries," wrote Richard White in a history about Lakeside for the local historical society. "They were also skilled in making pottery, weaving baskets and making jewelry from shells, seeds, hollow bones and small stones."

Lindo Lake is one of the county's only natural lakes.

The Kumeyaay called the natural freshwater lagoon "Aha-Ta-Munk," which translates to mean "to fill with water." Quail Creek, Los Coches Creek, and occasionally flood waters from San Diego River filled the lagoon then. With the arrival of Spanish missionaries in 1769, the padres named the lagoon Lindo Lago, meaning "pretty lake."

During the Mexican regime, when lands were granted to private citizens, the Estudillo family of Old Town in 1845 was granted the nearly 48,800-acre El Cajon Rancho, the era's second largest land grant rancho in San Diego County. It encompassed all of El Cajon as well as Lakeside and Lindo Lake.

By 1869, the Estudillo family began selling its lands, including 10,000 acres to Benjamin Hill. In 1886 Hill sold 3,000 acres to El Cajon Valley Company, which laid out the town of Lakeside, named for its location on Lindo Lake. That company built a grand 80-room Victorian hotel in 1887 that resembled the Hotel del Coronado, and it opened in February 1888. The historic boat house was built on the lake in 1887 and still sits on the lake today.

The railroad came to Lakeside in 1889, ushering in a new era of prosperity to the town centered at the inn as well as Maine Street, where several historic buildings still exist. But by 1920, the grand Lakeside Inn had fallen into disrepair and was torn down. Lakeside's post office sits on its site today. The San Diego, Cuyamaca, and Eastern Railway tracks that connected Lakeside and Santee to San Diego were destroyed in the 1930s.

To see photographs of the grand old Lakeside Inn, head a couple of blocks west to Lakeside's historic Maine Avenue to the Lakeside Historical Society's buildings at the Community Presbyterian Church at the corner of Maine and Parkside. This 1895 church was Lakeside's first, and it became the local historical society's headquarters in 1994. Its neighboring Manse, built in 1915 for the church pastors, is open on Saturday afternoons, and photos of the Lakeside Inn can be viewed, along with many other fascinating relics of yesteryear, including old telephone systems, spinning wheels, historic gowns, furs, jewelry, furnishings, and historic photos and publications. Enthusiastic docents are on hand Saturdays from 11:00 a.m. to 3:00 p.m. to share the collections.

Lindo Lake flooded the town on occasion, such as in 1927 and 1941. It also would go dry during long periods of drought. Wells were drilled to keep it full. Lake Jennings' Chet Harritt Dam and the redirection of Los Coches Creek have adversely affected Lindo Lake, but today the County Parks Department works at keeping it full. Half of the lake remains dry today, and the loop trail takes in both sections.

Begin the loop near the Community Center on Vine Street just off Woodside Avenue, heading counterclockwise. In winter, the migrating water fowl make this hike especially interesting. A large flock of wonderful white pelicans was there the day I strolled the flat path. There were also several Canada geese and lots of domestic geese, both white and banded with gray. A few great blue herons waded in the shallows. Many American coots and mallard duck pairs floated on the blue water. Double-crested cormorants held open their wings to dry. A yellow warbler sang in a pepper tree, a cinnamon teal duck curled up on shore, and American bitterns strutted their pretty striped selves.

The pepper trees are fine specimens today, and wonderful willows make for yellow fall color here.

In sight of that historic boat house is an exercise area where 17 physical fitness stations invite people to work out for free with lovely views. A power rower, a stationary bike, a four-person leg press, a two-person arm press, balance steps, and an assisted row/push-up contraption are among the offerings.

Just past the small peninsula where the boat house is located, head off to the right to walk around that dry part of the lake, where a few unpaved paths pass under those willows and several colorful cottonwoods. The path connects to the one around the water-filled lake to make that entire loop. The pathways are very flat and easy, and they invite hikers, bicyclists, dogs on leashes, and lots of baby strollers.

Boats are no longer allowed on Lindo Lake, but fishing from shore is still available.

Crime used to be a big problem at Lindo Lake County Park, but not so much today. The County Parks rangers and local police have worked hard in the last few years to rid the lovely spot of gangs and criminals. Bird photographers are more common there now.

Thomas Brothers Map: Page 1232, B-3.

Before You Go: Download a copy of the trail map at the county's parks page for Lindo Lake County Park: http://www.co.san-diego.ca.us/reusable_components/images/parks/doc/LindoLake/LindoLakeParkMap.pdf.

For more information, go to the county page: http://www.sandiegocounty.gov/parks/picnic/lindolake.html.

This lake loop trail is open to hikers, bicyclists, and dogs on leashes.

Trailhead: From Highway 67 heading north, exit at Winter Gardens Boulevard and head east, turning left at Woodside Avenue. Woodside dead-ends at Vine Street, where you turn left to head into the parking area. From Highway 67 heading south, exit at Mapleview Street heading east. Turn right onto Vine Street and park just before reaching Woodside.

Distance/Difficulty: A 1.5-mile total loop; very easy.

7-16. Silverwood Offers Excellent Education

Take a guided hike at Silverwood Wildlife Sanctuary in Lakeside and learn how nature rebounds after a disastrous fire. Every Sunday at 10:00 a.m. and 1:30 p.m. (except July through September due to heat), the wildlife sanctuary offers free guided hikes. The sanctuary is also open Sundays from 9:00 a.m. to 4:00 p.m. for self-guided hikes on its 4.0 miles of trails. Pick up sheets at the entry that identify lettered markers on the Self-Guided Geology Trail, as well as numbered markers on the Self-Guided Chaparral Trail.

On a Sunday in October, I hiked with resident manager Phillip Lambert, who shared his impressive knowledge on a range of topics. That weekend marked 10 years after the catastrophic Cedar Fire of 2003 destroyed this entire area—and a lot more. Some 280,278 acres were burned from Cuyamaca to Scripps Ranch, and 15 people were killed, making it the deadliest as well as the largest fire in California recorded history.

"The Cedar Fire was the first time this area ever experienced a fire like that," he said. "It was a Santa Ana wind-driven fire with 30–60 mph gusts. The shrubs just exploded. We had slicks that dated back 400 years, but the fire was so hot, exfoliating sheets in these rocks just exploded, so now there is no evidence of those sites." He shared photos of the area right after the fire; it looked like a gray moonscape. Today, oaks have resprouted, and ceanothus, yuccas, sugar bush, and laurel sumac have all come back. Lichens have also returned to the rocks.

Markers inform about geology and chaparral at Silverwood.

"We learned a lot after the fire," Lambert, who has been resident manager at Silverwood since 1996. He escaped the fire in the middle of the night with little time to spare. Every structure on the property was destroyed.

He pointed out that ecosystems need fire "every once in a while," to turn dead fuel into ash for nutrients for the soil. "It's always more fertile for 10 years after a fire," he pointed out, noting that after 10 years, the heightened growth slows again.

Lots of "fire followers," especially wildflowers, emerge after a fire. "We had California poppies, Parry's phacelia, golden eardrops (a species of poppy), and slimy monkey flowers that no one had ever seen here until after the fire. Our plant list now numbers 343 species since the fire."

The 757-acre Silverwood is owned and maintained by the San Diego Audubon Society. Its members have also recorded 124 bird species on the property as well as many reptiles and mammals, including mule deer, bobcats, raccoons, coyotes, and cottontails.

The property dates back to 1936 when its owner, Harry Woodward, built a summer cottage on his 85 acres here. He named it Silverwood for the way sunlight shines off the leaves of coast live oak trees. Woodward deeded his property to San Diego Audubon in 1965, and the organization has added additional acreage ever since. The sanctuary's purpose is to preserve most of its acreage as wilderness, "an exceptionally diverse assemblage of chaparral and streamside riparian flora and fauna," it says.

Its first resident manager, Frank Gander, with help from Howie Wheeler, put together a plant list in 1966 of 287 species as well as a bird list. Gander, formerly a longtime botanist at the San Diego Natural History Museum, even has a species of hybrid oak named after him: Gander oak. Gander was resident manager for 10 years until he passed away. Some facilities and trails are named after Gander and Wheeler.

As I followed Lambert around the compact collection of lower-elevation trails, he talked about the mixed chaparral and the riparian oaks here and how they've recovered since the Cedar Fire. "In the skeletal remains of oaks, you can still see the direction the fire burned," he pointed out. The thick bark of the oaks help insulate their living tissue. Even if the tree burns, the "heat from the fire activates new trunks at the base of these old oak trees," he said. But the oaks are stressed today because of the drought over the last few years. "Unless we get a lot of rain, they can't produce sap to protect themselves against the oak borer," a dreaded beetle that's killing oaks all over the county.

He showed me some historic sites used by the Kumeyaay hundreds of years ago, including one considered a female puberty ceremonial site that may have been a hunters' site in a native culture that preceded the Kumeyaay by 8,000 years. He took me to another Kumeyaay shaman site where the huge boulders did seem specially formed; one looked like a lion head, and another looked like a snake or whale.

We saw tracks made in soft sand by desert cottontail rabbits, California towhees and quails, and coyotes.

Lambert shared how the natives used yucca to make fibers for mats, ropes, and bow strings, and how they used their roots and leaves for soap. Then he pointed the way up the Circuit Trail so I could see the amazing Silverdome. It's widely considered the biggest granite monolith in Southern California, and it is impressive. As you reach the top ridge on the Circuit Trail—a fairly steep climb of several hundred feet in a half-mile or so—there it is, a huge, rounded granite dome covered by lichen, rising some 500 feet to its elevation of 2,388 feet and backdropped by rocky peaks like Rock Mountain and El Capitan. The views from that Circuit Trail are truly panoramic; on a clear day, you can see the ocean, Mount Soledad to the west, and plenty of peaks to the north and east.

See what you can learn at Silverwood.

Thomas Brothers Map: Page 1212, F-2, where all the trails begin off Wildcat Canyon Road.

Before You Go: Visit the sanctuary's website, http://www.sandiegoaudubon.org/our-work/sanctuaries/silverwood-wildlife-sanctuary, to learn more.

Trails are open only to hikers. No pets allowed.

The sanctuary is open only on Sundays, 9:00 a.m. to 4:00 p.m., from October to June. Guided hikes are free and are offered on Sundays at 10:00 a.m. and 1:30 p.m. during those months.

There are lots of interesting displays on flora, fauna, and the fire at the Frank Gander Nature Education Center. Up the short Wright McConnell Trail from the entrance, there is an Observation Center with several bird feeders, where I saw yellow goldfinches and red house finches.

Pick up a trail map at the sanctuary entrance area where you sign in.

Trailhead: From Highway 67, turn east onto Mapleview Street and then left (north) onto Ashwood, which turns into Wildcat Canyon Road. After Ashwood, go 4.8 miles to Silverwood's entrance on the right (east).

Distance/Difficulty: The loop Circuit Trail is about 2.0 miles total, with an elevation change of nearly 1,200 feet; moderately difficult. The other trails are fairly flat and easy.

7-17. Learn about Local Flora in Stelzer County Park

One of the best places to learn about local flora is Louis Stelzer County Park in Lakeside. Along its easy, 0.7-mile-long Riparian Trail that follows a stream through Wildcat Canyon are several plaques that identify trees and plants, also sharing their Native American uses. With the main park's picnic facilities, barbecues and playgrounds, it's an ideal outdoor destination for children. In fact, parents named this Lakeside park the 2009 Best Family Park in all of San Diego County in Nickelodeon's Parents' Picks Awards.

"We also have an award-winning Discovery Kit program that's correlated with California's science framework," Ranger Patty Heyden told us. "Teachers love it." That Discovery Kit is a hands-on course that includes field trip activities in the park and pretrip and follow-up activities for the classroom and the home. Kits are available for grades K-6.

The Stelzer County Park trails are among the best for children.

The educational programs are designed to encourage kids to explore and appreciate nature, and its namesake would be proud.

Louis Stelzer bought this 310-acre parcel in the 1940s for a weekend retreat, according to a sign in the park. He called it Shadow Mountain Ranch, which he deeded to the county upon his death in 1972 with the request that it "be developed into a park so that the children of San Diego be provided a place for outdoor education and recreational opportunities." Adults will learn as well by just taking a walk along that main trail.

The two main habitats here are coastal sage scrub and oak woodland. Coastal sage scrub consists mainly of low-growing, aromatic, soft-leaved shrubs. Oak woodlands are usually near stream canyons and often include stands of pine trees as well as sycamores. Both of these habitats suffered in the 2003 Cedar Fire, which burned 95 percent of

Stelzer County Park. Plaques along the trail tell the story of such fires, and how the habitats recover along with the animals and birds that live there.

Another plaque identifies the splendid coast live oak, several of which form a beautiful shade canopy over the early part of the Riparian Trail. Native Americans used the acorns, bark, and stems of different kinds of oaks for food, basket weaving, fuel, and candle frames.

The western sycamore, the tree with the mottled bark, is always found near stream beds, another plaque says. Native Americans scraped the fuzz from the bottom of its leaves and mixed it with quail egg yolk to relieve sinus problems and asthma.

The arroyo willow, found along stream banks, makes a good nesting site for the endangered least Bell's vireo bird. This plaque notes that the salicin in its bark is an active ingredient in aspirin, and Native Americans chewed the bark to relieve headaches and pains. They also made bows, cradle pads, and skirts from the willow.

Plenty of poison oak is found here. Both poison oak and wild grape vines wrap around several of the oak trees along the trail. Avoid poison oak and its itchy rash by learning to identify it: "Leaves of three, let it be." A plaque identifying poison oak notes that Native Americans made it into a medicine to counteract rattlesnake bites.

They also made a strong tea out of California sagebrush to alleviate bronchial problems and used a strong wash of it to clean wounds and stop swelling. Wild cucumber seeds were made into necklaces and used as marbles. The roots of Jimson weed (named for its early identification at Jamestown in America's settler history) were made into a liquid used in rites of manhood, which is very toxic and can even cause death.

Once you've ingested all these interesting facts from the Riparian Trail, take the Wooten Loop at its end to go up the sunny hillside. In just 0.9 miles, you'll reach an observation deck that affords a fine view of Wildcat Canyon. In another 0.28 miles, you'll reach the Stelzer Ridge Trail. Take a left here and return in a little more than a half-mile back to the main park.

The most amazing sight in the park is right in the middle of the picnic area. It's an enormous coast live oak whose limbs extend every which way, some of which are now supported. "We call it Moses," said Ranger Heyden. "It's 200 to 300 years old. The Cedar Fire actually went around this main park on both sides, so the tree wasn't even singed." It's also sometimes called the Wedding Tree because lots of happy nuptials take place under its enormous canopy.

There's a lot to love about Stelzer County Park.

Thomas Brothers Map: Page 1232, C-1.

Before You Go: For more information about the park, its Discovery Kit program and facilities, go to http://www.co.san-diego.ca.us/parks/picnic/stelzer.html.

At that website, download a map (http://www.sandiegocounty.gov/content/dam/sdc/parks/LouisStelzerCountyPark/Documents/LouisStelzerMap.pdf).

This trail is open only to hikers and dogs on leashes. The park is open from 7 a.m. to sunset. There is a $3 fee to park here; self-pay at the entry points in the envelopes provided.

Trailhead: To reach Louis Stelzer County Park, go east on Interstate 8 and then north on Highway 67. When Highway 67 ends, turn right onto Mapleview Street. Turn left onto Ashwood Street, which becomes Wildcat Canyon Road. The park is on the right at 11470 Wildcat Canyon Road.

Distance/Difficulty: It is 1.5 miles for the round-trip loop Riparian and Wooten trails. The Riparian Trail is very easy; the Wooten Loop requires a small elevation gain and is totally exposed to the sun.

7-18. Two Trails Combine Hills and Lake Views

Combining a portion of the California Riding and Hiking Trail with a meander around Loveland Reservoir makes for a fine hike in Alpine's backcountry with blue-water views. About 12 miles of the CR&H Trail, established statewide in 1945, wind through

Alpine between Crest and Dehesa. That's a fraction of the 108 miles of that historic trail in San Diego County, of which only about 76 miles are currently in use. Statewide, some 1,060 miles of the CR&H trail have been completed.

The hike highlighted here begins at the parking area for Sweetwater Authority's Loveland Reservoir on Japatul Road. The CR&H trail goes both north and south from here, immediately west of the parking area entrance. You'll see the yellow-topped metal posts that mark the CR&H trail throughout its course. It's open to hikers, equestrians, and mountain bikers, but no dogs or motorized vehicles.

This portion of the CR&H trail is little used, as evidenced by the high growth of grasses that significantly obscure the trail in some places.

Loveland Reservoir views are the reward in this chaparral.

As you head to the northeast after crossing Japatul Road, the trail winds through thick chaparral habitat, a lot of which is in bloom in June. Here is one of the best opportunities to distinguish buckwheat from chamise, two of the most abundant shrubs in our chaparral that can appear very similar when they're not blooming. When they are blooming in late spring and summer, they're easy to tell apart. Buckwheat's flowers, white in summer and turning rust in fall, are clustered in rounded bouquets on long stems. Chamise flowers are cream colored in spring and early summer, and they extend from the ends of stems in cone shapes. Chamise is probably San Diego County's most abundant shrub, according to James

Lightner in his book *San Diego County Native Plants,* and it is so dominant in chaparral that the habitat is often called chamise chaparral. Sprinkled along with these blooming shrubs are some lovely yellow mariposa lilies, bright fuchsia-colored canchalagua, and golden yarrow.

The trail winds uphill a bit from the road as it climbs its way north along switchbacks. I had planned to take it about 2.0 to 3.0 miles one-way to its northern junction at Via Dieguenos Street, where I expected to see views of Palo Verde Lake. But after about a mile, the grasses had grown so thick that I began to lose sight of the trail.

At that mile point, the trail had turned north alongside a beautiful riparian canyon below of the Sweetwater River, the source that feeds Loveland Reservoir. The trail here also hugs the edge of the hill, in some cases so narrow with steep drop-offs that I would think it might be a bit dicey for horses. With that hard-to-see edge and the fact that the overgrowth might hide some rattlesnakes, I decided to turn back. Views to the south take in a remarkably green valley along the very eastern edge of Loveland Reservoir, with lots of layers of hills on all horizons.

When I got back to the parking area, I talked to one of the watershed caretakers of Sweetwater Authority, the governing body of the reservoir, who told me about snake chaps, a safety item of clothing for outdoor workers. I want to get some now. Do a search, and you'll find many choices of snake-proof chaps and gaiters.

I continued my hike down to Loveland Reservoir, a lovely manmade lake that is one of two made by dams along the Sweetwater River—the same river that begins in Cleveland National Forest and runs through Cuyamaca Rancho State Park all the way to the ocean, through a 230-square-mile watershed. Loveland Reservoir, completed in 1945, has a capacity of 25,400 acre-feet of water and supplies drinking water to Chula Vista, National City, and Bonita residents. It's open only to shoreline fishing for bass, catfish, bluegill, red-eared sunfish and crappie. Boats, swimming, and dogs are not allowed here.

There are about 4.5 miles of trail along the southern edge of Loveland, with another 2.5 miles along the northern edge. But again, these trails aren't always obvious, and you sometimes have to find your way to the next segment. However, you can't get lost because the lake remains the marker here.

I walked down the well-worn path to the lake and then headed to the left along Loveland's southern shoreline. Generally, take the higher path for easier going. I went only about a half-mile here before turning back, making for about 3.0 miles total on this hike.

Before You Go: Download a map of some of the CR&H Trail as well as Loveland Reservoir from Sweetwater Authority: http://www.sweetwater.org/Modules/ShowDocument.aspx?documentid=41.
Check another map at Alpine Trails Brochure: http://whiteoakwildnights.com/alpineTrails.pdf.
The best map I've found of this entire segment of the CR&H Trail is in Jerry Schad's excellent hiking guidebook, *Afoot and Afield in San Diego County,* for the hike around Loveland Reservoir.
This trail is open only to hikers, equestrians, and bicyclists; no dogs.

Trailhead: From Interstate 8 heading east, exit at Tavern Road in Alpine, heading south 2.7 miles to its junction with Dehesa Road to the right. Stay straight ahead, where Tavern Road turns into Japatul Road. Go about 1.0 mile to the Loveland Reservoir parking area on the right.

The CR&H Trail, going both north and south from here, is immediately to the west of (before) that parking area on both sides of Japatul Road. Cross Japatul Road to begin the northern section of the trail described here.

Distance/Difficulty: The CR&H Trail heads north from Japatul Road about 3.0 miles to its junction with Via Dieguenos, where it also continues north past Interstate 8. The trail around Loveland Reservoir hugs the shoreline in both upper and lower segments for about 4.5 miles along the south shore and 2.5 miles along the north shore. For the 3.0 miles I hiked, I logged an elevation gain of about 630 feet; moderate.

7-19. Old Chaparral, Views of Riparian Ribbons on Bell Bluff Trail

Hike the Bell Bluff Trail in Alpine through 45-year-old chaparral, where red-trunked, big-berry manzanita rise some 15 feet high and where views extend a couple of hundred feet below into the green riparian ribbon of the Sweetwater River. The trail follows the old Spanish Bit Drive, an abandoned dirt road that is open to hikers, equestrians, mountain bikers, and dogs on leashes. The trail's first mile is also part of the California Riding and Hiking Trail, whose yellow-topped metal markers you'll see at the trailhead and along the trail.

The trail begins between two homes in the Palo Verde Ranch development, where many homes have horses ready to ride on the nearby trails. The trail quickly crosses the Sweetwater River, which is totally dry here in late summer. It passes through that riparian habitat of willows and old oaks, and then it climbs up about 180 feet in elevation into chaparral. After you've gone just a third of a mile or so, you'll leave views of Alpine homes behind and head into the wilderness, where layers of hills stretch on the horizon.

Bell Bluff Trail leaves the city behind.

At this point, below the trail on the right, you get the first great glimpse of the Sweetwater River's rich riparian ribbon of green live oaks hugging the water source as it weaves southwest toward Loveland Reservoir, which you can't see from here. There are less-traveled trails that veer off from the main one, but I stuck to the obvious main trail heading straight ahead.

Soon you'll reach the tallest of the lovely red-trunked manzanita that flank the trail, some at least 15 feet tall. The big-berry manzanita is one of the "Essential Chaparral Six," the most characteristic shrubs in the chaparral according to the California Chaparral Institute based in Escondido. The others are ceanothus (wild lilac), scrub oak, chamise, silk tassel bush, and mountain mahogany.

A few mountain mahogany bushes on this trail were in full feathery glow in mid-August, when their "silvery, feather-like styles (projections from ovaries) appear in summer after flowers drop, giving plants beautiful ghostly aspect," writes James Lightner in *San Diego County Native Plants*. These specimens were so filled with the feathery styles that they appeared to be covered in white blooms until close-up inspection revealed the fascinating tendrils.

The Alpine Trails brochure is published by the Alpine Planning Group Trails Subcommittee, which is part of San Diego County's Alpine Community Trails Pathways Plan. The brochure notes that the Bell Bluff Trail "travels through 35-year-old chaparral, offering great views." However, I think the chaparral is now 45 years old, ever since the enormous 1970 Laguna fire wove its path of destruction through this area. Santa Ana winds reaching 50 miles per hour had blown a tree against a power line, which fell into dry brush near Sunrise Highway and Interstate 8 in the early morning of September 26, 1970. The fire "raged at unbelievable speed toward Alpine" and "roared through Harbison Canyon, Jamul and Crest ... consuming 4,000 acres an hour," according to a report recalling the disaster in the *San Diego Union* on October 9, 1987. The fire had traveled 32 miles in 30 hours, approaching El Cajon. When it was over on October 3, the Laguna Mountain Fire had scorched 185,000 acres, now counted as the fourth worst wildfire in California history.

There is little sign of that fire on the Bell Bluff Trail today. The California Chaparral Institute defines "old-growth chaparral" as 50 years old or more, so this area is nearing that status as a "vigorous plant community that supports a dynamic population of animals."

After a little more than 1.0 mile on the trail, it reaches an intersection with the California Riding and Hiking Trail heading off to the right, and the Bell Bluff Trail continuing straight ahead a bit to the left. Near this junction, you'll also see on the left a small grove of tall eucalyptus trees.

At about 1.7 miles from the start, you'll see a trail heading off to the right, with the main trail still heading straight. At this point, the main trail gets a lot rockier as it climbs toward Bell Bluff itself, a round, rocky promontory that's part of the Cuyamaca Mountains.

Bell Bluff is No. 95 on the Sierra Club's 100 San Diego Peaks list, rising to 3,409 feet in elevation. The Alpine Trails Brochure notes that the hike "to the peak of Bell Bluff may be closed because of private property at the top," but there are reports of some who have bushwhacked their way there. I stopped after about 1.85 miles from the start and headed back, after climbing only about 340 feet in elevation. Then I took that trail heading off to the right that I'd noticed on the way up. It went only about 0.15 mile to a sweeping vista down into Japatul Valley to the southeast, where I could see construction on the Sunrise Powerlink project.

I headed back from here, noticing the many new and old chaparral yucca plants along the way.

Thomas Brothers Map: Page 1254, E-2, intersection of Via Dieguenos and Spanish Bit Drive.

Before You Go: Download a copy of the Alpine Trails Brochure with its general map: http://whiteoakwildnights.com/alpineTrails.pdf.

The trail is labeled "Bell Bluff Trail" on the Cleveland National Forest map, available at the Descanso Ranger Station, 3348 Alpine Blvd., Alpine 91901, as well as at CNF's website (http://www.fs.usda.gov/cleveland).

You may also download a copy of the Google map of Spanish Bit Drive off Via Dieguenos in Alpine.

It is open to hikers, bicyclists, equestrians, and dogs on leashes.

Trailhead: From Interstate 8, exit at Alpine Boulevard/Willows Road, heading south. Turn right (west) on Alpine Boulevard. Go about 1.5 miles and turn left (south) on South Grade Road. Turn left onto Via Viejas (entrance to Palo Verde Ranch), left on Via Belota, and then right onto Via Dieguenos. Park at the wide spot on the road before you reach the trail between 2728 and 2732 Via Dieguenos.

Distance/Difficulty: I went a little more than 4.0 miles round-trip; fairly easy.

7-20. Granite Slabs, Rivers Mark Sloan Canyon

The hike down into Sloan Canyon in Alpine presents a fine lookout into the backcountry, where the Sweetwater River carves its way through some lofty mountains. The terrain here is largely undeveloped, save for a small enclave of trailer homes near the bottom of the canyon. From the beginning of the trail at an elevation of about 1,575 feet, you can see all the way down to the riparian ribbons of cottonwoods, oaks, and willows that line both sides of the Sweetwater River, which sits at about 825 feet in elevation.

Reach the trailhead for the California Riding and Hiking Trail, which begins this hike off the Sequan Truck Trail Road. The first thing to view as you drive to the trailhead is a lovely overview of Loveland Reservoir, created by a dam on the Sweetwater River. Once you find the beginning of the CR&HT here, begin the descent down the single-track trail toward the river bottom. Big slabs of smooth granite, exposed and free from vegetation, dot the landscape.

Jerry Schad, in *Afoot and Afield San Diego County,* describes these as exfoliated granite slabs. According to geologic experts, exfoliation is a process in which rocks weather by peeling off in sheets rather than eroding little by little. Yosemite's Half Dome is an example of exfoliation, whereby molten plutons that formed deep underground and rose with the Sierra Nevada range acquired fine cracks through pressure-relief jointing. When weathering opened up those joints, loosened slabs broke off, creating such monumental rocks like Half Dome. Although the low-lying granite slabs in Sloan Canyon do not in any way resemble Half Dome, they evidently were formed in much the same way.

The CR&HT continues its fairly steep way down the slope for about a half mile, when it reaches the Sloan Ranch Road. Turn right to continue downhill toward the river. The trail is deeply cut by water and is sandy, so watch your footing.

The road is easier going than the CR&HT here because it's wider and gentler in grade. Continue to descend to that riparian habitat along the river. Backdropping the Sweetwater River here is Sycuan Peak, at 2,801 feet high.

In about 1.37 miles from the beginning, you'll see a rusted remnant of an old jalopy's frame, marking a spur road that leads to the left (south) into the remote rural homes. National Geographic's topography map of the area cites a "gauging station" near this point, which measures water flow presumably from Loveland Reservoir into the continuing Sweetwater River.

When you look straight ahead toward the south, you'll see a riparian habitat that is essentially perpendicular to that along the Sweetwater River below. That southern

Riparian ribbon views dress up Sloan Canyon.

riparian ribbon is home to Lawson Creek in Lawson Valley, headed toward Lawson Peak (3,660 feet) to the southeast. According to the map, Sloan Ranch sits near the confluence of Lawson Creek and Sweetwater River.

Abundant water sources, including several springs, were among the draws to this area for both Kumeyaay people and settlers who followed. Archaeological evidence of Kumeyaay villages can be found throughout Alpine, according to the Alpine Historical Society.

One of those early settlers was George Washington Webb, who built the Julian-to-Banner Toll Road in 1871. Webb moved to his Alpine Ranch in what is now called

Harbison Canyon in 1872; Harbison Canyon is next to Sloan Canyon. Webb's Alpine Ranch is largely credited with giving Alpine its name.

John Stewart Harbison moved here in 1874 and became the county's leading beekeeper, keeping more than 2,000 hives. He is credited with making San Diego County the leading honey-producing county in California, and making California the leading honey-producing state in the nation at that time, says the historical society. Today, North Dakota is the leading honey-producing state, followed by California, according to 2011 statistics kept by the USDA.

At that spur road, keep to the right, continuing on the Sloan Ranch Road, sometimes called the Sloan Canyon Road. At about 2.2 miles from your start, you reach the river. In autumn, the heart-shaped leaves of the cottonwood trees are bright yellow, making for our fall color. Along the river are also a few live oaks, stately sycamores, and willows; the latter two also show color as they lose their leaves. Look for western bluebirds and scrub jays along this riparian habitat.

A wooden plank bridge takes the road across the river, where a locked road gate stops further vehicle traffic along Sloan Canyon Road. However, there is a horse gate you may open to continue if you wish; it goes for about 3.0 more miles on the Sloan Canyon Road until it intersects with Dehesa Road. I turned around and retraced my steps back up after reaching the gate.

Going back up those 800 feet in elevation is hardest along the CR&HT, where a few short parts are quite steep. When you get back to the Sequan Truck Trail road (obviously a variation on Sycuan), where you started, another bonus awaits. On the clearest days, look from the top to the west, and you'll spy Point Loma behind downtown's skyline.

Thomas Brothers Map: Page 1253, F-6, G-6.where Sequan Truck Trail becomes more dotted …

Before You Go: Download a map of this Sloan Valley Trail from *The Reader,* where Jerry Schad's column on it appeared in 2007: http://www.sandiegoreader.com/photos/2007/feb/15/481/.

Another, longer view of this trail is available at the San Diego Horse Trails website: http://www.sdhorsetrails.com/sloancanyon.html.

For more information and another map, go to the Alpine Trails brochure: http://whiteoakwildnights.com/alpineTrails.pdf.

It is open to hikers, bicyclists, equestrians, and dogs on leashes.

Trailhead: From Interstate 8, exit at Tavern Road, heading south for 2.7 miles until it ends at Dehesa Road on the right and Japatul Road straight ahead. Continue on Japatul Road for 0.3 miles and then turn right on Sequan Truck Trail. Sequan Truck Trail is paved for about 2.8 miles, when the pavement ends. Continue 0.2 miles to a sharp right bend, where there is space to park off the road.

Walk up the road straight ahead for about 0.25 miles. Private homes line each side, but the road continues straight ahead where it is paved again for a short way. Look for the CR&HT sign on the left, passing a dirt road that goes uphill to the left. The CR&HT descends.

Distance/Difficulty: From the parking area to the gate at the river and back is about 4.45 miles round-trip. Moderately strenuous.

7-21. Wright's Field Invites Detailed Exploration

At first glance, Wright's Field in Alpine appears to be little more than a wide-open field of grasses, which is dry brown during summer. But explore it a little bit, and the crisscrossing trails that cover this preserve will take you to a hill or two, to a small Engelmann oak woodland among boulders, and even to an ancient rock wall that dates from Spanish Colonial days here in the early 1800s.

The field was preserved in the 1990s, when the Back Country Land Trust was able to buy about 230 acres, with ongoing plans to add about 140 acres more "of the most significant part of the preserve," it says. The native grassland in Wright's Field is one of the highest quality in the state, according to the BCLT's web page. The preserve is also part of the county's Multiple Species Conservation Project (MSCP). More than 300 plant species and 100 bird species have been identified here. The grasses would have been important to the early rancheros, who raised cattle here. In fact, the old Spanish name for this area found on an 1846 map was Mesa del Arroz, or "grassy mesa." "More grain was produced here than anywhere else in the county" in 1848, according to the historical society's timeline of Alpine history.

Look for ancient rock wall in Wright's Field.

You'll find that old rock wall almost straight ahead from the main entrance to Wright's Field, off Tavern Road. Archaeologists believe the wall dates to the area's missionary period from about 1780 to 1830. The local Kumeyaay were coerced into adopting the agricultural practices of the Spanish missionaries in order to survive. The rock wall is believed to have enclosed a 10-acre agricultural site, and evidence of olive groves, vineyards, fruit orchards, and grain fields has been found. According to an article written by Albert Simonson for Alpine Historical Society, the rock wall used to be over four feet high, but local builders of fireplaces probably stole many of the rocks in the early 20th century.

"These so-call dry (or unmortared) rounded-stone field walls are not known to exist anywhere else around here," writes Simonson, "but they are found in different parts of Latin America.... The discovery of Alpine's field walls aroused great interest among academics in California. Not only is it apparently a rare relic of our Indian and Hispanic past, but the enormity of effort required for its construction amazes all who see it."

You could miss the rock wall if you aren't attuned to finding it, because it blends in with the grasses. That's part of the appeal of exploring Wright's Field: the more you look, the more you discover. Dig a little deeper and look for details, and that wide-open grassland reveals a bounty of nature.

There are loads of wildflowers, including sunflowers, buckwheat, sugar bush, canchalagua, wallflowers, and more. The lighter green Engelmann oak, compared to the darker green coast live oak, shows up along the preserve's southern and eastern edges. There are also two rare butterflies that have found an abundance of their favorite host plants in Wright's Field. The Quino checkerspot butterfly feeds on the erect plantain and owl's clover, both abundant in this preserve. The Hermes copper butterfly's host plant is the spiny redberry, and it feeds on buckwheat, also prevalent in this coastal sage scrub habitat. I noticed lots of small bright yellow butterflies flitting around.

I began from the main entrance and took the perimeter trail to the right to head off in a counterclockwise direction. I climbed the nearest hill to the south, looking back over the field spreading below me and the 4,197-foot-high Viejas Mountain looming to the north. I wandered up to the eastern edge, where those fine old oak trees held court among some big old boulders. There appear to be other entries into the preserve from these east-side neighborhoods. There are many main trails that crisscross and intersect, making it a fun destination for bicyclists too.

Here's another detail to look for. There are countless wildlife trails heading off from the main ones; these are far narrower, fainter trails where the grasses have basically been tamped down by wildlife. I always wonder why the coyotes and bobcats and such don't use the main trails too, but they may see more details I'm missing.

I did see lots of rabbits and so many grasshoppers among those grasses; perhaps the critters are the ones who really know all the best routes.

Thomas Brothers Map: Page 1234, A-7, the unnamed private road immediately above MID (middle school) to right of Tavern Road.

Before You Go: For more information about the Back Country Land Trust, go to http://www.bclt.org.
   For a basic map and more information, go to the Alpine Trails brochure: http://whiteoak wildnights.com/alpineTrails.pdf.
   The preserve is free and is open from sunrise to sunset to hikers, bicyclists, equestrians, and dogs on leashes.
   To read Albert Simonson's article on Wright's Field, go to http://www.alpinehistory.org/ our_nature_park_wrights_field.html.

Trailhead: From Interstate 8, exit at Tavern Road, heading south for about one mile. When you reach the Joan MacQueen Middle School on your left, park on Tavern Road where you can.

Access to Wright's Field is immediately next to the school's northern edge. From Tavern Road, walk east up the paved, private road (no vehicles allowed here) that borders the north side of the school and its parking area. The entry to Wright's Field is at the end of this private road.

Distance/Difficulty: The trails crisscross for several miles if you explore them all. The perimeter loop route is about 1.5 miles. I wandered around for about an hour and a half. Easy.

7-22. Short but Steep Climb to Top of Sycuan Peak

The hike up an old Jeep road to the top of Sycuan Peak near Jamul is steep but short. In just about a mile, you reach the top of this lone promontory, where your view will take in a full 360 degrees extending to Dehesa and Lawson Valleys, Loveland Reservoir and several other singular peaks, downtown, Point Loma, San Diego Bay and the Pacific.

Begin off Lawson Valley Road on an unmarked, old dirt road heading north uphill to the 2,810-foot-high Sycuan Peak. The peak is in the center of the Sycuan Peak Ecological Reserve, an area now managed by the California Department of Fish and Wildlife.

Sycuan Peak was once a lookout.

Just to the northwest of the peak lies Sycuan Indian Reservation, home to one of 13 Kumeyaay bands in San Diego County, which also include Campo, Viejas, Barona, San Pasqual, Santa Ysabel, La Posta, Jamul, Mesa Grande, Inaja Cosmit, Capitan Grande, Ewiiaapaayp, and Manzanita. The name Sycuan derives from the Kumeyaay word for a yellow primrose flower indigenous to San Diego. "Sycuan" means "primrose," which translates to "life" in the Kumeyaay language, according to the Sycuan tribe. Look for the four-petaled flower in spring.

Also found on the slopes of Sycuan Peak are the uncommon dehesa nolina, also known as dehesa beargrass, a plant consisting of rosettes of fibrous blue-green, serrated leaves somewhat similar to agave. It puts forth a showy white-flowered single stalk rising to six feet high, according to *San Diego County Native Plants* by James Lightner. These plants are endemic to this area, spreading only about 15 miles around Dehesa Valley, notably on Sycuan Peak and nearby McGinty Mountain.

Sycuan Peak Ecological Reserve came into existence in the late 1990s, when it was acquired by the Department of Fish and Wildlife, according to Phyllis M. Faber's *California's Wild Gardens: A Guide to Favorite Botanical Sites.* California's Ecological Reserve System was authorized by the state legislature in 1968. The first such acquisition and designation was the Buena Vista Lagoon Ecological Reserve in Carlsbad. Today, the state's ecological reserve system encompasses 130 properties totaling about 216,000 acres, conserving California's biological diversity by protecting important species and habitats. Sycuan Peak was once largely privately owned, and developments were planned until this land was purchased by the state for conservation.

The steep trail up to the top offers a truly panoramic survey of this swath of the lightly populated area between Alpine and Jamul.

As you stand at the top, look southeast for 3,738-foot-high Lyons Peak with its communication towers. A little farther east from Lyons Peak is 3,660-foot-high Lawson Peak. Lawson Valley stretches below to the east. Then blue-water Loveland Reservoir comes into view, a dammed lake formed along the Sweetwater River that continues its flow west through Sloan Canyon and Dehesa Valley. Almost immediately to the west is 2,183-foot-high McGinty Mountain, another, smaller ecological reserve that also offers a steep trail to its top. To the southwest, you'll see another antennae-topped peak, the 2,565-foot-high San Miguel Mountain. All these peaks stand out (or up) on the landscape, making for an interesting survey of the backcountry's peak topography from here.

At the top of Sycuan Peak is a lone old telephone poll with old electrical lines still attached; none of it is active anymore, however. A Jamul resident I encountered on the trail told me that Sycuan Peak was once a lookout during World War II. You can still see plenty of airplanes heading to Lindbergh Field. That local hiker also told me that he hikes this trail as a loop, continuing along a ridge at the top to another trail that returns back to Lawson Valley Road. I looked for this ridgetop trail at the top but didn't find anything. Upon consulting Google Earth maps of the area, it looked like some bushwhacking would be required to connect to trails off Choukair Drive.

When I reached the top, I marveled at the views, imagining a far clearer vision of downtown and the ocean on very clear days. I turned around and retraced my way back.

This old road is quite steep to climb, and its gravelly portions make for hard parts on the way down as well. Parts of it are also very badly eroded, so it's just as well it's open only to hikers as well as dogs on leashes. But remember it's short, and those views are very long.

Thomas Brothers Map: Page 1273, G-4, Lawson Valley Road.

Before You Go: For (only a little) information on Sycuan Peak Ecological Reserve, go to the Department of Fish and Wildlife's website for it: https://www.wildlife.ca.gov/Lands/Places-to-Visit/Sycuan-Peak-ER.

This trail is open only to hikers and dogs on leashes.

The directions to the reserve on this website take you to the northern reaches of the reserve, not the peak trail described here.

Download a Google Earth map of the trail up Sycuan Peak. Go to http://maps.google.com and search for Sycuan Peak, CA.

Trailhead: From Highway 94, a.k.a. Campo Road (note right turn onto Campo Road to continue on Highway 94 East when highway enters stoplight area), in Jamul, turn left (east) onto Lyons Valley Road. At a four-way stop-sign intersection where Lyons Valley Road turns right and Skyline Truck Trail continues straight ahead, continue on Skyline Truck Trail straight ahead. Turn left onto Lawson Valley Road and go 2.5 miles. Immediately beyond the 2.5-mile marker on the left (north) is the unmarked, steep dirt road that heads up Sycuan Peak. Park nearby where you can on the road shoulder.

Distance/Difficulty: It's about 1.1 miles and about 750 feet in elevation gain to the top, making for a 2.2-mile round-trip. It's steep and so is moderately strenuous.

7-23. Classic Backcountry Trails Feature Lots of Wildflowers

Mount Gower Open Space Preserve in Ramona is a nearly pristine wilderness that evokes a classic San Diego County landscape. As part of the County of San Diego's parks system, it presents "San Diego's backcountry as it was centuries ago," notes the county. Over 95 percent of this 1,600-acre preserve was burned in the devastating 2003 Cedar Fire. The largest wildfire in the state of California's recorded history, San Diego County's Cedar Fire occurred in October 2003 during extremely hot temperatures, low humidity, and Santa Ana winds. It burned over 280,000 acres, destroyed over 2,200 homes, killed 15 people (including one firefighter), injured 104 firefighters, and resulted in the arrest of a man accused of arson. "Yet, only months later, plants began to sprout new growth," notes a placard on the Mount Gower trail.

Most of Mount Gower is chaparral habitat, one of the most widespread vegetation communities in San Diego County. Chaparral has adapted to wildfire by either resprouting from underground roots or regrowing from seeds after a fire. "This new growth has less competition for resources such as sunlight and water, and thrives once a fire has cleared an area," states the placard.

Chaparral habitat features dense, hard-stemmed, leathery leaved shrubs, typically including manzanita, chamise, and ceanothus (also called wild lilac). All three are evident on the Mount Gower trails. In late spring, there is also an amazing abundance of wildflower blooms, especially yellow varieties. Parts of the western trail are even obscured by the bounty of yellow blooming plants.

Using the book *San Diego County Native Plants,* by James Lightner, I tried to identify the several wildflowers I spotted: yellow monkeyflowers, yellow wallflowers, yellow rock roses, bush sunflowers, golden yarrow, yellow pincushions, and yellow and orange deerweed. I also spotted the arresting bright pink canchalagua, white chamise, white morning glories, white osmadenia, and light-blue-blooming black sage. Several flowering stalks of yucca also captured my attention. Whatever their names, the wildflowers' bounty of color added a lot to appreciate on this otherwise relatively barren hillside. They are certainly the main attraction in late spring.

Wildflowers aplenty found on Mount Gower.

There are two main trails offered at Mount Gower. One is relatively easier for a bit less than 2.0 miles one-way, and it heads northwest from the main trailhead. Another heads nearly 4.0 miles one-way to the southeast. A couple of short spur trails to viewpoints make the total trail mileage here almost 8.0 miles. I took the northwest trail.

The large staging area at the trailhead also has primitive restrooms and water for horses. The trails are popular with equestrians and are also open to mountain bikers. After hiking a short ways, you will come to an intersection of the two trails. Take the left turn for the northwest trail. Cross the dirt roads that service the power lines and continue on the northwest trail, where a metal stake shows its continuance.

This trail actually descends along a switchback into a dry ravine before climbing, again by switchbacks, to a viewpoint at about 2,300 feet in elevation. There's a wooden bench at the end for a rest break. Views extend through the San Vicente Valley to the west and south, and they also take in some of the development of San Diego Country Estates.

The longer, more difficult southeast trail, according to the Mount Gower Open Space Preserve brochure, leads through Swartz Canyon with its sycamores, willows, and oaks. Then it rises to a high ridge, two meadows, and a rock shelf to an upper meadow. "Unusual rock formations are a scenic attraction here," it says, including two large boulders that lean against each other, known locally as Teepee Rock.

The day I was there in early June, it reached 90 degrees Fahrenheit. It is very hot here during the summer, and there are few respites of shade—none on the northwest trail I chose. But for that glimpse of typical county terrain, complete with sweeping views, go to Mount Gower.

Thomas Brothers Map: Page 1173, E-2 and F-2 (where Gunn Stage Road ends at Equestrian Center red dot)

Before You Go: Download a copy of the brochure, with a trail map, at the county's parks page for Mount Gower: http://www.co.san-diego.ca.us/parks/openspace/Mt_Gower.html.
   This trail is open only to hikers, bicyclists, equestrians, and dogs on leashes.
   It is closed from August 1 to September 1 because of extreme summer heat. It's free.

Trailhead: From Highway 67/78 in downtown Ramona, go south on Tenth Street, which turns into San Vicente Road. Continue on San Vicente Road for about seven or eight miles, turning left at the intersection of Gunn Stage Road. Continue to the end of Gunn Stage Road, where the Mount Gower Open Space Preserve begins. You may continue through the open gate up the hard-packed gravel road to the upper staging area, where the restrooms are and the trails begin.

Distance/Difficulty: The northwest trail is about 4.0 miles round-trip; moderate.

7-24. Simon Preserve Trail Climbs to Ramona Peak

The hike up to Ramona Peak in Simon Preserve is a fairly steep, 550-foot climb that results in wide views over the backcountry and its many peaks on the horizon. Ramona Peak stands at 2,128 feet in elevation and is a grassy wide ridge reached by an old, rocky dirt road. There is another narrower trail that goes virtually straight up to the top—an old goat trail, some say—but it is off-limits because the 2003 Cedar Fire destroyed some 95 percent of Simon Preserve. It is hoped that vegetation will restore itself better without human interference.

Simon Preserve, a 650-acre parcel, is in southeast Ramona and is just west of San Diego Country Estates, a housing development that began in 1972. The preserve's acreage was acquired by the County of San Diego in 1995 from the sons of former U.S. Secretary of the Treasury William E. Simon, with the stipulation that it be used as open space for recreational purposes and that it be named the William E. and Carol G. Simon Preserve, after their parents. The elder Simon was treasury secretary from 1974 to 1977 under Presidents Nixon and Ford. A financial guru at the time, the fiscally conservative Simon was known as the Energy Czar during the 1974-1975 oil crisis.

The goat trail and a few others are sometimes referred to as pioneer trails, suggesting the preserve's earlier life. It straddles the historic boundaries of Rancho Santa Maria and Rancho San Vicente and was home to settlers since at least the 1840s, according to an archaeological survey of the preserve done for the county.

The valleys of Santa Maria and San Vicente were part of land grant ranchos, Rancho Santa Maria and Rancho San Vicente, respectively. Rancho Santa Maria was granted by Mexican Governor Pio Pico to Californio Jose Joaquin Ortega, who had married Pico's sister, Maria; Ortega was known to have lived on the rancho in 1844 and 1845, harvesting wheat and raising horses and cattle. The Mexican government granted Rancho San Vicente to Juan Lopez in 1846. The lands eventually fell into the hands of other owners by the 1880s. The Santa Maria Valley developed into the town of Ramona, and the San Vicente Valley remained largely agricultural until the construction of San Diego Country Estates in the 1970s. An eastern part of Simon Preserve's land was used for Chester Gunn's express pony mail service in 1871, but its steepness proved difficult, and so other routes were established by the 1880s.

Lots of history lives in Simon Preserve.

Horses are still welcome on Simon Preserve's 5.0 miles of trails. Mountain bikers also should note that the climb up to the ridge top is fairly steep and rocky.

The old dirt road reaches Ramona Peak in nearly 2.0 miles, where the trail straddles the ridge both to the east and to the west. From the top, looking southeast back over San Diego Country Estates, you can also spy nearby Mount Gower. Beyond the housing development are more peaks. When I reached the top, upon noting a small pile of rocks, I took a left, heading toward the more undeveloped views to the north and west, into the peaks and valleys toward Ramona and Julian, including some verdant avocado groves. I walked to two water tanks, which were at the end of this part of the main trail. Going back the other direction on the ridge takes you all the way to the top of Ramona Peak. To the east are views of the peaks of Cuyamaca.

The main trail continues over that ridge saddle up and down into the northern reaches of the preserve. I simply went back down the way I'd come, making for about a four-mile round-trip hike. Walking back down a rocky, steep road is almost as hard as walking up one.

Fall and winter are perfect seasons for this climb because it gets very hot in the summer.

Thomas Brothers Map: Page 1173, D-3, just east past intersection of Spangler Peak Road and Bassett Way.

Before You Go: For more information as well as a map of the preserve and its trails, go to http://www.co.san-diego.ca.us/parks/openspace/Simon.html.

Simon Preserve trails are open to hikers, equestrians, mountain bikers, and dogs on leashes. It's free and is open from 8:00 a.m. to 5:00 p.m.

Trailhead: From the north, from Highway 78 in downtown Ramona, take the San Vicente Road/Tenth Street south. Make a left on Arena, a left on Spangler Peak, and then a right on Bassett Street.

From the south, take Wildcat Canyon Road north. Turn left onto San Vicente Road, left on Arena, left on Spangler Peak, and then right on Bassett.

Just after that turn onto Bassett, you'll see a trail on the left in an open area between homes, noted simply with a horsehead silhouette marker. You'll see the boundary and kiosk of Simon Preserve a little way up this trail.

Distance/Difficulty: The preserve has five miles of trails. My route was about 2.0 miles one-way, for 4.0 miles round-trip. Moderately difficult.

7-25. Barber Mountain Looks to Lyons Peak

While winding around the backroads of Jamul, my friend and I were looking for an unmarked trail off Skyline Truck Trail, but there was nothing obvious except private driveways. Then we came upon CalFire's Lyons Valley unit on Skyline Truck Trail and went in to ask the firefighters. They couldn't really recommend the dirt road we were seeking when I showed them my map, and so they offered a few other nearby trails to hike. They directed us to Barber Mountain Road, an old dirt road that headed toward the 3,257-foot-high peak. The road lies mostly on Cleveland National Forest land, so access is no problem, unlike a lot of private property in this area.

We reached Barber Mountain Road by continuing on Skyline Truck Trail, heading straight through the four-way intersection with Lyons Valley Road and Honey Springs Road. At the top of the hill, Barber Mountain Road is on the left, marked by two gates. We hiked on the main road behind the biggest gate and headed east on this old dirt truck trail.

Views from Barber Mountain extend to Lyons Peak.

Behind us were lofty views of Lyons Peak, the boulder-strewn, 3,642-high peak with a handful of communication towers and an old fire lookout tower that dates from 1913. That fire lookout tower is no longer in use, and access to the top of the peak and its communications towers is limited to helicopter or law enforcement escort because the road leading to the top is on private property. The firefighters in the Lyons Valley unit told us that property owner is very vigilant about not allowing access, so forget trying to bag that peak—it is not on the San Diego County Peaks list.

However, it does have an interesting history. It's named for Captain Nathaniel Lyon, an army captain who was seeking a new route east to the desert in 1851, according to Richard F. Pourade's *The History of San Diego*. Looking east from San Diego, Lyon "saw two mountains, one covered with vegetation which he believed was named San Miguel, and the other, higher and appearing white with granite boulders piled in huge masses and noticed the inviting appearance of a depression on the north side which 'determined me to attempt a passage.'" At the base of what became Lyons Peak, Lyon discovered an old Indian trail, which he followed southeast into "one of the most remarkable mountain gorges in nature, having on either side high, steep mountains covered with huge granite blocks ... the trail opened into a fine valley, having grass and water and beautiful oak groves."

This description could almost apply today. The Barber Mountain Road heads southeast from Lyons Peak, where views extend into pastoral Lyons Valley. The 3,660-foot-high Lawson Peak hugs that valley to the north, and to the east are Pine Creek Wilderness and Hauser Wilderness.

It is very quiet here on Barber Mountain Road, and those views go wide across the layers of hills and valleys in every direction. There is very little in the way of buildings, so it might not appear all that different from Lyon's day.

A patch of the hillside immediately north of the valley is still scarred by the Lyons Valley brushfire that burned about 450 acres here in September 2013. The 2007 Harris Fire that burned more than 90,000 acres during that October burned through this area as well, but vegetation since then has made a strong comeback along this old dirt truck trail.

In late August, we saw a lot of those late-summer bloomers, California goldenrod, with clusters of bright yellow flowers, lining the road. Very abundant were shrubs of felt-leaf yerba santa, a native with a gray cast and thick, serrated-edge leaves, sporting lavender flowers in spring.

Check out www.naturebytesvideo.com for a wealth of videos about San Diego County's habitats, plants, birds, and animals. The videos were produced by a handful of local naturalists. Henry Shenkman, one of its founders, offers lots of information about yerba santa. "The taxonomy name means 'woolly leaf,'" says Shenkman on the video. The plant was very important to native people: "It was called 'Great Medicine,' by the natives and the Spanish name is 'sainted herb.'" Native people made the leaves and flowers into teas and poultices, which they used to fight coughs, colds, sore throats, asthma, tuberculosis, and more.

We also saw a very tiny desert horned lizard with its crown and rows of spines. It relies on camouflage to elude capture, and while it sat motionless in the brush, it sported hues of terra cotta and green.

We went about 2.0 miles on Barber Mountain Road and then turned back to retrace our route. The road itself is only about 3.0 miles long before it intersects to the south with Honey Springs Road.

Thomas Brothers Map: Page 1294, E-3.

Before You Go: The best map of this Barber Mountain Road trail is on the Cleveland National Forest map, southern region. Go to the CNF website to get a map: http://www.fs.usda.gov/main/cleveland/maps-pubs. This is a great map to have of the entire county.

It is open to hikers, bicyclists, equestrians, and dogs on leashes.

Trailhead: From Interstate 5 heading south, exit at Highway 94 and head east. After 13.9 miles, turn right onto Campo Road to continue on Highway 94 east. After 4.5 miles, turn left onto Lyons Valley Road. In 1.6 miles, continue straight where the road becomes Skyline Truck Trail. In about 5.0 miles you'll reach that four-way intersection with Lyons Valley Road (again) and Honey Springs Road; continue straight ahead. At the top of the hill on the left is Barber Mountain Road, a dirt road with street sign and two gates.

Distance/Difficulty: We went about 4.0 miles round-trip; the total on this road could be about 6.0 miles out and back. An elevation gain of about 450 feet makes it pretty easy.

7-26. Trees Are the Treat in Hollenbeck Canyon

Hollenbeck Canyon Wildlife Area joined the county's hiking opportunities in 2001 when California's Wildlife Conservation Board acquired 3,200 acres of former Daley Ranch property. Now managed by the state Department of Fish and Wildlife, the canyon offers a wonderful walk under huge old coast live oaks and sycamores along a little stream that sometimes floods. Over time, the stream created the narrow canyon.

This trail was once part of the California Riding and Hiking Trail, and it still makes a good destination for horseback riders. I met three equestrians on the trail: Joe Thunder on his horse Lacey, Dick Huddleston on Chief Crazy Horse, and Kathy Gray on Bo. They were excited to tell me about the two coyotes they'd seen earlier, sitting on rocks above the trail watching them.

The only wildlife I saw were lots of squirrels, several hawks soaring overhead, and a number of ants moving in and out of their colonies on the trail.

This area known as Jamul Valley, then about 9,000 acres, was granted to the Mexican governor of California, Pio Pico, in 1831 as Rancho Jamul. The Burton family held the land after Pio Pico until the end of the 1850s, according to the Department of Fish and Wildlife's history on Hollenbeck Canyon. Farmers then began settling here believing the land was available for homesteading.

In the late 1890s, John D. Spreckels, a sugar fortune heir, gained control of the land and formed the Southern California Mountain Water Company, which constructed the

Morena, Barrett, and Otay dams. In 1916 Spreckels sold the land to former San Diego Mayor Louis J. Wilde, who hoped to convert the property into a dude ranch and movie studio, but that never happened. Wilde planted tobacco here instead. In 1929, George R. Daley bought the property and turned it into a cattle ranch. His heirs made the deal with California's Wildlife Conservation Board for the property.

A beautiful trail winds through Hollenbeck Canyon.

This parcel was joined with a second 1,979-acre parcel in 2003 known as Honey Springs Ranch. Today's Hollenbeck Canyon Wildlife Area is a 5,189-acre parcel. It is described as a "unique opportunity to provide compatible wildlife-dependent recreation and to conserve, restore and protect declining sensitive species and their associated habitats in one of the largest blocks of contiguous land available in San Diego County," said the California Department of Fish and Wildlife in its documentation on the Hollenbeck Canyon acquisition. This parcel is also adjacent to the Rancho Jamul Ecological Reserve to the west and the Otay Mountain Wildlife Management Area to the south, providing a core of undisturbed habitat in south-central San Diego County.

The document also notes much historic evidence of native Kumeyaay people here, including village sites, rock art, a quarry, and morteros and metates used to grind acorn and other foods.

For most of the way, the trail joins an old ranch dirt road, so it's easygoing for mountain bikers. Past a yellow-topped post early on the trail, you descend from the wide-open and parched grassy meadows into the Jamul Creek stream corridor with its ancient oaks and sycamores. At one-third of a mile, the first real marker is at a T intersection. Go right to continue through the canyon.

Wander through the oaks, sycamores, willow bushes, and occasional datura and morning glory blooms as you go deeper into the canyon. There are a couple of places where the trail has been diverted to avoid deeper stream crossings, but these are easy and obvious. Note the grassy marshes near the stream. The enormous oaks (with their nubby cubbyholes where limbs once were) and the tall sycamores make it a worthwhile destination by themselves. The trees survived the most recent wildfires and probably have lived hundreds of years.

After about a mile, the trail begins to ascend a hill, affording great views of the oak-studded canyon you've just walked through, with a few giant boulders begging to be picnic seats. You'll see on the left the brick remnants of an old fireplace—all that's left of a cabin.

The highest point on the horizon ahead is Lyons Peak, which has an elevation of 3,738 feet. The Hollenbeck website at Fish and Wildlife says the canyon area's lowest point is 750 feet elevation, and its highest is 2,100 feet.

At the next marker (1.5 miles), the main trail goes left. A spur to the right will take you farther into the narrowing canyon, and at about half a mile, fences mark the end of the wildlife area and the trail. I continued only on the main trail, heading to the left at the marker. It climbs more steeply to the end point at about half a mile. You could turn back at the marker and avoid the steepest section. In either case, turn back, and retrace your way to the parking area.

Maybe you'll see those coyotes.

Thomas Brothers Map: Page 1293, subpage 1313, E-1.

Before You Go: The best trail map here is to search for a satellite view of Hollenbeck Canyon on Google.

For more information from the state's Department of Fish and Game, go to https://www.wildlife.ca.gov/Lands/Places-to-Visit/Hollenbeck-Canyon-WA.

This trail is open to hikers, bicyclists, equestrians, and dogs on leashes.

Trailhead: From Highway 94, drive four miles east of Jamul and turn left (north) onto Honey Springs Road. The Hollenbeck Canyon parking lot is on the left.

Distance/Difficulty: This hike is about 4.0 miles round-trip; moderate.

7-27. Easy Lake Morena Trail Has Vast Views

Lake Morena County Park is a hidden gem for hiking. It's popular for fishing, but its 8.0 miles of trails are lightly trod. It's an easy amble along a lovely lake leading to an upper meadow with old pine and oak trees, along with vast views into the wilderness. Its 3,250 acres of chaparral, oak woods, and grasslands lie just southwest of the Laguna Mountains. The centerpiece is Lake Morena, a reservoir owned by the City of San Diego that is the highest and most remote of the city's reservoirs.

Lake Morena is also one of the oldest reservoirs in the region. Work on Morena Dam began in 1897 on Cottonwood Creek, but it wasn't completed until 1912. By comparison, only Lake Cuyamaca (built in 1887), Sweetwater Reservoir (1888), and Upper Otay Lake (1901) are older. With a water storage capacity of 50,694 acre-feet,

Morena Reservoir is the third largest in the city, below El Capitan (112,807 acre-feet) and San Vicente (90,230 acre-feet).

But few reservoirs can claim as colorful a history as Lake Morena.

Skirt the edge of one of county's oldest reservoirs.

The Morena Reservoir was about 18 years old in 1915 when the City of San Diego's councilmen became concerned about area water shortages. The Morena Reservoir had never been filled to its capacity, according to a 1970 article in the *Journal of San Diego History,* "Hatfield the Rainmaker" by Thomas W. Patterson. Some of the councilmen had heard of Charley Hatfield, who had made a name for himself with his efforts to make rain in Hemet and Texas. Though there were skeptics, on December 13, 1915, the city engaged Hatfield and agreed to pay him $10,000 if he could fill the Morena Reservoir by December 20, 1916.

Hatfield constructed his tower there in early January 1916 for his proprietary methods of "moisture acceleration," as he called it, which involved evaporating things from shallow pans and shooting puffs of stuff into the air.

From January 10 to January 18, 1916, it rained in torrents. San Diego River and Tijuana River flooded, killing people and cattle. The existing Otay Reservoir overflowed. The Santa Fe and San Diego-Arizona rail connections were put out of operation, as was the Pacific Coast Highway. Morena Reservoir spilled over.

To this day that historic rainfall of 1916 is called Hatfield's Flood. The city council, which was sued for flood damage by several, refused to pay Hatfield because then it could be held liable.

You can learn even more about this history inside the ranger station at Lake Morena, including information about the Kumeyaay tribes who lived here for hundreds of years before the Spanish priests arrived in the late 1700s. Lots of historic artifacts are on display, including genuine arrowheads and guest books from the 1950s from the old lodge that was here then.

Begin hiking at Ward's Flat Trail, which heads south just before the lower boat ramp into the lake. This trail quickly joins the dirt road that skirts to the west around the lake. After about the first mile, you'll come to an abandoned barn on the left, where an old sign announces the camping fee of one dollar. A short ways later, also on the left, is only the chimney of that old lodge. Just beyond that chimney is an intersection with another dirt road heading to the left. Take that road to head up to the meadow and Morena Butte Trail.

This road is far less traveled, and it winds through old live oaks and some fine specimens of Coulter, Jeffrey, and pinyon pines. Near where the road takes a U-turn to head back, you'll note a sign to the Morena Butte Trail. Take this single-track trail for those amazing views into the vast wilderness to the southwest. Near here too is a marker for a spur trail that leads you to the Pacific Crest Trail in 1.5 miles.

I headed back the way I came. Then when I reached the main Ward's Flat road, I headed further west before retracing my steps again. The road goes along the lake again and eventually comes to a gate. If you pass through that gate, you come to the short spur Hauser Overlook Trail that takes you to the dam. Head back the way you came.

Thomas Brothers Map: Page 1296, C-5, the dotted line for Morena Reservoir Road is actually the trail.

Before You Go: Go to the county parks page for Lake Morena County Park for more information about camping, fishing, and renting boats, and for the trail map: http://www.co.san-diego.ca.us/parks/Camping/lake_morena.html.
  There is a $3 day-use fee to park here, payable at that ranger station.
  Open to hikers, bicyclists, equestrians, and dogs on leashes.

Trailhead: From Interstate 8 east, exit at Buckman Springs Road, heading south for seven miles. Turn right onto Oak Drive, heading west for two miles to Lake Morena Drive, straight into the park.

Distance/Difficulty: About 4.0 miles round-trip; easy.

8. Fallbrook and Palomar

Fallbrook, famous for avocados, has a handful of trails, one of which even secrets a sandy beach along a creek. Palomar is truly one of the best places countywide for the biggest, oldest trees. While fire has occurred there, it hasn't decimated these historic oaks and pines, which are enormous. It is said that Palomar features the most Sierra Nevada–like atmosphere in the county, and it's also one of the best places for fall color from the black oak trees. There are several stunning trails inside Palomar Mountain State Park, and other trails surround Palomar's famous telescope in the Cleveland National Forest.

8-1. Hellers Bend Offers Views into Bonsall, Fallbrook

Hellers Bend Preserve is one of seven preserves owned and managed by the Fallbrook Land Conservancy (FLC) that offer hiking trails through a variety of riparian and coastal sage scrub scenery. Hellers Bend is a 48.5-acre property acquired in 1996 by the conservancy, and it features a steep paved trail culminating in panoramic views of Bonsall and Fallbrook.

The first part of the trail crosses a year-round stream studded with live oak and sycamore trees. This riparian habitat also has lots of wild grape vines growing up the trunks of the trees and several native willow bushes like those that long-ago natives used in basket weaving. Immediately after this stream, a short, unpaved spur trail takes off to the left of the main trail. After passing through those willows and wild grape vines, it stops in short order at a serene sylvan scene. Here, in the shade of oaks, sycamores, and willows, you can see and hear only the rushing stream and maybe an occasional black phoebe or tree swallow rustling in the trees.

The Hellers Bend trail heads up for views.

The FLC has an extensive list on its website (www.fallbrooklandconservancy.org; go to "Native Animals of FLC Preserves" on its "Our Preserves" page) of over 150 species of birds that have been sighted at each of its preserves. I saw only the American crow, which is not as big a thrill as if I had spotted a turkey vulture, a calliope hummingbird (the world's smallest bird), or even a greater roadrunner, all of which have been documented at Hellers. (Most references to Hellers omit the apostrophe that seems missing. But at the actual entrance, the main sign has no apostrophe. Another sign calls it Heller's Bend Preserve. We're sticking with no apostrophe here.)

Ten different mammals have also been spotted at Hellers, including the coyote, mountain lion, bobcat, raccoon, and skunk. I saw only some squirrels. And happily, I didn't see any rattlesnakes, though both the western and red diamond of that species have been seen here.

The steep paved portion of the trail winds straight up the hill for about a half-mile. At the top are two benches inviting hikers to sit a spell and take in the 180-degree view that spreads south across Bonsall and Fallbrook. There are many houses in that view today, including some large longtime properties with horse corrals and trails, as well as some avocado orchards. It is surely quite a bit more developed than it was when the FLC was formed in 1988.

"Much of Fallbrook's land was undeveloped when the FLC formed," says an article on the history of the organization on its website. "A frequent comment was, 'We have plenty of open space, so why do we need a land conservancy?'"

When a map was drawn up to show how much green space existed in the 30,000 acres that made up Fallbrook, some residents were alarmed to learn that only three protected open space areas then existed: the private Pala Mesa golf course, the county's Live Oak Park, and a small 10-acre parcel inside a gated development.

After public town meetings, some concerned residents formed the FLC with an eye toward protecting the rural environment they loved. Today the FLC owns more than 1,850 acres of permanently protected open space in 10 parks and preserves, and it has planted more than 4,000 trees and maintains several miles of trails open for public exploration.

One summer, the FLC's Environmental Education program involved 220 students from La Paloma and Live Oak Elementary Schools in restoring the native coastal sage scrub habitat in Hellers Bend. Fourth- and fifth-grade students planted rooted cuttings or seedlings into pots grown in the FLC nursery before being planted at Hellers. Flags identifying the areas of the habitat restoration may still be found about midway up the paved part of the trail.

Past the end of the pavement where the two benches are, the trail becomes an old dirt road and eventually turns into a narrow unpaved trail. This area has fewer trees and so is far less shaded, but with every foot of elevation gained, the views become broader. The trail ends at the top near the preserve's fence, and you retrace your steps back down.

As you walk back down the hill past those views, imagine how Fallbrook and Bonsall probably looked just 25 years ago, and tip your cap to the leaders of the FLC for preserving these spaces for contemplation.

Thomas Brothers Map: Page 1047, H-4 (in the middle of this square where the unmarked road crosses the little blue line (stream)).

Before You Go: Download bird lists or other information from the Fallbrook Land Conservancy website before you go: www.fallbrooklandconservancy.org.
This trail is open only to hikers and dogs on leashes.

Trailhead: Take Interstate 15 north to Highway 76 at Bonsall. Turn west on Highway 76, go about 4.5 miles, and take a right onto South Mission Road. After about 1.5 miles, turn left onto Hellers Bend. After about 0.3 miles, note the entry to Hellers Bend Preserve; park on the road shoulder and walk into the preserve.

Distance/Difficulty: About a half-mile to the top, of 1.0 mile round-trip. Moderate only due to steepness.

8-2. Los Jilgueros Has Ponds, Firescape Garden Advice

The ponds in Fallbrook's Los Jilgueros Preserve are fairly full after rains, making this hiking destination especially attractive when that happens. The 46-acre preserve offers a 1.5-mile loop trail that's very easy and very popular with dogs walking their people. Joggers and bicyclists are welcome here too.

Locals love Los Jilgueros.

The name comes from an 1889 map that identified the stream that runs through here as "Arroyo de los Jilgueros," which translates from Spanish to mean "Stream of the Goldfinches." It was a farm owned by Arthur Anthony in the 1920s, who built the dams along the stream to create the two ponds to store water for irrigation. In 1990, the Fallbrook Real Estate Company donated the land to the Fallbrook Land Conservancy, which currently operates the preserve.

The level trail winds through lots of green grasses now. Some 400 native oaks, sycamores, and alders have been planted recently, along with cacti, shrubs, and other native plants.

Locals come here frequently, it seems. One man who lives nearby, Chuck Fuller, is 85 years young, and his 6-year-old boxer,

Tasha, befriended me at the beginning of the trail. "Come with us," said Chuck, "and we'll show you the ponds. There might be some egrets there." Chuck and Tasha accompanied me the whole way, greeting other friends along the trail. Tasha was especially pleased to see Lynn Lenell and her beagle/golden retriever mix, Lady Bug, and her coyote hybrid, Rusty, because Lynn always carries treats for all her canine friends here.

The ponds attract lots of waterfowl. The day I was there, flocks of American coots scooted across the water. The egrets come in the early mornings, Chuck told me. Several benches along the trail invite hikers to linger, especially by those ponds.

The Peppertree Homes development has made the preserve a little less pristine than it used to be. Eventually 265 homes on 162 acres will wrap around the preserve.

One especially interesting feature of Los Jilgueros is its Firescape Demonstration Garden, the second such garden ever built in California. The first Firescape Garden was built in Santa Barbara in the 1970s after a disastrous fire there. The North County Fire Department wanted some form of "fire safety belt" on the northern border of the preserve to protect neighboring homes.

Roger Boddaert had seen the garden in Santa Barbara and proposed such a project here. In 1995 it became a reality, and today it features over 100 different species of plants that create a "fire-resistant landscape."

Many of the plants in this garden are labeled. Zone one, nearest the homes (or maybe your own house), contains low-growing plants with low fuel volume, kept thinned and adequately watered. These include day lilies, Santa Barbara daisies, and star jasmine.

Zone two contains low-growing ground covers that are resistant to fire and low in fuel volume. These include aeonium, agave, aloe, ice plant, jade, and wild strawberries.

Zone three is a transition area planted with low shrubs and perennials that are low fuel-volume, including coyote brush, penstemon, yarrows, and California poppies.

Zone four is native vegetation thinned to reduce fuel volume and includes coastal live oak, sycamores, and ceanothus (wild lilac).

"The Firescape Garden is a model of how Southern Californians can landscape around their homes with plants that provide safety from fires, require low maintenance, and at the same time blend in with the natural environment," says the Fallbrook Land Conservancy. This garden has inspired others to be created at Quail Botanical Gardens in Encinitas and in the Elfin Forest area.

Even though Los Jilgueros is popular for dog walking, the preserve stresses that it was created to preserve and protect open, natural space. "It was not created to be a dog park," it says. It has strict rules and responsibilities for dog walkers.

- Dogs must be on leashes.
- Pick up your dog's poop. Period. Pick up other poop when you see it.
- Do not let your dog approach any person or dog without the person's permission.
- Stay on trails. It is your responsibility to protect wildlife and wetlands.

- Do not let your dog disturb birds or wildlife. Do not let your dog dig; there are several ground-nesting birds in the preserve that must be protected, and rabbits sometimes nest their newborns in holes just barely underground.

Bicyclists must always give pedestrians right of way, and bicyclists must ride only at reasonable speeds.

Whether or not you have a dog, Los Jilgueros is a very pleasant preserve offering an easy hike along with some landscaping advice through its firescape garden. Maybe you'll even see some goldfinches.

Thomas Brothers Map: Page 1027, G-6

Before You Go: Check the conservancy's website for more information: www.fallbrookland conservancy.org.

This trail is open only to hikers and dogs on leashes.

Trailhead: From Interstate 15, exit at Highway 76, head west 4.5 miles to South Mission Road, and turn right (north). Continue about 4.0 miles, passing Stage Coach Lane. About 0.3 miles farther is the driveway to Los Jilgueros on the right.

Distance/Difficulty: A 1.5-mile loop. Easy.

8-3. Surprising Inland Beach on Santa Margarita River

It seemed improbable, but I came upon one of the county's sandiest waterfront beaches some 15 miles east of the Pacific Ocean. It was wide open with deep, soft sand, lots of shells, and not a single beachgoer in sight. It fronted the Santa Margarita River in Fallbrook and was the highlight of the 2.0-mile-long trail in the Santa Margarita County Preserve.

The 220-acre Santa Margarita County Preserve is part of the County of San Diego's Multiple Species Conservation Program. In partnership with the Fallbrook Land Conservancy, the trail is open to equestrians, mountain bikers, hikers, and dogs on leashes.

However, I can't imagine mountain biking, at least on the part of the trail I hiked, because it was so deeply sandy most of the way.

From the trail's southern entry point off De Luz Road, hikers enter a dense riparian habitat, where arroyo willow make bushwhacking off the trail virtually impossible, and where big old sycamore trees and coast live oaks provide some welcome shade. Lots of yellow wallflower blooms add color to the trail, with an occasional purple phacelia and evergreen wild grape vines clinging everywhere. A little more color popped in with a blue western scrub jay, and a little black crested phainopepla bird perched on a limb.

Friends of the Santa Margarita River's website (http://www.friendsoftheriver. org/site/PageServer?pagename=FORCalRiversSantaMargarita) notes that the Santa

Margarita River basin boasts impressive diversity, including more than 500 plants, 236 species of birds, 52 species of mammals, 43 species of reptiles, 24 species of aquatic invertebrates, and 26 species of fish.

Sandy beach surprise lies on the Santa Margarita.

I hiked on the sandy trail, heading straight ahead for about a mile, crossing the river at one point across a line of rocks, and following the map offered at the trailhead. The dense willow and other foliage made it impassable beyond that point. I retraced my steps and followed a trail spur to the west, where a sign is posted with the preserve rules. This short spur led directly to that wide-open beach and the free-flowing river—a genuine surprise.

I didn't see any during my midday hike, but deer and other large mammals are said to make their homes here, relying on the fresh water from the Santa Margarita River. It's one of the last free-flowing rivers in Southern California, according to Friends of the Santa Margarita River. The river's upper watershed begins at the confluence of Temecula and Murrietta Creeks in the Santa Margarita Mountains, Santa Rosa Plateau, and Palomar Mountain, eventually emptying into the ocean on the lands of Camp Pendleton.

It's also one of the largest riparian systems in Southern California, according to the county, covering some 1,500 acres along its 27 miles. A primer on its ecology on the Friends of the Santa Margarita River website notes that riparian is derived from the Latin word, "ripa," meaning bank or shore. A riparian habitat characteristically surrounds a stream, creek, or river. "Nowhere else in Southern California is there a comparable unbroken length of riparian environment and its complement of plant and wildlife species," says the FSMR website.

After walking the length of the sandy beach, I had to return to my entry point and continue back along the main trail. Upon reaching the parking area again, I took the smaller trail just to the south of the main trail to see where it led. Again I went through thick willow groves and headed right at the T intersection. This trail was far rockier, as though it were once a creek bed. It quickly ends up back at another point on the river itself, where I could see a tantalizing trail on the other side of the deep water but couldn't navigate my way there.

I retraced my steps and this time took the left at that T intersection, which wasn't a very good idea. This was a short spur filled with spider webs and dense foliage—evidence that it doesn't get much traffic. It quickly dead-ended anyway.

There is another entry to this trail, which I didn't explore, but the map suggests it connects to this main trail while also crossing the river to the other side, perhaps where I saw it from that one point.

Thomas Brothers Map: Page 997, F-7.

Before You Go: Check for more information and download a copy of the trail map from the county's parks page: http://www.sandiegocounty.gov/parks/openspace/santamargarita.html.
This trail is open to hikers, bicyclists, equestrians, and dogs on leashes.

Trailhead: To reach the main trailhead where I began, from Interstate 15 north, exit at Mission Road/Fallbrook, heading west. At the light, turn right onto Mission Road. Continue for about five miles, turning right onto Pico Avenue (one block after Main Street), which immediately turns into De Luz Road. Continue about two miles; at the intersection with Sandia Creek Road, stay on De Luz Road (which curves left), where you'll see the sign for the Santa Margarita Preserve.
To reach the northern trail entry, at that intersection with Sandia Creek Road, turn right onto Sandia Creek Road and continue for about a mile. You should reach another preserve parking area.

Distance/Difficulty: About 2.0 miles one-way, or 4.0 miles round-trip; easy.

8-4. Wilderness Gardens: County's First Still One of the Best

Wilderness Gardens near Pala was San Diego County Parks' very first open space preserve established in 1973. The nearly 700 acres here offer four habitats: oak woodland, riparian, chaparral, and coastal sage scrub. There are about five miles of easy hiking trails through lovely grounds, as well as some historic sites that recall a few very different eras.

It's often called a hidden gem because of its natural beauty and interesting cultural history, all tucked away in the northern part of the county. Even the drive on Highway 76 is notably appealing—and interesting when you come upon the large Pala casino operation in an otherwise rural area.

There are five trails covering those five miles in the preserve, all heading out from the same main trailhead. I hit four of them as an interconnected wander and found a lot to admire here.

I started on the Main Trail and quickly connected to the Upper Meadow Trail, which is clearly marked at its entry. The park brochure calls this the most scenic trail in the preserve. It climbs a little hill from where you can see the San Luis Rey River region (often totally dry), as well as the impressive Pala Mountain to the south and the Palomar range to the northeast. There are old, dry ponds up there that recall the preserve's days as a ranch.

The county's first open-space preserve is a hidden gem.

Back down to the Pond Loop Trail, there is a working pond that still attracts lots of waterfowl. The existing pond, surrounded by such tall cattails that it's hard to see a lot of the water, was created in the 1960s by then-owner Manchester Boddy, noted publisher of the *Los Angeles Daily News*. He also founded the Descanso Gardens in La Cañada and bought this land in 1954 for horticulture propagation; he named it Wilderness Gardens. It is said Boddy built the pond to offer water to indigenous wildlife. It still seems to be working. I've never seen as much scat of all kinds on any other trail. Dogs are not allowed here to protect the wildlife, which must be flourishing if this abundant evidence is any indication. I didn't see any critters while I was there, but coyotes, raccoons, bobcats, deer, and snakes are commonly seen here.

The Camellia Trail winds around another abandoned pond that once irrigated hundreds of camellia plants. They aren't here any longer, but there are mighty live oaks, the striking white-limbed sycamores, several blooming oleanders, and the fragrant sages.

This loop trail connects back to the Main Trail, which is really an old, graded dirt road. It passes the ranger's headquarters housed in a charming 1930 ranch house, where old photographs and artifacts share a little more history. Take a look inside if the rangers have it open when you are there. Near the headquarters are remains of the county's first grist mill, which was built by the Sickler Brothers, who owned this land in the 1880s. Farmers from the area would come here to grind their wheat and corn into flour, camping and visiting with their neighbors during the weeks this task would take.

A little farther on, protected by some wooden fencing and identified with a sign showing a wagon wheel and arrowhead (which designates it as a historical marker), is a mortero, a grinding rock where even earlier generations ground acorns. The Luiseño

Indians lived here for thousands of years, migrating along the river banks from the mountains to the coast according to the seasons.

There's much to admire still in the county's first open-space preserve.

Thomas Brothers Map: Page 1030, F6.

Before You Go: Wilderness Gardens is open only 8:00 a.m. to 4:00 p.m. Fridays through Mondays; it is closed Tuesdays, Wednesdays, and Thursdays. It is closed in August because of the heat.

Download a copy of the trail map at the San Diego County parks pages for Wilderness Gardens: http://www.sandiegocounty.gov/reusable_components/images/parks/doc/Trails_Wilderness_Gardens.pdf.

This trail is open to hikers, bicyclists, equestrians, and dogs on leashes.

For more information, go to its county park page: http://www.sandiegocounty.gov/parks/openspace/wildernessgardens.html.

Trailhead: From Interstate 15, exit at Highway 76 and head east for 9.5 miles. Wilderness Gardens Preserve is on the right.

Distance/Difficulty: About 3.0 miles for this loop of several trails; easy.

8-5. Easy Trail Features Native Flora, History

The River View Trail in Wilderness Gardens Preserve near Pala offers one of the best introductions to hiking in our county. It's an easy, wide, and flat old dirt road that harbors few risks, but it covers some scenic territory with lively historical artifacts. This round-trip loop of nearly 3.5 miles is among the 5.0 miles of easy to moderate trails in Wilderness Gardens, the county's very first open-space preserve established in 1973. Named Wilderness Gardens by Manchester Boddy, who owned the property from about 1954 to 1967, it is located along the San Luis Rey River.

In Boddy's old ranch house, built around 1930 and now the park ranger headquarters, several exhibits share various historic periods of life here. One collection displays woven grass baskets and arrows that depict staples in the lives of local native American people who lived here for thousands of years, migrating from the mountains to the coasts with the seasons. Their lives changed dramatically in 1798 when Spanish Franciscans established a mission at the mouth of the San Luis Rey River near Oceanside, as well as satellite missions east in Pala. Native people of the area came to be known as the Luiseño, abbreviated Spanish for "people of San Luis Rey."

On the River View Trail not far from the old ranch house, one Luiseño mortero is highlighted with a sign pointing to its historic interest. Grinding rocks such as these (for pounding acorns into meal) were located along the river.

Grinding became another benchmark in Wilderness Gardens' history when the Sickler brothers of Missouri purchased this land in 1880 to establish the first grist mill in northern San Diego County. While it operated for about 10 years, Sicklers' Grist Mill was a social gathering place where farmers and families from all over the region brought their corn and wheat crops to be ground into flour. On display in the ranch house is a recreated model of what the grist mill looked like in its heyday. Today the only things left of the grist mill are its stone foundation and lone water wheel, which helped power the grinding stones. Water was brought to the mill by a flume diverting water from the river, but the flume is gone now.

Easy trail along San Luis Rey River.

Even the water in the San Luis Rey River is gone except during hard winter rains. Ever since Lake Henshaw was dammed in 1923 on the upper part of the river, and the Escondido Canal diverted most of its midstream flow, the middle portion of the river is largely dry much of the year.

Interestingly, according to a report prepared in 1827 by Father Antonio Peyri, who had served in the local mission since its founding in 1798, the San Luis Rey River "has abundant water only in the rainy season, from the month of October or November to May or June of the next year, when it is again lost in the sand."

When you walk along the River View Trail, also called the Main Trail, it's especially easy to imagine life here during the Boddy years. Boddy had been owner of the *Los Angeles Daily News* and had also established Descanso Gardens. After he'd sold the newspaper and Descanso Gardens in the early 1950s, he bought Wilderness Gardens, first called the Old Mill Ranch, in 1954. He hoped to create another Descanso Gardens attraction. He planted some 100,000 camellias, azaleas, rhododendrons, lavender, and lilac, but after he died in 1967, the property declined. Almost all the plants Boddy planted are gone now, with the property returning to more native species. Boddy's heirs sold the property to investors, and eventually plans were made to develop it. Escondido residents Betty Morin and Peggy McBride spearheaded a move to raise funds, purchasing the property and creating the county's first open-space preserve.

At its western end, the River View Trail connects to the Camellia View Trail, where imagination fills in what it might have looked like during Boddy's day. The large pond that is a centerpiece of the main trail was one that Boddy built, and it still attracts lots of waterfowl and wildlife. Don't try to approach the pond through its thickets of vegetation—most of it is poison oak.

With Palomar Mountain as its northeastern backdrop, Wilderness Gardens today is a picturesque, quiet place tucked into about 750 acres hidden in a steep canyon below 2,087-foot Pala Mountain. Vegetation today is highlighted by native oaks, sycamores, and wild grapevines, now preserved for many more years.

Thomas Brothers Map: Page 1030, F-6, where dotted line south of 76 is entry road.

Before You Go: Go to the county parks page: http://www.sandiegocounty.gov/parks/openspace/ wildernessgardens.html.

The preserve is open only Thursdays through Mondays, 8:00 a.m. to 4:00 p.m. There is a $3 parking fee charged.

This trail is open to hikers, bicyclists, equestrians, and dogs on leashes.

Trailhead: To reach Wilderness Gardens, from Interstate 15, exit onto Highway 76 and head east for 9.5 miles. The entrance to the preserve is on the right (south) side of the highway, about 4.0 miles east of Pala Casino.

Distance/Difficulty: The round-trip River View Trail is about 3.4 miles; easy.

8-6. Palomar's Boucher Trail Has Fall Color

Palomar Mountain is one of the best places in the county for fall color. The trail to Boucher's Lookout guided me along a surprisingly grassy green path through old-growth oaks as well as cedars and firs, where the golds and reds of fall cast a colorful glow in the sunshine. The black oaks, the most common deciduous tree in our local mountains, are the only oaks that drop their leaves in fall, turning golden when they do. The season's reddest leaves of all are from another oak—the poison oak, which is a shrub rather than a tree.

Black oaks bring fall color to Palomar.

Many canyon live oaks and coast live oaks are up on the mountain as well, and though you'll see some leaves on the ground, these oaks are not deciduous. The leaves of the black oaks have large cut-out lobes, whereas the leaves of the live oaks are more solidly oval with shallow spiny-teeth cutouts. The poison oak shrubs, which can also grow up the live oak tree trunks like vines, have less-lobed leaves that are more oval; they grow in bundles of three: "leaves of three, let it be."

The acorns of the black oaks are said to be the favorite acorn of the historic Luiseños, who lived on Palomar Mountain during the summer for hundreds of years. My hike started near Palomar Mountain State Park's Silvercrest picnic area, where there is said to be a granite ridge about 15 feet long that features some 24 grinding holes (morteros) that the natives used to transform acorns into meal.

From the Silvercrest parking area, walk along the State Park Road a short way (about 0.2 miles) until you reach a five-road intersection with Nate Harrison Grade and Boucher Road. In between the two one-way forks of Boucher Road (to your left) will be the trailhead for Boucher Trail. Boucher Trail is for hikers only and climbs uphill in 0.7 miles to the fire lookout that bears the same name. This part of the trail is the best for those black oaks in their golden fall phase. You'll also pass a bunch of native California incense cedar trees that you may mistake for redwoods, because their trunks feature similar reddish bark.

At Boucher Lookout (yes, you can also drive on that road to reach this), you'll have a truly panoramic view over Pauma Valley to the west. From this elevation at 5,438 feet, on the very clearest days you can see not only the ocean but Catalina Island. This fire lookout, built in 1949, is still one of the most important in Southern California because of this sweeping view.

Palomar Mountain is not a mountain peak but a mountain range, "a rolling plateau," wrote Marion Becker in the 1958 book *Palomar Mountain: Past and Present*. Peter Brueggeman has edited this gem for online accessibility (www.peterbrueggeman.com/palomarhistory/beckler.pdf). "Geologically, Palomar Mountain rests on a granite block, 25 miles long, six miles wide," wrote Beckler. "As we look down from Boucher Hill, we see a vast country of ridges and depressions, running northeast by southwest, like the grain in wood." Interestingly, she added, Palomar Mountain is surrounded by faults, including the San Andreas Fault, the Agua Caliente Fault, and the Temecula-Elsinor Fault. "But Palomar, on its granite base without fault, is made invulnerable to earthquakes," Beckler wrote.

The Boucher lookout is named for a Palomar pioneer, William Bougher, who homesteaded here when it was called Smith Mountain in the early 1900s. Leland Fetzer explains in his 2005 book *San Diego County Place Names A to Z* that the different spelling of the lookout from its namesake "probably reflects the pronunciation of the family name (BOO-ker) ... mapmakers seemed to have obtained their place-name information from interviews, not from printed sources."

From the lookout, keep going on the Boucher Trail, which continues across the road to the north. This part of the trail features more amazing views down the mountain to the west, where you'll see the winding Nate Harrison Grade Road below that commemorates the former slave who homesteaded on Palomar for decades in the late 1800s, raising hay and hogs "despite numerous run-ins with bears and mountain lions," according to the state park's website. The bears are gone, but mountain lions still live here.

Where the trail intersects the Nate Harrison Grade Road, continue straight ahead on the Adams Trail to Cedar Grove Campground. Lots of that bright red (in fall) poison oak is found here, as is a bracken fern meadow that offers its own brown shade of fall color.

From the Cedar Grove campground, I would have liked to continue on the Scott's Cabin Trail back, but the ranger at the entrance told me that area of the park was effectively off-limits because workers were busy chainsawing and cleaning up dead trees. He advised me to walk along the State Park Road back to the Silvercrest Picnic Area parking.

Thomas Brothers Map: Page 1052, A-1, where all those little roads meet ...

Before You Go: For more information about the state park as well as a trail map, go to http://www.parks.ca.gov/pages/637/files/palomarmountain2009.pdf.
  This trail is open only to hikers. Dogs are not allowed on state park trails.
  There is an $8 vehicle day-use fee to enter the state park.

Trailhead: From Highway 76, take S6 (also called South Grade Road) up to the top of Palomar Mountain. Turn left onto S7 to Palomar Mountain State Park's entrance.
  Park at the Silvercrest Picnic Area and walk a short way down State Park Road to the five-road intersection, where Boucher Trail begins between the two forks of Boucher Road.

Distance/Difficulty: About a 3.0-mile loop. With about 600 feet in elevation gain, it's easy to moderate.

8-7. Mighty Oaks on Palomar's French Valley Trail

Some of the most magnificent oak trees in the entire county flank the French Valley Trail in Palomar Mountain State Park. These amazing giants—some with a circumference that must measure at least 20 feet around—have undoubtedly witnessed hundreds of years of life on top of Palomar Mountain, from the time when the Luiseño people came here each fall to harvest the acorns of these canyon live oaks, as well as those of the coast live oaks and black oaks that abound up here.

The ancient oaks aren't the only attraction on this gorgeous trail. As it winds through French Valley and then Doane Valley, the views across the bunchgrass meadows (natural preserves) to the rising hills covered by evergreen trees are simply beautiful.

It has been said that Palomar possesses one of the few Sierra Nevada–like atmospheres in Southern California. With elevations rising to about 6,000 feet, its plentiful pine, cedar, and fir trees make it a true mountain experience.

Palomar Mountain State Park was created in the 1930s when 1,683 acres of "the most attractive part of the mountain" was acquired for a state park. Today the park covers 1,832 acres. Many of the roads and trails here were built during the 1930s by the Civilian Conservation Corps.

Some of county's biggest, oldest oaks are on French Valley Trail.

Village sites and 10 smaller gathering areas of the Luiseño have been identified in this area including Doane Valley. These mountain camps were used during summer and early autumn for gathering and grinding acorns, pine seeds, elderberries, and grass seeds, according to the state park. The main Luiseño village lay at the foot of the mountain and is called Pauma.

The Luiseños called this area Wavamai, but when the Spaniards arrived in the late 18th century, they named it Palomar, or "place of the pigeons," because thousands of band-tailed pigeons once nested here, according to the state park.

Marion Beckler offered another tale in her 1958 book *Palomar Mountain: Past and Present,* presented online by Peter Brueggeman (http://www.peterbrueggeman.com/palomarhistory/beckler.pdf). She wrote that Palomar had been known as "Paauw" for endless centuries by the local Indian tribes. "The name blended the idea of 'mother' with 'mountain,'" she wrote. She said Palomar was also known as "Smith Mountain" for 50 years after the violent death about 1867 of Joseph Smith, the first European settler on Palomar. Smith's death "remains a mystery that still inspires sleuthing."

There is no specific reference to how French Valley got its name, but perhaps it came from the days of Smith, who settled on Palomar in 1859. Smith had been overseer of the 1858 Butterfield Stagecoach road that traveled to Warner's Ranch at the foot of Palomar. Smith was a former sea captain who came west with Colonel Cave Couts in 1848 for the survey of California's southern border, according to Beckler's book. Smith began ranching on Palomar's valleys, where he harvested the natural grass for his cattle, sheep, horses, and hogs. He had bought several French Percheron horses, which were popular at the time as draft horses. Maybe those hardy horses of yesteryear gave French Valley its name.

Today, go to French Valley for those awesome oaks. You'll be dwarfed by them fairly early on the French Valley Trail, which leaves from the Doane Valley campground. The French Valley Trail intersects soon with the Doane Valley Nature Trail. Continue to the right on the French Valley Trail. You'll soon come to the first oak grove that graces both sides of this trail. Some of these specimens are impressive with their large spreading, horizontal branches, but they are juniors compared to the ones still ahead.

After emerging into a clearing with views of conifers ahead, the trail hits another intersection, this time with the Lower Doane Valley Trail. Stay to the right on the French Valley Trail; you'll come back via that Lower Doane Valley Trail later. Soon you'll pass through a lot of bracken ferns that make the ground really green in summer. These ferns, which were prized food when young by those Luiseños, according to the Doane Valley Nature Trail guide, turn yellow in fall. Look for the member of the mint family called heal all, with its blue-purple flower tips; its medicinal properties have been used ever since the time of the Luiseños.

The next grove of oaks is nothing short of astonishing. These canyon live oaks are huge. Some wind their roots around enormous boulders, adding to the other-worldly atmosphere.

Then you'll reach the meadows, abloom with tiny white forget-me-nots and yellow rock roses. At points, the grasses are so thick they almost obscure the trail. Among these protected meadow grasses is an herb called horkelia clevelandii, or Cleveland's horkelia, a member of the rose family. On this plant, the endangered Laguna Mountains Skipper butterfly lays its eggs. This butterfly is found only in the high mountain meadows of Palomar and Laguna. I saw lots of colorful, variously patterned butterflies, so maybe one of these skippers was among them.

The French Valley Trail eventually ends near its meeting with French Creek. To make this trail a loop, join the intersection near that end with the Lower Doane Valley Trail and hike back to the campground.

Thomas Brothers Map: Page 1052, B-1, the entrance to Palomar Mountain State Park.

Before You Go: Go to the state parks page for Palomar to get a complete trail map, including one for this French Valley loop: http://www.parks.ca.gov/pages/637/files/palomarmountain2009.pdf.

For more information, check the website of Friends of Palomar Mountain State Park: http://www.palomarsp.org.

This trail is open only to hikers; no dogs allowed on state park trails.

Trailhead: From Interstate 15, exit at Highway 76, heading east for about 20 miles. Turn left onto South Grade Road, also known as S6, heading up to Palomar. At the top of the hill called Crestline, where S6 intersects with S7, take a left onto State Park Road to the park entrance. There is an $8 day-use fee.

Once inside the park, follow the signs to Doane Valley Pond and Campground. Park only in the day-use area. Walk from that parking lot north into the campground. The trailhead for the French Valley Trail is found at camp site No. 25.

Distance/Difficulty: The French Valley Trail is about 1.3 miles one-way, making for about a 2.6-mile round-trip loop. Easy.

8-8. Learn to Identify Biggest Trees on Palomar's Fry Creek Trail

The Fry Creek Trail in Palomar's Cleveland National Forest meanders through some of the biggest, oldest trees in San Diego County. This trail provides a good opportunity to learn to identify some of these giant oak and pine trees that make this mountain region appear more like the Sierra Nevada than any other place in Southern California. Note that this trail atop Palomar Mountain is not in the state park but is in the adjacent CNF lands.

According to the Cleveland National Forest's ecological description of Palomar and its neighboring Cuyamaca region, the predominant trees here at this elevation between 5,000 and 6,000 feet include Douglas fir, white fir, Coulter pine, Jeffrey pine, incense cedar, black oak, and canyon live oak.

Some of the county's biggest, oldest trees are found on Fry Creek Trail.

Here are some characteristics to look for, gleaned from James Lightner's book *San Diego County Native Plants* and other sources.

The Douglas fir is a dark-green tree that can reach 120 feet high, with horizontal branches and short (under three inches) singular needles. Fir trees' needles are always singular.

The white fir is light-colored, has smooth bark, and is silver-blue, with short, singular needles on stiffly horizontal branches. These trees can reach 120 feet high, are the most widespread of the western firs, and can live for 350 years.

Coulter pine has needles that form in bundles, and the Coulter (sometimes called big-cone pine) is the stockiest of mountain pine trees, growing in a pyramidal shape to 75 feet high. Needles are long, are grey-green, and grow in bundles of three.

The Jeffrey pine, sometimes called yellow pine for its yellow-colored wood, is symmetrical, rising up to 150 feet high with thick grey or brown bark. Peeled bark has a vanilla aroma (similar ponderosa pine bark smells of pitch). Needles are 10 inches long and in bundles of three.

The incense cedar is most easily recognized by its thick, reddish bark; it is often mistaken for a redwood. It can reach 120 feet high and appears conical or pyramidal. Its needles are flat and like evergreen paddles, and they have a cedar aroma.

The California black oak is deciduous. Its leaves turn golden yellow before dropping in autumn; they are bronze in spring and green in summer and have prominent, thumb-sized lobes. It can grow to 75 feet high, and its bark appears black in the shade. Its acorns, completely covered by spherical cups until they mature in their second year, were favored by indigenous people as well as the band-tailed pigeons.

The canyon live oak is an evergreen tree that can reach 70 feet high; its trunks can be 20 feet wide with several large branches. Its leaves are not lobed like the black oak, but are oval with spiny edges.

Those band-tailed pigeons are Palomar's current namesake. The Luiseño Indians lived seasonally on this mountain for centuries, calling it Wavamai. When the Spaniards arrived in the late 18th and early 19th centuries, they named it Palomar, meaning "place of pigeons," referring to the thousands of band-tailed pigeons that nested here then.

Many of the trails in this Cleveland National Forest follow the old ones used by the indigenous people. When I started out on the Fry Creek Trail, I scampered up a wrong turn onto a little-used trail that may have been one of those old ones—or perhaps just a current-day path used by wildlife.

From the trailhead at the day-use parking area, the path goes uphill and shortly comes to a three-way intersection. I mistakenly kept going straight, but that trail (faint all the way) climbed straight uphill and pretty much petered out near the top of the ridge. I went back downhill to try to find the real trail back where I'd seen a fork. I found that fork, which actually is the three-way intersection. Turn left when you first reach that intersection to stay on the real Fry Creek Trail. It's far more obvious, and big wooden posts, along with a few wooden trail signs, tell you this is the correct path.

The trail makes a wide circle around the Fry Creek campgrounds and eventually ends at an old dirt road. Turn left onto that road, which becomes the paved road of the campground, until you are back to the trailhead parking area.

When I got back to the trailhead map, I noticed the trail crosses that road and continues on the southwest side of the campground back to the beginning, but I missed that part.

Thomas Brothers Map: Page 1032, D-6.

Before You Go: For a map of the southern region of the Cleveland National Forest, go to its website (http://www.fs.usda.gov/cleveland) to order one. This is a very good map to have for the entire county.

For more information about CNF areas in Southern California, including Palomar, visit http://www.fs.usda.gov/Internet/FSE_DOCUMENTS/stelprdb5277346.pdf.

You need an Adventure Pass to park here ($5 day use or $30 annual fee, obtainable at national forest ranger stations, outdoor equipment firms like REI, and the Palomar Mountain general store.) You may also pay a $5 day-use fee at the parking area.

For more information on CNF's Adventure Pass, go to http://www.fs.usda.gov/detailfull/r5/passes-permits/recreation/?cid=stelprdb5208699&width=full.

This trail is open only to hikers as well as dogs on leashes.

Trailhead: From state Highway 76, take either S6 (also called South Grade Road) or S7 (East Grade Road) up to the top of Palomar. At the Crestline summit intersection, continue on S6 (also called Canfield Road) a few miles to the Fry Creek Campground entrance on the left. Just inside the entry is the first parking area for day use and the Fry Creek trailhead.

Distance/Difficulty: About 2.0-mile loop; easy.

8-9. Long Live Palomar and Its Big-Tree Trails

You may have read about the state budget woes that threatened to close Palomar Mountain State Park in 2012. After help from many local supporters, that ax never fell, and we are all the richer for the trails that remain open in some of the most beautiful mountain scenery in our county.

The 1,862-acre state park averages 5,000 feet in elevation with the highest point, High Point, rising to 6,140 feet, just east of the world-famous Palomar Observatory. Some 40 inches of rainfall each year support the fine conifer forest atop Palomar with old-growth trees including Douglas fir, white fir, reddish-barked incense cedar, live oak, black oak, Coulter pine, and yellow pine.

Myers Fire Road is the only trail in Palomar State Park that allows leashed dogs.

The black oak trees (which are the only oaks in San Diego County to lose leaves in the fall, coloring the landscape with gold) show off new leaves in a bright spring green color. Interestingly, when those new leaves begin to sprout, they are tinged a bronze-red.

You'll see all of these towering trees on all the trails in Palomar. The Doane Valley Nature Trail is a great introduction to the region with its downloadable nature guide to take along as it interprets numbered posts on the 1.0-mile loop. The Thunder Spring

Trail wanders through some of the best fir and pine forests on the mountain. The French Valley Trail is an all-time favorite for massive old oaks that have thrived here for hundreds of years, as well as wide-open meadows that surround a creek.

I've enjoyed hiking on almost every mile of the dozen trails in Palomar Mountain State Park. There are a few other tree-rich trails to explore on the adjacent Cleveland National Forest (CNF) lands, which include the observatory, operated by California Institute of Technology and open every day free of charge from 9:00 a.m. to 4:00 p.m.

When I went to Palomar Mountain State Park recently to hike, I planned to follow the Doane Valley to Fry Creek Trail, which connects the state park to the CNF Fry Creek campground. But after checking in at the Palomar entry, the excellent chief ranger, Jessica Murany, informed me that trail is all but obliterated, requiring more bushwhacking through poison oak than I like. She also noted that a family recently got lost (and found) in that area. That was enough information for me to seek a different route. She directed me to Myers Fire Road, which proved to be another excellent foray through the forests of Palomar.

Upon leaving from the Doane Valley Campground (some of the biggest and oldest oaks and firs make this a very popular camping destination), I followed Myers Fire Road uphill through thick stands of black oaks, incense cedars, and pines. I spotted the bright blue flashes of both western bluebirds and Steller's jays. I marveled at those bronzed-red baby leaves of a young black oak sapling. I was astounded at the size of the pine cones of the Coulter pine, which is also called the big-cone pine. Coulter pine cones are the largest of any pine, measuring from eight to 16 inches long and weighing up to 10 pounds. It's little wonder they're called widowmakers if they fall on anyone's head.

In early May, wildflowers were showing off too, including the purple chaparral pea, scarlet bugler, blue ceanothus (wild lilac), tiny yellow hairy lotus mixed in with white popcorn flowers, purple lupine, white blooming stems of the western choke cherry, the short, low-growing blue Bajada lupine, and lots of tiny baby blue eyes.

As you wind up the fire road, after about the first half-mile, you'll come to a faint road that goes off to the right; don't take that. It's an old driveway that goes to private property where fire claimed the home in the 2007 fire. Continue straight ahead on the Myers Fire Road. After about 1.2 miles from your start, the main road makes a sharp hairpin turn to the right, and a fainter road continues at the left. Follow that hairpin turn to the right. In another half-mile or so, you'll reach the road's end, where some old cabin ruins tell of a previous life up here. Turn around and go back the way you came. You'll note you've crossed from the state park into CNF lands on this road.

If you now take that faint road you passed at the hairpin turn, this continuation of Myers Fire Road dips downhill, and in about another three-quarters of a mile, it ends at a gate.

The views from Myers Fire Road are another bonus. On a very clear day, you can probably see the ocean. On any other day, you have up-high views down onto Palomar itself—the meadows and distant ridges covered in pines.

Myers Fire Road is the only trail in the state park where you can take your dog, always leashed. Dogs are also allowed on CNF lands but not on state park trails (though they can be in state park campgrounds).

More than $83,000 had been raised through private donations to help keep Palomar Mountain State Park operating. To continue to donate, go to http://www.palomarsp.org.

Thomas Brothers Map: Page 1052, B-1.

Before You Go: Download a map of all the Palomar Mountain State Park trails, including Myers Fire Road, at http://www.palomarsp.org/pmsp/printer_friendly.pdf.

The map of the fire road shows a spur trail off the right near the end of that road; that's where the hairpin turn goes right to the cabin ruins.

There is an $8 day-use fee to park in Palomar Mountain State Park, paid at the ranger station entry.

Trails are open only to hikers. No dogs allowed on state park trails.

Trailhead: From Interstate 15, head east on Highway 76. Follow signs to Palomar, going left on South Grade Road (S6). When you reach the top of the mountain, follow signs and take two left turns to reach Highway S7 to Palomar Mountain State Park.

Once in the state park, park at the Doane Pond day-use parking area. Walk to the campground and the beginning of Myers Fire Road near campsite No. 9. You'll see a gate across the road and a sign noting "No Hunting Access."

Distance/Difficulty: This route on Myers Fire Road was about 1.9 miles one way, making a 3.8-mile round-trip hike, with an elevation gain of about 700 feet. Moderate.

8-10. Observatory Trail Winds through Forest to Scope

The Observatory Trail on Palomar Mountain winds through some of the thickest forests of old-growth pine, fir, cedar, and oak trees found in San Diego County. The October 2007 Poomacha Fire did destroy about 1,000 acres in the adjacent 1,862-acre Palomar Mountain State Park, but this trail lies in the Cleveland National Forest, where there remain more stately California incense cedars, Douglas firs, white firs, canyon live oaks, and black oaks than in most other places countywide.

Palomar's elevation is above 5,000 feet, so summer is a good time to visit this beautiful mountain top because it's always about 10 degrees cooler than at sea level.

An added allure of this trail is its termination at Palomar Observatory, home of what famed NBC radio newscaster Lowell Thomas reported in 1934 was "the largest glass casting ever made, for the costliest scientific instrument ever designed, the biggest telescope in the world, an instrument designed to see farther into the cosmos than had ever been possible." It is no longer the biggest telescope in the world (that would be the Gran Telescopio Canarias in Spain's Canary Islands today, twice as big as Palomar's), but the 200-inch Hale Telescope in Palomar Observatory "may be the most productive astronomical instrument in the world," wrote Ronald Florence in "Palomar, After 50 Years," in the San Diego Historical Society's *Journal of San Diego History* in 1998.

Even with the advances in technology of the last quarter century, he wrote, "the 200-inch remains a premier research instrument ... a monumental tribute to men of extraordinary insights ... and to an era when the remarkable American 'can-do' spirit in a time of widespread economic hardship brought the skills and energy of a nation together to create an enduring masterpiece of science and technology."

Wonderful views of Mendenhall Valley are seen from Observatory Trail.

The construction of Palomar's Hale Telescope captured America's imagination for 20 years, from its beginnings in 1928 when astronomer George Ellery Hale secured a $6 million grant from the Rockefeller Foundation for its painstaking and perilous delivery up the mountain in 1947, to the beginning of its full-time scientific observations in 1949. "Never before, and perhaps never again, would such widespread attention be devoted to a scientific instrument with such benign aims," wrote Florence.

The historic milestones of the telescope are nicely documented in the small museum at the observatory. The observatory itself is open daily (except December 24–25) from 9:00 a.m. to 4:00 p.m. during daylight savings time, and from 9:00 a.m. to 3:00 p.m. during standard time. Newly available is a podcast for a self-guided tour; go to http://www.astro.caltech.edu/palomar/visitor/media/haletourpodcast.mp3 to listen to or download the 10-minute audio tour. One-hour tours of the observatory are offered Saturdays and Sundays from April through October at 11:00 a.m. and 1:30 p.m. for $5 per person; buy tickets in the gift shop.

You might want to time your hike for those tours. The Observatory Trail's southern end begins at the Observatory Campground in the state park. It's 2.2 miles to reach the trail's northern end, which lies just outside the observatory parking area. This mountain trail—one of the few National Recreation Trails in the county—lies next to the S6 road that leads up to the observatory, but it's a much prettier journey to hike on this narrow, rocky path. After about the first three-quarters of a mile, you come to a wooden platform that offers a splendid view into Mendenhall Valley, where pastures and ponds create an idyllic pastoral landscape.

As the trail winds through those forests punctuated with several outcroppings of huge boulders, note the many wildflowers that add vibrant colors: magenta wine cups, pink California roses, baby blue eyes, yellow monkeyflowers, scarlet buglers, light blue leaf daisies, purple showy penstemons, and red paintbrushes, all plentiful in spring.

Walking from the campground to the observatory is the uphill direction, with an elevation gain of some 700 feet. Retracing your way back down is the easier way to go.

Thomas Brothers Map: Page 1032, D-6.

Before You Go: For a map from federal recreation pages in national forests of this Observatory Trail leaving the campground, go to http://www.recreation.gov/webphotos/facilitymaps/72310_OBSC.pdf.

You may also go for a Google satellite map of the area.

You can view a map of the Observatory NRT (National Recreation Trail) on the southern Cleveland National Forest map; go to http://www.fs.usda.gov/main/cleveland/maps-pubs to order a map.

The Observatory Trail is open only to hikers, and because it's on national forest lands, dogs on leashes are permitted. (They are not permitted on Palomar Mountain State Park trails.)

For the state parks brochure on Palomar Mountain State Park, go to http://www.parks.ca.gov/pages/637/files/palomarmountain.pdf.

You can pay a $5 day-use fee at the entrance to the Observatory Campground parking area, or display your Adventure Pass on your dashboard. Purchase a $30 annual or $5 day-use Adventure Pass for parking on forest lands at the Palomar Mountain General Store, the Cleveland National Forest ranger headquarters at 10845 Rancho Bernardo Road, San Diego, or other ranger stations, as well as outdoor outfitters such as REI and Adventure 16.

Trailhead: From Interstate 15, exit at Highway 76 and head east to Palomar. After about 15 miles, follow signs to Palomar Mountain, going north (left) on S6 (also called South Grade Road). At the mountain top Crestline intersection of four roads, continue straight on S6, then called Canfield Road. The Observatory Campground entrance is on the right, about 2.5 miles from this intersection.

Distance: It's 2.2 miles one-way, or 4.4 miles round-trip. Easy to moderate.

8-11. Loop Tour on Palomar Features Many Highlights

A four-trail loop hike in Palomar Mountain State Park provides a lovely sampler of the forests, meadows, and springs that have drawn people here for centuries. Resident Luiseño Indians, who called this area Wavamai, hunted deer and gathered acorns, pine seeds, and elderberries during summer and fall for hundreds of years. When the Spaniards arrived in the very late 18th century, they named the area Palomar, or "place of pigeons," after the many band-tailed pigeons that once thrived here.

The mule deer are still in residence; I saw a family of three. The pigeons continue to feast on the acorns of the black oak trees. One of the only sounds in this pristine state park is the constant knocking of the redheaded acorn woodpeckers. They like those acorns too and store them in holes they peck out, usually in mature or dead pines or Douglas firs.

As I was walking along these tree-lined trails, the footpaths were nearly obscured from all the fallen leaves from the black oaks, the only oak in the area that loses all its leaves, offering golden fall color in these mountains. There were lots of acorns on the ground now too, so the woodpeckers were busy sheltering their supplies.

Hike this excellent sampler loop for Palomar's beauties.

Palomar boasts one of our county's thickest forests, filled with black oaks, live oaks, and some very large old pines, firs, and cedars. Its highest point, High Point, 6,142 feet in elevation, is one of San Diego County's half-dozen peaks over 6,000 feet; the majority of the state park area averages about 5,000 feet above sea level. On the clearest days, you can see Catalina Island from the lookouts on S6, the road winding up to Palomar.

I began my loop route at the Silvercrest Picnic Area, immediately beyond the state park entry. Most of this entire loop was closed for a long time for fire hazard reduction work; it reopened in late January 2011. I started on Scott's Cabin Trail immediately across the road from Silvercrest's facilities. This spur trail is still a work in progress as park crews try to recreate it, but it's easy to follow. Look for the white poles that currently mark its route through the debris-strewn area.

After only a half mile or so, this spur trail connects to the main Scott's Cabin Trail. From this intersection, the paltry remains of Scott's Cabin are only 0.1 miles to the left, but you'll pass them on the way back if you complete this full loop.

I turned right onto the Scott's Cabin Trail, heading toward Chimney Flats Trail. Wooden post markers at each intersection give the mileage to the next one.

After crossing the park's maintenance road, the trail becomes the Chimney Flats Trail and goes down an old dirt road through lots of oaks and conifers. Eventually it reaches Chimney Flats, identified by its own wooden marker, a big meadow covered with grasses and bracken fern.

Meadows like Chimney Flats were favorite hideaways up here in the late 1800s for cattle and horse thieves to shelter their stolen animals before taking them to Mexico.

Bracken fern is toxic to livestock, according to James Lightner's *San Diego County Native Plants* book, so I wonder how that turned out.

Soon you start to hear the gurgling of Chimney Creek, which the trail crosses before reaching Thunder Spring Trail. That trail begins to follow the larger Doane Creek, and you can see the vast meadows of Doane Valley, named for George Edwin Doane, who raised hay, cattle, and hogs here in the 1880s.

Thunder Spring itself is noted with a wooden marker. You'll soon spot Doane Pond, a favorite for fishermen because it's stocked with trout twice a year. At the west end of the pond, the trail intersects with the Cedar Trail, which climbs back up to Scott's Cabin Trail. This is the steepest, hardest part of this loop.

At the next intersection, turn left onto Scott's Cabin Trail and keep a lookout for the remains of that cabin. Scott was a homesteader here in the 1880s, and he also planted apple orchards, some of which still remain. I couldn't find any other information about that person.

The state park's new ranger, Jessica Murany, has lots of plans to make her mark on Palomar. One of them is to learn who Scott was. Another is to seek a grant to restore his cabin, which now consists only of a few foundation logs (noted with another wooden marker). If anyone has photographs of the old cabin before it fell victim to vandals and age, she'd appreciate a copy to help restore it.

Just after the cabin remnants, the spur trail back to Silvercrest Picnic Area intersects to the right. Again, follow the white poles through the rough terrain. You will have made a grand loop through a lot of Palomar's montane attractions.

Thomas Brothers Map: Page 1052, B-1—where State Park Road goes west from S6, into Palomar Mountain State Park.

Before You Go: Download an excellent trail map at http://www.parks.ca.gov/pages/637/files/palomarmountain2009.pdf, which will show this entire loop route.

Dogs, horses, and mountain bikes are not allowed on Palomar Mountain State Park trails; hikers only.

Trailhead: From Highway 76, go north on S6, also known as South Grade Road. You can also reach Palomar's summit from the East Grade Road farther east off Highway 76.

Once at the summit, take the State Park Road west into Palomar Mountain State Park. Vehicles pay an $8 day-use fee at the park entrance.

Park at the Silvercrest Picnic Area immediately past the park entrance. Begin on Scott's Cabin Trail just across the road.

Distance/Difficulty: The loop is 4.1 miles total and is easy to moderate in difficulty with about 800 feet in elevation change.

8-12. Be Happy in Palomar's Love Valley Meadow

Take your valentine any month to Love Valley Meadow at the base of Palomar Mountain to wander a classic San Diego County landscape. From your perch at about 3,500 feet elevation along the southern flank of Palomar, you'll find sweeping views of the wide-open Valle de San Jose and its flats surrounding the west and east forks of the San Luis Rey River, all leading to the sparkling blue waters of Lake Henshaw. The 6,150-high Aguanga Mountain surrounds the vast valley to the southeast.

Love Valley Meadow is a much smaller pastoral sweep of grasslands, where I encountered a bevy of black cattle lazily grazing the day away.

Laze the day away in Love Valley.

There's plenty of shade for them among the several kinds of gnarly oaks—coast live oaks, black oaks, and Engelmann oaks—that spread their mighty branches across the land.

This trail is really an old dirt road that forks off East Grade Road and leads up to Palomar's peak. It's easy to find the trailhead, which is marked with a big sign courtesy of Cleveland National Forest.

I also enjoyed the loop drive to this trail, heading north on Interstate 15, exiting on Highway 76 heading east. From the intersection of Interstate 15 and Highway 76, it's about 31 miles to East Grade Road, also known as S7, which is a left (north) turn off Highway 76 from this direction. When I returned, from East Grade Road I turned left onto Highway 76 and headed into Santa Ysabel, connecting to Highways 79 and then 67. The drive was itself a lovely foray into San Diego's backcountry.

In order to park on National Forest lands, you need to place an Adventure Pass on your dashboard. You can purchase day-use ($5) or annual passes ($30) at any Cleveland National Forest office or at most outdoor and sports equipment outlets, including REI or Adventure 16.

Horseback riders, bicyclists, hikers, and dogs on leashes are all welcome on this trail, and because it's a wide, graded dirt road, all such activities are relatively easy. There's a small elevation gain of about 300 feet from trailhead to meadowlands, but the road's grade and route make the walk easy for virtually any fitness level.

As the road descends into the meadow, near the low point is a Y intersection where the road splits, and both directions become less maintained. I took the fork to the left and walked under many mighty oaks, still glimpsing those views into the huge valley and Lake Henshaw below. When I reached a small rise, where huge granite boulders gave picturesque foregrounds to the lake views beyond, I also evidently breached the comfort zone of those bovine chow hounds, some of which ran farther afield. At least I didn't cause a stampede.

They watched as I turned around and returned the way I came. When I reached that Y intersection again, I took the other fork to check out an old oxidized metal-sided barn, whose corrals may still have some role in the lives of the cattle I met. It was empty of any activity when I was there, but it added another point of interest to photograph.

Also attracting the eye are the bright red trunks of manzanita, the improbable spiny round bases of yucca plants, and plenty of brittle bush and buckwheat that promise yellow and white wildflowers come spring. Then there are what I like the call the ghost trees—dead trunks that have become sculptural marvels. Enormous boulders offer some of the best places to sit while contemplating those expansive views.

Surprise your valentine with a picnic and be peaceful in Love Valley.

Thomas Brothers Map: Page 1052, J-6.

Before You Go: Hikers, bicyclists, equestrians, and dogs on leashes are all welcome here.

You need an Adventure Pass to park at the trailhead because it's Cleveland National Forest land. For more information on the Adventure Pass and where to buy one, go to the Cleveland National Forest website (www.fs.usda.gov/main/cleveland) and go to passes and permits.

For a map that locates the old road into Love Valley, purchase the Cleveland National Forest Visitor Map/South; for details, go to its website: http://www.fs.usda.gov/main/cleveland/maps-pubs.

Trailhead: Take Highway 76 to East Grade Road, turning north (the only possible direction to turn). Near the 3.3 mile marker is a large unpaved parking area marked by a sign: "Love Valley Meadow."

Distance/Difficulty: About 2.0 to 3.0 miles round-trip. Easy.

8-13. Doane Valley: Huge Trees, Historic Sights, and Peaceful Valleys

There are few wilderness areas in San Diego County that have such majestic, old trees as Palomar Mountain. In its elevation of about 5,000 feet are large pine, fir, and cedar forests as well as gnarly oak groves along its wide-open valleys. In fact, Palomar Mountain State Park notes it's one of the few areas in Southern California with a Sierra Nevada–like atmosphere.

One of the best trails to familiarize yourself with the flora is the Doane Valley Nature Trail. This 0.75-mile loop has 30 markers along its path that accompany a brochure you should download before you go (http://www.parks.ca.gov/pages/637/files/DoaneValleyforWeb.pdf). The markers will identify such natural features as the wild rose (marker #2), life in a log (#5), white fir (#7), lichen and moss (#11), incense cedar (#14), canyon live oak (#17) and Ponderosa pine (#18). I combined some of this trail with a couple of others to create a 2.5-mile loop that included some historic sites, magnificent forests, a peaceful valley, and a couple of lively streams.

Huge trees, meadows and streams are on Palomar trails.

I began on the Doane Valley Nature Trail, which starts out along Doane Creek. A short distance from the trailhead, I took a left-hand, uphill turn onto the Weir Historic Trail (following trail markers; the right turn continues on the nature trail). I was dwarfed by the huge old cedars and pines whose fallen needles carpeted the trail.

These forests were home to the Luiseño Indians for centuries. They hunted game and ground acorns in the morteros found on some granite slabs. They used to call this mountain area Wavamai, but when the Spanish came in the 18th century, they named it Palomar, or "place of pigeons," for the thousands of band-tailed pigeons that nest here.

Pines and firs from Palomar were used to build the Mission San Luis Rey in 1798, four miles upstream. The missionaries worked with the local Indians until 1834, when Governor Figueroa ordered all California missions to be secularized. By then, disease and cultural change had devastated the Luiseño population, but descendants still live on nearby reservations.

In the 1860s, Nathan Harrison, a freed black slave, made his home in Doane Valley, where he raised hogs and grew hay. When he died in 1920, he was believed to be 101 years old. The old road to Pauma is named after him.

George Edwin Doane came in the early 1880s and built a shake-roof log cabin in what is now Doane Valley Campground. You'll see a placard about him and his search for a wife who could stand the whiskers of his enormous beard. His cabin has been restored into a park ranger residence.

Palomar Mountain State Park was created in the 1930s when 1,683 acres were bought for a state park. In 2013 it marked its 80th anniversary.

I stayed on the trail to the historic weir, but at one point fallen trees and landslides had obliterated it. I could see another trail on the other side of the creek, so I took a log crossing and connected to that trail, still headed to the weir. The historic weir is a stone dam constructed in the 1920s to see if the creeks here could support a power plant. There wasn't enough water for such a project, so the only thing left is a stone column atop a small dam. It stands at the confluence of French Valley, Pauma, and Doane Creeks. The stone column makes for an interesting exploration among the boulder-lined creeks and ponds made by the old dam.

After tracing back on that north side of Doane Creek, I followed trail markers to connect to the Lower Doane Trail and French Valley Trail, both of which head back to Doane Valley Campground and the pond parking lot. Here I entered those oak groves, with enormous old canyon live oaks spreading huge limbs. The trail here is thickly cushioned with fallen acorns, the favorite food of the acorn woodpecker. I didn't see one this time, but I did see the brilliant turquoise blue flash of what I think was a mountain bluebird.

It will probably be even more beautiful here in spring, when dogwood, azalea, and wild lilac all bloom.

Thomas Brothers Map: Page 1052, 1A.

Before You Go: For more information about Palomar Mountain State Park, go to its state park pages: http://www.parks.ca.gov/?page_id=637. You'll find links to the Doane Valley Nature Trail Guide noted above, as well as trail maps, which are located in the park's brochure.

There is an $8 day-use fee. Hikers only; mountain bikes, and equestrians are not allowed on these park trails. Dogs are generally not allowed in state parks, except in campground areas. But in Palomar, leashed dogs are welcome on paved roads, the trail only around Doane Pond, or on Myers Fire Road.

Trailhead: Head east on Highway 76 from Interstate 15. From that intersection, go 26 miles and turn left onto S6, also known as South Grade Road. Follow signs to Palomar Mountain State Park.

At the mountaintop known as Crestline, go left onto East Grade Road, again following signs to Palomar Mountain State Park (not the observatory).

From the park entry, take right-hand turns on paved roads for about 1.7 miles, following signs to "Camps." Park in the Doane Valley Pond day-use parking lot.

There are two trailheads here; take the one on the right marked to Doane Valley Nature Trail and Historic Weir Trail.

Distance/Difficulty: From 0.75 mile to over 3.0 miles total, depending on which trails and how far you go. Fairly easy.

8-14. Oak Grove Climbs for Long Peak Views

Near the center of the northern reaches of San Diego County is the oldest established trail in the Palomar Ranger District, which climbs up the backside of Palomar Mountain to reach lofty peak views. The Oak Grove Trail in the tiny community of Oak Grove on Highway 79, very close to Riverside County's border, is a rocky, narrow trek that switchbacks and soars straight up several hundred feet on the flanks of Palomar.

The trail connects after nearly 2.0 miles to the rough dirt roads of Oak Grove Truck Trail, where you can continue another five miles to High Point Truck Trail and Palomar Divide Road. Even from the top of the foot trail, the views extend far and wide.

High Point is Palomar's highest elevation at 6,142 feet. The real giants you can see from up here are the two highest peaks in Southern California: San Gorgonio Mountain, 11,503 feet in the San Bernardino Mountains; and Mount San Jacinto, 10,834 feet in the San Jacinto Mountains. Both are usually snow-capped until April or May each year, which makes them especially easy to locate during winter.

One of the hardest trails has the longest views.

Both of these peaks are also notably prominent because they stand so far above their surrounding terrain. San Jacinto is ranked 17th, and San Gorgonio 18th in a list of "129 ultra-prominent mountain peaks of the United States" on Wikipedia.

To reach these views requires some effort on the Oak Grove Trail. According to the Cleveland National Forest, the 1.9-mile-long trail climbs 1,440 feet from 2,760 to 4,200 feet in elevation. First, you have to find the trailhead behind the fire department compound in Oak Grove on the left side of Highway 79 when heading north. Park to the left of the main building here just off the highway, then start walking behind that building to the northwest. You'll pass between other buildings and eventually reach the end of the blacktop road, where a dirt road intersects on the left. A sign alerting "Resident and Official Vehicles beyond This Sign Only" is the first clue. Turn left onto that dirt road, and you'll soon see wooden posts with red-painted tops pointing to "Trail." Follow those trail markers, cross a rocky stream bed, and continue on a dirt road a short way until another trail marker points to a pass-through in a fence.

The trail is easygoing until you start to climb those Palomar flanks. It switchbacks up a few times and then goes straight up. After I'd come really close to the intersection with the dirt roads and was rewarded with those views, I turned around after about an hour of climbing, retracing my steps back with care.

There are some large, old manzanita bushes along the trail, as well as some of specimen chaparral yucca known as our Lord's candle; before it blooms, it's just a perfectly round rosette composed of sharp, bayonet-like leaf spears.

The snow-capped peaks are a special sight, and the views to the south and east are far-reaching. There are large swaths of green pastureland in Grove Valley, surrounded by 4,837-foot-high Tule Mountain and 5,548-foot-high Beauty Mountain. Immediately below lies Oak Grove, and you can easily see from here how it got its name.

There are two historic markers in Oak Grove. One sits in front of the Oak Grove Stage Station, the only remaining station on the Butterfield Overland Mail Route that operated between San Francisco, St. Louis, and Memphis from 1858 to 1861. The other marker is for Camp Wright, which moved to the Oak Grove Stage Station in 1861 during the Civil War to protect this route between Arizona and California. The California State Military Museum offers an interesting note about this area: "The Oak Grove Stage Station was where Camp Wright moved in December 1861 because wind near Warner's Ranch 'blows in a perfect gale (not a moderate breeze) more than half the time driving the dust in clouds and blinding the eyes of everyone and infiltrating every coffee pot, camp kettle, etc.,' the [Camp Wright] surgeon reported." I found it breezy on the trail.

According to the Temecula Historical Society newsletter in July 2010, the owner of the Oak Grove station property, Mark Shook, had threatened to demolish the historic building over disagreements with county officials about his property. After preservation officials statewide rallied to save the station, Shook stopped that plan and has opened the building to the public on Saturdays and Sundays from 9:00 a.m. to 5:00 p.m. He and his late father, Miles Shook, have been owners since 1986 and restored and stocked it with period antiques and artifacts, including sculptural oxen and horse teams drawing wagons outside.

The Oak Grove Stage Station today is a National Historic Landmark.

Thomas Brothers Map: Page 409, H-5.

Before You Go: For more information, go to the Cleveland National Forest website on day hiking (http://www.fs.usda.gov/activity/cleveland/recreation/hiking/?recid=47396&actid=50) and click on the Oak Grove Trail in the Palomar North Side Area.

For a map of the trail, order the Cleveland National Forest map for its southern section: http://www.fs.usda.gov/main/cleveland/maps-pubs. This is a good map to have on hand

This trail is open only to hikers and dogs on leashes.

Trailhead: Oak Grove is located on Highway 79, either twenty-seven miles north of Santa Ysabel or twenty-five miles south from Interstate 15 in Temecula. You may also reach Highway 79 from Highway 76 from Pala, turning north on Highway 79.

Park in the fire department compound; the trail is behind the buildings to the northwest.

Distance/Difficulty: The Oak Grove Trail is 1.9 miles one-way, or 3.8 miles round-trip. Strenuous.

8-15. Birds, Tracks Abound around Lake Henshaw

Hike around Lake Henshaw for some excellent birding and tracking opportunities, or just for beautiful scenery. When I was there on the last day of September, when winter migration of many bird species had already begun, I spotted many lovely water fowl floating and foraging in the blue waters of the pretty lake. During this time of year, the water level was quite low—currently only at about 10 percent capacity. One can also see lots of animal tracks heading for the water.

I began hiking counterclockwise from the lake's entrance, heading out near the water's edge. There isn't really a trail, but there is easy access for shoreline fishing as well as walking. Because the water level is low, along the shoreline lies hard-packed mud, especially during these drought years. That means tracks from various wildlife are exceptionally visible. I saw those of coyote, bobcats, deer, cattle, and even wild turkey.

I also spotted what appeared to be skidded landings of birds—perhaps a hawk caught something, or one of the great blue herons landed. Tracking isn't usually this easy, so take your renderings of footprints and see what you can figure out.

Standing nearly four feet tall, the majestic great blue herons, which are mostly gray, were abundant. You can get fairly close to the herons, who usually are wading near shore as they fish—but get too close, and they'll soar away with their six-foot wingspan.

I also saw a lovely white snowy egret with its yellow legs; lots of long-billed black-necked stilts with their pink legs; a trio of double-crested cormorants on a set of pilings; several black-and-white killdeer with their two black breast bands; American avocets with their black-and-white striped wings, long upturned bills, and light blue

Identify tracks in your trek around Lake Henshaw.

legs; long-billed dowitchers with long straight bills and white eyebrows, who wade near shore probing the sand constantly like sewing machines; our smallest shorebirds, the least sandpipers, with their yellow legs and mottled backs; northern shoveler ducks with their large bills; and black American coots with their white beaks.

I marveled at all this bird life while I walked around the edge of the lake. It was very easygoing. At the opposite side of the lake from its entrance, there are some lovely oak-studded hills that harbor more bird life, notably hawks. Views of nature all around extend to Mesa Grande and Palomar Mountain.

One especially exciting bird I saw was a white pelican near the far side of the lake. They migrate here beginning in September and leave by February, according to the *San Diego County Bird Atlas* by Philip Unitt and the San Diego Natural History Museum. The white pelican is normally "gregarious ... foraging in teams," according to Unitt, but the one I saw was alone. The fairly rare species might nest at Lake Henshaw "if not persecuted by fishermen," says Unitt.

When I reached a little more than 2.0 miles around the lake, I decided to turn back instead of trying to go all the way around the lake. The lake is said to be about five miles around, but the man at the store who gave me my day-use permit said a creek (I believe it's the San Luis Rey River) on the northeast side of the dam is sometimes hard to cross.

Lake Henshaw's dam on the San Luis Rey River was constructed in 1923, making it the sixth oldest dam to create a reservoir in San Diego County. The older ones are Lake Cuyamaca and Sweetwater Reservoir, both in 1888; Lake Morena in 1912; Lake Hodges in 1918; and Lower Otay Reservoir in 1919 (begun in 1897 and reconstructed after the disastrous 1916 flood destroyed it).

William Griffith Henshaw was the visionary behind Lake Henshaw. Born in 1860 in Illinois, he came with his widowed mother and two brothers to Oakland, California, in 1873. He was a very successful businessman, having founded companies to manufacture improved illuminating gas, a ferry system between Oakland and San Francisco, and the Union Savings Bank of Oakland, including the first skyscraper for that city. He also formed cement, salt, oil, and mining companies, according to *The History of Warner's Ranch and its Environs* by Joseph J. Hill in 1927.

In 1911 Henshaw purchased the Warner's Ranch lands from former California governor John G. Downey, as well as the ranch's hydro-electric power rights from H. E. Huntington. Henshaw also controlled the water rights and lands along the Santa Ysabel Creek, which empties into the San Dieguito River. Henshaw organized the San Dieguito Mutual Water Company and built the Lake Hodges dam.

After forming the San Diego County Water Company, Henshaw built Lake Henshaw's dam and eventually sold its operations to the City of San Diego, including land that would become the Lake Sutherland reservoir in 1928.

"This region, which had lain dormant from the end of the boom in 1890 until this water was distributed on it over 30 years later, has been brought to life and is now in a condition of vigorous growth," wrote Hill in 1927. "It is not only suitable for citrus culture, but it is particularly adapted to the avocado. In no other section of the Southwest can this fruit be produced in such quantities and to such perfection."

After I reached the starting point of my hike again, I continued on to the dam, hiking clockwise from the boat dock. This section involves an actual trail that heads up from the shoreline, climbing about 100 feet or so and winding its way through oak groves. You get some very lovely lake views from this vantage point. You can walk across the dam and farther, according to the man at the store, but I turned back after reaching the dam.

It's about a half-mile to the dam from the parking area. Find that unpaved trail at the northern edge of the lower parking area, just past a sign stating, "No Vehicles Allowed Beyond This Point."

Today, Lake Henshaw is operated by the Vista Irrigation District, a member of the San Diego County Water Authority. Fishing for crappie, bluegill, catfish, and bass is popular here, and the lake is open every day. Rental boats are available, and you may also launch your own boat here. But simply hiking here to see all the birds, animal tracks, and unblemished backcountry is worth driving the winding backroads.

Thomas Brothers Map: Page D, the lake near the intersection of Highways 76 and 79.

Before You Go: Download a copy of the map of Lake Henshaw (trails not noted) at http://www. sdfish.com/places-to-fish/lakes/lake-henshaw.

Also, go to www.lakehenshawresort.com for information on the cabins and camping available at the resort across the highway from the lake, and for more information about lake rules.

You must purchase a day-use permit to enter the coded gates of Lake Henshaw from the store at the resort across the highway. It's $7.50 per adult, and free for kids 12 and under with adult.

This trail is open only to hikers.

Trailhead: Lake Henshaw is located on Highway 76, about 3.6 miles west from its intersection at Highway 79, if you come from Ramona or Julian through Santa Ysabel. Lake Henshaw is about 31.5 miles east on Highway 76 from its intersection at Interstate 15 near Pala.

Distance/Difficulty: I went about 5.0 miles total, including the 2.0 miles one-way around the lake and back, and the half-mile to the dam and back. Easy.

9. Santa Ysabel, Julian, and Warner Springs

Santa Ysabel, Julian, and Warner Springs are home to several of my personal favorite trails, including Santa Ysabel Open Space Preserves East and West and Volcan Mountain. Add several segments of the Pacific Crest Trail—every piece of it is beautiful—and you have some gorgeous hiking waiting for you here.

It will take about one to two hours to drive to these areas from the center of the city, but you will find some of San Diego County's finest scenes well worth that effort.

9-1. Black Canyon Offers Journey and Destination

Getting there is half the thrill of hiking in Black Canyon. To reach this fine trail through a deep canyon where a creek sports some small waterfalls that tumble into placid swimming holes, you travel Black Canyon Road, a spectacular backcountry graded dirt road.

Residents of Mesa Grande use Black Canyon Road to reach Ramona. It's maintained by the county, so you don't need four-wheel drive to navigate it. However, it's narrow and hugs the edge of this steep canyon, where sheer drops are obvious hazards. Signs advise, "Use horn at one-lane curves," so take care around its hairpin turns in case you do encounter oncoming traffic that often seems to go too fast for these conditions.

The Black Canyon trail leads to a lovely pond.

Views from the road itself are awesome as it winds through this undeveloped chaparral along the east flank of 4,051-foot-high Black Mountain. Here the riparian ribbons that skirt both Black Canyon Creek and Santa Ysabel Creek stand out below in the canyon bottoms.

According to Jack Brandais's book *Weekend Driver San Diego,* Black Canyon Road is an old one. "I did a bit of research and found it not only pre-dates the Automobile Age, it probably goes back to the Native Americans who lived in the area before European settlers came in the late 1700s," he writes. There's even an old bridge (replaced just a few years ago and no longer used) that was constructed in 1913; it sits just beside the new bridge near the road's junction with Sutherland Dam Road.

From Highway 78 just east of downtown Ramona, turn left (north) onto Magnolia, which soon turns into Black Canyon Road. You reach the intersection with Sutherland Dam Road at about 7.3 miles from Highway 78, but keep going straight ahead on Black Canyon Road, across the new bridge. Very shortly you'll reach the intersection on the left with Santa Ysabel Truck Trail, a gated dirt road that goes sharply downhill. Park either at the top here along Black Canyon Road and walk down that Santa Ysabel Truck Trail for less than a half-mile, or drive down that steep, rockier road if the gate is open and park at the bottom. In either case, be sure to park off the roads and display an Adventure Pass, allowing you to park on Cleveland National Forest lands.

At the bottom, walk along the Santa Ysabel Truck Trail road east for a short way. "This was once the entrance to the Black Canyon Campground, closed about 30 years ago," reports Jerry Schad in his excellent hiking guide, *Afoot and Afield in San Diego County.* You'll see remnants of this old campground, where about a dozen campsites used to be located along this creek. You'll soon see where the road crosses the creek and backtracks to climb up the northern slope of Santa Ysabel gorge. Don't cross the creek; stay to the right, and you'll see an old wooden placard that signals the beginning of the trail.

The trail is not heavily traveled, so it's a little faint in places but is still visible. It winds through some fine old oaks as it weaves along the south side of Black Canyon Creek. In a bit less than a mile, you'll reach the biggest of the pools, where you can see evidence of a small waterfall, but it's nonexistent in late summer. Even so, it's a lovely pool with huge boulders lining its edges and lots of shade from oaks and willows.

The trail ends here, so retrace your steps back to your car. Note the fire damage on some of those hearty old oaks; this area was hit by the 2007 Witch Creek Fire.

When you head back out the way you came on Black Canyon Road, take a left onto Sutherland Dam Road, where it intersects at the old and new bridges, and enjoy that blue-water view of Lake Sutherland on the way back to Highway 78.

Thomas Brothers Map: Page 409, H-11.

Before You Go: Jerry Schad's book *Afoot and Afield in San Diego County* has the best map of this trail and the roads that lead to it.

You can search for Black Canyon on Google satellite maps.

You can also find the road route on the Cleveland National Forest map, which you can order through the CNF website at http://www.fs.usda.gov/cleveland/.

This trail is open to hikers, bicyclists, equestrians, and dogs on leashes.

In order to park on any CNF lands, you must display an Adventure Pass, available at ranger stations as well as outdoor stores like REI and Adventure 16. They're $5 for day use or $30 for an annual pass. For more information on the CNF Adventure Pass, go to http://www.fs.usda.gov/detailfull/r5/passes-permits/recreation/?cid=stelprdb5208699&width=full.

There's a ranger station at 1634 Black Canyon Road in Ramona, just a few blocks north of Highway 78.

Trailhead: While traveling east on Highway 78, just beyond downtown Ramona, turn left (north) onto Magnolia, which turns into Black Canyon Road. About 7.4 miles from Highway 78, just beyond the new and old bridges, you'll reach the intersection on the left with Santa Ysabel Truck Trail. Park off the roads here and hike down SYTT to the trailhead, which is on your right just before that road crosses the creek.

Distance/Difficulty: About 2.0 miles round-trip; easy except for boulder scrambling along the creek and pools.

9-2. Santa Ysabel Open Space Is a Painterly Place

With its meadows of wildflowers, woodlands of oaks and sycamores, and grasslands that wave in the breeze, Santa Ysabel Open Space Preserve East is one of the prettiest places in the county for a hike. It's also one of the more recent. It opened as a preserve in 2006 after the Nature Conservancy bought the old ranch land from local owners in 1999. The county acquired title when the state of California bought it from the conservancy in 2001 with help from the state Wildlife Conservation Board grants.

Today there are 13 miles of multi-use trails for hikers, bicyclists, and equestrians, and dogs on leashes in the 3,800-acre preserve. There's a West Vista Loop Trail that starts off Highway 79 just north of Santa Ysabel, and the Kanaka Loop Trail in the eastern section begins off Farmer Road just north of Julian. Both of these loop trails connect via a portion of the Coast-to-Crest Trail, which will eventually extend 70 miles from the beach in Del Mar to Volcan Mountain in Julian. The Coast-to-Crest Trail and this preserve are part of the San Dieguito River Park.

Santa Ysabel is one of prettiest places to hike.

I took the eastern Kanaka Loop Trail, which follows Santa Ysabel Creek for about a mile and a half of its nearly five-mile, one-way length. I found the scenery here to be lovely at every turn.

The trail follows old ranch roads the entire way, so the going is relatively easy. As I meandered near the creek, I marveled at the wildflower meadows that spread their colors across the landscape in March, April, and May. Painterly swaths of purple are created by countless blooming miniature lupine, one of our county's best-known native wildflowers that can be profuse in open meadows. Interspersed with these violet-colored colonies were lots of little white popcorn flowers, occasional yellow wallflowers, pink phlox, and the adorable baby blue eyes. Enjoying this springtime bounty were many black-speckled red ladybugs. The tall grass made a fascinating show when the gentle breezes created undulating waves of green that swelled across the landscape.

About a half-mile after these wide-open meadows, the trail goes under a canopy of huge old live oak trees, which never fail to impress. Still near the creek, the trail then passes by several enormous sycamores, just beginning to leaf out in spring.

One of the few signs on this trail informs the hiker that these are American sycamores, which can grow 75 to 100 feet tall and live for 500 to 600 years. They are distinguished by whitish, peeling bark. The Kumeyaay natives, who called this trees 'ehpuull, used the inner bark as a remedy for coughs and colds, according to the sign. It was under these old sycamores where I glimpsed a lone wild turkey, who seemed to disappear moments later in the tall grass.

After 1.5 miles, where the trail takes a sharp left near a locked gate, I turned around and retraced my steps back. The trail does continue another 3.3 miles in a more strenuous loop, and it also connects to that Coast-to-Crest Trail that heads into the western portion of the preserve.

The area has long been favored by locals. History reveals that Father Juan Mariner was the first European to visit the valley in 1795, when it had a large Kumeyaay Indian population. By 1818, Father Mariner returned to the area and built the Santa Ysabel Asistencia, also known as the Santa Ysabel Mission, which still stands today on Highway 79 near the western entry to Santa Ysabel Open Space Preserve East.

In 1844, Jose Joaquin Ortega and his son-in-law, Edward Stokes, were granted the 17,719-acre Santa Ysabel Rancho by the Mexican governor at the time.

During December 1846, General Stephen Watts Kearny and his army passed through here on their march to the Battle of San Pasqual during the Mexican-American War. A year later in 1847, Jean Baptiste Charbonneau, son of Sacagawea, guided the Mormon Battalion from New Mexico through here to fight in that war. By 1848, the war had ended, the United States had won, and California prepared for statehood in 1850.

By the 1860s, Santa Ysabel Rancho passed into the hands of various new owners through the 1920s, who pursued dairy and cattle ranching. The last owners before the Nature Conservancy purchase in 1999 were the Cauzza brothers, immigrants from Switzerland who built Santa Ysabel Ranch into three dairies and who passed the property down through four generations.

I encountered three other hikers on the trail who agreed this was one of the most beautiful places we'd seen in the county.

Thomas Brothers Map: Page 1136, A-1.

Before You Go: Download a copy of the trail map for Santa Ysabel Open Space Preserve East at the county's parks website: http://www.sandiegocounty.gov/content/dam/sdc/parks/SantaYsabelPreserve/Documents/Santa_Ysabel_East_Brochure.pdf.

You may also download a trail map at the San Dieguito River Park website: http://www.sdrp.org/wordpress/wp-content/uploads/10.14-Trail-Map-SYP-East.pdf.

This trail is open to hikers, bicyclists, equestrians, and dogs on leashes.

County preserve staff members frequently lead hikes here on select weekends throughout the year. Check the Program Guide at the San Diego County Parks website for details on hikes in Santa Ysabel, as well as other county parks: http://www.sandiegocounty.gov/content/dam/sdc/parks/ProgramGuides/DPRProgramGuide.pdf.

Trailhead: To reach the Kanaka Loop Trail in Santa Ysabel Open Space Preserve East, take Highway 78/79 into Julian to Main Street. Head north on Main Street, which turns into Farmer Road. Take Farmer Road to Wynola Road and turn right; then make a quick left back onto Farmer Road. Pass the Volcan Mountain Wilderness Preserve sign on your right. Santa Ysabel Preserve will be on your left, about one mile from the Volcan Mountain sign. Park in the staging area.

Distance/Difficulty: For the first part described, about 3.0 miles round-trip; easy. For the entire 5.5-mile loop, it is moderate.

9-3. West Vista Loop of Santa Ysabel East Has Mighty Oak Canopies, Views

Some of the grandest oak woodlands are found in the Santa Ysabel Open Space Preserve East, one of the most scenic places to hike in the county. The West Vista Loop Trail there features several oak species and panoramic views that sweep north and west into the Santa Ysabel valley. This trail follows an old road that was once part of the Edwards Ranch, which grazed cattle here for some 75 years. In 1998 and 1999, the Nature Conservancy acquired the 5,400 acres of that family's ranch and incorporated it as the Santa Ysabel Ranch Open Space Preserve. Ownership titles to both the 3,890-acre Santa Ysabel East parcel and the 1,512-acre West parcel were transferred to San Diego County in 2001, which currently manages both.

Santa Ysabel Open Space Preserve is also part of the San Dieguito River Park (www.sdrp.org/wordpress), a joint powers authority formed in 1989 by the County of San Diego and the cities of Del Mar, Escondido, Poway, San Diego, and Solana Beach to preserve and restore land along the San Dieguito River Valley. The river park's goal is to create and maintain preserved lands in this valley offering hiking, equestrian, and biking trails from the ocean to the river's source on Volcan Mountain.

Partnering in this endeavor is the San Dieguito River Valley Conservancy (http:// sdrvc.org), a nonprofit, citizen-based organization helping to implement the river park's planned Coast-to-Crest Trail, which will eventually stretch 70 miles from Volcan Mountain near Julian to the ocean between Del Mar and Solana Beach. Part of that Coast-to-Crest Trail is open for hiking in the Santa Ysabel Open Space Preserve East parcel. A three-mile section of it continues from the West Vista Loop Trail to the Kanaka Loop Trail at the eastern edge of this part of the preserve.

Oaks and views abound in western part of Santa Ysabel East.

This time, I stuck to the West Vista Loop Trail, where old Engelmann and coast live oaks spread their canopies over the trail, one of my favorite sights when hiking in our county's backcountry.

Several signs are posted along the way that identify these native species, also offering their names in Kumeyaay as well as a few interesting facts.

The Engelmann oak—one of the most endangered oak species due to urbanization, reports the sign—is typically smaller than the live oaks, growing to about 40 feet and living 100 to 200 years. It features blue-green leaves and deeply furrowed bark. By dropping its leaves during summer, water is conserved, making Engelmanns "drought-deciduous."

The coast live oak can grow to 75 feet, lives 125 to 250 years, and is more fire adapted than other oaks.

Over 30 percent of the Santa Ysabel Open Space Preserve East was burned in the devastating Cedar Fire of 2003, the largest wildfire in California's recorded history, claiming over 280,000 acres. According to an extensive survey conducted in 2004 for the Nature Conservancy and the county (http://www.co.san-diego.ca.us/ reusable_components/images/parks/doc/Appendix_B.pdf) regarding the impact of the Cedar Fire on Santa Ysabel East, Engelmann oaks suffered the most mortality among oak trees, killing about 30 percent of them. In comparison, live oaks often resprout from their trunks after fires. Oaks are generally more fire adapted than pines.

The West Vista Loop Trail offers one of the best chances to note the differences between Engelmann and live oak species, because you often see the far bluer-leaved Engelmann right next to the greener-leaved live oak.

Poison oak is also identified with a sign on this trail ("leaves of three, let it be"), as is scrub oak, whose name in Spanish is chaparro, from which chaparral is derived. Another sign points out basket bush, which looks similar to poison oak, both of which were used in Native American basketry.

Areas of nonnative grasses are also frequent on this trail, which may eventually be removed according to another 2004 survey done on the biodiversity of Santa Ysabel Ranch Open Space Preserve (http://www.co.san-diego.ca.us/reusable_components/ images/parks/doc/Appendix_D.pdf). This biodiversity survey is especially interesting for its cataloguing of wildlife, including mountain lions, bobcats, coyotes, deer, birds, reptiles, and insects. Several cameras have been set up on the preserve that have captured images of the lions and bobcats, among other species.

I saw a large deer bounding through the trees, but thankfully no mountain lion was in pursuit. I noticed many industrious ant colonies on this old ranch road, and in the distance I spotted the red-tiled roof of the historic Santa Ysabel Mission, which originated in this valley in 1818; its current church dates from 1924.

See what you can spot from this beautiful trail.

Thomas Brothers Map: Page 1135, B-1.

Before You Go: Download a map of the West Vista Loop Trail in the Santa Ysabel Open Space Preserve East on the San Dieguito River Park's website: www.sdrp.org/wordpress.
  This trail is open to hikers, bicyclists, equestrians, and dogs on leashes from 8:00 a.m. to 5:00 p.m. every day in winter; it is open until 7:00 p.m. in summer. It's free.

Trailhead: Go north on Highway 79 about one mile from the town of Santa Ysabel, just before you reach the historic Santa Ysabel Mission. Park on the side of the road.

Distance: The round-trip for the West Vista Loop Trail is 4.4 miles. Moderately difficult.

9-4. Trails Open through Splendid Santa Ysabel West

In 2010, Santa Ysabel West Open Space Preserve opened its gorgeous trails for hikers, bicyclists, equestrians, and dogs on leashes. Although not yet connected, it joins Santa Ysabel East Open Space Preserve to offer one of the most beautiful foothill landscapes available in the county for hiking.

Both the west and east parcels were part of the old Santa Ysabel Ranch and are still leased for cattle grazing. The Nature Conservancy bought the 1,512-acre Santa Ysabel West parcel in October 1999, and a year later it purchased the 3,890-acre Santa Ysabel East. San Diego County acquired title to both parcels in 2001 and currently manages their trails. East opened in 2006, and West in early 2010.

The trails in East and West Santa Ysabel Open Space Preserves are part of the San Dieguito River Park's Coast-to-Crest Trail, a 70-mile-long trail that eventually will traverse the county from the beach at Del Mar to Volcan Mountain near Julian. As you might assume, Santa Ysabel East Open Space Preserve is east of the town of Santa Ysabel and continues from there to the base of Volcan Mountain. Santa Ysabel West Open Space Preserve's trailhead lies about 1.5 miles west of the town of Santa Ysabel.

Gorgeous foothills landscape awaits in Santa Ysabel West.

The trails in Santa Ysabel West, which follow the old ranch road, are much more difficult than those in Santa Ysabel East, because they take several steep up-and-down dips to make for some hilly navigation. I met a couple, Fred and Pattie Hight, riding their pretty palominos, Ronnie and Pie. They were taking it easy because the steep terrain was a bit hard on their horses. But let me hasten to add it's no mountain climb; take it easy like the horses, and you won't be taxed that much. I rate it only moderately difficult. The trailhead begins at an elevation of about 3,000 feet.

The ascents afford fantastic views throughout the lovely Santa Ysabel Valley. To the east, you can see through pastureland all the way to Volcan Mountain. The terrain is beautiful, with its rolling grasslands dotted with cattle, splendid oak trees, occasional boulder outcroppings, and a few glimpses of bright blue water.

At the beginning of the Santa Ysabel West trail, you'll spot an old stock pond. Some of those cattle might be around here, and spring is calving season, so be ready to see plenty of baby cows then. This area has been cattle land for at least 200 years. Native Americans, including Kumeyaay ancestors of those on the current Santa Ysabel and Mesa Grande reservations, seasonally occupied these grasslands and meadows.

Santa Ysabel Creek is full whenever we have abundant rains, and it runs through Santa Ysabel West. In fact, the trail crosses the creek; when I was there, it was quite full. Some hikers could jump across via some boulders, but I took off my shoes to wade through the water at the trail. County plans eventually call for a bridge to cross this creek.

The steep rise from the creek takes you up to a small loop that continues right onto Ridge Trail, left onto a short segment of the Coast-to-Crest Trail, and left onto Upper Creek Trail and back to the main Lower Creek Trail.

On the Ridge Trail, where again you are rewarded with magnificent valley to mountain views, lots of bright yellow mountain violets sway in the breezy meadow. From this vantage point, you can also get a glimpse of Lake Sutherland to the northwest. Lots of wildflowers are adding their colors to this peaceful panorama, including the tiny white forget-me-not, the purple canchalagua, baby blue eyes, and yellow lotus or California broom. By April and May, there might also be abundant purple lupine, because those are plentiful in Santa Ysabel East in spring.

The Engelmann oak is the dominant tree in Santa Ysabel West, according to a county report on its flora and fauna. There are also plentiful coast live oaks here, the most common large tree in San Diego County. They bloom from March to April with flowers called catkins. It can be hard to distinguish between the Engelmann and the live oak. The Engelmann is usually wider than it is tall; its scaly bark is whitish gray and brittle; its branches are crooked; and it leaves are grey-blue or green, though new leaves can be golden, according to James Lightner in *San Diego County Native Plants*. The live oak can be taller, reaching 75 feet; its main branches can be massive and twisting, and its leaves are yellow-green and convex.

Spring is a splendid season to explore the magnificent hiking trails through Santa Ysabel West Open Space Preserve.

Thomas Brothers Map: Page D, just west of the intersection of Highways 78 and 79.

Before You Go: Check the county parks website and download a trail map at http://www.co.san-diego.ca.us/reusable_components/images/parks/doc/SantaYsabelWest_Trails.pdf.
You might also want to check San Dieguito River Park's page (www.sdrp.org/wordpress) for more information.
This trail is open to hikers, bicyclists, equestrians, and dogs on leashes. Santa Ysabel West Open Space Preserve is open every day from 8:00 a.m. to 5:00 p.m. during fall and winter, and from 8:00 a.m. to 7:00 p.m. during spring and summer.

Trailhead: From downtown Ramona, on Highway 78, drive 13.8 miles east and look for the Santa Ysabel Open Space Preserve West sign on the left, just before going downhill to Santa Ysabel.

Distance/Difficulty: The main Lower Creek Trail is about 1.84 miles long or 3.68 miles long round-trip, combining with the Upper Creek Trail, Coast-to-Crest Trail, and Ridge Trail for a total round-trip of about 5.5 miles. Moderate to strenuous.

9-5. Cedar Creek Falls Draws Crowds

Some of San Diego's most dramatic backcountry landscapes are viewed from the trail to Cedar Creek Falls, a cascade that falls more than 80 feet into a 50-foot-wide pool. This popular trail has had a long history. In his masterful book, *Afoot and Afield San*

Diego County, the late Jerry Schad reports that the falls were a popular destination for Sunday outings in the early 1930s, before the El Capitan Dam was built (in 1934) and when auto access was easy from Lakeside.

You can no longer drive here, but the east entry trail at Saddleback Trailhead that follows the old Eagle Peak Road from Julian remains very popular on weekends. There is another trail that reaches Cedar Creek Falls from the San Diego Country Estates neighborhood in Ramona from the west, called the San Diego River Gorge Trailhead. I took the trail from the Saddleback Trailhead.

Cedar Creek Falls is popular and dangerous.

Both trails to the falls were closed for about nine months from July 2011 until April 1, 2012, while the Cleveland National Forest officials determined whether they were safe. Today, a visitor use permit is required to visit the Cedar Creek Falls area, and hikers must have proof of the permit and photo ID in their possession while in that area. The trails to Cedar Creek Falls were closed because a 16-year-old boy from El Cajon died in July 2011 after falling from a cliff near the falls. Such fatalities have occurred several times over the years here, often from people diving into the pool from the top of the falls—a difficult task not only because of the height but because of the rocks that extend out at the bottom and the shallow depth of the pool. Jumping from the top of the falls is now prohibited (all cliff areas around the falls are closed), and U.S. Forest Service rangers are on-site to enforce that ban. Alcohol is also prohibited here, which sometimes contributed to fatalities.

Falling from cliffs isn't the only hazard. One man was airlifted to a hospital from heat exhaustion. Over the July 4 weekend in 2012, eight people were airlifted for various injuries, and several more were transported by ambulance.

Inexperienced hikers may not have brought enough water, especially for the return trip back up that sometimes narrow and rocky fire road. There is no shade along this road, and the steady climb back up (about a 1,000-foot elevation gain) might prove harder than some estimate. "The strenuous hike from Cedar Creek Falls back up to both trailheads requires more than two miles of consistent, challenging uphill hiking," says the CNF. "This hike is not advised for those who are not regularly active or anyone with previous health conditions that can be aggravated by heat or intense physical activity."

If you use common sense and caution, carry plenty of water, and are at least somewhat experienced at hiking, this trail is one of the county's most appealing on many levels. That dramatic scenery is one immediate reward. Cedar Creek is a tributary that feeds into the San Diego River, whose riparian ribbon is on splendid view some 1,000 feet below after about the first half-mile.

When descending to the river bed from the Saddleback Trailhead, look to the north (to your right), and you'll see Mildred Falls, or at least the sheer drop in the cliff where Mildred Falls sometimes cascades. When we were there in late April, there wasn't a drop falling, though the dark coloration of its granite face was just as obvious. If Mildred Falls does have water, it's one of San Diego County's highest waterfalls at more than 100 feet.

This trail also passes by some of the best wildflower displays you will find: red Indian paintbrush, purple lupine and a deeper purple larkspur, yellow monkeyflowers, white California everlasting, tiny purple asters, blue dicks, yellow lotus, yellow and white tidy tips, and even a lovely, round, and radiating head of the purple blooms of what may be wild onion.

As it follows the old fire road (which in places has eroded significantly into the steep cliff below), the trail winds downhill to that river bed fairly gradually, making the significant elevation gain a bit easier to handle. About 1.5 miles down from the trailhead, you'll note a spur trail to the left that used to take hikers to the top of the falls. As posted, this spur trail is now closed. When you reach the San Diego River bed at the bottom, follow the signs to the waterfall directing you to the left. You must cross Cedar Creek twice over placed-stone paths that test your balance.

Soon you'll hear that mighty waterfall and then see it through the cottonwood and sycamore trees. When we were there on an April Sunday afternoon, there were dozens of people crowded at the pond, sitting on the rocks that surround it and swimming in the cool water.

Retrace your steps and hike back up the way you came, making sure you have plenty of water so you can truly enjoy the beautiful scenery in this upper San Diego River gorge.

Thomas Brothers Map: Page 1174, G-4 (where the dotted Eagle Peak Road intersects with itself—this intersection should be where the road stops, and the trail begins on the long leg of Eagle Peak Road that heads west ...)

Before You Go: For details on the visitor permit required here, go to Cleveland National Forest's page on its recreation opportunities at Cedar Creek Falls: http://www.recreation.gov/permits/Cedar_Creek_Falls/r/wildernessAreaDetails.do?contractCode=NRSO&parkId=109033. At this website, go to Permit Area Map, where you can also download a copy of the trail map.

There is no permit fee, but there is a nonrefundable transaction fee of $6 required for each permit reservation; you must enter all names of the people in your hiking group on each permit reservation. You can book these permits online at that website. Up to five people can be included on one visitor permit. Each day allows seventy-five visitor use permits.

For questions and answers about this visitor permit, go to http://www.fs.usda.gov/Internet/ FSE_DOCUMENTS/stelprdb5415400.pdf.

This trail is open to hikers, bicyclists, and equestrians, but it is advised only for hikers. Dogs on leashes are permitted, but "dogs are not advised in this area due to the high number of canine deaths caused by heat stroke each year," says CNF. "Conditions that lead to heat stroke in dogs include exercising in hot weather in areas without shade." Don't go during extremely hot weather, and of you do bring your dog, bring plenty of water for him or her.

Trailhead: To reach the east entry trail at Saddleback Trailhead, from Highway 78 heading into Julian from Ramona, turn right (south) onto Pine Hills Road, about 1.0 mile west of Julian. After about 1.5 miles, veer right (southwest) onto Eagle Peak Road. After about another 1.4 miles, shortly after Silver Cloud road, bear right again to stay on Eagle Peak Road at its intersection with Boulder Creek Road (the road sign is a little turned here and might confuse you). Continue on Eagle Peak Road for another 8.2 miles of dirt road, navigable for most regular passenger cars, until you reach the end, where parking is available only on the sides of the road. Take caution not to block the road. The hiking trail continues on down the old road.

To reach the San Diego River Gorge Trailhead, from Interstate 8, exit at Highway 67 and head north. Turn right onto Mapleview Street and then left onto Ashwood Street, which turns into Wildcat Canyon Road. After 12.2 miles, turn right onto San Vicente Road for 2.6 miles, left onto Ramona Oaks Road for 2.9 miles, and then right onto Thornbush Road; the parking area is at the end of Thornbush.

Distance/Difficulty: Cleveland National Forest estimates both trails are about 6.0 miles round-trip. We found the mileage from the Saddleback Trailhead to be about 2.6 miles one-way, or about 5.2 miles round-trip, with an elevation gain of about 1,000 feet; moderately strenuous.

9-6. William Heise County Park Offers Panoramic View

It seemed especially appropriate that I spied a wild turkey when I hiked in William Heise County Park in November. Fall is a great time of year to visit this 1,000-acre county park for several reasons. It's located just a mile west of Julian, known for apple pie that time of year. The crisper weather suits the higher elevation, and skies tend to be clearer in the fall, so the panoramic views are really astounding.

Hopefully forest fires will remain absent, which can also occur during Santa Ana conditions in fall. Placards at the trails' start point out that over 70 percent of this park was burned in the 2003 Cedar Fire in late October/early November. "As devastating as the fire was, however, our visitors now have the opportunity to witness nature's way of rejuvenating," says the park's brochure and map, available at the park entrance.

There are four main trails here, three of them looping and interconnected, with the Cedar Trail by itself closer to the park entrance. All the trails cover a little more than 5.0 miles. Also here is the northern end of the Kelly Ditch Trail, a 5.5-mile-long equestrian, biking, and hiking trail that heads south into Cuyamaca Rancho State Park.

I started at the Self-Guided Nature Trail, an easy half-mile loop, connecting about midway around to the Desert View Trail to reach Glenn's View. On the Self-Guided

Nature Trail, which has two starting points, meander through oak, pine and cedar forests. It's remarkably lush and green, though burned trunks are dramatic reminders of the fire's devastation.

Climb to Glenn's View for panoramas.

Along this trail several of the trees and shrubs are labeled, offering a little course in local botany. You'll see coast live oak, Jeffrey pine, eastwood manzanita, incense cedar, and silver sage. See if you can find a Coulter pine, identified at the starting point placard. The Coulter pine can grow to 70 feet tall and has the heaviest pine cones in the world.

I took the right fork counterclockwise up the Desert View Trail, which is noted on the map as steeper than the other loop up this trail. For a gentler climb, go up Desert View Trail clockwise, coming down on the steeper part. I took the steeper trail up and came back the same way, which is shorter in distance than the entire Desert View Trail loop (2.25 miles total), finishing on the rest of the Self-Guided Nature Trail.

To reach Glenn's View, the trail passes through several climate and vegetation zones. From the lower elevations of mixed forest, riparian, and chaparral, you reach the high desert, which you'll recognize when you start seeing yuccas and agaves in the tree-free higher zone. In fact, you'll have climbed 900 feet to reach 4,939 feet in elevation.

The reward is an amazing view. Cuyamaca and Laguna mountains are to the south. Anza-Borrego Desert is to the east, as is the faintly blue expanse of Salton Sea. When you look back from where you started, the layers of forested hills and mountains extend all the way west to the ocean. There's a little eyeglass at the trail's end, which didn't seem to bring the distances any closer but still felt like a prize after the climb. It is placed there in memory of Glenn Wyatt, a park ranger here during the 1970s.

William Heise was a Los Angeles inventor of the gurney locking mechanism, and he owned this property with his wife. They had no children and gave the land for a small price to San Diego County in the 1960s.

This county park is also a well-kept campground, with about 70 campsites—some with little wilderness cabins, some with RV hookups, some for tents, and some for groups. There is water available as well as facilities, including some hot showers for campers. But just a day hike here makes a great fall getaway.

Thomas Brothers Map: Page 1156, C-5.

Before You Go: Download a copy of the park map at the San Diego County's website for William Heise County Park: http://www.sandiegocounty.gov/content/sdc/parks/Camping/heise.html.

These main trails are open only to hikers and leashed dogs. Bikes are allowed only on the Kelly Ditch Trail. Pick up a trail map at the park entrance.

For more information as well as campground reservations, visit www.sdparks.org. You can also make online reservations at the county's website, noted above.

Trailhead: On Highway 78/79, just one mile west of Julian, turn south onto Pine Hills Road. Follow the signs to William Heise County Park and take a left on Frisius Road, which dead-ends at the park entrance.

Once you enter the park, locate a brochure and map where you pay the $3 day-use parking fee. Drive through the campground area to Campsite Area 3, where there are some day-use trail parking spaces.

Distance/Difficulty: About 2.0 to 3.0 miles round-trip; easy to moderate depending on trail choice.

9-7. Fragrant Cedar Trail Comes Back in Heise

If you hike the Cedar Trail in William Heise County Park, the fragrance of these aromatic cypress-family trees will add to its forested allure. There are 10 miles on seven trails in William Heise County Park, which lies just south of Julian. The trails travel through mixed forest, riparian, and chaparral habitats, offering some sweeping views along the way. The 2.25-mile Desert View Trail is a loop in the park's northern section that, as its name implies, offers a panoramic vista into the desert.

This time, I headed to the park's southern section and combined the 1.0-mile Cedar Trail with the 1.0-mile Potter Loop Trail and a portion of the Harrison Park Trail (an access road). That made a fine loop through those cedar forests and chaparral areas, where wide views take in the hills to the south and southeast of Julian.

This entire area was hit hard by the disastrous Cedar Fire, the 2003 conflagration that remains the largest fire in recorded California history. It burned more than 280,000 acres in October 2003, killed 15 people, and destroyed 2,232 homes, including some 750 in Julian alone. About 70 percent of William Heise County Park was destroyed in the blaze.

Now, more than 10 years later, you will see many cedar saplings growing along the Cedar Trail itself. Identify the incense cedar tree by its reddish-brown, deeply furrowed bark, as well as its leaves, which are not like the singular needles of a pine tree. Cedar "leaves" are evergreen, but are many-branched and rather flat, webbed, and bright green.

You'll also find lots of Jeffrey and Coulter pines here, as well as coast live oaks.

One of the biggest thrills along the Cedar Trail during the July my friend and I were there was the sighting of a Humboldt tiger lily, the first one I've seen on any trail. This showstopper features several large orange-yellow flowers with dark red spots whose petals curve strongly back toward the stem.

Find the beginning of the Cedar Trail south of Areas 1 and 2. Look for the connector trails south of both the RV Loop and the Cabin Loop (for cabins 3–14) and Campsites 41–60.

We hiked the Cedar Trail loop clockwise, which makes for a slightly easier incline. Follow the signs to the Potter Loop Trail, which lies south off that Harrison Park Trail

Cedars make a comeback on Heise's Cedar Trail.

road, and head to the left there for a clockwise loop as well, which makes for a much easier incline on this steep trail. These are fairly steep trails; my GPS unit logged more than 950 feet elevation change for the entire route. The Potter Loop Trail heads out of the forest and into the chaparral hillsides. Although there is little shade in this area with just a few scattered oaks, the views extend across the hills both south and east. The Kumeyaay enjoyed these views, too, and William Heise County Park is home to some morteros where ancient women once ground acorns into flour.

This land was also home to two gold mines (long ago abandoned and sealed). Julian reaped worldwide fame in 1870 when Fred Coleman found gold in Coleman Creek just west of Julian. The gold boom ended by 1876, though mining in the area continued into the early 20th century. The heyday of Julian's gold mining occurred from 1870 to 1876, during which time 240,000 ounces (15,000 pounds) had been mined, worth some $362 million in today's dollars, according to a Junior Ranger publication at William Heise park.

Many of this area's cedars were harvested during the building of Julian, and a large sawmill once stood just south of the Heise park's main restroom.

William Heise was a businessman from Los Angeles. In 1932 he invented the "electric three-way casket table," which was used to transport caskets in ambulances and hearses. In 1941, he bought some 900 acres just south of Julian, which he sold to the County of San Diego in 1967 for $67,000. In 1988, the Woolman family sold the land to the south of the current picnic area, and today William Heise County Park consists of 929 acres.

William Heise County Park was officially opened in 1970 and was actually the county's first fully functioning campground. Today the county park offers 14 year-round wooden cabins, 20 partial hookup sites for RVs and campers, 37 non-hookup sites, and 42 tent-only sites.

These loop trails offer an excellent survey of the montane beauties—evergreen trees, oaks, and hilltop views—that define Julian. They can also connect to the 5.75-mile Kelly Ditch Trail that connects to Cuyamaca Rancho State Park to the south.

Thomas Brothers Map: Page 1156, C-5, where Frisius Drive dead-ends into Heise Park Road.

Before You Go: Download a copy of the trail map from the county's parks website: http://www. co.san-diego.ca.us/reusable_components/images/parks/doc/Trails_Heise.pdf.
The Cedar Trail is hikers only, but the Potter Loop Trail, Harrison Park Trail, and Kelly Ditch Trail are also open to mountain bikers and equestrians. Dogs on leashes are permitted on all the trails.
There is a $3 day-use fee, and parking is available in day-use areas only, not in marked campsite or cabin spots.

Trailhead: From Highway 78 heading east into Julian from Ramona, turn right (south) onto Pine Hills Road (following signs for William Heise County Park). Turn left (east) onto Frisius Road until it stops at the county park.

Distance/Difficulty: Combining the Cedar Trail and the Potter Loop Trail with a short foray onto the Kelly Ditch Trail made for a little less than 3.0 miles total; moderately strenuous with some 900 feet in elevation gain.

9-8. Inaja Memorial Is Easy Intro to Local Hiking

The Inaja Memorial Trail, one of four National Recreation Trails in San Diego County, offers an easy introduction to hiking here. It's a half-mile loop trail with 11 markers, accompanied by an interpretive brochure that points out natural features, views, and even some history.

Between Santa Ysabel and Julian, the Inaja trail was constructed in 1962 and is a memorial to 11 firefighters who lost their lives here in the 43,611-acre Inaja Forest Fire of 1956. It was designated a National Recreation Trail in 1980. There are over 1,000 National Recreation Trails in the 50 states. The National Trail System Act of 1968 authorized creation of this system of trails, and new trails are added every year. Designation provides benefits such as technical assistance and access to funding. The four National Recreation Trails in San Diego County are Inaja Memorial Trail, Bayside at Cabrillo National Monument, Noble Canyon in Laguna, and Observatory in Palomar.

The Inaja Memorial Trail leaves a popular picnic park and carves through a chaparral habitat that sits at about 4,000 feet elevation. The trail weaves through enormous granite boulders and lots of live oaks. Pick up a copy of the brochure at the trailhead. Marker No. 2 points out that the live oak trees are evergreens, whose acorns were a food staple for the Diegueño Indians who lived here. The acorn of the black oak at higher elevations was their favorite, with the live oak acorn their second choice. The acorns were dried, shelled, and ground into a coarse meal.

Children will enjoy Inaja Memorial Trail.

Marker No. 3 sits next to a scrub oak, a typical plant in chaparral. "Chaparro is the Spanish name for a small shrubby oak … Chaparral means thicket of chaparros," says the brochure. Deer and other animals eat these acorns.

Marker No. 5 offers a fantastic view across Santa Ysabel Valley. The brochure says that in 1795, Father Juan Mariner and Sergeant Pablo Grijalva led a Spanish party of explorers here, where they found the friendly village of Elcuanan. Mariner named this valley Santa Ysabel, "Saint Elizabeth." In fall of 1818, an adobe chapel was built near the site of Santa Ysabel's present church.

Rancho Santa Ysabel was granted to Jose Joaquin Ortega in 1834, who kept sheep and cattle here. General Kearny and Kit Carson found provisions at Santa Ysabel when they led a small contingent of the American army here during the Mexican-American War in 1846, just before going to San Pasqual, where they were defeated by the Mexican Lancers.

The manzanitas found near Marker No. 6 are full of tiny red berries during fall. The name comes from the Spanish manzana, meaning "apple," referring to these fruits that were favored by the Diegueños—and still are by coyotes and deer.

Just beyond this marker, another marker instructs hikers that the trail turns a hard right. This part of the trail affords fine views to the southwest into the San Diego River Canyon as well as to the east into the Pine Hills neighborhood of Julian. I didn't see the final five markers, so when I reached the end, I retraced my steps to find them. It turns out that where that sign points to the trail going right, the original trail actually continues to the left, where markers 7–11 are found, pointing out chamise plants that "are very important to fire ecology," that white sage and buckwheat are both good honey producers, that the granite boulders consist mainly of quartz diorite and granodiorite and host lots of lichen, and that views into Julian recall gold discoveries there in 1870.

Also on this part of the original trail is a lookout with a scope and directional plaque that points to Mount Woodson, Mount Gower, the San Miguel Mountains, San Diego River, and Cuyamaca Peak.

The entire loop is only about a half-mile, but when you take the two routes back, you've added another quarter-mile or so. The extra explorations and discoveries are well worth doubling that last half.

Thomas Brothers Map: Page 1135, C-4.

Before You Go: For more information, go to Cleveland National Forest's website for day hiking (http://www.fs.usda.gov/activity/cleveland/recreation/hiking/?recid=47396&actid=50) and find Inaja Trail in the Capitan Back Country Area.

You can also find Inaja Memorial Picnic Site at http://www.fs.usda.gov/recarea/cleveland/recreation/recarea/?recid=47546&actid=70.

For more information on the National Recreation Trails program, go to http://www.nps.gov/nts/index.htm.

This trail is open to hikers and dogs on leashes.

Even though it's on Cleveland National Forest lands, where an Adventure Pass is usually required to park, there is no pass required at Inaja.

Trailhead: On Highway 78/79 between Ramona and Julian, the well-marked Inaja Memorial Picnic Area is located 1.0 mile east of Santa Ysabel or about 6.0 miles west of Julian.

Distance/Difficulty: About 0.5 mile to 0.75 mile round-trip; easy.

9-9. Vast Views, Wildflowers in Eagle Peak Preserve

Eagle Peak Preserve is called the flagship of the San Diego River Park Foundation. It is its original open-space preserve, established in 2003. This 516-acre preserve is located just above the popular Cedar Creek Falls eastern trailhead and includes some of those remarkably dramatic views down into the San Diego River gorge. The preserve is located off Eagle Peak Road a half-mile before its end at Saddleback Trailhead, where the trail begins to Cedar Creek Falls. There are three entrances to Eagle Peak Preserve, but the second is the one with the main trail and limited parking off the road.

The Historic Trail, so named by a trail map at the trailhead, follows an old road that was once the main road into Julian. The first mail was carried to Julian on horseback over the Eagle Peak Trail by Chester Gunn in the fall of 1870, according to a plaque at the trailhead.

Gunn, who was also engineer of the Owens Mine in Julian in 1869, ran the pony express service between Julian and San Diego, making one trip a week on the Indian trails, according to a memoir by his sister, Anna Lee Gunn Marston, in the San Diego History Center's archives.

When stagecoaches entered the picture, the pony express was no longer needed, so Gunn opened the first store in Julian, where he was also postmaster and a Wells

Fargo Express agent. He shipped out all the gold that miners had discovered, receiving a percentage. By 1873 he had taken up fruit raising, planting the first apple orchard in Julian.

The old road into Julian is now a fine hiking trail.

The Historic Trail on Eagle Peak Preserve follows that old road, which is really easy to spot where many of its rock walls remain intact. It follows the route of an old Indian trail. "The indigenous people in the San Diego area have used the San Diego River as a water resource for millennia," writes John H. Minan, law professor at USD School of Law, in a San Diego Law Review 2004 article about the San Diego River. "During the Kumeyaay Period (8000 B.C.–1769 A.D.), the Kumeyaay lived along the banks of the river for at least 10,000 years," he writes. Village sites from this period include two at the river's headwaters, near Eagle Peak Preserve. The preserve is said to include some archaeologically significant historic sites of Kumeyaay people, including some sites dating back as much as 4,000 years.

The preserve is also the site of an early homesteader's ranch, the historic 800-acre Marcks Ranch. William H. Marcks was an early Julian pioneer who homesteaded this property in 1899, according to that trailhead plaque. The German native and his family raised bees here as well as some cattle.

The bees would have loved all the wildflowers thriving in this open-space preserve. In mid-May, that old road itself was sprouting many blooms of white and yellow pincushions and blue sapphire woolly-stars. I also saw beautiful blue larkspur, purple Parry's phacelia, violet showy penstemon, red Indian paintbrush, yellow splendid mariposa lily, pink bush mallow, purple lupine, yellow monkeyflowers, and lots of fragrant white sage.

The habitats located on the preserve include native grasslands, coastal sage scrub, riparian, and chaparral. You'll see lots of chamise, buckwheat, and scrub oak. You'll also see some Engelmann oaks, considered one of California's rarest oak trees that usually features a lighter green leaf than that of the more common coast live oaks.

The trail follows that old road for a steady elevation gain of about 750 feet in its first 2.0 miles. The trail map at the plaque shows two other trails, Two Sons Trail heading south from Historic Trail and Pond Trail heading north from it, before you log the first mile. I didn't see either of those trails (perhaps they have overgrown; maintenance and signs might be good here).

I went about 1.75 miles on the Historic Trail before it became more overgrown than I wanted to hike. This distance appears about a half-mile farther than the plaque map indicates. I turned around and retraced my route back along that old road, marveling at the astounding backcountry views afforded from this elevation. It really is beautiful up here, near where San Diego River begins on Volcan Mountain near Julian.

Both San Diego and San Dieguito rivers begin on Volcan Mountain. The San Diego River Watershed covers about 440 square miles and has the greatest population of any watershed in San Diego County. Five reservoirs—El Capitan, San Vicente, Lake Cuyamaca, Lake Jennings, and Lake Murray—are located on the river and supply water to some 760,000 residents.

Someday, the San Diego River Park will complete a continuous trail along the entire 52 miles of the river itself. That will one day connect with both the San Diego County Trans-County Trail and the San Dieguito River Park Coast-to-Crest Trail. Also, nine miles of its headwaters, beginning immediately south of Inaja Memorial Park outside Julian and continuing just before its confluence with Cedar Creek, are proposed for federal Wild and Scenic River designation, meaning the river would be preserved in its free-flowing condition, and its surrounding environment would be protected. The astounding views down into the San Diego River gorge from Eagle Peak Preserve look like they'll be here for a long time.

Thomas Brothers Map: Page 1174, H-3.

Before You Go: Download information and directions to Eagle Peak Preserve from the San Diego River Park Foundation (www.sandiegoriver.org). Under "Get Involved," go to "Explore on Your Own" and then to Eagle Peak Preserve. You can download a Google map of it here.

You can also download a photograph of the map on the trailhead's plaque at http://www.efghmaps.com/blog/20120310d.jpg. Go to www.efgh.com/maps for a website hosted by Philip Erdelsky, who posts several San Diego County public domain maps.

This trail is open to hikers, bicyclists, equestrians, and dogs on leashes.

Trailhead: From Highway 78/79 heading from Ramona into Julian, turn right (south) onto Pine Hills Road, which lies just a mile or two west of downtown Julian. After about 1.5 miles on Pine Hills Road, turn right onto Eagle Peak Road. Stay on Eagle Peak Road, which soon becomes a well-maintained dirt road; continue past its intersection with Boulder Creek Road. From your turn off Pine Hills Road, continue on Eagle Peak Road for about 8.5 miles to the second entrance of Eagle Peak Preserve. You will have seen the first entrance's sign about 1.0 mile earlier, then this second one, where parking is available off the road.

Distance/Difficulty: I went about 1.75 miles for a round-trip of about 3.5 miles, with an elevation change of about 750 feet; easy to moderate.

9-10. Old Banner Toll Road Still Glitters Today

The trail down the Old Banner Toll Road near Julian shares that city's illustrious history with gold in more ways than one. First, the trail winds down the western slopes of Banner Canyon, where several mines were established in the storied rush to find gold here in 1870. The trail leads to one of them, the Warlock Mine.

Second, the trail follows the old toll road that was essentially created to aid those miners and remains an impressive feat in itself.

Third, the quartz rocks here all along the trail are pretty and surprisingly sparkly. Some slabs appear to be painted metallic gold, and some rocks hold deposits that reflect the sun just the way they must have done in 1869 when rancher Fred Coleman, a former slave, let his horse drink from a creek, where he saw some bright yellow particles.

It remains an exciting exploration today for all these reasons.

Old Banner Toll Road still gleams.

The trail begins off a private road off Highway 78, the current steep switchback route from Julian down to the desert, often called the Banner Grade. Private property surrounds this Bureau of Land Management (BLM) land, so hikers and equestrians must be respectful here and observe those boundaries. Once you're on the trail, the remnants of the old toll road, the views down into Banner and ahead into the desert and Granite Mountain are splendid, as are the return views coming back up the hill of imposing Volcan Mountain, whose highest point rises to 5,850 feet.

Very near the beginning of the trail, a placard tells the story of "The Historical Wilcox Toll Road, Julian to Banner." The road was built by Horace Wilcox and opened in 1871, a full year after reports of gold brought lots of prospectors to the Julian area. The nation was hard hit after the Civil War, and many Southerners fled to California in search of a better life.

Before the road was built, mining machinery in this area, as well as provisions for the miners, were lowered more than 1,000 feet down these steep slopes by a "stone sled," says the placard, "attached to ropes with a tree tied behind the sled to serve as a brake."

Wilcox charged 3 cents per head of cattle, sheep, goats, and other livestock; 12.5 cents for saddle horses; 25 cents for one-horse carts and wagons; 50 cents for two-horse rigs, and $1 for a loaded four-horse wagon. The road was purchased by the County of San Diego in 1874 and declared a "free" road. It was in use until the present-day Banner Grade highway was opened in 1925, according to the placard. The old road was still passable, it says, until the rains of 1979–80 washed out most of it. Now only a trail remains.

After about a half-mile on the trail, a photo is displayed above the first point, where you can see the remains of the Warlock Mine. The photo shows what it looked like before the Pines Fire of 2002 destroyed most of its wooden structures. You can still see the metal fittings of an old tower and the concrete forms surrounding some openings.

Also near here, to the right of trail when heading down, you'll see an old mine opening. This narrow, short entry heads into the Golden Gem mine, but these old holes look to me more like homes for lions and coyotes than places to explore, where claustrophobia must be a constant.

At nearly a mile on the trail, a sharp left downhill takes you to that old mine in another quarter-mile to half-mile. Beware of exploring the old mine because a lot of its tunnels have collapsed, and the area remains an active fault. The Warlock Mine was worked intermittently until 1957. Interestingly, the county declared the Warlock Mine a fallout shelter in 1962, but the collapse nixed that idea.

The entire canyon is part of the Elsinore Fault, which runs from Pala through Santa Ysabel and Julian down into Banner Canyon and the desert, according to Richard F. Pourade's seven-book series *The History of San Diego*. Pourade was editor emeritus of the San Diego Union when James and Helen Copley commissioned him to write this series from 1960 to 1977.

The earthquake fault is one of the reasons Julian's gold fortunes lasted for only a few decades before petering out. "Where the Mother Lode (of the Sierra Nevada) was formed as a mesothermal deposit of great masses of gold-bearing rock moved into position under relatively low pressures, San Diego's deposits were of hypothermal origin of small amounts of mineral-bearing rock forced into tiny cracks under extreme pressures," wrote Pourade. Julian's miners were never assured of finding big gold deposits. The exception, he said, was the Stonewall Mine, just several miles south in Cuyamaca, which mined a "huge and consistent pocket of ore" until it petered out in 1901.

When you reach that spur trail down to the Warlock Mine, a sign is posted stating private property and no trespassing. While the old road continues, more no-trespassing signs make it clear hikers should not continue. I turned around and went back up, marveling at those views of Volcan Mountain but even more transfixed by those sparkling rocks that made my imagination soar.

Thomas Brothers Map: Page 1136, D-7, where Woodland Road ends and then appears to keep going, turning into dotted line …

Before You Go: The best map of this trail is in Jerry Schad's book *Afoot and Afield, San Diego County.* You may also download a Google satellite map for the Old Banner Toll Road Trail in Julian.

Trailhead: From Highway 78 heading east about 1.0 mile outside of Julian, turn right at Whispering Pines Road. Immediately after turning, turn right on Banner Road and then left on Woodland Road to its end at a cul-de-sac, where you can park.

Walk ahead on the unpaved road, marked private, about 0.5 miles to an intersection on the left with a trail sign pointing to the left. Follow that road into the BLM land and the trail straight ahead.

Distance/Difficulty: Add 1.0 mile round-trip for the walk along the unpaved private road to the trailhead. The distance from here to the junction with the Warlock Mine spur trail is about 0.9 miles, with the Warlock Mine trail about another 0.4 miles. Total distance round-trip is about 3.6 miles. Moderate with an elevation gain of about 750 feet.

9-11. Wildflowers, Vast Views Highlight Volcan Mountain

Pass through the James Hubbell Gateway to hike up Volcan Mountain in spring. There you'll see expansive meadows blanketed in cream cups, those tiny, tufted, yellow-and-white wildflowers that often appear in our local mountains but rarely so many at once. When you reach the 5,353-foot-high summit on the main trail, at the southeastern end of the tiny summit loop, you'll also find some large colonies of bright orange California poppies, our state flower, on a hillside looking down over Julian.

At the top are panoramic views to the east, where you'll see the Banner Grade of Highway 78 descending to Earthquake Valley in Anza-Borrego and, on a very clear day, the Salton Sea. To the west, views extend across the rolling pastures of Santa Ysabel and even to the ocean.

Vast views and bountiful wildflowers are atop Volcan Mountain.

Volcan Mountain is actually a horseshoe-shaped series of ridges that extend north to south for about 15 miles, according to a report made by Susan M. Hector for CalFire of the California Department of Forestry (to see full report, go to http://calfire. ca.gov/resource_mgt/archaeology-volcan_report.php). Its highest point at Oak Ridge, a bit farther north from the summit trail's, reaches 5,510 feet high.

The main trail up to Volcan's easily accessible southern summit is open all the way to the top only on weekends from April through November. During the rest of the week, however, you can hike up the main trail (an old Jeep road) to the midsummit gate, about 1.5 miles one-way. You may also hike up the Five Oaks Trail, the only other trail located on Volcan Mountain so far, which is a single-track trail open only to hikers that begins off the main trail after about 0.35 miles and then connects again to the main trail after 1.1 miles. The main fire road summit trail is open to hikers, bicyclists, and equestrians, but dogs are not allowed in this wilderness preserve.

The climb to the top is fairly steep. When you reach that second intersection with the Five Oaks Trail after about 1.4 miles, you will already have logged an elevation gain of about 730 feet. To reach the summit, the elevation gain is about 1,100 feet in about 2.5 miles. You will have passed through some lovely old oak groves along the road, forests of conifers, and some mountain meadows complete with lots of spring wildflowers, including blue lupine, scarlet buglers, tiny yellow mountain violets, purple filaree, yellow fiddlenecks, and bright white fleabane daisies invariably visited by tiny, gossamer-winged butterflies.

After that first really steep stretch, the trail evens out a bit, and though it still climbs, the grade isn't as hard. A short way after the midsummit gate, you'll begin to see the cream cups covering the hillsides. Near the summit, you'll reach an area known as Simmons Flat, a high-mountain meadow punctuated by a few huge live oaks.

In fact, some of the largest canyon live oaks in the state are found on Volcan Mountain, according to Hector's report. In spring, you'll pick out the new bright green, deeply lobed leaves of the black oaks, the only native oak here that loses its leaves in the fall.

Black oak acorns were favored by early native people who populated Volcan Mountain for thousands of years. The Kumeyaay-Ipai Indians made Volcan Mountain their home, and the area was also important to the Luiseño people, who lived just north of the Kumeyaay. Archaeological studies conducted on Volcan Mountain since the 1990s have identified more than 60 sites of late prehistoric (about 1,500 years ago) inhabitants. Among them are many milling areas in bedrock that feature deep morteros, shallower metates and slicks, rock walls and rock enclosures, several boulders with cupules, lots of pottery remnants, and more. The cupules are small, cup-shaped depressions that have been ground onto rocks. These forms are found all over the world, but little is understood about their purpose. They are usually found near morteros and may also occur with pictographs in rock shelters. They may have been associated with religious activities or even fertility ceremonies, posits Hector.

Although you won't see these archaeological sites on Volcan's main trails, you will see a more recent artifact of the past. Near the summit you'll walk past an old rock chimney with a placard that notes it was once part of a cabin built when Volcan Mountain was on the short list of locations tested between 1928 and 1932 for placement of the Hale Telescope, which ultimately landed on Palomar Mountain.

The Volcan Mountain Wilderness Preserve is part of the San Diego County Parks Department. Guided hikes up Volcan Mountain are offered frequently on weekends from spring through fall. Check Volcan Mountain Foundation's website for a schedule: www.volcanmt.org.

Volcan's main trail is the eastern end of San Dieguito River Park's Coast-to-Crest Trail that will one day stretch 70 miles from here to the ocean at Del Mar. Volcan Mountain is home to the headwaters of the San Dieguito River. Volcan's Ironside Spring feeds Santa Ysabel Creek, which 25 miles farther west meets Santa Maria Creek in San Pasqual Valley to become the San Dieguito River.

Climb up to its source for one of the finest hikes in the county.

Thomas Brothers Map: Page 1136, 3-B, where the dotted line road intersects with Farmer Road just north of Wynola Road.

Before You Go: Download a copy of the trail map from the San Dieguito River Park's website: http://www.sdrp.org/wordpress/trails/.

The main trail all the way to the summit is open only on Saturdays and Sundays from April through November, 9:00 a.m. to 5:00 p.m. The trail to the midsummit gate and the Five Oaks Trail (hikers only) are open sunrise to sunset, year-round.

Dogs are not allowed. The main trail is open to hikers, bicyclists, and equestrians.

Trailhead: From the main intersection in downtown Julian, turn north on Main Street, which soon turns into Farmer Road. When Farmer Road dead-ends at Wynola, turn right and then go one hundred yards; turn left to continue on Farmer Road again. The sign for Volcan Mountain appears shortly on the right. Park on the shoulder of Farmer Road by the preserve's sign.

Distance/Difficulty: The main summit trail is about 5.0 miles round-trip with about 1,100 feet in elevation gain; fairly strenuous.

9-12. Volcan's Five Oaks Trail Is a County Jewel

For hiking to some of the finest oak woodlands, native grassland meadows, and sweeping views of the backcountry, Five Oaks Trail in the Volcan Mountain Wilderness Preserve near Julian is hard to beat. Opened in 2004, the narrow, hikers-only, 1.3-mile trail was built with help from the California Conservation Corps. According to the sign at its trailhead, it offers a "more intimate hiking experience under oak canopies, through chaparral and across open meadows, revealing stunning vistas of the San Diego County backcountry."

The other main trail through Volcan Mountain's preserve follows a fire road up to the summit.

The lovely Five Oaks Trail offers an opportunity to try to identify the five oak species that give the trail its name. According to Tom Chester's comprehensive plant guide to the trails on Volcan Mountain (http://tchester.org/sd/plants/guides/lagunas/volcan_mtn.html), the five oak tree species found here are black oak, canyon live oak, coast live oak, Engelmann oak, and interior live oak. There are also lots of scrub oak and even poison oak, but interestingly, poison oak is a type of sumac rather than an oak species.

Five Oaks Trail is among the most alluring trails countywide.

Several signs along the trail identify some of these oak species, along with other plants that are typical of the habitats found here (coastal sage scrub, chaparral, and oak woodland). This trail's signs are among the best I've seen for learning to identify these plants; they also reveal the plant's name in Kumeyaay and the uses the native people had for them. One sign in the middle of the white-blooming California buckwheat says it is the dominant plant of coastal sage scrub, flowering from June through October. It was used by natives for medicine and food. Another sign identifying scrub oak points out that the word chaparral is derived from the Spanish word *chaparro*, meaning scrub oak. The sign identifying white sage, with its smooth white leaves and lovely fragrance, points out that natives used it to purify and cleanse.

The first massive oak tree you'll notice is on the fire road that proceeds uphill from the trailhead that begins at the splendid carved wooden gates created by Julian's famed artist, James Hubbell. You hike up about 0.4 miles on this road before you reach the trailhead to the Five Oaks Trail. Just before that junction, you'll see an enormous coast live oak whose characteristic large, spreading branches give it a huge canopy. Its relatively short trunk is massive, and the tree is surely over 60 feet tall. This species can often grow as old as 250 years, according to another sign on the trail, and this one must be very old. The infamous Cedar Fire of October 2003 burned 20 percent of this 2,600-acre preserve, but oaks remarkably often survive after fires.

Another reason Five Oaks Trail offers such a beautiful foray is because its native vegetation is virtually undisturbed.

Early peoples, including the Kumeyaay, Ipai, Cupeno, Cahuilla, and Luiseño, hunted and gathered on Volcan Mountain for some 11,000 years, according to the Volcan Mountain Preserve Foundation's web site. When the Spaniards arrived in Southern California in the late 18th century and later when gold was discovered in Julian in the 1870s, Anglo-Americans poured into this area. In the early 20th century, Volcan was homesteaded, mined, and logged, "but to a lesser degree than other mountains in Southern California," says the foundation.

The trail switchbacks up the mountain, gaining about 400 feet elevation and offering several spots for panoramic views over Julian's apple and wine country. On a very clear day, you may even see the Pacific Ocean. Volcan Mountain is the eastern terminus of the Coast-to-Crest Trail, the 70-mile trail spearheaded by the San Dieguito River Park and its conservancy that will one day reach the beach at Del Mar. The end of the Five Oaks Trail is marked by a stone bench that offers yet another striking vista, this one to the east, past Banner Grade to the threshold of the Anza-Borrego Desert.

The trail continues a short way to a junction with the main Fire Road Trail, which is a bit shorter for a return route. I retraced my way back along this lovely Five Oaks Trail, enjoying those views once more. This trail has now made my top-ten list.

Thomas Brothers Map: 1136, B-3.

Before You Go: Download a trail map at either the San Diego County Parks & Recreation page (http://www.co.san-diego.ca.us/reusable_components/images/parks/doc/Trails_Volcan. pdf), or at the San Dieguito River Park's website (http://www.sdrp.org/wordpress/wp-content/ uploads/10.14-Trail-Map-Volcan-Mountain.pdf).

Operated by San Diego County, Volcan Mountain Wilderness Preserve is open seven days a week, dawn to dusk, for hiking only on its Five Oaks Trail (no dogs allowed), or for hiking, biking, and horseback riding on its Fire Road Trail to midsummit.

Full summit hikes are offered only on weekends, April through November.

For more information, check the Volcan Mountain Preserve Foundation's website: http:// www.volcanmt.org.

Trailhead: Head to Julian on Highway 79. At the main intersection in town, turn north onto Main Street, which soon becomes Farmer Road. After about 2.2 miles, turn right onto Wynola Road for only about 100 yards; then turn left back onto the continuation of Farmer Road. In another 100 yards, the entrance to Volcan Mountain is on the right. Park outside the preserve along the side of Farmer Road.

Distance/Difficulty: About 3.4 miles round-trip. Moderate.

9-13. PCT Near Warner Springs Surveys Historic Lands

The Pacific Crest National Scenic Trail carves through a lot of San Diego County's backcountry. About 300 people annually make the entire 2,650-mile expedition from the border of Mexico to Canada through California, Oregon, and Washington, but we less intrepid hikers can still enjoy several of its scenic segments.

The Caliente Wilderness section of the PCT offers an exciting adventure, starting with the road to reach its trailhead. The views here are sweeping as you hike along a ridge that offers an unobstructed vantage point over the vast Valle de San Jose as well as Lake Henshaw to the south, while 4,000-foot-high peaks, including Rocky Mountain and Pine Mountain, are immediately to the west of the trail. There is little sign of development in this part of the county, and there is virtually no sound of any kind. Lots of boulder outcroppings add interest.

Caliente Wilderness views extend to peaks and lake.

The road off Highway 79 leading to the trailhead is called Indian Flats Road (on some maps also called Lost Valley Road), and though it's paved for the full seven miles to the very nice, primitive Indian Flats campground (after which the road becomes dirt), it is a very narrow, essentially one-lane road where you hope you don't encounter any oncoming traffic.

The PCT trailhead here begins with a large map showing the trail both north and south from this starting point. After a short half-mile hike on the old access road, you reach the PCT junction; watch for the stacks of rocks to alert you. The trail's southerly direction is practically behind you, so you could miss it if the signs signifying the PCT weren't placed here. The southern route descends for about 3.0 miles to Agua Caliente Creek.

I took the northern route, which essentially meant I kept walking straight ahead at that PCT junction. The trail was narrower there and carved its way along the ridge.

There are no trees here, which may be why there were virtually no birds—hence, the exceptionally quiet atmosphere. However, there are huge manzanita shrubs at least 10 feet tall, and they are lovely specimens with their smooth red bark and red berries in the fall. There are also equally tall shrubs with scruffier bark and more needlelike leaves that I think are goldenbushes. Both species are common natives in chaparral habitat.

As you scan the vast valley, still largely undeveloped, it's easy to imagine life here 160 years ago, when Warner Springs, the tiny town here, was once Warner's Ranch, the only inhabited stopping place between New Mexico and Los Angeles for wagon trains, gold seekers, and stagecoaches. The main business today is Warner Springs Ranch Resort, where ancient sulfur hot springs still draw visitors, along with golf and horseback riding. After bankruptcy and closure, the ranch resort is set to make a comeback during summer 2015 with a full remodel by summer 2016. Its namesake, according to the resort's website (https://www.warnerspringsranchresort.com), was John Warner, a 23-year-old New Englander who went west with famed mountain man Jedediah Smith. The six-foot-three-inch Warner was soon called Juan Largo (Long John), and he married an English sea captain's daughter, Anita Gale, who had been a ward of the widowed mother of Pio Pico, who would become the governor of California when it was under Mexican rule. Warner was awarded a land grant by Mexico for the 48,000-acre Valle de San Jose in 1844; he changed its name to Warner's Ranch and officially changed his own name to Juan Jose Warner. Though he and his two adopted Indian boys stood off an attack on the ranch by 100 Cahuilla Indians, who burned the ranch and stole all the livestock, Warner was ruined and never returned. He did eventually get elected to the California State Senate, where, despite his bitter experience at the ranch, he fought for Indians' rights and protections.

I hiked along the PCT for just a couple of miles, reaching the sign for water at a seasonal spring to the left, where I turned around. You can continue a couple of thousand miles farther north, or even just several more.

One of my favorite parts about this trail occurred on my way back. It was about 1:30 p.m. and the sun hit the trail just perfectly to illuminate the countless specks of shiny mica, making my return really sparkly, a fine ending to this exploration.

Thomas Brothers Map: Page 409, K-7, where Lost Valley Road intersects Highway 79.

Before You Go: The best maps of the entire Pacific Crest Trail are from The Halfmile Project; they are free PDF files. Go to http://www.pctmap.net/maps. For this Caliente Wilderness segment of the PCT, go the California Section B, Pages 1 and 2, of the Halfmile maps.

The Cleveland National Forest map, southern section, is also a good one for the PCT. Go to http://www.fs.usda.gov/cleveland to order a map or find the nearest ranger station to buy one.

Note that mountain bikers are not allowed on the Pacific Crest Trail, but this segment is open to hikers, equestrians, and dogs on leashes.

The website OhRanger.com, which offers information on all national and state parks as well as national forest lands, has a description of this Lost Valley section of the PCT as well. Go to http://www.ohranger.com/cleveland-natl-forest/poi/pacific-coast-trail-lost-valley-section.

For more information on the Pacific Crest Trail, go to its website: www.pcta.org.

Trailhead: On Highway 79 north of Santa Ysabel, drive 1.7 miles north from the main entry to Warner Springs Ranch Resort to the Indian Flats Road on your right. Drive 4.7 miles on this paved, narrow road to the PCT trailhead, marked by a large map placard. There is limited off-road parking around here. The trail begins to the left of that map, past the gate on the dirt road.

Distance/Difficulty: About 4.0 miles round-trip. Easy to moderate.

9-14. Agua Caliente Creek Section of PCT is Fairly Easy

The Agua Caliente Creek section of the Pacific Crest Trail near Warner Springs is a fairly easy meander through pretty riparian and chaparral habitats. The full mileage of this designated segment of the PCT is 9.0 miles from this trailhead to Indian Flats road, but of course you can make a round-trip of far less distance. When a friend and I were there in mid-August, it was hot enough to encourage us to turn around after about 2.0 miles one-way, but it was still quite scenic.

Starting at PCT signposts located immediately east of the Agua Caliente Creek bridge over Highway 79 (noting mile markers, about mile 36.6 on Highway 79), the trail heads east on the north side of the creek. During August there was a little water in the creek, but only near that bridge.

The Agua Caliente segment of PCT is often hot and scenic.

Agua Caliente means hot water in Spanish, and although the water in the creek isn't hot, it lies next to the historic mineral hot springs that still draw visitors to Warner Springs Ranch.

In 1795, according to the ranch, a Spanish expedition led by Fray Juan Mariner explored a beautiful valley here below the San Jacinto Mountains. "Besides the majestic grandeur, the adventurers were struck by a remarkable phenomenon, the gushing forth of 'Agua Caliente,' the hot mineral waters that would later bring thousands of visitors from all over the world."

The Aguanga geologic fault gives rise to the hot springs, according to the U.S. Forest Service's official map of the Pacific Crest National Scenic Trail. It says some 230,000 gallons of water flow out of the hot springs every day, with the water averaging 138 degrees Fahrenheit.

For centuries, Cupeño and Cahuilla Indians used these waters for healing purposes. The springs then became part of the 44,000-acre Mexican land grant given to John

Warner in 1844. Kit Carson visited the springs in 1846, and passengers from the Butterfield Stagecoach stopped at Warner's ranch from 1858 to 1861. In 1911, William Henshaw developed the ranch into a resort.

The Pala Band of Mission Indians tried for years to close a deal to buy the ranch from some 1,400 equity owners in the country-club-type property. The Pala Band considered the acquisition a restoration of its ancestral land, because the Cupeño were forced to leave their home here in 1903 to move to Pala, 40 miles north. After the ranch entered bankruptcy and closed in 2012, in 2013 Pacific Hospitality Group, a San Diego-based hotel management firm, bought the resort at auction. Pacific Hospitality said it spent $15 million to $18 million to acquire the property, and it planned another $50 million to fix it up. The 18-hole golf course and some of the guest rooms were expected to be open by summer 2015, with the full resort transformation complete by summer 2016.

The first mile or so of the Agua Caliente Creek section of the PCT crosses private Warner Ranch property on an easement before it enters Cleveland National Forest land. The PCT trail can be a little confusing because it intersects with an old ranch road and other horse trails that lead to the ranch. Much of the trail is marked with wooden posts bearing the Pacific Crest Trail logo, but there are a couple of places where there are three trails that head off ahead. In each of these cases, take the middle trail, and that will keep you on the PCT.

Hot Springs Mountain, 6,533 feet in elevation, is the highest peak in the county, and it looms on the horizon to the east. The first mile or so stays in the creek bed, where some fine old coast live oaks, sycamores, and cottonwoods provide some shade. The lighter green cottonwoods with their heart-shaped leaves are particularly pretty here.

You'll also come to a private campground area that is on ranch land, where signs ask that hikers respect the private property here. You might want to take a short break on the old rope swing that hangs from an oak tree.

After you cross the creek, which is dry during late summer, the trail begins to climb into chaparral, rich with the beautiful red-barked manzanita shrubs. Upon hiking up a few hundred feet on the switchback trail, you reach viewpoints that scan the creek bed all the way to the valley where Warner Springs Gliderport lies. Sky Sailing Inc. has been offering soaring flights in sailplanes, also known as gliders, since 1959. We saw several of the sleek white gliders being towed into the air and then gliding on their own thermals over this scenic land.

After reaching the crest of that chaparral ridge, we turned back and retraced our way, careful to take those middle trails on our return. In the heat of summer, the shade of those old oaks gave some lovely respite along the path.

Thomas Brothers Map: Page 409, K-7, right where blue Agua Caliente Creek crosses Highway 79.

Before You Go: The best maps of the entire Pacific Crest Trail are from The Halfmile Project; they are free PDF files. Go to http://www.pctmap.net/maps. For this Agua Caliente segment of the PCT, go the California Section B, Page 1, of the Halfmile maps.

The Cleveland National Forest map, southern section, is also a good one for the PCT. Go to http://www.fs.usda.gov/cleveland to order a map or find the nearest ranger station to buy one.

Note that mountain bikers are not allowed on the Pacific Crest Trail, but this segment is open to hikers, equestrians, and dogs on leashes.

The website OhRanger.com, which offers information on all national and state parks as well as national forest lands, has a description of this Agua Caliente section of the PCT. Go to http://www.ohranger.com/cleveland-natl-forest/poi/pacific-crest-trail-agua-caliente-section.

For more information on the Pacific Crest Trail, go to its website: www.pcta.org.

Trailhead: Heading north on Highway 79, the trailhead lies about 15 miles north from Highway 78 at Santa Ysabel. The parking turnouts off the highway are located just past the Agua Caliente Creek bridge, which is about 1.2 miles north on Highway 79 from Warner Springs, at mile marker 36.6. Park on either side of the highway in the turnouts. At the turnout closest to the bridge, walk back toward the bridge and through a wire fence, and look for the PCT wooden markers immediately east of the bridge.

Distance/Difficulty: We went about 2.0 miles for a 4.0-mile round-trip. Easy to moderate.

9-15. Extensive Oak Woodland on PCT Near Warner's

Few sights are finer to me than sun dappling on a trail through old oak woodlands. One of the most extensive such habitats can be found for some 2.0 miles on the Pacific Crest Trail near Warner Springs. This segment of the PCT begins immediately south of

One of the county's grandest oak groves is on PCT near Warner Springs.

the Warner Springs CDF Fire Station and heads southeast about 8.0 miles to Barrel Springs on Highway S22, a bit west of Ranchita. The PCT passes by Eagle Rock, a distinctive boulder outcropping that remarkably resembles its namesake.

It's about 3.6 miles one way to Eagle Rock from this trailhead of the PCT, making for more than 7.0 miles round-trip to that destination. But even if you have less time, the first 3.0 miles or so are well worth the effort.

From the trailhead, the PCT almost immediately enters that oak woodland. In keeping with the riparian habitat where the native oaks are usually found, the trail follows Canada Verde Creek for a couple of miles.

As you walk alongside the gurgling creek, the oaks that provide wonderful shade are simply breathtaking. The dominant species here are coast live oaks (the most common large tree in San Diego County) and canyon live oaks (sometimes considered the most beautiful oak). Although it can be hard to distinguish between these two oak species, the coast live oak can reach 75 feet high with massive trunks reaching 6 feet wide, whereas the canyon live oaks can be even taller, up to 100 feet, and sometimes feature multiple trunks that can spread 10 feet wide. Whether or not you determine the kind of oak, these specimens are huge and old, probably hundreds of years. They create lots of shelter as well as food sources for many forms of wildlife.

After those first 2.0 miles or so, the trail leaves that riparian stream habitat and moves into wide-open chaparral, where the views extend for miles and the boulder outcroppings begin to appear. On view from here in the distance to the southwest is Lake Henshaw, created in 1923 when the San Diego County Water Company dammed the San Luis Rey River.

William G. Henshaw (1860–1924) was a banker from San Francisco and Montecito who had been attracted to financial opportunities in these parts in the early 1900s, when he was in partnership with Colonel Ed Fletcher, one of the San Diego County's development and water pioneers. Henshaw bought the old Warner Ranch lands in about 1911 for the purpose of water rights, which he and Fletcher would develop ultimately into Lake Henshaw; they also developed the Lake Hodges reservoir.

The ownership of Warner Springs Ranch Resort has had its share of tales over 100 years. The Henshaw family long ago divested itself of that property, but San Diego County's Pala Band of Mission Indians tried for years (around 2010) to purchase this site of its ancestral village. Most of the 900 or so members of Pala live on their 12,270-acre reservation off Highway 76 near Pauma Valley. Their ancestors, the Cupeño, lived on Warner Springs Ranch lands for generations until the U.S. Supreme Court ruled in 1901 that they be removed. They were expelled in 1903 and forced to relocate to Pala, then a Luiseño reservation. That 40-mile journey took three days; the Cupeños call it their Trail of Tears.

The Pala band opened escrow on Warner Springs Ranch in 2010, but after failing to negotiate the sale with the ranch's several owners, the ranch fell into bankruptcy and was bought at auction in 2013 by Pacific Hospitality Group. Plans call for a summer 2015 partial reopening with full resort remodeling completed by summer 2016.

The property still includes two adobe buildings from 1849 and 1857, when John Warner, who held the Mexican land grant on these acres, operated a trading post here. The ranch was also a stopover for the Butterfield Overland Mail Stage Route from 1857 to 1861. The only surviving stage station building is the 1858 Oak Grove Butterfield Stage Station, a National Historic Landmark, located 13 miles northwest of Warner Springs on Highway 79 in Oak Grove.

The old oaks on this part of the PCT have been here during all these human dramas. Eagle Rock goes back even further, of course. Although I didn't have time to make it all the way to that outcropping, a couple of hikers I encountered on the trail showed me photos they'd taken of the amazing rocks that jumble into a huge spread eagle formation.

For me, the oaks were amazing enough.

Thomas Brothers Map: Page 409, K-7, where Warners is on Highway 79.

Before You Go: The best maps of the entire Pacific Crest Trail are from The Halfmile Project; they are free PDF files. Go to http://www.pctmap.net/maps. For this Eagle Rock segment of the PCT, go the California Section A, Page 13, of the Halfmile maps.

 The Cleveland National Forest map, southern section, is also a good one for the PCT. Go to http://www.fs.usda.gov/cleveland to order a map, or find the nearest ranger station to buy one.

 Note that mountain bikers are not allowed on the Pacific Crest Trail, but this segment is open to hikers, equestrians, and dogs on leashes.

 For more information on the Pacific Crest Trail, go to its website: www.pcta.org.

Trailhead: Head north on Highway 79, about 16 miles from Santa Ysabel. Park on the side of the road in front of the California Department of Forestry station in Warner Springs, just before Warner School.

 Immediately to the south of the entrance to the CDF is the PCT trailhead. Pass through the cattle guard gate and immediately turn right, crossing the wash that goes back under Highway 79. You'll see the yellow PCT signpost, heading southeast away from the road.

Distance/Difficulty: I went about 3.0 miles one-way for a 6.0-mile round-trip; it's about a 7.2-mile round-trip to Eagle Rock. Easy to moderate.

9-16. PCT in San Felipe Hills Another Great Trail

The wide-open backcountry of San Felipe Hills makes for an excellent outing on the Pacific Crest Trail. San Felipe Hills is a 5,325-acre parcel of public lands administrated by the Bureau of Land Management and consisting of a 6.5-mile-long ridge of rolling hills that rise steeply from surrounding valleys. Elevations here range from 2,800 feet to 4,660 feet, but the PCT sticks mostly to the ridge line, so its elevation change on this 3.0-mile stretch is only about 600 feet. The land is largely chaparral, filled with lots of chamise, buckwheat, and scrub oak, but because this ridge lies in a transition zone just above Anza-Borrego, you'll also see scattered beavertail and cane cholla cacti along with yucca.

Find "100" in rocks for the 100th mile of PCT on this segment.

In spring, you'll see patches of colorful wildflowers that paint the landscape pink. These are the fringed spineflower, a member of the buckwheat family, and they appear almost leafless as they spread low across the landscape, with lots of tiny pink flowers with six feathery, prickly petals. Also look for white forget-me-nots, yellow splendid mariposa lilies, tiny purple asters, white pincushions, deep purple larkspur, scarlet buglers, golden yarrow, sunflowers, and purple thistles.

This portion of the PCT was completed in 1985. The entire 2,650 miles of the Pacific Crest National Scenic Trail was not completed until 1993, though its first portions (including the John Muir Trail in California) had begun construction as early as the 1920s. By 1932, six segments of the system were completed: the Cascade Crest Trail in Washington, Oregon Skyline Trail, Lava Crest Trail in Northern California, Tahoe-Yosemite Trail, John Muir Trail, and Desert Crest Trail in Southern California. The PCT appeared on a federal government map for the first time in 1939, according to the Pacific Crest Trail Association.

"The forgotten outdoorsmen of today are those who like to walk, hike, ride, horseback or bicycle," said President Lyndon B. Johnson in 1965 when he called for a national system of scenic trails. "For them, we must have trails as well as highways. Nor should motor vehicles be permitted to tyrannize the more leisurely human traffic."

In order to be a National Scenic Trail, the trail must be 100 miles or longer, continuous, primarily nonmotorized routes of outstanding recreational opportunity. The trails are established by Acts of Congress. There are seven National Scenic Trails in the country today, including the Appalachian (2,158 miles), Pacific Crest (2,650 miles), Continental Divide (3,100 miles), and North Country (3,200 miles). The first two NSTs were Appalachian and Pacific Crest, both designated in 1968.

Every portion of the PCT in San Diego County fills the bill that its scenic qualities "are superior when compared to those of other trails." We have many gorgeous trails in our very large county, but the PCT is one of the most beautiful, no matter where you step on it.

Design of the PCT called for it to stick to ridge tops wherever possible to maximize long-range views. This section south of Barrel Springs is picture-perfect as it weaves atop the San Felipe Hills ridge, offering expansive views across a landscape that is largely undeveloped.

The only citified thing you'll see is the tiny town of Ranchita that lies on S22 (Montezuma Valley Road), right before it plunges down into the desert. Otherwise, it's all hills and valleys and riparian ribbons stretched out as far as the eye can see. To the northeast, you can even spot Hot Springs Mountain at 6,533 feet, San Diego County's highest peak, located on the Los Coyotes Indian Reservation.

This trail segment begins at the watering hole that is Barrel Springs—an old tub with a hose dripping water into it, as well as a sign that notes the water must be boiled for five minutes before drinking. This spot is very valuable to PCT thru-hikers, the 700 to 900 hearty folk every year who usually leave the Mexican border in April or May, with fewer than half of them reaching Canada at the end of September. Interestingly, fewer than 5 percent of thru-hikers go southbound.

The PCT winds south along the ridge and reaches Scissors Crossing, 1,200 feet lower and about 24 miles later. Three runners we encountered the day we were hiking had come up from Scissors Crossing to Barrel Springs for their weekly one-way, two-car outing.

My friend and I were content to hike slowly, enjoying the solitude and admiring the vast views down into Hoover Canyon to the east and up to Warner Springs to the north. One special moment on this segment was the number 100 spelled out in white rocks on the trail—the 100th mile of the PCT.

"The Pacific Crest National Scenic Trail is a treasured pathway through some of the most outstanding scenic terrain in the United States," says the USDA's Forest Service on its PCT pages. Indeed, the trail passes through 23 national forests, 16 national forest wildernesses, and three BLM districts as it winds from Washington's North Cascades to the Columbia River Gorge through the High Sierras and the great desert of Anza-Borrego.

Pick any portion, and you'll be happy.

Thomas Brothers Map: Page D, middle, near San Felipe Hills Wilderness Study Area.

Before You Go: The best maps of the entire Pacific Crest Trail are from the Halfmile Project; they are free PDF files and include notes about water sources and campsites as well as elevation plots for every half-mile of the entire trail. Go to http://www.pctmap.net/maps. For this San Felipe Hills segment of the PCT, go the California Section A, Page 12, of the Halfmile maps.

The Cleveland National Forest map, southern section, is also a good one for the PCT. Go to http://www.fs.usda.gov/cleveland to order a map, or find the nearest ranger station to buy one.

Note that mountain bikers are not allowed on the Pacific Crest Trail, but this segment is open to hikers, equestrians, and dogs on leashes.

For more information, go to the Pacific Crest Trail Association's website: www.pcta.org.

Trailhead: For this segment heading south from Barrel Springs, from Highway 79, head east onto S2, then east again on S22 (Montezuma Valley Road), following signs to Borrego Springs. Once on S22, the trailhead is at mile marker 1, where there is a large parking area on the south side of the highway. The trail heads both north and south from here; we went south.

Distance/Difficulty: We went about 3.0 miles one-way, turning back for a round-trip of 6.0 miles with an elevation gain just under 600 feet; fairly easy.

9-17. Wildflowers, Vast Views in Mountain to Desert Loop

Combine three trails for a wide loop from mountain meadows down toward the desert, and you'll see abundant spring wildflowers and vast views of wilderness. Begin at the Pedro Fages Monument near the northern end of Sunrise Highway, or S1. This California Historical Landmark No. 858 commemorates October 29, 1772, when Spanish Colonel Pedro Fages headed east from San Diego here searching for army deserters. "It was the first entry by Europeans into Oriflamme Canyon," says the monument. Fages led the first Europeans from here into the Colorado Desert, which stretches from Anza-Borrego north to Mojave, and eventually continued to San Luis Obispo. The Fages expedition might well have taken the route one follows here, or one very close to it, that would have followed an old Kumeyaay route between the Laguna Mountains and the desert.

From the Fages monument, head east on the California Riding and Hiking Trail. You'll begin this loop through this high-mountain meadow of Laguna, where spring wildflowers are truly abundant.

Three trails combine for wilderness outing.

If you hike here in early April, you should be treated to one of the mountains' annual spring glories: large colonies of goldfields (tiny yellow sunflowers) that virtually paint the landscape a soft yellow here just northeast of Lake Cuyamaca. Sprinkled among those goldfields are also lots of tiny pink red-stemmed filarees, yellow Johnny jump-ups, baby blue eyes, yellow and white cream cups, yellow fiddlenecks, pink bush mallow, and yellow baby stars.

Hiking along with me through those wildflowers was a coyote, watching me watch him.

After about 1.36 miles, you'll come to a junction with the Mason Valley Truck Trail, a dirt road that leads to the Pacific Crest Trail. You'll come back up via this road, but for now, go right at this junction and past the gate, and in just 0.09 miles, you'll reach the PCT. Head left (east) on the PCT, which heads down into the desert from here. Now you're gazing at the enormous desert below from this perch at about 4,700 feet in elevation. It's one of those wondrous sights of mountains and canyons and valleys afforded from the eastern side of Laguna down to the desert.

The PCT drops about 840 feet in elevation over about 1.3 miles here, making for a fairly steep grade along the single-track trail, open to hikers, equestrians, and dogs on leashes. Mountain bikes are not allowed on the PCT. The PCT doesn't travel through any state parks on this route, and so dogs are allowed here.

This steep descent on the PCT passes between Chariot Canyon and Oriflamme Canyon. Oriflamme Canyon sits below the eastern flank of 4,611-foot Oriflamme

Mountain. "Since the 1880s, people have claimed to have seen 'burning balls' or 'spirit flames' on Oriflamme's east side (oriflamme means 'golden flame')," says the U.S. Department of Agriculture's official map of the Pacific Crest Trail. "Hoping the mysterious sparkles were gold, many prospectors mined on Oriflamme—to no avail. One scientific explanation for the glimmers is that the dry desert wind blowing sand against the quartz boulders produces static electricity or sparks."

Along the PCT here, look for blue and white ceanothus (wild lilac), and in early spring you can see the bright pink flowers of red bud shrubs. You'll also see lots of bright yellow bush poppies.

When you reach the canyon bottom, go right on the Mason Valley Truck Trail, which heads toward the continuation of the PCT. Pass the PCT, which heads farther east, continuing straight ahead on the Mason Valley Truck Trail.

This old road is named for James E. Mason, according to Lowell and Diana Lindsay's *The Anza-Borrego Desert Region*. Mason was the stagecoach driver who took the first westbound overland mails on the initial run of the Jackass Mail route, which went up from the desert to Laguna. Mason acquired the first patent of the old Vallecito stagecoach mail and passenger station around 1878, after it had been abandoned in 1877. In 1891 he also acquired the 160 acres in the valley that now bears his name, where this old route eventually intersects with Highway S2 farther down in the desert.

In about 3.28 miles from your start, you'll reach the T intersection of the Mason Valley Truck Trail; this is a popular mountain biking trail. Go right here and head back up the switchback road that affords more of those sweeping views. When you finally reach the top, which is a slightly longer but more gradual ascent than going back up the PCT, look back over the route you've traveled. There's a lot of wilderness here that probably hasn't changed much even since Fages was here.

After about 5.2 miles total, you'll reach that first intersection with the PCT again. Continue straight ahead through the gate and then left back onto the CR&HT, through the meadows to the Fages monument where you started.

Thomas Brothers Map: Page 1176, 4-J, about where S1 makes a deep curve away from the northeast side of Lake Cuyamaca.

Before You Go: The best map I've found for this loop is Tom Harrison Maps' Cuyamaca Rancho State Park Trail Map, available at outdoor stores such as REI and Adventure 16, or online ($9.95, www.tomharrisonmaps.com).

The best maps of the entire Pacific Crest Trail are from The Halfmile Project. They are free PDF files and include notes about water sources and campsites, as well as elevation plots for every half-mile of the entire trail. Go to http://www.pctmap.net/maps. For this segment of the PCT, go the California Section A, Page 8, of the Halfmile maps.

The Cleveland National Forest map, southern section, is also a good one for the PCT and these other trails. Go to http://www.fs.usda.gov/cleveland to order a map, or find the nearest ranger station to buy one.

No bikes on the PCT; this segment allows hikers, equestrians, and dogs on leashes.

Trailhead: Park at the Pedro Fages Monument parking area off Sunrise Highway (S1), at the 36-mile marker, about 22.5 miles north of S1's intersection with Intersection 8, or about 1.7 miles south of S1's intersection with Highway 79, just north of Cuyamaca.

Distance/Difficulty: The total loop is about 6.7 miles with about 1,000 feet in elevation change. Moderately strenuous.

9-18. Culp Valley, CR&HT Loop Features Awesome Views

Hike the long loop combining the Old Culp Valley Road, the Jasper Trail, and the California Riding and Hiking Trail to gaze at one of the most characteristic landscapes in our county that appears nowhere else. It's a transitional habitat zone that moves from high chaparral of about 4,500 feet to desert canyon at about 3,000 feet, so you begin in a land of glowing cholla cacti and climb up through California juniper, scrub oak, sumac, and silk-tassel bush.

But what really makes this landscape so distinctively ours are the boulders. Huge piles of granite boulders dot most of this area, the likes of which are rarely seen outside this county. They make for a formidable, dramatic landscape, which you can survey from on high, viewing a huge swath of this historic valley. Capping the view on the clearest days is a bright blue line on the horizon that is the Salton Sea, another rare anomaly distinguishing the Anza-Borrego desert. From the CR&HT, you can also see the splash of green that is the town of Borrego Springs spread out below.

Hiking Culp Valley in winter is good not only because the temperatures are cooler but also because the snakes are usually less active. When you're around all those boulders, that's a good thing.

Boulderscapes and long views are found in Culp Valley.

I began this loop with a little bushwhacking from the parking area at the Culp Valley Primitive Campground. After crossing S-22 from the parking area just off the highway, I walked across the high-desert landscape, heading straight from the road to a ridge, where I could look for the Old Culp Valley Road. I found the Old Culp Valley Road, a dirt road, just to the west of that ridge, and I hiked to its spur end of a circle surrounded by wooden posts, about 0.75 miles from the start.

The main Old Culp Valley Road, heading southeast off this short spur, eventually connects to S-22 below Culp Valley Primitive Camp. I began hiking up that old road, catching glimpses of the Salton Sea behind me and marveling at the boulderscape spread out everywhere ahead of me.

Much of this area is scarred by the recent fire in 2012, but as a placard at the parking area notes, "productivity (in chaparral) is increased when fire sweeps through in its normal cycle of 10 to 25 years." Plants such as sugar bush and manzanita send up new growth from the root crown just below the surface. You'll see these sprouts on all the blackened remains of the manzanita.

At about 2.2 miles is an informational placard about the Culp Valley Cultural Preserve in Anza-Borrego Desert State Park. The preserve covers 1,277 acres within the 15-square-mile Culp Valley. "The main features of this area are exceptionally large numbers of rock-shelter dwellings, abundant springs and luxuriant vegetation—all factors in making this area an optimal intermediate stopping place on the seasonal round of Native People in the prehistoric and contact periods, as well as a favored place to graze cattle during the ranching era," says a paper on the cultural preserve for the state park.

According to the paper, in 1925 ethnographer John Peabody Harrington reported that natives named this area "Ackawaka," and there were still some native structures standing then. Ackawaca meant something like "where a stream of water flowed between two limestone rocks, or rock spring." The placard notes that the Cahuilla people who lived here were drawn by all the boulders that offered natural cover for storage and shelter, as well as the several springs that still attract wildlife.

The Paroli family, whose old homesite is just down the Culp Valley Road from where I began, homesteaded here in the early 1900s and ran cattle with Ralph Jasper and Alfred Wilson, both of whom have trails here named after them.

I continued uphill on the dirt road and past the intersection with the Wilson Trail. There was a spur road about 3.5 miles from the start leading to "The Slab," the foundation of an old house built of white granite rocks. According to Lowell and Diana Lindsay's *The Anza Borrego Desert Region,* this house was built by Bert Jones in the 1930s for its beautiful view of the Borrego Badlands, the eastern end of the Santa Rosa Mountains and the Salton Sea.

Back up the dirt road, in another mile (about 4.5 miles from start), the CR&HT intersects. I took that trail to the right (northeast). It then intersects with a dirt road, where I turned right, following the arrow on the CR&HT post. At one last fork with another dirt road, turn left (northeast), heading up the Jasper Trail to S-22.

When you reach S-22, cross the highway and look for the yellow-topped marker for the CR&HT. This trail now heads into that high chaparral, and as you climb up into the boulderscape, the views down into Borrego and over to the Salton Sea become even more dramatic. This single-track trail is harder and steeper than the dirt road. Look for those yellow-topped wooden markers to stay on the trail.

You'll eventually see the Culp Valley campground and parking area spread out below you. The trail descends steeply here until you reach that flat area. Turn right at the bottom to take the campground road back to your car. This is a long and fairly steep trail at the end, so be sure to leave plenty of time so you're not negotiating that descent in the dark. The whole loop took me nearly five hours, with nearly two hours of driving time to get there. Of course, you could do parts of this loop. Park off the highway at the upper end at the Jasper Trail, just shy of the seven-mile marker on S-22, and head down that dirt road. You can also cross the highway to hike the CR&HT, turning back on either one when you wish. The views from the CR&HT are the most amazing.

Thomas Brothers Map: On Page D, but there is no S-22 shown there. This area lies just off—to the west—of S-22 shown on Page 1098.

This route lies between mile markers 9 and 10 on S-22, Montezuma Grade Road.

Before You Go: The best map of this area is the *Recreation Map, Anza-Borrego Desert Region,* published by Wilderness Press and available at outdoor recreation stores such as REI or Adventure 16.

You can also download a copy of the map from the Anza-Borrego Desert State Park's website: http://www.parks.ca.gov/pages/638/files/abdspmap.pdf.

The CR&HT is open only to hikers and equestrians. The Old Culp Valley Road is also open to bicyclists. Dogs are not allowed on state park trails, and they'd probably prefer to avoid those cholla cacti anyway.

Trailhead: From Highway 79, go east on Highway S-22, Montezuma Grade Road, toward Borrego Springs. Park off the highway in the Culp Valley Primitive Campground, between mile markers 9 and 10 on S-22.

Jasper Trail is just before mile marker No. 7 on S-22 on the right; park off the highway at the beginning of this dirt road.

Distance/Difficulty: I went about 8.7 miles total with a total elevation gain of about 1,455 feet; moderately strenuous.

9-19. Short Spur to View on Way into Desert

One of the dramatic entries into Anza-Borrego Desert State Park is via Highway S-22, just east of Ranchita. As you wind down this road, dropping steadily over 3,000 feet in elevation until you reach the desert, one of the first possible stops is Culp Valley. This is a truly transitional landscape that stands at about 3,400 feet in elevation. It merges chaparral into the desert, with vegetation and geologic changes easily seen as you descend to the desert floor.

Culp Valley is a high-desert region of amazing boulderscapes. It is also an area long lived in by ancient peoples. Culp Valley is one of seven areas in Anza-Borrego

Desert State Park classified as Cultural Preserves in December 2010. The others are Coyote Canyon, Little Blair Valley, Angelina Spring, Vallecito, Piedras Grandes, and the Southern Overland Trail.

The actual boundary of the Culp Valley Cultural Preserve lies to the south of Highway S-22. Known by the Kumeyaay as Kish Kawish, Culp Valley on this side is said to preserve significant archaeological and historic features in this ridge-top valley. But the trail I explored here is on the north side of S-22, in the area that also holds primitive camping sites and Peña Spring, a natural artesian water source that was also an attraction to those ancient people. It offers an easy hike when you're on your way down to the desert.

View the desert from the short trail to a natural spring.

But first, a word about Highway S-22. It's also known as Montezuma Valley Road, and it begins off County Highway S-2, just a few miles west of Highway 79. It continues east through Borrego Springs and then becomes Borrego Salton Seaway until it ends at the Salton Sea, totaling 45.8 miles long.

Montezuma Valley Road originally went only about five miles, stopping at Ranchita, according to a short history about it by Tom Davis, a field engineer with the San Diego County Roads Department, now known as the Department of Public Works' Transportation Division. In the first half of the 20th century, Davis says, there were several prison camps in the backcountry, which provided much of the labor for road construction in the desert. Construction of the Montezuma Grade past Ranchita into Borrego Springs, a distance of about 12 miles, began in 1954 and took 10 years to complete. Some 160,000 tons of dynamite carved a way down San Ysidro Mountain. When the road was completed in 1964, the then honorary mayor of Borrego Springs, Gale Gordon, who was star of *The Lucy Show* on television at the time, declared June 24, 1964, a holiday to mark its completion.

Culp Valley is located at about mile 9.2 on Highway S-22. The turn-off to the spring, campgrounds, and this lookout trail is on the north side, a left turn when heading down into the desert. Drive in as far as you dare in a normal car; four-wheel drive is highly recommended.

This road ends with a circle parking area. Off the northeastern end of this parking area, you'll see a sign for Peña Springs and the California Riding and Hiking Trail. The CR&HT heads both north and south from here for 8.0 miles total, reaching from about 1.5 miles east of Ranchita off S-22 to about mile marker 16.5 off S-22, near the desert park headquarters.

For this short foray to the spring and a canyon overlook, take the trail to Peña Spring. You'll actually be heading north off that CR&HT, descending into a natural wash. You'll see Peña Spring, reportedly named for Peña Paroli, a female member of the Paroli family whose homestead site is part of that cultural reserve on the south side of S-22, in just about 0.4 miles on your left off the trail. It's obvious not only from the manmade rock arrow pointing to it from the trail but because of the bright green shrubs and grasses that thrive at this natural water source. Look for animal tracks in the mud here; coyotes, foxes, and bobcats like this spot because of the abundant birds and small animals that also come for the water.

Instead of continuing on the CR&HT, look for a trail and washes that head downhill, basically straight north from here. In another 0.7 miles or so, you'll continue downhill a bit until huge rock boulders will make your way farther much harder to navigate.

From this point, a fantastic viewpoint east down into Borrego and Hellhole Canyon is your reward. Go back the way you came.

Thomas Brothers Map: Page 1098, C-1.

Before You Go: Download a map of the Culp Valley Area Trails from the Anza-Borrego Desert State Park page: http://www.parks.ca.gov/pages/21299/files/anza_culp_valley_map.pdf.
It is open to hikers, bicyclists, and equestrians; no dogs on state park trails.

Trailhead: From Highway 79, head east onto S-2 and then east onto S-22, past Ranchita. At mile marker 9.2 on S-22, turn left (north) onto the dirt road marked as Culp Valley. This road forks left to Peña Spring (about 0.4 miles total) and right to campsites (about 0.3 miles total). Take the left to Peña Spring and park off the road. The trail is at the end of this dirt road, at the northern end of the parking area.

Distance/Difficulty: You could wander Culp Valley for several miles, but this short hike is about 1.0 mile one-way, for a 2.0-mile round-trip. Easy.

10. Cuyamaca Rancho State Park and Vicinity

Cuyamaca Rancho State Park is one of the county's most important and special natural treasures. More than 25,000 acres here feature several of our county's highest mountain peaks (including Cuyamaca Peak, 6,512 feet) along with forests and meadows. The effects of the disastrous 2003 Cedar Fire still are seen here, but in more than 10 years since, resurgence of the forest is also on view.

I always see more wildlife in Cuyamaca than anywhere else, including mule deer, wild turkeys, coyotes, bobcats, and foxes. When some of the springtime meadows are covered in wildflowers, you will find yourself in a hiker's paradise.

10-1. Airplane Monument Trail Honors Aviation Pioneers

The Airplane Monument Trail in Cuyamaca has far-reaching views from its Japacha Ridge vantage point, as well as a memorial that marks "the site of one of the most sought after crash sites in U.S. military history," wrote Alexander D. Bevil in the *Journal of San Diego History*.

After climbing uphill nearly 800 feet, the trail reaches the monument: A bronze plaque at the base of a battered, stone-mounted Liberty V-12 engine reads "In memory of Col. F. C. Marshall and 1st Lt. C. L. Webber who fell at this spot Dec. 7, 1922." The two military officers had left North Island in a twin-seat U.S. Army DeHaviland DH4B model biplane early that morning, Webber, 26, sat at the rear-seat controls with Marshall, 55, the forward-seat passenger on a fact-finding inspection tour of cavalry posts throughout the Southwest. Colonel Marshall was a decorated World War I veteran, and Lieutenant Webber was an expert pilot in what were still the early days of aviation. Their crash would also become associated with several notable people who went on to play major roles in U.S. military aviation history, Bevil said (http://www.sandiegohistory.org/journal/v51-3/pdf/v51-3_crash.pdf).

During a two-week period in July–August 1922, Webber and his copilot, First Lieutenant Virgil Hines, logged almost 4,000 miles in a DH4B exploring and mapping potential air routes. "Arguably, the most historic use of DH4Bs occurred on June 26, 1923, when North Island Army pilots Virgil Hine and Frank W. Seifert made the first successful aerial refueling from their plane to that of fellow pilots' Lieutenants Lowell H. Smith and John Paul Richter beneath them." Within just two months, Hine, Seifert, Smith, and Richter were establishing new world flight records for distance, speed, and duration, including flying some 1,250 miles over San Diego for 37 hours and 15 minutes, using in-flight refuelings.

All of these pilots had tried to help locate the crash site of Webber and Marshall when the two failed to reach their destination on December 7. "By Dec. 17, the search for Webber and Marshall had evolved into the largest combined air and ground search in U.S. military history during peacetime," wrote Bevil. It wasn't until May 4, 1923, that the wreckage and the pilots' remains were discovered by local rancher George W. McCain when he was riding on horseback along Japacha Ridge.

Early aviators are honored with a memorial on the Cuyamaca trail.

The memorial was dedicated in May 1923 and was also refurbished by Civilian Conservation Corps workers in 1934, who constructed the Airplane Monument Trail, and again in 1968 when the state parks improved the monument. Colonel Seifert was the only participant surviving then, and he talked about the search for the two men.

Colonel Seifert had also been a San Diego City Councilman from 1927 to 1929, during which time he led the campaign to develop Lindbergh Field for national civilian aviation by dredging San Diego Bay to create fill for the airfield, acquiring the unofficial title "the father of Lindbergh Field." He had also reenlisted in the air force in 1942, flying combat missions against Japanese forces in the Pacific, and after World War II ended, he served in Germany and saw duty with the Nuremberg War Crimes Commission. As it happens, he was the grandfather of one of my best friends since junior high school, Ellen Flentye Brice of La Jolla.

I can imagine how hard it would have been to locate this crash site before there was a trail here. It's even more amazing to imagine a little open-air biplane in 1922 trying to navigate these mountains in foggy weather, which contributed to the crash when the failing engine meant the plane couldn't climb high enough to avoid the trees on this ridge. Many of the trees are gone at the highest elevations on this ridge since the disastrous 2003 Cedar Fire, which destroyed much of Cuyamaca Rancho State Park.

The trail starts on the West Side Trail, where some fine old oaks and pines still thrive.

After 0.6 miles, it intersects with the Monument Trail, when the elevation gain really begins. The trail passes through a lot of goldenbush, whose yellow blooms enliven the chaparral habitat here in late summer. The only other wildflowers still blooming in late August included pretty pink asters and some delicate blue sapphire woolly-stars.

At about a mile up on the Monument Trail, you'll see views extending far to the west. At the top of the ridge where the monument sits, the views go long across Cuyamaca to the east, including a peek of Stonewall Peak.

You can make a 5.3-mile loop hike by continuing north on Monument Trail from the little spur trail to the actual monument. This trail becomes West Mesa Trail, and then it intersects on the right with the Japacha Fire Road to take you back to your starting point. Or you can climb to the monument and retrace your way back for about a 4.5-mile round-trip.

Either way, it's a fine place to "honor the memory of the two pioneer military aviators who died on this spot while flying outdated machines through treacherous skies over forbidding terrain."

Thomas Brothers Map: Page 1216, upper 6-E, right where 79 marks the highway just below the hairpin turn.

Before You Go: Download a map of the trail from the state parks website (http://www.parks. ca.gov/pages/667/files/CuyamacaWebLayout09301010.pdf), or pick up a copy of Tom Harrison Maps' Cuyamaca Rancho State Park Trail Map, available at the visitor center, open on Saturdays and Sundays.

This trail is open only to hikers and equestrians. Dogs are not allowed on state park trails.

Trailhead: From Interstate 8, take the Highway 79 exit, heading north toward Descanso and Julian. Cuyamaca Rancho State Park begins on Highway 79 about five miles north of Interstate 8, with the park headquarters about ten miles north.

On Highway 79, park in the large Sweetwater Trailhead parking area in Cuyamaca Rancho State Park, just north of the Green Valley campground and south of the visitor center. From this parking area, walk north across the bridge over Sweetwater River on Highway 79 to start on the West Side Trail on the west side of the road.

Distance/Difficulty: About a 4.5-mile out-and-back on the same trail, or about a 5.3-mile loop if continuing north on the Monument Trail as noted above; moderately strenuous.

10-2. Cuyamaca's Azalea Glen Shows Signs of Recovery

Bright green pine seedlings appear bountiful next to the blackened trunks of pines, cedars, and oaks that suffered mightily during the 2003 Cedar Fire in Cuyamaca Rancho State Park. Even more abundant is the new growth of the bushy ceanothus (wild lilac) that also boasts bright green twigs and branches. The Azalea Glen Loop Trail in the state park offers a great look at this remarkable resilience in nature. It's also a wonderful wander through classic coniferous forest and peaceful meadows, and you pass by a few sonorous streams.

One of the most entertaining sounds on my hike there was the *knock-knock-knock* of an acorn woodpecker. Upon hearing it, I'd try to find it, locating its little bobbing red head on a tall pine or even dead oak with lots of holes in it—perfect for storing those acorns.

Such signs of health seem to celebrate the state park's 80th anniversary, which took place officially in October 2013.

The California State Park system was very small in 1928 when its first bond act was passed, allowing the purchase of land for Cuyamaca Rancho and Palomar Mountain State Parks. Ralph Dyar, namesake of a trail here as well as the old visitors' building that sadly burned in the 2003 fire, sold the state 20,000 acres of his ranch, which became Cuyamaca Rancho State Park in 1933. CRSP now has nearly 25,000 acres, almost 90 percent of which were badly burned in the devastating Cedar Fire. To help recovery, the park has planted over 5,000 trees using seedlings from stock gathered in the area.

But even among the "ghost" trees, the vast meadows and streams remain relatively unchanged in the park's 80-plus years. It's easy to imagine hundreds of years earlier, with the native Kumeyaay gathering acorns and grinding them in their holes on the flat granite slabs. In fact, about a half-mile in on the Azalea Glen Trail there are two such slabs dotted with several morteros (grinding holes) that were used by Kumeyaay women for grinding the acorns into flour.

Cuyamaca is an anglicized version of ah-ha'Kwe-ah-mac, a Kumeyaay word meaning "water behind the clouds." There are four main peaks here, the highest of which is Cuyamaca Peak at 6,512 feet. The others are North Peak, 5,993 feet; Middle

Wonderful morteros found on Azalea Glen Trail.

Peak, 5,883 feet; and Stonewall Peak, 5,730 feet. These peaks gather rains from storm systems coming from both the Gulf of California and the Pacific Ocean. Most of the park is at an elevation of about 4,800 feet, so it's much cooler here than on the coast. Wear layers to protect yourself against the chill, even on a sunny day.

The Azalea Glen Loop Trail connects to both the California Riding and Hiking Trail and the Paso Picacho Loop Trail, and there are obvious signposts along the way to guide you. The Azalea Glen trail passes through that mortero-bordered meadow up through more forest, then through a lovely glen of the Azalea Creek. Note the bright red branches of manzanita here. The trail then climbs uphill through lots of rocks to reach Azalea Spring at the top. From here are sweeping views toward Stonewall Peak and the sparking blue waters of Lake Cuyamaca. After joining the Azalea Glen Fire Road for a short time, the Azalea Glen Loop Trail continues downhill to its starting point.

This is mountain lion country, though they are rarely seen. To reduce the chances of encountering one, the park's best advice is avoid hiking alone, especially between dusk and dawn; make noise while hiking to reduce chances of surprising a lion; always keep children in sight and within arm's reach; and hike with a good walking stick, which can help ward off a lion. If you do encounter one, stay calm and face it; do not turn your back or run because this could trigger its instinct to attack. Try to appear larger by raising your arms; throw rocks or sticks without bending over or crouching; fight back if attacked.

Cuyamaca is a true Southern California treasure, and Azalea Glen will show you why.

Thomas Brothers Map: Page 1176, 2E.

Before You Go: For information about Cuyamaca Rancho State Park, go to the state park website: http://www.parks.ca.gov/?page_id=667. Download a copy of the trail map that is in the park's brochure (http://www.parks.ca.gov/pages/667/files/CuyamacaWebLayout2010Rev.pdf).

Also check the website of Cuyamaca Rancho State Park Interpretive Association (www.crspia.org) for news. It usually posts if any trails are temporarily closed.

The best map of all Cuyamaca Rancho trails is Tom Harrison Maps' Cuyamaca *Rancho State Park Trail Map*, available at outdoor stores including REI and Adventure 16, as well as online at www.tomharrisonmaps.com.

This trail is open only to hikers and equestrians. Dogs are not allowed on state park trails.

There is an $8 day-use fee in the park's campground areas, including Paso Picacho Campground where this trailhead is located.

Trailhead: On Highway 79, twelve miles north of the Descanso exit off Interstate 8, enter the Paso Picacho Campground in Cuyamaca Rancho State Park. Park in the day-use parking area. The Azalea Glen Loop Trail begins at the west edge of the picnic area, just a short distance from the day-use parking area; signposts mark it.

Distance/Difficulty: About 3.6 miles total loop; moderate.

10-3. Oaks Make Comeback along Blue Ribbon Trail

Every trail in Cuyamaca Rancho State Park offers beauty and worthy exploration, and every trail there also shows the devastation that still exists more than a decade after the Cedar Fire of 2003. Combine part of the South Boundary Fire Road and the Blue Ribbon Trail to survey the ecological status of this historic land, where you'll also enjoy some long views.

Park in the East Mesa parking area off Highway 79 and cross the highway to begin on the South Boundary Fire Road. This wide dirt road is open to hikers, equestrians, and mountain bikers (dogs are not allowed on state park trails), and it winds uphill from the highway a few hundred feet, where you'll have fine views over the East Mesa of the state park. Look for Oakzanita Peak on that eastern horizon; this rocky point stands at 5,054 feet in elevation.

About halfway along the South Boundary Fire Road segment of this hike, the road makes a deep U-turn. As soon as you round the bend, you'll encounter the big western views afforded on this road. You can see a few layers of distant peaks to the west and a high-mountain meadow to the south, all past a deep green valley. On the other side of the ridge to the west is the Sweetwater River that runs through the state park. To the north and northeast are Cuyamaca and Stonewall peaks.

The forest rebounds along Blue Ribbon Trail.

After 1.3 miles on the South Boundary Fire Road, the Blue Ribbon Trail (hikers and equestrians only) intersects on your left and heads down into that valley. Most of this southern area of the park remains chaparral, and its shrubs are clearly making a comeback. Lots of manzanita, chamise, ceanothus, sugar bush, and scrub oak seem to be thriving on the Blue Ribbon Trail. Look for the spring blooms of manzanita, chamise, and ceanothus here in March and April. Manzanita, chamise, and scrub oak all resprout from their bases after a fire, and you'll see that evidence on this trail.

But most striking is the comeback of the coast live oaks. They are nowhere near what they once were here in Cuyamaca, but the burned trunks have clearly resprouted with new growth.

Virtually all the pines and other conifers throughout Cuyamaca were killed by the 2003 conflagration that destroyed 95 percent of the nearly 25,000-acre state park, and they don't resprout.

In 2008, American Forests partnered with California State Parks, CAL Fire, and Conoco-Phillips to reforest Cuyamaca. In that first year, 9,000 pine seedlings (mostly Jeffrey pines) were planted across 25 acres of the park, followed by 78,000 more seedlings in 2009 and 2010 over 331 acres. Plans still call for more planting across 2,500 acres over the next decade.

In spring 2010, the Cuyamaca Rancho State Park Reforestation Project became the first public land project to be listed in the Climate Action Reserve for offsetting carbon.

Local environmentalists and scientists disagree that part of that reforestation should involve the grinding, mastication, and burning of acres of ceanothus to plant those trees. This issue is ongoing, according to the California Chaparral Institute.

In spite of attempts to remove it, ceanothus continues to resprout from its underground burls and germinates from new seedlings, according to the institute. However, when it has just been removed, exposed soil becomes fertile for invasive weeds. According to a study sponsored by California State Parks, two biologists from San Diego State University, Linnea Spears and Erin Bergman, studied ceanothus (particularly Palmer Lilac) and its comeback in the fire-devastated park. "On a landscape scale, I recommend no vegetation management of ceanothus palmeri dominated stands," wrote Spears. "Ceanothus is a nitrogen fixing genus of California shrubs that serves an important ecosystem function, especially following fire in California's montane forests. These shrub stands will naturally thin over time … allowing establishment of conifers. Ceanothus is also known to be an intermediate host for mycorrhyzal fungi associated with conifer species and necessary for their survival."

Ceanothus (wild lilac) is also one of the great blooming beauties of Cuyamaca in the springtime, with various species sporting white or blue flowers. Its leaves and twigs are food for deer and cottontail rabbits, and its seeds are consumed by birds and small mammals, including wood rats and squirrels.

After about 0.7 miles on the Blue Ribbon Trail, look for a trio of interesting cairns. After about a mile on the Blue Ribbon Trail, it intersects with a trail that heads left (east) to a private property. The trail itself continues to the right just another half-mile to its end at the Merigan Fire Road. Turn back and retrace your route.

The state park and the Cuyamaca Rancho State Park Interpretive Association are discussing a proposal to rename the Blue Ribbon Trail in Jerry Schad's honor, the Cuyamaca Equestrian Association (CEA) reported in October 2011. Schad, who died at 61 in September 2011, was the author of the seminal local hiking guidebook *Afoot and Afield San Diego County*.

"Other local agencies are also looking to rename other familiar hiking trails in his honor," said CEA. I'd like to hear if and when any of that happens to honor the late local hiking legend.

Thomas Brothers Map: Page 1216, F-5, where S. Boundary Fire Road intersects Highway 79.

Before You Go: Download a map of this route from the state parks brochure on Cuyamaca Rancho State Park: http://www.parks.ca.gov/pages/667/files/CuyamacaWebLayout2010Rev.pdf.

The best map of all Cuyamaca Rancho trails is Tom Harrison Maps' *Cuyamaca Rancho State Park Trail Map*, available at outdoor stores including REI and Adventure 16, as well as online at www.tomharrisonmaps.com.

The Blue Ribbon Trail is open only to hikers and equestrians. Dogs are not allowed on state park trails.

Trailhead: From Interstate 8, take the Highway 79 exit, heading north toward Descanso and Julian. Cuyamaca Rancho State Park begins on Highway 79 about five miles north of Interstate 8, with the park headquarters about ten miles north.

Park at the East Mesa parking area in the state park, on Highway 79, right past the Oakzanita parking area and before Green Valley Campground. On foot, cross the highway to begin on the South Boundary Fire Road, just a short way south from the parking area.

Distance/Difficulty: The combined route here of part of the South Boundary Fire Road and the entire Blue Ribbon Trail totals 5.6 miles round-trip, with an elevation gain of a bit more than 700 feet. Easy to moderate.

10-4. Cuyamaca Sampler on Cold Spring Loop Hike

A fine sampler of many of Cuyamaca Rancho State Park's natural attractions can be had on a loop combining the Cold Spring Trail with the Stonewall Creek Fire Road and the Cold Stream Trail. This hike highlights the resilience of oak trees after the disastrous 2003 Cedar Fire, the wide-open meadows that can be carpeted with wildflowers in spring, views of rocky Stonewall Peak and Little Stonewall Peak, and a lovely look at Stonewall Creek and its hard-rock gorge.

Begin by heading northeast on the Cold Spring Trail off the West Mesa parking area. This trail is open only to hikers and equestrians; dogs are not allowed on state park trails. At the very beginning, you'll see a cement container with a sign posting "non-potable water"—that is Cold Spring itself.

The Kumeyaay people who lived here for thousands of years before the Spaniards arrived in the late 18th century called this cold spring Ah-Ha Wi-Ah-Ha, meaning "water colder water," according to a list of Indian place names in the Ipai language.

Walk through forest where legends once reigned.

Mary Elizabeth Johnson wrote a booklet in 1914 titled *Indian Legends of the Cuyamaca Mountains,* and she tells the story of Cold Spring, or Ah-Ha Wi-Ah-Ha. Johnson notes that the Cuyamacas are full of "myths and legends handed down from generation to generation by tribal song and squaw-tale.... Yet so swiftly has the hand of civilization wiped out the old traditions and customs that but few Indians remain who remember them, and fewer still are those willing to divulge them. Only when one comes into intimate contact with them is one accorded the privilege and honor of hearing the tales of their ancestors." Evidently, Johnson was honored, and she dedicated her booklet to "Kwa-mi'e (Maria Alto) whose friendship has been a revelation of the poetic instinct, the dramatic impulse and the nobility of character hidden beneath the stoical mask of our primitive people." You can read her entire booklet online for free at Google e-books.

The Kumeyaay legend of Water Colder Water centers on Hum-am' Kwish'wash (Whip to Kill People), an evil giant among many who ages ago ruled Cuyamaca lands. Living near Green Valley, Hum-am' Kwish-wash had an innate sense of beauty, Johnson wrote. "He not only selected the most delightful places in which to live, but ... he stole the fairest of the Indian maids and required them to weave the most exquisite designs in their art of basket making ... He wanted nothing but the coldest water to drink so he created for himself a spring of colder water." According to legend, he created this spring of cold water in one of "the most alluring spots on the mountain side, in the dense shade of the fragrant forest of pines and cedars."

Most of those pines and cedars were lost in the 2003 Cedar Fire, but the oaks were far more adaptive to fire. You'll see lots of oaks resprouting now, more than a decade later, into full trees.

However, the greater threat to the oaks today is the goldspotted oak borer, an insect first detected here in 2008 that is proving devastating to coast live oaks, canyon live oaks, and black oaks in Cuyamaca as well as in Cleveland National Forest lands in the Laguna Mountains. Research continues about the efficacy of insecticides. For now, officials say the most important way to curb its infestation is by not bringing outside firewood into the state park, which is how they think the insects got here in the first place.

The Cold Spring Trail winds uphill through oak forest and chaparral for 1.4 miles, where it intersects with the Stonewall Creek Fire Road (open to hikers, equestrians, and mountain bikers), where you turn right for this loop. Just before that intersection, you'll hear and see and even cross over Stonewall Creek, which winds down through its canyon along a low, rocky path. There are some fine old oaks here too, including some that appear to have escaped the big fire.

Hike along the fire road for 1.0 mile until it intersects with Upper Green Valley Fire Road, where you turn right. Now you have reached some wide-open meadow lands, which could be ablaze in spring wildflowers this March, April, and even May. Note a bench by a placard showcasing birds in this area, inviting you to "listen for the deep croak of the common raven or the sharp scream of the red-tailed hawk, the raucous rant of the western scrub-jay or the whistling melody of the mountain chickadee." I saw a western scrub jay as well as a Steller's jay. I heard the laughing "wake up, wake up" call of the redheaded acorn woodpecker and saw a bunch of them in the ghost trees along the trail in this meadow land.

When you reach the Hill Trail, a short connector between Upper Green Valley Fire Road and the Cold Stream Trail, turn right (no bikers on this connector). Follow this uphill for 0.3 miles, where it intersects with the Cold Stream Trail. Turn right, heading back to the West Mesa parking area in about 0.7 miles.

Before I headed out on the Cold Stream Trail, I stopped to admire Grandfather Oak, which lies just below this last trail intersection on the edge of a huge meadow. This fine old coast live oak is estimated to be over 300 years old, and it escaped the fire. It also escaped the ax, whose head remains embedded in the base of its trunk after it failed to fell this lovely giant.

Some Cuyamaca giants are good.

Thomas Brothers Map: Page 1176 (bottom to page 1196), G-5, where West Mesa Loop Fire Road intersects Highway 79.

Before You Go: Download a copy of the map from the state park brochure on Cuyamaca: http://www.parks.ca.gov/pages/667/files/CuyamacaWebLayout2010Rev.pdf.
The best map of all Cuyamaca Rancho trails is Tom Harrison Maps' *Cuyamaca Rancho State Park Trail Map*, available at outdoor stores such as REI and Adventure 16, as well as online at www.tomharrisonmaps.com.
The Cold Spring Trail and Cold Stream Trail are open only to hikers and equestrians. Dogs are not allowed on state park trails.
Generally, bicyclists are allowed on the fire roads in Cuyamaca, including Stonewall Creek Fire Road and Upper Green Valley Fire Road.

Trailhead: From Interstate 8, take the Highway 79 exit, heading north toward Descanso and Julian. Cuyamaca Rancho State Park begins on Highway 79 about five miles north of Interstate 8, with the park headquarters about ten miles north.
Park in the West Mesa parking area, which is between the park's visitor center and Paso Picacho campground. Head northeast from that parking area on Cold Spring Trail. It's free to park here.

Distance/Difficulty: This loop hike is about 3.8 miles with about a 700-foot elevation gain; easy to moderate.

10-5. Wildlife, Oaks Abound on Cuyamaca's Cold Stream

For viewing wildlife, Cuyamaca is the county's premier destination. On its Cold Stream Trail in late November, I saw a bobcat, a troop of wild turkeys, bright blue scrub jays, flocks of redheaded acorn woodpeckers, and even a gaggle of sixth graders.

This trail leaves from the Dyar House Trailhead at the visitor center of Cuyamaca Rancho State Park. From the parking area, you will certainly notice the stone-walled shell of the once-grand house built by the Ralph Dyar family in 1923. This historic home was once the park's headquarters and visitor center, and it even included a small museum. However, it was destroyed during the 2003 Cedar Fire. That fire destroyed over 280,000 acres of San Diego County, including more than 24,000 acres of Cuyamaca

Rancho State Park. Fire crews fought to save historic structures in the park, but the Dyar House and all the historic buildings at Camp Hual-cu-Cuish were destroyed in the huge blaze, reported the *CSPRA Wave* (the newsletter of the California State Parks Rangers Association) in its January–February 2004 issue.

Camp Hual-cu-Cuish, used for years by local scouting troops, was first developed in the 1930s by the California Conservation Corps, and it "represented some of the best examples of CCC-era park rustic architecture in California State Parks," said the *Wave.*

Find Grandfather Oak by Cold Stream Trail.

The Dyar house was the mountain cabin of wealthy Beverly Hills residents Ralph and Helen Dyar. They had bought 20,000 acres that was Rancho Cuyamaca in 1923, selling it to the state in 1933 when it became Cuyamaca Rancho State Park.

Sadly, especially with the state's budget woes, restoration of the Dyar House will probably never occur. The day I was there, Val Bradshaw, facilities manager for the entire state park system, happened to be reviewing Cuyamaca's condition. I asked her about the Dyar House. She said funds will probably not be available to bring it back to its former glory, but the stone shell will likely at least be protected from further destruction.

The fire also devastated flora and fauna. "Ancient stands of stately sugar pines on Middle Peak and Cuyamaca Peaks were reduced to ash," said the *Wave.* "These old-growth trees were as large as six feet in diameter and perhaps 500 years old. Very few survived the blaze." Oak trees are far more resilient; 75 percent of them survived. Most of the wildlife was able to escape. Evidence of that 2003 fire is still there, but rejuvenation is also hard at work. Bradshaw remarked how Cuyamaca is an excellent example of the resilience of nature after such a catastrophic fire.

I came upon the sixth graders gathered beneath one of the largest coast live oak trees in the park. They were attending the week-long camp for sixth graders from all over the county's public schools. I went to that sixth-grade camp myself decades ago, and I was delighted to see the tradition continues.

Holly Ellis-Austin, an outdoor education program specialist with the county schools' Cuyamaca Outdoor School, was spellbinding the kids with the legend of Jedediah Smith and the Grandfather Oak, a giant tree estimated to be from 300 to 600 years old, she said. The explorer credited with being the first white man to enter California from the east, Smith was indeed in the San Diego area around 1826. Ellis-Austin repeated the legend of how Smith and the local Kumeyaay people disagreed about how to use the land. One day Smith decided to chop down Grandfather Oak. He took one swing with his axe, and an earthquake struck at that exact moment. A huge limb fell from the tree onto Smith, knocking him unconscious. The medicine man of the Kumeyaay saved his life, and Smith declared he would never cut down the tree and understood its importance.

Ellis-Austin also told the students that the 2003 fire went in a virtual circle around Grandfather Oak, sparing its magnificent life.

Then she told the kids to look for an axe blade still stuck in the tree, which has grown around it over the years. Yes, that axe blade is there.

Grandfather Oak is just below the Cold Stream Trail, where some large boulders make perfect perches in front of it. It is No. 13 on the Kumeyaay Nature Trail, with views of the meadow and Stonewall Peak behind it.

Part of the Cold Stream Trail is also called the Indian Village Trail or the Kumeyaay Nature Trail, and those numbered posts correspond with a brochure explaining how the Kumeyaay people lived in this area. The brochures should be available in a box at the beginning of the trailhead.

Near the posts marked No. 5 (the brochure points out that the Kumeyaay made pots using clay from this stream), No. 6 (wild lilac sticks were used to kill rabbits), and No. 7 (willow branches were made into acorn storage baskets), several oak trees hosted dozens of black-and-white acorn woodpeckers, their red heads bobbing on the tree trunks when they'd knock-knock the holes—you'll surely hear them. I saw the bluebirds in this area, too.

The wild turkeys were chowing down in that wide-open meadow below Stonewall Peak, one of Cuyamaca's highest at 5,730 feet. But the bobcat was the best sighting. This rarely seen creature surprised me at the parking lot trailhead. It was just a bit larger than a house cat, with pointed ears and white-striped markings. When it saw me, it crouched down, watched for a minute, and then sped away.

At that trailhead entry, if you go south on Cold Stream Trail, you'll hit Sweetwater River in about a half-mile at the junction with East Side Trail. The river was too full to cross without taking off my shoes, so I turned around. Cold Stream Trail continues north for about 3.0 miles if you go all the way to its junction at Los Caballos.

Thomas Brothers Map: Page 1176 (bottom to page 1196), G-6, where the park headquarters is noted.

Before You Go: Download a copy of the trail map for Cuyamaca at its state park page brochure: http://www.parks.ca.gov/pages/667/files/CuyamacaWebLayout2010Rev.pdf

The best map of all Cuyamaca Rancho trails is Tom Harrison Maps' *Cuyamaca Rancho State Park Trail Map*, available at outdoor stores such as REI and Adventure 16, as well as online at www.tomharrisonmaps.com.

For more information, check Cuyamaca's website: www.parks.ca.gov/?page ID=667.

Visit www.crspia.org, the site of the Cuyamaca Rancho State Park Interpretive Association. The park's visitor center is open only on Saturdays and Sundays from 10:00 a.m. to 4:00 p.m. This trail is open only to hikers and equestrians. Dogs are not allowed on state park trails.

Trailhead: From Interstate 8, take the Highway 79 exit, heading north toward Descanso and Julian. Cuyamaca Rancho State Park begins about 5.0 miles north of Interstate 8, with the park headquarters about 10 miles north.

Park at the visitor center just off Highway 79 between Green Valley and Paso Picacho campgrounds. The trailhead for Cold Stream Trail is across from the placard for the Dyar House Trailhead parking area. The trail is well marked, so you don't have to have the map.

There is a $10 day-use fee to park in the visitor center lot.

Distance/Difficulty: The Cold Stream Trail totals about 3.0 miles one-way, or 6.0 miles round-trip. Easy.

10-6. Cuyamaca Meadows Home to Lots of Life

The mountain meadows of Cuyamaca Rancho State Park are one of our natural wonders. From a distance, they appear to be filled with nothing but yellow and green grasses across wide swaths of the mountain landscape that averages just over 4,000 feet in elevation. But walk through them during summer, and they're anything but dull. Life abounds here, both in resident critters and abundant, colorful wildflowers.

On a loop hike combining seven trail segments, I passed through the huge Green Valley that surrounds the Sweetwater River, marveling at the tiny beauties I saw here.

Wildflowers are abundant on Cuyamaca meadows.

There are over 100 miles of trails in Cuyamaca, many open only to hikers and equestrians, with several (including the old fire roads) open to mountain bikers too.

Dogs are not allowed on state park trails, including Cuyamaca's. The one trail here where you may take your leashed dog is the Cuyamaca Peak Fire Road.

I began at the parking area just opposite the park's visitor center and store, which is open only on Saturdays and Sundays, though the trails are open daily. From the west side of that parking area, begin on the Cold Stream Trail and head south to the Sweetwater River crossing; you'll come back on this trail through the old Indian Village.

The trail soon crosses that river thanks to a plank laid over it. At the next junction, after you've gone a total of 0.3 miles, head northeast (left) on the East Side Trail toward Dyar Spring for another 0.3 miles. This part of the hike passes through the highest ground on this loop, but it's not very high (total elevation gain on this loop is about 300 feet), winding through some old oak trees with vistas to the northwest into those meadows.

When you reach the Dyar Spring junction, head left again (northeast) on the East Side Trail, toward the Harvey Moore Trail, for about 0.8 miles. Now you're in that Green Valley mountain meadow. The trail carves its way through the tall grasses, where those wildflowers and other life forms invite close-ups. On several occasions, some larger than usual lizards darted out onto the trail in front of me, running ahead until they darted back into the brush. A squirrel popped up in the brush at one point. I saw a beautiful turquoise western bluebird fly out from the meadow too.

The wildflowers here were the surprise. You can't see some of them unless you look closely, but the rewards are great. I saw tall purple wine cups, pink bush mallow, lovely white and yellow cream cups, pink checkerbloom, white yarrow, yellow ranchers' fiddleneck, red-stemmed filaree, white California everlasting, blue miniature lupine, baby blue eyes, and pink splendid mariposa lilies.

After winding through the meadow for nearly a mile, the trail climbs a short way above the now-dry river bed, and then it intersects with the Harvey Moore Trail. Here I saw lots of snake tracks on the sandy trail. Instead of taking that long Harvey Moore trail to the right (east), take the unmarked trail to the left (northwest) for another 0.6 miles. You cross the river bed, but it's noticeably dry throughout this part of the valley. Head up just a bit until you go back into the mountain meadow again. On the way up, look for scarlet buglers, pink California roses, yellow wallflowers, and lots of blue elderberry shrubs, whose white flowers bunch all over the bush in showy clusters. After the 0.6 miles, the trail intersects with the Upper Green Valley Fire Road, where you take a left (southwest) for another 0.4 miles to continue this loop.

The next intersection offers a 0.3-mile connector trail to the Cold Stream Trail, where you started, or you can continue straight ahead on the fire road for another 0.4 miles to reach the visitor center again.

I took the connector trail to the Cold Stream Trail for good reason. That last 0.4 miles of the Cold Stream Trail back to your parking area has one of the grandest oak trees in the park: Grandfather Oak. You'll see it nearly straight ahead: the connector trail meets up again with Cold Stream Trail, where you turn left (south). A short way off the trail takes you right up to the great old oak, marker No. 13, the last marker on the Cold Stream Trail's Kumeyaay Nature Trail that you now backtrack on to return to the parking area.

"Many stories have been told under the shade of this tree," says the accompanying brochure for the Kumeyaay Nature Trail. "My grandparents told me they used to play under its branches and that their grandparents did, too." Look for the ax blade stuck in the base of its trunk for almost the last 100 years.

If you pick up the nature trail pamphlet at the visitor center before you head out, you can follow the numbered markers to learn about plants and trees used by the Kumeyaay, who lived here for generations.

Thomas Brothers Map: Page 1176, bottom to Page 1196, G-6, "park headquarters."

Before You Go: Download a map of Cuyamaca Rancho State Park from its state park pages (http://www.parks.ca.gov/pages/667/files/CuyamacaWebLayout09301010.pdf), but note this map does not show the (unmarked) connector trail from Harvey Moore Trail to the Upper Green Valley Fire Road. The Cuyamaca Rancho State Park Trail Map from Tom Harrison Maps does show all the trails mentioned here.

The best map of all Cuyamaca Rancho trails is Tom Harrison Maps' *Cuyamaca Rancho State Park Trail Map,* available at outdoor stores such as REI and Adventure 16, as well as online at www.tomharrisonmaps.com.

This loop is open only to hikers and equestrians. Dogs are not allowed on state park trails.

Trailhead: From Interstate 8, take the Highway 79 exit, heading north toward Descanso and Julian. Cuyamaca Rancho State Park begins on Highway 79 about five miles north of Interstate 8, with the park headquarters about ten miles north.

Park just opposite the visitor center, which lies between Green Valley and Paso Picacho campgrounds.

Distance/Difficulty: The entire loop is about 3.1 miles; easy.

10-7. Green Valley Falls Still Full in Summer

On a hot summer day, the easily accessed Green Valley Falls area in Cuyamaca is filled with folks enjoying the cool pools. Located on the Sweetwater River, the falls tumble down boulders and pool in several spots that beckon bathers to the shallow waters. Climbing around the boulders can be a bit tricky, but lots of families find perches for an afternoon of fun in the verdant valley of old oaks.

It can be so crowded that the Green Valley Falls Camp/Picnic Area in Cuyamaca Rancho State Park is often full with no parking available. Campers are already there, but if you're on a day trip, you'll need to arrive early to use the day-use parking areas.

When a friend and I were there on an August weekend, we lucked out with the last parking spot and took a look at the falls, which were amazingly abundant for summertime.

After seeking a quieter trail away from the crowds, we headed out on the Falls Fire Road to connect to the Sweetwater Trail, which follows the river to the south. You can join the fire road from the Green Valley Falls Trail by heading south from the falls.

The Falls Fire Road is an old dirt road that cuts through the oak woodlands of Cuyamaca, offering some pretty views as well as evidence of the hearty nature of oak trees after fires. The 2003 Cedar Fire, the worst in California recorded history, burned almost all of the nearly 25,000 acres of the state park (it claimed over 280,000 acres total), but about 75 percent of the oak trees survived. Pine trees were not so lucky. Since that devastation, 78,000 trees have been planted by Reforest California as of March 2010, according to KPBS news. "We want to maintain this level of effort for at least the next seven years," Mike Wells, reforestation project manager, told KPBS that year. "So say roughly about 75,000 trees a year."

Go beyond falls to escape summer crowds.

Cuyamaca Rancho State Park and Chino Hills State Park in San Bernardino County were the primary recipients of Reforest California's Million Tree Challenge, but Palomar Mountain State Park was another beneficiary of the replanting efforts. The goal was to reestablish patches of landscape with native trees that will allow for progression of reforestation on burned areas, according to Reforest California's website at the time. The website is no longer active, so presumably the project has been completed.

Restoring the coniferous forest habitat provides important protection for a wide variety of native mammal and bird species. About half of the $6 million budget was donated by private parties.

After about 0.8 miles, the Falls Fire Road connects to the South Boundary Fire Road, where you take a left. Go for only about 0.3 miles to the junction of Sweetwater Trail, where you take a right. Very near that junction, the trail crosses Sweetwater River, which is high enough that you'd need to wade knee-deep through the water to continue on the trail. Just to the left, look for a dry route across the river via a log that's been placed there. You need to balance yourself across that log and bushwhack a bit through the arroyo willows to reconnect to the Sweetwater Trail.

You can see the riparian habitat that follows the river—the arroyo willows and oaks, along with so many cattails that the water is hidden—but you never really see the river.

This trail continues for another 1.2 miles before it reaches the junction of the Merigan Fire Road (to the left) and the Saddleback Trail (to the right), and it eventually connects to the California Riding and Hiking Trail and back to the South Boundary Fire Road and the Falls Fire Road. About midway onto the Sweetwater Trail, we could hear another falls on the river. More giant boulders in this area obviously created this waterfall, but we couldn't see it from the trail's vantage point. Near here, we simply turned back and retraced our simpler route to our starting point.

The best map of the trails in Cuyamaca is the *Cuyamaca Rancho State Park Trail Map* by Tom Harrison Maps, which you can purchase at REI as well as other outlets, including the park's visitor center (a bit north on Highway 79 from Green Valley Falls), and the little store and produce market just past Descanso near where Highway 79 meets Old Highway 80.

Thomas Brothers Map: Page 1216, D-3.

Before You Go: For more information about the Green Valley Falls area in Cuyamaca Rancho State Park, visit http://www.parks.ca.gov/?page_id=24895 and http://www.parks.ca.gov/?page_id=667.

Download the trail map from the state park brochure on Cuyamaca: http://www.parks.ca.gov/pages/667/files/CuyamacaWebLayout09301010.pdf.

The Sweetwater Trail is open only to hikers and equestrians. Dogs are not allowed on state park trails. Generally, bicyclists are allowed only on the fire roads in Cuyamaca.

Trailhead: From Interstate 8, take the Highway 79 exit, heading north toward Descanso and Julian. Cuyamaca Rancho State Park begins on Highway 79 about five miles north of Interstate 8, with the park headquarters about ten miles north.

Park in the Green Valley Campground, the southern-most campground in the park. To reach the Green Valley Falls and Falls Fire Road, head to the day-use parking area at the southern end of the campground, near camping spot 70.

Day-use fee is $8 per vehicle, payable at the entrance to the campground.

Distance/Difficulty: About 5.0 miles round-trip; easy.

10-8. Hike Harvey Moore Trail for Cuyamaca Meadows

The Harvey Moore Trail in Cuyamaca Rancho State Park offers a 9.0-mile loop hike through some or our high country's prettiest oaks, pines, and meadows. The entire loop can begin at the Sweetwater Trailhead just north of Green Valley campground, winding around to Granite Spring and then circling back along Harper Creek to the park's visitor center. At a little more than the halfway point, the Harvey Moore Trail intersects with the Deer Park Trail, which heads east into the Laguna Mountain Recreation Area of Cleveland National Forest.

Consider a two-car outing for that Cuyamaca-to-Laguna hike; it's about 12 miles one-way from the Sweetwater Trailhead in Cuyamaca to the Penny Pines Trailhead on S1 (Sunrise Highway) in Laguna. Even if you hike only a portion of the Harvey Moore

Trail, like we did, you'll find yourself in the pastoral sweep of Cuyamaca's beauties that have attracted people here for a long time.

Harvey Moore Trail winds through oaks and meadows.

We began at the Manzanita Trailhead, immediately north of the park's visitor center. There are no official trails leading from this parking area off Highway 79, but when the visitor center and store parking areas are full, this is the best overflow area. After walking across the meadow on the west side of the Sweetwater River, we headed back to the visitor center, where we picked up the Cold Stream Trail and headed north.

This section of the Cold Stream Trail is also known as the Kumeyaay Nature Trail, where 13 numbered wooden posts accompany a brochure that shares how the Kumeyaay lived here for hundreds of years. At the trail's beginning, there's a recreation of a traditional Kumeyaay hut, built out of willow branches. The Kumeyaay lived here during summers for at least 7,000 years before a Spanish military expedition came through here in 1782, according to the state park. The local Indians would migrate during winters down into the desert to the east or the foothills and ocean to the west. The Kumeyaay called this area Ah-he-K'we-ah-mac, meaning "the place where it rains" or "mist behind the clouds."

The numbered markers point to a wild rose, whose buds were eaten and petals were used to make tea; to pine trees, whose pitch was used for glue and to cure sores, and whose pine seeds were eaten; to manzanita, the red-trunked shrubs whose berries were an important food and whose leaves were brewed into medicinal teas and made into lotion to treat poison oak; and the black oak, whose acorns were favored and ground in morteros (deep holes in granite slabs) that are found in several places throughout Cuyamaca, including near marker No. 9 on this trail.

The last marker points to Grandfather Oak, a coast live oak tree that is estimated to be over 300 years old. Look for the ax blade embedded in its base for nearly 100 years now.

From here on the Cold Stream Trail, head east on the short 0.3-mile Hill Trail, which connects to the Upper Green Valley Fire Road. At that junction, head north (left) on the fire road 0.4 miles to the junction with the Harvey Moore Trail, which lies on the right (east) immediately beyond a placard off the fire road about the Birds of Cuyamaca. We saw several flocks of wild turkeys here, as well as the bright blue Steller's jay, the blue-and-white western scrub jay, and an ash-throated flycatcher with its pale yellow belly.

The Harvey Moore Trail hugs the northern side of Harper Creek, which is very dry during this third year of drought. This trail is not open to bicyclists but only to hikers and horses. Cuyamaca is a state park, and so no dogs are allowed on trails. Generally, bicyclists are welcome on Cuyamaca's fire roads, several miles of which crisscross the park.

Harvey Moore was Cuyamaca Rancho State Park's first park ranger in 1933 until he retired in 1955. Moore had been ranch foreman for Mr. and Mrs. Ralph M. Dyar of Los Angeles, who had purchased the old rancho in 1923 with plans to develop around Lake Cuyamaca. The Dyars built a beautiful stone home in Green Valley, probably using stones that had previously been used to build the 1857 stone home of James Lassator and his family, who had purchased 160 acres in Green Valley from the last hereditary Kumeyaay chief in the region. The Great Depression forced the Dyars to sell the rancho to the state in 1933 (reportedly for half its appraised value). The Dyar home was the park's headquarters and museum until the Cedar Fire reduced it to rubble in 2003.

Harvey Moore is believed to have created many of the park's trails with help from the young men employed by the California Conservation Corps of the 1930s. Today there are more than 100 miles of trails in Cuyamaca.

After crossing a wide-open meadow and heading into the oaks and pines (notably coming back after 2003's disastrous Cedar Fire), the Harvey Moore Trail crosses Harper Creek (still no water) and heads south toward its intersection with the Deer Park Trail into Laguna. We didn't follow the trail there but continued for a bit up Harper Creek. In its dry form today, you can maneuver up its granite slabs through this riparian area of old oaks. It's a nice spot for a picnic.

We headed back the way we came, looking for those wild turkeys and mule deer and bobcats. We didn't see them this time, but we did see their tracks.

Thomas Brothers Map: Page 1176 to Page 1196, G-6.

Before You Go: Download a copy of the trail map for Cuyamaca Rancho State Park from the state park's brochure pages: http://www.parks.ca.gov/pages/667/files/CuyamacaWeb Layout2010Rev.pdf.

The best map of all Cuyamaca Rancho trails is Tom Harrison Maps' *Cuyamaca Rancho State Park Trail Map*, available at outdoor stores such as REI and Adventure 16, as well as online at www.tomharrisonmaps.com.

This trail is open to hikers and equestrians.

For the latest park news, check the website of the Cuyamaca Rancho State Park Interpretive Association: www.crspia.org.

The visitor center and store is open from 10:00 a.m. to 4:00 p.m. Saturdays and Sundays.

Trailhead: From Interstate 8, take the Highway 79 exit, heading north toward Descanso and Julian. Cuyamaca Rancho State Park begins on Highway 79 about five miles north of Interstate 8, with the park headquarters about ten miles north.

From Julian heading south on Highway 79, park headquarters is about fifteen miles south.

Park in Cuyamaca's Visitor Center parking area ($10 day-use fee) or in the Manzanita Trailhead parking area (free) immediately to the north of the visitor center.

From either point, begin on the Cold Stream Trail (a.k.a. the Kumeyaay Nature Trail), which heads north from the visitor center and store.

Distance/Difficulty: We went on the Cold Stream, Hill Connector, Upper Green Valley Fire Road, and Harvey Moore trails for a round-trip total of about 5.0 miles with an elevation gain of about 500 feet; fairly easy.

10-9. Oaks, Berries, and Horses Enliven Juaquapin Trail

Cuyamaca's Juaquapin Trail is a scenic loop trail, much of it along the Juaquapin Creek. While listening to the soothing sounds of flowing water, you'll pass through riparian and oak woodland habitats. This trail also affords views of huge meadows, and to the west, Oakzanita Peak, which rises over 5,000 feet in elevation.

Those oak woodlands seem particularly thick on this eastern portion of Cuyamaca compared to the western section. Although most of the grand old oak trees survived the devastating 2003 Cedar Fire here (unlike the conifers), many of the oaks are now being slowly killed by the goldspotted oak borer, a deadly pest. Identified in 2008, the borer's threat to oaks in San Diego County is particularly acute in Cuyamaca Rancho State Park and Cleveland National Forest areas in Laguna and Palomar, according to a recent pest alert report to the USDA Forest Service written by Tom Coleman and Steven Seybold.

Some 20,000 coast live oaks, canyon live oaks, and black oaks have died here in the last several years, says the report. The researchers believe the goldspotted oak borer arrived here during the last 15 years through oak firewood brought in by campers, which is currently prohibited in both Cuyamaca and Palomar state parks and is the single most important effort to control the problem.

The magnificent old oaks along the Juaquapin Trail aren't the only attraction here, however. With fall around the corner, I spotted quite a few berries, including the red hollyleaf cherry and the especially bountiful blue elderberry.

I also saw a bright blue western bluebird and a bright yellow oriole, as well as several tiny butterflies that I think were dainty sulphurs feasting on miniature purple asters.

This area is home to much wildlife, including deer and their predator, the mountain lion—one of which had been spotted in this area just a couple of days earlier. But I saw only horses with their riders, because this is a popular equestrian trail. A group of 12 equestrians greeted me at the beginning of my loop on the East Side Trail. Proper trail conduct calls for hikers to yield to horseback riders by stepping off to the lower side of the trail and speaking normally so horses don't get spooked by hikers' presence.

The East Side Trail hits a junction where I took the right turn on the trail, named Connector to Juaquapin Trail. In less than a half-mile, it connects to the Juaquapin Trail loop, which goes both ways. I took the right turn, heading southeast on the Juaquapin Trail, and I hit another junction, where I took a left toward the Dyar Spring Trail.

Berries, bluebirds, and butterflies abound on Juaquapin Trail.

When maneuvering on this loop trail with so many connectors, a good map really helps. Look for the *Cuyamaca Rancho State Park Trail Map* by Tom Harrison Maps, or the state park's Cuyamaca Rancho State Park map of hiking and riding trails; both are available at various retail outlets such as REI and Adventure 16, as well as the visitor center in the state park.

While heading toward Dyar Spring Trail, I encountered another group of horseback riders. I learned they were members of Cuyamaca's Mounted Assistance Unit, a volunteer group of equestrians who patrol trails in the park to help and educate visitors. Veteran members were taking along four interested riders to see how they and their horses performed. Ted Van Arsdale, who keeps his horses at home in Del Mar, has been riding with the MAU since 1996 and was very helpful to hikers on this trail, removing a fallen limb and offering assistance.

After my hike, I went to the visitor center in the park, open only on weekends from 10:00 a.m. to 4:00 p.m., where I met Lee Hieronymus, one of 17 who started the MAU in 1976. The MAU was the first volunteer group in the park, and Hieronymus has been volunteering there for 34 years now. Also in the visitor center were Suzie and Walt Kirkwood of Descanso, who have been involved in the MAU for 17 years. Suzie is the coordinator of the MAU's patrols and events.

"There have been a lot of good times, and I've made a lot of good friends," Hieronymus, who turned 70 that October, told me of his years in the MAU. For information about joining, go to the website for all volunteer groups in Cuyamaca Rancho State Park: www.crspia.org.

Thomas Brothers Map: Page 1216, F-6, where hiking trail starts to right of Highway 79.

Before You Go: Download a copy of the map from the state park brochure on Cuyamaca: http://www.parks.ca.gov/pages/667/files/CuyamacaWebLayout2010Rev.pdf.

The best map of all Cuyamaca Rancho trails is Tom Harrison Maps' *Cuyamaca Rancho State Park Trail Map*, available at outdoor stores such as REI and Adventure 16, as well as online at www.tomharrisonmaps.com.

For more information, go to the state park's page: http://www.parks.ca.gov/?page_id=667. This trail open only to hikers and equestrians. Dogs are not allowed on trails in state parks.

Trailhead: From Interstate 8, take the Highway 79 exit, heading north toward Descanso and Julian. Cuyamaca Rancho State Park begins on Highway 79 about five miles north of Interstate 8, with the park headquarters about ten miles north.

Park in the Sweetwater parking area, the first largest parking area north of Green Valley Falls campground. There is no fee to park here, and it's open dawn to dusk.

Begin on the left-hand spur of the East Side Trail.

Distance/Difficulty: I went about 2.0 miles before retracing my steps back. The entire Juaquapin Loop is about 5.0 miles round-trip. Easy to moderate.

10-10. Kelly's Ditch Trail Is Work in Progress

Combining the western portion of the Marty Minshall Trail with the southern portion of the Kelly's Ditch Trail in Cuyamaca Rancho State Park offers blue-water Lake Cuyamaca views and lots of wildflowers in spring and summer. Begin at the Trout

View old pines and lake from trail that connects to Heise Park.

Pond parking area off Highway 79 and head west across the highway to find the Minshall Trail at the highway's junction with Milk Ranch Road. Hikers, equestrians, and bikers skirt the west side of Highway 79 on the Minshall Trail for a little more than a mile before reaching the trailhead for Kelly's Ditch Trail. Note that dogs are not allowed on state park trails.

This part of the Marty Minshall Trail winds through deep grasses, where wildflowers such as splendid mariposa lilies and blue-eyed grasses are sprinkled along the way. At some points, the grasses are so thick that they obscure the trail. If you lose the trail, look around for it uphill, and you should find it again.

The Minshall Trail here climbs a bit above the road and wanders into some old oaks and conifers, including some mighty specimens that clearly escaped the destruction of the 2003 Cedar Fire. Parts of the trail are even covered in pine cones from some very tall, mature pine trees.

This part of the Minshall Trail—named after longtime park volunteer Marty Minshall, who once lived by Lake Cuyamaca—eventually connects to the Sugar Pine Trail that heads to 5,883-foot Middle Peak. Cross this connection and continue straight ahead, still winding along the west side of Highway 79, passing the Lake Cuyamaca store and restaurant on the shoreline. Near the lake's actual dam at its northwest edge, the Minshall Trail will end at the highway, where you walk along its shoulder a short way north to the Kelly's Ditch Trail on the left.

The Kelly's Ditch Trail heads northwest from here around the western flanks of 5,993-foot North Peak for about 1.1 miles to its junction with paved Engineers Road; this portion is open only to hikers and equestrians. From Engineers Road, Kelly's Ditch Trail (from here open to hikers, equestrians, and bikers) heads north about 4.8 miles to William Heise County Park in Julian. This latter portion of Kelly's Ditch Trail had been closed for some time due to impassable brush.

As it happened, I was able to go on Kelly's Ditch Trail only about two-thirds of its way to Engineers Road, where a huge dead tree had fallen, making the trail impassable.

But there are lots of wildflowers along this hike, also including purple bush lupine, yellow velvety false lupine, wine cups clarkia, bush mallow, pink wild pea, pink rock rose, wild blue flax, purple thistle, red Indian paintbrush, and yellow mule's ears. I also saw lots of butterflies, including a mylitta crescent, a West Coast lady, an orange sulphur, a Pacific fritillary, and a couple of great spangled fritillaries.

The wooden signpost for the trail spells it Kelly's Ditch Trail, but I have also seen it on many maps as Kelley's Ditch Trail. Jerry Schad, in his book *Afoot and Afield San Diego County*, notes that the trail follows "a diversion ditch well over a century old."

"As far as the identity of Mr. (or Ms.) Kelly, I don't know," replied Dave McClure, current president of Cuyamaca Rancho State Park Interpretive Association and head of its volunteer trails maintenance unit, to my inquiry. "But the ditch was originally constructed to provide water to the Stonewall Mine. It was fed by a number of wells on North Peak to the mine. You can still see sections of the original stone-lined Kelly's Ditch Flume as you hike along this trail."

After copious research to learn who Kelly (or Kelley) was, I found the most likely candidate to be Robert Kelly, who was a cattle rancher in Cuyamaca Valley in 1871, according to "240 Years of Ranching … in the San Diego Region" by Sue A. Wade, Stephen R. Van Wormer, and Heather Thomson.

Gold was discovered around Julian in March 1870, and by 1871 Stonewall Mine in Cuyamaca was fully operational; water flow to the mine was critical. Robert W. Waterman purchased Stonewall Mine in 1886, and in 1887 he became governor of California. Gold production in the mine was especially strong from 1886 to 1892—"the most productive gold mine in San Diego County with a total yield of approximately $2 million over its entire span of operation," according to the state park's history pages.

When Ralph Dyar bought the land in 1923 that would become in 1933 Cuyamaca Rancho State Park, he filled in the old mine shafts.

Meanwhile, the earthen Cuyamaca dam was built in 1886 to form Lake Cuyamaca. Its water was then diverted to San Diego by way of a 37-mile redwood flume to El Cajon Valley, completed in 1888.

McClure noted that Kelly's Ditch Trail is still a work in progress. "We've been struggling over the past year to get the upper section of this trail to Heise Park open; we're almost there but have about a quarter-mile left to go." He pointed out that all Cuyamaca trails—some 130 miles of them—are maintained by volunteers. "We attempt to get out at least twice a week to do maintenance work." They also respond to reports like mine about the downed tree, he said. "And we are always looking for volunteers. Many of us are retirees, so it's a great opportunity for people looking to get out of the house into the fresh mountain air. No experience necessary."

A few weeks later, Mr. McClure told me those valuable volunteers had indeed cleared the trail all the way to William Heise Park in Julian.

Thomas Brothers Map: Page 1176, D-5, where Highway 79 makes sharp curve to east; trailhead is off Highway 79 just before Engineers Road.

Before You Go: Download a copy of the map from the state park brochure on Cuyamaca: http://www.parks.ca.gov/pages/667/files/CuyamacaWebLayout2010Rev.pdf.

The best map of all Cuyamaca Rancho trails is Tom Harrison Maps' *Cuyamaca Rancho State Park Trail Map*, available at outdoor stores including REI and Adventure 16, as well as online at www.tomharrisonmaps.com.

For more information, go to the state park's page: http://www.parks.ca.gov/?page_id=667.

Most of this trail is open to hikers, bicyclists and equestrians, except the portion of the Kelly Ditch Trail noted above that excludes bicyclists. Note that dogs are not allowed on state park trails.

Trailhead: From Interstate 8, take the Highway 79 exit, heading north toward Descanso and Julian. Cuyamaca Rancho State Park begins on Highway 79 about five miles north of Interstate 8, with the park headquarters about ten miles north.

Park at the Trout Pond parking area, which is past the headquarters and on Highway 79 where it intersects with Milk Ranch Road (Thomas Brothers map, Page 1176, 7-E).   Cross the highway to find the Marty Minshall Trail's western portion, where it intersects with Milk Ranch Road just off Highway 79.

Continue about 1.3 miles to Kelly's Ditch Trail, on the west side of Highway 79 a short way past the lake's dam.

Distance/Difficulty: About 4.0 miles round-trip; fairly easy with about 400 feet elevation gain.

10-11. Loop around Mountain Lake in Cuyamaca

Hike the perimeter of Lake Cuyamaca for a lovely foray around a mountain lake, one of the few actual mountain lakes in the county. Lake Cuyamaca sits at about 4,600 feet in elevation. It's an easy ramble near the water's edge that is especially picturesque on Fletcher Island, which sits at the lake's northern end. It's also one of the few places in

Cuyamaca where you can take your dog on a leash. Lake Cuyamaca is surrounded on three sides by Cuyamaca Rancho State Park, where dogs are not allowed on state park trails. Lake Cuyamaca is owned and operated by the Helix Water District, so leashed dogs are welcome on the Lake Trail.

To park on lake district lands, you need a day pass, which is $6 payable at the Tackle Shop next to the Lake Cuyamaca Restaurant on Highway 79.

I began the lake loop at Chambers Park near the lake's northwestern end, where condominiums, cabins, and sites for RV and tent camping are available for campers and fishermen.

Take an easy amble around Lake Cuyamaca.

After parking here with that day pass, I simply walked toward shore and began on the Lake Trail. You'll see several wooden post markers for the Lake Trail along its way. I went clockwise, across the dike toward Fletcher Island.

Fletcher Island gets its name from Colonel Ed Fletcher (1872–1955), one of the most influential men in early San Diego County, a noted land and water developer who also served in the California State Senate. Fletcher was born in Massachusetts and came to San Diego in 1888 with $6.10, according to the Ed Fletcher papers archived at UCSD's Mandeville Special Collections Library. His first job here was with M. T. Gilmore, a prominent local banker who made Fletcher an agent for a produce merchant. Fletcher traveled all over the county in this role, and he soon learned its geography as well as the population's dependence on development of water resources.

T. S. Van Dyke had begun to build the dam on Lake Cuyamaca in 1885, establishing the San Diego Flume Company in 1886. Cuyamaca Dam was completed in 1887, making it the oldest dam in San Diego County. From Cuyamaca, San Diego River water was diverted to a wooden flume, which was completed in 1888, taking the water all the way to La Mesa and to what would eventually become Lake Murray.

In 1910, Ed Fletcher and Montana banker James Murray bought the San Diego Flume Company, renamed it Cuyamaca Water Company, and upgraded the flume. Fletcher and various partners ultimately also built the dams at Lake Henshaw and Lake Hodges as well.

Interestingly, Fletcher's title of "Colonel" stemmed from California Governor George Pardee appointing him in 1907 as a lieutenant colonel in the California National Guard, according to the San Diego History Center. "The title stuck. It fitted his vigorous, dramatic kind of leadership," said the local newspaper decades later.

Lake Cuyamaca suffered many years of dry spells and water shortages, and it was virtually unused until Fletcher's son, Willis "Wig" Fletcher, formed the Lake Cuyamaca Recreation and Park District in the mid-1960s to preserve the lake. The dike was built to create a smaller, deeper lake that could better resist drought. The district began stocking trout in cooperation with the California Department of Fish and Game in 1974. Today some 38,000 pounds of trout are stocked in Lake Cuyamaca every year.

Fletcher Island is the prettiest part of this perimeter hike around the lake. Here, the trail winds through lots of old Jeffrey and Coulter pine trees that frame views of the water. The lake district has planted maple trees here too. Winter is a good time for bird watching on the lake, with flocks of Canada geese spending time here. I also saw several stately great blue herons, many mallard duck pairs, plenty of American coots, and several little sparrows on shore.

Continuing on from Fletcher Island, the Lake Trail winds across a wide-open grassy plain at the western end of the lake, where Cuyamaca Rancho State Park connects. You'll see 5,700-foot-high Stonewall Peak ahead as well as Cuyamaca's highest point, 6,512-foot-high Cuyamaca Peak, the county's second highest summit after Hot Springs Mountain.

During the drought years, the lake was at only about 5 percent capacity, according to the San Diego County Water Authority, so all of this area can be very dry. When you reach the lake's restaurant, you can continue on the lake perimeter trail until you get to the dam. You cannot walk across the dam, so the trail will take you up to Highway 79, where you must walk along the road shoulder for a short way until you see the single-track trail continuing toward the lake just past the dam. You'll walk along the shore by the lake's Lone Pine camp site, where RV and tent camping is offered. Soon you'll reach Chambers Park again, where you started.

Lots of fishermen try their luck from the shoreline or in small boats on the lake. In addition to trout, they're fishing for bass, bluegill, catfish, crappie, and sturgeon. The most successful fisher I saw was a great blue heron right off shore below the camping area. He nabbed a tasty trout, which struggled to get free but was no match for the mighty, hungry bird.

Thomas Brothers Map: Page 1176, restaurant about D-5, Chambers Park about F-2.

Before You Go: There isn't a good trail map available of the Lake Trail around Lake Cuyamaca, but you can download a copy of the map of the lake from the Lake Cuyamaca Recreation and Park District: www.lakecuyamaca.org.

This lake trail is open only to hikers and dogs on leashes.

To download a map of all the trails in Cuyamaca Rancho State Park, go to the brochure of the park from the state parks' pages: http://www.parks.ca.gov/pages/667/files/CuyamacaWeb Layout2010Rev.pdf.

Trailhead: On Highway 79, Lake Cuyamaca is about 9.0 miles south of Julian and 16 miles north of Interstate 8 via the Japatul/Descanso/Highway 79 exit. The lake lies immediately north of Cuyamaca Rancho State Park boundaries. Find the tackle shop next door to the Lake Cuyamaca Restaurant and Store.

Chambers Park lies off Highway 79 just a short way north of the restaurant and store.

Distance/Difficulty: The total loop around the lake is about 3.2 miles, with an elevation gain of only about 250 feet; easy.

10-12. Stonewall Peak Loop Surveys Cuyamaca

A loop hike up the backside of Stonewall Peak in Cuyamaca Rancho State Park passes through several of the state park's classic features: pine forests, expansive meadows, views of Lake Cuyamaca, and those giant granite boulders that characterize this Southern California Batholith, the rocky core of these Peninsular Range Mountains. Be on the lookout for Cuyamaca's year-round residents, including mule deer, wild turkeys, more than 100 species of birds, and rattlesnakes.

This loop is about 5.0 miles total, with an elevation gain of nearly 1,000 feet in the last 1.5 miles, making it fairly strenuous even though switchback trails climbing up the peak both ways make it easier.

Hike up the back side of Stonewall Peak too.

You won't miss the evidence of fire here, especially the devastation from the 2003 Cedar Fire that destroyed some 90 percent of the park's 24,700 acres. But even more recent fires are the result of controlled burns, a practice undertaken in the state park with CalFire. A series of controlled burns has been conducted over the past few years near the park's Paso Picacho campground. Because of the most recent burns, the popular Azalea Glen trail loop and a portion of the California Riding and Hiking Trail that connects to it have been closed. The fires destroyed some bridges along these trails, so they are closed until the facilities can be repaired. Check with the park to see when these trails will be open.

"Fighting fire with fire has been given the green light by a new study of techniques used to reduce the risk of catastrophic wildfires. And with a rise in wildfires predicted in many parts of the country, researchers say controlled burns and other treatments to manage this risk should be stepped up," says a paper published in June 2013 in *BioScience*, a peer-reviewed journal. The paper was led by UC Berkeley researchers and included scientists from the U.S. Forest Service and six research universities in the United States and Australia. "Some question if these fuel-reduction treatments are causing substantial harm, and this paper says no," said Scott Stephens, lead author and UC Berkeley associate professor of fire science. "The few effects we did see were usually transient. Based upon what we've found, forest managers can increase the scale and pace of necessary fuel treatments without worrying about unintended ecological consequences."

I began on the Cold Stream Trail heading north. This trailhead is across Highway 79 from the entrance to Paso Picacho campground. As you begin on the trailhead for Stonewall Peak, the Cold Stream Trail heads north (left) very shortly, where the main Stonewall Peak trail takes a sharp southern (right) turn to head uphill. This portion of the Cold Stream Trail is an easy meander through pine forests and burned ghost oaks, and it affords blue-water views of Lake Cuyamaca farther north.

After 1.0 mile on the Cold Stream Trail, it intersects with an open portion of the CR&HT that heads east (right) for a half-mile to its intersection with the Stonewall Peak Trail's northern end. When I was hiking along this portion of the CR&HT, I spied an entire herd of mule deer—at least a dozen of them cruising through the forest. I didn't see any males with antlers (bucks develop antlers in summer), but I was thrilled with this sighting of the big-eared natives. Mule deer's "Black-tailed race of Coast Ranges is smaller, darker (than the Sierran species)," according to the National Audubon Society's Field Guide to California. They have black tails that stand out against their white rumps, and their ears really are large, like mules'. They watched me as carefully as I watched them.

Look for that Stonewall Peak trail intersection on the right (south) just before the CR&HT splits to the Los Vaqueros Trail to the left and the Vern Whittaker Trail to the right. Now head up the back side of Stonewall Peak. There aren't as many switchbacks until the top on this part of the Stonewall Peak Trail compared to its main ascent opposite Paso Picacho campground. It's somewhat of a grind to get up there.

In spring you'll see lots of color from the blue-blooming ceanothus (wild lilac), the adorable baby blue eyes, the yellow blooms of Douglas' violet, the even tinier yellow blooms of hairy lotus, the deep pink of San Diego sweet pea, and the showy white bonanza of summer snow. On the long tubular red blooms of a scarlet bugler, I spotted the flash of a remarkably orange hummingbird, probably Allen's hummingbird, with its bright green crown. I also marveled at many redheaded acorn woodpeckers (as well as their storage of acorns in hundreds of holes in old pine trees), yellow-rumped warblers, and bright blue western bluebirds with their rust-colored breasts. But my favorite sighting this time was a female California quail, our state bird, which posed on a branch for me as I climbed up Stonewall Peak Trail. Her topknot crown with her black-and-white patterned belly made her especially lovely. On the way into the park in a meadow near the visitor center, I also saw those wild turkeys, but this time I saw several males displaying their really gorgeous tail feathers, a special sight.

When you near the top of Stonewall Peak, look for the trail that heads off to the right to go back down before reaching the actual summit. Now it's all downhill from here, as they say, and it's another beautiful day in Cuyamaca.

Thomas Brothers Map: Page 1176, subpage 1196, 2-E, Paso Picacho off Highway 79.

Before You Go: State park trails do not allow dogs. The Stonewall Peak Trail is also closed to bicyclists.

Download a copy of the park map from the state parks' page for Cuyamaca Rancho State Park: http://www.parks.ca.gov/pages/667/files/CuyamacaWebLayout2010Rev.pdf.

My favorite map of Cuyamaca trails, however, is published by Tom Harrison Maps, *Cuyamaca Rancho State Parks Trail Map*. It is available online or at the park's visitor center (open only Saturdays and Sundays) for $10.

Trailhead: The Cold Stream Trail and the Stonewall Peak Trail share the same trailhead, immediately opposite the entrance to the Paso Picacho campground in Cuyamaca. The campground is off Highway 79, about 11 miles south of Julian or about 12 miles north of Interstate 8's exit for Japatul Valley/Descanso.

Park in the Paso Picacho campground; it's $8 per vehicle for day use.

Distance/Difficulty: The loop from Cold Stream to CR&HT to Stonewall Peak and down is about a 5.0-mile loop; fairly strenuous.

10-13. Los Vaqueros, Los Caballos Trails Trek Horse Country

Joining Los Caballos Trail with Los Vaqueros Trail in Cuyamaca takes hikers through wide-open meadows with views of Lake Cuyamaca to pine-filled forests sparked in fall with the orange and yellow leaves of black oaks.

In the middle of these trails is Los Vaqueros Group Horse Camp, a facility that was closed for years following the disastrous 2003 Cedar Fire that destroyed most of Cuyamaca Rancho State Park (CRSP). It reopened in 2011 and now offers camping accommodations for up to 80 people and 45 horses in corrals. Many local equestrian groups rent the facilities for weekends in spring, summer, and fall. Several miles of various trails open to horseback riders connect to the group horse camp, including about 12 miles of the California Riding and Hiking Trail. We saw several horses with their riders on the loop between the trails of Los Caballos, which means horses in Spanish, and Los Vaqueros, which means cowboys in Spanish, on a crisp fall weekend afternoon. Most were members of an equestrian group from Lakeside who gathered here for a four-day weekend.

I began the trail at the Trout Pond parking area at the north end of Cuyamaca Rancho State Park, just before reaching Lake Cuyamaca. From Trout Pond, begin on the Marty Minshall Trail (named for a longtime CRSP volunteer), which skirts a large meadow at the southern edge of Lake Cuyamaca. Much of that meadow is submerged by the lake during very wet years when the water level rises. This trail intersects to the right with the Los Caballos Trail in about 0.4 miles. It continues through the meadow, the northern section of the Cuyamaca Meadow Natural Preserve, which receives the highest level of protection in state park lands. It should be covered in wildflowers in spring. In the grasses of this meadow, I saw several wild turkeys bobbing for bugs, their iridescent feathers shining in the sun.

After another half-mile or so, the trail intersects with a dirt road that simply leads to a camp electrical facility. Cross this road to continue on the trail straight ahead, where it now becomes the Vern Whitaker Trail. An avid horseman in Southern California, Vern Whitaker is the namesake of the Vern

Popular horse trail offers meadows, pines.

Whitaker Horse Camp in Anza-Borrego Desert State Park, which lies about 8.0 miles north of Borrego Springs. In the early 1980s, it was said that he wintered in that desert camp and summered in the Los Vaqueros Horse Camp of Cuyamaca.

It is generally accepted that the Spanish explorers brought domesticated horses to California in the late 1700s. Very near here on the California Riding and Hiking Trail that extends from Cuyamaca to Anza-Borrego is the Pedro Fages Monument on S1, which commemorates that Spanish colonel's route through this area down into the Oriflamme Canyon and on to the Mojave and Central Valley in 1772.

In the 2012 exhibition *The Horse* at the San Diego Natural History Museum, I learned that prehistoric horses roamed coastal San Diego between 37 million and 43 million years ago. The museum's collections hold several horse fossils, including teeth from Oceanside's Lawrence Canyon as well as horse teeth and foot bones found in Chula Vista, some dating back as recently as 100,000 years ago.

When you begin on the Vern Whitaker Trail, you'll also begin to see the facilities of the horse camp. It was here I smelled something foul, and I later learned what it was.

The trail hugs the south perimeter of the horse camp's corrals. It continues about a half-mile past the horse camp until it intersects with the Stonewall Creek Fire Road. A left at that intersection will take you up the hill to another intersection with the Soapstone Grade Fire Road in just about 0.1 mile. This short spur is worth the view at the top of the huge meadow that spreads below and reaches all the way to the edge of the desert.

From here, I turned around and retraced my way back to the horse camp, where I took the Los Vaqueros Trail to make a different return loop to where I began.

A trio of volunteer horsewomen with the CRSP mounted patrol greeted me on this trail and told the story of the odor. A very old horse—he was 30—had died on that trail. His owner had no choice but to leave him there to return to nature, because his 1,200-pound remains couldn't be removed. It was a bittersweet tale because the horse loved trail riding here, they said, and he would have wanted to end that way.

I had photographed another 30-year-old horse and her rider earlier that day—a white beauty named Crystal, ridden by Paul Bitondo, joined by his wife, Theresa, on her bay, Safire. Thirty is a lot of years for a horse, but Crystal was in fine form, Theresa told us.

As I wound our way back through the pines and the meadow, I saw several deer, wild turkeys, and many colorful birds, including acorn woodpeckers, western bluebirds, and northern flickers. I always see more wildlife in Cuyamaca than anywhere else in the county.

The horses fit in perfectly.

Thomas Brothers Map: Page 1176, E-7 on the top map—where the hard right turn on Highway 79 at the bottom of the lake (where Highway 79 intersects with Milk Ranch Road) continues up "Cuyamaca Highway."

Before You Go: Download a map of Cuyamaca Rancho State Park trails at the state park's brochure page: http://www.parks.ca.gov/pages/667/files/CuyamacaWebLayout09301010.pdf.

One of the best maps of CRSP trails is Tom Harrison Maps' *Cuyamaca Rancho State Park Trail Map*, which is available at the park's visitor center on weekends as well as outdoor stores such as REI or Adventure 16.

These trails are open only to hikers and equestrians. Dogs are not allowed on state park trails.

Trailhead: From Interstate 8 heading east, exit at Descanso/Japatul Valley and head north on Highway 79. Near the northern end of CRSP, just before reaching Lake Cuyamaca, at the sharp right turn of the highway, you'll see the large Trout Pond parking area, near the intersection with Milk Ranch Road.

Begin on the Marty Minshall Trail here and then connect with Los Caballos and Vern Whitaker trails before returning along Los Vaqueros Trail back to Marty Minshall.

Distance/Difficulty: About a 4.5-mile, round-trip loop; easy.

10-14. Two Waterfalls, Yellow Willows in Southwest Cuyamaca

The southwestern corner of Cuyamaca Rancho State Park is usually a very quiet place. It is off the beaten path of the main camping and hiking areas of the park, with its trailhead in Descanso off Viejas Boulevard. It was so quiet that I could hear the wings flapping of a red-tailed hawk flying above me.

One sound was decidedly loud: the rain-swollen Sweetwater River. In mid-November 2011, when I was there, the river was in full force after a few heavy rains.

The highlights of my hike were two full-fledged waterfalls. Neither was as big a cascade as nearby Green Valley Falls, but these tucked-away marvels didn't attract the crowds either. One flowed into a natural basin, and the other was an "artificial" waterfall created by a man-made diversion dam.

Two waterfalls are seen from Merigan Fire Road.

I began this exploration on the Merigan Fire Road, which is open to hikers, equestrians, and mountain bikers. The fire road was once the main ranch road for a 1,800-acre ranch sold by Dr. Haig Merigan to the State of California in 1977 to be added to Cuyamaca Rancho State Park (CRSP). Dr. Merigan, a San Diego dentist, and his family were "gentleman ranchers," and he hoped his land would be developed into a horse camp in the park. Dr. Merigan was third in a long line of gentleman ranchers to own this historic ranch, according to a report on the equestrian facilities in the CRSP.

Allen T. Hawley, the scion of a pioneer ranching family in El Cajon since 1884, bought over 2,200 acres here in 1929. It was Hawley who had the charming native stone cottage built in 1929, which you see when you start out on the Merigan Fire Road; it's now a ranger's residence.

Hawley sold the ranch in 1941 to Mary and Lawrence Oliver. Oliver was a prominent player in San Diego's economic and social scene, having emigrated to San Diego from the Azores Islands in 1903. He built companies involved in oil, fishing, and canning. The Olivers sold the ranch in 1958 to the Merigans.

The first trail that connects to the Merigan Fire Road is the Dead Horse Trail, about 0.7 miles from the trailhead. I couldn't find any stories about the origin of that trail's name, but considering this area was long in ranching, it might be obvious.

The Dead Horse Trail, open only to hikers and horseback riders, descends down a steep narrow drop to the Sweetwater River in just about 0.1 mile from its beginning. When you get to the bottom, you'll see a very small wooden post with an arrow pointing to the left, where three trails intersect. The arrow shows where the main trail continues. Follow either of the other two trails to the right to reach that first waterfall. In short order, you'll see a fine tumble of crystal clear river falling about 6 feet down boulders into a big deep pool. I spent some time here admiring the lovely scene.

Head back to that arrow for the rest of the trail. In a very short distance, I reached the Sweetwater River again, which was too deep for me to cross and awfully deep for horses too—several feet. Perhaps in the heat of summer, and probably during the long drought, the water is low enough to forge this crossing. The other side of the trail looked pretty overgrown, so I'm not sure how easy it is to continue. The map notes that Dead Horse Trail is 2.4 miles long before intersecting with the California Riding and Hiking Trail. According to the CRSP, the Dead Horse Trail is considered a technically advanced riding trail that crosses the river and climbs steeply up rocky chaparral with a 600-foot elevation gain.

I hiked back up to the Merigan Fire Road and continued ahead. The fire road continues for another 1.2 miles before reaching an intersection with the Saddleback Trail. The views along the road are lovely in fall. They are expansive across the boulder-strewn hills on either side, and as the road rises and falls before reaching the river again, it passes through old oaks that even frame Cuyamaca Peak, the county's second highest at 6,512 feet. The rich riparian habitat along the Sweetwater River becomes a golden ribbon through this landscape during autumn when the extensive arroyo willow trees turn yellow.

About midway along this part of the road, before it heads up a steep incline, look for a spur trail on the left. You will hear that sound of cascading water to alert you again. Down this spur you'll reach that second waterfall, this one higher and mightier as it flows over a cement wall.

At the junction with the Saddleback Trail, I retraced my way back along the Merigan Fire Road, where I ran into the only other users I'd seen: four horses and their riders, all alive and well.

Thomas Brothers Map: Page 1236, B-2, immediately to the left of Mitzpah Lane off Viejas Boulevard, to the north into the park.

Before You Go: Download a trail map of the entire park from the state parks' page, http://www.parks.ca.gov/pages/667/files/CuyamacaWebLayout09301010.pdf.

You may also buy a map of Cuyamaca Rancho State Park from the CRSP Interpretive Association; check its web site, www.crspia.org, or buy one at the park's visitor center off Highway 79. Another good map to purchase is the Cuyamaca Rancho State Park Trail Map by Tom Harrison Maps; look for this one at REI and Adventure 16.

This trail is open to hikers, bicyclists and equestrians; dogs are not allowed on state park trails.

Trailhead: To reach the Merigan Fire Road parking and staging area, from Interstate 8 heading east, take the Japatul/Descanso/Highway 79 exit, heading north on Highway 79. Just after Highway 79 turns left where it intersects with Old Highway 80 heading to Guatay – 3.0 miles after Interstate 8 – turn left onto Viejas Boulevard. In 1.1 miles, just beyond Mitzpah Lane, park in the trailhead parking on the right.

There is a self-pay, $8 day-use fee here.

Distance/Difficulty: The round-trip is about 4.0 miles total. Much of the fire road is flat with a few steep inclines. Easy to moderate.

10-15. History, Butterflies, and Views on Milk Ranch Road

The Milk Ranch Road connects with the Black Oak Trail loop and the Middle Peak Fire Road to offer peak views in a very historic portion of Cuyamaca Rancho State Park. Milk Ranch Road is a wide-open dirt road that is closed to public vehicles, and it makes an easy trail into this Middle Peak area of Cuyamaca, just west of Lake Cuyamaca. It's popular with mountain bikers and equestrians as well, but dogs are not allowed on state park trails.

Hike the Middle Peak section of Cuyamaca.

The equestrian staging area just off the beginning of Milk Ranch Road near its intersection with Highway 79 is the old site of the Boy Scouts' Camp Hual Cu-Cuish. That camp was operated from 1940 until 1998, and then it was totally destroyed in the devastating Cedar Fire of 2003, the largest wildfire in California's recorded history.

The Boy Scouts had named their Cuyamaca camp after the Native American name for Middle Peak, which stands 5,883 feet in elevation just to the northwest. Hual Cu-Cuish in the natives' California Yuman language means "tough, strong." In the historic Native American story, according to a wooden board at the Milk Ranch Road trailhead, Middle Peak or Hual Cu-Cuish was known as the strong brother in the battle that ensued over a mountain spring, known as a maiden. Cuyamaca Peak, which stands at 6,512 feet due south of here (the second highest peak in San Diego County), was then known as "crooked neck," the result of this battle.

The Kumeyaay people lived in this part of Cuyamaca for thousands of years during the summers, and in this old Boy Scout campsite, lots of evidence has been found by archeologists of the villages that once thrived here. There are many morteros, the deep depressions in granite rock that were used to grind acorns into meal. The Kumeyaay favored the acorns of the black oaks.

Milk Ranch Road winds west from Lake Cuyamaca to La Puerta Springs, perhaps one of those "maidens" in the old Kumeyaay stories. It's a gradual elevation gain of about 500 feet to the first major intersection with Azalea Springs Fire Road and those two loops of the Black Oak Trail.

With views to the south to Cuyamaca Peak and to the southeast to Stonewall Peak, the devastation of that Cedar Fire is still much in evidence. Middle Peak used to be home to the county's largest conifers, but mostly ghost stumps remain. There is evidence of regrowth, and many of the oaks, which typically survive fire better than conifers, still stand.

The Black Oak Trail's western loop was closed a few years ago so workers could remove much of this dead fire fuel.

The old Milk Ranch, according to the map, lies a short way farther on Milk Ranch Road beyond that major intersection. It was the Milk Cattle Ranch in about 1870 when John Treat homesteaded here to raise Durham cattle and horses. Treat, along with other landowners at the time, were involved in the notorious Cuyamaca Land Grant Trial, over disputed borders and Julian gold mines. For a full accounting, read the 1971 issue of the *Journal of San Diego History* about this historic dispute.

That major intersection is anchored by a beautiful old black oak tree befitting the junction with the Black Oak Trail. The trees are laden with acorns during fall. The eastern segment of the Black Oak Trail (the first one you'll encounter) is harder to spot because it backtracks to the right off Milk Ranch Road.

From the western segment, even if you go a short way up that single track, you'll see sweeping views all the way to the ocean on a very clear day. One of the loveliest sights on this trail were the dozens of tiny blue butterflies feeding on the bright yellow California goldenrod right on the edge of Milk Ranch Road.

Thomas Brothers Map: Page 1176, D-7.

Before You Go: Download a good map of these trails in the Cuyamaca Rancho State Park brochure at the state park's website: http://www.parks.ca.gov/pages/667/files/CuyamacaWebLayout09301010.pdf.

For trail updates, check the CRSPIA website: www.crspia.org.

These trails are open to hikers, bicyclists, and equestrians. No dogs on state park trails.

Trailhead: Park in the Trout Pond parking area on the east side of Highway 79, across the highway from the Milk Ranch Road trailhead. The Trout Pond parking area is located on Highway 79 at the southern end of Lake Cuyamaca, about 1.5 miles north from the Paso Picacho campground, just before Highway 79 makes a hard right.

Distance/Difficulty: Milk Ranch Road is about 1.5 miles to the major junction, making a 3.0-mile round-trip up and back. Combining it with the Black Oak Trail's eastern segment and Middle Peak Fire Road makes about a 4.8-mile loop. Fairly easy.

10-16. Minshall-Mine Trail Has Fall Color and Wildlife

Cuyamaca Rancho State Park is especially alluring during the crisp, clear days of fall. The leaves of the black oak trees turn golden, making them one of our few trees worthy of leaf peeping. When I was there in late October, I exclaimed with excitement because I saw more wildlife than on any other trail. The species I saw even seemed to go with the season.

I combined two trails for a loop with views of Lake Cuyamaca and the Cuyamaca Meadows Natural Preserve, as well as some history of the Stonewall Mine that once produced a lot of gold.

Find golden history and gorgeous meadows on this Cuyamaca favorite.

I started at the Trout Pond Trailhead. Note that there isn't actually a trout pond trail, and before you reach this trailhead (going north on Highway 79), you will see a sign pointing east for the Stonewall Mine. You can drive to the mine on that road, but the trail described here is a much more rewarding way to reach it. The Trout Pond Trailhead is a popular staging area for horseback riders, and it's the beginning of three trails. I began on the Minshall Trail. Named for Marty Minshall, a legendary park volunteer, this trail was her favorite. It skirts the southern edge of Lake Cuyamaca and is also the northern boundary of the Cuyamaca Meadow Natural Preserve, which receives the highest level of protection in state park lands.

At one of the first meadowland areas, I saw a group of animals migrating through the tall grasses. It was a flock of wild turkeys, bobbing through the grass and feeding along the way. There were nearly a dozen of them, their red wattles and iridescent feathers sparkling in the sun.

I came to a trail intersection with a big sign saying, "Danger: Hunting Occurs by this trail, Wed & Sun." The sign refers to waterfowl hunting on Lake Cuyamaca on Wednesdays and Sundays during the season, according to regulations. For more information, go to the Lake Cuyamaca Recreation and Park District website: www. lakecuyamaca.org. The lake is also popular for fishing and is stocked with trout all year long.

At that danger sign, I followed the main trail to the left toward the lake. The Minshall Trail (there are periodic posts identifying it) skirts an old road here and then goes through the oak woodlands. I saw another flock of wild turkeys, this group crossing the trail behind me.

You'll note a trail intersection that goes to the right up to Stonewall Mine. Don't take that turn; you will come back down on this trail. Going straight ahead here on the Minshall Trail offers an easier route to the mine.

The Minshall Trail intersects later with the Stonewall Mine Trail at a service road. You'll see a trail signpost prohibiting horses on this section and directing hikers to Stonewall Mine just 0.1 miles ahead. Stay straight on this paved road, past the dumping ground for dumpsters. At the top of the hill, you'll find the Stonewall Mine remains, including a little cabin that presents fascinating old photographs and information about those mining days.

Gold was discovered in the Julian area in the 1860s. At the height of the gold mining operations here (1886–1891), more than 500 people lived in Cuyamaca City, a company town that operated the Stonewall Mine.

California Governor Robert Whitney Waterman owned the mine, which produced about $2 million in gold, equivalent today to more than $60 million. He provided the town with one of the nation's first long-distance telephone lines, one of the region's first public libraries, piped water, and mail service. The mine was closed in 1892.

To return, take the Stonewall Mine Trail that goes up the hill to the west of the mine, past the restrooms. Near here, I saw a young mule deer, its large ears perked up as it lay down in the woodlands some distance away, watching me.

On this return loop, you'll come to two four-way trail intersections that aren't marked. Take the right turn at each, heading back toward Lake Cuyamaca. You'll soon reach that intersection you noted earlier on the Minshall Trail. Turn left to retrace your steps back to the parking area.

When I reached that wide-open meadow where I first saw the wild turkeys, I saw more movement in those tall grasses. This time it was a coyote. It was pretty far away, but I was still thrilled to see it. I watched it a long time and saw it leap onto some potential meal in the grass.

The trail eventually headed in his direction, and there was that coyote, about to intersect my trail not more than 20 yards away. When he saw me, he turned around and ran away.

Marty Minshall was right: This is a splendid trail.

Thomas Brothers Map: 1176, 7-E on top half of page, at the very southern end of the lake, where the highway makes a left then a hard right (right where Milk Ranch Road goes off to the west).

Before You Go: Download a good map of these trails in the Cuyamaca Rancho State Park brochure at the state park's website: http://www.parks.ca.gov/pages/667/files/CuyamacaWeb Layout09301010.pdf.

The visitor center at Cuyamaca Rancho State Park is open only on Saturdays and Sundays from 10:00 a.m. to 4:00 p.m.

There is no fee to park on the road shoulder by this Trout Pond Trailhead. These trails are open only to hikers and equestrians. Dogs are not allowed on state park trails.

Trailhead: Go east on Interstate 8, taking the Descanso/Highway 79 exit. Head north on Highway 79. At the 10.7 miles marker in Cuyamaca Rancho State Park, where the highway takes a left turn then a hard right, just before Lake Cuyamaca. Park next to the Trout Pond Trailhead sign.

Distance/Difficulty: About 2.0 miles round-trip; easy.

10-17. Views Can Be Vast from Oakzanita Peak

On a clear day, 5,054-foot-high Oakzanita Peak in Cuyamaca reveals a stunning, 360-degree view. You can see peaks of Mexico to the south, high country meadows and Laguna peaks to the east, the peaks of Stonewall and Cuyamaca to the north, and the downtown skyline and Coronado Islands in the ocean to the west. It's an amazing panorama if you're lucky enough to climb to the top right after a good rain seems to clean the air of haze.

Cuyamaca Rancho State Park is sometimes called "the rooftop of San Diego County" because several peaks higher than 5,000 feet are within its boundaries. From Oakzanita Peak, you really feel you are near that top. It's a fairly moderate climb, even though it involves a 1,134-foot elevation gain over about 3.2 miles one-way, thanks to a switchback trail.

According to the Tom Harrison Maps' *Cuyamaca Rancho State Park Trail Map,* the climb starts out at 3,920 feet elevation at the beginning of the Lower Descanso Creek Trail. Crossing that creek a couple of times on that 0.7-mile leg, the trail passes through lovely riparian habitat with black oaks and sycamores, both losing their leaves in fall in a cascade of gold.

This trail joins the East Mesa Fire Road for just 0.1 miles, and then it connects to the Upper Descanso Creek Trail for 1.8 miles up with switchbacks making the climb a bit gentler. After turning right at the junction with the Oakzanita Peak Trail, you'll reach the top in another 0.6 mile. Views on the way up to the top are pretty amazing.

About halfway up the Upper Descanso Creek Trail, you begin to see peaks on the northern horizon.

Oakzanita Peak is relatively easy for rooftop views.

Very clear are views of Cuyamaca's highest peak, Cuyamaca Peak, which stands at 6,512 feet elevation. It ranks as the second highest in San Diego County, with Hot Springs Mountain at 6,533 feet near Warner Springs the highest. Also to the north, you can see Stonewall Peak in Cuyamaca, which rises to 5,730 feet. To the east, Laguna's highest point, Monument Peak, stands at 6,271 feet. Almost all these peaks are on the Sierra Club's 100 San Diego County Peaks, except for the summit of Hot Springs Mountain — but there is a lower point on Hot Springs on the list. When it's so clear you can see the ocean and downtown San Diego some 50 miles to the west, that's a true thrill.

Also worth the climb are the high-mountain meadows. A big one at the junction of the Upper Descanso Creek Trail and Oakzanita Trail seems to be a fine place for mule deer to graze. Evidence of the disastrous 2003 Cedar Fire is still evident here, though manzanita is making a comeback near the summit. Many of the oaks survived, including lots of scrub oak sporting little acorns during fall. Yellow blooms of goldenbush still color the scene in fall.

The native Kumeyaay lived here for thousands of years, migrating especially in the fall to harvest those black oak acorns. They called Cuyamaca "ah-ha-Kwe-ah-muc," meaning generally "the place where it rains." With an average rainfall of about 35 inches a year, it's one of the wetter places in the county.

I'd recommend waiting a day or two to climb up Oakzanita Peak after one of those rainfalls, because the Upper Descanso Creek Trail is fairly rocky and narrow and could be more treacherous if it's muddy and slick. Equestrians and hikers are welcome on both the Lower and Upper Descanso Creek trails, but mountain bikers are not allowed on these segments. Mountain bikers can make it to the top of Oakzanita Peak via the East Mesa Fire Road, which offers a more gradual ascent/descent. Its mileage is longer at 4.0 miles one-way (8.0 miles round-trip) from Highway 79. You may also take that route up or back as a loop trail with the Descanso Creek trails, adding a bit more than a mile to the round-trip.

Time it sometime in fall, winter, or spring, when the air is clear, and you'll find the views make that climb especially worthwhile.

Thomas Brothers Map: Page 1216, F-5.

Before You Go: Download a trails map from the state parks brochure of Cuyamaca Rancho State Park at http://www.parks.ca.gov/pages/667/files/CuyamacaWebLayout09301010.pdf.

You may want to buy the Tom Harrison Maps' *Cuyamaca Rancho State Park Trail Map* at REI, Adventure 16, or online. You can also buy state park maps at the visitor center, open Saturdays and Sundays from 10:00 a.m. to 4:00 p.m., located inside the state park about three miles north on Highway 79 from the trailhead.

The Lower and Upper Descanso Creek Trails are open only to hikers and equestrians; the East Mesa Fire Road and Oakzanita Peak Trail are open also to bicyclists. No dogs are allowed on state park trails.

Trailhead: From Interstate 8 east, head north on Highway 79 toward Julian. About 6.0 miles north from I-8 is the Oakzanita parking area just off the highway on the right, past the 3.0-mile marker and before Green Valley Falls campground.

Begin this route on the Lower Descanso Creek Trail, connect right onto the East Mesa Fire Road, and then turn right onto Upper Descanso Creek Trail. Turn right onto Oakzanita Peak Trail.

Distance/Difficulty: About 6.4 miles round-trip. Moderately strenuous.

10-18. Cuyamaca's Pine Ridge Trail Looks Both East And West

For some of the best views looking both east and west in Cuyamaca, head to the Pine Ridge Trail in the southern part of the state park. This trail ascends about 600 feet from its trailhead as it follows a ridge that sits about 4,500 feet above sea level. Within the first half-mile or so, you hike up to reach the first views to the west, looking into the Sweetwater River canyon and beyond into the pine-dotted rises that diffuse into layers of shadowy hills. The panoramic display is a fine reward. There is very little shade on this ridge, so you might want to wear a hat and be sure to bring plenty of water. It's hot here during the summer.

After continuing upward, the trail does give some respite with flat expanses. It heads northwest and soon reveals the eastern meadows and peaks. This vantage point affords sweeping views of the West Mesa, Green Valley, and the highest point in Cuyamaca, Cuyamaca Peak, at 6,512 feet high.

According to Jerry Schad in his masterful book, *Afoot and Afield San Diego County*, the name "Pine Ridge" refers to the Coulter pines that covered these slopes before the Cedar Fire of October 2003. There remains much evidence of that fire here. Most of the manzanita bushes are blackened skeletal remains bordering both sides of the trail. A few of the pines have returned, and new seedlings are showing promise.

When you get into the highest parts of this trail, a few wildflowers still show some color, including the yellow daisy-like hulsea, a San Diego native, and some Cleveland sage, which is the most fragrant of the sages. In fact, parts of this ridge seem to be among the most fragrant in the county.

Pines tend to suffer more than oaks in huge forest fires.

After about 2.2 miles, Pine Ridge Trail intersects with the South Boundary Road, also marked as the California Riding and Hiking Trail; turn right at this intersection. Just a little farther is another T intersection with the Arroyo Seco Fire Road. Turn right again here to make the loop back to Green Valley campground.

The Arroyo Seco Fire Road is an easy walk back another mile or so to the campground. It's an entirely different world with lots of huge live oak trees that offer plenty of welcome shade. The oaks are clearly less devastated by fire. As I was ambling along this old dirt road, I saw a very unusual sight: two owls flying in the trees. Usually owls are on the move at night, and this was practically high noon. But though they flew away from me pretty quickly, they were so distinctive and large that I'm almost certain they were owls—probably spotted owls, which grow to 19 inches and live in old-growth coniferous forests along the West Coast.

It was a fine day in the forest, but then I hit a snag. When I returned to my car, I had been ticketed for parking outside the day-use parking area, receiving a $64 fine. I had my day-use ticket attached to my windshield, but because the park was literally empty, I parked near the trailhead at an empty campsite. All the campsites were empty in practically the entire campground on this Monday afternoon. Even the ranger at the entrance said there were only four people in the park that day.

So be advised: park only in the day-use lots and walk to the trailhead.

Thomas Brothers Map: Page 1216, 3-D &E, where it says Green Valley Campground.

Before You Go: Download a trails map from the state parks brochure of Cuyamaca Rancho State Park at http://www.parks.ca.gov/pages/667/files/CuyamacaWebLayout09301010.pdf.

You may want to buy the Tom Harrison Maps' *Cuyamaca Rancho State Park Trail Map* at REI, Adventure 16, or online. You can also buy state park maps at the Cuyamaca visitor center, open Saturdays and Sundays from 10:00 a.m. to 4:00 p.m., located inside the state park about 3.0 miles north on Highway 79 from the trailhead.

This is a hikers-only trail—no horses, mountain bikes, or dogs allowed.

There is an $8 day-use fee, paid at the campground entrance.

Trailhead: From Interstate 8, exit at Descanso/Japatul Valley and head north onto Highway 79. About 7.0 miles north on Highway 79, turn left into the Green Valley Campground and Picnic Area. Park in the day-use parking area and head to campsite No. 38, where the trail begins.

Distance/Difficulty: About 3.2 miles round-trip; moderate.

10-19. Bird's-Eye Panorama atop Stonewall Peak

The trail up Stonewall Peak in Cuyamaca Rancho State Park is one of the most popular in that nearly 25,000-acre park. When you reach the top, there is a 360-degree view over of the forested peaks and wide-open meadows below, including an excellent bird's-eye view of Lake Cuyamaca.

It's almost 2.0 miles one-way with a gain of about 800 feet in elevation, but it's a more moderate climb than that might suggest because of the trail's many switchbacks. If you climb in spring, the blooms of the ceanothus (wild lilac) will dominate the landscape almost everywhere. In mid-May, when I was there, the blue lilacs were nearly finished blooming, but the white Palmer's lilacs were amazingly abundant. The white lilacs should continue blooming until about mid-June.

Stonewall Peak is among Cuyamaca's most popular trails for good reason.

You'll note from the beginning of the trail that the landscape still appears ravaged from the catastrophic 2003 Cedar Fire that burned over 280,000 acres countywide, making it the largest wildfire in recorded California history. In that fire, most of Cuyamaca's fir and pine trees, along with many of its oaks, were destroyed.

But within five years of the fire, lots of white fir, sugar pine, Coulter pine, Jeffrey pine, and incense cedar saplings were thriving. At the beginning of the trail, you'll also see several little mesh screens protecting seedlings of Jeffrey pines that have been planted. And if you look closely at all the ghost oak trees along the trail—those sculptural forms that once were black oaks as well as canyon and coast live oaks—you'll see that they're sprouting new growth at their bases. Some of these old trees were enormous specimens.

Stonewall Peak, at 5,730 feet high, is the most picturesque peak in Cuyamaca Rancho State Park, owing to its sharp rock walls that from a true peak at the top, visible from miles around. According to a geologic history of San Diego County from the San Diego Natural History Museum, Stonewall Peak is in the western part of the Peninsular Ranges Batholith, an exposed irregular igneous mass. Stonewall Peak is formed from light-colored, bouldery outcrops of a type of granite that contains a lot of (gray) quartz and (whitish) feldspar. "The abundance of chemically resistant quartz slows the chemical weathering and leaves these rock types high above more easily weathered igneous materials."

From the top of Stonewall Peak, you can see all three of Cuyamaca's highest peaks, which are composed of a slightly different kind of rock, "the coarse-grained equivalent of basaltic rocks that are found in ocean basins" and that weathers slowly. From that Stonewall summit, look to the west and north, and from left to right you'll see these three peaks: 6,512-foot Cuyamaca Peak, 5,883-foot Middle Peak, and 5,993-foot North Peak, the latter looming directly behind and above Lake Cuyamaca.

You really notice the granite too when you reach that Stonewall summit. At the end of the trail, there is nothing to hike up but rock. A hand rail aids as you ascend carved steps at the very top, where a railing also surrounds the narrow rocky point.

Lake Cuyamaca is one of the prettiest parts of the view from up here, and in spring you'll also see the patches of yellow goldfields wildflowers coloring the meadows.

The second oldest dam built in California created Lake Cuyamaca in 1888. During that same time, the Stonewall Mine, which lies between Stonewall Peak and Lake Cuyamaca, was flourishing. Stonewall Mine was "the richest gold mine ever worked in today's San Diego County," wrote Leland Fetzer in the San Diego History Center's 2006 *Journal of San Diego History*. The gold mine was discovered in 1870 and was named the Stonewall Jackson Mine, in honor of the Confederate general, according to Fetzer. But anti-Southern sentiments quickly abbreviated that name to the Stonewall Mine, which was also then given to the nearby peak. In 1886, the mine was owned by Robert W. Waterman, who would become California governor. The mine was closed in 1892, shortly after Waterman died and the mine proved unproductive. During Waterman's ownership, the Stonewall Mine produced more than $2 million in gold and supported some 200 miners and their families, who lived in Cuyamaca then.

Of course, the Kumeyaay had already occupied Cuyamaca seasonally for generations by then, and its name was derived from their name for this area, "Ah-ha'-Kwe-ah-mac'," meaning "what the rain left behind" or "mist behind the clouds." Their largest village in the area was near the road that today goes to Stonewall Mine, north of Stonewall Peak.

Just shy of the summit, the trail intersects with its northeast spur heading to Los Caballos (or Los Vaqueros) Horse Camp in 1.5 miles. You could make this a longer loop (probably about 5.0 or 6.0 miles total) if you take that route, connecting to the Vern Whitaker Trail to the Cold Stream Trail to return to Paso Picacho's parking area.

Thomas Brothers Map: Page 1176, bottom Page 1196, E-2, Paso Picacho campground.

Before You Go: Download a map and brochure from the state parks' page for Cuyamaca: http://www.parks.ca.gov/pages/667/files/CuyamacaWebLayout09301010.pdf.
  Day-use parking in the Paso Picacho Campground is $8.
  Only hikers are allowed on the Stonewall Peak trail—no bikes, horses, or dogs.

Trailhead: From Interstate 8, exit at Descanso/Japatul Valley to head north on Highway 79. Travel about 12 miles north to reach the Paso Picacho Campground in Cuyamaca, on the left. The Stonewall Peak Trail begins across Highway 79 on the east side, immediately opposite the Paso Picacho Campground.

Distance/Difficulty: The 2.0-mile trail makes a 4.0-mile round trip that's moderate with an 800-foot elevation gain.

10-20. Sugar Pine Trail Still Shows Fire Devastation

Fire devastation is still visible on Sugar Pine Trail.

The Sugar Pine Trail in Cuyamaca that climbs up to Middle Peak was once home to some of the grandest old pine and fir trees in the county. Its namesake, the sugar pine, is the largest native pine in our region, sometimes attaining a height of up to 160 feet with a diameter up to 8 feet; "the current champion is 10 feet in diameter," says the National Audubon Society's *Field Guide to Trees, Western Region*.

Middle Peak, the third highest in Cuyamaca at 5,883 feet (behind North Peak at 5,993 feet and Cuyamaca Peak at 6,512 feet), was also home to large stands of Coulter pines (with the largest pine cones), Ponderosa pines, and Jeffrey pines, as well as incense cedars and white firs. Coast live oaks and black oaks were also abundant. However, the Cedar Fire of 2003 claimed nearly all of them here.

"The Cedar Fire destroyed 99 percent of the 25,000-acre Cuyamaca Rancho State Park, including 500-year-old growth pine forests in the vicinity of Cuyamaca Lake," reports the San Diego Wildfires Education Project produced for teachers by San Diego State University and the San Diego County Water Authority.

Fire plays in important role in maintenance of mixed conifer forests, like the one on Middle Peak, but it is advantageous typically when fire is frequent and of low intensity, when it has minimal effect on large trees. Some trees, like the Coulter pine whose cones usually don't open to release seeds unless heated by fire, are adapted to or even require fire to reproduce.

"Prior to October 2003, much of CRSP had not burned since at least 1911 (when fire records were first kept) due to a policy of fire suppression in the park," says the SDSU project. As a result, the increase in tree density and abundance of available fuel turned the Cedar Fire into a "stand-replacing, crown fire ... the largest mapped fire in California history." Climbing up Middle Peak by way of the Sugar Pine Trail reveals this stunning devastation. Almost all the trees are either gone or standing dead like ghost trees. The underbrush, however, has come back with a vengeance.

The trail leaves from the west end of the Marty Minshall Trail that parallels Highway 79 for about 0.7 mile. Here the grasses are so thick that the trail is sometimes obscured. I found it easier to walk along the edge of the highway, but note there's no shoulder on the road, so be careful of oncoming vehicles.

I began to search for the Minshall Trail when I reached the old foundation of the former Lakeland restaurant that also burned to the ground in that Cedar Fire. While heading west, you can pick up the trail just beyond that foundation; head north (right) when you find it. Soon enough you'll see a signpost designating it as the Marty Minshall Connector to the Sugar Pine Trail.

The Sugar Pine Trail then heads uphill to the west (left), generally following an old road. The trail winds uphill through those ghost trees and a lot of sugar bush; the latter frequently creates canopies over the trail and virtually obscures any other view. There is also a lot of poison oak, so watch for that.

At about 1.3 miles of uphill climbing, you'll note an intersection on the left that heads to a red-and-white CalTrans sawhorse; this leads immediately to the Middle Peak Fire Road, which can return you in another 1.5 miles or so to your parking spot. I pressed on ahead on Sugar Pine Trail, winding another 0.8 miles up that hill through that brush, finally coming upon that same Middle Peak Fire Road. A post marker points the way to the left to the Black Oak Trail in just 100 feet from this intersection.

The road then comes to a T intersection with the west half of the Black Oak Trail to the right and the Middle Peak Fire Road heading to the east half of the Black Oak Trail to the left. You could take either one of these routes; the Black Oak Trail, both east and west, emerges at virtually the same spot on the Milk Ranch Road, which the Middle Peak Fire Road also eventually intersects.

I went left on the Middle Peak Fire Road and wound my way downhill.

Views from the trail take in all the peaks—Cuyamaca, North, and even Stonewall—and you'll also see glimpses of Lake Cuyamaca.

When you reach lower elevations, the oak trees seem to be coming back. Severe fires like the Cedar Fire kill young coast live oaks, but "mature trees have high fire survival rates, even with severe fire," says the SDSU project. "Coast live oak sprouts from the trunk, branches and/or root crown after fire ... A tree may appear dead a whole year after a fire, but may still be alive and resprout." Canyon live oaks and black oaks also resprout.

Cuyamaca Rancho State Park is site of a reforestation project that was the first of its kind to be approved for funding through carbon offset programs, conducted by the California Department of Parks and Recreation in partnership with American Forests, the California Department of Forestry and Fire Protection, SDSU, and UCSB. The fourth and final phase of tree plantings was completed in March 2012. I saw lots of Jeffrey pine seedlings in this program on the Stonewall Peak trail on another outing.

Thomas Brothers Map: Page 1176, D-5.

Before You Go: Download a copy of the trail map for CRSP from the state parks page: http://www.parks.ca.gov/pages/667/files/CuyamacaWebLayout09301010.pdf. Note that dogs are not allowed on state park trails, and the Sugar Pine Trail is open only to hikers and equestrians.

Trailhead: From Interstate 8, exit at Japatul/Descanso, heading north on Highway 79. After about 14 miles, at a sharp right-hand curve in the highway, park at the Trout Pond trailhead parking area off the road.

Cross the highway and begin on the Marty Minshall Trail heading north, parallel to Highway 79. In 0.7 miles, head west and north on the Marty Minshall Connector Trail to the Sugar Pine Trail. At the Middle Peak Fire Road intersection, go left to return to the parking area. Black Oak Trail (east and west segments) take you back as well. When the Black Oak trails or the Middle Peak Fire Road intersects with Milk Ranch Road, go left to return to the parking area.

Distance/Difficulty: I went a total of about 5.5 miles; the longest version going the entire Sugar Pine Trail to Black Oak Trail to Milk Ranch Road would be about 6.0 miles.

With an elevation gain of nearly 1,000 feet, it's moderately strenuous.

10-21. Loop through Two State Parks for Springtime Wildflower Fest

Following four parts of different trails, a fine loop hike can be made that takes you through both Anza-Borrego Desert State Park and Cuyamaca Rancho State Park over a transitional chaparral habitat loaded with wildflowers in spring. The two state parks actually border each other in this area. At about 600,000 acres, Anza-Borrego Desert State Park is the largest state park in California and the second largest in the country (after New York's Adirondack Park). Cuyamaca Rancho, with about 25,000 acres, is the sixth largest out of 279 state parks in California.

Spring is an excellent time to explore this area because the wildflowers put on a lovely show, and with little shade here, it gets a lot hotter in summer.

This loop begins at the very western edge of Anza-Borrego Desert State Park off Highway S1, just northeast of Lake Cuyamaca. Begin on the California Riding and Hiking Trail that crosses S1 near mile marker 36, at the Pedro Fages Monument. Head southwest on the trail, across the highway from the historic monument. The monument honors Spanish Colonel Pedro Fages, who discovered the Colorado Desert and the San Joaquin Valley in 1772, when he headed east along this route from San Diego searching for army deserters. He rode into Oriflamme Canyon in Anza-Borrego and then traveled through the Central Valley until reaching Mission San Luis Obispo. He served as governor of Las Californias (then Alta and Baja) from 1782 to 1791.

Some of the best wildflower shows appear on this loop through two state parks.

The California Riding and Hiking Trail (CRHT) has its own interesting history. The vision for it began in 1945 when the State Legislature passed the California Riding and Hiking Trails Act, calling for a single 3,000-mile loop trail between the Mexico and Oregon borders. The state Department of Parks and Recreation worked on developing the CRHT through the 1960s. After funding and planning difficulties made the single trail seem impossible, that act was repealed in 1974 and replaced with the California Recreational Trails Act, which focused on pursuing shorter trail segments statewide. "Though never finished, the now historic CRHT still serves as one of California's earliest and most successful models of trail building on a county, regional and statewide scale," wrote Ann Compton for the Equine Land Conservation Resource.

By the 1960s, some 1,060 miles of the CRHT had been completed statewide. In San Diego, 108 miles of the CRHT exist, with only 76 miles of it in use.

The wildflowers begin appearing as soon as you start hiking on the CRHT here. When I was there in early April, one of the first I saw were yellow Johnny jump-ups, a type of native violet that is a treat to see anywhere. They were accompanied by many tiny pink red-stemmed filarees.

Soon you will also see the blue-water view of Lake Cuyamaca to the northwest. The surrounding area here is dominated by huge mountain meadows, splashed with large patches of yellow flowers; they are goldfields, a native sunflower that's only a few inches high. These colonies of goldfields near Lake Cuyamaca are one of the county's spring wonders, notes James Lightner in his book, *San Diego County Native Plants.* San Diego County counts more than 2,000 native plant species, "more wild species than in any comparable area in the continental United States," writes Lightner.

Indeed, on this hike alone, in this transitional chaparral habitat lying at nearly 5,000 feet elevation, I also saw baby blue eyes, white and blue ceanothus (wild lilac), pink-blooming manzanita, yellow and white cream cups, yellow fiddlenecks, pink bush mallow, yellow hairy lotus, yellow baby stars, and white summer snow—a springtime bonanza.

After 2.4 miles on the CRHT, a fairly easy hike with only about a 200-foot elevation gain, turn left at the junction with the Soapstone Grade Fire Road. Follow this rocky dirt road downhill for 0.6 mile until you reach the creek bed at the bottom and the intersection with the Upper Green Valley Fire Road. This downhill leg of the loop is the steepest, so I was glad I chose the counterclockwise route. Here I also saw the singular blooms of our lord's candle, a type of yucca.

When you reach the oak woodland along the creek bed at the bottom, take a left onto the Upper Green Valley Trail. There is an unmarked wooden post here. To the right, a marked post points the way to the Upper Green Valley Fire Road. On the Upper Green Valley Trail, there were more blooms of the yuccas, some not yet in full flower, and lots of ceanothus.

Follow the Upper Green Valley Trail uphill (gradually) for 1.3 miles until you reach a large wooden sign pointing to the trail you just took. At this wooden sign, take the upper trail to the left heading northeast to continue 1.2 miles on the (unmarked here) La Cima Trail. The La Cima Trail hugs Highway S1 until you return to the Pedro Fages Monument, where you started.

Thomas Brothers Map: Page 1176, H-4.

Before You Go: Download a map of this loop from the state parks' brochure page for Cuyamaca Rancho State Park: http://www.parks.ca.gov/pages/667/files/CuyamacaWebLayout09301010. pdf. This loop is also shown on Tom Harrison Maps' *Cuyamaca Rancho State Park Trail Map.*
    This loop is open to hikers, bicyclists, and equestrians. Dogs are not allowed on state park trails.

Trailhead: On Highway S1, Sunrise Highway, 1.7 miles southeast of its intersection with Highway 79 through Cuyamaca, park at the Pedro Fages historical monument at mile marker 36. Begin on the California Riding and Hiking Trail across the highway from the monument.
    Reach this trailhead from Interstate 8 heading east, exiting at Sunrise Highway, heading north on S1 to Laguna Mountain Recreation Area and proceeding to mile marker 36 on S1.
    If you are heading south on Highway 79 from Julian, turn left onto S1 and go just 1.7 miles to the monument parking area.

Distance/Difficulty: The total loop is about 5.6 miles; easy to moderate.

10-22. West Side Loop Shows Oaks Rebounding to Deer's Delight

Hiking a loop of Cuyamaca's West Side Trail with its Cold Stream Trail still reveals the long-lasting impact of the 2003 Cedar Fire that burned almost all of that state park. The landscape remains studded with the ghosts of former pine trees, but the black oaks are making a comeback.

The West Mesa area of Cuyamaca Rancho State Park was studied from 2004 to 2009 by SDSU biologists for California State Parks to determine the effects of that disastrous fire, the largest wildfire in California's recorded history. Some 98 percent of pine trees were killed by the fire, whereas most of the oak trees were killed only above-ground and resprouted from their bases.

Ceanothus (wild lilac), especially Palmer lilac, has resprouted, and the West Side Trail is home to lots of it, which should sport profuse white blossoms in spring. Ceanothus is a host for a type of fungus that is necessary for survival of conifers, according to the studies, and it "plays an important nutrient cycling role post-fire in California ecosystems."

You'll see many oak trees resprouting from their old bases into new trees. "Oaks may be the single most important genus used by wildlife for food and cover in California forests and rangelands," according to a study on the California black oak for the U.S. Department of Agriculture's Forest Service in 2007 (http://www.fs.fed.us/database/feis/plants/tree/quekel/all.html). The native Kumeyaay who used to live here during summer and fall depended on oak acorns for their meals, and they preferred black oak acorns over all others. "Its acorns are the largest of the western oaks, and are heavily consumed by livestock, mule deer, feral pig, rodents, mountain quail, wild turkey, jays and woodpeckers," according to the study.

Mule deer share the Kumeyaay's taste for the acorns of black oaks. That study reported that mule deer in Cuyamaca "preferred California black oak acorns over any other forage." Fawn survival rates tend to increase or decrease with the size of local black oak acorn crops. Chipmunks, squirrels, and raccoons also consume the acorns. And where there are deer, there are mountain lions as well.

I saw so many deer tracks on the West Side Trail that I expected to see some, and soon enough two bounded across the trail

Look for morteros and views of Stonewall Peak from West Side Trail.

into the heavy growth of ceanothus, probably looking for those acorns, which they'll eat from fall through spring when new green forage is more scarce.

I began at the West Mesa Trailhead, which lies on Highway 79 between the park's visitor center and Paso Picacho campground. Cross the highway to begin on the West Side Trail, which heads off to the right from the West Mesa Fire Road.

That trail winds up about 600 feet in elevation as it heads 1.8 miles north toward Paso Picacho. Views of the rocky Stonewall Peak are plentiful. It's a fairly narrow trail and is open to hikers and equestrians. Bikers are not allowed on this trail—usually they stick to Cuyamaca's several fire roads—and dogs are not allowed on state park trails.

Just to the south of the West Mesa Fire Road, which is where this portion of the West Side Trail begins, is Arrowmakers Ridge, a site known for yielding more than 1,300 projectile points for archaeological studies done in the 1930s for the San Diego Museum of Man. The West Mesa area was site of a large Kumeyaay village that dated from AD 500, perhaps due to all the streams, springs, and oaks here.

The trail crosses a flowing Cold Stream a little more than halfway up this part of the West Side Trail, where it soon opens to a meadow area that's part of Fern Flat. At that 1.8 miles point, the trail intersects with a connector trail to Paso Picacho on the right. You'll see lots of mesh screens protecting fledgling Jeffrey pine seedlings planted by the park.

After walking past the fire station and park headquarters buildings, cross the highway in front of Paso Picacho campground entrance to begin the next segment on the Stonewall Peak Trail. A short way up that trail will take you to the intersection with the Cold Stream Trail on the right. This part of the Cold Stream Trail—about 1.8 miles as well from the Stonewall Peak Trail to West Mesa Trailhead—is currently not recommended for equestrians, so it is open only to hikers. The trail here is very narrow and heavily rutted, which might make it hard for horses to secure their footing. But for hikers, this trail offers some big views to the south over mountain meadows to southern peaks as it winds along with the free-flowing Cold Stream. In fall, the black oak leaves are turning yellow, mountain mahoganies sport feathery styles, and even winter currants are red and ripe for the picking.

One of the coolest attractions here is the large granite slab just to the south of the trail that holds a few morteros, evidence that the Kumeyaay who once lived here were grinding those black acorns for meals.

When the Cold Stream Trail intersects with the Cold Spring Trail, you'll see a bubbling tank filling with water that is the Cold Spring. Just 0.2 miles after this intersection is the connector trail to the right back to the West Mesa Trailhead parking area.

Thomas Brothers Map: Page 1176—bottom half that is page 1196, G-5, where the dotted West Mesa Fire Road hits Highway 79—that's West Mesa Trailhead parking area.

Before You Go: Download a copy of the trail map in the brochure of Cuyamaca Rancho State Park from its state park website: http://www.parks.ca.gov/pages/667/files/CuyamacaWeb Layout09301010.pdf.

Or buy a copy of the Cuyamaca Rancho State Park Trail Map by Tom Harrison Maps at the visitor center, which is open only on Saturdays and Sundays from 10:00 a.m. to 4:00 p.m.

This trail is open only to hikers and equestrians.

Trailhead: From Interstate 8, exit at Descanso/Japatul Valley and head north on Highway 79 to Cuyamaca Rancho State Park. Park in the West Mesa Trailhead parking area just off Highway 79, between the park's visitor center and its Paso Picacho campground. Walk across the highway to its west side, beginning on the West Mesa Fire Road for a very short way to the West Side Trail on the right.

Distance/Difficulty: About a 4.5-mile loop combining the West Side Trail with the Cold Stream Trail; easy to moderate.

10-23. Two Parts of Roberts Ranch Feature Healthy Oak Woodlands

Whoosh! A huge hawk soared so close to me that I could hear it slicing through the air. It landed on a limb of a giant canyon live oak tree that I had been admiring in silence. I broke that silence myself with a "Whoa!" Then the hawk was off in a flash before I could take its photo. It was one of my most thrilling moments on the trails, this time on the northern section of Roberts Ranch in Japatul Valley, where mature live oak groves thrive among meadows that are surely blanketed in wildflowers in spring.

There are two sections of Roberts Ranch, separated by Interstate 8 at the Descanso/Japatul Valley Road exit. They were added to the Cleveland National Forest after Descanso cabinetmaker Duncan McFetridge, affectionately known by some as the Robin Hood of Cleveland Forest, crusaded to stop housing development plans there and raised money to help purchase and add them to the national forest lands, according to Jerry Schad in *Afoot and Afield San Diego County.*

Two separate trails lead to mighty oaks.

In 1992 the U.S. Forest Service got congressional approval to allocate $2 million to buy about 285 acres, preserving wildlife corridors in the area. Trails were opened there in 1998.

I began on the southern section, immediately north of a CalTrans maintenance facility and through a metal gate (open when I was there) to a dirt road where more CalTrans vehicles sat. Walk down that dirt road about 100 yards until you see an obvious trail cut through the thick meadow grasses to the east. Follow the trail as it winds through large meadows and into several healthy oak groves.

Cows evidently continue to graze there on land remarkably free from fire destruction, considering how close it lies to scene of the disastrous 2003 Cedar Fire. That wild firestorm was the largest in California recorded history, burning 422 square miles, including most of the 25,000-acre Cuyamaca Rancho State Park that lies just several miles to the north from Roberts Ranch.

Lots of Engelmann oaks, as well as coast and canyon live oaks, some very old and very large, are dotted among the ranch's meadows. Engelmann oaks, named for St. Louis botanist George Engelmann (1809–1884), can reach about 60 feet high. They are usually smaller than coast or canyon live oaks, and their evergreen leaves are lighter in color, appearing blue-green or grey-green compared to the other two species.

Coast live oaks can reach some 80 feet high, and canyon live oaks can rise to 100 feet. Both have leaves that are dark green and oblong with spiny teeth, making it hard to tell the two species apart. The coast live oak leaves tend to be more convex (edges turned under), whereas canyon live oak leaves tend to be flat. If you see a huge specimen whose several horizontal limbs extend enormously, it's probably a canyon live oak and may be more than 200 years old.

I followed the most obvious trail and eventually reached the remnant of an old ranch road as I continued hiking to the east and south. There are actually several trails here, so one could wander around, but I stuck to the main one, usually choosing the high road. Sometimes I marked an X on the sandy surface at those multiple-choice trails so I could find the same return route. It might not matter because they all likely lead back to the same general area.

I eventually reached a T intersection with another road, and I had gone about 1.75 miles one-way. That road to the right ended shortly at a locked gate, and to the left it continued into the backcountry. According to San Diego Horse Trails, the road is a continuation of the fire road from Horsethief Canyon and continues for about 3.0 miles from here.

I went a short ways and then turned back to retrace my steps, trying to follow my original path.

Then I drove to the northern section of the ranch, which lies on the north side of that same Interstate 8 exit. This trail begins across the highway from the park-and-ride lot, at a metal gate across a dirt road. The trail dissipates near an old collection of ranch corrals. I stuck close to those and continued next to them to the right a bit uphill, where I soon saw an obvious trail heading off to the left. I took that and wandered through some even older, thicker oak groves.

I went only about 0.6 mile here before turning around, when I reached another T intersection with a little-used road. I was happy to go back into those oak groves again, and it was here where I admired that enormous live oak tree with its huge spreading limbs, perfect for a hawk perch.

Thomas Brothers Map: Page 1235, J-6 and J-7. J-6 is where the northern section is, on the east side of Highway 79 from that parking "P." The southern section begins just south of this freeway intersection and just east of Japatul Valley Road.

Before You Go: If you go to http://www.trails.com/topomap.aspx?trailid=HGS043-159, you can view a satellite map of the area, zooming in until you see the trails on either side of Interstate 8 at that Descanso/Japatul Valley Road exit.

You need an Adventure Pass from Cleveland National Forest to park on the road for the southern section. For a $5 day pass or $30 annual pass, go to the forest ranger station in Alpine or at outdoor stores (including REI and Adventure 16). For more information about the Adventure Pass, go to http://www.fs.usda.gov/main/cleveland/passes-permits/recreation.

These trails are open to hikers and dogs on leashes.

Trailhead: For the southern section of Roberts Ranch, from Interstate 8, exit at Descanso/Japatul Valley Road and head south. Go 0.2 miles and turn right before the intersection of Campbell Ranch Road. Park on either side of the road here. On the east side of the road, immediately north of the CalTrans maintenance facility, walk through the gate onto the dirt road about 100 yards until you see an obvious trail cut through the meadow grasses on the right.

For the northern section, head north at that same exit and park in the park-and-ride lot on the west side of Highway 79. Walk (or run) across the highway and enter through the metal gate on the east side of the Highway 79 to begin on the dirt road.

Distance/Difficulty: I went for a little more than 5.0 miles round-trip on both sections; easy.

10-24. Find This Hidden Wilderness Valley

Horsethief Canyon Trail goes almost straight down about 500 feet to one of the loveliest oak- and sycamore-studded creek valleys anywhere. That drop requires the requisite slog back up, but the boulder-strewn canyon complete with rushing Pine Valley Creek makes it well worth the effort.

Horsethief Canyon is in the Pine Creek Wilderness, which is part of Cleveland National Forest. Just south of Interstate 8 where Highway 79 heads north to Julian, the Pine Creek Wilderness encompasses 13,000 acres designated by Congress in 1984 as part of the National Wilderness System.

"A wilderness, in contrast with those areas where man and his work dominate the landscape, is hereby recognized as an area where earth and its community of life are untrammeled by man, where man himself is a visitor who does not remain," declares the Wilderness Act of 1964, as cited on Cleveland National Forest's website.

Although there are several trails in this wilderness, I saw no other signs of man-made activity, and that made for an almost pristine experience in nature. The only reminder of exactly where I was occurred when a Border Patrol helicopter buzzed me overhead.

Jerry Schad reports in his 2007 edition of *Afoot and Afield San Diego County,* a masterful hiking guidebook, that illegal immigrants have generally moved farther east than Pine Creek, though it was an active migrating area in the 1990s. The helicopters are evidently still keeping tabs. Schad also points out that Horsethief Canyon itself was used in the 1880s by thieves who stashed their stolen horses before taking them south across the border.

Drop down into Horsethief Canyon to reach Pine Valley Creek.

It's easy to imagine that history in this deep canyon that virtually hides in the folds of mountains that rise some 1,000 feet higher to reach nearly 4,000 feet. Horses and men could surely hide here, and with Pine Valley Creek providing water (not potable today without sterilizing), they could survive.

The trail down to the creek valley basically follows a runoff that empties into Pine Valley Creek. If heavy rains have occurred, parts of the trail could be wet. That may also make for the steady sound of water flowing as you head down the hill.

The vegetation at the top is mostly chaparral with fragrant sage and evergreen chamise, along with occasional yucca and dudleya (the latter similar to aeonium found in local succulent nurseries). At the bottom are habitats of riparian (surrounding a creek or river canyon) and oak woodland with lots of grasses. The decibel level of Pine Valley Creek rises audibly as you get closer to it. Cleveland National Forest says rainbow trout and bass are found in Pine Valley Creek.

When I made the climb back up, I noticed other trails in the area. At one point, I reached a fork where the left turn seemed to be the main trail, and the right turn was a much smaller trail. I realized I hadn't noticed this switch on my way down and had to catch my bearings by scanning the scenery to determine which way I should go. I took the smaller fork to the right, and it proved to be the same way I'd come down. Be observant so you don't get lost. According to the map at the trailhead, they probably all head back to the same spot, but you might have more ground to cover.

At the Horsethief Canyon trailhead parking area, there are two trailheads. The nearest one across the road from the map sign heads right to Espinosa and Secret Canyon

Trails. For the Horsethief Canyon trail, take the one that goes off to the left of the map sign and connects after the road gates onto a graded dirt road. A short way down that road (about 300 yards) is a wooden post marked "Trail." Just to the right of that marker are two trail forks; one goes uphill and the other goes down. I took the downhill trail, which is also marked at its top with a metal marker saying "Wilderness."

No matter how you reach the bottom of Horsethief Canyon, you'll be rewarded by that beautiful creek valley in the wilderness.

Thomas Brothers Map: Page 1275, 4E.

Before You Go: The best trail map of the entire Pine Creek Wilderness is published by Cleveland National Forest and is available at its district offices in the county, or often at outdoor stores such as REI and Adventure 16. Seek *A Guide to the Pine Creek Wilderness and Hauser Wilderness* ($8) from the Cleveland National Forest website, http://www.fs.usda.gov/detail/cleveland/maps-pubs.

You may see the Horsethief Trail on the map in the Cleveland National Forest Visitors Guide: http://www.fs.usda.gov/Internet/FSE_DOCUMENTS/stelprdb5277346.pdf. Horsethief Canyon is in the Descanso Ranger District.

You may also download a satellite map of the trail the from Cleveland National Forest website: http://www.fs.usda.gov/recarea/cleveland/recreation/recarea/?recid=47468&actid=50.

Find more information on the area from CNF's Pine Creek/Hauser Wilderness Area pages: http://www.fs.usda.gov/recarea/cleveland/recarea/?recid=75032.

You need an Adventure Pass to park on CNF lands. You can buy a $5 day-use pass or a $30 annual pass through CNF ranger stations (also online) or various retail outlets, including REI or Adventure 16. For more information about the Adventure Pass, go to http://www.fs.usda.gov/main/cleveland/passes-permits/recreation.

This trail is open to hikers, equestrians, and dogs on leashes.

Trailhead: From Interstate 8 heading east, exit at Highway 79/Japatul Valley Road, turning right (south) onto Japatul Valley Road. Travel south on this road for about 5.0 miles, then turn left onto Lyons Valley Road. After about 1.5 miles, turn left at the Japatul Fire Station road, making another immediate left into the Horsethief Canyon parking area.

Distance/Difficulty: About 3.0 miles round-trip; moderate.

10-25. Espinosa Trail Explores Pine Creek Wilderness

The Espinosa Trail in the Pine Creek Wilderness is a classic example of what the national Wilderness Act of 1964 mandated. It called for securing "for the American people of present and future generations the benefits of an enduring resource of wilderness, untrammeled by man," where we can all enjoy "challenging recreational activities like hiking … and extraordinary opportunities for solitude."

Pine Creek Wilderness covers 13,480 acres and was designated by Congress in 1984. It is bordered on the south by the Hauser Wilderness, an 8,000-acre parcel of steep mountainous terrain studded with granite boulders and outcroppings. The original 1964 Wilderness Act also created the National Wilderness Preservation System, and the act put only 9.1 million acres into its fold. Since then, the system has grown every year and now totals more than 109 million acres in 662 wilderness areas in 44 states.

True wilderness can be found on Espinosa Trail.

The sign at the Espinosa trailhead warns that "smuggling and/or illegal entry is common in this area due to the proximity of the international border," but trammeling here is legally allowed only by hikers, equestrians, and dogs on leashes (no bikes).

The trail heads into the steep canyons of the Pine Valley Creek, where views take in the 4,657-foot-high Corte Madera Mountain to the northeast and the sheltered, peak-surrounded Skye Valley to the south. The Espinosa Trail is rocky and steep in parts, but it is mostly dominated by chaparral and scrub oak habitats, with riparian and oak woodlands along the year-round Pine Valley Creek itself as well as some tributaries. During rainy years, the usually dry Espinosa Creek (sometimes spelled Espinoza) gurgles alongside as you wind down into the creek valley.

The entire Espinosa Trail covers about 6.4 miles from west to east, but only about 2.9 miles of it are located in Pine Creek Wilderness, where only hikers and horseback riders and dogs are allowed. The eastern portion of the trail is open to vehicles and other such uses.

I wanted to experience that solitude and natural beauty, so I kept to the western end. The first part here ascends for a brief time until reaching the top of the ridge with those long southern and northern views. Then it descends several hundred feet in about 1.75 miles before reaching Pine Valley Creek, sometimes called simply Pine Creek. Always a rushing stream, Pine Valley Creek is surrounded by oaks with occasional sycamores and willows. It's a lovely place.

Espinosa Trail then crosses that creek (either by wading through or trying to find a rock route across) and continues to a junction, with the Secret Canyon Trail heading north or the other half of Espinosa heading east through the wilderness. I chose to stop at the creek and retrace my steps back up.

Such a bountiful water source here certainly suggests that it has been home to man long before it was declared a wilderness. Cleveland National Forest, which manages it, notes that the Kumeyaay and their ancestors occupied these areas for over 10,000 years. "The Kumeyaay were primarily a hunter/gatherer culture that practiced a unique form of land management that may have included agriculture," says the CNF on a page about Pine Creek Wilderness. "The Kumeyaay also developed a fairly advanced ceramic technology, which is relatively rare among hunter/gatherer cultures."

The oak trees would have provided acorns, and the sugar bush and toyon (Christmas berry) provided berries in the winter. Today these foodstuffs are enjoyed by birds as well as mammals, including coyotes. I saw lots of sugar bush and toyon, both of which produce their colorful pink and red berries, respectively, in the fall and winter.

I also enjoyed serene solitude and appreciated the efforts of the Wilderness Society (http://wilderness.org), founded in 1935, whose early members were responsible for the creation of the Wilderness Act. The society continues to be a leading American conservation organization working to protect our public lands. "Wilderness clears our air and filters our water," says the society. "Wilderness provides essential habitat for wildlife. And wilderness is a natural retreat from the stress of our everyday lives."

It's as close as the Espinosa Trail.

Thomas Brothers Map: Page 1275, E-3,4.

Before You Go: The Cleveland National Forest's website offers information on the entire Espinosa Trail: http://www.fs.usda.gov/recarea/cleveland/recreation/hiking/recarea/?recid= 47448&actid=50. The wilderness portion is the Japatul end.

The best trail map of the entire Pine Creek Wilderness is published by Cleveland National Forest and is available at its district offices in the county or often at outdoor stores, including REI and Adventure 16. Seek *A Guide to the Pine Creek Wilderness and Hauser Wilderness* ($8) from the Cleveland National Forest website: http://www.fs.usda.gov/detail/cleveland/maps-pubs.

You need an Adventure Pass to park on CNF lands. You can buy a $5 day-use pass or a $30 annual pass through CNF ranger stations (also online) or various retail outlets, including REI or Adventure 16. For more information about the Adventure Pass, go to http://www.fs.usda.gov/main/cleveland/passes-permits/recreation.

Open to hikers, equestrians, and dogs on leashes.

Trailhead: From Interstate 8, exit at Descanso, Highway 79/Japatul Valley Road and head south on Japatul Valley Road for about 5.6 miles. Turn left onto Lyons Valley Road for about 1.6 miles; then turn left at the Japatul Fire Station turnoff, where the parking area is just to the left.

This is the Horsethief Canyon trailhead area. The Espinosa trailhead is the one heading straight up immediately east from that parking area, where the smuggling warning sign is located.

Distance/Difficulty: It's about 1.75 miles one-way to Pine Valley Creek, for a 3.5-mile round-trip hike. Moderately difficult.

10-26. Quiet Secret Canyon Has Creek, Bridge

Hike even a portion of the northern segment of the 15.6-mile-long Secret Canyon Trail in the Pine Creek Wilderness for wonderful river-gorge views. The trail winds along pretty Pine Valley Creek, which typically flows freely all year long. In deeper sections the creek is home to rainbow trout and bass. In this northern part of the trail, you'll likely see only some small minnows in the shallower sections here. The trail flanks the river gorge a few hundred feet above it as it takes hikers through some fine old live oaks as well as Jeffrey pines. These Jeffrey pines that follow Pine Valley Creek gave the town of Pine Valley its name.

This lovely mountain valley was known before 1869 as "El Valle de los Pinos," according to "Pine Valley—A Mountain Oasis," an article by Todd Gilbert in the *Mountain Empire Country Living Magazine*. This "oasis dense with pines, manzanita and centuries-old oak trees once shaded only the Indians that inhabited the region," he wrote. Captain William S. Emery, a former Butterfield stagecoach driver, and his wife settled in this area in 1869 and renamed the area Pine Valley, "one of the oldest names in the county," said Gilbert. Emery became a cattleman here as well as a family newspaper publisher.

Lovely Secret Canyon Trail looks down onto river gorge.

This northern section of the Secret Canyon trail follows the path of an old stone flume that was never completed (around 1895), according to Jerry Schad's *Afoot and Afield San Diego County*. It would have carried water to a proposed reservoir in Pine Valley from King Creek, a tributary of the San Diego River just west of the Cuyamaca Mountains. I didn't see any evidence of that project on the hike.

Pretty quickly on the trail, though, I did see ongoing evidence of this area's historic residents: cows. Smack dab on the trail were a bunch of big bovines, just lounging on the path. There wasn't really a way around them, so I kept approaching gently until they lumbered along their own path down to the creek.

Cattle grazing is permitted in wilderness areas by permit, but otherwise, this 13,000-acre Pine Creek Wilderness Area, so designated by Congress in 1984, "is an area of undeveloped federal land retaining its primeval character and influence, without permanent improvements or human habitation, which is protected and managed so as to preserve its natural conditions" (Wilderness Act of 1964). Because it is designated wilderness, only hikers, equestrians, and dogs on leashes are permitted here.

I saw a lot of poison oak and several wildflowers, including Indian pink, Indian paintbrush, scarlet bugler, pink California wild rose, splendid mariposa lilies, and lots of yerba mansa, their white petals surrounding a tall showy yellow bracht, especially down in the wetter areas right beside the creek. The trail heads down to the creek, with two crossings made easier by well-placed boulders.

There is evidence of fire damage in this area, but from the Laguna-Kitchen Creek Fire of 1970 as opposed to the enormously devastating Cedar Fire of 2003 that consumed most of nearby Cuyamaca. The Laguna-Kitchen Creek Fire of September 1970 burned 185,000 acres, 388 homes, and 1,000 other structures. By comparison, the Cedar Fire of 2003 burned 280,278 acres, 2,820 buildings including 2,232 homes, and killed 15 people, making it the largest fire in recorded California history. According to the Cleveland National Forest, the Tragedy Springs Hazardous Fuels Reduction Project served as a fuel break that stopped the Cedar Fire's eastern spread as it neared Guatay and Pine Valley, saving those communities as well as much of Mount Laguna.

After about 1.7 miles from the Pine Creek Trailhead, you reach the impressive Pine Valley Creek Bridge that carries Interstate 8 over this river valley. Built in 1974, it was the first bridge built in the United States using the segmental balanced cantilever method. It rises 450 feet above the valley floor and is over 1,700 feet long. It is also known as the Nello Irwin Greer Bridge in honor of its project engineer. Greer's design is credited for rerouting the freeway to save Pine Valley and many of the native pines, as well as two miles of freeway construction, requiring this enormous bridge over the Pine Valley Creek canyon.

Interstate 8 was officially designated in 1964 as it slowly replaced U.S. Highway 80. Interstate 8 in California was completed in 1975 to the Arizona border, and to its eastern terminus at the Interstate 10 interchange at Casa Grande just before Tucson in 1973.

A short way beyond the bridge, as the trail climbs above the creek, I turned around where a small tributary crossing tumbles over a few boulders. The trail dissipates a bit here. I have read it might be hard to follow from this point, but it continues until it reaches the trailheads for Horsethief Canyon, Espinosa Trail, and the southern end of Secret Canyon Trail, near the Japatul Fire Station on Lyons Valley Road.

I walked silently in this lovely wilderness where even the cows seem quieter.

Thomas Brothers Map: Page 1237, A-4, where dotted Pine Valley-Las Bancas Road intersects Old Highway 80.

Before You Go: Download a satellite map of the entire Secret Canyon Trail, also noted here as Pine Creek Trail, from Cleveland National Forest's website on Pine Creek Wilderness Area: http://www.fs.usda.gov/recarea/cleveland/recreation/hiking/recarea/?recid=47496&actid=50. Another page on Pine Creek Wilderness has a map of this trail too: http://www.fs.usda.gov/detail/cleveland/recreation/?cid=stelprdb5286397#pine.

The CNF page on the Secret Canyon Trail is http://www.fs.usda.gov/recarea/cleveland/recreation/hiking/recarea/?recid=47502&actid=50.

You need an Adventure Pass to park in the Pine Creek Wilderness staging areas. For a $5 day pass or a $30 annual pass, go to http://www.fs.usda.gov/main/cleveland/passes-permits. You may buy the passes at the CNF ranger station in Alpine just off Interstate 8, at outdoor recreations stores (including REI and Adventure 16), or at the Pine Valley Store on Old Highway 80.

It is open to hikers, equestrians, and dogs on leashes.

Trailhead: To reach the Pine Creek Valley Wilderness Trailhead, from Interstate 8, exit at Pine Valley and head north. Turn left onto Old Highway 80, go about 1.5 miles to the trailhead on the left, and turn left, heading about 0.5 miles to the parking area. The Secret Canyon Trail is well marked, just beyond the restroom.

Distance/Difficulty: I went about 4.2 miles round-trip with about 630 feet in elevation change; fairly easy.

11. Laguna Mountain and Vicinity

Laguna Mountain Recreation Area is another mountain gem in San Diego County. On Cleveland National Forest land, Laguna features Big Laguna Lake and a few other ponds, some scattered peaks, and several more segments of the Pacific Crest Trail. Some of the healthiest pine forests remain in Laguna, which has largely escaped the desecration of the biggest wildfires.

The PCT in Laguna is breathtaking for its views of the desert that lies practically straight down from this mountain range; you will believe the PCT surely got its name here for being on the edge.

11-1. Grand Loop of Laguna Has Lakes, Meadows

A grand tour of Laguna's beautiful mountain landscapes can be had on a Big Laguna Trail loop. This hike travels to three lakes, across the vast Laguna Meadow where the Kumeyaay once had a summer camp, and through pine and oak forests that provide some welcome summer shade.

Big Laguna Lake is one of county's only natural lakes.

I began this loop at the Laguna Campground off Sunrise Highway, S1, where there are a few day-use parking spots. If there are no day-use parking spots, you can park just off Sunrise Highway and hike in to the campground area. The trail heads off from the southern end of the Meadow Loop Laguna Campground, and also from the southern end of the main campground near the parking area by the amphitheater. I began at the Meadow Loop trailhead.

492

The trails are all signposted as the Big Laguna Trail (BLT, as it's known by locals). Watch for these signposts along the way.

From the trailhead, I hiked south, heading to Little Laguna Lake, the first of those three lakes. During years of drought, however, the lake is so low that it appears to be just an especially green, wet meadow.

Heading south along the western edge of this (sometimes dry) lake, you'll soon come to the first intersection, which is actually with the BLT coming from that other trailhead in Laguna Campground, where a wooden platform bolsters the trail for a short way. Head to the right here, going west. On your left (south) is that giant Laguna Meadow, a 900-acre wet meadow that's a remnant of seasonally wet meadows that were once extensive in the Palomar and Laguna Mountain areas, according to the Cleveland National Forest, which governs this recreational area.

Cleveland National Forest (CNF) was one of the nation's earliest forest reserves established under the Forest Reserve Act of 1891. The act originated to slow wasteful and illegal timber cutting, but in Southern California, where the state had established the California Forestry Commission even earlier in 1886, the act was used to protect watersheds. The thinking was "lack of protection from fire was causing serious damage to irrigation works of the late 1880s," according to a history of Cleveland National Forest (http://www.fs.usda.gov/detail/cleveland/learning/history-culture/?cid=stelprdb5278297).

Cleveland National Forest (named for President Grover Cleveland) began with the Trabuco Cañon Forest Reserve in the Santa Ana Mountains, created by President Henry Harrison in 1893. In 1897, President Cleveland created the 700,000-acre San Jacinto Forest Reserve. In 1907, the forest reserves were changed to national forests and transferred to a new Bureau of Forestry (now Forest Service) in the U.S. Department of Agriculture. Also in 1907, President Teddy Roosevelt added Palomar and Laguna Mountains to the Southern California forest reserves, and in 1908 he combined them to form the new 1,904,826-acre Cleveland National Forest. Over the next 20 years, several deletions were made to CNF, returning nonforest value lands to the public. Today CNF consists of about 460,000 acres of forest land across Southern California.

By the mid-1920s, emphasis in forest reserves shifted from watershed protection to recreation. The Laguna Mountain Recreation Area was designated within CNF in 1926, according to a 1975 article, "Cleveland National Forest: San Diego's Watershed" by Michael Sakarias in the *Journal of San Diego History* (http://www.sandiegohistory.org/journal/75fall/cleveland.htm).

There was opposition to the national administration of these forests, notably from cattlemen who didn't want restrictions on grazing. It's interesting to note that cattle grazing still takes place in Laguna, though only in fenced areas. Laguna Meadow is one of those now-protected areas, because grazing here was eliminating the Cleveland horkelia, the only host plant that sustains the endangered Laguna skipper butterfly. This butterfly is thought to exist only in Palomar Mountain and Laguna, though it hasn't been seen in Laguna in several years. I saw lots of butterflies in that meadow, though I don't think any were Laguna skippers. The ones I saw were feeding on yellow nuttall cinquefoil, which is in the rose family like the horkelia. They were also flitting around pink checkerbloom and blue dicks.

The trail soon hits Big Laguna Lake, one of the largest natural lakes in our area that's usually filled with water all year long. The BLT loops entirely around Big Laguna Lake, but I kept heading essentially straight (taking a left at both lake loop intersections) along its southern end, heading toward Water of the Woods, the third lake in this loop.

Between Big Laguna Lake and Water of the Woods, the trail goes right by a slab of granite filled with several morteros. A hiker I met on the trail, George Jillich of Point Loma, told me this area was the site of a Kumeyaay summer camp.

CNF lands have indeed been inhabited by humans for at least 10,000 years, including those of the Late Prehistoric Period (from 500 BC to AD 1769, the year the Spanish came through here), which included the Kumeyaay. Pottery was first used during this period, as were mortars and pestles to grind acorns and other seeds. These deep morteros in the granite slabs were used to grind acorns of the favored black oaks.

The trail soon winds around the lovely Water of the Woods Lake. Continuing around that small lake and past the Sunset Trail, the BLT skirts the southern edge of Laguna Meadow. Now you are on a Big Laguna Trail spur trail, this one No. 6, the Kemp Spur. Follow the BLT signposts with the No. 6 on the bottom.

Pass an intersection with Spur Trail No. 3, continuing on No. 6. When the trail intersects with a gate, continue to the left (north) on the BLT, now winding through pine and oak forests. At the last intersection with a cattle guard crossing, take a right over that cattle guard to head back to the Laguna Campground. You can continue straight ahead and find yourself back on the trail's wooden platform at the first intersection. That dry Little Laguna Lake should lead your way back.

Thomas Brothers Map: Page 1218, 4,5-B,C–Laguna Campground.

Before You Go: Download a map of Laguna Mountain Recreation Area and most of its trails from the Laguna Mountain Volunteer Association (www.lmva.net).

You may also want to buy *Laguna Mountain Recreation Area Trail Map,* also published by the LMVA and available at the visitor center (open on weekends) or often at the Mount Laguna Lodge.

You need an Adventure Pass to park on CNF lands in Laguna. A $5 day pass or a $30 annual pass may be purchased at the CNF Ranger Office in Alpine, at the Mount Laguna Lodge, or at outdoor stores including REI or Adventure 16. For more information about the Adventure Pass, go to http://www.fs.usda.gov/main/cleveland/passes-permits/recreation.

Additionally, there is a $7 day-use parking fee in the campgrounds.

These trails are open to hikers, bicyclists, equestrians, and dogs on leashes.

Trailhead: From Interstate 8 heading east, exit at Sunrise Highway, S1, heading north to Laguna. About 12.7 miles from that freeway intersection, just past the mile marker 26, Laguna Campground is on the left. Park in the day-use areas of the Laguna Campground or just off Sunrise Highway, near that campground entrance.

Distance/Difficulty: This total loop is nearly 5.0 miles; easy, with a total elevation gain of about 350 feet.

11-2. Lake Views Amid Forests Of Laguna Mountain

Big Laguna Trail in the Laguna Mountain Recreation Area reaps many wilderness rewards. At nearly 6,000 feet in elevation, the area is home to lots of wildlife. In late April, with patches of snow still on the ground after all the spring storms, I saw a coyote, squirrels, a green garter snake, bright blue mountain bluebirds, the bigger blue Steller's jay, and a pale golden hawk soaring above the coniferous forest. There are many Jeffrey pine trees with their thick, patchwork-looking bark, mixed with black oak trees, whose leaves fall annually, budding out in spring.

Start at the Penny Pines trailhead area on S1 a few miles north of the town of Mount Laguna. You'll see markers on the right (east) side of the road citing the Penny Pines plantation effort.

Big Laguna Trail is a natural county wonder.

The Penny Pines plantation plan gathers donations from individuals and groups to plant seedlings in the national forest lands throughout California. According to the markers here, many people have given funds for this effort in Laguna. Individuals or groups donate $68 toward the cost of planting seedlings on one acre of national forest land statewide. The forest service plants the seedlings on national forest land nearest you or in the forest of your choice.

"Over the last 20 years, wildfires have burned an average of 100,000 acres of national forest land in California each year," says the Penny Pines program brochure. "Fortunately, natural reseeding occurs on some of this burned land. But much of it must be replanted."

A healthy forest is critical for all the wild animals and birds that live here. Grasses and shrubs are equally important, but the trees help hold the soil in place. Since the Penny Pines program began in 1941, donations have surpassed $1 million. When combined with federal forest planting funds, they have been used to plant more than 2 million seedlings on 88,000 acres of national forest land statewide. For more information or to participate, visit http://www.fs.usda.gov/detailfull/cleveland/about-forest/?cid=FS BDEV7 016685&width=full.

Cleveland National Forest, where Laguna lies, covers some 460,000 acres. It's a treasure trove of wilderness. By hiking on its trails, we can all learn to appreciate and protect the montane beauty that exists just an hour's drive from the urban core.

When you start out on Big Laguna Trail, for the first mile or so the landscape is littered with fallen and felled trees. There hasn't been an enormous fire here in recent years (Laguna largely escaped the devastating 2003 Cedar Fire), but there have been storms that may have destroyed many of these trees. The reforestation efforts are clearly important in this area.

Even with the patches of snow still on the ground, wildflowers can be profuse. I saw lots of lavender mountain phacelia, yellow violets, and baby blue eyes. After that first mile, the trees and shrubs seem a lot more abundant.

You soon reach the vast Laguna Meadow, a wide-open space of grasslands with very few trees. Right in the middle of this huge meadow is the trail's best scenic reward: Big Laguna Lake, full after rainfalls. Laguna is translated from Spanish to mean pond or lagoon or lake; it might be a diminutive version of "lago," which means lake in Spanish as well. Perhaps it might be translated to mean "big little lagoon lake," just to confuse things. Whatever its name means, it's a magnet for all kinds of wildlife.

You can continue on Big Laguna Trail, which covers 6.7 miles one-way, crosses Sunrise Highway (S1), and then stops at its intersection with the Pacific Crest Trail. The PCT continues north and will return you to your starting point in another 3.5 miles or so. Or you can follow signs to El Prado and Laguna campgrounds. The one-way distance to Laguna campground is about 4.0 miles. You might have another car here or walk back to your original parking place.

I chose to backtrack on the same trail after I reached Big Laguna Lake, which made for about a 5.0-mile round-trip hike, following the signs to Noble Canyon and then Penny Pines.

Thomas Brothers Map: Page 1218, about A-2, a bit north of Oasis Road off Sunrise Highway.

Before You Go: Download a map of Big Laguna Trail from the Laguna Mountain Volunteer Association's website: http://www.lmva.net/id3.html.

Also check http://www.fs.usda.gov/activity/cleveland/recreation/hiking/?recid=47396 &actid=50.

You must display a Cleveland National Forest Adventure Pass to park anywhere on the roads in Laguna Mountain Recreation Area. You can buy an annual pass for $30 or a day pass for $5 at the Descanso Ranger District Office on Alpine Road in Alpine off Interstate 8, or at Mount Laguna Lodge or the Mount Laguna Visitors Information Center (the latter open only on the weekends). For more information about the Adventure Pass, go to http://www.fs.usda.gov/main/cleveland/ passes-permits/recreation.

These trails are open to hikers, bicyclists, equestrians, and dogs on leashes.

Trailhead: From Interstate 8, exit at S1, Sunrise Highway, heading north for about 14.3 miles, past the town of Mount Laguna, and a little past mile marker 27. You'll see a sign for Penny Pines; park on either side of the road. The trail begins on the west side of S1 and starts out on the Noble Canyon Trail. After about 100 yards, you reach the junction with Big Laguna Trail; turn left onto it.

Distance/Difficulty: From 5.0 to 10 miles round-trip. Easy.

11-3. Laguna's Chico Spur Trail Offers Meadow, Forest

It always seems a surprise to encounter snow in our mountains in April, but on Laguna Mountain, where the most snowfall occurs in our county, it can even happen until June. With its highest elevation just over 6,200 feet, most of Laguna's trails are over 5,000 feet, where snow levels can persist. When I hit the Chico Spur of the Big Laguna Trail there in mid-April, there were some six to eight inches of snow still on the ground. It had melted enough that navigating the trail was no problem, but it made the going much slower in some areas. Even when there was no snow, that terrain was also fairly wet, with the trail acting sometimes like a creek from melting snow. Waterproof boots really made a difference. With bright sunshine warming the air to the mid 70s Fahrenheit, this white landscape seemed to sparkle.

One really fun thing about hiking in snowy or wet conditions is spotting wildlife footprints. In snow or mud, I saw prints of raccoons, deer, coyotes, and even quail, our state bird. I may even have seen mountain lion prints; the biggest ones I saw were deep in snow and about fist-sized, but there wasn't much definition.

Chico Spur is one of eight Big Laguna spur trails.

The Chico Spur is one of eight spur trails off the Big Laguna Trail. That entire trail complex covers 17 miles, making lots of options possible because all the trails link ultimately to each other. (The Big Laguna Trail itself connects with the Noble Canyon Trail as well as the Pacific Crest Trail, so you could go thousands of miles from here.) I made a loop hike of about 4.0 miles combining spurs Nos. 1, 7, and 2, and the Old County Road.

I began at the Sunset Trail trailhead, which is just opposite the Meadows Information Center near mile marker 19 on Sunrise Highway, S1. Start out on that Sunset Trail, passing the intersection to the right with the Old County Road (where you'll return), and in only another one-tenth of a mile or so, veer right onto Spur No. 1, where the wooden post marks the Big Laguna Trail with the No. 1 on the bottom.

In less than a half-mile, you'll reach the intersection with the Sunset/Kemp Spur, No. 7, where you turn right. Straight ahead is the giant Laguna Meadow, a huge, treeless, open space that should be awash in wildflowers once all the snow has melted. In about another half-mile, you'll reach that meadow as well as the next intersection with two spur trails, No. 6 heading northwest, or left, and No. 2 heading southeast, or right. Go right onto Spur No. 2, Chico Spur.

The trail follows a fence line with Laguna Ranch, private property up here in the Cleveland National Forest. It meanders through that meadow, where some hardy white and yellow cream cups, yellow southern buttercup, tiny purple red-stemmed filaree, and yellow-and-white tidy tips have pushed themselves up. Cleveland National Forest notes that the best time to view wildflowers in Laguna Meadow is in May and June, when you should also see some purple lupine standing tall here.

Soon you leave the meadow and enter the pine forests of Laguna. Most of the evergreen trees in Laguna are Jeffrey pines, according to the Laguna Mountain Volunteer Association (LMVA). They may be identified by their five-inch-long needles in bundles of three, with rounded pine cones four to six inches long and their fragrant bark that smells like vanilla or butterscotch.

You might see some Jeffrey pines covered with holes in the bark. "This is the work of the acorn woodpecker," says the LMVA. This redheaded bird digs out the holes with his beak and fills them with acorns from the many black oaks here. The trees with these storage holes (even dead trees) are also called granary trees.

The acorns of the black oaks were also favored by the Kumeyaay who used to live here. "Generally, only women gathered wild plants and seeds, but men and older children helped with gathering acorns," says the LMVA. Each family kept acorns in storage granaries that were baskets woven usually from willow branches. The acorn crop produced by any oak is called a mast.

The Chico Spur's No. 2 trail continues through Chico Ravine, following a creek, and in about 2.0 miles it connects to the Old County Road, where you turn right heading back another mile or so to that intersection with the trail where you started. On the way back on the Old County Road, I saw a bunch of those colorful acorn woodpeckers, making calls and showing off their black-and-white wings as they flew back and forth between those pines. I also spotted a black-and-white mountain chickadee and a really lovely western bluebird with its pale rust-colored breast.

Even with snow, there's lots of color in Laguna.

Thomas Brothers Map: Page D, between maps 1237 and 1218.

Before You Go: Download a trail map from the Laguna Mountain Volunteer Association: http://www.lmva.net/id3.html.

You may also buy the *Trail Guide of the Laguna Mountain Recreation Area,* available for purchase at the Laguna Mountain Visitors Information center near the Mount Laguna general store (which may also carry it).

The spur trails are open to hikers, mountain bikers, equestrians, and dogs on leashes.

You need an Adventure Pass to park in Cleveland National Forest lands, including Laguna. Purchase a day use pass for $5 or an annual one for $30 at the visitor center or general store in Laguna, or at outdoor equipment stores including REI or Adventure 16. For more information about the Adventure Pass, go to http://www.fs.usda.gov/main/cleveland/passes-permits/recreation.

Trailhead: From Interstate 8 heading east, exit at Sunrise Highway, S1, heading north. In about 5.6 miles from the freeway, near mile marker 19.1, park along the wide shoulder near the Meadow Information Center. The Sunset Trail start is on the west side of S1, across the highway from the Meadow information kiosk.

Distance/Difficulty: This loop is about 4.0 miles total; easy.

11-4. Butterflies, Wildflowers on Easy Trail to Waterfall

The hike to Cottonwood Creek Falls in Laguna is one of the easiest to a waterfall in San Diego County. In just under a mile one-way, descending about 500 feet down through dense and bushy chaparral, you reach the wide-open riparian habitat of cottonwood, arroyo willow, and oak trees that line Cottonwood Creek. That dense brushy beginning is accompanied by an annoyance everyone on the trail mentioned: flies. Most of them won't hurt you, but they will likely bother you with their persistent buzzing around your body. Add a few big horseflies who *do* bite, and complaints can be louder. But soon enough, you've reached the bottom of this creek bed, and the breezes and sounds of running water put those pesky flies behind you. The willows wave their spring green leaves down here, and the scenery becomes quite pretty along Cottonwood Creek.

The creek lies in a deep canyon in Cleveland National Forest here on the Laguna mountain plateau. According to a 2005 land management study for CNF, Cottonwood Creek is one of three rivers in Laguna being considered for Wild and Scenic River designation (the other two are the San Luis Rey River and San Mateo Creek). Such designation as part of the National Wild and Scenic River System comes if a river is free-flowing and possesses one or more outstandingly remarkable values, including scenery, geology, fish and wildlife, and history.

Cottonwood Creek certainly offers lovely scenery, it flows year-round—though to a far lesser degree in late summer—and several sites in its 11.9-mile corridor have been found to have prehistoric evidence. "Some (sites) have exhibited evidence of contact between the local inhabitants and the Hohokam pueblo builders of Arizona, which is a rare finding for California," says the CNF study. "The cultural resources found within the creek corridor are therefore considered to be outstandingly remarkable and the creek is found to be eligible for designation as a recreational river."

Several people had braved their way through the flies on the day we were there in late May. They were hiking upstream to explore the handful of falls along Cottonwood Creek. The first small cascade is reached just after you make a sharp left at the canyon bottom to follow the creek upstream. Another small falls occurs a little farther, and finally the third can be reached with some boulder scrambling. The third cascade is the largest, falling about 10 feet into a deep pool of water. Be careful getting there, however, because the boulders can be worn smooth, making them slippery. Slip into the water, and the algae grasses will make it even harder to step out.

Cottonwood Creek is one of easiest trails to a mountain waterfall.

I watched a few hikers spread themselves out over the creek's boulders, and it was easy to imagine such a scene occurring here over thousands of years.

After retracing my way back up the trail, I took note of the colorful wildflowers sprucing up that scenery: mountain blue curls, purple lupine, red Indian paintbrush, tiny yellow snakeweed, and bright white milkmaids hidden in the shade. I also spotted several butterflies along the trail, adding their own scenic beauty. I did some research on the butterfly identification website (www.discoverlife.org), and I think the tiny ones I spotted were an orange banded and spotted type of Lycaena. According to the CNF land management study, another species found here is the Laguna Mountain skipper butterfly (pyrgus ruralis lagunae), which is endangered. This butterfly is a small (one inch), black-and-white checkered one found only from about 4,000 to 6,000 feet elevation in the Laguna Mountains and Palomar Mountain.

Concentrate on the pretty insects instead of the annoying ones, try to identify the colorful wildflowers, and note the many shades of green among the oaks, cottonwoods, and willow trees at the canyon bottom. You'll discover why this creek canyon has been visited for millennia.

Thomas Brothers Map: Page 1237, F-6. No trail is marked here, but this is about where it is—close to Cottonwood Creek.

Before You Go: For information about this trail, go to the Laguna Mountain Volunteer Association's website: http://www.lmva.net/id46.html.

The best trail map for Cottonwood Creek is to search for it on Google satellite maps. You'll find it heading south from Sunrise Highway (S1), near two big turnout areas.

You must display a CNF Adventure Pass to park on these forest lands. A $5 day-use of $30 annual pass may be purchased from a Cleveland National Forest ranger station or at some retail shops, including REI, or the Mount Laguna general store farther up the mountain road. For more information about the Adventure Pass, go to http://www.fs.usda.gov/main/cleveland/passes-permits/recreation.

This trail is open to hikers, bicyclists, and dogs on leashes.

Trailhead: From Interstate 8 heading east, exit at S1 (Sunrise Highway), heading north. From this intersection, go about 1.8 miles, or just past mile marker 15, and park in the large turnout on the east side of S1. The trail begins at the northern edge of this parking area, near the power lines.

The trail basically follows the power lines down the canyon. When you reach the canyon bottom, follow the trail as it turns sharply left to join Cottonwood Creek. Follow the creek upstream to reach the upper falls, taking care on the slippery boulders.

Distance/Difficulty: About 2.0 miles round-trip; moderate.

11-5. Wildflowers, Desert Views on Laguna's Edge of PCT

One of the most bountiful displays of wildflowers is on view during spring in Laguna along the Pacific Crest Trail. Add the astounding vistas afforded on this actual edge of the Laguna Mountains, where the land drops dramatically some 4,000 feet to the desert below, and you'll enjoy one of the best trail experiences in the county.

When we hiked there in mid-May, we saw big patches of summer snow, the clumps of tiny white flowers with yellow centers that sometimes seem to cover the mountain meadows (usually through July). We also saw violet mountain phacelia, dark purple chaparral nightshade, yellow western wallflower, red scarlet bugler, blue dicks, western blue flax, red Indian paintbrush, blue lupine, pink checkerbloom, and deep pink San Diego sweet pea. There were also lots of Lemmon's linanthus, another tiny white flower with bright yellow centers that appears in low clumps, and the very tiny, hairy lotus groundcover whose yellow blooms resemble those of sweet peas.

We began on the Foster Point Trail, which heads east on remnants of an old dirt road from Sunrise Highway, S1, before intersecting with the Pacific Crest Trail in about 0.3 mile. For the first part of the hike, the trail goes through an area called Flathead Flats, dotted with old oaks and pines. Many of the wildflowers are in this area, where you might also see blue scrub jays and even bluer Steller's jays, the latter with their crested heads. When we hit the PCT, we turned north to continue to Foster Point.

The day we hiked there was also the day of the 34th annual PCT 50-Mile Trail Run, a competition among some 200 runners who began at 6:00 a.m. at Buckman Springs and climbed more than 7,500 feet in up-and-down elevation from 3,000 feet to Laguna's 6,000 feet, turning around at Penny Pines and going back to the starting point. In 2014 the winners were Michael Alfred, who clocked the run at 7:22:04, and Margaret Nelsen, at 8:14:00.

We were happier walking along this single-track rocky trail, feasting our eyes on those expansive desert views on this mountain crest. "The belt of granitic gneisses exposed in the Laguna Mountains essentially divides the county into two zones of plutonic igneous rocks," says the San Diego Natural History Museum's "Geologic History of San Diego County." "To the west, the rocks are much more diverse in composition and character and form what is referred to as the western zone of the Peninsular Ranges Batholith (PRB)."

Foster Point points out all the peaks on the horizon.

Immediately to the east of Laguna is the Eastern PRB, which drops down steeply into Anza-Borrego. The two zones were caused by collision of the two tectonic plates, one carrying the western zone arc and the other the North American continent. Among the consequences of this ancient land formation were the gem minerals that have made Southern California famous, says SDNHM. Pink and green tourmaline, aquamarine, golden topaz, and blood-red garnet are "but a few of the gems found in these earliest igneous rocks of the eastern zone." The event also deposited gold between the quartz grains that made nearby Julian so famous in its mining heyday from about 1870 to 1900.

When you join the PCT heading north from Foster Point Trail's beginnings, you'll also soon see evidence of the Chariot Fire that burned about 7,000 acres in Laguna in July 2013. That fire destroyed the historic Al Bahr Shrine Lodge on the other side of Sunrise Highway, as well as a 1927 cabin that was part of Foster Lodge, the Sierra Club's historic facility on this eastern side of Sunrise Highway.

After you head north on the PCT, in about 0.4 mile you'll see the wooden sign pointing east for Foster Point between two metal post signs for the PCT. Take that short spur to reach a rock pillar that holds a metal direction-finder map that points to 17 peaks in view from here, including (on the clearest days) 11,502-foot-high San Gorgonio Mountain, 82 miles away; and 10,821-foot-high Mount San Jacinto, 63 miles away. Even closer are 5,850-foot-high Garnet Peak, just 2.0 miles away; and all three peaks of Cuyamaca, between 8.0 and 9.0 miles away. Almost immediately to the south, just 1.0 mile away, is 6,271-foot-high Monument Peak on Laguna, the county's fourth-highest peak after Hot Springs Mountain (6,533 feet), Cuyamaca Peak (6,512 feet), and Laguna's Cuyapaipe Mountain (6,381 feet).

Both the Sierra Club lodge and this metal direction finder are named for Loris and Ivy Foster, founders of the Sierra Club's San Diego chapter in 1948. In 1951 the local club had been given the two 1927 summer cabins by their builders, E. T. Guymon Sr. and E. T. "Ned" Guymon Jr., who had been permitted the first and only lots for homes in Laguna, which was designated a recreation area in 1926 within Cleveland National Forest.

Beautiful views, bountiful wildflowers, and fascinating natural and human history abound on Laguna's part of the PCT.

Thomas Brothers Map: Page 1218, C-4.

Before You Go: Download a trail map of the Laguna area from the Laguna Mountain Volunteer Association: http://www.lmva.net/id3.html. You'll see Foster Point on this map but not the trail leading to it.

For the best map, go to Jerry Schad's *Afoot and Afield in San Diego County* for the trail to Foster Point and its intersection at PCT.

For maps of the Pacific Crest Trail, go to the Pacific Crest Trail Association: http://www.pctmap.net (California Section A, Page 6).

The PCT is open only to hikers, equestrians, and dogs on leashes.

You must display a CNF Adventure Pass to park on these forest lands. A $5 day-use pass or a $30 annual pass may be purchased from a Cleveland National Forest ranger station, at some retail shops, or at the Mount Laguna general store farther up the mountain road. For more information about the Adventure Pass, go to http://www.fs.usda.gov/main/cleveland/passes-permits/recreation.

Trailhead: From Interstate 8 heading east, exit at Sunrise Highway (S1) and go north. At about mile 25.7, where a road heads west to Horse Heaven Group Camp, park on the east side of S1 in the large shoulder area. Look for the opening in the barbed wire fence, immediately to the left of the gates, and head east on the old road.

Distance/Difficulty: The distance from the trailhead to Foster Point's directional map is only about 1.4 miles round-trip with only a few hundred feet in elevation gain; but the PCT invites you to hike all you want on its 2,650 miles from Mexico to Canada. This little part is easy.

11-6. Views All the Way Around from Garnet Peak Top

Garnet Peak in Laguna Mountain Recreation Area is one of the county's easier peaks to summit, and its 360-degree views from the top are a fine reward. It lies on the eastern ridge of Laguna that drops down dramatically some 4,000 feet to the desert floor. On the clearest days, you can see the Salton Sea 60 miles away to the southeast, the 10,400-foot peaks of San Gorgonio and San Jacinto to the northwest, and all four main peaks of Cuyamaca to the west. The direct trail to Garnet Peak begins off Sunrise Highway

(S1) at mile marker 27.8, about a half-mile past the Penny Pines parking area, where you can also reach the Garnet Peak trail heading north from the Pacific Crest Trail (PCT).

From the direct Garnet Peak trailhead, the trail crosses the PCT at a little more than a half-mile. The peak trail then begins an earnest climb, with about a 550-foot elevation gain. It's a fairly straight shot up with virtually no switchbacks, but that elevation gain is not terribly strenuous.

Windy Garnet Peak offers truly sweeping views.

At the beginning of the trail, you'll notice lots of healthy Jeffrey pine seedlings. This area was affected by both the 2002 Pines Fire of Julian and the historically huge 2003 Cedar Fire, and the Jeffrey pines were hit hard. These seedlings show the resilience of forests some 10 years later. Jeffrey pines are the most common conifer of the higher elevations on Laguna Mountain, according to James Lightner in *San Diego County Native Plants*. When the bark of a Jeffrey pine is crushed, its fragrance has been compared to vanilla.

As the Garnet Peak trail continues to climb higher, reaching its ultimate elevation of 5,900 feet, the trees disappear and chaparral shrubs take over. A virtual sea of manzanita covers the flanks of Garnet Peak, brightening the fall landscape with red bark and the last of its red berries.

Sprinkled in with the manzanita are ceanothus, chamise, chaparral yucca, and lots of mountain mahogany. This area of Laguna harbors some of the biggest colonies of mountain mahogany, which is especially recognizable in the fall when its ghostly, feathery projections appear all over the plant after its yellow flowers have fallen. In spring, many wildflowers should be found on this trail, including yellow mariposa lilies, purple clarkia, golden yarrow, and scarlet buglers.

When the trail nears the top of the first peaklet, it continues on a short saddle to the actual peak. At this point, the views down into the desert are simply amazing. The actual top of the peak is a jumble of big rocks, making the final ascent harder than the trail, which itself is quite rocky. Adding to the difficulty, it is extremely windy up there on this edge overlooking the desert. As Jerry Schad noted in *Afoot and Afield San Diego County,* "This must be one of the windiest places in the county."

Those rocks on top of Garnet Peak are actually quite colorful. The peak was named for the crystallized silicate gemstones that once were mined in this area, according to the Cleveland National Forest, which oversees Laguna. Some lower-quality garnet outcroppings may still be found.

Spend a moment at the top to survey that 360-degree view and see how many peaks you recognize on all the horizons. Perhaps most obvious are all the peaks of Cuyamaca. From left to right when looking from Garnet Peak to the southwest, on the horizon above the PCT below, they are Cuyamaca Peak (6,512 feet), Stonewall Peak (5,730 feet), Middle Peak (5,883 feet), and North Peak (5,993 feet).

Garnet Peak was one of the original 100 peaks of Southern California first listed— and climbed—by 1946 by Weldon Heald of the Angeles chapter of the Sierra Club. He climbed Garnet Peak in 1940. All peaks on that list had to be over 5,000 feet in elevation. Today that HPS (Hundred Peaks Section) list contains 275 named summits in Southern California.

There is another list of 100 San Diego County Peaks compiled by the San Diego chapter of the Sierra Club (http://sandiegosierraclub.org/get-outdoors/hike/peaks-list/peak-list), and Garnet Peak is No. 59 on that list. The 100 San Diego County Peaks list includes several that are well below 5,000 feet in elevation, but they were all selected "based on their accessibility, topography, variety of terrain, prominence and ability to offer climbers a well-rounded representation of the entire county," from the Anza-Borrego desert to the mountains of Palomar, Cuyamaca, and Laguna.

Garnet Peak may have one of the best views of all.

Thomas Brothers Map: Page 1218, A-1

Before You Go: Download a map from the Laguna Mountain Volunteers Association website: http://lmva.net/id3.html.
 The Garnet Peak trail is open to hikers and dogs on leashes.
 You need an adventure pass to park on Cleveland National Forest lands, including Laguna. A $5 day pass or a $30 annual pass may be purchased at outdoor stores (including REI and Adventure 16), the Mount Laguna store, or the CNF ranger station in Alpine.
 For more information about the Adventure Pass, go to http://www.fs.usda.gov/main/cleveland/passes-permits/recreation.

Trailhead: From Interstate 8 heading east, exit at Sunrise Highway (S1) and head north. Park off the highway on the dirt shoulder area in front of the Garnet Peak trail head at mile marker 27.8, about a half-mile past the Penny Pines parking area.

Distance/Difficulty: The round-trip direct hike to Garnet Peak's summit and back is about 2.4 miles; moderate.

11-7. Laguna's Gatos Spur Is True Walk in the Woods

The Gatos Spur of the Big Laguna Trail offers a classic walk in the woods. It's also a popular mountain biking trail complete with several log jumps for extra excitement. It's a narrow single-track trail for most of the way, so hikers should be prepared to jump off the trail if those mountain bikers whiz by. Otherwise, it's a pretty quiet amble in the Laguna Mountain Recreation Area, one of the most heavily used areas of the Cleveland National Forest.

The 460,000-acre Cleveland National Forest has been so designated since 1908, and that protection has afforded long life to the now tall Jeffrey and Coulter pines, cedars, and fir trees. However, the bark beetle is an infestation problem that's killing the weaker pines.

Gatos Spur has extra enticements for mountain bikers.

The Gatos Spur meanders through some thickly forested areas, where the trail weaves among the various conifers as well as an amazing abundance of black oaks. There are far more black oaks here than coast or canyon live oaks; the black oaks are readily distinguished by their deeply lobed leaves (coast and canyon live oaks have oblong leaves). The black oaks also are the only oaks here whose leaves turn yellow and drop in the fall, so this trail could be quite colorful come autumn.

Begin this hike at the Agua Dulce Equestrian Trailhead, where you'll walk along the Old County Road for less than a half-mile before reaching the Gatos Spur trailhead. There are a handful of spur trails off the main Big Laguna Trail in this area; each has a numbered designation, which you should see on each trailhead signpost. The Gatos Spur is No. 3. You'll see the trailhead signpost for the Gatos Spur, shown only as the No. 3 on a Big Laguna Trail marker, on your right just inside a pair of posts marking a gravel road off that Old County Road. This part of the trail is open to hikers, bikers, equestrians, and dogs on leashes.

One of the first things I noticed was the abundance of scarlet buglers, casting a red tint across large swaths of the landscape. This trail also is home to lots of tiny purple asters, smaller baby blue eyes, large patches of pink wood roses, and healthy stands of red Indian paintbrush. Flying among the pines and oaks were dark blue Steller's jays, the ones with the crested head. I also found a bright orange feather, perhaps from a red-tailed hawk.

After about the first half-mile or so, the trail winds up out of the woods and onto a more wide-open crest, where views pan to nearby peaks. Soon it hits an intersection on your left with spur No. 7 to Chico Ravine. Stay to the right to continue onto Gatos Spur, No. 3. Later, No. 7 can be part of your loop return.

After this intersection where the signpost reads Gatos Ravine, equestrians are no longer allowed on this part of the No. 3 trail. That signpost also notes this part is "most difficult" for mountain bikers, and a second signpost here reads, "Caution: Jumps Ahead." The terrain isn't really harder for hikers here. The elevation gains are not great, but the trail does wind a lot through the forests. Those jumps for mountain bikers consist of logs piled up for a bit of airborne thrill. One of the jumps continues onto a long-fallen log that's been cut flat on top.

This second part of No. 3 goes for a little more than a half-mile before connecting to the Kemp Spur, No. 6. But before I reached that intersection, the clouds of some summer monsoons were beginning to threaten, so I turned back.

When I again reached that intersection with No. 7, called the Connector Spur, I took that trail to the right. After less than a half-mile, it intersects with the Chico Spur No. 2 trail. Go left to go back to your parking area, or go right into Chico Ravine, which leads all the way to Laguna Meadow. I wandered into the ravine for a while before turning around and heading back to that No. 2 trail to Sunrise Highway. Upon intersecting with that Old County Road again, I turned left to walk back to the Agua Dulce parking area.

It was a fine walk in the woods, ravines, and meadows.

Thomas Brothers Map: Page D, between maps 1237 and 1218.

Before You Go: Download a copy of the trails map from the Laguna Mountain Volunteer Association's website: http://lmva.net/id3.html.

You may also buy *Laguna Mountain Recreation Area Trail Map,* published by the CNF and the Laguna Mountain Volunteer Association at Laguna's visitor center and at the Mount Laguna general store.

You need an adventure pass to park on Cleveland National Forest lands, including Laguna. A $5 day pass or a $30 annual pass may be purchased at outdoor stores, the Mount Laguna store, or the CNF ranger station in Alpine.

For more information about the Adventure Pass, go to http://www.fs.usda.gov/main/cleveland/passes-permits/recreation.

These spur trails generally are open to hikers, bicyclists, equestrians, and dogs on leashes, but note that part of Gatos Spur No. 3 is closed to equestrians for safety.

Trailhead: From Interstate 8, exit at Sunrise Highway (S1), heading north to Laguna Mountain Recreation Area. About 8.4 miles from I-8, just past mile marker 21.5, turn left off Sunrise Highway onto the Wooded Hill Campground Road. Go about 0.7 miles to the Agua Dulce parking area, just to the right of the gate that stops further vehicle traffic on the main road.

Walk on that old road past the gate about a half-mile to the trailhead on your right, to the No. 3 Gatos Spur trail of the Big Laguna Trail.

Distance/Difficulty: I hiked about 5.0 miles total. Easy to moderate.

11-8. Indian Creek Has Lots of Cures

A hike down Indian Creek Trail in Laguna takes you to a year-round creek that is surprising for its lack of surrounding riparian habitat. No oaks, cottonwoods, or willows line this creek bed; rather, the stream flows through an area dominated by low grasses and shrubs, where the sound of frogs flows unimpeded. It's still pretty, though, and the hike to get there winds through some fine old Jeffrey pine forests that have escaped the wildfires that decimated them almost entirely in nearby Cuyamaca.

To reach the Indian Creek Trail, you must start on either the Noble Canyon Trail or the Pine Mountain Trail. The Pine Mountain Trail is about a 1.5-mile hike to its junction with the Indian Creek Trail near Champagne Pass Viewpoint, Indian Creek Trail's halfway mark. Hike the Noble Canyon Trail for about 2.0 miles to reach its intersection with the Indian Creek Trail.

The pine forests on way to Indian Creek Trail remain healthy.

I took Noble Canyon Trail, which offers a pretty walk through those pines, along with lots of black oaks whose deciduous leaves were not yet budding in mid-March. Several of the black oaks also appeared completely denuded of bark, which may mean they have succumbed to the dreaded goldspotted oak borer, a pest that has killed an estimated 21,500 oak trees covering 1,893 square miles in San Diego County as of 2010, according to the University of California Cooperative Extension.

A few scattered coast live oaks along the trail appeared in fine health, along with scrub oak, green-limbed ceanothus, chamise, and manzanita. When you get closer to Indian Creek, look for the light green, almost gray-blue artemisia, also known as big sagebrush, a very fragrant shrub that was eaten by early pioneers. Native people used it to line the floors of their homes for fragrance and to ward off insects, to make a tonic to ward off colds and flus, and to treat stomach aches.

At the top of the Noble Canyon Trail, before you reach Indian Creek Trail, you'll see a lone home below in the meadows by Filaree Flat. The private property is known as the Lucas Ranch, home of the last Kwaaymii Indian, Thomas Lucas, who was born here. He died in 1989, but his daughter, Carmen, who retired from a career in the marines, still lives here with her family in the only building left after the 2003 Cedar Fire burned others to the ground.

You can choose some longer options with the Indian Creek Trail. From the start at Penny Pines parking area, hike 2.0 miles of Noble Canyon Trail to Indian Creek Trail, and then 2.0 miles to Champagne Pass Viewpoint. Then connect to Pine Mountain Trail for its 1.5-mile length to Pioneer Mail parking area. Connect to the Pacific Crest Trail (PCT) for about 3.5 miles back to Penny Pines for a total loop hike of about 9.0 miles. Alternatively, you can hike the 2.0 miles of Noble Canyon to Indian Creek Trail and then hike the entire 4.0 miles of Indian Creek Trail, which intersects with the Deer Park Trail that heads into Cuyamaca Rancho State Park and connects with the Harvey Moore Trail for a total one-way hike of about 10.5 miles, perhaps arranging a two-car setup.

The Noble Canyon Trail is one of four National Recreation Trails in San Diego County. It's a 10-mile trail that begins here and continues southwest to Pine Valley. Portions of this trail were established long ago by miners and ranchers, according to the Laguna Mountain Volunteer Association. The other National Recreation Trails here are Bayside Trail at Cabrillo National Monument in Point Loma, the Inaja Memorial Nature Trail outside Julian, and the Observatory Trail in Palomar. There are more than 1.000 National Recreation Trails in the 50 states (for more information, go to http://www.americantrails.org/nationalrecreationtrails/about.htm). Unlike National Scenic Trails (there are 11, including the PCT) or National Historic Trails (there are 19, including the Juan Bautista de Anza National Historic Trail), which must be approved by acts of Congress, National Recreation Trails may be designated by the secretary of the interior or the secretary of agriculture, and applications are taken every year.

After 2.0 miles on Noble Canyon Trail, it intersects with the Indian Creek Trail on the right. Indian Creek Trail winds downhill to the creek in about 1.0 mile, and then it heads back up through chaparral for another mile to Champagne Pass Viewpoint and its intersection with the Pine Mountain Trail. When I reached Indian Creek, I turned back because some 6.0 miles round-trip was enough for me. It gave me a chance to wander through those Jeffrey pines again. According to the U.S. Department of Agriculture, Jeffrey pines can live 400 to 500 years, reaching 200 feet in height. Jeffrey pine needles are in bundles of three, seven to 11 inches long. Its cones are six to 10 inches long, and its spines are tucked inward so they are not prickly.

The Ponderosa pine is a very similar species, but its pinecones are prickly. Whereas Jeffrey pine bark is deeply furrowed, is reddish-brown, and smells like vanilla, Ponderosa pine bark is more orange in color and has an odor of pitch. Jeffrey pines are far more common here than Ponderosas; the seeds in its pinecones are eaten by birds, squirrels, and chipmunks.

The resin from all pine trees has an antiseptic, diuretic turpentine that was long ago used to treat kidney and bladder ailments, as a rub for rheumatic problems, or for respiratory complaints from colds and flus.

Inhale deeply on the Indian Creek Trail in Laguna.

Thomas Brothers Map: Page 1218, 2-A.

Before You Go: Download a copy of the trail map from the Laguna Mountain Volunteer Association (http://www.lmva.net/id3.html).

You must display an Adventure Pass from the Cleveland National Forest to park on Laguna Mountain lands. You can buy a $5 day pass or a $30 annual pass from the Ranger Station in Alpine, at outdoor recreation stores such as REI or Adventure 16, or at the Mount Laguna store or visitor center.

For more information about the Adventure Pass, go to http://www.fs.usda.gov/main/cleveland/passes-permits/recreation.

The Indian Creek Trail is open to hikers, mountain bikers, equestrians, and dogs on leashes.

Trailhead: From Interstate 8, exit at Sunrise Highway (S1), and head north about 14 miles, between mile marker 27.0 and 27.5, and park at the Penny Pines parking area.

Distance/Difficulty: I went about 6.3 miles round-trip, from Penny Pines to Noble Canyon Trail to Indian Creek Trail and back; about 800 feet elevation change. Moderate.

11-9. Kwaaymii/Desert View: Two Trails in Laguna Offer Self-Guided Lessons

Two trails in the Laguna Mountain Recreation Area offer an excellent self-guided lesson in the flora and history of the native people of the area. The trails are about a mile apart, and both have printed trail guides corresponding to numbered posts discussing the trails, illuminating trees, plants, and lifestyles of the people who used to migrate seasonally between here and the desert. You can easily hike both trails in under two hours. The first is the Kwaaymii Trail, which is a half-mile loop, and the second is the Desert View Trail, which is another loop covering about 1.3 miles.

The Kwaaymii Trail begins right next to the Mount Laguna visitor center. The Kwaaymii (pronounced Kwhy-me) were a sub-tribe of the Kumeyaay (Ku-me-I) Native Americans. The Kwaaymii migrated from the desert to the mountains each spring, where several hundred people lived in three villages near Laguna Meadow, according to the trail guide. They would come to grow crops and hunt game before returning to the desert for winter.

There are 10 markers on this trail that share information about how the native people lived here. Marker No. 1 points to the wooden cabins that dot this area today, and it says the Kwaaymii built their homes from pine and juniper branches with doors made from deer hide or woven reeds.

Marker No. 2 states deer grass was a favorite for making baskets. Acorns (marker No. 3), gathered from black oak trees, were stored in huge baskets for the journey back to the desert. The branches of wild lilac (ceanothus), says marker No. 4, were used as throwing sticks to kill rabbits, whose meat was stewed with acorn flour and whose hides were used for clothing and blankets.

The beautiful, red-barked manzanita was favored for its berries (No. 5), which are high in vitamin C and were also used in medicinal teas.

No. 6 shows the morteros (deep holes) and metates (shallow holes) on a large outcropping of bedrock, where women gathered to visit while they ground their acorns and other seeds into fine meal. The trail guide says most of these large mortars had a ramada built over them for sun and wind protection.

The Desert View Trail, just about a mile back on Sunset Highway in the Burnt Rancheria Campground, has 19 markers corresponding to its trail guide. This trail meanders through oak and pine forests, joins the Pacific Crest Trail for about a mile, and rewards hikers with a fantastic view of that desert, as promised.

There is a lot to learn on the Kwaaymii and Desert View Trails.

At marker No. 2, note the mistletoe on the California black oak tree, which is a parasite but won't kill the oak. Conversely, dwarf mistletoe, another species, infects only the coniferous trees in the forest and is a true parasite, causing stunting and early death of Jeffrey pine trees.

No. 3 points out that oak trees grow toward the light, so oak branches are irregular. "This characteristic of growing toward the light is known as phototropism," says the guide. Pine trees, by contrast, grow straight up, responding to gravity, which is known as "geotropism," typical of all conifers.

Besides Native Americans, 45 species consume acorns, says the trail guide, including woodpeckers, Steller's jays, raccoons, and squirrels. An oak with a 17-inch diameter is about 100 years old and produces 60 pounds of acorns each year, compared to five pounds a year from a 50-year-old oak with a nine-inch diameter.

Mountain mahogany (No. 6), a member of the rose family, is a favored food of the mule deer. The deer also feed on several grass plants (No. 10).

The Pinyon pine (No. 7), was favored by the Kwaaymii for its nutlike seeds, which we know today as pine nuts. They were roasted and then eaten whole or ground and mixed with sage and chia seeds. Pinyon pines were more prevalent in Laguna until a fire in the 1940s destroyed most of them.

The hundreds of holes in "Old Windy" (No. 13), a Jeffrey pine, are made by the acorn woodpecker. This redheaded bird digs out the holes and fills them with acorns, into which wasps lay their larvae, which the woodpecker returns to harvest. These trees are called granary trees, says the guide. "The holes, in the bark of the tree, do not harm the Jeffrey pine trees."

You'll encounter splendid views from the ridge of Thing Valley, into La Posta Creek Canyon, and then to the In-Ko-Pah Mountains and finally the desert. On a really clear day, you should be able to glimpse the faint blue of the Salton Sea. From the desert viewpoint (No. 15), you'll also notice an FAA radar station on nearby Stephenson Peak.

At the end of the trail, I was deposited in a different part of the campground with no obvious route to return to my car. Follow the numbered camping spots in descending order to return to the entrance of the campground and the parking area.

Thomas Brothers Map: Page 1218, F-6 and G-7.

Before You Go: Download a copy of both of these trail maps at the Laguna Mountain Volunteer Association's website: http://www.lmva.net/id3.html.

The trail guides are not available for downloading, so you'll have to hope the trail guide boxes located at the beginning of each trail are stocked. You may also visit the visitor information center at Mount Laguna to get the trail guides; the office is open on Friday afternoons and on weekends.

You need an Adventure Pass to park anywhere in Laguna, which lies on Cleveland National Forest lands. You can buy day passes for $5 or annual passes for $30 at the general store in Mount Laguna, at the visitor center when it's open, and at outdoor equipment stores. For more information on Adventure Passes, go to the national forest pages for Cleveland National Forest: http://www.fs.usda.gov/detailfull/r5/passes-permits/recreation/?cid=stelprdb5208699&width=full.

Both of these trails are open to hikers and leashed dogs.

Trailhead: From Interstate 8, exit at Sunrise Highway (S-1) and head north to the village of Mount Laguna, about eleven miles. Park in the Visitor Center parking lot, where the Kwaaymii Trail begins.

Desert View Trail is about a mile south on S-1 from the visitor center, in the Burnt Rancheria Campground. When entering the campground, turn left and park in the Nature Trail parking lot, where the Desert View Trail begins.

Distance/Difficulty: Kwaaymii Trail is 0.5 miles, and Desert View Trail is 1.3 miles. Both are round-trip loops. Easy.

11-10. Laguna's Lightning Ridge Offers Snowy Views

You know you've reached another world when you see the road sign that says, "Unlawful to throw snowballs at vehicles or occupants." Less than an hour from the beach are the Laguna Mountains, where winter snows blanket the landscape for a few weeks at a time nearly every year. Several trails beckon in these pine and oak forests; in fact, there are about 70 miles of trails in Laguna. I sought Lightning Ridge Trail for its Laguna Meadow views and found a lovely walk through woods that haven't been as devastated recently by huge wild fires, compared to neighboring Cuyamaca.

Laguna's forests are not as damaged from fire as Cuyamaca's.

Lightning Ridge Trail is fairly easy, with an elevation change of about 250 feet. Switchbacks along the way make it even easier to handle. Find the trailhead near Horse Heaven campground in the Laguna Mountain Recreation Area. Off S1 (also called Sunrise Highway) at about mile 25.7 (note mile markers on the road) is the entry to Horse Heaven campground. In winter, the road gates are closed to the campground. Park just outside the gates off S1, being careful not to block the gates if they need to be opened.

You need a National Forest Adventure Pass to park here or on any national forest lands. Adventure Passes may be purchased in Laguna at the Visitor Center, which is open only on Friday afternoons and Saturdays and Sundays. Passes are $5 a day or $30 for an annual pass.

You can also buy Adventure Passes from Laguna Mountain Lodge and Market, at REI or Adventure 16 stores countywide, or at Cleveland National Forest ranger stations; the closest one to Laguna is at 3348 Alpine Boulevard in Alpine, just before you reach Sunrise Highway. That office has lots of information on area trails too.

From your car, walk around the campground gates and take the dirt road that immediately forks to the right off the paved road to the campground. Walk along that dirt road for about two-tenths of a mile. You'll notice two trailhead markers on either side of the dirt road, which are just wooden posts each marked with a white arrow at the tops. Take the right-hand trail to wind up the hill to a water tank. From the top of the hill you can see Little Laguna Lake and an expansive view of Laguna Meadow.

It is pretty in winter with a dusting of snow, and it's colorful in spring with a show of wildflowers.

Continue down the dirt road until you reach that original marker on the other side from your starting point, now on your right. Follow that trail covered in pine needles, making for a cushioned path, and meander through mighty oaks and tall Coulter pines (those with the biggest pine cones). This part of the trail descends to Laguna Meadow as it switchbacks down the ridge.

It doesn't take long to reach the bottom for closer views of the meadow through the trees. At the bottom is a T intersection where you turn left, following the sign to Horse Heaven Group Camp and back to your car. Turn right, and it will take you to Laguna Campground, which offers another entry point to this trail. Or you can always climb back up the way you came and retrace your steps. Notice some evidence of lightning: the dead and blackened tree trunks give proof that this ridge is named well.

When I got back to my car one winter, some folks were enjoying another kind of recreation here: sliding down the little hills on their garbage can lids or boogie boards. Leave it to San Diego County to offer a snow day for boogie boards.

Thomas Brothers Map: Page 1218, C-4.

Before You Go: Download a copy of the trail map through the Laguna Mountain Volunteer Association (www.lmva.net).

You must have an Adventure Pass to park here ($5 day use; $30 annual). For more information on Adventure Passes, go to the national forest pages for Cleveland National Forest, http://www.fs.usda.gov/detailfull/r5/passes-permits/recreation/?cid=stelprdb5208699&width=full.

This trail is hikers only, but leashed dogs are okay, and it's an easy one for kids.

Trailhead: Travel 40 miles east of San Diego on Interstate 8, exiting onto Sunrise Highway (S1). Go 10 miles north past mile marker 25.5. Just inside the road gates to Horse Heaven Group Camp, take the dirt road that forks to the right. About 0.2 miles later, find the wooden trail arrow markers.

Distance/Difficulty: About 1.3 miles loop trail; easy.

11-11. Lucky Five Trail Preserves Views from the Crest

Near the confluence of Cleveland National Forest's Laguna Mountain Recreation Area, Anza-Borrego Desert State Park, and Cuyamaca Rancho State Park is a precious area where a few trails beckon. These trails are lightly traveled compared to those closer to the centers of each of those three recreational gems. They all begin at the Sunrise Trailhead of the Anza-Borrego Desert State Park, a large parking area complete with facilities and horse tie-ups. You can connect to the Upper Green Valley Trail, the California Riding and Hiking Trail, and La Cima Trail from here.

This time I took the Lucky Five Trail, which heads south along the edge of Sunrise Highway, taking hikers to the Lucky Five Ranch and then across that highway to the Pacific Crest Trail for a loop with jaw-dropping views. Few places give the sense that you are really on the edge more than the eastern slope of the Laguna Mountains, where they drop steeply into the desert. The Pacific Crest Trail really earns its name here.

When you're on the PCT here at nearly 5,000 feet elevation, panoramic vistas go to the northern and eastern horizons, where they take in the mountain ranges that flank Anza-Borrego's desert on all sides.

The Lucky Five Ranch site occupies a lovely wide-open meadow, seen to the south of the trail just before you reach the highway to head to the PCT. The whole area is an important wildlife corridor between Cuyamaca, Anza-Borrego, and Laguna, as well as a beautiful open space where chaparral and cismontane habitats are home to lovely wildflowers in June, including the fascinating native deer's ears, which are not seen anywhere very often.

Lucky Five has history, views, and wildflowers.

Along the Lucky Five Trail, I also saw lots of golden yarrow and yellow bush poppies, as well as purple lupine, purple penstemon, scarlet bugler, purple thistle, and the small purple chaparral nightshade with its bright yellow cone-like centers.

Thanks to conservation efforts from a wide group of concerned citizens, the 2,675-acre Lucky Five Ranch was acquired in 2001 by the Anza-Borrego Foundation with help from the Conservation Land Group of Sausalito. An anonymous donor kicked in $2 million of the $5.59 million purchase price, also funded by Proposition Twelve, Habitat Conservation Funds, the Land and Water Conservation Fund, and the Transportation Equity Act.

The Lucky Five Ranch land was then transferred to California State Parks "to form a critical land bridge between Anza-Borrego Desert and Cuyamaca Rancho State Parks." The ranch centerpiece was known as the Little Valley to the Kwaaymii Laguna Band of Mission Indians, who lived on this land for generations. Carmen Lucas is a Kwaaymii who lives on the homeland of her people on Laguna Mountain, and she works as an archaeology technician, Indian monitor, and consultant. She was asked to weigh in on the Lucky Five Ranch purchase in 2001 when the state parks considered putting horse camps there. "As a kid, I wondered about that land, the former reservation of my ancestors," Lucas told the Planning and Conservation League in Sacramento for one of its publications (http://www.pcl.org/pcl_files/12_Historical_Cultural_Resources.pdf). "I was excited to finally walk on this land."

She found many traditional plant resources there, "including chokecherry (which was eaten), oaks (acorns were a food source), penstemon (which was smoked), and sumac (important for basket making)," she said. "I also saw visible cultural resources: rock rings, milling sites near a natural spring, midden soil areas (indicating former living places), pottery shards and manos and metates (rock tools for preparing food). Developing the site would endanger plants and cultural resources."

Her efforts and those of others, as well as the devastating 2003 Cedar Fire that touched this area, scrapped those horse camp plans. The Lucky Five Ranch remains an open-space jewel today.

The Lucky Five Ranch borders the southeastern edge of Lake Cuyamaca as well as the historic Rancho Cuyamaca, which borders the northern edge of that lake. This 2,117-acre Rancho Cuyamaca property was purchased by the Nature Conservancy from its former owners, who were aided by the Conservation Land Group in the 2002 sale. Rancho Cuyamaca, also known as Cuyamaca Ranch and Tulloch Ranch, was a cattle ranch ever since George Sawday, great-grandfather of Margaret Alice Tulloch, purchased the property in 1943; it had been held in the family since then.

Now all these lands are added to the open spaces that we hikers love. Explore that lucky land of plenty, where big backcountry views haven't changed much—and won't—for generations.

Thomas Brothers Map: Page 1177 (on page 1176), B-6.

Before You Go: Note that the PCT allows only hikers and equestrians—no bikes. Dogs are not allowed because the PCT goes through state parks here.

The only map I've found that shows this trail is Tom Harrison Maps' *Cuyamaca Rancho State Park Trail Map*, which you can usually find at REI or Adventure 16. Tom Harrison Maps may also be ordered online at www.tomharrisonmaps.com for $9.95 each.

This trail doesn't appear on the regular trail maps for Laguna, Cuyamaca Rancho, or Anza-Borrego Desert state parks.

You need an Adventure Pass to park anywhere in Laguna, which lies on Cleveland National Forest lands. You can buy day passes for $5 or annual passes for $30 at the general store in Mount Laguna, at the visitor center when it's open, and at outdoor equipment stores. For more information on Adventure Passes, go to the national forest pages for Cleveland National Forest, http://www.fs.usda.gov/detailfull/r5/passes-permits/recreation/?cid=stelprdb5208699&width=full.

Trailhead: From Interstate 8, exit at S1 (Sunrise Highway), heading north to Laguna. About 21.5 miles from that highway intersection, just past mile marker 34, park in the Sunrise Trailhead parking area in the Anza-Borrego Desert State Park on the left. When heading south on S1 from its junction at Highway 79, the parking area is about 3.6 miles from that intersection.

It's free to park here, and there are facilities. The Lucky Five Trail is at the southern end of the parking area. It heads south about 1.1 miles to the S1 highway, where you'll see a private, closed gate into Lucky Five Ranch. Cross the S1 highway and continue on the dirt road that heads uphill. In about another half-mile, this road intersects with the PCT; go left on the PCT to head north back to your parking area. You'll come to another intersection after about a total of 3.6 miles, where a sign directs you to the left to the Sunrise Parking area.

Distance/Difficulty: The Lucky Five Trail loop with the PCT is about 3.85 miles total with about a 550-foot elevation gain. Except for one moderate, short climb, it's easy.

11-12. Bag the Easy Monument Peak for Amazing Views

A hike to Monument Peak in Laguna takes you to the one of the highest elevations in that portion of the Cleveland National Forest at 6,271 feet, affording a panoramic view east into the Anza-Borrego Desert. On a clear day, you can even see the massive Salton Sea. It's a surprisingly easy hike, with an elevation gain of only about 500 feet from its trailhead.

Monument Peak is on the local Sierra Club's 100 peaks list, (http://sandiegosierraclub. org/get-outdoors/hike/peaks-list/peak-list), which consists of peaks in San Diego County that offer nontechnical, publicly accessible climbs "to encourage outings to less traveled areas, to explore remote high points, to develop navigational skills and to instill within climbers a sense of stewardship of the land," says the Sierra Club.

Monument Peak is one of easiest peaks in county to summit.

The trail to the peak is not on the map at the trailhead, and neither is it typically found on hiking trail maps of the Laguna Mountain Recreation Area, where it is located. But Jerry Schad, in his comprehensive hiking guidebook *Afoot and Afield in San Diego County,* maps the route and guides hikers to the right trail. Since Schad wrote his book, the trail is now easier to locate and navigate than it was a few years ago.

Begin on the eastern-most spur of the Big Laguna Trail, passing among some fine examples of Jeffrey pines and black oaks. Some of the oak trees, with their splendid gnarly trunks, are great examples of anthropomorphic shapes; see if you can find one whose protruding former limb makes it look like a fish.

In about a half-mile, the Big Laguna Trail intersects with the Pacific Crest Trail, where you turn left heading north. In about another half-mile, where the PCT makes a sharp left turn, you'll notice two trail markers directing you to that left turn to continue on PCT. In between these markers is an unmarked trail that heads straight ahead (east) to Monument Peak. These trail markers make the trail intersection to Monument Peak really easy to locate. You are heading straight for the antennae you see on the top of Monument Peak.

This part of the trail climbs uphill and is fairly rocky. It also passes through one of the county's densest colonies of manzanita, a dominant shrub in chaparral habitat known for its beautiful red-brown bark. This area offers one of the best collections of manzanita I've seen, notably because they haven't been burned in disastrous fires. Manzanita is very drought-tolerant and resprouts after fires, but in some of our county's backcountry, you see only the twisty remnants of this beautiful shrub.

During fall, the red-barked manzanita also features small red berries that native Kumeyaay from hundreds of years ago dried and ground into meal or steeped in water for tea. They prepared medicines from manzanita leaves and used its bark for firewood and housing materials, according to a fascinating essay on the Kumeyaay in Southern California by Michael Baksh for Palomar Community College (http://www.kumeyaay. info/kumeyaay_way/).

At the top of this trail, you'll reach the first of those antennae, where you head left around the fencing that encloses some of the equipment. Just beyond that fencing, join the paved road and turn left; that takes you to the top of Monument Peak, where there are more antennae. These antennae are part of NASA's Satellite Laser Ranging international network. Additionally, some of the equipment here on Monument Peak is part of the Scripps Orbit and Permanent Array Center (SOPAC at UCSD) and an EarthScope geophysical station, both of which gather seismic records for earthquake studies.

After taking in the 360-degree views into the desert as well as across Laguna to the west—on a very clear day you should be able to see the ocean—head back the same way you came.

When you go back down, after the fenced area, you are heading down a natural rocky ravine and could miss the left turn onto the proper trail home. Look for the small stack of rocks to guide you to that left.

Thomas Brothers Map: Page 1218, E-5

Before You Go: Download a map of the Big Laguna Trail and its intersection with Pacific Crest Trail at http://www.lmva.net/id3.html.

For a map of the trail to Monument Peak, get a copy of Jerry Schad's *Afoot and Afield in San Diego County.*

You need an Adventure Pass to park on Cleveland National Forest lands. Buy a $5 day-use pass or a $30 annual pass at the Mount Laguna general store, at outdoor equipment stores such as REI, or at the Cleveland National Forest ranger station on Alpine Road in Alpine, which is on the way. For more information on Adventure Passes, go to the national forest pages for Cleveland National Forest: http://www.fs.usda.gov/detailfull/r5/passes-permits/recreation/?cid=stelprdb5208699&width=full.

This trail is open to hikers and dogs on leashes.

Trailhead: From Interstate 8 east, exit at Sunrise Highway (S1), heading north. Just beyond mile marker 25 (about 25.2), there is a large parking area off the road with the trailhead for Big Laguna Trail. Head east on the Big Laguna Trail from S1.

Distance/Difficulty: About 2.6 miles round-trip; easy to moderate.

11-13. Oasis Spring Has Surprise Vegetation, Big Views

One of the shortest, easiest trails in Laguna Mountain Recreation Area features some unusual attractions. After walking through old pine forests and glimpsing the vast desert below, a verdant watery scene emerges with flora not commonly found in this area. It's aptly named Oasis Spring, and although the trail is not marked or maintained, it is easily navigated until you reach the very last segment to the old pump house. Begin by heading north on the Pacific Crest Trail just below the Desert View Overlook Deck at mile 26.5 on Sunrise Highway.

See unusual vegetation, canyon views from Oasis Spring Trail.

The PCT really earns its name as it cuts through Laguna. The trail seems to carve its way along the edge of this Peninsular Range of mountains, which rise over 6,000 feet, dropping precipitously down jagged cliffs thousands of feet below to the enormous Anza-Borrego desert. It's a classic ecotone, a transitional area between two ecosystems or habitats, viewed here more dramatically than most.

The views below take in Storm Canyon, a neighborhood where people have lived for more than 10,000 years. According to a placard at the Desert View Overlook, the

Kumeyaay and Diegueño people used a route through this canyon during their seasonal migrations. They would live in the Laguna Mountains in summer and then travel to the desert to live there during winter. "Every spring they carried baskets of dried fish, melons, beans and other desert foodstuffs up the canyon to the summer mountain retreat," says the placard.

The route through Storm Canyon continued to be important because it was the only wagon road into Southern California during the Gold Rush days of 1849. It was also the route for mail carriers in 1857 when the nation received its first overland Atlantic to Pacific mail service, when James Birch's San Diego–San Antonio mail began operation, according to an article on the Legends of America website (www.legendsofamerica.com/ca-vallecito.html).

Westbound stagecoaches dropped mail at the Vallecito Stage Station near Agua Caliente Springs (still a historic site operated by the county on Highway S2); pack mules carried it over the mountains to Descanso, where another stage continued the delivery to San Diego. As the forerunner of the Pony Express and Northern stage lines, this mail route was known as the Great Southern Overland, but after a San Francisco joke about San Diego's "Jackass Mail Route," that name stuck. In 1858, this canyon also became part of the Butterfield Overland Stage Route that traveled between Missouri and San Francisco.

After about a half-mile on the trail, the PCT heads a bit inland away from that desert view. When it takes a very sharp left, with two PCT signs marking this turn, instead go straight ahead onto an unmarked trail, stepping over a line of rocks that keeps hikers on the PCT. This is the Oasis Spring trail, which now steadily descends for nearly another half-mile to a large concrete water tank on your right.

It is here at the water tank that the vegetation becomes different with the steady spring water. Bright green ferns, tall brown cattails, yellow lilies, and vibrant red California fuchsias surround this tank.

The trail switchbacks down to the bottom of the tank, where the ground is pretty wet from the running stream. The trail guide of the Laguna Mountain Recreation Area (available at the visitor center on weekends) points out that heavy vegetation and burned trees obscure the trail almost completely, but if you "look for faint trails under the canopy, which will take some 'bush whacking' to stay on, you will see the roof of the pump house."

I could just see the roof of the pump house below, once the original water source for most of Laguna Mountain. The trail guide points out the big leaf maples and grapevines, which are not native here. The big leaf maple patriarch tree burned several years ago, but its descendants "are rising from the ashes."

I also noticed a lot of poison oak, turning bright orange in fall, just below the water tank where the trail becomes virtually unidentifiable, if not impassable. I declined to bushwhack my way farther. I also preferred to see the trail to avoid any encounters with snakes that might be hiding.

I turned around and retraced my way back, enjoying those panoramic views into Storm Canyon once again.

Thomas Brothers Map: Page 1218, 3-B

Before You Go: For a description of the trail, go to the Laguna Mountain Volunteer Association's website: http://www.lmva.net/id44.html.

Download a copy of the trail map from the LMVA: http://www.lmva.net/id3.html.

You need an Adventure Pass to park here on Cleveland National Forest lands. The pass is $5 for day-use or $30 annually, and it can be purchased at the visitor center in Laguna, the Laguna Mountain Lodge, or REI and other retailers. For more information on Adventure Passes, go to the national forest pages for Cleveland National Forest: http://www.fs.usda.gov/detailfull/r5/passes-permits/recreation/?cid=stelprdb5208699&width=full.

This trail is open to hikers, bicyclists, equestrians, and dogs on leashes.

Trailhead: From Interstate 8, exit onto Sunrise Highway (S1), heading north to Laguna Mountain Recreation Area. At mile marker 26.5, park off the pavement at the Desert View Overlook Deck and begin on the Pacific Crest Trail, heading north, just below the deck.

Distance/Difficulty: It's about 2.0 miles round-trip; easy.

11-14. PCT's Transition to Desert Offers Sweeping Views

Upon exploring another leg of the Pacific Crest Trail just north and east of Laguna, you'll find shrubby chaparral terrain with vast desert views. Only a few miles north from the mountains of Laguna, this part of the PCT is actually in the northwestern corner of Anza-Borrego Desert State Park. At about 5,000 feet—some 1,000 feet lower in elevation from Laguna's pine and cedar forests—this transitional landscape from mountains to desert is a stark change in scenery. The PCT is one of 11 national scenic trails, which also include the Appalachian National Scenic Trail (NST), the Arizona NST, the Continental Divide NST, the Florida NST, the Ice Age NST, Natchez Trace NST, New England NST, North Country NST, the Pacific Northwest NST, and the Potomoc Heritage NST. The PCT and Appalachian NST were the first two national scenic trails established in 1968.

The PCT is 2,650 miles long, from the Mexican border to the Canadian border through California, Oregon, and Washington. However, it's not the longest of the national scenic trails. That distinction goes to the North Country NST, which stretches 4,600 miles through seven states along the northern U.S. border from New York to North Dakota.

We are currently in the "Decade for the National Trails," leading to the 50th anniversary of the National Trails System Act in 2018.

This mountain-to-desert portion of the PCT winds through classic chaparral habitat, where no trees impede those far-reaching views. The land is thick with shrubs that carpet the landscape in green. Dominant among these shrubs are mountain mahogany, a native that's a member of the rose family that sports little yellow blooms in spring followed by its most distinctive feathery curls; chamise and red shank, both members of the rose family that have little white flowers in spring; and manzanita, a member of the heath family with its leaves that are more gray-green, its white or pink spring blooms, and its beautiful reddish bark that colors the hills year-round.

Scan sweeping views from PCT in the very high desert.

In keeping with this transition to the desert, you'll also see scattered brittlebush that blooms yellow in spring, the classic yucca or nolina, and the chaparral yucca, also known as our lord's candle. The latter, with its very tightly wound rosette base, is monocarpic, meaning it dies after it blooms its single, eight-foot-tall flower stalk.

The other most arresting sight on this part of the PCT is a large quartz outcropping that sits right next to the trail about a half-mile or so from this trailhead. Quartz is second most abundant mineral found on the planet after feldspar. Quartz is especially common among granite, and it can be translucent, white, or almost any other color. The quartz outcropping here gleams mostly white with veins of red-orange running through it. It stands about three to four feet high and about 10 to 15 feet long, most of it on the north side of the east-bound trail.

After about 1.5 miles, large mountain meadows appear in the distance, where grasses take over those shrubs. You'll also catch a glimpse to the northwest of a blue corner of Lake Cuyamaca.

You can continue on this trail for a couple thousand miles, but I turned back after about 2.0 miles, making a 4.0-mile round-trip hike. This part of the PCT has a fairly gradual and relatively small elevation gain.

Upon returning to the Sunrise Trail parking area, I noticed two other trailheads here that I'll explore another time. La Cima Trail connects to the Upper Green Valley Trail and the California Riding and Hiking Trail from here. The Lucky Five Trail heads to the south to connect with another portion of the PCT.

Thomas Brothers Map: Page 1177 (on 1176), C-7.

Before You Go: Note that the PCT allows only hikers and equestrians—no bikes. Leashed dogs are allowed here because this segment of the PCT doesn't go through any state parks.

The best map I've found of the trails in this area is Tom Harrison Maps' *Cuyamaca Rancho State Park Trail Map,* which you can usually find at REI or Adventure 16. Tom Harrison Maps may also be ordered online at www.tomharrisonmaps.com, for $9.95 each.

These trails don't appear on the regular maps for Cuyamaca Rancho State Park or Anza-Borrego Desert State Park.

You need an Adventure Pass to park here on Cleveland National Forest lands. The pass is $5 for day use or $30 annually, and it can be purchased at the visitor center in Laguna, the Laguna Mountain Lodge, or REI and other retailers. For more information on Adventure Passes, go to the national forest pages for Cleveland National Forest: http://www.fs.usda.gov/detailfull/r5/passes-permits/recreation/?cid=stelprdb5208699&width=full.

Trailhead: From Interstate 8, exit at S1 (Sunrise Highway), heading north to Laguna. About 21.5 miles from that highway intersection, just after mile marker 34 on S1, the Sunrise Trailhead parking area in the Anza-Borrego Desert State Park is on the left. After heading south on S1 from its junction with Highway 79, the parking area is about 3.6 miles from that intersection.

The trailhead is across the highway from this parking area. A signed spur trail of about a quarter-mile takes you to the PCT, where I headed to the left (north).

It is free to park here, and there are facilities.

Distance/Difficulty: I went about 2.0 miles for a 4.0-mile round-trip hike; easy.

11-15. Picture Boulders, Oaks on PCT South From I-8

Hike the Pacific Crest Trail south from the Boulder Oaks campground, and you'll encounter (appropriately) big boulders and beautiful oaks. Lining the few riparian habitats along streams—mostly dry in the fall—are the stately cottonwood trees with their heart-shaped leaves as well as the arroyo willow trees, both of which color the landscape yellow in the fall.

The PCT is open to equestrians and hikers as well as dogs on leashes here, because it's on Cleveland National Forest land. Dogs are not allowed on state park lands, including the PCT where it crosses state parks. Bicycles are not allowed on the PCT.

From Boulder Oaks to Lake Morena County Park, the PCT covers a bit more than 5.5 miles. I went a little more than 2.8 miles one-way, making a round-trip of about 5.65 miles. From Boulder Oaks to its southern terminus near Campo, the PCT covers about 22 miles.

Of course, these mileages are nothing compared to hiking the entire PCT, which zigzags 2,650 miles from the Mexican border near Campo to the border of Canada in Washington. According to the Pacific Crest National Scenic Trail Map published by the U.S. Department of Agriculture, the PCT crosses national monuments, national parks, national forests, Bureau of Land Management land, federally designated wilderness areas, state and county parks, and tribal lands along the way. It ascends more than 57 major mountain passes. Temperatures can exceed 100 degrees Fahrenheit in the Anza-Borrego Desert State Park and drop below freezing in the Sierra Nevada Mountains.

Of the 11 national scenic trails, the PCT encompasses the greatest elevation range, from 140 feet above sea level in the Columbia River Gorge between Oregon and Washington to 13,200 feet at Forester Pass in California's Sierra Nevada. It goes through six of North America's seven ecozones: alpine tundra, subalpine forest, upper montane forest, lower montane forest, upper Sonoran, and lower Sonoran. For more information on the national scenic as well as national historic trails, go to http://www.nps.gov/nts/nts_trails.html.

Boulders and oaks characterize this segment of the PCT.

This portion of the PCT south from Boulder Oaks offers a very easy, practically flat grade for most of the way. Shortly after the campground, the trail dips into one of those riparian stream areas loaded with yellow cottonwoods and willows in autumn. Then it heads up a bit as it winds east toward Buckman Springs Road. It follows along the east of that road and passes through some fine old oak groves before reaching an enormous meadow area. When I stopped to photograph one of the massive coast live oak trees, the most common large tree in our county, a huge, dark orange flash flew out of that tree. It flew away too fast to make identification, but it may have been a great horned or barn owl, whose daytime slumber was disturbed.

At nearly 2.0 miles from Boulder Oaks, the PCT reaches a bridge that holds Buckman Springs Road. It's easy to make a wrong turn here. To stay on the PCT, go to the eastern end of that bridge and follow the PCT signs. After you cross under the bridge near its eastern end, the trail climbs uphill for the most elevation gain on this section (about 400 more feet) as it heads toward Lake Morena.

I did make that wrong turn and went too soon under the bridge along the continuation of a trail. I followed this very sandy trail that crosses several dry stream beds for another half-mile or so. At that point I reached a truly splendid, old oak grove that was worth the short detour. I turned around because I never saw another PCT sign, and I began to wonder whether I'd missed the trail at the bridge. When I went back to the bridge, I saw where the signs continued at the east end of the bridge, and I followed the PCT there up the ridge toward Lake Morena, eventually turning back after I'd gone nearly 3.0 miles one-way.

The views from that ridge extend north into Laguna, where the PCT gains about 3,000 feet in elevation in about 23 miles, from Boulder Oaks to Monument Peak, one of the highest peaks in the county. As I retraced my steps back on that gentle section of the PCT, I noticed all the blue-green sagebrush bushes that were a lovely foil to the yellow cottonwoods and willows.

The oaks are my favorite tree to ponder, and this time I was on the lookout for anything huge that might fly out of one.

Thomas Brothers Map: Page D, off I-8, just to right of Pine Creek Wilderness and Hauser Wilderness, where I-8 makes that deep dip before turning east.

Before You Go: The best trail maps of the entire Pacific Crest Trail are its Halfmile PCT Maps, now available online: http://www.pctmap.net. This segment is on California Section A, Campo to Warner Springs, Page 3.

View the entire Pacific Crest Trail from the forest service's website: http://www.fs.usda.gov/Internet/FSE_DOCUMENTS/stelprdb5353107.html. This is an interactive map, so find the southern end of the trail and zoom in until you get the close-up view of this portion at Boulder Oaks, where Interstate 8 meets Old Highway 80 near Buckman Springs Road. You'll see the PCT cross I-8 near here.

You might also want to purchase a big PCT map, available at outdoor stores such as REI and Adventure 16, or from the Pacific Crest Trail Association's website (http://www.pcta.org).

This trail is open to hikers, equestrians, and dogs on leashes.

Trailhead: From Interstate 8, exit and head east at Buckman Springs Road. Go south at the exit until the first stop at Old Highway 80, where you turn left, heading east. Go 2.0 miles to the Boulder Oaks Campground on the right.

There is PCT parking just inside the campground. You must display your Adventure Pass to park on Cleveland National Forest lands. Buy a $5 day use or $30 annual Adventure Pass at the nearest CNF ranger station in Alpine, at outdoor stores like REI or Adventure 16, or from the CNF's website. For more information on Adventure Passes, go to the national forest pages for Cleveland National Forest: http://www.fs.usda.gov/detailfull/r5/passes-permits/recreation/?cid=stelprdb5208699&width=full.

Distance/Difficulty: I went about 2.85 miles one-way for a 5.65-mile round-trip; mostly easy with a total elevation gain of about 500 feet.

11-16. Another PCT Segment, Another Great Day

Every time I hike a different segment of the Pacific Crest Trail, I find something fascinating. In every case, the views are wonderful. Sometimes they are even breathtaking, especially on the eastern flank of the Laguna Mountains, where the trail really hugs the edge and the land drops steeply down into the desert. The trail explores the backcountry every step of the way, so even if you might see signs of civilization, they tend to be far away, and you are usually surrounded by wilderness.

These observations were in full force on my latest segment from Kitchen Creek Road to a little above Cibbets Flat, a 3.0-mile hike one-way creating a 6.0-mile round-trip.

As you head north on the PCT from Kitchen Creek Road, the trail quickly hugs that edge, but does not yet look down into Anza-Borrego. Here, the land drops sharply but down into canyons and valleys covered in chaparral. The eastern horizon takes in the In-Ko-Pah Mountains, where Interstate 8 fingers its way through a pass far away. Just below are Fred Canyon and, a bit farther, Antone Canyon, where seasonal creeks form riparian ribbons of live oak trees.

Find unusual rock formations, long views on Cibbets Flat segment of PCT.

The trail leaves the road, curves east, and then heads north, and that feeling of the edge comes into play. Here's where something fascinating caught my eye. The trail winds through chaparral filled with that habitat's characteristic low-growing, drought-resistant shrubs, including chamise, manzanita, ceanothus (wild lilac), scrub oak, and laurel sumac. There is no shade. Then suddenly, virtually vertical rock formations thrust upwards in overlapping plates. They are kind of a dark red and seem like sentinels on the trail. They led me to research what they could be, and I learned some geologic history along the way.

According to the "Geologic History of San Diego County" from the San Diego Natural History Museum, during the Jurassic Period (about 160 million–170 million years ago), deeply buried sedimentary rock layers were disrupted at least twice by rising magmas from volcanic actions, and they were twisted into the steeply tilted segments now exposed throughout the central and western part of San Diego County. "Along Sunrise Highway in the Laguna Mountains, near-vertical layers of mudstone and sandstone, now schist and quartzite, attest to the uplift and metamorphism that must have accompanied these magmas," the museum says.

Along Sunrise Highway is a belt of granitic rocks called the Cuyamaca-Laguna Mountain Shear Zone. It is usually described as gneiss, which is metamorphic rock (changed rock formed deep in the earth after high temperatures and pressures) with elongated clusters of dark minerals. "What makes these rocks different is that the darker minerals, biotite mica and hornblende, have been recrystallized into tiny rod-like aggregates by large-scale tectonic forces."

The trail is generally quite rocky along this segment, and you'll also see a lot of white quartz (even large running outcrops of it to the east), as well as shiny mica embedded in it. There are also colorful, red-banded rocks, and gneiss is usually a banded formation.

After about 1.8 miles and 414 feet in elevation gain, the trail crosses a dry creek bed in Fred Canyon. There are many old live oaks here, even if there is no surface water, so this is the only shady spot on this segment. It is a lovely quiet picnic site. At about 2.3 miles and 570 feet in elevation gain, the trail intersects with Fred Canyon Road, a popular dirt road for mountain bikers and backroad enthusiasts. To the west about 0.6 mile lies Cibbets Flat Campground with water and toilet facilities, as well as 25 campsites for $14 a night.

I continued straight ahead on the PCT, noting the very unusual sign here: "Safety Hazard: Unexploded Military Ordnance in this area; Stay on Road and Trails." These devices were onboard a military Super Cobra helicopter that crashed around here in 2009. The two pilots were killed, and the wreckage spread over about two acres. The helicopter was carrying several rockets 2.75 inches in diameter. If by chance you see any such thing, don't touch or approach it but call 911, advises the sign. Stay on the trail, and you're safe.

The last part of this segment climbs more steeply now, rising another 215 feet in about a half-mile. At the top of this area, you'll look back down onto the trail you've hiked which you can see for a very long way as it winds through the passes of the hills on either side. Layers of blue hills on the horizon make a lovely scene. I turned around and headed back, noting all the yuccas that have yet to form their single blooms, as well as the last of the ceanothus blossoms becoming seed vessels. I spotted a few bright blue scrub jays and some red-winged blackbirds, and I heard the soft sounds of California quail. Soaring overhead was something unusual that I think was a prairie falcon, which nests on cliff ledges, so it might be at home here.

Once again, another fascinating hike on the Pacific Crest Trail.

Thomas Brothers Map: Page D, Interstate 8, just east of Pine Creek Wilderness where freeway takes a dip before heading on to intersection with Highway 94.

Before You Go: The best trail maps of the entire Pacific Crest Trail are its Halfmile PCT Maps, now available online: http://www.pctmap.net. This segment is on California Section A, Campo to Warner Springs, Page 4.

View the entire Pacific Crest Trail from the forest service's website: http://www.fs.usda.gov/Internet/FSE_DOCUMENTS/stelprdb5353107.html. This is an interactive map, so find the southern end of the trail and zoom in until you get the close-up view of this portion near Kitchen Creek and Fred Canyon Roads.

You might also want to purchase a big PCT map, available at outdoor stores such as REI and Adventure 16, or from the Pacific Crest Trail Association's website: http://www.pcta.org.

You must display your Adventure Pass to park on Cleveland National Forest lands. Buy a $5 day use or a $30 annual Adventure Pass at the nearest CNF ranger station in Alpine, at outdoor stores like REI or Adventure 16, or from the CNF's website. For more information on Adventure Passes, go to the national forest pages for Cleveland National Forest: http://www.fs.usda.gov/detailfull/r5/passes-permits/recreation/?cid=stelprdb5208699&width=full.

This trail is open to hikers, equestrians, and dogs on leashes.

Trailhead: From Interstate 8, exit at Cameron Station/Kitchen Creek Road (about 7.0 miles east of Laguna's Sunrise Highway) and head north on Kitchen Creek Road. At about 2.5 miles, you'll see the PCT markers on either side of the road near gates and a painted cattle guard on the road pavement. Park here off the road in the wide shoulder area and cross the road to start heading north on the PCT.

Distance/Difficulty: I went about 3.0 miles north on the PCT, retracing my steps back for a 6.0-mile round-trip hike with about 960 feet in total elevation gain. Moderate.

You could arrange for a second car pickup in Laguna if you want a longer, steeper hike. From Kitchen Creek Road to Thing Valley Road, the next available parking area near the PCT heading north, it's about 10.1 miles on the PCT with an elevation gain of nearly 2,000 feet.

11-17. Pioneer Mail PCT Views Both Desert, Mountains

This segment of the Pacific Crest Trail on the eastern edge of the Laguna Mountains offers panoramic views down some 4,000 feet into the desert and across to the Oriflamme and Sawtooth mountain ranges. At a few points on this piece of the PCT, you really feel as though you are on the rim of the world, with the narrowest part of the trail truly hugging that cliff on its vertical edge. This part of the PCT has passed through Laguna Mountains proper with its lovely pine and fir trees. Here you are in a transition zone between mountains and desert, a treeless chaparral habitat filled with lots of blooming buckwheat, chamise (not blooming in summer), and manzanita.

Where the PCT hugs a dramatic edge, hang gliders take to the air.

The red-barked manzanita in midsummer to late summer sports bright orange berries. The mountain mahogany shrub displays its feathery styles that appear after its flowers have dropped, "giving plants beautiful ghostly aspect," notes James Lightner in his book *San Diego County Native Plants*. Some of the mountain mahogany I saw were covered in so many of those feathery tendrils that their flowers must have been thick a few months earlier.

I began this hike at the Pioneer Mail Picnic Area off Highway S1, or Sunrise Highway, at about the 29.3 mile marker. With its large parking area, it's a good equestrian staging spot, and the PCT invites horseback riders as well as hikers. Bikers are not allowed on the PCT. Dogs on leashes are allowed on this part of the PCT; the only parts of the PCT where you cannot take dogs are when it passes through national or state parks.

The first half-mile of this hike takes you to Kwaaymii Point, a 5,440-foot-high rocky promontory that looks down into Cottonwood Canyon, which separates the Oriflamme from the Sawtooth Mountains. The views extend to Little Blair Valley and Vallecito Valley in the desert, backdropped by (from north to south) 5,432-foot-high Granite Mountain, the Pinyon Mountains, and the Vallecito Mountains.

The Kwaaymii Laguna Band of Mission Indians lived here during summers in Laguna for thousands of years, spending winters in the desert below. The Kwaaymii are a subgroup of the Kumeyaay, formerly called Diegueño. The Kumeyaay consist of two related groups: the Ipai, extending north of San Diego River to Escondido and Lake Henshaw, and the Tipai, extending south of San Diego River (including the Laguna Mountains) and down into northern Baja California.

After an 1860 smallpox outbreak and the 1918 influenza epidemic, most of the Kwaaymii were wiped out. Tom Lucas, the last full-blooded Kwaaymii, died in 1989. Born here in Laguna in 1903, as the only Kwaaymii remaining, he petitioned the U.S. government to have the reservation deeded to him as private property. The 320-acre Lucas Ranch, where his daughter, Carmen (whose mother's heritage included German, French, Irish, and Scottish), still lives, was badly burned in the 2003 Cedar Fire, but the cabin her father had built there in the 1920s remains. Carmen often serves as a local native archaeological consultant.

Just before Kwaaymii Point, you'll note a couple of concrete barricades holding up that cliffside edge. This portion is actually a former segment of Sunrise Highway, according to Jerry Schad in *Afoot and Afield San Diego County*. "Before 1975, this was a hair-raising part of Sunrise Highway; but that was before the road was bypassed and replaced by a new, wider and less spectacular stretch of roadway," wrote Schad.

This wide part of the trail hosts a popular launching pad for local hang gliders, a few of whom I saw the Sunday I was there. There are three markers here that memorialize three local pilots: Ray Petersen, Richard M. Zadorozny, and Tab Kennedy. A present-day pilot getting ready for takeoff was one of two, Bill Helliwell and Mike Tryon, who set a hang gliding altitude record here at Laguna of 16,500 feet high. The pilots told me they were planning that day to go down near the Butterfield Stage marker in the desert below, about a 45-mile drive but just a 3.0-mile flight. I saw them later from the trail soaring high above this awesome landscape.

I also encountered a group of four adults with a four-year-old child in a backpack carrier. Daniel Cimarosti, Rosalind Haselbeck, Allison Renshaw, and Rich Williams, with Atticus (the son of Renshaw and Williams), were continuing a segmented hike along the PCT, with Williams blogging about it along the way. The Leucadia residents started at the Mexico border in June and are day-hiking 6.0- to 18-mile segments intermittently. "We're at mile 53.85 today," Williams told me. Their blog can be found at http://hikingpct.blogspot.com.

When the trail begins to turn inland away from that edge, at about the 2.0-mile point from Pioneer Mail, you'll notice lots of burned manzanita that look like ghost shrubs. With the less interesting views, I went a bit farther, turned around, and retraced my way back.

Pioneer Mail, a sign says at the trailhead, is dedicated to the pioneers of the first transcontinental mail route from Texas to San Diego. Known as the Birch Overland Pioneer Mail Trail, it began operation in 1857. The actual route was located north of this facility. The first men who crossed these mountains used pack animals, so it was dubbed the Jackass Mail Route.

Mules are still invited here.

Thomas Brothers Map: Page 1197, on page 1176, G-6.

Before You Go: Download a copy of the trail map at the Laguna Mountain Volunteer Association website: http://www.lmva.net/id3.html.

The best trail maps of the entire Pacific Crest Trail are its Halfmile PCT Maps, now available online: http://www.pctmap.net. This segment is on California Section A, Campo to Warner Springs, Page 7.

You must display your Adventure Pass to park on Cleveland National Forest lands. Buy a $5 day use or a $30 annual Adventure Pass at the nearest CNF ranger station in Alpine, at outdoor stores like REI or Adventure 16, or from the CNF's website. For more information on Adventure Passes, go to the national forest pages for Cleveland National Forest: http://www.fs.usda.gov/detailfull/r5/passes-permits/recreation/?cid=stelprdb5208699&width=full.

This trail is open to hikers, equestrians, and dogs on leashes.

Trailhead: To reach the Pioneer Mail Picnic Area and PCT trail head, from Interstate 8, exit at S1 (Sunrise Highway), heading north to Laguna Mountain Recreation Area. The Pioneer Mail area is on the right, just past mile marker 29.

Distance/Difficulty: I went about 2.2 miles one-way, for about a 4.4-mile round-trip. The total elevation gain was about 600 feet and was very gradual. Mostly easy.

11-18. On Top of the World on Pine Mountain Trail

When you're on the Pine Mountain Trail in Laguna, it seems as though you're on top of the world. The trail stays on the rim edge most of the way and affords splendid mountaintop views to the south and west. The trail begins across Sunrise Highway from the Pioneer Mail equestrian parking area in the Laguna Mountain Recreation Area, part of Cleveland National Forest. The Pioneer Mail area is home to a historic route that once was traveled by stage coaches.

Across the highway from that parking area and immediately to the north is an unnamed road that drops into the valley to the west; its gates are usually open. The trailhead begins immediately to the north of those gates; look for the Pine Mountain Trail's wooden marker.

Stay on the edge on Pine Mountain Trail.

The trail descends a bit and continues a short way along the western fenced edge of Sunrise Highway. What caught my attention from the start were lots of little blue butterflies darting in and out of the shrubs lining both sides of the narrow trail. There are virtually no trees here and therefore no respite from the sun, but many flowering plants color the scene, including bright red scarlet buglers, light purple western asters, purple California thistles turning into wish flowers, beautiful yellow mariposa lilies, and tiny baby blue eyes. About midway along, a virtual white sea of chamise and buckwheat bushes covers the descending terrain in late spring.

Down in the valley below, you can see more evidence of the fire, as well as a home that's on private property in this national forest area, sometimes noted on maps as the Laguna Indian Reservation. The Kumeyaay used to live on these lands for hundreds of years before European explorers and settlers came to this area in the 1769 Gaspar de Portola expedition that rode through here on the way from San Diego to Monterey, naming many places. Laguna means pond, lagoon, or little lake in Spanish.

The Cedar Fire of October 2003, the largest fire in recorded California history that destroyed more than 280,000 acres and killed 15 people, tore through this northern edge of the Laguna Mountain Recreation Area. Remnants of its destruction are still visible, especially in the burned sculptural forms of manzanita, but a lot of the low chaparral vegetation is again robust.

The last major fire here was the 1970 Laguna Fire that burned more than 175,000 acres and killed eight people. It was the largest fire in California's recorded history until it was surpassed by the 2003 Cedar Fire and then the Witch Creek Fire in 2007 (now the second largest).

As you continue along the rim trail, in about a mile it intersects a dirt road. Cross this road and continue on the trail where you see another wooden post marker. Shortly after that dirt road intersection, you'll note some actual pine trees on the highest ridge visible to the northwest. The trail doesn't take you there, but they reside on Pine Mountain, a peak that rises to 5,640 feet in elevation. The highest point in Laguna is Cuyapaipe Mountain, at 6,378 feet.

After about another 1.5 miles, the trail ends at an intersection with Indian Creek Trail. I turned around at this point and retraced my steps back, making for about a 5.0-mile hike round-trip.

Do try to make it all the way to this intersection. The narrow trail gets rockier, but the views get better around every corner, and the best ones are at the end. There are also several options here to make longer treks. Indian Creek Trail (turning right at the intersection with Pine Mountain Trail) to the west actually continues into Cuyamaca Rancho State Park. According to the Trail Guide pamphlet available at the Laguna Mountain Recreation Area's visitor center, a left turn onto Indian Creek Trail intersects at 0.93 miles to the Noble Canyon Trail, where another left intersects in 1.9 miles to the Penny Pines Parking Area, where you can connect to the Pacific Crest Trail in 0.2 miles, taking a left for a 3.6-mile hike back to the Pioneer Mail parking area, totaling about a 9.0-mile loop hike.

Thomas Brothers Map: Page 1197, on Page 1176, G-6.

Before You Go: Download a copy of the trail map at the Laguna Mountain Volunteer Association website: http://www.lmva.net/id3.html.

You must display your Adventure Pass to park on Cleveland National Forest lands. Buy a $5 day use or a $30 annual Adventure Pass at the nearest CNF ranger station in Alpine, at outdoor stores like REI or Adventure 16, or from the CNF's website. For more information on Adventure Passes, go to the national forest pages for Cleveland National Forest: http://www.fs.usda.gov/detailfull/r5/passes-permits/recreation/?cid=stelprdb5208699&width=full.

Dogs are allowed on leashes, and Pine Mountain Trail is open to hikers, equestrians, and mountain bikers.

Trailhead: Take Interstate 8 east, exiting at Sunrise Highway (S1), heading north into Laguna. A few miles north of the small town of Mount Laguna and the visitor center (open only on weekends), between the 29.0 and 29.5 mile markers, park in the Pioneer Mail equestrian area or on either side of the road. Cross the road to reach this trailhead.

Distance/Difficulty: About 2.5 miles one-way, or 5.0 miles round-trip. Easy.

11-19. Hike through the Snow on Laguna's Red-Tailed Roost

It was nearing 70 degrees under sunny, blue skies, and I was tromping through snow sometimes two feet deep. I was on the Red-Tailed Roost Spur in Laguna, a lovely trail through conifer and black oak forests any time of year, but in winter it's sometimes blanketed with that white fluff we seldom associate with San Diego. It had been more than a week when it had snowed in Laguna, and enough had melted so that the trail was still visible—a key factor when trying to navigate the mountain routes in winter. Wait a while for some of the snow to melt to reveal the trails, and you'll wander through a landscape that's unusual here and very cool in every sense of the word.

Laguna has snow even when it's 70 degrees outside.

The trail is a loop that covers about 3.0 miles round-trip. On a normal day, it can be hiked in about 1.5 hours, but when trudging through thick snow, add another 30 to 60 minutes. Both ends of the loop converge at about the same spot, so you may choose to hike the trail either clockwise or counterclockwise. In terms of uphill exertion, the clockwise route is a little easier.

I took the counterclockwise route, and although parts of the trail were definitely covered in snow, I never lost sight of it. Footprints that had gone before me also helped show me the way.

The Red-Tailed Roost Spur Trail is No. 4 of the spur trails off the Big Laguna Trail, a trail complex on Laguna Mountain that totals 17 miles, consisting of the main trail and eight named spur trails. The spur trails are marked with wooden signposts with Big Laguna Trail pictured on top, and the spur name and number below. Sometimes you'll see only the Big Laguna name and spur number, so know what number your spur trail is before you start.

The first leg of the Red-Tailed Roost Spur Trail when going counterclockwise is the prettiest meander through conifer and old oak forest. There are coast live oaks here as well as pines and cedars. One of the most notable of these conifers is the incense cedar, with its distinctive reddish bark that one might mistake for a redwood. A California native tree, the incense cedar is fairly easy to distinguish among the conifers: Its bright green leaves are flattened, like its seed cones, according to James Lightner's *San Diego County Native Plants*.

Pines, by comparison, have needles rather than those flat evergreen leaves, and they have pine cones rather than flat seed cones. Common pines in Laguna to look for on this trail include the Jeffrey pine, another native that has thick gray, brown, or pinkish bark with 10-inch-long needles in bundles of three. Its peeled bark smells like vanilla. The native Ponderosa pine can be one of the tallest, up to 175 feet, with thick somewhat reddish bark that has the odor of pitch. On short branches, its needles are also in bundles of three. The sugar pine, another native, is the tallest and can grow to 200 feet, with smooth, pale bark and needles in bundles of five. It's particularly inviting walking through this conifer forest when the white snow illuminates the landscape.

After about the first 0.75 mile when hiking the loop counterclockwise, the trail descends about 300 feet and then connects with Escondido Ravine Road, a dirt road that services some private cabins you'll see. Take a left onto that road (heading northwest) and pass around a locked gate, following the trail signposts. Continue along that road for about another 0.75 mile. The snow was thickest here on the road, the lowest elevation on this trail route. Below the road, look for the Escondido Creek, which flows through here all year.

When you reach a cattle guard on the road, you'll see the trail marker on your left. Follow the Red-Tailed Roost No. 4 signpost uphill, now gaining about 400 feet in elevation through more forest. At the top of this ridge, you'll encounter lots of black oak trees—the only oaks here to lose their leaves in winter. I also saw several people sledding on the sparse but still slick snow patches.

The trail then descends about 135 feet back to the parking area where you started. Your feet might be a bit wet if you tromped in the snow, but you'll have walked through yet again another fascinating landscape experience in our remarkable county.

Thomas Brothers Map: Page 1218, F7.

Before You Go: Download a copy of the trail map at the Laguna Mountain Volunteer Association website: http://www.lmva.net/id3.html.

You must display your Adventure Pass to park on Cleveland National Forest lands. Buy a $5 day use or a $30 annual Adventure Pass at the nearest CNF ranger station in Alpine, at outdoor stores like REI or Adventure 16, or from the CNF's website. For more information on Adventure Passes, go to the national forest pages for Cleveland National Forest: http://www.fs.usda.gov/detailfull/r5/passes-permits/recreation/?cid=stelprdb5208699&width=full.

This trail is open to hikers, bicyclists, equestrians, and dogs on leashes.

Trailhead: From Interstate 8, exit at Sunrise Highway (Highway S1), heading north. Just beyond the 22.5-mile marker, across from the Mount Laguna Fire Station, turn left into the Red-Tailed Roost parking area. The trailhead for both ends of the loop is located at the western end of the parking area.

Distance/Difficulty: A 3.0-mile round-trip loop; easy to moderate.

11-20. Valley Views and a Pond Make Sunset Trail Special

Sunset Trail in Laguna is one of the prettiest mountain trails in the county, complete with a pond in its middle. The trail winds through pine and oak forests studded with giant granite boulders, offers two splendid viewpoints that cast your eye over distant valleys and peaks, and reveals the wide-open Laguna Meadow, where that little pond lies. I stopped at the pond and retraced my route back, but you can continue for several miles, even reaching Big Laguna Lake if you have the inclination.

Sunset Trail is in the Laguna Mountain Recreation Area, part of Cleveland National Forest, which was named for President Grover Cleveland. President Cleveland had championed public lands and greatly increased forest reserves in the West.

Sunset Trail is a Laguna favorite for forests, meadows, and a pond.

It all started in 1891 when Congress passed the Forest Reserve Act to protect the nation's forests from wasteful and illegal timber cutting. In Southern California, the critical issue was water, and so in the 1890s, several forest reserves were set aside here for watershed protection. Two of these parcels formed Cleveland National Forest, designated in 1908 by President Theodore Roosevelt.

Today, Cleveland National Forest includes about 460,000 acres in three separate areas within Orange, Riverside, and San Diego Counties. Its diverse landscape supports more than 260 species of birds, 57 species of mammals, and six distinct ecosystems: conifer forests, mountain, riparian, oak woodlands, chaparral, and coastal sage scrub.

Sunset Trail winds through those conifer forests of tall evergreen trees, including Coulter and Jeffrey pines and incense cedars. Most notable perhaps are the Jeffrey pines, a native tree that can grow to 150 feet tall and whose peeled bark smells like vanilla, making this walk pleasantly fragrant. There are also lots of black oaks, another native that can grow to 75 feet tall with acorns that are said to have superior flavor. No wonder natives have lived in these forests for at least 10,000 years, long ago migrating between here and the desert according to the seasons. I noticed many oak seedlings along this trail, so those acorns are working that way now. The forest seemed really healthy, sporting several blooming wildflowers even late in the summer season. I spotted tiny yellow asters, scarlet monkeyflowers, and tall yellow goldenrod.

The first viewpoint occurs pretty quickly—after about three-quarters of a mile from the trailhead. Suddenly to the west is the wide-open Crouch Valley, home to the Crouch Ranch according to the map, which is surrounded by layers of shadowy hills to the west. At an elevation of about 5,460 feet, if the day is very clear, you can see the ocean from here.

After winding a little farther through the forested trail, you come to the other view, this time looking northwest to Cuyamaca peaks on the horizon. The trail then becomes rockier as it weaves through boulders and drops a few hundred feet down. By about 1.5 miles from the trailhead, you come onto the lower edge of the huge Laguna Meadow and that little pond, Water of the Woods (sometimes referred to as Lake of the Woods). The sign marking Water of the Woods has been obliterated mostly by bird droppings, so the lake is pretty healthy. According to a detailed map near the trailhead, Water of the Woods is fed by the Agua Dulce Creek and ultimately connects to Big Laguna Lake and Little Laguna Lake, both to the east of Sunset Trail.

If you wish to continue past Water of the Woods, the Big Laguna Trail heads east from the pond and goes to Big Laguna Lake. You may also continue about 3.0 more miles on Sunset Trail, which connects at 4.6 miles to the northern edge of Big Laguna Trail. You'll note at the trailhead where you started that the first fork splits the trails, both of which are marked: the left one is Sunset Trail, and the right is Big Laguna. It looks like you can loop those trails at the pond.

Again, I stayed on Sunset Trail to the pond and then turned around and retraced my steps back, making for about a 3.0-mile round-trip hike that offers some beautiful nature to appreciate.

Thomas Brothers Map: Page D, between pages 1218 and 1237.

Before You Go: Download a copy of the trail map at the Laguna Mountain Volunteer Association website: http://www.lmva.net/id3.html.

Go to the Cleveland National Forest pages for general information on Sunset Trail, in the Descanso District. This page lists most of the hiking trails in CNF: http://www.fs.usda.gov/detailfull/cleveland/recreation/?cid=stelprdb5288896&width=full.

You will need an Adventure Pass to park here. You can purchase a $5 day pass or a $30 annual pass at local outdoor equipment stores, including REI and Adventure 16; at Cleveland National Forest Ranger Stations, including one in Alpine on the way; or at the general store in Laguna, a few miles farther north on Sunrise Highway from the trailhead. For more information on Adventure Passes, go to the national forest pages for Cleveland National Forest: http://www.fs.usda.gov/detailfull/r5/passes-permits/recreation/?cid=stelprdb5208699&width=full.

This trail is open to hikers and dogs on leashes.

Trailhead: Take Interstate 8 east and exit onto Sunrise Highway (S-1). Note mile markers, and between 19.0 and 19.5 miles on the markers, you'll see the Meadows Information Station with several informative placards. Notice the sample footprints (paw prints) in the cement there that show local wildlife; the paw prints of mountain lions are a lot bigger than those of the deer, raccoon, or coyote.

The trailhead is across the highway from this Meadows Information Station and a few yards north. Look for a wooden sign that marks the entrance to both Sunset and Big Laguna trails.

Park on either side of the road shoulder.

Distance/Difficulty: From 3.0 to 9.0 miles round-trip, depending on how far you go on the Sunset Trail. Easy.

11-21. Northern Sunset Trail Views Earn the Name

The bright blue flash of a Steller's jay, the yellow and orange leaves of black oaks, and views all the way to Point Loma are reasons to find Laguna's Sunset Trail in autumn. The Sunset Trail is one of the prettiest in Laguna for its big trees and big views. In the months of October, November, and December, it's especially rewarding because the skies tend to be clearer for those glimpses of the ocean some 65 miles to the west.

Part of the Cleveland National Forest, Laguna Mountain was declared a recreation area by presidential proclamation in 1926, but its Sunset Trail wasn't opened until 1993. The trail is aptly named because it traverses the entire western rim of the Laguna Mountain plateau, according to Jerry Schad in *Afoot and Afield in San Diego County*, and it offers potentially amazing views of the sunset over the ocean on those very clear days.

View all the way to the ocean from Sunset Trail in Laguna.

The entire Sunset Trail is about 4.5 miles one-way. I've done the southern portion of the trail from the Meadows Information Station to Water of the Woods, about a 3.2-mile round-trip hike up and back, and it's one of my personal favorites.

This time, I started at its northern end from the Penny Pines parking area beginning on the Big Laguna Trail. Actually, beginning on the Noble Canyon Trail for a very short time, the Big Laguna Trail heads south (left) from there. At about 1.0 mile, past a junction with the No. 5 spur trail to the right, the Sunset Trail intersects on the right, heading west. In about another 0.3 miles, another intersection occurs between the Sunset Trail to the right and the western Big Laguna Trail to the left. Follow the signposts with the sunset picture at the top to stay on the Sunset Trail. You could take that Big Laguna Trail, follow it through the huge Laguna Meadow along the western edge of Big Laguna Lake, and then take the eastern Big Laguna Trail back to Penny Pines. This would be an easier, flatter route. But take the Sunset Trail for those amazing views on clear days, as well as a walk through some beautiful black oak and pine forests that cover the hills above Laguna Meadow.

The Sunset Trail is open only to hikers, whereas the Big Laguna trails are also popular with mountain bikers. These trails are one-track and narrow, and so the Sunset Trail is also a welcome relief from jumping off the trail for the bikers on busy weekends.

After a little more than 2.0 miles from the start, you'll reach the crest of the Sunset Trail at about 5,775 feet elevation, having climbed about 420 feet in elevation to get there. Those black oaks are the oak trees that lose their leaves in the fall, so they add some fine yellow and orange color to the landscape then. Coast live oaks and canyon live oaks don't lose all their leaves and so remain evergreen. Black oaks' leaves are deeply lobed, quite unlike the oblong leaves of both live oaks.

In about 3.1 miles from the start, you'll reach the lovely pond, Water of the Woods. Fall and winter bring more birds here, so look for colorful ducks. Follow the connecting trail heading left at the north end of the Water of the Woods to reach the easternmost Big Laguna Trail. Pass the first Big Laguna Trail, which winds up the western side of the lake, and cross the meadow below the lake to reach the second (east side) Big Laguna Trail. Take a left (north) there to head back to your starting point at Penny Pines.

There is very little water in Big Laguna Lake by October. By spring, it is a much bigger lake, and the wildflowers in that enormous Laguna Meadow are bountiful. The 900-acre Laguna Meadow is a remnant of a series of seasonally wet meadows that were once extensive in the Palomar and Laguna Mountain areas, according to the CNF. Its two seasonal lakes attract waterfowl and shorebirds, and I saw lots of American coots and mallard ducks.

In the fall, the beauty is in those black oaks because the Big Laguna Trail climbs just a bit up through boulders and pines and oaks, never far from those lake and meadow expanses. You might spot a beautiful blue scrub jay or a paler blue western bluebird with its ruddy red breast. You will surely hear the *knock, knock, knock* of redheaded acorn woodpeckers. More than 200 resident and migratory birds are found here. Hikers I encountered on the trail also reported they had seen deer.

The really amazing sight on the crest of the Sunset Trail was the unmistakable finger of Point Loma extending into San Diego Bay, fronted by a faint but recognizable downtown skyline. On a clear day, you can see forever from here.

Thomas Brothers Map: Page 1218, A-2.

Before You Go: Download a copy of the trail map of the Laguna Mountain Recreation Area from the Laguna Mountain Volunteer Association: http://lmva.net/id3.html.

For lots of information about Cleveland National Forest and Laguna Mountain Recreation Area, go to the CNF visitors' guide: http://www.fs.usda.gov/Internet/FSE_DOCUMENTS/stelprdb5277346.pdf.

You need an Adventure Pass to park on CNF lands. Buy a $5 day-use or a $30 annual pass at the Descanso Ranger Station in Alpine, at Mount Laguna's general store, or outdoor stores (including REI and Adventure 16). For more information on Adventure Passes, go to the national forest pages for Cleveland National Forest: http://www.fs.usda.gov/detailfull/r5/passes-permits/recreation/?cid=stelprdb5208699&width=full.

The Sunset Trail is open to hikers and dogs on leashes.

Trailhead: From Interstate 8, exit at Sunrise Highway (S1) and head north. At about mile marker 27.3, park in the Penny Pines parking area off S1. Off the western side of the highway, the Noble Canyon Trail begins. It connects to Big Laguna and then Sunset Trails.

Distance/Difficulty: My total loop from Penny Pines on the Big Laguna to Sunset to eastern Big Laguna was about 6.75 miles, with a total elevation gain of about 900 feet; moderate.

11-22. Self-Guided Walk in the Woods Has Panoramic Views

Wooded Hill Nature Trail in Laguna is a wonderful walk in the woods with a rewarding view that spans as far west as a clear day allows. It's also a self-guided trail whose 31 numbered markers painted on rocks inform the hiker along the way. Spring is especially colorful on this trail with lots of wildflowers in bloom, including tiny baby blue eyes covering the ground, bright red pine paintbrush popping up along with yellow wallflowers, and one of the largest concentrations of blooming white wild lilac shrubs. Most of the evergreen trees in Laguna are Jeffrey pines, the trail guide says. Needles of the Jeffrey pine are in bundles of three.

Numbered markers share knowledge of nature on Wooded Hill trail.

There are also lots of black oak trees here, which help provide cover for the Jeffrey pines, according to the trail guide. Some 45 species eat the oak's acorns, including woodpeckers, Steller's jays, raccoons, and squirrels.

The trail weaves through giant granite boulders too, which are constantly being eroded by the green lichens that live on their surface. Another kind of lichen also grows on the pine trees. "These lichens, like those found on rocks, are not parasites but merely use the trees as places to grow," says the trail guide.

At the first half-mile on the trail, there is an intersection that offers a choice of returning to the parking area if you want a short half-mile loop, or continuing to the left for a full 1.5-mile hike and those panoramic views. I took the left fork and continued up the hill.

Wooded Hill is one of the highest points on Laguna Mountain at 6,223 feet. When you reach the summit on the trail, the views sweep 180 degrees across the western landscape. The day I was there wasn't so clear that I could see the ocean, but simply viewing the several layers of hills beyond the forest was a fine reward. On a very clear day, one may even see the Channel Islands from this elevation.

When you near the 10,000-gallon water tank, the No. 21 marker on the trail guide, there is a confusing fork in the trail. There are several trails here created evidently for access to that water tank, and I took a couple of very wrong turns. After I went pretty steeply downhill on one, I decided it probably wasn't right, so I backtracked and went back to the water tank area. I took yet another wrong fork and eventually went back again to the water tank. I returned to the trail point where I was first confused and took the right fork, which was the right choice.

When you hit that intersection near the water tank, take the right fork. You should see markers No. 22 and 23 right away, and you'll know you're on the right trail.

When you reach marker No. 27, you'll begin to notice many Ceanothus palmeri (wild lilac) blooming profusely with white flowers. Their fragrance is another bonus. If you see hollow knots in the old oak trees, you might also see some animals. The trail guide says the squirrels and raccoons live in four-inch-diameter holes about 20 to 30 feet above ground, whereas woodpeckers use smaller holes about 10 to 20 feet above ground.

The final marker, No. 31, points to a large tree stump and says its rings show its life history. Light rings mark wood grown during spring and early summer; darker rings are evidence of growth in late summer and autumn. Together they make an annual ring.

Such interesting facts make this walk in the woods even better.

Thomas Brothers Map: Page D, between pages 1218 and 1237.

Before You Go: Download a copy of the trail map from Cleveland National Forest's visitors guide, which includes a section on Laguna Mountain Recreation Area: http://www.fs.usda.gov/Internet/FSE_DOCUMENTS/stelprdb5277346.pdf. In the visitors guide, go to the Descanso Region for the map of Laguna trails.

You may also download a copy of the trail map of the Laguna Mountain Recreation Area from the Laguna Mountain Volunteer Association: http://lmva.net/id3.html.

The accompanying trail guide cannot be downloaded, but pick up a copy at the Visitor Information Center in Laguna, open on Friday afternoons and weekends. It is also stocked in the box at the trailhead.

You must post an Adventure Pass to park here on Cleveland National Forest lands. Buy a $5 day-use pass or a $30 annual pass at the Mount Laguna store, at the visitor center, or at outdoor recreation stores like REI and Adventure 16. For more information on Adventure Passes, go to the national forest pages for Cleveland National Forest: http://www.fs.usda.gov/detailfull/r5/passes-permits/recreation/?cid=stelprdb5208699&width=full.

This trail is open to hikers and dogs on leashes.

Trailhead: From Interstate 8 east, exit at Sunrise Highway (S1) and head north. Just after the 21.5-mile marker, take a sharp left turn into the Wooded Hill campground area. Go about 0.3

miles on this road until you see the Wooded Hill Trailer Circle turn on your right; directly across the road from this campground turn is the parking area for Wooded Hill Nature Trail on your left.

Distance/Difficulty: About 1.5-mile loop; easy.

11-23. Potrero Has Oaks, Owls, and Bonus Side Trips

Here is a short, easy hike accompanied by some bonus attractions. It's the nature trail at Potrero Regional Park, a surprisingly interesting place that lies at the southern edge of the county, just a few miles from the Mexican border. The drive to get there winds through some lovely backcountry filled with big boulders, oak groves, and seasonal creeks. There are two routes to get there, making for a fine driving loop exploration.

Begin by going east on Interstate 8, past Pine Valley and Sunrise Highway, and exiting at Buckman Springs Road. Head south from here about 20 miles, past Lake Morena and through Campo. Campo is where those bonus attractions await. The first is the Campo Stone Store, on a list of "San Diego County Historical Treasures," acquired and restored by the county as a museum in 1948. Also known as the Gaskill Brothers Stone Store, this lovely old stone building that sits right on Highway 94 is now a small museum operated by the county and open only on weekends. It recreates what a general store might have offered in the late 1800s (http://www.sandiegocounty.gov/parks/campostone.html). The Gaskill Brothers had originally built a wooden frame store here in 1868, according to a plaque on-site, but after border bandits raided it in 1875, the brothers built this fort-like replacement in 1885. You can read all about the border bandits' attack in the Potrero park ranger's office by the campgrounds.

Just across the highway from that historic old general store lies the Pacific Southwest Railway Museum, home to more than 80 pieces of old railroad equipment, including historic steam locomotives, passenger and freight cars, and cabooses, some of which are open inside for viewing. The railway museum is generally open on Saturdays and Sundays; check the website (www.psrm.org) for specific times because they change with the seasons.

The museum also offers 90-minute rides on the Golden State Limited, a railway excursion on the San Diego and Arizona Railway for just 12 miles. Golden State departures are at 11:00 a.m. and 2:30 p.m. on weekends except during summer, when they are at 5:00 p.m. on Saturdays only. Other railway excursions depart seasonally on weekend days too; check the website.

After continuing on Highway 94 to Potrero Regional Park, you'll see its impressive coast live oak groves as soon as you round the bend and head down to that tiny town.

When I arrived at the regional park, I saw a huge barn owl fly into one of those majestic old oak trees—an uncommon sight, especially in the daytime. I parked immediately, but it had already escaped further view. I headed to the park's northeast corner to hike its self-guided nature trail through chaparral country.

At the very beginning of the trail, you'll see a very short spur leading to an excellent example of morteros; in one big slab of bedrock are several of those deep acorn-grinding holes used long ago by Kumeyaay women who once lived here. The trail covers a loop of only about 1.0 mile as it dips up and down in the boulder-strewn chaparral, covered with lots of buckwheat, chamise, and a few scattered oaks. Potrero in Spanish translates to mean "pasturing place," and this area served that purpose for a long time.

More than 800 oaks live in Potrero Regional Park.

After the Kumeyaay lived in this acorn-rich area, Charlie McAlmond, a ship captain from San Diego, settled in Potrero Valley in 1868 and established a cattle ranch, according to the county's park brochure. Other ranchers followed, and horse-drawn wagons hauled oak firewood from here to San Diego.

The county has recently acquired an additional adjacent parcel northeast of the current park boundaries, where there may be additional trails in the future. "We are in the process of identifying opportunities for new trails up there, but we want to be sure we do it right," said Scott Hoover, district manager for the County of San Diego Department of Parks and Recreation. "We acquired these lands as part of the Multiple Species Conservation Program (MSCP), so we need to determine what needs to be protected. But if we are able to put in trails there, we'll establish an equestrian and hiking staging area—this may be several years out."

Meanwhile, I finished the loop hike and headed back to the hundreds of oak trees that dominate this park. I simply wandered around the many old trees, looking up in the towering limbs for those owls. I didn't see them, but I asked Park Ranger Jeff Dart about them, and he told me there were many barn owls, great-horned owls, and long-eared owls living in these trees. "Lots of hawks too," he said, including a pair of red-shouldered hawks that nest by the baseball field. "There are more than 800 oak trees in this grove alone," he told me.

The owls are primarily nocturnal, so the best way to see them would be to camp here—and that's available too. Potrero Regional Park offers 39 RV camping sites and an additional seven tent-only sites. To make reservations, visit www.sdparks.org.

Return via Highway 94 to Interstate 5 for that full loop backcountry exploration.

Thomas Brothers Map: Page D, where Highway 94 nearly touches the Mexican border.

Before You Go: Download a copy of the nature trail map from the San Diego County parks' page for Potrero Regional Park: http://www.sdcounty.ca.gov/parks/Camping/potrero.html.

The trail is open to hikers and bicyclists, as well as dogs on leashes.

Trailhead: From Interstate 8, head east, exiting at Buckman Springs Road and heading south. Follow signs for Campo, passing Lake Morena. At the intersection with Highway 94, turn right, heading west. Follow signs for Potrero County Park, turning right onto Potrero Valley Road then right onto Potrero Park Road.

To return a different way, head west on Highway 94 to Interstate 805 and Interstate 5 near downtown San Diego.

Distance/Difficulty: The loop trail is about 1.0 mile total; easy.

12. Anza-Borrego and Vicinity

One of the largest state parks in America covering some 600,000 acres, Anza-Borrego Desert State Park is a wonderland of other-worldly landscapes. This is the land of naked geology, of folds and faults and badlands, of slot canyons and palm-tree oases. You will see sights here that are decidedly different from anything you will see anywhere else. If you're very lucky, you may even see the peninsula bighorn sheep, which helped give the desert its name.

Do not make the mistake that the desert is devoid of life. Its denizens abound, despite the arid conditions. Wildflowers are a major draw during spring, but even during other times of the year, if you look closely, you will see plants, animals, and birds that thrive here. The details of the desert will surely open your eyes to this other world that helps make San Diego County one of the most diverse places in the nation.

Generally, the trails in the desert are open only to hikers; dogs are not allowed on any of these state park trails. Many trails are best suited to hikers only, especially the sandy washes.

Bicyclists can travel both primitive Jeep roads and paved roads in the desert state park; go to http://abdnha.org/biking/index.htm.

Equestrians are welcome on all primitive roads as well as equestrian trails in Coyote Canyon and on the California Riding and Hiking Trail. There are two equestrian camps in Anza-Borrego. For horseback trails, visit http://www.desertusa.com/thingstodo/du_absp_horse.html.

12-1. Borrego Palm Canyon Natives Greet Hikers

Nothing will amaze you more about the diversity of San Diego County's natural wonders than a hike in the Anza-Borrego Desert State Park. There are few places on the planet quite like it. This vast region—California's largest state park and the nation's second largest, next to Adirondack Park in New York—encompasses some 600,000 acres, or about 1,000 square miles of wilderness. It offers 500 miles of dirt roads, 110 miles of hiking trails, and a unique geology with fossils that prove it was a tropical sea some 6 million years ago. About 3 million years later, the sea had turned into a savannah landscape populated by mammoths, giant camels, saber-toothed cats and cheetahs, and giant sloths. It is said that Anza-Borrego offers the ability to track geological time divisions by fossils better than any other North American area.

Today it is a timeless wonder of palm-tree oases, astounding rock formations, eroded badlands, and seasonal wildflowers that paint its naked geology with color. And if you're very lucky, you'll get to see its namesake.

The park's name "captures the relationship of man and the land in the southwestern desert of California," write Lowell and Diana Lindsay in their seminal guidebook *The Anza-Borrego Desert Region*, which offers detailed, tenth-of-a-mile directions about the region. "Juan

Bautista de Anza was the Spanish captain of the epic 1776 San Francisco colonial expedition. Borrego, the Spanish word for bighorn sheep, is the very symbol of desert wilderness."

Peninsula bighorn sheep are an uncommon thrill to see in Anza-Borrego.

The peninsular bighorn sheep is the park's namesake. This endangered hoofed mammal is surprisingly adapted to navigating the rocky slopes above the desert floor. It is rarely seen; in all the years I've hiked in Anza-Borrego, I'd never seen one before.

But on a November day in Borrego Palm Canyon, where one of the easiest and most traveled trails in the desert beckons, I saw several, including some impressive males with their extremely thick, ridged, and backward-curving horns; some females with their shorter and more slender horns; and a couple of youngsters. According to the *National Audubon Society's Field Guide to the Southwestern States,* after breeding from October to December, the ewe gives birth to one lamb around May or June. Therefore the youngest sheep I saw was likely less than six months old.

Several of us who were on that trail that day bonded as we were transfixed by the sightings. One delightful couple from Cincinnati, who had bought a home in Borrego for their retirement, were the first to point them out to me. The sheep can be very hard to spot because they are camouflaged among the colors of the rocks. Their very white rumps are usually their giveaway. We were at the end of the Borrego Palm Canyon trail at the palm tree oasis, a fascinating sight in itself.

Borrego Palm Canyon offers a trail guide with numbered posts along the way. Marker No. 15, the last one, points out that the California fan palms in this oasis (*Washingtonia filifera*) are the only palm trees native to California. The long skirts of palm fronds protect the bark from water loss and insect predators, says the guide. The oasis is filled with water, which attracts all the wildlife that make their home here, including mountain lions, coyotes, and the sheep.

"Remarkable animals, the sheep are sure-footed and have keen hearing and eyesight," says the trail guide. "Humans on this trail don't seem to bother them, but the sight or scent of dogs (wild or domestic) stresses them greatly." That's one of the reasons dogs aren't allowed on desert state park trails.

Other posts on the trail tell how the beavertail and cholla cacti store water, how the orange-blooming ocotillo sprouts leaves within 24 hours of rainfall, and how the desert lavender (blooming from October through May) attracts hundreds of bees. I also saw several Costa's hummingbirds dart among the chuparosa's red flowers, one of their favorites according to a sign at the trail's start.

The several of us on that trail watched the sheep traversing the exceedingly rocky terrain for nearly an hour. Spotting them up in the rocks was thrilling enough, but when they came down for a snack on krameria and acacia bushes and a little water, they were practically in our midst. At one point, I was virtually surrounded with one on a rock right above me and several others just yards away.

Finally I had to go back. Instead of the Main Trail, I took the Alternate Trail, according to a signpost on the return trip. This trail was less traveled and a little higher on the edge of the desert wash, making it rockier and a bit harder to negotiate. It eventually joins Main Trail.

The Borrego Palm Canyon trail is one of the desert's most popular—even one of the most populated trails in the county. I hadn't been on it in many years, but I was reminded again why it is so worthy.

Thomas Brothers Map: Page 1078, on Page 1058, F-2.

Before You Go: Check the Anza-Borrego Desert State Park's official website at http://www.parks.ca.gov/default.asp?page_id=638. You can download a map of the Borrego Palm Canyon trail (http://www.parks.ca.gov/pages/638/files/ABDSPmap.pdf) and learn other information about this specific trail. It is open only to hikers.

An excellent map worth adding to your library is the Recreation Map of the Anza-Borrego Desert Region published by Wilderness Press: www.wildernesspress.com. It is often available at REI, Adventure 16, and the desert state park's visitor center.

Trailhead: It's about a two-hour drive one-way from central San Diego to the state park headquarters area. Take Interstate 8 east to the Descanso exit, Highway 79. Head north on 79, then east on Highway 78, and then north on S3 to Borrego Springs. You can also get there from the north via State Routes 2 and 22, or Highway 67 through Julian to Highway 78 east.

Once in Borrego Springs, follow signs to the state park's visitor center and Borrego Palm Canyon Campgrounds, which lie at the town's western end of Palm Canyon Drive (S22). Go to the campground and park at the trail parking area.

There is a $10 day-use fee.

Distance/Difficulty: About 3.0 miles round-trip; fairly easy even with about a 600-foot elevation gain and rocky trail.

12-2. Three Short Trails Survey the Desert

Hike three short desert trails, each remarkably different, for a fine survey of Anza-Borrego's higher country. All located near Tamarisk Grove Campground and at about

1,300 to 1,750 feet in elevation, two of these three trails can be combined in a single hike; the third is just a 1.6-mile drive up the steep, no-shoulder road. Two of the trails also offer brochures at the trailheads that accompany numbered markers to identify many of the plants and share how they survive in this extreme climate.

Scope the desert high country from three short trails.

I began on the Cactus Loop Trail, immediately across Highway S3 from the campground. This trail climbs about 250 feet up a rocky and somewhat steep slope through a desert garden of glowing jumping cholla, beavertail, fishhook, hedgehog, and barrel cacti, along with ocotillo, agave, catclaw, and creosote bushes. It's a classic desert trail of rocks, ridges, overlooks, and views down into washes, with a high-point panorama that looks across the desert in every direction. There are also some very tall (and sometimes very welcome) cairns, those piles of single rocks that point the way to the trail. The brochure calls this a 1.0-mile loop, but my GPS unit measured it closer to 0.75 mile.

In spring, the chuparosa bush, marker No. 1, sports its long tubular red blossoms, which gives it its other name, hummingbird bush. Both year-round desert residents, Anna's and Costa's hummingbirds seek out these red blossoms.

Marker No. 2 points to the hook-shaped thorns of the catclaw bush, whose tiny leaves help prevent water loss, a common desert plant feature.

I am always thrilled when I see a beavertail cactus in bloom. Its bright fuchsia blossoms pop in the muted desert landscape. Just a few were blooming when I was there in late March; they should bloom through April.

Many of the fishhook cacti on this trail were blooming. They feature small cream-colored blooms with pink details, and they are often found nestled next to rocks. Also look for hedgehog cactus, "also called 'calico cactus' because of its multi-colored spines," says the brochure. "Like other cacti, the hedgehog's spines are actually modified leaves that create needed shade for the plant while deterring potential browsers." It sports bright purple flowers in late spring.

Even higher above this trail is Pinyon Ridge. "Look carefully for peninsular bighorn sheep," says the brochure. I wished I had seen some.

I thought they might be visiting my next trail, the Yaqui Well Trail, which lies just a short distance west on S3, still across from Tamarisk Grove Campground and immediately west of the ranger's residence. "Yaqui Well is a naturally occurring spring that has supported plant growth, wildlife, centuries of Kumeyaay people, pioneers, ranchers and travelers of all kinds," says its brochure. Places of year-round water are rare in the desert, so Yaqui Well has been an important drinking hole for lots of life. The well itself certainly appeared dry to me, but a "Closed for Renovation" sign in front of it gives hope. In any case, its surroundings attest to a water source in this area, because forests of very green bushes line up along this trail.

Marker No. 2 on this trail points to the creosote bush, "the most common shrub around." Small yellow flowers in spring, followed by fuzzy seed balls, were dressing them up in late March. "The local Kumeyaay Indians developed dozens of medicines from this plant. Creosote tonics cured colds, healed wounds, prevented infections, relieved pain and even got rid of dandruff."

Also sporting long, fuzzy yellow blooms were honey mesquite shrubs. These long blooms will become seedpods by early summer, one of the most important food sources for the Kumeyaay, who ground them into flour for cakes and cereals, says the brochure. "All parts of the plant were used to make food, beverages, clothing, tools, medicines and more."

Yaqui Well is also a birder's destination, thanks to the water source. I spotted some bright common yellowthroat warblers as well a pair of house finches (the male sporting a lovely red head and breast) on the red blooms of ocotillo. Hummingbirds also like these blooms.

"Because it grows extremely slowly, the tallest ocotillos may be hundreds of years old," says the brochure. Its tiny leaves sprout after rain, but they fall until more rains bring them back to life again.

I also saw lots of shiny black phainopeplas (females are gray), a common desert bird who loves to feast on red mistletoe berries, according to the brochure. Desert mistletoe is a parasite on catclaw, mesquite, and ironwood, and its red berries appeared in late March. Some years are better than others for spring wildflowers in the desert, depending on rainfall. When I was there, I marveled at all these blooms as well as tiny gold poppies, purple phacelias, and pink palefaces.

I drove to the final trail, the William L. Kenyon Overlook Trail, about 1.6 miles northeast on Highway S3. Although you could hike it, the no-shoulder road here is very narrow and steep and could be hazardous to pedestrians. Totally different from the lower two trails, the Kenyon overlook trail winds through an area of granitic rock with some interesting formations that even appear to be painted. As explained on one of the other trails' brochures, "the rust-colored stain covering these rocks is known as desert varnish. This mysterious coating appears on rocks after thousands of years of exposure to the desert ... we believe microscopic bacteria living on the rocks absorb manganese and iron oxide causing them to become blackish or reddish."

But the real reward on this short hike is the astounding view that spreads below when you reach the cliff-hanging end of the trail.

A plaque at the trail's viewpoint end notes that Bill Kenyon was superintendent of the state's District Six, covering beaches and parks, from 1947 to 1959. He was "tireless in his efforts to acquire and preserve these magnificent desert lands." Also at the viewpoint is a placard describing Mescal Bajada, which stretches for miles below this high-point overlook. "Mescal Bajada is the piedmont lying at the north base of the Vallecito Mountains," say Lowell and Diana Lindsay in *The Anza-Borrego Desert Region*. "It is about four square miles, extending from Stag Cove on the west to The Narrows along Highway 78 on the east. Three major washes drain from the Pinyon Mountains across the area." Flash floods can occur in these washes, which deposit sand and gravel in the alluvial fans (bajadas in Spanish) that give the area its name. Lots of agave (mescal) cover this terrain.

You can make the Kenyon Overlook a loop hike by continuing east from the markers to reach Yaqui Pass Primitive Campground. Then walk along S3 back to your car, or avoid walking on that highway and go in and back out on the trail. You will have enjoyed a splendid survey of the astounding Anza-Borrego Desert.

Thomas Brothers Map: Page 1118, on Page 1098, J-5, where Highway 78 joins Yaqui Pass Road, also known as Highway S3.

Before You Go: For a state parks map of the Anza-Borrego Desert Region, go to its website: http://www.parks.ca.gov/pages/638/files/ABDSPmap.pdf.

Robin Halford's *Hiking in Anza-Borrego Desert, Over 100 Half-Day Hikes,* has good maps of all three trails.

These are hikers-only trails.

You might also want to purchase the recreation map and guide *Anza-Borrego Desert Region*, published by the Anza-Borrego Desert Natural History Association for $9.95 (http://www. abdnha.org/store/products_books/Map-of-the-anza-borrego-region.htm).

Trailheads: Each of these trails is well marked from Highway S3, also known as Yaqui Pass Road. From Highway 78 heading east, turn left (northeast) onto S3 toward Borrego Springs. Very shortly after this intersection is the Tamarisk Grove Campground, which has been refurbished and reopened in 2014. You may pay a $5 day-use fee to park in the campground, or you may park just outside it on the road shoulder.

The Cactus Loop and Yaqui Well Trails have accompanying brochures at the trailheads, both of which are across S3 from the campground entrance. Cactus Loop is immediately across from the entrance, and Yaqui Well is a bit to the west, just past the ranger's residence.

William Kenyon Overlook Trail is 1.6 miles farther northeast on S3 from the campground, and it is well marked with an off-road parking area near a call box.

These trails are best for hikers; no dogs allowed on state park trails.

Distance/Difficulty: Cactus Loop Trail is about 0.75 mile round-trip and is moderate; Yaqui Well is about 1.75 miles round-trip and is easy. Kenyon Overlook is about 0.75 mile out and back, or about 1.2 miles as a loop; fairly easy.

12-3. Illustrious History and a Slot Canyon

Close to the eastern edge of San Diego County, Anza-Borrego's Calcite Mine trail offers a wealth of desert beauty: vast views, painted hills, a little history, and one of the coolest slot canyons. The first wonder is the enormous Salton Sea, which lies 228 feet below sea level just beyond the county line in Imperial County. It is the first thing to see from the Calcite Mine trailhead.

A marker at the trailhead shares some of the story of the mine's history. "Soon after the surprise attack on Pearl Harbor, the U.S. government sent specialists to this region to inspect a deposit of calcite. It was to be used in bomb sights and anti-aircraft weaponry."

Fascinating history and splendid slot canyon await on Calcite Mine Trail.

The land was then owned by John W. Hilton (1904–1983), a fascinating character who became an expert gemologist, botanist, geologist and miner, zoologist, adviser to General George S. Patton, friend of President Dwight Eisenhower, master of guitar and song, a very good writer, and an exceptional landscape painter. Hilton is widely considered one of the best plein air desert landscape oil painters of the 20th century, and his masterful works regularly fetch well over $10,000 apiece. View several of his desert landscapes for sale at http://bodegabayheritagegallery.com/Hilton_John_W_.htm.

Hilton, along with Dr. Harry Berman, a mineralogist from Harvard, discovered the "optical" calcite, a common crystal deposited in veins in the desert's sandstone. This high-grade calcite crystal sharpened the targeting accuracy of gun sights so well that it raised the survival rate of allied bombing patrol missions. Hilton and his friend Guy Hazen first mined the calcite themselves, but they soon sold the mine to the Polaroid Corporation, which sent 30 miners and machinery to gouge out trenches. The mine was worked until a synthetic substitute was invented, and mining stopped around 1945.

The Calcite Mine Trail follows an old, difficult rocky road that can also be traveled by expert, intrepid Jeep drivers. It's actually much easier to walk this road the 2.0 miles to the Calcite Mine area. The road first drops into the sandy valley of Palm Wash, and then it climbs to a narrow ridge gradually ascending some 800 feet in elevation to reach the Calcite Mine area. There is little vegetation in this area of naked geology except for occasional, very tall ocotillo and stubby creosote bushes.

As you walk along the ridge above the Palm Wash below, note the colorful strata of the sandstone and granite hills that rise hundreds of feet above the valley floor. Although not as dramatically colored as some desert landscapes elsewhere, this area still seems to be painted in pastels of green, pink, and salmon, which are caused by various minerals in the soils and rocks.

At the trail's end in the Calcite Mine area (noted with a sign), you can see the holes and trenches carved out of the sandstone cliffs in its mining heyday. But even more rewarding are those vast panoramic views from this vantage point at 1,100 feet in elevation, taking in the blue Salton Sea to the east and the Borrego Badlands and Borrego Mountain to the southwest.

I returned on the same road with the intention of exploring the area I had passed about a half-mile from the road's end. Here, where the road descends sharply to the canyon floor, is a sign in front of a wash proclaiming "Foot Travel Only; No Vehicles." Don't miss this side trip because it goes to one of the most amazing slot canyons in Borrego.

It's the Middle Fork of Palm Wash and begins with its sandy passage along Palm Wash, soon entering a slot canyon that is so narrow, only one person can pass through at a time. The passageway through this canyon goes through tight, undulating curves of smooth sandstone and rock, making for an amazing desert adventure. I climbed over a couple of huge, round boulders that were wedged in this narrow slot, and I considered how strong, forceful, and deadly the flash floods could be that must rush through here. Eventually (probably less than a quarter-mile), when a bunch of those boulders made the passage through much harder, I turned back.

The views and the gradual descent made the return trip just as worthwhile.

Thomas Brothers Map: Page D, east of Page 1058.

Before You Go: For more information, check the Anza-Borrego Desert Natural History Association's page on Calcite Mine at http://www.abdnha.org/pages/06 exploring/north/roads/022/calcitemine.htm.

For a general map of the state park, including this trail, go to http://www.parks.ca.gov/pages/638/files/ABDSPmap.pdf.

This trail is best for hikers; dogs are not allowed.

Trailhead: On S22 going east from the town of Borrego Springs, also known as Borrego-Salton Seaway, go to mile marker 38 and park in the parking area on the north side of the road. Find the narrow footpath that leaves from the northeast corner of that parking area as it follows along the north side of S22, until you reach the Calcite Mine history marker and the trailhead/dirt road.

Distance/Difficulty: About 4.0 miles round-trip; moderate.

12-4. Colorful Rock Walls and a Slot Canyon

Canyon Sin Nombre in Anza-Borrego stands out for its colorful metamorphic and granitic rock walls, but it also leads to a cool slot canyon that's a desert wonder to explore. Taking the main signed canyon dirt road is one of the easier routes to follow in Anza-Borrego. From the parking area just off Highway S2, the old sandy Jeep road dips down at the beginning and then begins a very gradual descent into the canyon itself. The road is very soft sand and is not recommended for anything but four-wheel-drive vehicles. Don't take any risks; park your car just off the highway and hike the entire route on foot. You'll appreciate more details that way, especially if it's during spring wildflower season.

The first 0.7 mile or so is a wide-open approach to the canyon itself. In this section, there are many ocotillo, a native shrub that's unlike anything else. In fact, according to James Lightner's *San Diego County Native Plants,* it is the sole genus in its botanical family. In this first section, there are also some cholla and lots of barrel cactus, whose spring blooms are amazingly pretty for such a formidable plant. Both the ocotillo and barrel cactus were blooming when I was there in very late February.

Then you reach the canyon's entry, which you'll recognize when the road turns sharply left and the walls close in. The colors in those cliffs also really pop in shades of brown, gray, rusty red, and white. The bands of white rock that virtually stripe the brown or red rock in which they're embedded are called dikes or sills in geology. According to www.geology.about.com, both are intrusions of magma between layers of another kind of rock; a dike tends to be vertical, and a sill is usually more horizontal.

The narrow canyon winds around through these hard-rock cliffs that soon change into mudstone and sandstone cliffs.

Colorful cliffs lead to another slot canyon in Canyon Sin Nombre.

The vegetation changes too. Instead of the ocotillo and cactus, there are lots of blue-green smoke trees, white-blooming wishbone bushes, yellow-blooming brittlebush, and an unusual sight of red-berried mistletoes in mesquite shrubs.

After about 2.0 miles from the trailhead, where the canyon walls begin to widen, you'll notice four metal posts (to keep out vehicles) on the left with a sign that reads, "Fire in metal container only." Here is the opening to that slot canyon. You'll pass by a couple of rock-circled fire pits (some obviously ignored that sign), and then you'll enter a slot canyon that's one of those desert highlights. As you wind through the slot canyon, the walls get narrower and the going gets tougher. I went in only about a quarter-mile or so and then turned around and retraced my way back.

I continued on the main canyon road, but when it opened up considerably with less exciting scenery, I turned around after going a little more than 2.5 miles one-way and retraced my way back the way I'd come. Canyon Sin Nombre runs north for about 4.0 miles total, eventually connecting at its northern end with the Carrizo Canyon Wash.

When I returned to the parking area, a group of hikers came out of the canyon at the same time. I had seen them on a ridge above the canyon right before I reached the slot canyon, and I wondered if they'd come out from that narrow tributary. They had. They told me they'd wandered through that slot canyon, which is very narrow at the end; their arms touched both sides as they climbed up boulders to reach the top. Once out of the slot canyon, they were on top of a ridge overlooking Canyon Sin Nombre. An old, narrow trail follows that ridge top until you can walk down a wash to join the main Canyon Sin Nombre dirt road about 0.5 miles from the trailhead. Their round-trip mileage was 5.25 miles, just a bit longer than going in and back the way I had done. For a map and photos of their hike through Canyon Sin Nombre, go to Bill Bamberger's website: www.travelswithbillandnancy.com.

Thomas Brothers Map: Page D, south of Page 1138.

Before You Go: For a state parks map of the Anza-Borrego Desert Region, go to its website: http://www.parks.ca.gov/pages/638/files/ABDSPmap.pdf.
   Also check the website of the Anza-Borrego Desert Natural History Association for the southern area: http://www.abdnha.org/pages/06_exploring/south/south_drivehike.htm.
   This trail is open to hikers, bicyclists, and equestrians; no dogs allowed on state park trails.

Trailhead: From Interstate 8 east, exit at Ocotillo and head north on S2 (Imperial Highway). About 13.5 miles from that freeway intersection, just past mile marker 51 and the Carrizo Badlands Overlook, look for the sign posted for Canyon Sin Nombre on the right. Turn right and park on the ridge to the right, just off the main sandy road that enters the canyon.

Distance/Difficulty: About 5.0 miles round-trip; easy to moderate.

12-5. Borrego Ablaze in Wildflower Blooms

If winter brings heavy rainfall, spring brings an outstanding wildflower bloom in Anza-Borrego. One of the best trails for a variety of blooms is the Elephant Tree Trail, sometimes called the Elephant Trees Discovery Trail or the Elephant Trees Nature Trail. It's an easy, 1.5-mile loop on a well-marked sandy trail. Few other trails in recent memory have offered such a wealth of blooms, from those bright fuchsia flowers on beavertail cactus to the tiny yellow gold poppies that dot the desert floor. To make the most of your walk on the Elephant Tree Trail, stop by Anza-Borrego's headquarters and visitor center in Borrego Springs first to pick up a brochure that accompanies the numbered markers on the trail.

Elephant Tree Discovery Trail is a fine primer on wildflowers.

At the turnoff to the trailhead, you'll note a sign that tells the story of "The Lost Herd of Elephant Trees." Anza-Borrego is the only place in California where this rare tree grows. On the Elephant Tree Trail today, only one remains (which may be why it's now called Elephant Tree Trail—no plurals anymore). More of this species can be found farther into the Alma Wash that extends several miles to the southwest from the Elephant Tree loop trail, and they're abundant in Baja California and the Sonoran Desert. You'll also find them in Torote Canyon in Indian Valley.

The elephant tree stores water in its trunk and lower branches, which appear bulky, just like its namesake. It's one of the desert's larger specimens and can reach 10 feet tall. "It even bleeds when injured. A fragrant, gummy sap that is," says the sign. Desert natives of yesteryear revered the tree for this red sap, which was believed to cure skin diseases and to bring luck.

The accompanying brochure will point out the creosote bush, with its little yellow flowers, that is the "oldest living plant," able to last two years with no water at all and able to stay alive for 11,000 years because its small leaves are covered with oil, much like sunscreen.

The brittlebush, one of the most prolific any year of the desert bloomers, is often ablaze with its yellow flowers. It's a survivor, says the brochure. "When it rains, chemicals wash off its leaves into the ground below (keeping) other plants from sprouting nearby and competing for water."

The tall, long-lived ocotillo is usually in full orange bloom on this trail by mid-March to late March. It can live to be 200 years old.

One of the loveliest of the blooming beauties here is the wild heliotrope, with its purple flowers abundant all over this trail. You'll also find the fragrant desert lavender, as well as the deep purple indigo plant that natives favored as a dye.

It can be hard to distinguish the indigo bush from the smoke tree. Both have very spiky, thorny pale gray, almost whitish leaves that might even appear dead. They also both have those deep purple blooms.

The cheesebush is another bloomer, sporting its pale green, whitish flowers that you might miss because they blend into the bush's leaves.

Nothing is as exciting to me as the bright fuchsia blooms of the beavertail cactus, as well as those of the barrel cactus with gorgeous pale green petals with bright yellow and orange center stamens. You'll also see blooms on the fishhook cactus as well as the cholla.

Among the amazing discoveries in a spring desert wildflower season are the tiny blooms that cover the sandy desert floor. You have to look closely for these little wonders. See if you can spot the yellow and pink sand verbena, the bright yellow gold poppies, and the tiny white rock daisies.

There are several resources for locating the wildflower blooms in Anza-Borrego on any given day. Check the state park's official website (http://www.parks. ca.gov/?page_id=638) for flower area updates and map. Also check the wildflower pages of the Anza Borrego Foundation (http://theabf.org/wildflowers) for dates of guided hikes to the blooms, as well as a wildflower hotline phone number.

It's a good idea to stop in the visitor center in Borrego Springs to ask the volunteers there for the latest bloom reports.

Thomas Brothers Map: Page D, just east of Page 1100.

Before You Go: For a state parks map of the Anza-Borrego Desert Region, go to its website: http://www.parks.ca.gov/pages/638/files/ABDSPmap.pdf.
This trail is open to hikers; no dogs allowed on state park trails.

Trailhead: Stay on Highway 78, heading east all the way from Julian. At Ocotillo Wells, turn south (right) onto Split Mountain Road and proceed about 6.0 miles to the Elephant Tree Trail entrance.
You must travel nearly a mile on a dirt road, which can be passable in an ordinary passenger car with care; it's better in a four-wheel drive to navigate the sand and the rocks. You can park sooner than its end to avoid the rockiest part of this sandy road. It's free to park here.
If you stop at the visitor center in Borrego Springs first, head to the town by turning north on S3 from Highway 78 (follow sign to Borrego Springs). The center is at the west end of Palm Canyon Drive through the center of town.

Distance/Difficulty: It's a 1.5-mile loop. Easy.

12-6. Hike into the Desert's Colorful Cliffs and a Narrow Slot

Some of the most colorful cliffs in the desert are found in Hawk Canyon, a sliver in the west mesa of Borrego Mountain. Nearby is another desert wonder known as the Slot, a narrow passageway through the eroded badlands. Both Hawk Canyon and the Slot can be reached via a four-wheel-drive vehicle on the soft sand dirt road that heads into this West Butte area of Anza-Borrego. If you don't have four-wheel drive, negotiating that soft sand may be harder than it looks, so travel on foot and immerse yourself in these desert scenes.

Off Highway 78, Buttes Pass Road is the name of the dirt road that leads to both these attractions. Park your car off this road as far in from the highway as you dare. I started hiking after going on this road for about a half-mile.

Hike this canyon of color with another narrow passageway.

At 1.0 mile from the highway, Buttes Pass Road forks, with the right continuing as Buttes Pass Road and the left signed Borrego Mountain Wash. To reach Hawk Canyon, take the right fork to continue on Buttes Pass Road. Pass an intersection with Goat Trail, where the road begins to descend, offering the first glimpse of the colorful canyon ahead as well as a panoramic vista of this vast desert. In about 0.9 mile from the fork, you'll see a sign for Hawk Canyon to the left. This dirt road enters the colorful cliff bowl, which is also a popular primitive camping site. The road into Hawk Canyon dead-ends in a circle around the bowl after about a half-mile.

The sandstone walls of the cliffs here are colored salmon and a shade of green very much like the smoke trees that dot this area. There are also some mighty desert ironwood trees that seem improbably green, reaching heights of 20 to 30 feet, the tallest native tree in the desert. Ironwood trees can live to 1,500 years, according to the Anza-Borrego Desert Natural History Association.

The sandstone cliffs here are evidence of an ancient marine environment, says the ABDNHA. "The Coyote Creek earthquake fault runs north and south on the east side of the east mesa of Borrego Mountain in the highly active San Jacinto Fault Zone," it notes on a website about Hawk Canyon. In 1968, the Borrego Mountain earthquake registered 6.5 on the Richter Scale.

The smoke trees and ironwood trees are late bloomers in the desert, with the ironwood trees blossoming in white or pink in May and June and the smoke trees in purple in June and July. I looked for hawks but didn't see any this time, though they and golden eagles are said to come here. I did see a wintering black-throated gray warbler on an ocotillo that promised to bloom in orange by March.

To reach the Slot, head back to that first fork in the road and take the left branch to Borrego Mountain Wash. In another mile from that fork, you'll come to Desert Lookout, a large circular parking area on the dirt road where you begin to see another desert panorama, this one peering down into the badlands and far ahead to the green belt of the town of Borrego Springs and the Santa Rosa Mountains to the north.

The Borrego Mountain Wash dirt road takes a sharp left here. In that large circular parking area, look for a picture sign noting no dogs. Just to the left of this sign, you'll see a way to hike down into that wash below, which is the beginning of the Slot. You can walk through this narrow passageway for about 0.7 mile, according to Lowell and Diana Lindsay's guidebook, *The Anza-Borrego Desert Region*. You can reach that Borrego Mountain Wash road again, or you can simply explore a ways and head back out the way you came. As you peer down into this area of the badlands, you'll note several washes that carve their way through these 50-foot-high sandstone cliffs. The area is surely a natural maze if ever there was one.

I headed back on foot the way I came to reach my car, marveling at these fascinating desert highlights. You can choose to do either Hawk Canyon or the Slot alone, if you want fine exploration of a shorter distance.

Combining both, I hiked about 5.0 miles total round-trip.

Thomas Brothers Map: Page 1100/1120 (bottom left half of page 1100), J-1.

Before You Go: Download a map of this area from the Anza-Borrego Desert State Park page: http://www.parks.ca.gov/pages/638/files/ABDSPmap.pdf.

    For a bit of information about Hawk Canyon, check the Anza-Borrego Desert Natural History Association's page (www.abdnha.org) and go to the central region.

    It is open to hikers, bicyclists, and equestrians. No dogs are allowed on state park trails.

Trailhead: Buttes Pass Road, signed for four-wheel drive, heads north off Highway 78 at about mile marker 87.2, about 28 miles east of Julian. This marked dirt road is about 1.5 miles east of the intersection with Borrego Springs Road, or about 5.2 miles west of Ocotillo Wells.

Distance/Difficulty: From about 3.0 to 7.0 miles round-trip; fairly easy.

12-7. Indian Gorge Leads to Two Trails, Maybe Sheep

Indian Gorge in Anza-Borrego Desert State Park seems like one of the quietest places on the planet. Your footfalls on the sandy trail are about the only sound you'll hear. Occasional bird calls might puncture that silence, and if you're really lucky, you might hear some rocks tumbling down the steep walls of the gorge itself. That would be because you are in the company of bighorn sheep, the namesake of Anza-Borrego, The name is the combination of Anza, for Juan Bautista Anza, the Spanish explorer who forged a trail through here from Mexico to San Francisco in 1774, and borrego, the Spanish word for bighorn sheep, according to Lowell and Diana Lindsay's book, *The Anza-Borrego Desert Region: A Guide to the State Park.*

In late December on Indian Gorge Trail, I encountered a couple hiking out when I was hiking in. I didn't get their names, but they gave me some fascinating information. They had been seeking the sheep too, because they'd heard from fellow campers that a herd had been spotted here just two days earlier.

Look for bighorn sheep in Indian Gorge.

The gentleman told me to be on the lookout for their tracks. As we looked around in our immediate area, by coincidence there were some hoof prints easily distinguished in that sandy soil. He also said to scout the horizon of the rising gorge walls, because that's where you tend to spot the sheep first as they make their way over the ridges. "And listen for rocks falling," he told me, because the sheep can't help but displace them as they navigate the steep inclines.

He also pointed out to me a barrel cactus that had its top knocked off. A male bighorn with his heavy set of curved horns will ram the top off of barrel cactus to tear away the spines and reveal the soft, wet flesh that the herd enjoys. I was unlucky that day and didn't see any sheep. However, I did spot some fresh black pellet scat that was undoubtedly left by a herd.

The Indian Gorge dirt road that I was hiking leads to vast Indian Valley as well as two hiking-only trails: Torote Canyon and a spur trail to Palm Bowl, one of the palm groves also reached via Mountain Palm Springs just to the south of here. If you're in a four-wheel-drive vehicle, as the sign posted at the entrance to Indian Gorge urges, you may drive through the gorge and into Indian Valley, reaching those other two trailheads. The sandy road might seem easy even for regular passenger vehicles, but allow me to offer an anecdote.

Many years ago, a friend and I drove this dirt road to reach that Palm Bowl trail. Shortly we hit a rock, not realizing how bad it was until we'd gone those two miles and my small car's oil light began flashing. We'd punctured the oil pan. Luckily, some other hikers gave us a ride back to Ocotillo, where we could call for a tow truck.

The tow truck came, though the driver was extremely reluctant to go on this sandy dirt road at all. When he reached my car, we were able to load it onto his flat bed, but then the tow truck got stuck perpendicularly across the road. We tried to dig it out for a couple of hours, to no avail.

Then two separate caravans of hikers happened upon us from either direction, both unable to proceed because the truck was blocking the road. Some 16 men pushed that truck around on the road, which was now heading backward toward S2. My friend walked in front to guide the truck driver on his backward course. It was a very expensive towing and repair charge. I never risk driving my car on these sandy desert roads anymore.

I hiked in Indian Gorge just beyond that S2 entry. In 1.8 miles from S2, the Torote Canyon trail is on the right, marked with a wooden stake sign. I hiked up that narrow, rocky wash for another half-mile or so before turning around. Torote is the Spanish word for elephant tree, a relatively rare sight with its bulbous trunks and tiny, paired, fernlike leaves. Lots of small elephant trees cling to the walls of Torote Canyon.

Back at the Indian Gorge road, I continued farther from Torote Canyon in search of that trail to Palm Bowl, which should be about 2.0 miles from S2 (only 0.2 miles from Torote Canyon trailhead), on the left. The Lindsays say a "small rock monument marks the beginning of this trail, which is at first very faint." I missed it this time.

I kept hiking on the road until it forked, with the right turn heading into North Indian Valley and the left into South Indian Valley. I marveled at the gray smoke trees, tall green desert willows, and glowing jumping cholla cactus. I turned back just beyond that fork and retraced my way to my safe and sound car.

Thomas Brothers Map: Page D, west of the Carrizo Gorge Wilderness area.

Before You Go: Download a copy of the Anza-Borrego Desert State Park map from the state park page: http://www.parks.ca.gov/pages/638/files/ABDSPmap.pdf.
   Dogs aren't allowed on California state park trails.

Trailhead: From Interstate 8 east, exit at Ocotillo and head north on S2. About 18.6 miles from I-8, at about the 46.1-mile marker, turn left (west) onto Indian Gorge's dirt road. Unless you have a four-wheel-drive vehicle, park just off the road on hard-packed sand.
   The Torote Canyon trailhead is 1.8 miles from S2, on the right.
   The Palm Wash trail is supposed to be 2.0 miles from S2, on the left. The fork into North and South Indian Valley is 2.7 miles from S2.

Distance/Difficulty: From 4.0 to 8.0 miles round-trip, depending on how far you go. Easy to moderate (the rocky washes).

12-8. High-Desert Lizard Wash Has Flowers and Views

Nothing seems more striking than the bright fuchsia blooms of a beavertail cactus in spring in Anza-Borrego Desert State Park. They are among the largest blooms in the desert and are so shockingly deep pink, they really stick out. They are a bit precious, unlike the more prolific cholla or barrel cacti.

In search of this year's wildflowers, I went to Lizard Wash in very late March and found a few of those beautiful beavertails, but only one in bloom with a few others promising to burst within another month. Banner years for desert wildflowers vary with winter's rainfalls. Both the state park pages (www.parks.ca.gov/?page_id=638)

Find wildflowers in desert washes.

and those for the Anza-Borrego Foundation (www.theabf.org) offer seasonal updates on wildflowers and where to find them.

Still, if you look very closely, you will see a lot of detail even during those years when rains have been sparse. That's surely one of the amazing attractions of the desert: The landscape may appear monochromatically beige to many, but if you are willing to examine it closely, the tiny blooms and the striated rocks make it far more interesting than at first blush. Indeed, even though the blooms were tiny and sparse on this hike, I counted yellow desert dandelions, Parish's gold poppies, yellow blooming barrel cactus, tiny blue chia, white desert chicory, desert pincushion, and even the blue berries of California juniper.

The most abundant bloomers were the chuparosas, which appear almost lifeless most of the year with their pale green branches until they start sending out red, trumpetlike blossoms in winter. Chuparosa is Spanish for hummingbird, which these long flowers definitely attract. The other biggest show came from the purple mat, a very low-growing, tiny purple bloom that spreads all over the desert floor here. And ocotillos were sending forth lots of their bright orange blossoms too.

Another fascinating bloomer here is the desert agave, sometimes called the century plant, which sends up just one tall yellow-flowering stock that can soar 12 feet above the two- or three-foot-high plant. Like most agaves, it's monocarpic, meaning it dies after it sends up its single flowering stalk. But it may take from eight to 20 years for that flowering stalk to appear, and the plant has ensured survival because it has spread lots of babies around it.

Lizard Wash is usually a good bet for wildflowers simply because it's a wash; more water occurs there than other parts of the desert. The Lizard Wash Trail follows an old rocky dirt road just off Highway 78. This road is not really negotiable for anything but very high-clearance cars or four-wheel drive, so I parked just off the highway and started hiking on the road.

After about 0.8 miles, the road forks, with the main road continuing to the left, to Lizard Canyon East Fork, and an even rockier road heading right, to Lizard Canyon West Fork, which should be traveled only on foot.

I stayed on the east fork, going a total of about 1.5 miles until the road ended and the narrow wash itself became hard to navigate. Then I retraced my steps back and took that west fork road, which dissipated into random trails after about half a mile up the rocky canyon. I went up there only about 0.75 mile from the fork and back.

Lizard Wash offers a lovely foray into the high desert. Its elevation here starts at about 1,540 feet and goes up to over 2,500 feet. Views back to the north extend to 4,573-foot-high Pinyon Ridge all the way to 8,716-foot Toro Peak in the Santa Rosa Mountains.

I liked hiking this wide road in spring because it's easier to see snakes. I didn't see any, but often the rattlesnakes come out of their winter hibernation a bit ornery in March, April, and May, so I prefer to avoid those rocky, narrow trails that snakes like so much. "Reptiles are abundant in deserts because the high average temperatures and the intense sunshine found in North American desert are ideal for 'cold-blooded' animals," wrote Chris Smith in "Reptiles of the Anza-Borrego Desert" for the California State Parks in 2000. "All reptiles are ectotherms," he added, meaning they use heat sources outside their bodies to maintain preferred temperatures. With all that heat in the desert, they thrive there. When a lizard or snake crawls out of its refuge in the morning, it immediately tries to maximize absorption from the sun, Smith said. Then it moves back and forth between sun and shade (like the inside of a rock crevice) to regulate that temperature.

Smith said the most frequently seen lizard in Anza-Borrego is the zebra-tailed lizard, which is also North America's fastest lizard, sprinting at up to 18 miles per hour. Western whiptails are another commonly seen lizard. "Like most lizards, they have a breakaway tail that wiggles violently when pulled off," said Smith. "This remarkable adaptation allows the lizard to distract the attacking predator long enough to escape." Even in Lizard Wash, I didn't see any lizards, though they are usually most active in the daytime.

The sidewinder is one of four species of rattlesnakes found the Anza-Borrego, along with red-diamond rattlesnake, speckled rattlesnake, and western rattlesnake. "During the warm months of late spring and summer, rattlesnakes are completely nocturnal, preferring moonless nights for stalking their prey," said Smith.

Even so, I like to make vibrations with my hiking stick to warn snakes to slither away before I even see them.

Thomas Brothers Map: Page 1098/1118, H-5 on page 1118, just before S3 intersects with Highway 78.

Before You Go: Download a map of the Anza-Borrego Desert State Park from the state parks page: http://www.parks.ca.gov/pages/638/files/abdspmap.pdf. This map does not show the east and west forks; find that detailed map in either Jerry Schad's *Afoot and Afield San Diego County,* or in Robin Halford's *Hiking in Anza-Borrego Desert, Over 100 Half-Day Hikes.*
This trail is best for hiking; no dogs allowed on state park trails.

Trailhead: Park just off Highway 78, near the 75.9 mile marker, about 17 miles east of Julian and about 6.1 miles east of Scissors Crossing, where you'll see a posted sign for Lizard Wash.

Distance/Difficulty: I covered about 4.5 miles round-trip, but you may add another 1.5 miles total if you continue up the west fork; moderate.

12-9. Desert Explorers Head to Moly Mine

The hike to the Moly Mine in Anza-Borrego will appeal to bushwhackers and explorers who relish the unscripted hunt. There is not really a trail to follow in the Palo Verde Canyon that leads to the mine. The northern part of the Palo Verde Wash has many dry tributaries that can make the journey an adventure—or an ordeal. You may even follow this wash to a ridge on the east, which will lead you into Smoke Tree Canyon and Wonderstone Wash. Or so I've read. I never found the mine or the traversing trail to the east, but even my shorter exploration had its rewards.

Try to find Moly Mine.

The first reward is the palo verde tree, one of the most beautiful in the desert because of its bright green trunks and limbs. In spring, palo verde trees are covered with delicate yellow blooms. Palo verde means "green sticks" in Spanish, and they are green-limbed trees that photosynthesize in the bark as well as the leaves, wrote Jerry Schad in *Afoot and Afield San Diego County,* which makes them especially suitable for the dry desert.

This adaptation is also true of ocotillo, which also blooms in April and is also found in the Palo Verde Canyon wash.

Begin the hike on the north side of Highway S22, immediately across the highway from the Palo Verde Wash sign and parking area at mile marker 32.9. You will see the light-green palo verde trees ahead in the wash. These trees are plentiful in this wash but not outside it, so they are a good clue. Head north toward the Santa Rosa Mountains, gaining elevation very gradually.

Schad writes, "Head north, not straying off course into the smaller canyon to the east of Palo Verde ... The canyon narrows at about 1.5 miles. Begin looking for a steep rocky trail up the granitic canyon wall on the right (east) side of the canyon where a large palo verde tree is found in a small alcove ... This ancient Cahuilla trail ascends the ridge separating Palo Verde from Smoke Tree Canyon. It is part of a Native American trail leading to Wonderstone Wash, where rocks were quarried. If taking this trail to Smoke Tree Canyon, the Moly Mine is visible to the north from the trail."

Robin Halford, in *Hiking in Anza-Borrego Desert*, writes, "Follow the trees in the sandy and rocky wash that goes in a north-by-northwest direction. After 0.3 mile, the wash cuts between two low mud hills. Now follow the wash as it turns toward the west and skirts the north side of one of the mud hills. Near the west end of the hill, the wash turns to the north ... After 0.9 mile, the wash begins to narrow. After another 0.5 mile, the wash narrows even more and there is a large patch of exposed white rock on the left hillside. Walk around the rock outcrop on the right side and look for a faint trail that goes up the hillside on the right side of the wash. This 0.3-mile trail goes to Moly Mine."

To get to the traverse trail to Smoke Tree Canyon, Halford advises that after that 0.9-mile point, "stay near the ridge on the right side of the wash. After another 0.3 mile, look for the palo verde tree on the right with several rock cairns next to it that mark the beginning of the traverse trail."

The Moly Mine may really have been the Mollie Mine, according to Lowell and Diana Lindsay in *The Anza-Borrego Desert Region*. Phil Brigandi, author of *Borrego Beginnings: Early Days in the Borrego Valley 1910–1960*, believes the Mollie Mine is its proper name.

Mollie Clark, a niece of Borrego pioneer "Doc" Beaty, and her husband, Frank, had a home in Palo Verde around 1930, Brigandi wrote. Frank had found a promising vein of quartz on the east side of Palo Verde Wash, and he blasted two 50-foot-long tunnels on either side of it, but he gave up around 1932. "Over the years, Mollie became Molly, then Moly, and some people decided it must have been a molybdenum mine," wrote Brigandi. The Cahuilla mined too, when they went to Wonderstone Wash to collect wonderstones to make arrowheads.

I made it about 1.75 miles up the canyon, but I never saw those other faint trails. When the wash became increasingly rocky and harder to follow, I decided to turn back. I found my way that far with the help of those rock cairns, or ducks—stacked rocks that hikers have left to show the way. "Cairns have likely marked human travel routes from time immemorial," says the National Park Service. The word *cairn* is Scottish and simply means a pile of rocks. Cairns, according to some definitions, are larger man-made piles that may rise two feet or higher, whereas ducks or duckies are man-made stacks, usually of three, that may include a pointed rock that points the trail direction. I followed several rock stacks of three or four that were very reassuring as I navigated through the multitude of wash paths. Finding the way back was made clearer when finding those ducks. It was easy to get off the track, however, and dragging my stick to leave my own trail helped too.

I saw two cacti that are somewhat rare overall but fairly common in the Palo Verde Canyon, according to the Anza-Borrego Desert Natural History Association (www.abdnha.org): the diamond cactus, also called the pencil cholla, which caught me when I brushed too close and had to pull out its vicious spines from my leg; and the cottontop cactus, also called Mohave mound cactus, which grows in spreading clumps of tiny barrel shapes. Both of these sport yellow blooms in spring.

Even though I made my way back a little differently than the way I'd come, finding the highway is a thankfully easy destination.

Thomas Brothers Map: Page D, east of page 1058 marked, near end of SD County on Highway S22 (mile marker 32.9 on S22).

Before You Go: You can buy a map of the Anza-Borrego Desert Region from the ABDNHA online for $9.95 (http://www.abdnha.org/store/products_books/Map-of-the-anza-borrego-region.htm). Halford's book, the Lindsays' guidebook, and Schad's book have maps of the Moly Mine hike.
You may download a copy of the state parks' Anza-Borrego map, which shows only Palo Verde Canyon: http://www.parks.ca.gov/pages/638/files/ABDSPmap.pdf.
This trail open to hikers, bicyclists, and equestrians; no dogs on state park trails.

Trailhead: About 13.4 miles east of Borrego Springs' Christmas Circle on Highway S22, park on the south side off the highway near the Palo Verde Wash sign. Cross the highway and begin hiking north through the Palo Verde Canyon wash.

Distance/Difficulty: I went about 3.5 miles round-trip, covering about a 500-foot elevation gain. Easy to moderate.

12-10. Walk Like the Sheep in Moonlight Canyon

I felt a bit like a borrego myself during the first part of the Moonlight Canyon Trail in Agua Caliente Regional Park. Borrego translates from Spanish to bighorn sheep, the hardy residents of Anza-Borrego Desert State Park, which surrounds the 910 acres of Agua Caliente.

The bighorn sheep traverse the rocky cliffs of the desert with amazing agility, but I picked my way up the Moonlight Canyon Trail's rocky ascent a little more gingerly. The park ranger had told me when I paid my day-use fee that bighorn sheep had recently been sighted on this trail. I constantly surveyed the rocky landscape to spot them, but they didn't come to the water on the afternoon I was there. That natural spring water attracts all kinds of wildlife, including coyotes, bobcats, and foxes, as well as people who camp here to soak in the three therapeutic pools that are the popular draw at Agua Caliente.

The Kumeyaay Indians started coming to these natural mineral springs centuries ago. Spanish explorer Juan Bautista de Anza was the first European to explore the area in 1775. The desert region takes its name from Anza and the bighorn sheep, and *agua caliente* means hot water in Spanish.

Natural springs draw visitors to Agua Caliente.

Earthquakes that long ago shaped the nearby Tierra Blanca Mountains, as well as the Elsinore fault that runs underneath the park, enabled water to come to the surface here, according to the county.

Highway S2, which passes through this area, is also a historic route through the desert. It basically follows the same path that the Mormon Battalion marched in 1846 from Iowa to California to help defend California in the U.S.-Mexican War of that year. General Stephen Kearny marched with his troops along this same route from Kansas that summer, and he would soon face defeat at San Pasqual near Escondido.

Hopeful prospectors came through here during the gold rush of the 1840s and 1850s, and the old Butterfield Mail Route, which began in 1851, followed this route too.

Imperial County paved part of the road in 1951, but much of it was still unpaved until 1959, when San Diego County responded to a group of property owners for road improvements. "The petitioners also asked for a name change, from Imperial Highway to the Great Overland Stage Route of 1849," reports the county. "The supervisors agreed, despite the fact that the Overland Mail Route was never known as 'Great,' the route was not 'Southern' and it didn't exist in 1849." Today, S2 here is still marked with road signs that read, "Great Overland Stage Route of 1849."

Hiking the Moonlight Canyon Trail is much easier than that 2,000-mile march the Mormons endured. The 2.5-mile loop starts with a scramble up the rocky trail, rising some 350 feet to a saddle ridge. It then passes through a narrow wash, with parts of the trail requiring a scramble down some huge boulders. Past the midpoint, it winds through a riparian area where arroyo willows stand tall among water seeps. This wet area is not a true oasis like some palm-studded ones with running streams in the desert, but it is nonetheless notable for the different riparian vegetation.

Just beyond the wet depression, the trail widens and flattens as it heads back to the caravan area of the regional park. Walk through the campground area back to the start of the loop trail where you parked. The landscape here is rich with colorful granite and mineral crystals, including those Tierra Blanca Mountains. Abundant cholla cactus sparkle in the sun, and lots of tall ocotillo grow here, especially in the flat area near the end of the loop trail. Barrel cactus, creosote, and brittlebush promise lots of blooms here in the spring.

The regional park is open only from Labor Day weekend through the last weekend in May; it's closed during summer. Should you wish to stay longer, camping fees range from $19 for tents per day to $28 for full hookups.

Thomas Brothers Map: Page D, south of page 1138.

Before You Go: Check the county parks' page (http://www.co.san-diego.ca.us/parks/Camping/agua_caliente.html) for full information on the campgrounds. You may also download a trail map.
Download a copy of the Anza-Borrego Desert State Park map from the state park page: http://www.parks.ca.gov/pages/638/files/ABDSPmap.pdf.
Dogs and bikes are not allowed on this trail.
There is a $5 day-use fee per vehicle, paid at the ranger kiosk at the camping park's entrance. Day-use hours are 9:30 a.m. to 5:00 p.m.

Trailhead: From Julian, head east on Highway 78 to Scissors Crossing, turning south onto Highway S2 and heading 26 miles to the park entrance on the right.
You can also reach the park from Interstate 8 east, exiting at Ocotillo and heading 22 miles north on Highway S2 to the park entrance on the left.
Once inside the park, head to the shuffleboard courts, where day users find parking; it's near campsite #140. Look for the sign identifying the start of Moonlight Canyon Trail.

Distance/Difficulty: A 2.5-mile loop, easy to moderate.

12-11. Morteros, Rock Art Beckon In Blair Valley

Blair Valley in Anza-Borrego has one of the desert's most interesting set of trails for their varied cultural histories. There are three main trails that take you to different periods of the past. They are part of the 4,757-acre Little Blair Valley Cultural Preserve in Anza-Borrego Desert State Park, which contains 60 recorded cultural sites, including agave roasting pits, extensive bedrock grinding features, and elaborate pictograph panels of the native Californians who wintered here, the Kumeyaay. There are also ruins from more recent times of a well-known family that lived here in the 1930s and 1940s.

The trails begin off the Blair Valley Road, accessed at the turnoff 6.0 miles south of Scissors Crossing on Highway S2. The dirt road to these trails is decently maintained and is suitable for regular cars (without four-wheel drive). It is sandy and rutted in places, so drive slowly and carefully to avoid hitting rocks or getting stuck in the sand.

I was especially interested in the Morteros Trail, the middle of the three trails, which begins after about 3.5 miles on that main dirt road. The Morteros Trail has an interpretive brochure available at the trailhead that accompanies numbered markers on the trail.

The brochure calls it the "Ehmuu-Morteros Trail." Ehmuu is the Kumeyaay word for "bedrock hole," and mortero is the Spanish word for mortar. These are deep holes in bedrock that once were the Kumeyaay "stone food processor," says the brochure, in which women would grind seeds and nuts. There are several surprisingly deep morteros on this trail.

The first marker points out what may have been an agave roasting pit. The Kumeyaay word for agave is "emally," and the plant was a main staple for the early people here. "Note the dark soil and scatter of rocks in this area ... It could be the remains of an agave-roasting pit," says the brochure. Kumeyaay men would dig a deep pit and line it with rocks and a layer of hot coals. Then they placed agave heads, stalks, and leaves on

Little Blair Valley Cultural Preserve holds a lot of history.

the hot bed of coals and covered them with sand. After three days, they would dig them up and eat them. Lots of juniper and Mohave yucca grow in this area. Juniper berries were eaten ripe or dried and were another important food source for the Kumeyaay.

When I was there in early April, the beavertail cacti were sporting their gloriously bright fuchsia-pink blooms, as were the hedgehog cacti, sometimes right next to each other.

Marker No. 4 on the trail takes you to the first mortero, a deep one of at least eight inches that sits back near the base of a hill. No. 5 reveals "a Kumeyaay kitchen," a food preparation area with several morteros as well as metates (which are shallower, basin-shaped depressions) and slicks (which are smooth, flat surfaces). "Each was used for a purpose best suited for its shape and size," says the brochure. "Imagine dozens of Kumeyaay women at these rock stations pounding, grinding, drying, mixing or making cakes of the numerous wild foods gathered in this area." In addition to agave, yucca, and juniper, you'll also see creosote, jojoba, ephedra, and several kinds of cacti that "provided Kumeyaay residents with food, medicine, tools, shelter and clothing."

No. 7, the farthest marker, points to a clear painting of Indian rock art; this one is in black. "Black paint was commonly made by grinding up charcoal and adding oil from roasted wild cucumber seeds," says the brochure. "Paintbrushes were made from yucca and agave fibers."

No. 8 takes you to a rock shelter that may have functioned as food storage. "Look about the hill above this village area and you'll find many rock openings used for shelter and storage."

The Pictograph Trail is about 1.5 miles farther on that main dirt road (about 5.0 miles from the S2 turnoff on the main dirt road). From its parking area, this trail is about 1.0 mile one-way through a small valley to a large rock containing more Kumeyaay rock art; these examples are in red paint, which was usually made from iron oxide.

Head back out along the main Blair Valley dirt road. The first of the three trails (about 2.7 miles from S-2) takes you to the parking area for the Yaquitepec Trail on Ghost Mountain. Yaquitepec is the name the Marshal South family gave to the small adobe they built here, the ruins of which remain. This trail climbs up about 0.7 mile to reach a hollow near the top of Ghost Mountain, where the skeletal remains of the house and its large adobe oven still command a sweeping view.

"Here is where poet, author and artist Marshal South and his family lived from 1930 to 1947, pursuing a primitive and natural lifestyle that became well-known through South's monthly columns written for Desert Magazine," writes Diana Lindsay in her foreword for the book *Marshal South and the Ghost Mountain Chronicles*, which includes 102 articles and poems that South wrote for *Desert Magazine*. South "had a very loyal following, deservedly so," she writes. "South wrote with a lyric quality, painting word pictures as only a poet or artist could. He wrote with passion about the desert—its silence, beauty and natural history; its healthful qualities; its early inhabitants and their lifestyle."

Thomas Brothers Map: Page 1138/1158 (bottom half of page 1138), F-4, about where the road bends.

Before You Go: No bikes, horses, or dogs are allowed on this state park trail. Download a copy of the map from the state parks page on Little Blair Valley cultural area: http://www.parks.ca.gov/pages/21299/files/anza_little_blair_valley_map.pdf.

Trailhead: From Scissors Crossing, which is the intersection of Highway 78 and S2, go south on S2 about 6.0 miles to the turnoff on the left (east) to Blair Valley. On this well-maintained dirt road, drive 2.7 miles to the Yaquitepec Trail, 3.5 miles to the Morteros Trail, and 5.0 miles to the Pictograph Trail.

Distance/Difficulty: The Morteros Trail is about 1.0 mile round-trip; easy. The Yaquitepec Trail is steeper and about 1.5 miles round-trip. The Pictograph Trail is about 2.0 miles round-trip.

12-12. Mountain Palm Springs Offers One of the Best Palm Oases

There is no better time to visit the Anza-Borrego Desert region than spring. Wildflowers are blooming, the temperatures are moderate but warm, and the landscapes are nothing short of amazing. Palm oases are the biggest surprise. Whether it's your first or 50th time, when you round a bend in a relatively barren landscape to discover groups of tall palm trees, they take your breath away. They are taller than any plant around and live in tight groups. They seem secreted, hidden in washes among the faults and folds of the landscape. And they're always accompanied by water—sometimes bubbling creeks or even little waterfalls—in the otherwise parched environment.

There are about 20 canyons in Anza-Borrego that are home to the native California fan palms (also known as Washingtonia filifera). One of the most beautiful collections of these is in the Mountain Palm Springs area, where a primitive campground is located, as well as two connecting trails that lead to clusters of seven palm groves.

Mountain Palm Springs is a desert favorite for palm tree oases.

Even the drive to get to this trail is awesome. While heading east on Interstate 8, past Pine Valley between Campo and Ocotillo are boulder-strewn landscapes that appear otherworldly, where countless rocks perch precariously on other rocks, forming tableaus straight out of Dr. Seuss.

Pull off Interstate 8 at Ocotillo and head north on S2 to Mountain Palm Springs. The road is lined with the blooms of bright purple lupine and yellow brittlebush. The Carrizo Badlands reveal nature's erosion over millennia and amazing naked geology.

Some years are better than others for wildflower blooms. When I was there one spring in late March, it had a less than banner bloom, but there was still plenty of color on that road as well as the trail. Brittlebush blazes with its yellow blossoms, the barrel cactus heads show off their lime-green flowers, the hedgehog and beavertail cacti burst with their fuchsia-colored blooms, and the tall stalks of the ocotillo are aflame with orange flowers. One of my favorites is the apricot mallow, a native in these desert regions that features that pretty color surprise. Lots of little white and yellow desert daisies, sunflowers, and dandelions are sprinkled across the arid landscape.

Even if you go when the blooms have passed, the palm tree oases will still be a marvelous draw. "Among the tallest of desert trees, they live only where water is close to the surface," says a placard at the beginning of the trail to the Southwest Grove in Mountain Palm Springs. "They have survived thousands of years, remnants of times when horses, mastodons and saber-toothed tigers roamed through grasslands and mixed scrub forests ... Water and shade attract scores of bird species (as well as) coyotes, raccoons and bighorn sheep."

I didn't see those bigger forms of wildlife this time, but I did spot a couple of beige foot-long lizards that were nearly camouflaged on the desert floor.

As the trail meanders up the canyon wash, you arrive first at the Pygmy Grove, where about 50 stunted California fan palms reside. If you go another half-mile up the canyon and around another bend, you come upon the impressive Southwest Grove, where nearly 100 palms live tightly together. The water wasn't rushing but was clearly evident in each of these groves. Just beyond the Southwest Grove is Torote Bowl, another gathering of fan palms.

I didn't take the north fork trail to the other groves, Surprise Canyon and Palm Bowl, which have another hundred palms, but I will another day.

Go explore this landscape to discover another natural wonder in our county.

Thomas Brothers Map: Page D, west of the Carrizo Gorge Wilderness area.

Before You Go: Download a map from Anza-Borrego Desert State Park pages: http://www.parks.ca.gov/pages/638/files/ABDSPmap.pdf.
As in most state parks, dogs are not allowed on the trails.

Trailhead: Go east on Interstate 8, exit at Ocotillo, and head north onto S2. About 17 miles north, near the No. 47 mile marker, take a left into the Mountain Palm Springs primitive campground area. Go about 0.6 miles on this sandy, unpaved road to the end, where there is day parking. At the western end of this parking area is the trailhead to Southwest Grove; it's not marked as such, but you'll see the placard about Native Palm Groves.

Distance/Difficulty: About 3.0 miles round-trip. Easy.

12-13. Painted Gorge Lives Up To Its Glorious Name

Explore one of the most amazing natural landscapes in our southern desert region in Painted Gorge. Located in the southeast corner of the Coyote Mountains (not to be confused with Coyote Mountain and Coyote Canyon, just north of Borrego Springs), Painted Gorge lies just north of the town of Ocotillo. Painted Gorge is in Imperial County. Although the Anza-Borrego Desert State Park boundary stops at the eastern San Diego County boundary, the desert itself continues farther east into our neighboring county. Painted Gorge is located in BLM lands, some of which are designated open to recreational uses. Wilderness boundaries generally lie just beyond the dirt road that leads hikers to the colorful canyon gorge.

Reaching Painted Gorge is not the easiest of navigational tasks. The dirt road is signed and named Painted Gorge off County Route S80, and there are some signed wooden markers pointing the way, but there are other unnamed dirt roads here that could easily take you off course.

Painted Gorge is worth the effort to get there.

While heading east on County Route S80, just north of the Ocotillo exit off Interstate 8, take the marked Painted Gorge dirt road north. A regular passenger car may be able to navigate the road for a short ways, but reaching the gorge itself some 8.5 miles later requires four-wheel drive. We were able to take GPS readings, but cell phone service was not available here, so be sure you are playing it safe with your vehicle or you could be stuck a very long way inside the wilderness.

We headed north on the Painted Gorge dirt road, also called EC236, which we eventually learned is a BLM road designation referring to El Centro 236 for this area's jurisdiction headquarters. We then took a left at EC214, following a Painted Gorge directional, even though EC214 wasn't marked on any map we had. We finally reached a gate that marks the entrance to Painted Gorge. This gate is closed to motor vehicles from January to June "to protect lambing of peninsular bighorn sheep." We began hiking on foot from here. We also took those GPS readings at this gate: roughly +32.8 N latitude and -115.9 W longitude.

Getting there was half of this journey, but the landscape on the road and on the hike was awesome. The canyon's walls seem truly painted in colors of deep reds, yellows, greens, and browns, all caused by rocks containing copper, sulfur, and iron.

The gorge is also said to contain marine fossils from the ancient coral reefs that once inhabited this area when it was underwater some 5 million years ago. Indeed, just to the west of Painted Gorge is another worthy desert destination called Fossil Canyon, sometimes known as Shell Canyon. This entire area, according to the San Diego Natural History Museum, was once in the Imperial Sea from about 7 million to 2 million years ago.

We hiked along the dirt road and eventually started exploring the ridges of the area on far smaller trails—possibly those trod by bighorn sheep, which we didn't see.

Cross-country exploration here is fun but a bit challenging, because the rocks can be slippery on the steep inclines. Just don't lose your bearings.

We did see a couple of mountain bike enthusiasts, as well as a couple of campers who were shooting at their own targets. Such activities are allowed in the BLM areas here, which are open to recreational use.

When we got back to our vehicle, we headed out and took a left turn, where we had come in to the gate area, believing it was an unmarked road on our map that would take us back in a different loop. It wasn't. We don't know what road it was, but we ended up going farther east than we intended, and came probably very close to a U.S. Navy reservation area that's off-limits for a different kind of target shooting. There were lots of dirt roads crisscrossing each other; we eventually entered the off-road vehicle areas of Plaster City, where we headed for major power lines we could see that we'd gone under on our way into Painted Gorge. Best advice: Retrace your route back out the way you came to avoid getting that kind of lost.

We asked at the visitor center for a good map, and if anyone knew about the EC roads. Park Ranger Steve Bier finally had an answer. The BLM WECO (for Western Colorado Desert, El Centro) maps are the best for these off-road routes. Go to http://www.blm.gov/ca/st/en/fo/elcentro/wecd.html and then go to page four for Painted Gorge.

The beauty of this Painted Gorge is well worth the effort.

Thomas Brothers Map: Page D, just east of Coyote Mountains Wilderness.

Before You Go: One of the best maps of the region is *Anza-Borrego Desert Region Recreation Map* for Wilderness Press. It's $9.95 from the Anza-Borrego Foundation (http://www.theabf.org/anza-borrego-desert-region-recreation-map), or at retail stores like REI and Adventure 16.

You may also zoom in on the map found at http://www.anzaborrego.net/Travel/AnzaBorrego/page/Anza-Borrego-Desert-Maps.aspx, honing in just northeast of Ocotillo off County Route S80.

Trailhead: From Interstate 8, exit at Ocotillo and head north. Just beyond I-8 here, turn east onto County Route S80. In about 4.0 miles, turn north onto the marked Painted Gorge Road and head north. This road becomes EC236. Then turn onto EC214 to reach the gate that marks entry to Painted Gorge.

Difficulty: Mileage will vary; moderate. Allow a couple of hours to drive this rocky road in and out, and a couple of hours to hike around the area.

12-14. Lots of History, Green at Desert's Palm Spring

When you hike the trail in Anza-Borrego to Palm Spring, be on the lookout for the phantom stagecoach that is reportedly sometimes seen here. It's one of the ghostly legends that live on along this storied trail, which has figured prominently in several eras of our county's history.

Palm Spring oasis, where water still bubbles up to the surface today, was probably the site of the first palm tree oasis described in California by Spanish explorer Pedro

Fages in 1782, according to Lowell and Diana Lindsay's excellent book, *The Anza-Borrego Desert Region*. Fages noted this "small spring of good water, near which there were three or four very tall palm trees." This watering hole was favored by Native Americans for a very long time before Fages brought those early Europeans through the desert seeking routes from Mexico to California.

This historic watering hole still attracts.

The route here then was used by Kit Carson when he guided General Stephen Kearny and his Army of the West in 1846 from New Mexico to the infamous Battle of San Pasqual during the Mexican-American War. (San Dieguito River Park trails there.) Several weeks later, Lt. Col. Philip St. George Cooke and his Mormon Battalion, aiming to help the Americans in that war, came through here during their 2,000-mile march from Council Bluffs, Iowa, to San Diego, becoming the first group to pass through here on wagons.

During California's Gold Rush of 1849, this route became known as the Southern Emigrant Trail, when thousands of people flocked to California. Known locally as the Carrizo Corridor, this route that included Palm Spring then became part of the country's first overland mail and passenger service between California and the East from 1856 until 1858, then known as Jackass Mail for its use of mules. In 1858 it became the Butterfield Overland Mail route and was used by Butterfield stages carrying mail and passengers from Missouri to San Francisco.

"The Palm Spring station was built beside an all-year freshwater spring on the edge of the badlands halfway between Carrizo and Vallecito," write the Lindsays. "Before the station was built, a grove of tall palms grew around the spring and the oasis was a favorite resting place for soldiers, emigrants and mountain men. But by the time the station was built in 1858, all the palms had been chopped down to feed travelers' campfires."

This southern overland mail route ceased here in 1861 due to the beginning of the Civil War, as well as the coming of the railroad, making "the old emigrant road and Butterfield Overland Mail route virtually a ghost trail," write the Lindsays. There are no remnants of the station anymore today, except for a stone marker designating Palm Spring as California Registered Historical Landmark No. 639. The striking scenery is surely little changed, except for the lack of palms.

The trail to Palm Spring begins off Highway S2 and winds through a very sandy wash. You might be tempted to drive the Jeep road to the spring, but don't try it without four-wheel drive. A road sign warns drivers, "Soft Sand Ahead," which can render regular cars very stuck.

The old dirt road passes by lots of gray-blue smoke trees, cholla cactus, and ocotillo sprinkled with barrel cactus. The ocotillo were nearly finished blooming by the last week in March, but the barrel cacti were in full bloom with more to come, and the cholla showed blooms still a few weeks away. Look for bushes with the dense blooms of yellow head and spot the tiny purple sand verbena on that sandy floor.

The most color this spring came from creosote bushes sporting many yellow blooms. The Lindsays note that creosote is the most common plant of the Colorado Desert here, and it is also one of the oldest. In fact, because of the way it propagates through slow cloning, some creosote plants may be 10,000 years old, according to the Anza-Borrego Desert Natural History Association. Its yellow blooms are shaped like windmills, which become fuzzy seed balls later.

The most notable green here comes from the abundant mesquite trees that can reach 15 to 20 feet tall with long yellow blooms in spring. Those blooms eventually become beans, which were important to resident natives long ago and remain so to wildlife today.

Those mesquite trees congregate below the hill folds of the badlands beyond in a wide band of green that is truly notable in the desert. That bright green swath would have alerted those travelers long ago that water was probably here. Many animal and bird footprints in that soft sand around the spring reveal that wildlife still visit this water source.

From the start of the trail, hike about half a mile on the soft-sand Jeep road, and you'll come to a large intersection. Continue ahead toward the right; you will come back on the road at left. After about a mile from the start, the road forks again; go left following the sign to Palm Spring. In another 0.6 mile, you'll reach Palm Spring itself.

When you leave the spring, turn right to continue on the loop. In about 0.4 mile, you'll come to an intersection with a sign to the right for Mesquite Oasis. Stay left here and continue straight ahead for about 0.7 mile more. At the road intersection, turn left and hike for about 0.2 mile. You'll reach that first junction you passed, where you turn right to head back to the parking area in another 0.5 mile.

That apparition of the stagecoach comes from the legend that the stage was robbed and the driver killed, but the stage and its horses still tried to make it to Vallecito, say the Lindsays. Carry plenty of water, and you should have no problem here.

Thomas Brothers Map: Page D, near Carrizo Gorge Wilderness, southeast corner of San Diego County.

Before You Go: Download a copy of the Anza-Borrego Desert State Park map from the state park page: http://www.parks.ca.gov/pages/638/files/ABDSPmap.pdf.

A map of this trail loop is in Robin Halford's *Hiking in Anza-Borrego Dessert: Over 100 Half-Day Hikes.*

This trail is open to hikers and equestrians. It is too sandy for bicyclists, and no dogs are allowed on state park trails.

Trailhead: Park just off Highway S2 at the 43-mile marker, which is 26.4 miles south of Scissors Crossing (where S2 intersects Highway 78 from Julian), or 21.6 miles north of Ocotillo (at Interstate 8).

Distance/Difficulty: The loop totals about 3.4 miles. Though sandy, it's fairly flat and is mostly easy.

12-15. Rainbow Canyon Shows Off Marbled Metamorphic Rock

Rainbow Canyon in Anza-Borrego Desert State Park offers an amazing exploration of metamorphic rock. Colorful bands of various minerals create splendid slabs of marbled schist and gneiss that are evidence of changes over millions of years. Rainbow Canyon is also home to some of the desert's great stands of teddy bear or jumping cholla cactus, which seem to glow in sunlight. Tall ocotillo and barrel cactus are here too, and some of spring's finest wildflower shows can happen in this canyon as well.

It's not a true trail, so there isn't a trailhead to tell you you're on the right path. But there is a natural wash to follow that is as good as a trail once you find it. Before you enter the canyon itself, make your way over a metal fence that's been tamped down on the left. While following the wash, you'll need to scramble up about eight dry falls that entirely plug the narrow canyon. The first of these dry falls features one of the most beautiful examples of that metamorphic rock.

Striated, colorful rock formations are a draw for Rainbow Canyon.

Metamorphism means to change form, says Lisa Tauxe, a professor of geophysics at UCSD's Scripps Institution of Oceanography in an online lecture on igneous and metamorphic rocks (http://topex.ucsd.edu/es10/lectures/lecture16/lecture16.html). In geology, metamorphism refers to changes in rocks that occur over millions of years from heat, pressure, and fluids. An example of metamorphic rock is the transformation of clay to shale to slate then to schist, which has large mica flakes in it as well. "Under the most intense metamorphism," says Tauxe, minerals segregate into bands of light and dark minerals, characteristic of gneiss."

That first dry falls appears to be gneiss, with its wavy bands of dark and light rocks that suggest it was cooking millions of years ago. Take your time in this canyon to ponder these colorful rocks and how they formed.

Anza-Borrego desert was once under the ocean, write Lowell and Diana Lindsay in their book, *The Anza-Borrego Desert Region, A Guide to the State Park and Adjacent Areas.* "It changed from part of an ocean to verdant grassland to the present desert largely because of dynamic forces along the great San Andreas fault system," they say.

This part of Anza-Borrego is also interesting for a much more recent chapter in history. About 1.4 miles west of Rainbow Canyon on Highway S2 is a historic marker noting the Mormon Battalion marched through here in January 1847. (The stone pillar has lost its plaque, but the wooden sign citing the Mormon Battalion Trail is still there.) While marching from Council Bluffs, Iowa, to San Diego to assist General Stephen Kearny in the San Pasqual battles of the Mexican-American War, the Mormon Battalion had to hack out with axes a path for their wagons through the rocky chasms near here (Box Canyon, another nearby historic marker). Box Canyon then became the first wagon road into Southern California, following a route used for thousands of years by the native Kumeyaay and Kwaaymii people. This historic trail is known as the Southern Overland Trail, which was just approved in December 2010 by the California State Park and Recreation Commission as one of seven new cultural preserves in Anza-Borrego Desert State Park. (See http://www.parks.ca.gov/?page_id=21314 for a complete list and more information.)

As for the cholla cactus, they don't really jump at you, and they're not cuddly like teddy bears. But if you get too close to their sharp spines, they will attach painfully, making you believe they jumped onto your leg.

To find all these natural wonders, go east on Highway 78 from Julian to Scissors Crossing, the intersection of 78 and S2, where you turn southeast onto Highway S2. Drive about 11 miles. At mile marker 27.7, where the road makes a sharp right turn, park on the east side of the road, off the pavement, in front of a sign showing that sharp turn. This point is about 2.0 miles southeast on S2 from the Box Canyon marker, and about 1.4 miles southeast on S2 from the stone marker and wooden sign for the Mormon Battalion Trail.

From this parking spot, look northeast for the depression between two hills; this is Rainbow Canyon. Head toward that canyon, and soon you'll pick up a wide wash that will serve as the trail. Head up the canyon, scrambling over those dry falls. At about 0.7 mile, stay right at a canyon fork. At about a mile, turn back and retrace your way out.

Thomas Brothers Map: Page D, south of page 1138.

Before You Go: You can download maps of Anza-Borrego Desert State Park from its state park page (www.parks.ca.gov/?page_id=25225) or from the desert's Natural History Association (www.abdsp.org), but neither of these maps actually show Rainbow Canyon.

You may want to buy the *Anza-Borrego Desert Region Recreation Map*, published by Wilderness Press and available at outdoor recreation stores such as REI and Adventure 16, as well as online through the Anza-Borrego Foundation (http://www.theabf.org/anza-borrego-desert-region-recreation-map) The map shows Rainbow Canyon.

No dogs are allowed on state park trails.

Trailhead: From Julian, head east on Highway 78 to Scissors Crossing, and then turn southeast onto Highway S-2. Drive about 11 miles to mile marker 27.7, just past the turnoff to Oriflamme. Park on the east side off the pavement.

Distance/Difficulty: About 2.0 miles round-trip; easy with moderate scrambling.

12-16. Sentenac Birding Trail Full of Desert Wonder

The Sentenac Birding Trail in Anza-Borrego's Scissors Crossing area is a desert wonderland of unusual plants and, of course, birds and wildlife. It's a desert transition area that sits at nearly 3,000 feet in elevation, and it's centered on San Felipe Creek, making for a riparian area that mixes low-desert and high-desert plants that normally attract a variety of birds. The trail crosses Sentenac Cienega, or Sentenac Marsh, which connects to Sentenac Canyon, both near the historic Scissors Crossing where State Scenic Highway 78 intersects with County Route S2.

Marshy area in desert attracts lots of birds.

It's an easy loop trail of about 1.4 miles through a remarkably wet area for the desert. This trail also intersects with the Pacific Crest Trail, which passes through here.

I began by exploring the PCT for about a mile on the west side of S2. The PCT parallels S2 for about a half-mile or so before it heads west to climb the lower northeastern flanks of 5,633-foot-high Granite Mountain. The remarkable thing about this segment of the PCT was the variety of cactus in this area. I spotted several kinds of cholla, including jumping cholla and snake cholla, both of which should bloom in spring with yellow flowers; hedgehog cactus, which looks like clusters of small barrel cactus featuring bright magenta blooms; fishhook cactus, with its mounds of columns that sport tiny, hooked spines and the smallest (red and white) blooms of any local cactus, according to James Lightner's *San Diego County Native Plants*; and beavertail cactus, with its flat paddles that brighten the landscape in spring with bright fuchsia-colored flowers, which are the largest blooms among local cacti.

I turned back on the PCT to head toward the Sentenac Birding Trail, which lies across S2 on its east side. Begin on the PCT here, which heads into Sentenac Cienega and the San Felipe Creek area. In a very short distance (about 0.1 mile or so), the PCT dips down into a large wash, where you'll see a sign for the Sentenac Birding Trail heading off to the right.

"Anza-Borrego Desert State Park's lower San Felipe Valley and Sentenac Cienega comprise highly significant historical, cultural and natural areas," states the Land Conversation, an organization that helps restore ecosystems and revitalize languages and cultures, in a proposal to the state park to help restore this area. The group proposed a five-year program to enhance riparian plant and animal habitat here, particularly pruning and burning the willows to enhance growth following age-old Native American practices. "Lying along the Southern Emigrant Trail, the area was traversed and settled by an ethnically diverse set of native peoples for many centuries before it became a stop on the major land route into Southern California for 19th-century Euroamerican travelers," says the proposal (http://www.borregospringschamber.com/abdsp/documents/sentenacfinal.pdf). "Today it forms part of a critically important migratory route for birds and habitat for several rare and endangered species."

The San Felipe Valley was part of an ancient trade route among Cahuilla, Kumeyaay, Kamia, and Luiseño people, according to Lowell and Diana Lindsay's book, *The Anza-Borrego Desert Region*. The Butterfield Overland Mail route had a San Felipe Station at Scissors Crossing near here from 1858 to 1861. That station was later used by Banning stagecoaches and by the military during the Civil War.

Sentenac Cienega and Sentenac Canyon were named for Paul Sentenac, a Frenchman who homesteaded 160 acres here in the 1880s, where he built a stone cabin "atop the rocky little hill at the mouth of Sentenac Canyon," write the Lindsays. Sentenac raised cattle, goats, and sheep here.

"The abundance of water supports a lush plant growth, with many mesquite trees rimming the canyon and the cienega. In the canyon are cottonwoods, willows, a dense growth of carrizon grass and a great variety of other plants," write the Lindsays.

It is obvious that fire has gone through this area somewhat recently. It may be from a brushfire that burned here in April 2012 or from a larger fire in this area a few years ago.

From the start of the Sentenac Birding Trail, head south through lots of mesquite and catclaw, both of which can prick you with their sharp thorns. The trail skirts the area that was burned the most, where old mesquite is dead and hard to navigate. Follow the wooden posts that mark the trail to stay on course; if you think you've lost it, look for one of those posts ahead.

In a little more than a half-mile, the trail loops to head back north, this time heading into a remarkably tall grouping of cottonwood trees along the creek. Here I also saw some old coyote melon, which are like gourds in late winter—a very interesting sight in the desert.

Sadly, I saw very few birds, but perhaps mid-February is too early for that spring migration, which takes place closer to April and May. The wildflowers are probably blooming here by mid to late March. According to Mary Beth Stowe's birding blog (http:www.miriameaglemon.com), this riparian area is visited by Nuttall's woodpeckers, northern flickers, blue-gray gnatcatchers, wrentits, western scrub jays, black phoebes, white-crowned sparrows, Bullock's orioles, Bell's vireo, western tanagers, and California quail (our state bird), among others.

The trail connects again to the PCT near the San Felipe Bridge over Highway 78. Follow the PCT back to S2 where you started.

Thomas Brothers Map: Page D, between Pages 1136 and 1138.

Before You Go: The map that accompanies the Lindsays' excellent guidebook, *The Anza-Borrego Desert Region,* shows the Sentenac Birding Trail at Scissors Crossing.

You may also want to buy the *Anza-Borrego Desert Region Recreation Map,* published by Wilderness Press and available at outdoor recreation stores such as REI and Adventure 16, as well as online through the Anza-Borrego Foundation (http://www.theabf.org/anza-borrego-desert-region-recreation-map).

Also, Robin Halford's *Hiking in Anza-Borrego Desert State Park: Over 100 Half-Day Hikes* has a map of the Sentenac Birding Trail.

This trail is not on the state park map (http://www.parks.ca.gov/pages/638/files/abdspmap.pdf), but Scissors Crossing is where Highway 78 intersects State Route S2.

This trail is open to hikers but would be difficult for equestrians or bicyclists. Dogs are not allowed on state park trails.

Trailhead: Heading east out of Julian on Highway 78, turn south (right) onto State Route S2 (where these two roads intersect is Scissors Crossing). In just 0.2 mile, you'll see the PCT on both sides of S2. Park here off the highway. The Sentenac Birding Trail begins just off the PCT on the east side of S2.

Distance/Difficulty: The Sentenac Birding Loop is about 1.4 miles total; easy. The Pacific Crest Trail is 2,650 miles, but you can enjoy it however long you wish on either side of S2 here. Easy.

12-17. Seventeen Palms Wants Your Notes

Seventeen Palms is one of those surprising sights in one of the most desolate areas of Anza-Borrego Desert State Park. It's a watering hole to the east of the Borrego Badlands, where several sandy washes testify to water that sometimes roars through here. Today there are probably around 30 palms here, but Seventeen Palms gets its name from the original 17 that stood here decades ago, according to Diana and Lowell Lindsay in their comprehensive guidebook, *The Anza-Borrego Desert Region.*

In any desert oasis where water and shade are found, humans and animals have gathered for eons. Very long ago, mammoths and camels grazed here. "Many are the legends and superstitions surrounding the area, and the tales of lost mines and prospectors," write the Lindsays.

Today you'll also find tales from present-day travelers when you come upon the "post office" in Seventeen Palms. It's a wooden keg attached between two palm trunks in the middle of the oasis. Inside are several journals covering the past few years, filled with impressions from excited visitors who found themselves in this amazing place. There are also several pens in case you want to add your own notes.

Tales of the trails are found in Seventeen Palms.

"This desert post office was begun by early-day travelers and prospectors, who also used to leave a freshwater supply for those who followed," say the Lindsays.

The water in this oasis is certainly not running free, but it is present. The creek bed underlying these palms is mostly covered now with fallen fronds. Near a sign that reads, "Not for cooking or drinking," you can dip a stick into the depths and see that water is there.

Wildlife depends on this water source, so overnight camping is not allowed here, because most of the animals come to drink at night.

To reach Seventeen Palms, take the Arroyo Salado Camp turnoff from S22 and go through the primitive camping area; after 3.7 miles you'll reach the parking area. Four-wheel drive and high clearance are necessary here because the road is either very soft sand or very rocky. You can also hike in from the road and make this distance part of your hike. From that parking area, the palms are readily visible, and the walk to them is extremely short.

Arroyo Salado translates from Spanish to mean salty stream. The Lindsays note that the water in this oasis is very saline, so though it might not kill you, it "is highly laxative." According to the BLM, underlying clays and faults bring water close to the surface here.

You can hike along the Arroyo Salado road farther, but I simply hiked through the various washes around the Seventeen Palms. The views from here, especially when you climb the ridges, are spectacular. As you gaze north toward the Santa Rosa Mountains, the painted layers of the desert's hilly geology are simply beautiful.

There are also lots of wildflowers in this part of the park. Even in late January, blooms were beginning to show their colors. The bright orange blossoms of the tall ocotillo were budding. On the desert floor, purple sand verbena were beginning to carpet the ground. Big blooms of purple woody asters brightened their round bushes. Yellow desert sunflowers stuck up straight from their hairy white leaves. Dense bushes filled with tiny yellow and white pincushions yielded color upon close inspection. White popcorn flowers with their hairy foliage hugged the sandy ground. White desert chicory spread their daisy-like petals from pale yellow centers. My personal favorites were the desert lanterns, a type of evening primrose with red centers and yellow filaments that is a lovely addition to the stark landscape.

I never found any real trails to follow here and simply wandered along the easy washes and hiked cross-country up ridges to scope the views. On the lookout for other nearby palm oases, I never spied any others. According to the map, there are both Five Palms and Una Palma nearby, if you continue farther south on the Arroyo Salado dirt road.

Thomas Brothers Map: Page D, east of Page 1058.

Before You Go: For a good map of the Anza-Borrego Desert State Park, go to the state parks page: http://www.parks.ca.gov/pages/638/files/ABDSPmap.pdf.

The California State Parks also offers a good desert wildflower brochure: http://www.parks.ca.gov/pages/638/files/AnzaBorregoWildFlowers.pdf.

This trail is best for hikers; no dogs allowed on state park trails.

Trailhead: From Christmas Circle in downtown Borrego Springs, head east on S22 (also known as Borrego-Salton Seaway) for 15.7 miles to the Arroyo Salado Camp turnoff, which heads south at about the 34.8-mile marker. From there, it's 3.7 miles down the sandy, rocky dirt road to the parking area very near Seventeen Palms.

Distance/Difficulty: Easy. Allow a couple of hours to explore the area on foot.

12-18. Truckhaven Trail Has Sandstone Cannonballs

Truckhaven Trail in Anza-Borrego explores one of those classic desert landscapes of naked geology carved by wide washes, and it's dotted with smoke trees. Its other most interesting claim is historic: Thousands of years ago, Paleo-Indians lived in this land that then hosted many lakes and streams; in the early 1930s, it was a main thoroughfare here.

Begin just off the south side of Highway S22 at the sign marking Truckhaven Trail. A placard at the trail's beginning notes that Borrego's first trails consisted of those left by Native Americans.

The earliest inhabitants here are called Paleo-Indians, according to Lowell and Diana Lindsay's book *The Anza-Borrego Desert Region*. Paleo-Indians lived at least 9,000 years ago, "when the climate was milder and lakes and streams were plentiful." The Paleo-Indians of Anza-Borrego are called the San Dieguito Indians, and they were primarily fishermen and hunters.

Truckhaven Man, an archaeological figure found somewhere near here, where the Salton Sea was once ancient Lake Cahuilla, dates to some 3,000 years ago. Back then, people here were primarily seed gatherers who ground them in shallow metates (holes or slicks) that they fashioned from the rocks.

Thousands of years ago, the desert region presented a very different landscape.

From 2,000 to 1,500 years ago, the Yuman Indians lived here. They were the predecessors of the Kumeyaay, and they lived south of present-day S22, which is where Truckhaven Trail lies. Just north of S22, the Shoshoean Indians lived during the time of the Yuman, and their descendants are known as the Desert Cahuillas. Both the Kumeyaay and the Cahuillas were also seed gatherers who made and used pottery and ground their seeds in morteros (deep holes) with stone pestles.

Fast-forward to the time of early homesteaders, one of whom was Alfred Armstrong Beaty, who constructed this old Jeep road in 1929. According to the placard at the trailhead, Beaty led a mule-drawn scraper through the Borrego Badlands near here to the Truckhaven Cafe on old Highway 99, a cultural landmark in these parts that lasted at least until the late 1960s. "The 30 miles of road was not easy to build and almost impossible to maintain," says the placard. "Doc" Beaty obtained donations of food and money, as well as mules and labor, from supporters in Borrego and Coachella Valley to the north, where this road was a major route largely carrying farmers' bounty.

Truckhaven Trail was replaced by today's Borrego Salton Seaway, a.k.a. Highway S22, when it was completed in 1968. When you walk down Truckhaven Trail, imagine those mules carving out this route in 1929, only to have torrential rains gut it almost as soon as it was finished. It is still a Jeep road, but parts of it look very hard to navigate. For the most part, this trail follows those natural washes, except for two places where it climbs up out of them steeply. It's a mostly flat walk through washes.

In late April, despite the fact these are washes, there wasn't a wildflower to be found. There were several pale green smoke trees, whose purple blooms should add color here in June, and lots of big galleta, a very common grass that is found all over Anza-Borrego because it is especially good at extracting water from soil during dry periods. The muted colors you will find are in the sandstone cliffs that rise high above the washes.

And then there are the cannonballs.

From the trailhead at S22, follow the old Jeep road called Truckhaven Trail straight ahead to the south for about 0.7 mile, when it drops sharply down into the first wash for another 0.3 mile or so. At the bottom, you'll see the only wooden marker with an arrow pointing right, where Truckhaven Trail continues. But don't take that; you'll come back this way. Instead, turn left at this intersection, following the Jeep road.

Now you're in Cannonball Wash, named for the sandstone concretions that look like cannonballs that protrude out of the left side of the sandstone cliffs lining that wash. They are harder than the surrounding sandstone and are amazingly round.

After a bit less than a mile through Cannonball Wash, you'll come to a T intersection of the Jeep road; turn right on the Jeep road (unmarked, but it's the North Fork Arroyo Salado) and go through another wash, where you'll see a few more smoke trees and lots of that galleta grass.

In about another mile, you'll come to another unmarked intersection, where the right fork heads sharply uphill; take this right turn and go up over the hill. Then wind back down in another half-mile or so to that first intersection with the wooden arrow marker. Turn left and walk uphill to retrace your way back.

Contemplate the early Paleo-Indians, the homesteaders like Doc Beaty, and this land when Jeep roads were the only routes for Model As. Finally, take a look to the east at what many must have thought a mirage: the Salton Sea.

Thomas Brothers Map: Page D, east of Page 1058.

Before You Go: Download a map of Anza-Borrego from its state parks page: http://www.parks. ca.gov/pages/638/files/ABDSPmap.pdf. On this map, the route described here follows the loop south of S-22 from Truckhaven Rocks, including part of it named North Fork Arroyo Salado. This loop route is also on the map included in the Lindsays' book *The Anza-Borrego Desert Region*.

You may want to buy the *Anza-Borrego Desert Region Recreation Map*, published by Wilderness Press and available at outdoor recreation stores such as REI and Adventure 16, as well as online through the Anza-Borrego Foundation (http://www.theabf.org/anza-borrego-desert-region-recreation-map).

You can also find this route and map in *Hiking in Anza-Borrego Desert* by Robin Halford, listed as Cannonball Run.

This trail open to hikers, bicyclists, and equestrians, but dogs are not allowed on state park trails.

Trailhead: Travel east on Highway S22 (also named Borrego-Salton Seaway) about 18.5 miles east of Christmas Circle in Borrego Springs, just past mile marker 38. Park off the highway on the south side by the sign for Truckhaven Trail. This trailhead is immediately across the highway from the trailhead for Calcite Mines. You'll also note the microwave tower a bit farther to the east on that highway to the Salton Sea.

Distance/Difficulty: About 4.2 miles round-trip; easy to moderate (those two uphill climbs).

Bibliography

I used all of these books, pocket guides, and maps throughout my hiking adventures, and I recommend all of them. I would photograph birds and wildflowers and then return home to try to determine exactly what species they were. I learned a lot from each of these fine publications.

Books

Alden, Peter, and Fred Heath. *National Audubon Society Field Guide to California*. New York: Alfred A. Knopf Inc., 2008.

Alden, Peter, and Fred Heath. *National Audubon Society Field Guide to the Southwestern States*. New York: Alfred A. Knopf Inc., 1999.

Baughman, Mel, ed. *National Geographic Field Guide to Birds, California*. Washington, D.C.: National Geographic, 2004.

Burstein Hewitt, Lonnie, and Barbara Coffin Moore. *Walking San Diego: Where to Go to Get Away from It All*. Seattle: The Mountaineers Book, 2007.

Dunn, Jon L., and Jonathan Alderfer, eds. *National Geographic Field Guide to Birds of Western North America*. Washington, D.C.: National Geographic, 2008 edition.

Halford, Robin. *Hiking in Anza-Borrego Desert: Over 100 Half-day Hikes*. Borrego Springs, CA: Anza-Borrego Desert Natural History Association, 2005.

Lightner, James. *San Diego County Native Plants*. San Diego: San Diego Flora, 2011.

Little, Elbert L. *National Audubon Society Field Guide to Trees, Western Region*. New York: Alfred A. Knopf, 2000.

Lindsay, Lowell, and Diana Lindsay. *The Anza-Borrego Desert Region: A Guide to the State Park and Adjacent Areas*. Berkeley, CA: Wilderness Press, 1996.

Pryde, Philip R. *San Diego: An Introduction to the Region,* 4th ed. San Diego: Sunbelt Publications, 2007.

Schad, Jerry. *Afoot and Afield, San Diego County: A Comprehensive Hiking Guide.* Berkeley, CA: Wilderness Press, 2007.

Sibley, David Allen. *Sibley Field Guide to Birds of Western North America.* New York: Alfred A. Knopf Inc., 2003.

Spellenberg, Richard. *National Audubon Society Field Guide to Wildflowers, Western Region.* New York: Alfred A. Knopf Inc., 2001.

Udvardy, Miklos D. F., and John Farrand Jr. *National Audubon Society Field Guide to Birds, Western Region.* New York: Alfred A. Knopf, 2000.

Pocket Guides

Pocket Naturalist Guides from Waterford Press, www.waterfordpress.com:
    The Chaparral Scrublands of Southern California
    Birds of Prey
    California Trees & Wildflowers
    Western Backyard Birds
    California Trees & Wildflowers
    Hummingbirds
    California Butterflies & Moths
    Animal Tracks

Waterproof fold-out guides from Quick Reference Publishing Inc., www.quickreferencepublishing.com:
    Wildflowers of Southern California
    Butterflies of Southern California
    Birds of Southern California

Fold-out Guides from Local Wildflowers Local Birds Inc., www.localbirds.com:
    Quick Guide to Local Wildflowers of San Diego County
    Local Birds San Diego County
    Local Tracks of North America

Maps

Anza-Borrego Desert Region, Wilderness Press, www.wildernesspress.com.

Cleveland National Forest, US Department of Agriculture, www.fs.fed.us/r5/cleveland.

Laguna Mountain Recreation Area, Laguna Mountain Volunteer Association, www.lmva.net.

Pacific Crest National Scenic Trail, US Department of Agriculture, 2004 California Series—Southern California, www.pcta.org.

San Diego Backcountry, Anza-Borrego Desert State Park, Recreation Map, Tom Harrison Maps, www.tomharrisonmaps.com.

Cuyamaca Rancho State Park Trail Map, Tom Harrison Maps, www.tomharrisonmaps.com.

Index

About The Author

Photograph by Christopher Khoury, M.D.

Priscilla Lister is a native San Diegan and longtime journalist for local newspapers. She wrote the "Take a Hike" column for the *San Diego Union-Tribune* for more than six years. When Priscilla is not hiking, she travels the world and writes about those adventures. This is her first book.

Made in the USA
San Bernardino, CA
12 May 2016